SUBLIME HISTORICAL EXPERIENCE

Cultural Memory
in
the
Present

Mieke Bal and Hent de Vries, Editors

SUBLIME HISTORICAL EXPERIENCE

Frank Ankersmit

STANFORD UNIVERSITY PRESS

STANFORD, CALIFORNIA

2005

Stanford University Press
Stanford, California

Printed in the United States of America on acid-free, archival-quality paper

Library of Congress Cataloging-in-Publication Data

Ankersmit, F. R.
     Sublime historical experience / Frank Ankersmit.
          p. cm.
     Includes bibliographical references and index.
     ISBN 0-8047-4935-3 (hardcover : alk. paper)— ISBN 0-8047-4936-1 (pbk. : alk. paper)
     1. History—Philosophy.   I. Title.

D16.8.A639 2005
901—dc22

                                                            2004018557

Typeset by G&S Book Services in 11/13.5 Garamond

Original Printing 2005

Last figure below indicates year of this printing:
14   13   12   11   10   09   08   07   06   05

My bounty is as boundless as the sea,
My love as deep; the more I give to thee
The more I have, for both are infinite.
—(Shakespeare, *Romeo and Juliet,* Act II, Scene II)

So, because their natural form had been cut in two, each half
longed for what belonged to it and to engage with it; throwing
their arms around each other and locking themselves together,
because of their desire to grow back together.
—(Plato, *Symposium,* 191 a5).

CONTENTS

LIST OF ILLUSTRATIONS

ACKNOWLEDGMENTS

Sections 7.2 and 7.3 of Chapter 7 develop material that was previously published in F. R. Ankersmit, *De historische ervaring* (Groningen, 1993). Section 7.4 develops material previously published in F. R. Ankersmit, "Rococo as the dissipation of boredom," in C. Farrago and R. Zwijnenberg, eds., *Compelling Visuality* (Minneapolis, 2003), 132–156. Chapter 8 was previously published as F. R. Ankersmit, "The sublime dissociation of the past, or how to become what one is no longer," *History and Theory* 40 (2001): 295–323 (there are several adaptations in the present text).

Section 8.8 of Chapter 8 reworks and develops material that was previously published in F. R. Ankersmit, "Trauma und Leiden: Eine vergessene Quelle des westlichen historischen Bewusstseins," in J. Rüsen, ed., *Westliches Geschichtsdenken: Eine interkulturelle Debatte* (Göttingen, 1999), 127–146, and F. R. Ankersmit, "Trauma als bron van historisch besef," *Feit en Fictie* 4 (1999): 7–19.

I would like to thank the publishers of these texts for permitting me to use the material published by them in this book.

Two topics have been central to historical theory since World War II: the issue of historical truth and that of narrative or of historical representation. In the 1950s and the 1960s debate concentrated on the epistemological status of statements about the past and on the problem of historical explanation. The "covering law model," Collingwoodian hermeneutics, intentional or teleological explanation, the logical connection argument, and constructivism as defined by Oakeshott, Meiland, and Goldstein have been the rich harvest of this stage in the history of historical theory. But in the 1970s many theorists felt that all these discussions failed to take into account the fact that historical knowledge is expressed by texts rather than by individual statements or explanations. So in order to compensate for this lacuna, historical theorists started to investigate the historical text.

Two comments are due here. In the first place, theorists interested in the historical text were often called (and often called themselves) "narrativists." Even though it is undeniably true that most of historical writing has the character of being a narrative, this has caused a great deal of unnecessary confusion. The term *narrativism* suggested that the historical text is, essentially, a narrative, or a story as we may find it in novels, legends, or fairy tales. Many historians therefore distrusted narrativism from the start: They rightly pointed out that one cannot reduce the writing of history to mere storytelling. Moreover, they insisted that the historian's text is required to do justice to what the text is about and that this has no exact equivalent in novels, fiction, and so on. And their worries were all the more justified since several historical theorists allowed themselves as well to be misled by the term *narrativism* and to see historical writing as being merely a variant of the novel. They inferred from this the mistaken view that literary theory, that is, the discipline that had been developed for analyzing literature, could also tell us all that we need to know about the historical text. That the historical text should do justice to the past was thus wholly lost from view.

This, then, is why we had better speak of "(historical) representation" than of "narrative." Whereas we can tell narratives about what never actually took place, there is no representation without a represented. That is simply part of the etymological meaning of the word: you can only make something present again which is not present now (for whatever reason). So the term *historical representation* will never invite us to forget that the historian's text is a text about a past and that it should do justice to this past as well as it can. And this may also contribute to reducing the most unfortunate gap that has recently come into being between historical theory on the one hand and historians themselves on the other. Historical theory is in a sad state if the only dialogues it is capable of with the practitioners of the discipline itself are *dialogues des sourds*.

In the second place, the theories developed for understanding the nature of historical representation (or narrative) are a *supplement* to what was said in the 1950s and 1960s about the truth of statements about the past or about causal explanation and not a *replacement* of it. Theories of representation are, essentially, theories about how the whole of a historical text is related to the past that it is a representation of—and this is a problem that cannot be reduced to how a historical text's individual statements relate to the past. So there is no obvious and necessary link between theories of historical representation on the one hand and theories about the statement or explanation on the other. To put it provocatively—but precisely because of this with the clarity that is needed here—one can quite well be (as I happen to be myself) an adherent of positivist or empiricist accounts of historical writing for what takes place in the historical text on the level of the statement while being, at the same time, an adherent of a theory of historical representation for the text as a whole.

But when taken together, the kind of theories developed in the 1950s and 1960s and theories of historical representation make up all of historical writing. There is no aspect of what historians do when accounting for the past as we expect them to do that could not be reduced in one way or another to the kind of problems addressed in these two variants of historical theory.

Nevertheless, one aspect of how we relate to the past escapes the intellectual matrix of historical truth and representation. This is the dimension of historical consciousness or of historical awareness, that is, of where we are aware of there having been a past at all that is, somehow, part of who we presently are and to whose call we should respond in one way or another.

There are two ways to operationalize the challenges of historical consciousness. In the first, the practical variant, the crucial question is what could be learned from the past and be put to use for present purposes. Can we learn lessons from the past, as many authors since Thucydides, Cicero, Tacitus, and down to Machiavelli have argued? Can it contribute to an understanding of our collective identity, as had been argued by historists since Ranke? But there is also a more impractical and speculative way of looking at historical consciousness. Here the crucial question is, Why *should* we be aware of there having been a past at all? How and why does historical consciousness originate? Why should we not rather be like Nietzsche's cow herd, quietly moving around its meadow in a timeless present, "tightly bound to its present likes and dislikes, that is to say, to the stake of the moment," whom we will always ask in vain for the cause of its mindless happiness since it immediately forgets again how it wanted to answer our so very weird questions.

Again, two ways of dealing with this question will suggest themselves. One may take one's lead in the very notion of historical consciousness itself and ask oneself what state of mind we must be in, what the nature of our consciousness must be, if we are to consider the reflection about our collective past to be an urgent necessity. In short, the question will be, What will or must it mean to us to have an awareness of the past? But there is an alternative route to the issue of historical consciousness as well. Here we should ask ourselves, *What makes us aware of the past at all,* what should happen, or what must have happened to a nation or a collectivity to become fascinated by the problem of its past? This is the approach that will be adopted in the present study. And I shall try to answer the question of how and why we may become fascinated by our collective past in terms of the notion of "sublime historical experience." For a nation, a collectivity, a culture, or a civilization that has had such a sublime historical experience, the past and an awareness of this past will become ineluctable realities. The past will then be for them no less a part of what they are as our limbs are part of our bodies—and forgetting the past would then be an intellectual amputation.

Once again, this is a supremely impractical problem: It has no bearing whatsoever on what historians actually do and on the question of why they do what they do. Indeed, the kinds of issues to be dealt with in this book are as useless as they are meaningless from the perspective of the practice of historical writing. Nevertheless, no one taking the writing of history seriously can avoid asking him- or herself now and then this question of how we relate to our past. Moreover, one may well doubt the common wisdom that in philosophy of science and in philosophy of history nothing can be of interest that does not have an internal relationship to any aspect of the actual practice of science or of history. We would then automatically exclude from philosophical scrutiny those aspects of science and history that are compatible with any actual or imaginable way of doing science or history. And that there should be no such aspects to science or history is a mere dogma until independent proof has been given of its truth. Thus, as long as no such a priori proof has been given, there is room for a book like this one. Finally, this also has its implications for this book's pretensions. This book is not an endeavor to identify the cognitive instruments necessary for the acquisition of historical knowledge. It is not a blueprint of historical writing. It is rather like a painting that some may like and others may not. Most readers of this book will have an intuition of what the nature of history is and what we have it for. Some readers (as I hope) may conclude that this book has helped to deepen their intuitions, whereas others—for reasons that are easy enough to predict—will consider the book useless, "hyperbolic," or simply nonsensical. And I am content with this—for I am not trying to convince anybody of anything in this book. In this way it resembles Nietzsche's *Zarathustra;* it also is "ein Buch für Alle und Keine," a book for all and none.

I would like to thank several friends and colleagues for their most valuable help. To begin with, I thank Kiene Brillenburg Wurth. For several years we have discussed together the sublime and how the sublime manifests itself in music and in literature. I have been convinced by her critique of the Kantian sublime and fully accept what follows from this. I consider her book on the musically sublime to be among the best that has been written on the sublime in the last ten to fifteen years.[1] The traces of our so extremely fruitful discussions can be found in many pages of this book. She gave me the best that friendship and mutual interest can give us, and this is what I shall remember for the rest of my life. Hanneke van Brakel carefully read parts of the manuscript, and her suggestions for how I could improve my argument and its exposition have been most valuable. Arjo Vanderjagt's help has been indispensable to me for finding out how texts were read and interpreted in the Middle Ages and by sixteenth-century humanists. I am most grateful to Martin Jay; he showed me those parts of the manuscripts of his *Songs of Experience*[2] that were relevant to my own enterprise, and I have greatly benefited from this. We both know how desperate and lonely one can sometimes feel when having "to cross the swamps of experience," as he once so poignantly put it in a letter to me. My discussions with him have been for me an indispensable compass when trying to find my way through these treacherous swamps. No contemporary scholar has a greater erudition in the fields investigated in this study than he. Moreover, the reader's report he wrote for Stanford University Press has shown me how I could improve my argument on numerous occasions and to what other authors I could appeal in order to support it further. When preparing the final version of this book, I have also greatly benefited from Allan Megill's most valuable reader's report; and I would like to thank him here for his support and his continuing interest in my work. Another most important guide has been Craig Ireland's *Subaltern Appeal to Experience;*[3] I consider this book to be the best survey of contemporary attempts to rehabilitate the notion of experience. I read the manuscript of this book for Stanford University Press; since then we came into contact with each other, and we discovered how much we have in common. My debt to Arthur Danto is of a different kind: I came to the notion of historical experience by means of that of (historical) representation. And is there anything worth knowing about representation that does not have its antecedents in his oeuvre—an oeuvre that is unique in its combination of penetration and elegance? I would like to thank Kia Lindroos for checking what I have been saying on Benjamin; and both Lionel Gosman and Jörn Rüsen for doing the same for my account of Burckhardt. My colleague Eelco Runia, with whom I share a profound interest for the notion of historical experience, also commented on parts of this book, and his influence on my views are manifest throughout the text. And I have the greatest expectations for the future now that he joined me here in Groningen, together with Rik Peters. My cooperation with Jo Tollebeek during his stay for four years in Groningen belongs to the happiest memories of all of my academic career. In fact, Jo Tollebeek helped me with my first uncertain steps some ten years ago on the difficult path of historical experience. Hermien Lankhorst's help with the translation of the foreign quotes and with many other details of the text has simply been a *conditio sine qua non* for the completion of the text. I am deeply indebted to Henk de Jong, who most graciously and unselfishly put at my disposal the results of his archival research in the Bibliotheca Hertziana in Rome. Without his immensely valuable help I could not have written the sections on Eichendorff and Burckhardt in Chapter 4. Mimi Braverman copyedited the text, and she did so with an accuracy, a love of precision, and a devotion to the perfection of the text that are simply unequaled. My gratitude to her is greater than can be expressed in words. Finally, my cooperation with Leah McAleer, who supervised the production of the book and did so with a rare combination of efficiency and flexibility, belongs to the happiest memories that I shall have of the genesis of this book.

Groningen, December 2003

SUBLIME HISTORICAL EXPERIENCE

INTRODUCTION: EXPERIENCE
IN HISTORY AND IN PHILOSOPHY

Praeter haec duo cognitionis genera datur, ut in sequentibus os-
tendam, aliud tertium, quod scientiam intuitivam vocabimus.

Apart from these two ways of knowing there is, as I shall show, a
third one, that we shall call intuitive knowledge. (my translation)
—B. de Spinoza, *Ethica* (Pars Secunda, Prop. XL, Schol. II)

I.I THE "REBIRTH OF CENTRIPETALITY"

It has taken me far too long to complete this book. The explanation
is that I arrived at the notion of experience that is addressed in it from two
different perspectives—and it took me quite some time to adjust them to
each other in a satisfactory way.

The first perspective originated in recent developments in history
and historical theory and the other one originated in recent developments
in philosophy. In both of them one may observe a shift away from language
toward experience. This shift probably reflects a more general shift in our
contemporary culture; one could describe it as a moving away from comprehensive systems of meaning to meaning as bound to specific situations
and events.[1] But before turning to historical theory and philosophy, I want
to begin by saying a few words about this.

Meaning no longer travels as freely and easily through time and space
as it used to do: Its ties to its place of origin tend to become stronger than
ever before. Think, for example, of what is left of those comprehensive systems claiming to give meaning to all of humanity and to comprise all of the
past, the present and the future? It has been observed that in the contemporary world the present tends to "devour" both the future and the past
and that the "circles" of cultural, narrative, and textual meaning became

ever narrower to the point where they finally coincided with their center; that is, with the pure *experience* of the present.[2] Meaning now is centripetal rather than centrifugal. Recall, in this context, the contrast between the "centripetality" of the contemporary fascination for the (experience of the) event on the one hand, and the "centrifugality" of meaning in deconstructivism on the other. As a result meaning now tends to weaken its ties with "theory," that is, with the theoretical instruments we traditionally relied on to courageously expand the scope of cultural, narrative, and textual meaning;[3] it now preferably draws its content from how the world is given to us in *experience*. "Theory" and meaning no longer travel in the same direction; meaning has now found a new and more promising traveling companion in experience. And, needless to say, we can recognize this *renversement des alliances* and fathom its implications only to the extent that we are prepared to grant to experience an autonomy of its own in its relationship to "theory." Only then are we in the position to recognize that experience does really possess the capacity to explode the matrix within which "theory" has enclosed meaning.

If, then, experience now rebels against the imperialism of "theory" that has been so all-pervasive in all of contemporary philosophy of science and of language, we should ask ourselves how it could be successful in its revolt against "theory" and what we may associate with it. As we shall see in the course of this book, the role that is assigned to the subject is, in the end, decisive in this tug of war between "theory" and experience. If the role of the subject is negligible or even wholly nonexistent—as is the case in philosophy, language, and culture until quite recently—then "theory" will hold all the trumps and the game will be lost for experience. We will then find ourselves in the world of the post-structuralist's "language speaks man," where the subject, or the author, is, at best, a mere attribute of language—hence, in a world that is inhabited by almost all contemporary philosophers of language and culture, even if they would not hesitate to express their deeply felt repugnance to such hyperbolic post-structuralist locutions. So the rediscovery of experience is also the rediscovery of the subject, and vice versa—the one entails the other.

I.2 HISTORY AND HISTORICAL THEORY

This, then, brings me to the first perspective from which this book originates: history and historical theory. Undoubtedly one of the fascinating things about the writing of history—and where it so conspicuously differs from other disciplines—has always been that it does not feel in the least uncomfortable with a prominent position of the subject, that is, of the individual historian. The tie between name and theory is merely contingent in the case of, for example, the laws of Kirchhoff or of Maxwell, but a necessary one in the case of, for example, Tocqueville's *L'ancien régime et la révolution* or of Huizinga's *Waning of the Middle Ages*. A law of physics is cognitively wholly self-sufficient and, in this sense, independent of its discoverer, whereas a work of history is, at least in part, a self-expression of its author and in need of *this* author for its having been written at all. As soon as physics reached a certain stage, some great physicist was bound to discover the laws of Maxwell; if Maxwell had not formulated these laws, some other physicist would not have failed to do so sooner or later. But if Tocqueville had not been born, it is unthinkable that a book like *L'ancien régime et la révolution* would ever have been written. This is one of the reasons explaining why the practice of the writing of history may disrupt and put into question all that is always so much accepted as a matter of course in philosophy of science and of language and codified in the scientistic view of the world: Most historians will be ready to recognize the impossibility of eliminating the subject or the individual historian from the picture. But they will rarely infer from this that all their writings ought to be condemned to the wastepaper basket. For most historians the ineluctability of the category of the historical subject does not in the least reduce their discipline to idle and irrational speculation. And so it is with philosophy of history—as one might expect. Even more so, far from having been worried about the presence of the historical subject in their writings, much of philosophy of history regarded this presence as an asset rather than as the indubitable sign of the discipline's cognitive hopelessness. One need only think here of hermeneutics from Schleiermacher to Gadamer. And, as is also exemplified by hermeneutics, experience is then never far away as well.

But it is true, in the 1970s and 1980s both historians and philosophers of history have not remained insensitive to the siren song of scientism and of philosophy of science and language. However, since then the climate has changed dramatically, with the result that experience is no longer the unspeakable category that it used to be. With regard to history, the history of mentalities, *Alltagsgeschichte,* and much of cultural history can well be seen as a history of experience.[4] In these variants of historical writing the emphasis is on how people in the past experienced their world and in what way this experience may differ from how we relate to our own world. The focus is on what may seem to us strange or even simply impossible to imagine in the *expérience vécue* of our ancestors. Experience here is to be situated on the side of the object, on that the side of what is investigated by the historian.

But, next, in historical theory the emphasis on language has recently given rise to the question of whether the historian could ever successfully escape from the "prisonhouse of language" (to use Nietzsche's famous metaphor) and from how language determines our conceptions of the past. Can we rescue the past itself from how we speak about it? More specifically, can the historian enter into a real, authentic, and "experiential" relationship to the past—that is, into a relationship that is not contaminated by historiographical tradition, disciplinary presuppositions, and linguistic structures such as identified by Hayden White in his *Metahistory* of 1973?[5] When asking ourselves this kind of question, we have to do with "subjective experience," that is, with the historian's experience of the past. And then the crucial question is whether it is (historical) experience that may enable us to break through the walls of "the prisonhouse of language"— and this, in fact, is the main question to be addressed in this book.

Furthermore, these shifts from language to experience in both history and historical theory happily joined and mutually reinforced each other in the recent fascination for notions such as (collective) memory, trauma, Pierre Nora's *lieux de mémoire,* and (the representation of) the Holocaust—in sum, in all these tendencies in contemporary historical writing that can be taken together under the rubric of what I once referred to as "the privatization of the past."[6] Characteristic of this privatization of the past is that we now tend to use the term *memory* where we previously preferred to speak of "History" or of "the past."[7] This new idiom suggests an interesting shift in the nature of contemporary historical consciousness.

In the first place, the notion of "History" has the aura of the ineluctable and of a fate that we cannot escape; similarly, the notion of the past is suggestive of an objective reality outside our grasp and influence. This is different, of course, with memory. Ordinarily we remember things only if we wish to (trauma being the paradigmatic exception, of course); and we are all very much aware of the pliability of memory. Apparently the contemporary past is a much less fixed and final past than that of a generation ago.[8] It is no longer the massive objective reality that it used to be.

Second, the terms *History* and *the past* are suggestive of how a collectivity relates to its past, whereas *memory* is, strictly speaking, the domain of the individual only—"collective memory" being, in the end, a metaphor whose fruitfulness can always meaningfully be questioned. And, third, *memory* possesses a dimension of the experiential that is absent from the notions of "History" and of "the past." Within the context of what we traditionally associate with these words, it would make no sense (or even sound slightly ridiculous) to ask how we "experience" the past. Although the *remembered* past undoubtedly is a past that we "experience" in one way or another, memory gives us an experience or re-experience of the remembered past. Hence, when we start defining our relationship to the past in terms of "memory" rather than in terms of "history," we cannot avoid the question of whether we can *experience* the past and, if so, what meaning should be given to this notion of "the experience of the past" or to the idea of "historical experience."

So, in this way "experience" can be said to have been the polestar guiding both contemporary historical writing and historical theory in recent times.

1.3 PHILOSOPHY

The second perspective from which this book has been written originates in the state of affairs in contemporary philosophy. Twentieth-century philosophy has predominantly been a philosophy of language. And this is true not only of (Anglo-Saxon) analytical philosophy. The issue of language was, and is, no less prominent in (logical-positivist) philosophy of science, in phenomenology, in Heideggerian existential philosophy, in (post-)structuralism, and in deconstructivism, and so on. So, language has been the self-evident object and point of departure of almost all of twentieth-century philosophy. However, in the last ten to fifteen years we may observe in contemporary philosophy two developments signaling a move away from this exclusive emphasis on language.

In the first place, questions one used to formulate in the discourse of philosophy of language are now often reformulated in that of consciousness. We may think here of the writings of Dennett and Searle and of so many others who have dealt with the topic of consciousness since them.[9] And this can be interpreted as a movement toward experience. Let us try to imagine how these three notions—experience, consciousness, and language—are mutually related. The most obvious and natural way to think of their relationship is as follows: First, experience brings us into contact with the world; second, consciousness offers us representations of the world as we encounter it in experience; and, third, these representations can be expressed in terms of language.[10] Of course this is a most schematic way of putting it, and one may well say that four centuries of philosophical speculation since Descartes have been one sustained effort to put the flesh of philosophical detail on this bare skeleton.

But if we agree that this is how these three notions are basically related, it follows that this move from language to consciousness is, at least in part, a move toward experience. Indeed, language can do quite well without experience (although not without consciousness[11]): It is a system of socialized meanings and permits permutations of elements of itself that do not have counterparts in experience—the language of mathematics being, of course, the paramount example. But, in opposition to language, consciousness and its representations of the world could not exist without experience. The content of consciousness and its representations of the world are given to us in and by experience. Without experience, there is no consciousness. So, if we move from language to consciousness, the issue of experience becomes an ineluctable item on the philosopher's agenda.

And this brings me, more or less automatically, to a second feature of contemporary philosophy. I am thinking here of the more or less sudden elevation of aesthetics from a position of relative obscurity into a topic that is most eagerly and enthusiastically discussed in contemporary philosophy. It would, of course, be absurd to say that art has taken the place of science as the philosopher's preferred domain of inspiration, but it cannot be doubted that science has recently lost a good deal of terrain to art. Now, if we think again of these three notions—experience, consciousness, and language—who would doubt that art has its elective affinity with the first two rather than with language? Art is not a language—and all the efforts of Nelson Goodman to identify the grammar and the semantics of "the languages of art" are now seen as the *reductio ad absurdum* of the cognitivist approach to art rather than as a viable program for the philosophy of art. We feel much more at ease nowadays with Hans Georg Gadamer's, Richard Wollheim's, and Arthur Danto's openness to the experiential dimensions of the work of art and to how experience is expressed in and by artistic representation. And, indeed, is the success of the work of art, the impact it may have on us, not to be measured in terms of *experience?* Do we not see in the work of art primarily the expression of an authentic experience of the world by the artist? Moreover, is the genius of the work of art not primarily measured in terms of whether it can provoke a similar experience in us, as its spectators?

1.4 FROM THE RATIONALISM OF "THEORY" TO A NEW ROMANTICISM

So, in both history and philosophy we may observe an effort to rehabilitate the almost forgotten and thoroughly marginalized category of experience, a category that, if noticed at all, was regarded with so much contempt and disdain in most of the twentieth century's philosophy of language. The main topic of this book, therefore, is to contribute to the resuscitation of the notion of experience from its apparent death, to explore and to explain the parallelism of the relevant development in both historical writing and in philosophy, and, more specifically, to show what lessons historical writing can teach the philosopher.

Next, when hearing the word *experience* we immediately think of sensory experience, of how we get access to the world by seeing, hearing, tasting, touching, and smelling. And the fact that the sciences can be seen as a refinement of sensory perception still further contributed to our tendency to model experience on how the world is given to us in the experience of what we can see, hear, and so on. *This book, however, proposes the unusual thesis that there is also such a thing as "intellectual experience" and that our minds can function as a receptacle of experience no less than our eyes, ears, or fingers.* Our minds inhabit a world of potential objects of intellectual experience. These objects may be either as well defined as the objects of intellectual experience that Popper had in mind with his theory of "a third world of ideas"[12] or as vague but all-pervasive as what Carl Becker once described as "the climate of opinion" of a historical period.[13] And the objects in this "third world" are no less potential objects of (intellectual) experience than the objects of sensory experience constituting the daily reality we find around ourselves. The objection that these objects of intellectual experience should be mere constructions of more elementary components and can therefore never be experienced *as such*, is just as idle as the view that sensory experience is an illusion that should be reduced to and explained in terms of nerve-firings and of neurophysiological processes taking place in our brains. This is not how we experience the world. We should never allow ourselves to be unduly overawed by the specter of reductionism when dealing with the notion of experience.

This book defends an extreme variant of empiricism in the sense of claiming for experience a far more important role than tradition has granted to it. But on the other hand, the empiricism defended here will never go along with the transcendentalization of experience so characteristic of Western philosophy from Descartes, Bacon, and Kant down to contemporary variants of (neo-)positivism. One of the more interesting differences between science and history undoubtedly is that in science (and in philosophy of science) there is a natural alliance between empiricism and positivism, whereas in history the more empiricist one becomes, the farther one will move away from positivism. The explanation is that the relationship between experience and the subject of experience is different in science and in history. In science the subject of experience is defined transcendentally and because of this, in principle, it is compatible with any actual content of experience. It is compatible with any kind of experience, since the transcendental self processes the data of experience in such a way that it can digest them—and self-evidently experience has then lost its autonomy to the self's transcendental structures, to language, to "theory" (in all its variants), and so on. This is different in history. Since I cannot say the last word about this here, I must suffice with an appeal to the notion of *Bildung*. This basically Aristotelian notion is suggestive of what one might describe as "formative experience" (*Bildung* = formation) and of how our mental framework may be "formed" by experience. With *Bildung* experience enters into the definition of the subject of experience itself, whereas it will require no elucidation that science would immediately become impossible with such an intimate interaction between experience and the scientist. To put it succinctly, in science experience is an attribute of the world and in history it is both this and an attribute of the subject.

So in this way, in history, we can ascribe to the mind the faculty of experience as well, even though the mind does not possess any obvious equivalent to our eyes or ears for registering what is given to us; and it surely would be a sad and unforgivable mistake to see in this an invitation to reduce *intellectual* experience to some complicated combination of *sensory* experiences—as positivists and mainstream philosophers of science will probably be tempted to do.[14] I shall try to defend my proposal of an "intellectual empiricism" by focusing in this book on historical experience, that is, on how we experience the past and on how this experience of the past may come into being by a movement comprising at the same time the *discovery* and a *recovery* of the past. Historical experience involves, in the first place, a Gestalt-switch from a timeless present into a world consisting of things past and present. This gives us the discovery of the past as a reality that has somehow "broken off" from a timeless present. This is "the moment of loss." But at the same time historical experience aims at a recovery of the past by transcending again the barriers between past and present. And this could be characterized as "the moment of desire or of love." All of historical writing is to be situated in the space enclosed by these complementary movements of the discovery (loss) and the recovery of the past (love) that constitute together the realm of historical experience. Past and present are related to each other as man and wife in Plato's myth of the origin of the sexes referred to in the second epigraph of this book. *The sublimity of historical experience originates from this paradoxical union of the feelings of loss and love, that is, of the combination of pain and pleasure in how we relate to the past.*

The results of the reorientation recommended in the present study will be twofold. In the first place I hope to show that historical writing is a true gold mine for the philosopher, a gold mine that has been sadly neglected and ignored by philosophers since the death of neo-Kantianism and from which a number of new and exciting philosophical issues can be delved into. More specifically, I hope to show in this book that a set of new and important questions will demand the philosopher's attention, if we move from philosophy's traditional fixation on issues of truth to issues occasioned by the notion of experience, to assume a perspective from which we can consider truth and experience *ex aequo* and that will enable us to discuss experience independently from questions of truth. I am well aware that this places this book in direct opposition to most of contemporary philosophy. I do not know of any philosophers (with the possible exception of Dewey[15]) who have advocated this radical disconnection of truth and experience:[16] Experience is always seen (if it is seen at all) as the meek and obedient servant of truth. But the claim that there is a variant of experience preceding and transcending questions of truth and falsity is precisely the main thesis of this book.

In the second place, getting access to this philosophical gold mine will inevitably demand a readjustment of philosophy of history. Philosophy of history, in the last half-century, has predominantly been an attempt to translate the successes of philosophy of language to historical writing. Philosophy of history rather docilely allowed itself to be led and inspired by philosophy of language, and it never asked itself the question of whether other guides might not be more helpful in the endeavor to clarify our relationship to the past. I shall be the first to recognize that linguistic philosophy of history has achieved its indisputable triumphs. Hayden White's seminal work on the tropology of the historical text is the first and most obvious example to come to mind. We owe to this a new variant of the history of historical writing and this surely is a *ktèma eis aei.*[17]

Nevertheless, a high price had to be paid for this. The result was a historical theory for which *il n'y a pas dehors texte.*[18] The radical "otherness" of the past—and where it sometimes put to shame all our categories (linguistic or otherwise) for making sense of the world, or of the past—was thus eliminated. This book is mainly an attempt to rectify this and to do away with all the (quasi-)transcendentalist conceptions we may find not only in tropology but also in hermeneutics, deconstructivism, (post-)structuralism, or semiotics. It can therefore be seen as an uncompromising attack on all that came to be known over the last twenty to thirty years by the name of "theory." The "rationalism" that "theory" took over from transcendentalist philosophy of language will be rejected here in the name of the notion of *experience.* The intellectual bureaucracy of "theory" will in this book be replaced by the "Romanticism" of an approach to the past involving all of the historian's personality and not just (or even merely primarily) the formalism of his or her cognitive faculties. More specifically, this book is a rehabilitation of the romanticist's world of moods and feelings as constitutive of how we relate to the past. How we *feel* about the past is no less important than what we *know* about it—and probably even more so. "*Sentir, c'est penser,*" as Rousseau liked to say, and this is where I fully agree with him.

So I invite the reader of this book to enter the dark and sometimes even sinister Romantic world of the profoundest and quasi-existentialist layers in our relationship to the past—a dimension of historical consciousness that had effectively been filtered out by the transcendentalism and cognitivism of "theory," although I shall be the first to admit that, just like it was two centuries ago, one can only get to Romanticism after first having passed through rationalism and "theory." In this way the book will remain tributary to "theory" and the linguistic rationalism that it criticizes and wishes to transcend. I need only point out, in this context, that it will be a *literary* category—that is, that of the sublime[19]—that dominates the argument in this book and in terms of which this transition from rationalism to Romanticism will be performed. Indeed, the triumphs of "theory" no less deserve our admiration than the achievements of the Enlightenment. But, in the end, both the Enlightenment and "theory" resulted in an icy formalism, freezing all that may move the human heart. As the Dutch novelist Nicolaas Beets (1814–1903) amusingly put it in 1837, the Enlightenment "gave us the chilly formalism of A + B = C. The temperature decreased from that of human blood to that of frost. It literally snowed big ideas. It was a fresh but, in the end, uncomfortable cold."[20] So let us restore to our thinking about history and about historical writing at least something of the warmth of the human heart and of what has a resonance in the depths of our souls.

1.5 OUTLINE OF THE BOOK

Let me end this introduction with a brief sketch of what the reader may expect to find in this book. The first two chapters begin the rehabilitation of experience with an attack on its most redoubtable enemy: linguistic transcendentalism. An important theme running through all of the present study is the incompatibility of language and experience, as the latter word is understood here. No compromise is possible between language and experience, and the triumphs of the one are inevitably the defeats of the other. They truly are each other's mortal enemies: Where you have language, experience is not, and vice versa. We have language in order *not* to have experience and to avoid the fears and terrors that are typically provoked by experience; language is the shield protecting us against the terrors of a direct contact with the world as conveyed by experience. Language presents us with an image of the world, but as such it can offer only a shadow of the terrors inhabiting the world itself and of the fears that it may provoke. Language, the symbolic order, enables us to escape the perplexities of a direct confrontation with the world as it is given us in experience.

It is argued that Richard Rorty, who has done the most to undermine linguistic transcendentalism, in the end sides with it and against experience. The main purpose of the first two chapters is to place the issue of (historical) experience against the background of contemporary philosophical debate and to add, in this way, a *constructive* moment to Rorty's *destruction* of epistemology in his *Philosophy and the Mirror of Nature* of 1979. So, Rorty cleared the place on which the building of this book could be erected, to put it somewhat pompously, and without him this book could never have been written. This is why Rorty's linguistic transcendentalism is the appropriate point of departure for this book. Readers not interested in the pros and cons of linguistic transcendentalism had best skip Chapter 1 and start right away with Chapter 2, section 3. In the course of Chapter 2 the project that Rorty began with his critique of transcendentalism is carried to its logical conclusion, and the shortcomings of this bureaucracy[21] of "theory" (hermeneutics, [post-]structuralism, deconstructivism, semiotics, rhetoric, tropology, and so on) are expounded. Chapter 3 discusses Huizinga's notion of historical experience and how Huizinga translated his own historical experience of the culture of the late Middle Ages into language. In Chapter 4 it is shown that the preoccupation with historical experience is far from being of a recent date, and an account is given of what has been said about it by Herder and Goethe and, more elaborately, by Eichendorff, Burckhardt, and Benjamin.

Chapter 5 continues this account to the present with an analysis of Gadamer's conception of (historical) experience. Since Gadamer has undoubtedly been my most important discussion partner while writing this book, this chapter can be seen as the hinge around which all of my argument turns. The results of this chapter can be summarized with the following four claims. First, for a correct appreciation of the notion of historical experience investigated in this book, *we will be required to have the courage to disconnect truth and experience.* Second, this unconventional anti-cognitivist conception of experience thus automatically sidesteps all the familiar problems and issues occasioned by and discussed within cognitivist approaches to historical writings and historical consciousness—think, for example, of the perennial seesaw between historism[22] and universalism or of the objectivity issue. Third, the disjunction of experience and truth will require us to postulate a conception of experience that does not entail the existence of a subject of experience. Fourth, although these claims will sound most unbelievable, if not simply absurd, as long as we think of how we, as human individuals, experience the world, they will lose much of their provocativeness if we consider them from the perspective context of cultures or civilizations (as will be the case in the last chapter on sublime historical experience). These most peculiar entities simply *are* experiences without there being any subjects of experience around. Chapter 5 had begun with a discussion of how Gadamer relates aesthetic and historical experience in the first part of his *Wahrheit und Methode*. This issue is taken up again in Chapter 6; the aim of the chapter is to show that historical experience can best be understood from the perspective of Dewey's notion of pragmatist aesthetic experience.

Whereas these first six chapters are mainly theoretical in character, the last two attempt to give a practical illustration of what one can do with the notion of historical experience. Chapter 7 gives two examples of how historical experience may give us access to the past; a capriccio by Guardi and rococo ornament will be my examples for illustrating the nature of historical experience. What I readily confess to have experienced as *une terrible nécessité* demands that my argument shall be here, basically, autobiographical. Chapter 8, finally, suggests in what way the notion of historical experience may contribute to a better understanding of the emergence of Western historical consciousness and what its nature is. The notion of historical experience refers here to how a civilization may relate to its past as expressed in and by its historical consciousness. It is argued that if we wish to grasp the nature of (Western) historical consciousness, we shall have to focus on what one might call "experiences of rupture," in which a civilization discards a former identity while defining its new identity precisely in terms of what has been discarded and surrendered. The identification and investigation of these sublime experiences of rupture—think of the Renaissance and of the French Revolution—could be seen as the "research program" suggested or implied by this book. For other examples of these experiences of rupture one might think of how in the U.S. South the trauma of the Civil War can still be felt[23] and of how this may stimulate a feeling of loss and regret in even an occasional visitor to the South (like myself in 1985). Similarly, one might well ask the question of how the past is nowadays experienced in Russia after the two dramatic caesuras of 1917 and 1989. In sum, if we wish to understand how we relate to our past—and is this not the proper object of study of all historical theory?—we must carefully and painstakingly investigate the history of historical experience. That is, the epos of how Western man experienced his past all through the centuries.

And this epos will forever remain a secret to us as long as we restrict our gaze to the historical text and fail to address the question of what experience of the past it is meant to express—or to suppress, for that matter. Since experience has no voice of its own, since it depends on its mortal enemy—language—for its expression, we have remained deaf to it up until now and ignorant of how it determines our relationship to the past. So it will be the difficult but challenging future task of the historical theorist to liberate the history of historical experience from the heavy and oppressive weight of (the historian's) language and to unearth experience from the thick sedimentary strata of language covering it. What is the experience of the past underlying the language used by the historian? That is the question asked in this book. The book ends with an epilogue in which my argument about the nature of sublime historical experience is related to the Rousseau of the *Rêveries du promeneur solitaire* and, especially, to Hölderlin's novel *Hyperion*. This implies, in fact, the return to a stage before the victory of historism over natural law philosophy. In this way this book can be seen both as a moving beyond historism *and* as a comeback to what antedated historism.

1.6 DIRECTIONS FOR USE—AND A WARNING

Last but not least, I most emphatically insist that this is a book about sublime historical experience—*and not about anything else* (such as historical explanation, causality, narrative, or representation). This book is therefore not to be interpreted as a recantation of what I have said about such other topics in my previous writings. This book does not question the conviction that there is, or rather, has been a past existing independently of what we may say or write about it, that we can make statements about the past that are either true or false, that we can explain the past either by mentioning causes or in terms of texts representing the past, that all these things can rationally be discussed and, finally, that there is no occasion for historical skepticism and that there is such a thing as progress in historical writing. This is not a book on the philosophical problems of historical writing or on the relationship between historical writing and the past. It was, however, written on the assumption that there is a stage in how we relate to the past *preceding* the one in which historians dispassionately investigate a past that is objectively given to them. This is the stage of sublime historical experience,[24] the stage of the Gestalt-switch I mentioned a moment ago. It is the stage that may invite (admittedly highly impractical) questions about how the very notion of a historical past comes into being, about how we relate to the past, about whether we should believe the past to be important to us (or not), and about how the past may live on in our hearts and minds—in short, about *what is the nature and origin of historical consciousness.* It is a stage *preceding* all questions of historical truth and falsity. As I explained a moment ago, the conception of sublime experience discussed in this book cannot be related to questions of truth and falsity. This book's thesis can therefore not be criticized for being silent about how experience may help us attain the truth about the past—for this simply is not what this book is about. I am not implying by this that questions of truth and falsity should have no application to how we relate to the past. On the contrary, I hold in high regard what philosophers of history have had to say on this. But this book addresses a different topic.

So if anyone has the firm and indestructible conviction that questions about how we relate to the past effectively that resist reformulation in terms of truth and falsity can only be useless, meaningless, and not worthy of philosophical investigation, or worse still, that such questions simply do not exist, then he or she should close this book now and never open it again.[25]

1 ▨

LINGUISTIC TRANSCENDENTALISM IN EXTREMIS: [1]
THE CASE OF RICHARD RORTY

> Language goes all the way down.
> —(Richard Rorty)
>
> The scientific revolution of the seventeenth century perfectly suited
> an abstract, Cartesian view of experience that effectively denied the
> existence of primary experience. After Descartes, Western philoso-
> phers and scientists tended to replace the commonsense concepts of
> experience, wisdom, and know-how with an increasingly technical
> account of experience as made up of disconnected, subjective, sen-
> sory states. [2]

1.1 INTRODUCTION

Two different stories can be told about the recent history of philosophy and about Richard Rorty's place in that history. [3] According to the first
story, Rorty is the philosopher who broke in a revolutionary and radical
manner with what has been for several centuries, since Descartes and Kant,
the primary goal of most philosophical investigation. According to the alternative story, he is, on the contrary, the philosopher who—together with
some others like Derrida and Davidson—put the crown on that tradition
we associate with Descartes and Kant.

Let me start with the first story. This story runs as follows. Since the
days of Plato and Aristotle, Western philosophy was mainly interested in
the problem of the nature of our knowledge of reality; it was always concerned with the metaphysical, epistemological, rationalist, empiricist, or
linguistic foundations of our knowledge of reality and with the question
how this knowledge is acquired and can be legitimated. The main heroes
in this story are Descartes and Kant. As philosophers—and as epistemologists—they opted for what Putnam has called the *God's eye view,* that is,

for a point of view lying itself outside both observed reality and the subject of knowledge, and they hoped that from that "sublime"[4] point of view the relationship between the knowing subject and the object of our knowledge could be established in a neutral and undistorted way. Whatever their differences were, both Descartes and Kant—and the many philosophers who have continued their enterprise down to the present day—believed that all our most essential questions with regard to the nature, origin, "foundations," and legitimation of knowledge could be properly answered from the unassailable point of view of this transcendental self.

It is true that there have been philosophers such as Hegel or Marx who doubted the possibility of such an ahistorical, universalist transcendental point of view. But what philosophers like these effected, in the end, was a historicization of epistemology and a correction of the historical blindness of traditional epistemology rather than its destruction. As Gadamer has so brilliantly shown, historism, Hegel's experiment with the Absolute Spirit and Marx's conception of ideology were, in fact, attempts to continue the epistemological enterprise with even better and stronger, namely historical means rather than that these philosophers dealt the deathblow to epistemology, as they often liked to believe themselves. Historicization was for these philosophers not the destruction but the very perfection of epistemological certainty. Hence, we should not see the historists or the Hegelians as philosophers who were the first to abandon epistemology—as is so often done in accordance with how they liked to present themselves—but rather as those philosophers who have taken the epistemological enterprise to its very logical end. "History" now took the place of the transcendental ego; it offered the only point of view from which truth could be found and was thus expected to fulfill the same function as its more abstract and timeless predecessor.

In sum, it was not Hegel or Foucault but only Rorty, as the true heir to Heidegger, Gadamer, Derrida, and Davidson and to American pragmatism, who successfully tripped up the whole epistemological tradition. Rorty was the first who had the courage to abandon the transcendentalist point of view and all that went with it: The Rortyan pragmatist knows that such a point of view outside both reality and language is an impossibility and that all the illusions of modernist Western philosophy proceeded from the Enlightenment's dream of the transcendentalist point of view. Hence, with Rorty a long and important chapter in the history of Western philosophy has come to an end, and we may consider his oeuvre as the announcement of a new post-epistemological chapter in the book of that history. Now that the epistemological *anachoorèsis* from the world—the attempt to withdraw from the world to a transcendental point of view outside the world itself—has been abandoned, we may expect that this new chapter will deal with the direct interaction between subject and object, or between language and the world. And since human action is the favorite domain of this interaction between reality and our knowledge of reality, ethics and politics may be expected to become the main topics of this new chapter in the history of philosophy. Ethics and politics will thus take the place of the abstractions of traditional, foundationalist philosophy.[5] The *vivere privatim ac domestice* will be replaced once again by "civic humanism," just as the medieval obsession with the *civitas Dei* was replaced, in the works by Bruni or Salutati, by the compass of the *vivere civile*. And in his later writings Rorty was brilliantly successful in demonstrating what this shift ought to mean for contemporary philosophy.

But one can also tell a quite different story about the history of philosophy and Rorty's role in it. This story goes as follows. The Aristotle of *De Anima* experience and knowledge are the result of a union, interaction, or even outright identification of the subject and the object of knowledge. The subject may be said to possess (experiential) knowledge of the object if the subject succeeds in achieving a formal (that is, not a material) similarity to the object. One may think here of how our hands may come to "know" the form of an object by following its forms and thus by imitating these forms. Knowledge is, hence, a matter of the subject's being "formed" by the object and of a process in which the object leaves its indelible traces in or on the subject. This conception of knowledge is, obviously, captured far better by what we associate with the sense of touch than with the sense of sight. It makes no sense to say that what we see changes our eyes in some way or another. And, indeed, for Aristotle, just as for Merleau-Ponty in our own time, the sense of touch is prototypical of all experience and of all knowledge based on experience.[6] In this tradition experience articulates itself in how we are *formed* by it.

In the seventeenth century Descartes finally overturns this Aristotelian tradition because this tradition does not provide us with a reliable criterion for how to distinguish right from wrong. The criteria for distinguishing truth from falsity can be established only at a level that is free from our messy interactions with the world and with which Aristotelianism had been content. Aristotelianism may thus tempt us to take delusions for incontrovertible truths. And Descartes concludes that we should abandon the Aristotelian interaction between subject and object and withdraw within the silent and pure sanctuary of the inner *forum internum* of our rationalist self, judging, like a severe proto-Freudian censor, the reliability of the representations of reality that are offered to it. Only this severe censor, which will not allow itself to be compromised by the chaotic and untidy interactions between subject and object, can be a reliable guide on our way to indubitable certainties and can teach us how to distinguish between appearance and reality, between dream and waking.

Since Descartes and his seventeenth-century rationalist followers, the story of Western philosophy is, essentially, the story of what faculties of the subject, or of the mind, were proposed to assist this censor in our *forum internum* in its endeavor to distinguish between truth and falsehood and between appearance and reality. The empiricists of the century following Descartes abandoned reason for empirical observation, Berkeley turned to the notion of "the idea" as our transcendental guarantee for our access to reality, Kant primarily proposed thereto the imagination and his categories of the understanding—and Hegel and Marx gave the whole enterprise a new start by turning to history. However, in our own century, continental philosophy since Nietzsche and Anglo-Saxon philosophy since Frege consider *language* to be the key to most of the secrets surrounding the nature of our knowledge of reality. Whatever may separate Heidegger, Gadamer, and Derrida on the one hand from Russell, Wittgenstein, and Davidson on the other—this is where they are all in agreement. And the same is no less true for Rorty, for Rorty never really abandons this all-pervasive twentieth-century lingualism. Meaningful interaction with reality is, according to Rorty, impossible outside language; "language goes all the way down" as he puts it, and the explanation of this slogan is that we must think of ourselves "as never encountering reality except under a chosen description."[7]

But just as Hegel gave Kantianism its most convincing and optimal form by historicizing it, so Rorty optimizes lingualism by emphasizing with Davidson the continuous interaction of language and reality. And just as Hegel believed that his philosophical strategy meant a decisive rupture with Kantianism, while, in fact, he gave it its strongest and most convincing form, so is Rorty's pragmatism not the rupture with twentieth-century linguistic transcendentalism that it pretends to be but, in fact, its ultimate vindication.

These two stories about the recent history of philosophy define the plot of my argument in this chapter and the next. According to the first story, Rorty gave the deathblow to the transcendentalist tradition; but in the second story Rorty brought transcendentalism to its highest perfection: Even the domains of Aristotelian experience, the domain of the direct interaction of language and reality, are now no less subject to "the categories of language" as Kantian phenomenal reality was subject to "the categories of the understanding." For Rorty experience and knowledge without language are just as impossible as the experience of noumenal reality was for Kant.

Our question now, obviously, must be which of these two incompatible stories we shall have to prefer. Since Cartesianism initiated transcendentalism by rejecting the Aristotelian account of experience, then set on a path that would, three centuries later, grant to language the priority that experience had for Aristotle, we may expect the relationship between language and experience to give us the key to answering that question. And my story is, therefore, essentially a story about the relationship of language and experience.

1.2 ANTI-REPRESENTATIONALISM

Central in Rorty's thought is his so-called anti-representationalism, his view that we should not conceive of knowledge as a representation or reflection of reality—that is, knowledge and language should not be seen as a kind of *mirror of nature*—as common sense invites us to do. Rorty has several strong arguments against representationalism, but his most original and convincing critique is undoubtedly the one focusing on traditional conceptions of truth as a correspondence between language (that is, a proposition) and reality. His objection to a pre-Tarskian conception of the correspondence theory of truth[8] is that these conceptions inevitably presuppose the existence of some neutral background that is shared by language and reality and in terms of which truth as correspondence can only be established. There must be such a neutral background, for on the one hand we have such elusive things as sounds, sentences, or meanings and on the other, states of affairs, material things, and so on—and how could we be sure of moving correctly from the one to the other in the absence of such a neutral background that is shared by both? Just as money is, so to speak, the neutral background in terms of which we can argue from a commodity (reality) to its value (language) and, moreover, compare the value of different commodities, hence a background that is shared by commodity and value, so the correspondence theory of truth will inevitably presuppose some kind of formal scheme that will permit us to move from language to reality and vice versa.

However, as the pragmatist William James already observed, such a *tertium quid* behind or beneath both language and reality simply does not exist; language and reality are all that we have (and need), and it follows that traditional variants of the correspondence theory are founded on the mythology of a nonexisting and redundant "*tertium quid* intermediate between the facts *per se,* on the one hand, and all knowledge of them, actual or potential, on the other."[9] No such *tertia* are given to us, and the *tertia* that we believe might perform the job we expect them to do are always mere constructions based on intuitions we have with regard to either the facts themselves or the knowledge we have about them. They are intuitions that we, by circular argument, then invoke again in order to back up our claims to truth (in the same way that in a divorce case some people would say the husband's view gives you the truth, whereas others would hold that it is the wife's story that you should listen to). There is nothing beyond either reality or knowledge, and we should therefore abandon our search of a shared neutral background behind both knowledge and reality. The epistemological tradition, on the other hand, has always set great store by these *tertia,* and in the course of time epistemologists have developed the most ingenious *schemata* in order to define their nature. Paradigmatic here is the schematism of the categories of the understanding that Kant developed in his first *Critique.* These categories are the formal schemata within which the manifold of what experience presents to the mind is systematized in such a way that we shall be able to make true statements about (phenomenal) reality; the categories of the understanding function, so to speak, as the epistemological bridge between object and subject. But Rorty expresses his agreement with Davidson when Davidson, in a famous essay much admired by Rorty, categorically rejects the notion "of a conceptual scheme, a way of viewing things, a perspective (or a transcendental constitution of consciousness, or a language or a cultural tradition)." And Rorty concludes:

So I think that Davidson is telling us, once again, that less is more: we should not ask for more detail about the correspondence relation, but rather realize that the *tertia* which have made us have sceptical doubts about whether most of our beliefs are true are just not there.[10]

Indeed, one of the first fruits that we may expect from our abandonment of the correspondence theory and the schemata supporting it is that we can now vanquish the skepticist and the relativist. All problems occasioned by skepticism and relativism that, characteristically, arose in the wake of the triumph of the Cartesian epistemologist tradition have their common origins in the kind of schemata that I just referred to. In the first place these schemata gave rise to different "ways of worldmaking" (to use Goodman's terminology), suggesting that we can no longer hope for the existence of a "scheme-neutral" reality in terms of which our differences of opinion about what reality is like can be settled. The scheme, initially a mere modest and discrete *tertium quid* between reality and knowledge, rudely elbowed its way to the foreground while pushing aside both reality and knowledge. It was precisely the *tertia,* of which so much help was expected, that loosened the ties between language, knowledge, and reality—and since then skepticism has always accompanied Western philosophy just as Nietzsche's stroller is always accompanied by his own shadow: "That shadow all things cast whenever the sunlight of knowledge falls upon them—that shadow too am I."[11]

It is with knowledge as with the stock exchange: The more certain you want to be that you will not be losing your money and the more you are in need of the systems proposed by stock-exchange gurus and technical analysts, the less chances you will have of earning any money at all. And we can only be glad that scientists have been less afraid of their own Nietzschean "shadow" than philosophers professionally are, since only their so unphilosophical courage to set about without apriorist schemes and *tertia*[12] has brought science where it presently is. Second, and no less important, the schemata also generated the distinction between, on the one hand, what is still relatively close to the scheme and where the scheme itself is therefore still sufficient for establishing truth and, on the other hand, what is relatively remote from it, where the scheme itself gradually loses its control and where its application therefore gives rise to all the uncertainties typical of application. In this way the distinction between the analytically and the synthetically true came about, while the latter would never be able to completely escape skeptical doubt. Thus arose the strange situation that still causes utter amazement in the minds of undergraduate students when they are told by their philosophy professor explaining Hume to them that we are less certain of the fact that a thing that is dropped will actually fall to the ground than of the highly abstract and esoteric assertions that we may find in the works written by logicians or epistemologists. Surely, the epistemologist's schemata are widely at odds with our commonsensical conceptions of truth.

Furthermore, as soon as we abandon the schemata of the *tertia,* we can no longer properly say "that reality makes a statement true." The transcendentalist schematism always guaranteed the possibility of the identification of a certain chunk of reality corresponding to the statement, in the way that the zipcode in our addresses corresponds to a certain part of a city or village. And of this chunk of reality one could plausibly say that "it made the statement true" if the statement in question is a true statement. But, together with the schemata of the *tertia,* we shall also have to abandon this so-called confrontation model of the relationship between language and reality.[13] Now we can no longer conceive of a direct "confrontation" between language and reality. Rorty expresses his rejection of the confrontation model in the, at first sight, strange locution that truth "does not explain," that is, that we may not attribute explanatory force to truth. This peculiar way of putting it will become less strange to us as soon as we realize that, indeed, we could say about the *tertia* that they *explain* what will be the case when a statement and a state of affairs do actually correspond to each other, for the schematism of the *tertia* does actually (pretend to) introduce us to a deeper level where, and in terms of which, claims of correspondence can be legitimated and explained. Hence, thanks to the *tertia,* "truth" has just as much explanatory force as the laws of nature that will enable us to explain certain natural phenomena. Even more so, without this explanatory force the notion of truth as correspondence would have just as little solidity as a bridge without piers.

But for Rorty—and the pragmatists—truth cannot possess this explanatory force and, what is more, he is even prepared to accept the inevitable implication that truth is a *redundant* notion; the traditional conception of truth is for Rorty much like Wittgenstein's wheel in the machine that moves but without moving anything itself.[14] Rorty's argument against the explanatory force of the notion of truth is therefore that truth does not explain why we have true beliefs, for when we attribute to a statement the honorable predicate of being true, this does not mean anything more than that, provisionally at least, we have good reasons for saying the kind of thing that is expressed by the statement in question. And that is all there is to it; and we should get rid of the desire to associate all kinds of philosophical recondite speculations with this simple practical datum. More specifically, it is nonsense to believe that the statement in question is true because it fits into some aprioristically given scheme underlying both language and reality, as is suggested by the correspondence theory. Just as Newton's mechanics could succeed only after Newton renounced philosophical speculations about gravity and was content with asking himself the more modest question of how to fit the notion of gravity within the whole of his concept and theory formation, so philosophers should refrain from asking themselves how reality makes a statement true. Speculations about how to best answer this question can only result in the generation of these redundant *tertia* and the production of a useless intellectual overhead in our reflection about the origins of our correct opinions.

The consequences of this critique of pre-Tarskian variants of the correspondence theory go quite far, and Rorty never tires of pointing them out to his readers. For example, Rorty argues that a fixation or substantialization of language and reality was an unintended side effect of the introduction of transcendental schematisms. Against the background of the *tertia,* language and reality may obtain the same apparently well-defined but deceitful clear contours that clouds may have against the background of a blue sky, whereas we know them to be highly diffuse and volatile masses of vapor. If we consistently follow Rorty's rejection of the *tertia* and all that he associated with them, there is no longer room for the notion of a reality "out there," of a reality lying opposite to us (as transcendental egos) like a massive block or whole. Moreover—and this may sound a bit more untimely in our age that is so much fascinated by the phenomenon of language—Rorty also makes the amazing claim that "there is no room for the notion of 'thought' or 'language' as capable of being mostly out of phase with the environment."[15] With the abandonment of the schematisms of traditional transcendentalist epistemology and, more specifically, of our desire to lay down all knowledge on the cross of form (or schema) and content, we will also have to abandon the idea of "language as standing to the rest of the world as form to content."[16] This is why Rorty also rejects the view, which has recently been defended by so many textualists, that language is no less a thing than the things for which texts are the linguistic substitutes.[17]

Few philosophers have gone as far in this direction of the substantialization of language as Foucault: For Foucault, language does not just possess the same ontological status as the objects of this world; Foucault also assigns to language the same causal effectiveness as the forces of nature. According to Rorty, philosophers like Foucault can thus be said to demonstrate the unappetizing affinities between nineteenth-century idealism and twentieth-century textualism. Where the idealist argued that reality presents itself to us only insofar as it fits within the structure of the human mind[18] (thus requiring us to agree with Berkeley's claim that only an idea can refute an "idea"[19]), the textualist offers us a similar argument when saying that we have no access to reality outside language (thus requiring us to agree with the claim that only texts refute texts). Although Rorty is, on the whole, not unsympathetic to the textualist and his claims and although he would, with certain reservations, even be prepared to approve of Derrida's *il n'y a pas de hors texte,* he nevertheless sees in these similarities between idealism and textualism the decisive argument that ought to discourage us from surrendering to the idealist seductions of textualism. Indeed, if we argue from an acceptance of the schematisms of transcendentalism or from the cross of form and content to an interesting difference between language and reality, then the shell of the world will inexorably close itself around idea, language, or text — and then there will no longer be anything outside idea, language, or text.

Nevertheless, one may have one's doubts about Rorty's argument here. Certainly his argument is valid against the more irresponsible variants of Derridean textualism; surely textualism here becomes a contemporary metamorphosis of nineteenth-century idealism. However, when Foucault argues that language is a thing just like the more mundane things of reality, the movement is rather the *reverse:* For Foucault, instead of pulling all of reality into the realm of thought or language, language — or at least, the kind of language that we call "texts" — is taken up into the realm of objective reality. And this seems to be in agreement with Rorty's view that we must avoid a simplistic juxtaposition of language and the world. Additional confusion is created by the ambivalence of Rorty's own point of view. On the one hand, we shall see that there is a powerful strain in his argument that forces him to side with Derrida's latter-day variant of idealism. But on the other hand, he likes to say (much like Foucault) that there are no "interesting" differences between language on the one hand and the things in reality on the other — he believes that in our investigation of either texts or physical objects (*texts* and *lumps* in his colloquial vocabulary) we should not invoke different kinds of rationality, as is done by the advocates of the thesis that there exist a number of insurmountable differences between the natural and the human sciences.[20] Language is simply just one of the many components or aspects of reality, and the language about language (which we may find in the human sciences) therefore does not differ categorically from the language used for speaking about electrons or geological formations.[21] But, obviously, one can only say such a thing if one believes that there are no "interesting" ontological boundaries that separate things from language or text—and this is again, needless to say, the view of Foucault rather than the view of Derrida.

Thus, as a critic of Foucault, Rorty seems to reject the reification of language (with an argument that invites acceptance rather than rejection), whereas, as a disciple of Derrida, he seems to embrace it (but with an antiidealist argument suggesting rejection rather than acceptance). Surely, if one should wish to "deconstruct" Rorty or to discover in Rorty's writings what Paul de Man called "the text's point of undecidability," it might not be a bad idea to concentrate on his uncertain view of the ontological status of language, and it will therefore be worthwhile to investigate further Rorty's views of the relation between language and the world and his antirepresentationalist conception of that relation.

The point of departure here should be, once again, that truth must not be thought of in terms of a pre-Tarskian correspondence theory of truth or in terms of the view, for example, defended by Dummett, that truth always presupposes knowledge of the conditions that will make a statement true.[22] Such theories of truth will always result in a disconnecting of truth as a philosophical notion (and parasitic on the *tertia*) from how the notion functions in practical, daily discourse and thus, once again, in this redundancy of the notion of truth that we were already compelled to acknowledge because of our rejection of the *tertia*. But some further comments on this redundancy are possible. Rorty correctly observes that these redundancies will appear when truth is related to one-way traffic from object to subject or vice versa. In the first case we shall have to do with the (physicalist's) "making true" of a statement by reality that we discussed a moment ago already. In the second case we will have to do with what we might define as "representationalism," that is, with the (idealist's) view that the "representations" that we have of reality in terms of true statements are our only access to it. But both the former view and representationalism are founded on the questionable and unconsciously accepted intuition that language and reality should be seen as two parallel planes, while there is, ideally, a one-to-one correspondence of either reality to language (as in the former view) or of language to reality (as in representationalism). But this intuition, to pursue for a moment the spatial metaphor of the parallel planes that was just used, in its turn, presupposes a three-dimensional space in order to flesh out the metaphor of the two parallel planes and thus, *once again,* the introduction of such a *tertium quid* outside language and reality. Hence, this intuition of the two parallel planes is, once more, like the Wittgensteinian wheel moving itself while not moving anything else.

Having arrived at this stage, the ambivalence we noted a moment ago in Rorty's position can be seen to repeat itself. On the one hand, Rorty concludes that with the abandonment of the metaphor of the two parallel planes, we also have to abandon the reification of language, since there is no identifiable domain or platform (that is, the plane of language) where language could assume the substantiality that is attributed to it by those who want to reify language. On the other hand, and against Rorty, we might argue that precisely this abandonment of the spatial metaphor will turn language into just another element of reality (as is Foucault's position) and thus into the view that language or discourse is just as much a thing or an object as an electron or a geological formation.

However, if we have (with Rorty) the courage to dump this whole spatial metaphor of the two parallel planes and hence of the one-way traffic of either physicalism or of representationalism, this will show us how we ought to think about the notion of truth (according to Rorty)—namely, exclusively as a continuous, causally determined interaction between subject and object. Thus a gas chamber with individual, chaotically moving gas molecules all being labeled as either "language" or "reality" would be a far better and more appropriate metaphor than the one of the two parallel planes. And this truly is the heart of Rorty's pragmatism. According to Rorty, all that we can meaningfully say about truth is that it is always the result of this continuous and chaotic but causally explainable interaction between language and reality, for it is in this interaction that our beliefs originate. And at all times we should resist the temptation to exchange this modest and unassuming model for the proud apriorist schemes for the relationship between subject and object that were proposed by the physicalist or the representationalist.[23] Rorty formulates his *juste milieu* policy as follows: "We understand all there is to know about the relation of beliefs to the world when we understand these causal relations to the world; our knowledge of how to apply terms such as 'about' and 'true of' is fallout from a 'naturalistic' account of linguistic behavior."[24] And, I repeat, this is the essence of his philosophical program.

Now, precisely because this is so much the essence of his argument, it is all the more interesting to observe that the Rortyan model closely resembles Aristotle's epistemology. Just as Aristotle related knowledge exclusively to the causal interaction between our senses and reality, just as Aristotle emphasized again and again the continuity between reality and our senses as affected by reality, just as Aristotle defined knowledge as a becoming the same of the subject and the object (think again of how our hands may become acquainted with the form of a vase by imitating its curves), so Rorty is opposed to all attempts that have been made since Descartes to effect some artificial epistemological or metaphysical separation between the subject and the world. Indeed, at one (but, unfortunately, only one) place in his writings Rorty states *expressis verbis* that the Aristotelian conception of the interaction between subject and object will never put us on the wrong track that the majority of Western philosophers have so assiduously followed in the wake of the tradition initiated by Descartes.[25]

Furthermore, one may well discern in Rorty's interpretation of Davidson's conception of the relation of language and reality a reprisal of Aristotle's line of thought. It is all the more to be regretted that Rorty, unlike his pragmatist preceptors (such as Dewey), never felt tempted to explore the treasures that can be found in the Aristotelian tradition. More specifically, if in Aristotle's theory *experience* is the absolutely central notion, whereas Rorty, despite his anti-representationalist critique of lingualism, still essentially is a philosopher of *language,* the similarities between his own and Aristotle's position might have suggested to him that his own pragmatism is still a way station and that it is the notion of experience that will await him at the end of the route on which he had already set so many important and such courageous steps.

1.3 RORTY'S PRAGMATISM

Within Rorty's anti-representationalism we must not conceive of language as a kind of cushion between ourselves and reality, and that is also why we should no longer strive for "an ideal language . . . as an ultrathin cushion which translates the brutal thrust of reality into statement and action as directly as possible."[26] Language is for Rorty just another instrument that is available to us in our endeavor to cope with reality—albeit that language may well be our most successful instrument for the task. But, as such, language does not essentially differ from our thumb, which, in contrast to most mammals, we can place opposite to our other fingers—a faculty that has enabled us to transform reality with our hands according to our wishes to a degree that is, for simple anatomical reasons alone, unattainable to all these other mammals.

If, then, this is the central message of Rorty's pragmatism of language, the question immediately arises of where his pragmatism differs from instrumentalism. Both Rorty and the instrumentalist will agree with the nominalist view that language or concepts are not reflections of the true nature or essence of reality but mere guides or instruments in our effort to deal successfully with reality. Nevertheless Rorty wishes to distinguish his own position from that of the instrumentalist. His argument against the instrumentalist is that the latter hierarchizes reality into several ontological layers and that the criterion for their proper place in the hierarchy is the degree to which such a layer would still plausibly permit a realist interpretation of its language and concepts. In practice, as Rorty correctly observes, instrumentalists always reserve their nominalist asceticism for the more abstract theoretical concepts and they tend to become much less consistently nominalist when having to do with things like tables or goldfish. But, as Rorty would like to ask the instrumentalist, "Why do you attach more importance to the features which goldfish have and electrons lack than to the features which goldfish have and tables lack?"[27] Obviously the instrumentalist (still) believes that certain concepts are "closer to reality" than others. Rorty discovers in this privileging of the concepts of the things of daily reality a last remnant of Platonism that the pragmatist will have to do away with in order to make his own position as strong as possible.

It is in this context that Rorty really proves to have *le courage de ses opinions*. In opposition to the instrumentalist's hierarchy he defends the counterintuitive thesis "that we will feel in touch with reality all the time";[28] that is to say, this contiguity of language and reality, discussed in the previous paragraph, can be observed "*all the time*" (and when Rorty says "all the time" here, he really means what he says). This rather categorical claim has some surprising consequences. Thus Rorty now rashly rejects all the attempts that have been made since Vico and Dilthey to draw some boundary between the natural and the human sciences. The assumption behind all these attempts was always that either the natural sciences (as the physicalist believes) or the human sciences (as Vico believed) are closer to reality than the others. Rorty even goes as far as to contend that even if we move from the sciences to the realm of ethics and politics, no theoretically interesting boundary will have been crossed. Self-evidently, this risqué claim is at odds with all our intuitions, for undoubtedly there is an indisputable kernel of truth in the Vichian principle of "verum et factum convertuntur," that is, that we have a more direct access to the world of history and culture that we have made ourselves than to the world of nature, which is not of our making. And one wonders therefore whether Rorty's claim will not have the unintended effect on his readers of a *reductio ad absurdum*.

Even more so, would one not have expected that precisely the pragmatist ought to be preeminently appreciative of such facts that, whereas physicists normally agree about the meaning of a concept, this kind of agreement would automatically announce the death of a discipline like history? Disciplines like history can thrive and progress only as long as historical concepts such as "the French Revolution" or "Romanticism" can be given different contents and remain the "essentially contested concepts" that they are meant to be. That the meaning of such concepts is not fixed is the *conditio sine qua non* of the humanities. In history and the humanities progress is possible only on the condition of the inherent ambiguity of such concepts, whereas science would be unthinkable as soon as such a conceptual ambiguity became endemic in it. And this is only the tip of an iceberg of further differences, both less and more prominent, between the natural sciences and the humanities. Once again, is not the adogmatist and supremely practical pragmatist precisely the kind of theorist whom one would expect to be least inclined to wipe away all these practical differences with such a sovereign *air de dédain?* In what way is the cause of our understanding of the natural and the human sciences furthered by mixing them together into one indiscriminate cognitive soup? One may well begin to surmise that at least in this respect Rorty's variant of pragmatism is dogmatic rather than pragmatist. And would one not have believed that the pragmatist would always be the first to regard differences in practice with the greatest attention?

But on other occasions Rorty is certainly not indifferent to the question of how, in actual practice, the instrument of language is used by us in our attempt to deal with reality. Two answers to that question given by Rorty will require our attention here. First, if what philosophers used to associate with truth cannot, according to Rorty, be predicated on statements, this does not prevent us from characterizing them as "assertible." But one condition should not be lost from sight. Ordinarily one says that a statement is assertible when it is in agreement with the relevant syntactical rules and supported by additional information concerning the application of these rules.[29] And this can be understood in two ways. In the first place, one could decide to relate these criteria of "assertibility" to the ideal situation in which a complete transparence exists about these semantic rules and of a justified true belief about the world. Here, assertibility will have a *normative* character: This ideal situation will be our *norm* when discussing our actual claims to knowledge. But assertibility can also be defined in a *constative* way in the sense of describing under what circumstances, on the basis of what kind of conviction with regard to what aspect of reality, a proposition is actually considered to be assertible by a relevant community of language users. We will not be surprised that for Rorty only "constative assertibility" deserves our attention; "normative assertibility" would inevitably bring us back to epistemological conceptions of truth. And with the help of a similar argument Rorty also rejects the standard argument against pragmatism, that is, the argument that a statement is not "true" because it "works" but that it "works" because it is "true." It will need no elucidation that this standard argument can be effective only against the pragmatist after some epistemological conception of truth has been accepted *already.* And precisely this is what the pragmatist strategy so much urges us to avoid.

And this brings me to Rorty's second answer to the question in what way language is a useful instrument for coping with reality. As we all know, we should never be satisfied with what instruments are like at a certain moment but should always try to improve them for their tasks. And, says Rorty, it is the same with language: We shall always have to improve and further adapt our language and the concepts we use in order to make them serve our goals and purposes as best as they can. Language is not a mirror of reality but a complex and differentiated whole (almost like an organism) that, in a continuous Toynbee-like movement between challenge and response, always attempts to adapt itself as well as possible to changing circumstances—just like animal species whose evolution was described by Darwin. Hence, the philosopher should look for inspiration to Darwin rather than to Descartes.[30] The vocabularies that humanity has developed in the course of its history should be seen as a continuous *Darwinian* adaptation to ever-changing circumstances rather than as a *Cartesian* quest for the Grail of Truth about this world.

1.4 RORTY'S HISTORISM

Rorty's preference of Darwin to Descartes is suggestive of the historism of his pragmatism, a historism that is so absolutely crucial for a correct understanding of his thought that it would perhaps be better to characterize his position as a "historist pragmatism" rather than as "pragmatism" *tout court.*

Already in his *Philosophy and the Mirror of Nature* Rorty expressed his sympathy of historism. He says about this book—that can indeed best be seen as a deconstruction of the *history* of Western philosophy—that "the moral of this book is . . . historicist."[31] And in the last chapter of this decisive and magisterial attack on the transcendentalism of Western philosophy, Rorty elects Gadamer as his guide and discovers in the latter's *Truth and Method* the point of departure for a new (pragmatist) variant of philosophy aiming at *Bildung,* or *edification.* And of Gadamer one can certainly say that he has taken in, more than any other philosopher, all the implications of the historist point of view. Gadamer brought historism to its logical conclusion when he radicalized the still predominantly (neo-) Kantian historism of Dilthey by historicizing the historical subject itself with the help of his notion of *Wirkungsgeschichte.* Traditional historism from Ranke to the neo-Kantians historicized everything except the historical subject itself—and when philosophers finally came close to taking this ultimate step, historism had already disappeared in the morass of the so-called "crisis of historism."

The same positive appreciation of historism, although now supported by different arguments, is also found in Rorty's later writings. He praises Heidegger for his historism (whereas Derrida is not criticized for his anti-historism[32]), and he agrees with Heidegger's view that there exists no absolute and unchangeable "structure of rationality."[33] We must therefore, as Hegel already taught us to do, historicize Reason. And within such a historist philosophical matrix, interesting philosophy is not to be found in the smart knockdown argument in favor or against a certain philosophical view; of interest to Rorty are exclusively those aspects in the work done by philosophers that become visible from the perspective of the *history* of philosophy. Hegel's owls of Minerva, and not some timeless, universalist Reason, will decide what is of (lasting) value in the philosopher's work.

Paradigmatic of such new departures in the history of philosophy is when the philosopher (or the poet, for that matter) succeeds in developing a new vocabulary, a new manner of speaking in philosophy or, more specifically, in devising a surprising *re-description*[34] of how to think about ourselves and about the world. The idea is that the history of philosophy is, above all, the history of philosophical vocabularies and of the linguistic instruments humanity has used for dealing with reality. Philosophers are the functions of the vocabularies used by them, rather than the reverse. Or, as Rorty goes on to write, "to put the point in Heidegger's way, 'language speaks man'; languages change in the course of history, and so human beings cannot escape their historicity. The most they can do is to manipulate the tensions within their own epoch in order to produce the beginnings of the next epoch."[35] The really important philosophers were those who had a talent "for speaking differently" and thus succeeded in changing, to a certain extent, our linguistic habits.[36] Philosophy will therefore have to be practiced historistically: "Our relation to the tradition must be a rehearing of what can no longer be heard, rather than a speaking of what has not yet been spoken."[37] And one would, perhaps, do no injustice to Rorty by adding that for him the task of the philosopher is, just like that of the historian, to make the "silences of history" (as Michelet called them) speak and that precisely this is a "speaking of what has not yet been spoken."

And if historism is intrinsically related to Romanticism, Rorty does not hesitate to describe his own pragmatism "as a successor movement to Romanticism."[38] Like the Romantic, the pragmatist prefers spontaneity to receptivity—and this is also why romantic historism[39] was mainly a search for what is proper and peculiar to a historical epoch and for the thought and action of those personalities who best exemplify the idiosyncrasies of that epoch.[40] Finally, when romantic historism exchanged the grandiose systems, which the Enlightenment and its later disciples liked to project onto the past, for an interest in the small detail expressing the *Lokalvernunft* (Justus Möser) or the *couleur locale* (Barante, Thierry) of a historical epoch, Rorty repeats this movement when he celebrates Dickens as the greatest chronicler of the nineteenth century because of the innumerable, apparently "unnecessary details" which he confronts his audience with.[41]

Not only is there a striking resemblance between Rorty's position and the historism of the professional historian, there are, furthermore, some no less striking resemblances between Rorty's views and those developed by some recent historical theorists. I am thinking here of the anti-scientistic narrativism that has been proposed by historical theorists such as Hayden White and Paul Ricoeur and, second, of the interest in tropology and in metaphor that is characteristic of both Rorty and contemporary historical theory since White.

Let us start with narrative. Historical theorists believe that it is the primary task of the historian to bring order into the chaos of the data that the past has left us, and they often argue that the historian paradigmatically does so by telling a *story* about the past. Whereas *theory* is the most appropriate linguistic instrument of the natural scientist, the historian most often makes use of *narrative* in order to organize the manifold of historical contingencies into a (contingent) narrative whole.[42] And Rorty similarly described his own philosophical strategy as a movement "against theory and towards narrative."[43] He admires Heidegger for his unsurpassed talent for telling new and suggestive *stories* about the history of philosophy. Moreover, I do not think we would be doing an injustice to Heidegger by saying that Rorty is even more talented than he, or even any other contemporary philosopher, in narrativizing the history of philosophy in a challenging and thought-provoking way. Rorty truly is the undisputed master among the storytellers in contemporary philosophy. The influence and the cogency of his magnificent deconstruction of the epistemological tradition and, for example, his extremely powerful chapter on how Derrida fits into the history of philosophy (in my view still the best that has ever been said about that philosopher), strikingly demonstrate his almost uncanny capacity to use narrative as an instrument for undermining traditional certainties and, in this way, to show to what extent philosophical greatness effectively depends on this capacity. Do we not find, at the basis of the effort of the twenty to thirty philosophers that have dominated Western philosophy since Plato, the talent for renarrativizing the whole history of philosophy with their own contribution as the *peroratio* of that narrative?

Finally, Rorty emphasizes that his sympathy for narrative is in complete agreement with pragmatism: When we wish to decide about the purposefulness of our action(s), narrative is ordinarily our best guide. The kind of story that we hope to be able to tell to ourselves *ex post facto*—that is, after having opted for a certain course of action and having carried it out—is the crucial criterion for deciding whether this course of action may be said to be in a meaningful relationship to the rest of our life story. To take an example suggested by Rorty himself, when in Orwell's *1984* Winston realized that he would prefer to betray Julia than undergo O'Brien's torture, his life story had lost the coherence that it had possessed up to that moment. In a certain sense, after this betrayal there is no longer an identifiable place for Winston in this world, because he now lacks an adequate and consistent (moral) vocabulary in terms of which he could tell a meaningful *story* about himself that would enable him to define such a place.

Let us turn next to metaphor. Since Hayden White's influential *Metahistory* of 1973, many historical theorists have become aware of the figurative dimension of the historian's narrative language. They considered the tropes, especially metaphor, to be the most prominent and effective organizing principles in the historical text. Strong and convincing historical narratives or interpretations are typically supported by strong and imaginative metaphors. And those also have their analogues in Rorty's writings. However, where White needed four tropes for his historical theory—metaphor, synecdoche, metonymy, and irony—Rorty is content to tell us *his* narrative of the history of philosophy in terms of just metaphor and irony. In his view, these two tropes most adequately express the philosophical mentality of pragmatism.

With regard to metaphor Rorty agrees with Davidson's short, but seminal chapter on metaphor. Rorty follows Davidson in two respects. First, in opposition to Wittgenstein, Davidson (and Rorty) strictly distinguish here between the meaning and the use of language. And, second, on the basis of this distinction Davidson (and Rorty) argue that metaphor can be understood only from the perspective of use and not from that of meaning, for—and this is Davidson's and Rorty's main point—metaphor simply has no meaning apart from what the metaphor *literally* means. And that obviously does not help us to understand a metaphor. Hence, if metaphor nevertheless—as both Davidson and Rorty readily concede—is quite essential in our use of language, it can play its prominent role only because the metaphorical use of language functions as a causal stimulus for the development of new and surprising insights. Put differently, within the whole of our use of language metaphor deliberately creates a kind of semantic impasse that forces us to do something quite distinct from how we "normally" succeed in understanding language. As Rorty summarizes Davidson's conceptions:

Tossing a metaphor into a conversation is like suddenly breaking off the conversation long enough to make a face, or pulling a photograph out of your pocket and displaying it, or pointing at a feature of the surroundings, or slapping your interlocutor's face, or kissing him. Tossing a metaphor into a text is like using italics, or illustrations, or odd punctuations or formats.[44]

Metaphor is, for Davidson and Rorty, what one might call a "catastrophic" use of language; metaphor functions like a *deus ex machina;* it is like an intervention into language from *above* or from *outside* effecting a small rupture in the continuity of the normal use of language that may, at least for a certain part of language, announce a new dispensation. One may surmise that for Davidson metaphor mainly has a nuisance value. His acceptance of Tarski's truth theory left him without any room for metaphor in his philosophy of language, since metaphor would completely ruin all the Tarskian recursive definitions of the truth of statements. Davidson's catastrophe theory of metaphor should therefore be seen above all as an attempt to reduce metaphor to innocuousness and to make the world safe for Tarski.[45] Put provocatively, Davidson's chapter is not an attempt to explain metaphor but to explain it away. But this is different for Rorty. Rorty transforms Davidson's necessity into a virtue: If metaphor is such a linguistic *deus ex machina,* Rorty, much like Vico and Nietzsche before him, tends to see in it the *primum movens* of all linguistic change and evolution, and he thus grants to metaphor the honor of being "the growing point of language."[46]

Irony is the other important figure of speech in Rorty's tropological repertory. Unfortunately we will not find in Rorty's writings a systematic account of how he conceives of the relationship between metaphor and irony—and this is all the more regrettable since metaphor and irony often seem to perform much the same job in Rorty's account of the historical evolution of vocabularies. Both seem to be required for the adaptation of language to reality that is one of the major elements in Rorty's pragmatist (and Darwinist) philosophy of language. However, the following statement can nevertheless be made about the relationship between metaphor and irony in Rorty's philosophy. The Rortyan ironist is, first, always skeptical with regard to the vocabularies in use and, next, well aware of the fact that no vocabulary can be justified in terms of its own terminology; finally, the ironist is convinced that we could never say of any vocabulary that it is "closer to the truth" than an alternative vocabulary.[47]

Against this background the relationship between metaphor and irony can be defined as follows: Where metaphor should be associated primarily with the *constitution* of a new vocabulary or with changes in an existing one (one may recall here Rorty's metaphor of metaphor as "the growing point of language"), irony stimulates the *skeptical* and *adogmatic* attitude that we should carefully cultivate with regard to the language we happen to be using at a certain stage. Irony wipes out what the metaphor had written down, so to speak. And both together weave the texture of Penelope that the history of philosophy, and of the vocabularies adopted in its course, essentially is. Hence, one could describe Rorty's historism as a "deconstructivism" in the proper sense of that word: Contrary to the "construction" of vocabularies by metaphor, we have the "destruction" of vocabularies by irony, and the continuous movement between the two is, in the end, the intrigue of the history of philosophy.

But one comment should be added. Where ordinarily—and, especially, in historism—metaphor is the more powerful of the two tropes, in Rorty's writings irony clearly has the upper hand. Although Rorty praises metaphor for its creativity, he seems little inclined to investigate the sources of this creativity—and it is certainly true that Davidson's theory of metaphor leaves desperately little room for such an investigation, since it presents metaphor as a kind of linguistic miracle for which a satisfactory explanation is just as impossible as it would be to give to beings, living in an exclusively two-dimensional world, explanations of third-dimension intrusions into their world. On the other hand, it will need no clarification that irony sums up in itself the whole arsenal of Rorty's anti-foundationalist arguments: self-evidently, anti-foundationalism is intrinsically ironic.

In conclusion, in Rorty's case we encounter an unusual relationship between metaphor and irony, since irony, and together with it the element of "destruction," so strongly dominates the constructive efforts of metaphor—more about this in section 1.5. And, indeed, when Rorty presents the history of philosophy as a continuous dispute between constructive Kantian philosophers and parasitical anti-Kantian philosophers aiming at dislocation, the latter appear to have his special interest and sympathy.

Nevertheless, as Rorty would be the first to admit, we shall always need *both* the metaphorical and the ironical philosophers: "No constructors, no deconstructors. No norms, no perversions, Derrida (like Heidegger) would have no writing to do unless there were a 'metaphysics of presence' to overcome. . . . Everybody needs everybody else."[48]

It would be hard to think of a more striking illustration of Rorty's historism than this meditation on the nature of the history of philosophy. It is only from the perspective of this history of philosophy that we may arrive at such an assessment of the meaning and significance of both the metaphorical and the ironic philosopher's efforts. In this way, Rorty's affinities with the aims of the historian are obvious, and the historical perspective is always his compass for his orientation on the products of Western culture and of Western philosophy. And since the parallels with contemporary historical theory that were expounded on previously were not deliberately intended by Rorty, they are all the more striking. Even more so, one might argue that Rorty advocates a more daring and extreme variant of historism than the one that is propounded by most contemporary Anglo-Saxon historical theorists. Whereas the latter ordinarily wish to restrict their historist, narrativist, and tropological claims to the domain of the humanities only, Rorty radically universalizes these claims and wishes to uphold their validity for the domains of philosophy and the sciences as well. In this way the good old days of the *unity of science* seem, *mirabile dictu,* to have come back again. However, this time the imperialism of the unity of science does not have its *patria* in the natural sciences, for this time it is history from where the whole domain of science is colonized.

1.5 RORTY'S ABNEGATION OF HISTORISM

Historism is one of the most caustic intellectual acids that has ever been prepared by Western civilization. The historism of Nietzsche's *The Genealogy of Morals* and of Foucault's later writings offers striking illustrations. Religion, metaphysics, tradition, truth—all of them proved to be soluble in the acid of historism. Historism is even a stronger acid than logic, for logic can also be historicized with dramatic consequences for the pretensions of logic to offer timeless truths; and if one were to attempt the reverse and to rationalize history (in the way Hegel did in his *Phenomenology*), history will prove, once again, to be the stronger partner of the two.

Bearing this in mind, we must be struck once again by Rorty's apparent affinity with the historist picture of the world. Think of Rorty's view that intellectual history and the history of science could be seen as an endless exchange of old for new vocabularies. Obviously this raises the question of what this perennial and kaleidoscopic change of vocabularies (which was discussed in the preceding paragraph) is actually good for. And the no less obvious answer is (or, rather, has always been) that new vocabularies will bring us closer to what the world actually is like than the old ones succeeded in doing. This is how philosophers since the Enlightenment down to the (logical) positivists and their like of our own time liked to look at the matter. And this is also the view that was questioned by historism. Think, for example, of Ranke's well-known "each epoch is immediate to God," which suggests that "progress" is not the perspective from which we should look at historical evolution. Whether one ascribed to each historical epoch its own perfection or whether one rejected the idea of transhistorical standards (of truth, morality, or whatever), the implication always was that the notion of progress would inevitably violate the Truth about the past. Admittedly, historists, and Ranke first among them, rarely went as far as to actually practice such a completely agnostic attitude toward progress. Nineteenth-century historism most often cherished a resolutely "comic" view of the course of history, to use Hayden White's appropriate terminology, and it took pleasure in describing how the dissonances of the past always welded together in the harmonious chords of a world that was both later and better. In practice, historism remained much closer to the Hegelian conception of history than it believed itself.

Nevertheless, it remains true that historism had this unnerving capacity to make each conception of progress look foolish and parochial that I referred to a moment ago. Historism as a theory of history was forced to recognize as much in the so-called crisis of historism of the end of the nineteenth and the beginning of the twentieth centuries. And, as we know since Kuhn, even science, the domain of human endeavor where progress seemed to be wholly indubitable, became a victim of historist skepticism. So this is what I take the meaning and real challenge of historism to be.

Now, this historist skepticism can certainly be discerned in Rorty's writings and in how he deals with the question of what purpose is served by this endless single file of vocabularies. It cannot fail to strike us, in this context, that Rorty refrains from subscribing to the (logical) positivist view that later vocabularies are cognitively superior to older ones. This is not why he takes pleasure in this endless proliferation of vocabularies that history presents us with and what he expects from it. Instead, he suggests that the historical contingency of languages and vocabularies should serve a *political* purpose. That is to say, it serves the interests of a liberal and ironic openness and, in this manner, involves an abnegation of all dogmatic fixations. And, indeed, no reasonable person will deny that this is a good thing.

It is true, though, that on other occasions Rorty is also prepared to say about some vocabularies that they are "better" instruments for coping with reality than some others—for example, that Galilei's vocabulary is such a better instrument than the Aristotelian vocabulary preceding it.[49] But statements like these make sense only on the condition that Rorty explains to us why and under what circumstances one vocabulary can truly be said to be "better" than another. And this urgent question is stubbornly answered by Rorty with a persistent silence—undoubtedly because he fears that the attempt to answer it might result in a resuscitation of epistemological concerns. Here we can observe the thought-provoking intuition that if one rejects epistemology, historism is hard to avoid. And if we recall Rorty's eulogy of Gadamer with which *Philosophy and the Mirror of Nature* ends, it is clear that Rorty does welcome rather than fear all the historist implications of the main argument in that monumental and seminal work.

But perhaps we have been moving a bit too fast here. I would like to get back now for a moment to Ranke's "comic" conception, which I had presented as being basically at odds with the nature of historism. But this is only part of the whole truth about historism, as we shall recognize as soon as we realize ourselves that historism was both a theory about the past *and* a theory about the writing of history. As a theory about the past historism rejected the "progressivism" of the Enlightenment and of speculative philosophies of history such as Hegel's. This is historism as we ordinarily see it and as we encountered it earlier. But we get a different picture if we look at historism as a theory of historical writing. As a theory of historical writing, historism taught the historian how to bring order into the chaos and diversity of the past. This could be achieved, as Ranke and Humboldt argued, in terms of the so-called historical idea, a kind of entelechy in terms of which the historian should see the past itself. I deliberately formulated the role of the historical idea in the historist view of the nature and tasks of historical writing in terms of such a "seeing as," for this will make us aware of the affinity that historist thinking has always had with metaphor—

which is, as we all know, the trope inviting us "to see one thing in terms of another." This may go a long way to help us understand why Ranke ended up, despite his historist conception of the past itself, with this "comic" view of the past that I mentioned a moment ago. Ranke—and many of the historist historians of the nineteenth century—tended to project on the past itself the order they had brought about in their historical narrative with the help of metaphor. They believed that their narratives, and the order reigning there, mirrored what the past itself had been like. This is also what such a far more self-conscious and skeptical historist as Burckhardt found so objectionable in the historical writings of German historists such as Mommsen, and why Burckhardt himself preferably presented the past as a *spectacle coupé* always resisting the historian's (metaphorical) cognitive effort. This is what *he* believed to mirror the past "as it had actually been." This is also why Burckhardt's conception of history (and of his own time) was so much more pessimist than that of Ranke, who quite unproblematically read the so very impressive cognitive success of his own (metaphorical) historical writing into the past itself. In sum, we should not forget that we should always conceive of historism in terms of *two* tropes, that of metaphor no less than that of irony. Irony is the trope that is to be associated with historism's capacity to dissolve the past in individual episodes or epochs and therefore the trope that is responsible for the relativist and skepticist tendencies of historism. But there is also a constructive side to historism, where the historian's capacity of discerning unity in chaos and diversity is, or at least can be transfigured into, an attitude we may have toward life, the social world, and politics in general. This constructive side has its origin and support in metaphor—and that is no less part and parcel of historism than irony.

If, then, we consider Rorty's writings, there can be no doubt that irony is stronger than metaphor in his brand of historism (as had already been suggested in section 1.4); his outlook is closer to Burckhardt than to Ranke, so to speak. It would probably be more correct to say that both metaphor and irony have their job to perform in his thought but that he happens to subscribe to a theory of metaphor that robs it of its capacity to assert its rights against those of irony. Even more so, in Rorty's writings metaphor seems rather to be an unwilling accomplice of irony rather than playing the role of always and again constructing what is always and again destroyed by irony. Illustrative is that Rorty adopts Davidson's theory of metaphor (as we saw in section 1.4) and not the one advocated by theorists such as Max Black, Mary Hesse, or Gadamer. These theorists differ from Davidson in that they propose arguments to demonstrate the constructive role that metaphor can play in concept formation and, more generally, in our effort to achieve a cognitive grasp of the world as investigated both by scientists and in the humanities. Metaphorical "seeing as" is recognized by them to be one of our main and most powerful instruments for problem solving, both at the local and at the most general level. However, it would be an utterly hopeless task to account for the constructive character of metaphor (and for the roots it has in history) on the basis of Davidson's *deus ex machina* view of metaphor. So if we agree with much that Rorty has said about vocabularies and, especially, with his suggestion that metaphor can define the nature of their relationship and how they evolve out of each other in the course of the history of (a) science, then he adopted a theory of metaphor that prevented him from cashing in on the promises of this so valuable suggestion.

This is all the more to be regretted since on other occasions (when Davidson had not yet cast his spell over Rorty's argument) he seems to come much closer to a realization of these promises. In section 1.4 we observed that Rorty proposed a narrative criterion for how to decide between our practical options. And from there it would have been only a small step to apply this narrative criterion to the problem of how to decide which out of several competing vocabularies might reasonably be considered the best and most satisfactory one. More concretely, the criterion would thus be that we should prefer, in the case of a conflict of vocabularies, the vocabulary that will enable us to tell the most convincing narrative about the history of a discipline up to and including this last phase of the conflict between the warring vocabularies. Similar views have already been put forward by Alasdair MacIntyre and by Arthur Danto.[50] But although Rorty does indeed take some steps in this same direction, he does not go beyond an occasional suggestion. He thus writes about the protagonist of a new vocabulary:

His new vocabulary makes possible, for the first time, a formulation of its own purpose. It is a tool for doing something which could not have been envisaged prior to the development of a particular set of descriptions, those which itself helps to provide.[51]

In agreement with the ideas put forward by MacIntyre and Danto, the suggestion is clearly that we must, above all, expect a new vocabulary to be ca-

pable of optimally locating and defining itself narratively in regard to competing vocabularies. But, unfortunately, Rorty leaves it there and refrains
from elaborating on the intuition in greater detail.

Let us now make a temporary halt and take stock of our findings up
to now. To begin with, it cannot be doubted that a pronounced historism
has been the immediate result of Rorty's attack on epistemology and transcendentalism. As was to be expected, for is history not the obvious au-
thority to turn to as soon as we have become aware of the limitations of
trancendental Reason? Have history and historism not always been the
main source of trouble for all the aspirations of transcendental Reason?
Furthermore, we found that the notion of vocabulary is the scene on which
Rorty's historism primarily enacts itself: It is not so much religion, morals,
manners, or scientific debate but rather vocabularies that he requires us to
look at in order to appreciate the historist implications of his thought.
Next, it seemed worthwhile to distinguish between two components
and/or variants of historism: put schematically, the comic Rankean variant
on the one hand, and the darker and more pessimist ironical variant we can
associate with Burckhardt. And here an interesting asymmetry announces
itself. Although Rorty seems to be much closer to the Burckhardtian variant from a theoretical perspective than to that of Ranke because of the predominance of irony over metaphor in the relevant part of his writings, the
tonality of his work is, on the whole, conspicuously free from the pessimism of Burckhardt. And we shall certainly not find in it the kind of despair that had been so characteristic of the so-called crisis of historism of
the end of the nineteenth century.

Or, to add a more contemporary dimension to our present discussion, let us assume that postmodernism is in many respects the late twentieth century's way of dealing with the challenges of historism. As certainly
is a reasonable assumption:[52] Think, for example, of the striking parallelism between the historist's condemnation of the Enlightenment's conception of the past on the one hand, and the postmodernist rejection of
meta-narratives, on the other. But although Rorty has often, and sometimes with his own explicit approval, been associated with the cause of
postmodernism, we will not find in his writings much that might remind
us of how postmodernism did historism all over again. There is in his work
nothing of the shallow optimism of those postmodernists who so self-
complacently withdrew on the fully self-sufficient island of the present while

celebrating Ronald Reagan's "Don't worry, be happy." Nor does he seem to have any sympathy for the leaden seriousness of a postmodernist such as Lyotard, who attempts to crush the historist challenges of incommensurability implicit in his notion of the *différend* under the immense weight of our total moral condemnation of the Holocaust. Illustrative here is that Rorty prefers Derrida by far to Lyotard and that he unashamedly declares that he likes Derrida because Derrida is "funny" and has a sense of humor.

And this is not merely a matter of temperament (all the more so since the term *merely* naively underestimates the importance of mentality), for we may observe the same delicate light-spiritedness that Rorty attributed to Derrida in Rorty's own essay on ethnocentrism, an intellectual little gem in which he directly addresses the issue of moral relativism as provoked by historism. Historist relativism (Rorty does not use the term *historism* himself) does, in the end, require us to see Western liberal democracy as being somehow

"on a par" with that of the Vandals and the Ik. . . . If we continue this line of thought too long we become what are sometimes called "wet" liberals. We begin to lose any capacity for moral indignation, any capacity to feel contempt. Our sense of selfhood dissolves. We can no longer feel pride in being bourgeois liberals, in being part of a great tradition, a citizen of no mean culture. We have become so open-minded that our brains have fallen out.[53]

This is the moral predicament that historism faces us with—a predicament that was succinctly summed up by Rorty with the following words: "We would rather die than be ethnocentric, but ethnocentrism is precisely the conviction that one would rather die than share certain beliefs."[54] In order to overcome the impasses of ethnocentrism (or of historism), Rorty advocates an anti-anti-ethnocentrism, avoiding both the arrogance of ethnocentrism itself and the self-defeating relativism of anti-ethnocentrism. Anti-anti-ethnocentrism hopes to improve our present moral and political world not by means of the theoretical speculations of "specialists in universality as theologians and philosophers" but thanks to the effort of "the specialists in particularity—historians, novelists, ethnographers and muckraking journalists."[55]

Or, as he goes on to say a little later, anti-anti-ethnocentrism suggests that we "*should simply drop the distinction between rational judgment and cultural bias*" (my italics).[56] Now, let us be fully clear about this: In the context of the present discussion this truly is a most momentous declaration. Needless to say, summarized into one single sentence, this is precisely the whole issue with which historism had so fatefully and dramatically confronted Western civilization since the end of the eighteenth century! And by "simply dropping" the issue—as Rorty proposes we do—we do not so much solve the problem occasioned by historism but declare it—with Rorty—of no real relevance and significance. Thinking this over and taking this into consideration, we may now begin to surmise that Rorty's historism, despite his so clearly historist account of vocabularies and despite his insistence on irony, never went that deep and that it has always remained much on the surface of his thought.

1.6 DAVIDSON AS THE SOURCE
OF RORTY'S LATER ANTI-HISTORISM

In this section I shall deal with the question of what strands in Rorty's thought prevented historism from becoming solidly rooted in it. And we shall discover that Donald Davidson's philosophy of language—which leaves no room at all for historism, as will become clear—will provide us with a large part of the answer to that question. In order to deal with this question, we should focus, above all, on Davidson's notion of "radical interpretation"—and, indeed, the very notion of radical interpretation cannot fail to provoke in us associations with hermeneutics, with the issue of how historians may come (or not, of course) to an understanding of the actions and the speech of the people of the past. From this perspective we may expect not to move to a wholly different domain of philosophical speculation when moving from the problems occasioned by historism to those of radical interpretation.

So what does Davidson have in mind with radical interpretation?[57] Davidson emphasizes himself that his argument is a continuation of the famous second chapter of *Word and Object* where Quine deals with radical translation. So we should begin by saying a few words on Quine and on radical translation. Both Quine and Davidson require us to think (in Quine's words) of the "task of the linguist who, unaided by an interpreter, is out to penetrate and translate a language hitherto unknown. All the objective data he has to go on are the forces that he sees impinging on the native's surfaces and the observable behavior, vocal and otherwise, of the native."[58] However, when Quine and Davidson discuss the thought experiment of radical translation or interpretation, this is not out of sympathy for the predicament of the anthropologist or the linguist wishing to master an unknown and alien language.[59] The thought experiment is mainly intended, instead, to illustrate some basic points of their philosophy of language. In the case of Quine this has mainly to do with the implications of his linguistic holism, that is, of his anti-reductionist claim that "our statements about the external world face the tribunal of sense experience not individually but only as a corporate body."[60] In the case of a conflict between theory and observation we will not only have to take into account the theory in question but also all kinds of auxiliary hypotheses and theories used for the testing of it. The problem may have its origin in one of these theories just as well as in the theory in question. This introduces an indeterminacy in the relationship between (scientific) languages and the world that is explored in all its ramifications in Quine's writings and that can be considered to have been one of its main sources of inspiration.

To be more precise, this indeterminacy may actually take one of three different forms (which is not meant to imply that each of these indeterminacies should entail the other two): (1) the underdetermination of theory by evidence, (2) the inscrutability of reference, or (3) the indeterminacy of translation. Theories are underdetermined by evidence since different theories can account for the same evidence. Think of a theory T_1 that satisfactorily accounts for a certain body of evidence but fails to do so for new evidence, so that a new theory T_2 is required in order to do justice to both old and new evidence. Then both T_1 and T_2 can be said to fit the *old* evidence—*quod erat demonstrandum*. Next, Quine's thesis of the inscrutability of reference originates in his ontological relativity, that is, in the claim that our scientific theories fix "what there is." And then reference will share in the vicissitudes of theory. As Quine sums it up himself: "We now have a more explicit standard whereby to decide what ontology a given theory or form of discourse is committed to: a theory is committed to those and only those entities to which the bound variables of the theory must be capable of referring in order that the affirmations made in the theory be true."[61] Last, there is the indeterminacy of translation. The idea here is that if one has absolutely nothing to go on when translating an alien language into one's own, except to how both the speakers of the alien language and ourselves react to stimuli from the outside world (and this is what is at stake in so-called radical translation), we can never be sure about the accuracy of

translation, for these stimuli are compatible with logically different translations. For example, you see a rabbit scurrying by and then you hear the
native utter the sentence "Gavagai." We may infer from this that the terms
rabbit and *Gavagai* are synonymous. However, as Quine goes on to say,
"Who knows but that the objects to which this term applies are not rabbits
after all, but mere stages, or brief temporal segments, of rabbits? In either
event the stimulus situations that prompt assent to 'Gavagai' would be the
same as for 'Rabbit.' Or perhaps the objects to which 'gavagai' applies are
all and sundry undetached parts of rabbits; again the stimulus meaning
would register no difference." [62]

Now, even though it was emphatically not Quine's intention to develop a methodology or philosophy of linguistics or of the humanities, it
need not surprise us that Quine's philosophy of language was warmly welcomed by philosophers of history and the humanities. His holism, his anti-
reductionism, and his claims about the indeterminacy of the relationship
between language and the world undoubtedly have an elective affinity with
both the theory and practice of both the writing of history and large parts
of the humanities. And when the linguistic turn overtook most of the theoretical reflection on the nature of history and the humanities, the more responsible of these theorists often relied on indeterminacy claims to support
their case. More specifically, if historism traditionally emphasized the ineffable uniqueness of historical epochs (think of Ranke's famous "each epoch
is immediate to God") and the almost insurmountable barriers the historian would have to overcome in order to get access to the past, nobody
could fail to be struck by how close this did actually come to Quine's picture of how (different) languages relate to the world. Raymond Weiss could
therefore write some twenty years ago: "The seeds of historicism are present in his [that is, Quine's] theory of knowledge—in spite of the positivist
vestiges still there. He is, as it were, a half-way house between positivism
and historicism, thus exemplifying an ever growing tendency in philosophy to move towards historicism." [63]

Obviously, as long as Rorty remains close to Quine's philosophy of
language, his historism is not really jeopardized. Even more so, the historism resulting from his rejection of transcendentalism might have found
in Quine's thought a powerful ally, and in this way Rorty might have succeeded in obtaining for historism an intellectual status and respectability
that it so sadly lacks in the Anglo-Saxon world to the present day. How-

ever, in his later writings and after his discovery of Davidson, Rorty tends to exchange Quine for Davidson—and this meant the decisive end of all the historist promises of his writings of the early 1980s. Davidson's philosophy of language leaves no room at all for historism. I shall demonstrate this with a brief discussion of Davidson's variant of radical translation and of his influential attack on conceptual schemes.

When dealing with Davidson's theory of radical translation, it should be pointed out, to begin with, that Davidson speaks about radical *interpretation* rather than of radical *translation*. This puts a different complexion on the issue. As Davidson writes, in the case of radical translation we need three languages: (1) the object language (that is, the language to be translated), (2) the subject language (into which the object language is to be translated), and (3) a meta-language (of the theory stating what expressions in the subject language translate those in the object language). But we can conceive of a situation in which the meta-language and the subject language are identical; a situation that is characterized by Davidson as follows:

If the subject language happens to be identical with the language of the theory, then someone who understands the theory can no doubt use the translation manual to interpret alien utterances; but this is because he brings to bear two things and that the theory does not state: the fact that the subject language is his own, and his knowledge of how to interp(r)et the utterances in his own language."[64]

This is the context that Davidson has in mind with radical interpretation and that enables him to effectively deal with it. He now demands us to consider Tarski's recursive definitions of truth, that is, definitions given by T-sentences of the type

s is true (in the object language) if and only if p.

We can then say of such definitions that they provide us with the solution to radical interpretation in that s can be taken as a statement in the object language, whereas p gives us the merger of the subject language and of the theory of interpretation of sentences in the subject language. The problem of radical interpretation has thus been solved in terms of Tarski's theory of truth; or, as Davidson put it himself, "assuming translation, Tarski was able to define truth; the present idea is to take truth as basic and to extract and account of translation and of interpretation."[65]

So much then for theory, whereas, as far as the more practical dimension of Davidson's radical interpretation is concerned, we must realize, above all, that truth is decisive in his argument. Truth gives Davidson what the stimuli working on our senses could not achieve for Quine in his radical translation. Put differently, truth is the common background that is shared by both the speakers of the alien language and ourselves; and, obviously, if the speakers of the alien language did not primarily use language for making true statements and if the relationship between what they say and what the world is like is completely random (also for themselves), the effort of the radical translator or interpreter would be wholly hopeless. As Davidson comments, "What justifies the procedure is the fact that disagreement and agreement alike are intelligible only against a background of massive agreement. Applied to language, this principle reads: the more sentences we conspire to accept or to reject (whether or not through a medium of interpretation), the better we understand the rest, whether or not we agree about them." The principle in question is what he refers to a moment later as "the charity principle," that is, the principle that we shall assume the speakers of the alien language to be, on the whole, speakers of the truth. Or, as the principle was defined by Davidson's biographer Ramberg:

Certainly the field linguist will be exposed to error and deception but against a body of strongly supported T-sentences [that is, the sentences of a meta-language stating under what conditions the statements in its object language are true] she would probably recognize most of them. But should she be tempted to regard utterances of the subjects of interpretation as systematically false or random, she would merely be depriving her own theory of empirical bite. It is impossible to treat native speakers as anything but on the whole speakers of the truth.[66]

Thus, the possibility of a radical incommensurability of languages (or vocabularies) that still haunted Quine's philosophy of language could not possibly occur according to Davidson—a view reiterated by Rorty's slightly hyperbolic assertion that there is "a massive amount of true belief" that is shared by a Neanderthal man and the speaker of some highly sophisticated, physicalist language and which will prove to be a sufficient condition for the possibility of radical interpretation.[67]

I shall refrain from commenting on the philosophical merits of Davidson's conception of radical interpretation and restrict myself to the issue of how a historist may be expected to look at it. In this context we had best begin with recalling a well-known passage from Hume's "An enquiry concerning human understanding" (1748):

It is universally acknowledged that there is a great uniformity among the actions of men, in all nations and ages, and that human nature still remains the same, in its principles and operations. . . . Mankind are so much the same, in all times and places, that history informs us of nothing new or strange in this particular. Its chief use is only to discover the constant and universal principles of human nature, by showing men in all varieties of circumstances and situations, and furnishing us with materials from which we may form our observations and become acquainted with the regular springs of human action and behaviour.[68]

This passage is often quoted by historians attempting to explain where the historist's sense of the past differed from that of the Enlightenment. The difference is, to put it schematically, that for Hume "mankind are so much the same in all times and places," whereas the historist conceives of the past as a continuous kaleidoscopic change of forms. And I deliberately speak of a "change of forms" instead of mere "change." The difference between the prehistorist and the historist conception of the past is not that the prehistorist, say, David Hume, would be willing to deny the existence of change, whereas only the historist is open to the recognition of change when and where it occurs. One need only read Hume's *History of England* (or Gibbon's *Decline and Fall of the Roman Empire,* for that matter) to see that the issue is not as simple as this. Put differently, the difference between the prehistorist and the historist does not concern empirical issues, nor is it the case that the prehistorist would be unable or would deny to see change where it is seen by the historist; it is not a difference about *truth,* but about how to *conceptualize* the past and about what "forms" we should appeal to in order to account for the past. This is what urged historists such as Ranke and Humboldt to develop their notion of the historical idea, giving us the form of a historical epoch, nation, or institution, which we would nowadays describe as a representation of the past.

These historical ideas or representations of the past do not involve— or at least not necessarily so—disagreements about facts, about what has or has not been the case in the past. Representations of the past consist of true statements about the past; and the difference between individual representations of the past can therefore not be defined in terms of truth and falsity *but only in terms of the difference in sets of true statements about the past constituting these individual representations of the past.* Truth is taken for granted in the writing of history and is relegated to a mere preliminary phase in all that historical writing and discussion is about. In historical writing and in historical discussion the issue is not truth or falsity but what are the relevant truths. And what are the relevant truths or not can *sui generis* not be defined in terms of truth, since this concerns a fact about truth and hence is not something that can properly be analyzed in terms of truth itself.

It follows that Davidson's conception of radical interpretation does not qualify as a suitable model for the writing of history and that it will not enable us to penetrate the secrets of historical understanding.[69] If a historical representation is interpreted in terms of another one, truth is not at stake; and an appeal to Tarski's T-sentences to ensure interpretation would be useless. In the first place, what is expressed at the level of facts (that is, of truth) is rarely challenged in historical debate. Or, to be more precise, in historical representation (which is the historian's main cognitive instrument) the crucial question is what facts are to be cited in a historical representation and *not* the truth or falsity of statements describing facts. In his *The Social Interpretation of the French Revolution* Alfred Cobban nowhere questioned the facts that had been established by his Marxist opponents (such as Labrousse or Soboul);[70] stranger still, he made use of the *same* socioeconomic facts that had been dug up from the archives by his opponents in order to develop a powerful critique of their representation of the French Revolution. The point I wish to make here is that—as far as truth is concerned—there is in history a looseness in the relationship between fact and representation that is quite unlike the situation in the sciences. The writing of history simply does not have its equivalent of the theory-ladenness of empirical fact stating that empirical truth is always formulated in terms of theory. Admittedly, in some specialized fields of historical writing, such as Cliometrics, where econometrics is used to describe and explain the past, sometimes, but not always, a practice of historical writing may develop that resembles more or less what we know from the sciences. In such circumstances it may indeed happen that the level of the (historical) text—its quasi-theoretical dimension, so to speak—determines the nature of descriptions on the level of individual historical fact. And it may also be true that "theories," the kind of truisms that we know from daily life or value judgements, and so on will often do something similar in the more pedestrian kind of historical writing. But the scope of such "theories," truisms, and so on will be fairly restricted and will remain bound to the direct surroundings of the statement of individual fact. The semantic command of these "theories," truisms, and so on will never reach all the way to the highest level, that is, to that of the text *as a whole*. That level will always be beyond its scope. The level of fact does reach to this highest level in that the set of *all* the facts mentioned in a historical text defines the nature of the historical representation proposed in this text; but the power of the highest level—that is, that of the text *as a representation* of the past—does not reach as far down as to determine description. This is what theory can do but representation cannot. In sum, most often historical facts are like the air we breath: They are both the same to all of us and accessible to all of us, as historians. In most areas of historical research the description of historical facts owes little, if anything, to the representation(s) in which they are used. And then Davidsonian radical interpretation has nothing to go on.

When speaking a moment ago about this looseness in the relationship between fact and historical representation, I explicitly tied this looseness to the perspective of truth. However, from another perspective—viz. that of meaning—there exists no looseness at all in this relationship, and from that perspective historical writing presents us with all the precision that is needed for rational discussion. As I have argued elsewhere, the nature of a historical representation of the past or of a "narrative substance" (which is the technical term I introduced for referring to historical representations) is completely and unambiguously individuated by the descriptive statements constituting these representations or narrative substances.[71] It is therefore certainly not my aim to contribute to the all too familiar postmodernist claims about the complete indeterminacy in the relationship between historical language and what this language is about. On the contrary. But if one wishes to achieve precision in the issue of how in historical writing language and the world are related, models borrowed from the sciences are useless. If *this* is what the postmodernists have in mind, they are undoubtedly right and then I shall not disagree with them. The historian does not speak the language of science or of theory, and historical representations are not the historian's somewhat helpless and inarticulate equivalents of what theory is for the scientist. *The crucial difference is that theory determines the description of facts, whereas facts (viz. what is described by the statements contained by a historical representation or "narrative substance") determine historical representation.* In this way one could speak of "the fact-ladenness of historical representation." And in this sense the relationship between fact and representation can be said to be the exact reverse of that between fact and theory. *But that relationship is no less precise and determinate than is the case in the sciences.* From a logical point of view we can establish that the nature of a historical representation is determined by the historical facts that are mentioned in it. Precision in history comes "from below," so to speak, whereas it comes "from above" in the sciences. However, we can recognize it in historical writing only if we are prepared to accept the notion of historical representation as an indispensable logical entity and are willing to take stock of where it differs from the logical entities that we have learned to use from the philosophy of science and language. Without this logical entity historical writing can never be seen as anything more than either a hopeless cognitive muddle or as a forever helpless, inept, and ridiculous attempt to imitate the sciences.

At this stage a further fact about the writing of history needs to be taken into account that will add ammunition to our arsenal of arguments against a scientistic interpretation of historical writing (and therefore also against the utility of Davidson's radical interpretation as a model for the writing of history). As everybody will know from the practice of historical writing, there is always a large amount of overlap in the set of facts about the past that are mentioned in different representations of some part of the past. Even the most disparate representations of the French Revolution will not fail to mention July 14, 1789, the conflict between the Jacobins and the Girondists, the fall of the monarchy in August 1792, the Reign of Terror and Virtue, and, finally, Thermidor. Obviously, the nature of individual historical representations will therefore be determined by where they differ rather than by their shared overlap. The implication is that historical representations are at least partially and even predominantly defined by other representations, that is, by where they differ from these other representations. It follows that the dimension of meaning can never be eliminated from a satisfactory account of the nature of historical writing. In science, in Quine's radical translation, and in Davidson's radical interpretation, it certainly makes sense to try to eliminate all mentalistic language and to try to reduce meaning to truth. However, in the writing of history the effort is doomed to failure, and meaning will survive all attempts to completely reduce it to input from the world.

At this stage the following objection is to be expected. It may now be pointed out that there is an asymmetry between Davidson's argument and my own since I have been discussing historical representation, whereas

Davidson was speaking about the use of language in science. We should not forget that a large part of Davidson's philosophy of language originated from debates in the philosophy of science and, especially, from the debate on incommensurability that was occasioned by Thomas Kuhn's book on scientific revolutions. Put differently, Davidson was talking about what actually took place in the history of science (if seen, needless to say, from the sublime vantage point of the philosopher of language), whereas my discussion focuses on what can be said about historical representations. On the other hand, a case could also be made for the view that Davidsonian radical interpretation moves us firmly from the level of *res gestae* to that of the *historia rerum gestarum* (that is, that of representation). And there certainly is a message in the fact that in arguments like those of Quine, Davidson, and so many other philosophers of science, it is almost impossible to disentangle the level of the *res gestae* from that of the *historia rerum gestarum;* when reading these philosophers of science, you can never be sure whether they are talking about the relevant facts in *the past itself* (*res gestae*) or about a *history* of science (*historia rerum gestarum*). They tend to conflate both levels completely in their writings. And this message undoubtedly is that these philosophers of science and of language do, unwittingly, subscribe to a very naive and realist conception of the writing of history—that is, a conception according to which we can establish (with Ranke) "what actually happened in the past" and to which our accounts of the past will present us with exact copies of "what had actually happened in the past."

Another striking illustration of the realist temptation in contemporary philosophy of language is to be found in so-called causalist theories of reference, as have been proposed by Keith Donnellan, Saul Kripke, and Hilary Putnam. The challenge of incommensurability was met by these theorists by distinguishing between reference and what is attributed to the referent (at a later stage). For example, once upon a time in the past the reference of a term, say, *gold,* was fixed, and although physicists managed to say a great deal of sometime quite different things about gold since then, all these things are perfectly "commensurable" with each other since they are all pronouncements about one and the same thing, that is, gold. So the suggestion is that there is the stage of fixing the reference and then the rest is *simple comme bonjour,* for this is "merely" a matter of history and, on the basis of the tacitly realist view of history, history is not expected to be able to complicate the picture further. But historians and historical theorists know that history has the unnerving capacity to knock concepts loose from the anchors they have in their reference and to transform them into what Gallie dubbed "essentially contested concepts."[72] It may well be that the phenomenon is less prominent with the kind of concepts used in the sciences than if we have to do with concepts like "democracy," "art," or "justice" (Gallie's examples), and this may explain why philosophers of science and of language are such easy prey to the temptation of historical realism. But even in science, history will not fail to disturb the realist idylls of the advocates of causalist theories of reference.[73]

But let us grant the objection I mentioned a moment ago and see to what extent it affects my argument against radical translation or interpretation as a model for history. It will be my contention that the essence of my argument can be transposed without fatal adaptations from the level of historical representation to that of the past itself. The crucial datum is that the difference between past and present is, just like the difference between individual representations of some part of the past, not a difference to be defined in terms of the difference between truth and falsity but—once again—in terms of the difference between the sets of those true statements that we deem to be of relevance for positioning ourselves in our world and those we believe we can safely ignore or forget. This is what is at stake when we move, in agreement with the arrow of time, through the vicissitudes of our individual and collective life. Each year, each month, each week, each day adds a massive stock of new truths to the set of truths we rely on in our effort to cope with the challenges of individual and collective human existence, whereas each year, each month, and so on, a no less massive stock of truths is condemned to probably permanent oblivion. You read the newspapers not in order to find out what was wrong (or right) in what the newspapers stated yesterday, but in order to learn about what truths you should be aware of in order to understand the world you are living in.

And then it may sometimes happen in both our individual and our collective life that at a certain stage a critical stage arrives, that is, a stage in which we decide that a fundamentally new arrangement in this stock of truths that are of real relevance to us is needed. Think of an event such as the French Revolution. No fact about the ancien régime was denied by the Revolution. The Revolution was not like a new theory discomfirming a previous one; this is not how successive historical periods are related to each other, if only because historical evolution does not take place in order to disprove something. Historical evolution is not like an experiment in science we arrange in order to prove or disprove something; it has the characteristics of fate, it enacts itself even when we ourselves, like the French revolutionaries, believe to give form to the passive and malleable material out of which history is made. It is greater than ourselves and each attempt to reduce it to the model of science and of the scientific experiment will blind us to its nature. What the Revolution *did* effect, however, was a decisive rearrangement in the set of truths needed for a proper comprehension of the social and political world one was living in. The Revolution created a host of new historical truths, truths so dramatic and so ineluctable that no sensible person could suffice anymore with even the highest truths that were available under the ancien régime. So whole continents of truths now disappeared from the map of relevant knowledge of the world and were exchanged for the profoundly disquieting truths that the Revolution had produced. Or, to put it differently, the generation that lived through the Revolution moved from one representation of the world to another one; the change from one historical representation to another one that ordinarily is only enacted on the quiet and academic scene of historical writing now took place in real life. Normally historical writing "imitates" history (as Aristotle would have put it); here, however, history imitated historical writing, albeit in a strictly formal sense. And when thus moving from one representation to another one, one had to pass, if only for a moment, through the terrible void between individual representations and to experience the nakedness of momentarily having no self-representation at all. This, then, is the void in which sublime historical experience may announce itself, as will be demonstrated in Chapter 8.

But when History itself moved, during the French Revolution, from one representation to another, issues of truth and falsity are as immaterial to the transition as they are in the case of the opposition between two (or more) historical representations of one and the same part of the past. This is where historical change, as taking place in the past itself and as different from how it is conceptualized by historians, is at odds not only with Davidson's conceptions of radical interpretation, as expounded on earlier, but also with his no less influential attack on conceptual schemes.

In the present context two major aspects of Davidson's essay "On the very idea of a conceptual scheme" will demand our attention. In the first place, Davidson carefully distinguishes between total and partial incommensurability:

> In what follows I consider two kinds of case that might be expected to arise: complete, and partial failure of translatability. There would be complete failure if no significant range of sentences in one language [or conceptual scheme] could be translated into another; there would be partial failure if some range can be translated and some range could not (I shall neglect possible asymmetries). My strategy will be to argue that we cannot make sense of total failure, and then to examine more briefly cases of partial failure.[74]

It then becomes clear that partial untranslatability (or incommensurability) is fairly innocuous and that the real (relativist) challenge is occasioned by total untranslatability. So let's concentrate on total untranslatability. This brings us to the second and decisive stage in Davidson's argument. After having established that the issue of incommensurability and of the untranslatability of different languages (as spoken, for example, by the adherents of different Kuhnian paradigms) is often formulated in terms of the gap allegedly separating different "conceptual schemes," Davidson formulates his attack on the incommensurability thesis in terms of an attack "on the very idea of a conceptual scheme." Quoting Whorf and Kuhn, Davidson points out that claims about incommensurability and untranslatability are always based on the argument that there should be a neutral and common basis that is organized differently by different languages or conceptual schemes:

> The failure of intranslatability is a necessary condition for difference of conceptual schemes; the common relation to experience or to the evidence is what is supposed to help us make sense of the claim that it is languages or schemes that are under consideration when translation fails. It is essential to this idea that there be something neutral and common that lies outside all schemes. This common something cannot, of course, be the subject matter of contrasting languages, or translation would be possible.[75]

But, as Davidson implies rather than explicitly states, the idea of this "something neutral and common that lies outside all schemes" is just as useless and unwarranted a notion as the Kantian *Ding an sich* and for much the same reasons: It does no real work in the philosopher's account of how we acquire knowledge of the world, for we have never to do with a world (or experience, sense date, and so on) in complete isolation from the language we use for speaking about it. "Language goes all the way down," as Rorty would put it. The notion is therefore a wholly superfluous and redundant ornament in any account of knowledge, and one we had better do without. Belief in this "something neutral lying outside all schemes" is thus rejected by Davidson as the "third" and "perhaps the last dogma of empiricism."[76]

Now, both elements in Davidson's argument have neither meaning nor application in the writing of history and historical representation—and in both cases for much the same reasons. In the first place, it is hard to see how to distinguish between partial and total untranslatability in historical representation. The problem is that historical representation is always *both* at one and the same time. At the level of the facts mentioned in historical representations the gap separating them can properly be said to be merely "partial," for there always will be, as we have seen, a considerable amount of overlap, and it can be said with certainty what facts will have to be added to and deleted from each of the two in order to transform them into each other. However, representations are, *as representations and as distinct from being mere sets of statements describing facts,* not translatable in each other since each operation on them (such as the addition or elimination of one of the facts mentioned in them) will irrevocably transform them into a *different* representation. They are, so to speak, completely frozen with their forever inalienable identity and therefore are resistant to any attempt at translation. So this is the level where historical representations are always and totally untranslatable.

Next, there is Davidson's attack on "the third dogma of empiricism." And then we can observe, again, a telling asymmetry between Davidson's argument and the state of affairs in historical representation. In historical representation we do have this "something" that is "neutral and common that lies outside all schemes." This is what we can properly claim to be the case for the level of historical facts that may be mentioned in some historical representation and not in others. In the writing of history there is a large stock of historical facts about the past that had been established on the basis of historical research and from which individual historians can make their own selection when composing their own historical representation. Admittedly, this is a schematic way of putting it. Most historians will do their own historical research in the archives before composing their representations of the past, and in this way they may sometimes substantially enlarge our stock of facts about the past (so this commonage of historical facts is by no means fixed forever and unalterable; nevertheless, whatever set of facts it may contain, these facts can be used within the most disparate historical representations and, in this sense, they are "neutral and common"). We shall also have to take care of tense in the formulation of facts and of how temporal perspective may determine what can and what cannot be said, as was pointed out long ago by Arthur Danto in his argument about so-called narrative sentences (perhaps we should render them all tense-less).[77] But all this does not affect the logical point I am making here. Moreover, we can repeat here the same operation of a moment ago and move from what has been said just now about historical representations to the self-representations of individual historical epochs. The result is (in both cases) that the third dogma of empiricism gives a correct description of the factual basis of historical representation and that empiricism is the right philosophical account of this factual basis in the writing of history. Perhaps this goes a long way to explain why both historians themselves and historical theorists so often feel a natural affinity with empiricism, although I hasten to add that an empiricist account of all the writing of history—that is, including the dimension of representation—would surely be wrong.[78] The explanation is that at that level an asymmetry arises between the factual basis of representation and representation since we cannot equate the represented with this factual basis. Historians rely on facts, on evidence in their representations of the past but not in order to speak about these facts but about the represented past.

I come to a final consideration. Davidson expresses his agreement with Quine's rejection of the analytic/synthetic distinction, that is, of the conviction that questions of truth (what is synthetically true) can be distinguished from questions of meaning (what is analytically true). Now, if contemporary philosophy of language ever achieved results that should rejoice the heart of the historian and the historical theorist, this surely is the most obvious candidate. If we imagine a list on which all disciplines are arranged in agreement with their affinity with theoretical abstraction, the list beginning with theoretical physics and ending with the writing of history, it cannot be doubted that the intuitive plausibility of the rejection of the analytic/synthetic distinction increases as one moves down on this list of disciplines. The more theoretical a discipline is, the easier it seems to be to discern issues of truth from those of meaning, and the less a priori plausibility the rejection of the distinction will have. Think of mathematics: In science you cannot do a thing *without* mathematics, and in history you cannot do a thing *with* it. So does it not make sense to say that in science there is the synthetic part of the input of facts about the world on the one hand, and the analytical part when the a priori truths of mathematics come in on the other? Can we not say about the distinction between experiment (what is synthetically true) and mathematics (what is analytically true) that it is in agreement with our intuitions about the practice of disciplines such as theoretical physics? We all know that it often is wholly impossible to clearly discern between questions of truth and meaning in the case of historical writing. Think, for example, of a classic like Barrington Moore's *Social Origins of Dictatorship and Democracy:*[79] It will be practically impossible to say whether we admire this book because of how the notion of social revolution is defined or because of its exposition of the historical facts about the relevant periods in the past.[80] So it need not surprise us that Quine's attack on the analytic/synthetic distinction was warmly applauded in the humanities and received in these quarters as a benefaction from the gods of philosophy as welcome as it was unexpected. What had hitherto seemed to be the sure sign of the sad backwardness of these disciplines, now suddenly and unexpectedly became most respectable.

Put differently, the dissolution of the distinction was like a gift from God precisely in those disciplines where the notion of representation—that is, of what in these disciplines has always been the equivalent of the conceptual schemes as discussed here—is no less central than that of theory in the sciences. The notion of historical representation can reconcile the idea of conceptual schemes with why we should reject, with Quine and Davidson, the analytic/synthetic distinction. With regard to the analytic/synthetic distinction, we can truly say of a historical representation that meaning and truth could not possibly be tied together more intimately than is the case here, for the exchange of one truth in a representation for another will also change the meaning of the representation (or, if one wishes to be precise, of its proper name). With regard to the idea of conceptual schemes, a historical representation is a conceptual scheme in that it indicates what *language* we should use in order to understand some part of the past, namely, a language predicated on the kind of sentences that had been used for constructing this representation (or close variants of this kind of sentence). But, as such, this language is saturated with empirical truth and wholly free from the apriorism so often associated with it by philosophers of science and language for whom the language of mathematics was the natural thing to think of in the context of a discussion of conceptual schemes.

I would therefore agree with Nicholas Rescher's reservations about Davidson's rejection of conceptual schemes:

The idea that a conceptual scheme is altogether a priori and free from substantive commitments is thus clearly mistaken. But the conception of a conceptual scheme as such is patently strong enough to survive the abandonment of such mistaken conceptions. The fact that conceptual schemes can be misconceived is no reason for invalidating the very idea at issue.[81]

All the more so, since right at the beginning of his essay Rescher had emphasized what we would lose by abandoning conceptual schemes altogether. A discipline like descriptive sociology could not possibly do without conceptual schemes in order to "contrast e.g. kinship systems or other such mechanisms for the categorization and explanation of human affairs." And in a field like intellectual history they are no less indispensable for contrasting "different perspectives of understanding of different *Weltanschauungen.*" The suggestion clearly is that large parts of the social sciences and the humanities and, above all, the writing of history would immediately lose their point and purpose with the rejection of conceptual schemes. They are part and parcel of each well-considered effort to get a grasp of what people have been saying and doing in both the present and the past. As Rescher puts it, "There is, after all, something a bit eccentric about rejecting the idea of alternative conceptual schemes—something that smacks of the unrealism of one who closes one's mind toward what are people actually saying and doing."[82] Indeed, the writing of history would be impossible if one were to reject, with Davidson, the notion of conceptual schemes, for these are the historian's most obvious and important objects of investigation.

This section began with an exposition of the role of the notion of vocabulary in Rorty's writings. Needless to say, this notion—and certainly Rorty's use of it—smacks of the Kuhnian concept of paradigm, of how we can speak about the world in terms of different languages, of how these different languages may suggests that their users "live in different worlds" and can be said to have different *Weltanschauungen.* No less obviously, all this has a strong reminiscence of historist patterns of argument. And, as we would have expected, not only is there a pronounced historist basis in

Rorty's writings of the 1980s and early 1990s, but also on several occasions he explicitly expressed his agreement with the historist *Weltanschauung*. The best illustration is, undoubtedly, the final chapter of *Philosophy and the Mirror of Nature* in which Rorty embraces the radical historism of Gadamer's hermeneutics. Two ways were open to Rorty at this stage in the development of his thought—and this brings us to what from the perspective of the present study is the decisive turn in his intellectual career. He could decide to introduce historism—and all that goes with it—into Anglo-Saxon philosophy of language and science, or he could use all the intellectual sophistication of Anglo-Saxon philosophy of language for giving to historism a form that might, perhaps, convince his anti-historist Anglo-Saxon colleagues.

It is far from easy, and perhaps not even possible, to indicate the nature of the route that Rorty, in the end, followed when confronted with this dilemma. Moreover, the route that he ultimately chose is not without its paradoxes. One such paradox is how he negotiated his way between Quine and Davidson. There has always been in Rorty's writings an unmistakable tendency toward relativist or skepticist patterns of argument; perhaps he would not like this way of characterizing his position since we can speak only of relativism and skepticism after having availed ourselves of the epistemologist's discourse. But let's not insist on this. It is of more importance to note that Rorty's sympathies are clearly more with Davidson than with Quine, despite the fact Rorty's relativism is indisputably more congenial with the latter than with the former. Of course, it certainly is not my intention to put Quine on the scene as a relativist: His robust common sense and confidence in scientific rationality always preserved him from relativist exaggerations. Nevertheless, Quine's three indeterminacies—of the relationship between fact and theory, of reference, and of translation— are undeniably closer to Rorty's relativism than to Davidson's uncompromising and lifelong campaign against all variants of relativism and skepticism in the name of truth.

Be this as it may, when Rorty took Davidson rather than Quine as his guide, this meant the end of the historism so prominently present in his earlier work.[83] Let me add immediately what I wish and do not wish to imply with this. It is not my intention to pronounce on the wisdom of Rorty's choice. He may be right with this. My only point is that one cannot subscribe to Davidson's position on issues such as that of radical translation or interpretation, the relationship between meaning and truth or that of conceptual schemes *and still remain a historist.* This is what I have wanted to make clear in the substance of this section. And, again, if Rorty would then disdainfully riposte, "So much worse then for historism," I have no answer to him. There is, admittedly, something ineradicably "decisionist" about such all-encompassing positions as historism (*Weltanschauungen,* we had rather say with Mannheim [84]) in the sense that adherence or rejection of them is a matter of experience, character, or mentality rather than of argument.

Anyway, when thinking over all that has been said in this section, the historist will probably feel tempted to paraphrase the Marquis de Custine's remark on the Russians by saying that Rorty's oeuvre is an illustration of the general rule that however much an American scholar may have read Hegel, Nietzsche, Heidegger, Gadamer, or Foucault, when you scratch the surface, sooner or later an Enlightened and anti-historist Jeffersonian liberal will appear who is largely insensitive to the drama and the tragedy that is so much the essence of the past.[85] In Rorty's case it was Davidson's philosophy of language and, above all, Davidson's radical interpretation which drove out the historist tendencies in his earlier work. Jonathan Bennett once said that Rorty's position with regard to "radical interpretation" inevitably condemns him to "an incurious parochialism."[86] This is undoubtedly unfair to Rorty since he has gone further than any of his Anglo-Saxon colleagues in exposing the parochialism of contemporary philosophy of language. On the other hand, it is true that Rorty never really crossed the critical demarcation line between the anti-historism of the Anglo-Saxon countries and the historism of those of the European continent. Rorty may have often fought the battle with his Anglo-Saxon colleagues under the banner of history; but if push comes to shove he lives no less in a fundamentally ahistorical and eternal present than any other analytical philosopher. Historism and a sensitivity of the full weight of history have, in fact, always remained an affair of the European continent that never quite succeeded in conquering the Anglo-Saxon mind.[87] The explanation lies perhaps in the less violent and traumatic past of the Anglo-Saxon countries— a past that does not have its 1494 (and the disasters following it in sixteenth-century Italy), its wars of religion, its Thirty Years War, its 1789, its Napoleon, its Hitler, and so on.

Now that the United States and Europe are growing more and more apart, this may provide us with food for thought. There is no room for self-complacency on either side of the Atlantic, I believe. It may be that historism will prove, in the end, to have been or to express the reminiscence of Europe's deeply troubled and unhappy past and that it will therefore fade away with the memory of the horrors of the first part of the last century. As Shakespeare makes Prospero say in *The Tempest:*

> The charm dissolves apace,
> And as the morning steals upon the night,
> Melting the darkness, so their rising senses
> Begin to chase away the ignorant fumes that mantle
> Their clearer reason.

This passage gave Handel the inspiration for one of the most beautiful and most elegiac melodies in all of his oeuvre.[88] It may be that a new dawn has come for the Europeans in which they can afford to become "Americans." Conversely, it may be that the terrible weight of its responsibilities for this world's future will kindle in the American mind an increased susceptibility to the no less terrible weight of the past, for it is only against the background of history that our responsibilities may acquire their proper contours.

I.7 CONCLUSION

Twentieth-century philosophy has predominantly been a philosophy of language. Language became in our century the intellectual field on which all the movements were initiated and repeated that we know from the history of philosophy. Linguistic transcendentalism from Frege to Dummett saw in language the best and most sophisticated instrument for explaining the possibility of knowledge of the world. And under the influence of the later Wittgenstein, Kuhn, and the protagonists of the *linguistic turn* (such as Rorty in his first influential publication[89]), this linguistic transcendentalism was liberated from its scientist fetters and it invaded the domains of literature, art, history, and so on, in short, the whole of contemporary reflection on culture. However, (French) postmodernists like Foucault or Baudrillard opted, in the wake of Heidegger, for a different path. They reified language; being a *representation* of reality, language should be seen as a *substitute* for *represented reality* and being such a substitute it can be accorded only the same ontological status as represented reality itself: Language is a *thing*.

Rorty rejects both these strategies. Following Davidson he rejects the postmodernist reification of language: Language is neither a *thing* nor a *medium* between us and the world; he even shuns all speaking about "language," as if this word referred to some entity to which certain properties can be attributed. If one recalls Ryle's argument against "the ghost in the machine," one knows what one should do with the notion of "language," that latter-day variant of the notion of the Cartesian *res cogitans*. And in his own magisterial "deconstruction" of the epistemological tradition in Western philosophy since Descartes and Kant, Rorty tripped up all those who attempted to present language as our last and final *transcendentale*.

The paradox, however, is the following. However much Rorty robbed language of all the prestige and all the privileges that were granted to it in this century, he nevertheless remains, no less than his opponents, a philosopher of language. He continues to speak the same philosophical idiom as the philosophers of language whose activities he so ruthlessly condemned to irrelevance, and he refuses to develop a new philosophical "vocabulary"—if I am permitted to use his own vocabulary here. Rorty is not deterred by statements such as "human beings are simply incarnated vocabularies,"[90] and he praises Derrida because Derrida "does *not* contrast the way language works with the way 'the phenomenal world' works."[91] Even the most extreme linguistic transcendentalist would not know how he could improve on statements like these. Hence, just as Gibbon (according to his own slightly apocryphal account) decided to write the history of Rome when seated on the ruins of the Capitol, so Rorty wrote his own philosophy of language when seated on the remainders of a philosophy of language that he had so effectively destroyed himself. But after having emptied philosophy of language of all content, Rorty remains paradoxically fascinated by the empty shell that now stands in front of him. He must strangely remind us of Moses, who was not allowed to enter the land that he himself had promised to the people of Israel.

I deeply admire Rorty's work; I believe that few contemporary philosophers surpass him in depth, daring, and originality. In my view no contemporary philosophical oeuvre can give us a better idea of where philosophy presently is and where we should go from here. But even though Rorty succeeded in satisfying his own standards for philosophical greatness by giving us, with notions like anti-foundationalism, anti-representationalism, or the *tertia comparationis,* a new philosophical vocabulary, there is something strangely disappointing about his intervention in contemporary philosophy. Since this is a book on the philosophy of history, I may be forgiven when trying to find in history an appropriate metaphor: When Lamartine, after the stormy days of May 1848 had lost much of his former revolutionary élan, he was derided by the Parisian bourgeoisie as *un incendiaire, qui s'est fait pompier.* And Rorty likewise confronts us with the spectacle of an arsonist who turned into a firefighter, for aestheticism, aesthetic experience, a return to Aristotelian conceptions of experience, and the possibility of a direct and immediate contact with reality (more specifically, the past or the text) are so much the obvious revolutionary consequences following from his pragmatist destruction of the régime of transcendentalism and its *tertia,* that one can only be amazed by how he succeeded in avoiding them.

From the point of view of historical theory Rorty's reluctance to seriously consider the implications of his revolutionary activities is especially to be regretted, although not in the sense that a new kind of historical writing might take its point of departure in his conceptions; as I suggested a moment ago, they might add a new dimension to the history of mentalities by drawing our attention to the history of our experience of nature and reality. However, true revolutions can never be provoked, not even by revolutionary books, such as Rorty's books undoubtedly are. Revolutions just happen—or they don't. But what Rorty's writings can and even ought to effect in us is a new way of looking at the practice of history and of reading in general. Historians should learn to trust their most private and most intimate feelings on those rare occasions when what Huizinga called "the grace of historical experience" is given to them. They should realize that the best, the most sophisticated, and the most finely tuned instrument that they have at their disposal for understanding the past is themselves and their own experience insofar as this experience is not yet infected by the disciplinary historiographical epidemics that having infected the majority of their colleagues. This should not be taken to suggest a return to the hermeneuticist recommendation to historians to use their own life experiences for understanding the past and the actions of historical agents; quite the contrary, the experience of the past is not the experience of where it smugly fits a particular historian's own memories, expectations, and practical certainties but precisely where it defies all our intuitions about what the world is like. Only here we may encounter the past itself in its uncompromising and radical strangeness, that is, in its "sublimity," as this term will be understood later in this book. Only here do we discover a past, and a text, that can challenge all our categories for making sense of the world and that can make the past into the alien and wonderful world that it fundamentally is.

FROM LANGUAGE TO EXPERIENCE

Initially, the concept of experience will be left undetermined: only the presentation can concretize it.[1]

2.1 INTRODUCTION

In Chapter 1 we saw how Rorty's flirt with historism began with his discovery of Gadamer and ended with his discovery of Davidson. Language was the scene on which this short love affair was enacted. It was Gadamer's Heidegger-inspired conception of language and Quine's holism with regard to the language of science with which Rorty's fascination for historism began. And it was the anti-historism of Davidson's philosophy of language with which it ended a mere few years later.

In this chapter our focus will shift from language to experience. And such a shift is in agreement with the nature of historism. Historism was born from a preoccupation with differences between how we experience our world, on the one hand, and how people in the past experienced theirs, on the other. Think of the notion of *Lokalvernunft* (expressing how people of a specific time and place saw and experienced their world) of the proto-historist Justus Möser (1720–1794), think of Herder's "we cannot cut the ties with human feeling when we write history: its most sublime interest. Its value resides in this tie with human experience" (my translation).[2] And all of the historist program as it developed in the course of the nineteenth century was based on the assumption that each historical epoch is to be demarcated from others in terms of differences in how the world is experienced—even if it is true that historists rarely strove for a description of this experience of the world in all its fullness. From this perspective there certainly is more continuity between historism and contemporary historical writing than is often admitted. Historians nowadays wish to convey to their readers an inkling of "what is was like" or of "what is felt like" to be a thirteenth-century inhabitant of Montaillou (Le Roy Ladurie) or a nineteenth-century bourgeois (Gay)—and these are, in the end, typically historist questions. For historism, history is, essentially, the history of the *expérience vécue,* and experience is therefore the notion that is absolutely central in the historist conception of the aims and purposes of historical writing.

It seems quite likely, then, that the notion of experience will prove to be useful if we wish to get a clearer grasp of Rorty's abnegation of historism. This is why I begin this chapter with a brief analysis of Rorty's reponse to Thomas Nagel's much-discussed essay "What It Is Like to Be a Bat?" This essay focuses on the question of whether we can have any idea of "what it is like to be a bat." When we move around in our own daily world, the visual information our eyes give us is decisive for our orientation in the world, whereas bats, in order to find their way around in their world, have to rely on the radarlike sensors of theirs. And then the question arises—as Nagel insists—whether we can have any idea of what it is like to be a bat, given the fact that we must *experience* the world so completely differently from them because of these differences in sense organs. Although Nagel and Rorty were probably not aware of this themselves, their debate is, in fact, a reprisal of the venerable old debate about historism. A debate, moreover, in which all that is at stake with historism announces itself with an unusual force and clarity. These bats and how they experience their world offer, of course, a most dramatic variant of what may erect historist barriers between ourselves and our ancestors of a remote or more recent past. So, if one were to doubt, with Rorty, the existence of such "quasi-historist barriers" in the case of bats and of how they experience their world, there is, obviously, no room at all anymore for historism in how we relate to our collective past. What differentiates the different generations in the history of mankind from each other is a mere trifle in comparison with what differentiates our *expérience vécue* from that of bats. In sum, if there is no room for "bat historism," then there is certainly not room for historism in the ordinary sense of that term.

Although in this chapter the emphasis shifts from language to experience, language nevertheless has not yet wholly lost its hold of my argument. In this chapter language, viz. the texts that the past have left us, still is the only rendezvous between past and present. This chapter does not deal with the history of politics, the history of the nation; it does not deal with art, nor with the history of mentalities, and so on. The *text* and how we experience the *text* that the past has left us—this will be our exclusive concern here. More specifically, the leitmotif in this chapter is the question to what extent the authors to be discussed here—authors such as Rorty, Gadamer, and Derrida—are ready to leave room for the historist experience of the text. And, next, what useful intuitions about the experience of the text can be found in accounts about how texts were read and interpreted in the Middle Ages and in the sixteenth and seventeenth centuries.

2.2 RORTY AND NAGEL

In a famous and much discussed essay Nagel asks himself the question of "what it is like to be a bat."[3] One might argue that in this essay the problem of historism is formulated in a most dramatic way. All the questions that the historist (unlike Hume or Davidson) always likes to ask about the accessibility to the historians of how people in the past experienced their world present themselves most starkly when we ask ourselves, "What is it like to be a bat?" The bridge we have to cross in order to be able to answer the question "What was it like to be a peasant in Montaillou?" will certainly be an infinitely simpler and less pretentious construction than the one that will bring us to the experience of what it is like to be a bat. So all the problems that historism pretended to deal with will fully make themselves felt with the problem that Nagel put on the philosopher's agenda. And all the problems of historism can be said to culminate in a question such as "What is it like to be a bat?"

The crucial step in Nagel's chapter is his argument that the question of what it is like to be a bat is intimately related to the question of how organisms having consciousness *experience* their world: "The fact that an organism has conscious experience *at all* means basically, that there is something to be like that organism."[4] And Nagel goes on as follows: If we accept as true that a bat has consciousness—which seems to be a reasonable assumption—then the question of what it is like to be a bat presents us with the question of what it is like to have the perceptive faculties that the bat experiences its world with and that are, as we all know, so much different from ours. Nevertheless Nagel believes that we might, in the end, be able to get an idea of this, but then he adds the disheartening comment that, even if we were to succeed here, what we would have answered is the question what it would be *for us* to be like a bat. "But that is not the question," as Nagel reminds us. "I want to know what it is like for a *bat* to be like a bat."[5] The problem could be solved if we were to possess a neutral psychophysicalist language in terms of which subjective experiences and states of consciousness could objectively be described. Such a language could be the *tertium quid* enabling us to couple the experiences of bats to those of human beings.

Because of his critique of such *tertia*, we would expect Rorty to reject the possibility of such a language, although in a different context he appears to be more amenable to the idea. But Nagel categorically rejects such a possibility. His strong argument to that effect is that we can never be certain which mental states (subjective states of consciousness or experience) would correspond to that which is described in terms of the psychophysicalist language. There is not a reality that is neutral to both languages and in terms of which we could objectively compare what both languages refer to (in order to find out what matches with what). Thus, the idea of this psychophysicalist language will not be of any assistance to us in our question of what it is like to be a bat.[6] And we may derive from this argument the important conclusion that the question of what it is like to be a bat can be answered only—if it can *ever* be answered—if we succeed, in one way or another, in retaining the essentially subjective and perspectivist character of all experience and perception. It is *this*, and only this, that makes the experience of being a bat into the experience of being a bat. And because the *sub*jective nature of experience can be preserved only by assuming the point of view in question, each move into the direction of greater *ob*jectivity (as suggested by the point of viewlessness of psychophysicalist language) can only further remove us from an understanding of what it is like to be a bat, instead of bringing us closer to it.

Nevertheless, Nagel would not wish to imply that it would be a priori impossible to retain, in one way or other, the subjectivism of how the bat experiences its reality. At the end of his essay Nagel hazards some speculations about an "objective phenomenology" of experience that is not based on empathy or imagination. And about such a phenomenology, whose purpose would be "to describe, at least in part, the subjective character of experience in a form comprehensible to beings incapable of having those experiences,"[7] we could properly say that it must develop *concepts* that will enable us to do so. Put differently—and this is the crucial conclusion here—within the intended phenomenology, experience will necessarily precede language (and concept) and our point of departure will lie in a preverbal, nonlinguistic experience.

In a way this brings me to the essence of this chapter. Rorty's reaction to Nagel's argument will reveal to us the most crucial nonarticulated assumption of his philosophical position.[8] He disapprovingly comments that Nagel maneuvered himself in the same inexpedient position as Kant with his transcendental conditions of the possibility of knowledge. And insofar as Nagel's argument connects the subjectivism and the perspectivist character of "what it is like" to be a bat to a specific way of experiencing reality, the comparison with Kant undoubtedly makes sense. There certainly exists a close relationship between the notion of the (metaphorical) point of view on the one hand and transcendentalism on the other.[9]

But this is different with Rorty's accusation that Nagel is the prisoner of an "image," namely, the image of reality that is dictated by language. It is difficult to say what aspect of Nagel's argument could be Rorty's target here. More important, the accusation is, in fact, quite paradoxical. In this "age of linguistic transcendentalism" Nagel makes the unheard-of, unprecedented, and profoundly anti-Kantian move of allowing experience to precede language: "Reflection on what it is to be a bat seems to lead us, therefore, to the conclusion that there are facts that do not consist in the truth of propositions expressible in human language."[10] Rorty categorically rejects this possibility of prelinguistic experience (with the sole exception of pain as being prelinguistic[11]); and his conclusion is therefore that Nagel asked himself a meaningless question, since it leads to this absurdity of prelinguistic experience and thus to a profoundly mistaken view of the relationship between language and reality. And that means, in the end, that if Rorty is not prepared to go along with Nagel's, so to speak, "bat historism," he can have no sympathy for the indeed far more subtle and questionable variants of historism that demarcate the Herders from the Humes. If Rorty is right in asserting that the problem raised by Nagel is a nonproblem, it will be impossible for him to perceive the problems raised by traditional historism with even the strongest philosophical microscope.

I shall not enter into here a discussion of Nagel's and Rorty's disagreement—and I shall even be the first to concede that Nagel's argument has remained deplorably sketchy—but I now wish to return, instead, to the question that I asked at the beginning of my discussion of Rorty in the previous chapter. As you will recall, this concerned the question of whether we should tell about Rorty the story of the revolutionary who radically and uncompromisingly broke with all the more and less recent variants of the epistemological enterprise, or whether we should prefer, instead, the story that presents him as the most subtle *exponent* of this tradition. If we wish to answer that question, we shall have to concentrate on the relationship between language and experience—so much will, by now, be clear from the foregoing. For Rorty—after all has been said and done—language will remain "the measure of all things" in the literal sense of that phrase. "Language goes all the way down," as Rorty puts it himself in his reaction to Nagel—and one may add that his (and Davidson's) interaction model will indeed leave no room for the possibility of an experience of the world that is not predicated on language: Language and the world are as closely tied together here as the two sides of a sheet of paper, and there is just as little room for the autonomy (and the priority) of experience as there is between the front and the back of that sheet.

Even more so, one might argue that never has a philosophical position been defended that is more inimical to experience than Rorty's pragmatist interaction model. The more language and reality are integrated—and surely the interaction model is the *ne plus ultra* of this strategy—the more experience will be squeezed out of existence by it. It is against this background that Rorty's accusation that Nagel inadvertently invites a return to Cartesian and Kantian epistemology is both so surprising and so revealing. If there is one thing that we can be absolutely sure about with regard to the place of Descartes and Kant in the history of philosophy—and no one has made us more aware of the fact than Rorty himself!—it is that, in reaction to the Aristotelian conception of the sources of our experience and knowledge, they enclosed the transcendental subject of experience and knowledge within the narrow confines of a *forum internum*—a *forum internum* from which a contact with reality that is *not* mediated by either Reason, the Idea, the categories of the understanding, history, language, paradigm, or whatever you have, became forever impossible and inconceivable. Not Rorty's position but Nagel's thesis of the possibility of a preverbal and a prelinguistic experience of reality is therefore truly and fundamentally anti-Kantian and anti-epistemological. It is Rorty's interaction model, diligently guaranteeing the permanent omnipresence of language, that we should see as one of the so many latter-day variants of Kantianism or perhaps even as the ultimate perfection and culmination of Kantianism. If Rorty writes "Language goes all the way down," Kant could have said for exactly analogous reasons "The categories of the understanding go all the way down." The only exception that the Kantian system permitted to this rule was the sublime—and we no longer need be surprised that Rorty feels no sympathy at all for the category of the sublime.[12] From this point of view, Rorty can even be said to be *plus Kantianiste que Kant.*

2.3 THE PRISONHOUSE OF LANGUAGE: RORTY, GADAMER, AND DERRIDA

But could the attempt to emancipate experience from language ever be successful? Is the historist's program workable at all? Or is it a mere dream that we will immediately awake from if standing in the full daylight of contemporary philosophical wisdom? Perhaps. Rorty, whom one can hardly accuse of lack of interest for emancipatory causes in philosophy, was clearly unwilling to support the cause of experience. And that is a bad omen.

But maybe there are other contemporary theorists resisting the absolutism of language who favor the revolution of experience. I deliberately used here a political metaphor, for does transcendentalism not grant to language the right to pose as an omnipresent master (or tyrant?) from whom no escape is possible? Or, worse still, could language not be described as a "prisonhouse" from which thought and experience could never free themselves? Such was the bleak message that Roland Barthes presented to his audience in his notorious inaugural address at the Collège de France in 1978, two years before his premature death. The claim he defended there was aptly summarized by Christopher Prendergast as follows:

Barthes argued that oppression is intrinsic to the most fundamental representational system of all, our most basic medium for constructing the world and transacting with another, namely language. The predicative structures and operations of language impose attributes and identities that are not of our own choosing, a view the most notorious version of which is Barthes's claim in his introductory lecture at the Collège de France that language is fascist, imprisoning us in the frame of its own terms: the syntax of the sentence is like a sentence in the juridical sense, incarceration in what Nietzsche called the prisonhouse of language.[13]

When describing linguistic transcendentalism here as "fascist" or as an "incarceration of thought" and when referring to Nietzsche's metaphor of "the prisonhouse of language," Barthes surely chose the strongest invectives available to a French philosopher at that time. But since French philosophers of the period had a certain propensity to overstatement, we should certainly not blindly follow them in their love of alarmist and paranoic declarations.

Moreover, is not much to be said as well in favor of Herder's so much more optimistic view of language—to take an example from an author whose writings are considered with the greatest respect throughout the present study? Herder argued that the marvel of language precisely consists in its combination of being, on the one hand, an instrument accessible to us all, whereas, on the other hand, it allows us to express our innermost and most intimate feelings. This is what urged Herder to see in language even the model for the free and just society. If legislation were as successful as language in combining universality and (the respect of) individuality, the stone of wisdom that political philosophers since Hippodamus of Miletus have always vainly sought, would finally have been discovered. We would then know how to overcome the perennial opposition between the individual and society, between the private and the public, between freedom and compulsion that has always been the aim of political thought. Here we are, obviously, far removed form Barthes's pathetic picture of the fascism of language.

Nevertheless, Nietzsche's and Barthes's picture of the "prisonhouse of language" is suggestive enough to make us worry about it. Do we not all feel that language *has* a problem if confronted with the arts, with painting, with music, with the world of love (and hate), of all of our most intense and most personal feelings—and of our experiences?[14] And what about animals and children not yet having acquired the faculty of speech? Should we suffer the imperialism of language to condemn them to much the same world of mere automata in which Descartes had relegated all animals because of their not possessing *res cogitans?* So, there might well be some truth, after all, in this metaphor of the "prisonhouse of language." Since Rorty, in his fight against transcendentalism, so often relied on the help of Gadamer[15] (in *Philosophy and the Mirror of Nature*) and Derrida (in *Consequences of Pragmatism* and later writings), what is more natural than to ask ourselves now whether any help is, perhaps, to be expected from these philosophers? Surely, Derrida's extremism suggests that he can be expected to be more willing than "le bon Richard" to have *le courage de ses opinions;* and, as for Gadamer, his thought is immersed in historism—so should we not expect him to be more sympathetic to the cause of experience? More generally, what had attracted Rorty to these two philosophers was the anti-transcendentalism that he had rightly discerned in their writings; so let's follow Rorty's intuitions and chose them as our guides.

But, as we shall see, no such help will be forthcoming. Gadamer and Derrida confront us no less than Rorty with the paradox of combining a rejection of transcendentalism with a condemnation of disconnecting language and experience. And it is certainly distressing that the liberation of philosophy from the narrow constraints of transcendentalism that we may observe in their writings did change so desperately little that it left the world of history, of representation, of our experience of art, of music, and of the more existential aspects of the *condition humaine* as unexplained and as devoid of philosophical interest as had been the case in the heyday of logical positivism. It was as if our chains had been removed while we nevertheless kept on repeating the same movements as if we were still in prison—in the prisonhouse of language, that is. But one may draw an even darker picture. One could argue that in the days of logical positivism it was at least clear who was friend or foe. And we lost even this with Rorty, Derrida, and Gadamer. The battle lines between those who really wanted to get to grips with history, the humanities and political realities of the present and the future, and those who have only science before their eyes now seem to have been erased as well.

Think of this. The attack on transcendentalism necessarily had to take the form of dissolving the language/world barrier. This is what had always provided epistemology with its fuel: (Epistemological) transcendentalism dealt with the question of how to relate things to words—and, obviously, this question made sense only on the assumption that there is a clear barrier separating language from the world. Hence, doing away with transcendentalism resulted in a fusion of language and the world; language henceforward was just one more instrument for "coping" (Rorty's favorite term in this context) with the problems of human existence, not different from other such instruments such as hammers, screwdrivers, houses, television sets, airplanes, or computer programs—all things that we unhesitatingly see as items on the inventory of the world. Now, if we naturalize semantics by abandoning transcendentalism and see language as just one more item on this list, language is just as much taken up in the causal fabric of the world as these hammers and screwdrivers of a moment ago. This had two consequences. In the first place—as Rorty liked to point out so

often—within this picture it makes no sense to distinguish anymore between the sciences and the humanities. In both cases language merely is an
instrument for a pragmatist "coping with the world," and the causalistic interaction between language and the world is the last and only interesting
thing we could possibly say about how this instrument succeeds in deliver-
ing the goods we expect from it. So discussions about what is or is not peculiar to the humanities then become completely pointless.

But in the second place, this naturalization of semantics resulting
from the rejection of transcendentalism also entails that there could not be
any causalistic vacuums between language and the world (for what causalistic vacuum could exist among hammers, nails, and the boards we spike
together with them?). And if there are no such causalistic vacuums between
language and the world, our *experience* of the world must reflect this relationship between language and the world. Consequently, no content of experience could escape from this continuum of language and the world—a
fact that would irrevocably enclose experience within language. If not, what
could experience possibly be an experience *of,* given this fact of the absence
of any "vacuum" in this continuum of the causalistic interaction between
language and the world? Put differently, the naturalization of semantics (resulting from the rejection of transcendentalist epistemological transcendentalism) will lock up experience again within the same constraints (of
language) as had been the case under the dispensation of epistemology. In
this way the unwanted legacy of transcendentalism is carried over into post-
transcendentalist philosophical thought. Once again, the limits of language
are presented to us as the limits of experience as well; and, once again, our
hopes to disconnect language and experience are frustrated.[16]

Now, when dealing, as promised, with Gadamer and Derrida, I shall
be quite brief here about Gadamer since his views will be discussed more
comprehensively in Chapter 5. Gadamer presents us with the tack opposite
to the one preferred by Rorty. Unlike Rorty (who mentions the notion of
experience only in passing[17]), Gadamer is very much aware of the issue of
experience and he explicitly emphasizes in what manner language may violate experience, and we may even discern here a perennial conflict between language and experience:

We know how putting an experience into words helps us cope with it. It is as if its
threatening, even annihilating, immediacy is pushed into the background,
brought into proportions, made communicable, and hence dealt with.[18]

This truly is the heart of the issue, and I could not agree more with every word of the quote. Language is where experience is not, and experience is where language is not.[19] Gadamer is far more explicit about this than either Rorty or Derrida; and one may surmise that Gadamer, *nourri dans le serail* of historism and immersed in the whole historist tradition from its birth in the eighteenth century down to its interweaving with Heidegger's existentialism, was, unlike these two, very much sensitive to all the drama of the struggle between language and experience. It is all the more disappointing that Gadamer is no less prepared than Rorty to sacrifice experience to language. Or, rather, much to one's amazement, one will discover that Gadamer is even more careless and improvident about the issue than Rorty. Whereas Rorty takes us to this eternal present underlying all of history suggested by the Davidsonian notion of the charity principle and in this way retains in his account the shadow of a reality outside and beyond language that may function as an anchor for experience, authentic or not, within Gadamer's account reality must renounce all its claims in favor of (the language of) "effective history" or *Wirkungsgeschichte,* that is, basically, the history of how a text has been interpreted all through the centuries.

So, for Gadamer, there is nothing outside these interpretation-histories or outside the language of interpretation within which these histories are encapsulated. We can comprehend the past only insofar as it has been reduced to the "language" of these interpretation-histories, whereas the past itself (to which these histories owe their existence) no longer has any role to play in Gadamer's story. All of history, all of its drama, its tragedies, its triumphs, and its glories, are thus forced within the narrow frame of how it has been interpreted through the centuries in the historian's language. What is now left to us is only language, only the historian's language — this is the world within which we move, and there is nothing outside it. The obvious implication is, as Gadamer emphasizes in the third part of *Truth and Method,* that we can understand the past only insofar as it has obligingly taken on a linguistic appearance. Hence, language is "the House of Being that can be understood" (my translation), as Gadamer puts it; and what is outside this "house of language" necessarily exceeds our comprehension. Could we ever be further removed here from the historism of Burckhardt's "was einst Jubel und Jammer war, muss nun Erkenntis werden ("What once was joy and misery, must now become knowledge" [my translation])?[20]—which so movingly recognizes that the historian's main problem is to translate somehow the blood and tears, the joys and pains of human existence itself into the controlled and disciplined language of the historian. Surely, an almost impossible task, if ever there was one. But, all the same, a description of the historian's task indicating that all the successes (and failures) are to be situated on this trajectory between experience and language. So—once again we are enclosed within the prisonhouse of language, as was the case with Rorty already and as will be seen to be the case with Derrida again. *Erfahrung,* experience, is reduced once more to much the same pitiful status of obscurity and irrelevance as the *Ding an sich* of Kantian transcendentalism—and for much the same reason. So, Gadamer's attack on transcendentalism[21] paradoxically adds up, in the end, to a paving of the way for its final and ultimate triumph.

Before dealing with Derrida, we should recall that his thought is often described as "post-structuralist," which indicates that we cannot properly discuss Derrida without taking into account what he owes to the structuralist tradition as founded by Saussure. Now, the most striking difference between Frege's and Saussure's notion of "the sign" (a difference that may account for most of the frictions and misunderstandings between Anglo-Saxon philosophy of language and French [post-]structuralism) is that Saussure was not interested in the extensionalist dimension of the sign. For Saussure the sign is the conjunction of a signifier (thus a word, the sound we utter when pronouncing a word, an icon, and so on) and a signified (which is what the signifier "stands for").[22] And I deliberately use the somewhat ambiguous term *standing for* in order to indicate that Saussure does not clearly distinguish here between meaning and reference: The signifier may "stand for" both what is represented by the sign and its meaning. Obviously, Frege's distinction between *Sinn* and *Bedeutung,* between meaning and reference, between intension and extension, or between connotation and denotation, was intended to eliminate precisely this kind of ambiguity. Two consequences follow from this. In the first place, when people move from the idiolect of Anglo-Saxon philosophy (of language) to that of (post-)structuralism, there is always the danger of falling into the treacherous pit of this confusion of tongues and of unclarity about the proper meaning of the notions of reference and of meaning. In the second place, we should be aware that the referential dimension of the sign (or of language in general) is a matter that is more or less left open or undecided in the (post-)structuralist tradition. From the Fregean point of view this is, of course, an unpardonable weakness. But this indecision may well have its advantages if the (post-)structuralist notion of the sign is applied to the humanities, because reference is there profoundly problematic.[23] In the effort to understand the logic of the humanities, one had therefore best start with a notion of the sign which is as much as possible free from any a priori assumptions about reference—so that how we conceive this notion will not prejudice our dealings with the issue of reference here.[24] Indeed, if Anglo-Saxon philosophy of language was so singularly unsuccessful in mapping the logic of the humanities, the explanation is, in my view, that a conception of reference is always presupposed here that is admirably suited to our more pedestrian uses of language (and to its use in the sciences). However, what is unthinkingly presupposed here automatically prevents one from making any progress in the investigation of how reference functions in the humanities, and more specifically of how in the humanities the represented and its representation are related. On the other hand, I would not wish to suggest that the structuralist's conception of the sign should be without its problems if applied to the humanities. Far from it. The absence of a clear and generally recognized definition of the sign's referentiality has proven to be a rich source of unwarranted speculations by (post-)structuralist theorists, and one may well say that here lies the cause of most of the irritation that (post-)structuralism has rightly provoked among analytical philosophers of language.

A good example of the advantage that the Saussurian notion of the sign may sometimes have over Frege's is the post-structuralist notion of intertextuality. If stripped of its less relevant features, intertextuality comes down to the idea that linguistic meaning—hence the meaning of literary or of historical texts—is intertextual in the sense that these meanings mutually determine each other. To take history as an example, the meaning of one specific representation of the French Revolution is not exclusively dependent on *this* representation itself but also on what *other* representations of the French Revolution have to say about this most sublime historical drama. Everybody conversant with the realities of historical writing will be acquainted with this most peculiar and initially so counterintuitive phenomenon. Structuralism explains the phenomenon by taking into account the fact that we *recognize* signs by their being different from other signs: For example, when we recognize the letter *b,* this is not because we have been carefully scrutinizing *this* sign but because we immediately see where it (structurally) differs from other, structurally closely similar signs such as *p*, *q*, *d*, or *o*. But it is not easy to see how the phenomenon could be explained on the basis of the Fregean notion of the sign: Here, reference and meaning can in principle be fixed, independent of how *other* signs relate to (parts of) reality. And this seems to imply an insuperable gap between the Saussurian and the Fregean notion of the sign (although, in my opinion, the gap *can* be bridged in the end[25]).

After this brief detour through the domain of structuralism, I return to Derrida. I could not possibly do justice here to an oeuvre as huge and as variegated as Derrida's and restrict myself here to the so-called deconstructivism that is ordinarily associated with his name. Of relevance in the present context is the following. First, the structuralist notion of intertextuality as explained just now is also embraced in deconstructivism. But, second, the idea that the meaning of a text comes into being in its differences from other texts is here applied to one and the same text. That is to say, the paradoxical idea is that the meaning of a text is to be found in where it differs from itself. But how can we possibly say that a text differs from itself? The answer lies in the notion of context. It is often said that in order to understand a text, we must place it in its (proper) context. For example, in order to get the meaning of Hobbes's *Leviathan*, we should place it in the context of the religious civil wars of the sixteenth and seventeenth centuries. And we will then assign to the text its meaning by locating it in the web of frictions and tensions between the text itself and this specific context. This web is the mental world in which Hobbes's political thought originated. So, ordinarily context is something outside the text itself. It has been Derrida's revolutionary proposal to consider the text as providing its *own* context. So, all the frictions and tensions between text and context— which may help us clarify the text's meaning—are then pulled into the text *itself.* As a result, these frictions and tensions will now become part of the text itself; the text now no longer conveys one unitary and coherent meaning, but it now comes to be divided against itself. And in this way, it makes sense to say that the text differs from itself.

From the perspective of the struggle between language and experience, that is the topic of this chapter, deconstructivism is both promising and, in the end, disappointing. It is promising since the fact that text and language can be argued to be divided against themselves seems to leave room for a reading experience of the text in the proper sense of the word.

This being divided against itself of the text suggests a rupture in the otherwise smooth sheet of language, and hence this kind of disruption or discontinuity on the level of language that has in experience its natural counterpart insofar as experience, as understood here, is also suggestive of a movement outside or beyond language or the text. So does it not seem natural to situate the (reading) experience of the text, in the sense as meant in this chapter, in a following of the "trace" of these ruptures, of what has been left behind by these civil wars within the text and where language lost the war it waged against itself? Is the Derridean "trace" not to be situated in a realm outside language? In the case of Rorty's naturalized semantics, with its continuous causalistic interaction of language and the world, and in the case of Gadamer's quiet and unassuming self-perpetuation of *Wirkungsgeschiche,* we will find nothing even remotely resembling the drama of these textual civil wars that Derrida always makes us aware of. It may seem, therefore, that Derrida has come closer to an embrace of the notion of experience, as discussed here, than both Rorty and Gadamer have.

So much may be true. But that does not mean that deconstructivism really is open to the notion. Derrida is untypically explicit about this himself: Already in *Of grammatology* he rejects experience as an "unwieldy" concept that "belongs to the history of metaphysics and we can only use it under erasure *(sous rature).*"[26] And he marks his own distance from phenomenology by criticizing the latter for its infatuation with the notion of experience. In order to see why Derrida was never tempted to phrase the deconstructivist's insight into the text's being divided against itself in terms of experience, we should note that (inter-)textual conflict is for Derrida never suggestive of a move outside the (level of the) text. More specifically, within deconstructivism these divisions of the text against itself never really confront us with the dimension of the *unsayable,* of what could not possibly be expressed in language—and, indeed, only this would get us to what experience is all about. What must be said may sometimes be difficult to say and may require lots and lots of language—hence Derrida's endless logorrheas—but Derrida never raises his hands to Heaven in despair because his reading experience would exceed what he wishes to say. When deconstructivists have said about the text what they had to say, this is what, in their view, can or ought to be said about the text, however inconclusive that may be. And in this way what they have said is fully "adequate." So when they have finished talking, all that needed to be said *has* been said.

Surely, in deconstructivism meaning may proliferate endlessly because of these divisions producing ever new divisions. But deconstructivism never suggests that any phase in this continuous process of the proliferation of meaning might move us outside or beyond what can be expressed in language—as one might expect from a tradition having fought its victories under the banner of the notorious "il n'y pas dehors texte." Even more so, would such a phase really announce itself; the proliferation of meaning would come to a sudden stop, for only what can be expressed in language can keep the process going. But although in deconstructivism the interplay of texts with texts and of texts with themselves may become immensely complicated, this will never get us to a stage where language is, in principle, no longer transparent to itself. So deconstructivism necessarily excludes the conditions required for the possibility of experience; deconstructivism highlights and is most sensitive to semantic friction and conflict, but these tensions and conflicts never point to a dimension beyond their own linguistic circumscriptions and they can always be fathomed on their own, purely linguistic terms.[27] Or, to put it in the terminology to be adopted in the last chapters of this book, although certainly pointing in that direction (and for which I admire it!), deconstructivism never effectively acquires for itself the aura of the sublime—and only *this* gives us experience, as understood here, in its purest manifestation.[28]

2.4 EXPERIENCE AND THE TEXT: THREE PHASES

Section 2.3 dealt with how in the writings of Rorty, Gadamer, and Derrida experience (and nontextual historical reality) was ultimately pushed aside by linguistic or textual transcendentalism. In the remainder of this chapter I wish to do some preliminary work by preparing the terrain for what will be done in greater detail in the next chapters. That is, I wish to explain how we got caught in the prisonhouse of language, and I hope to do this in such a way to suggest how we might set ourselves free again and in what way the notion of experience can function as our guide on our way to freedom. As so often in such situations, much, if not all, depends on where one starts with one's story. For example, if we begin at the end of the eighteenth century, our story will inevitably become a repetition of the story told in the previous chapter and of what I have been saying in this one up to now. In order to avoid this, we had better move backward in time a little further and consider how the West dealt with texts from the Middle Ages down to the humanists of the fifteenth and sixteenth centuries.[29] The medieval scholastics and the Renaissance humanists were perhaps even more aware than us of the challenges posed by the text. And certainly the text never was taken more seriously. Texts were transcribed with an amazing accuracy and eagerly discussed, and the effort to do justice to the text was not merely a matter of academic interest (as presently is the case) but was even believed to have its impact on the salvation of the individual believer and of Christianity as a whole. Discussions of the text typically took the form of the commentary—of course I am well aware that this is an irresponsible simplification, but let us take it, nevertheless, as our point of departure here. Commentaries could take different forms. When printed books became widely available, the commentary would often have the form that we presently associate with the term. That is, one took care that the text was in an optimal form from a philological point of view and then one added learned references to related passages in other works. Each text thus became a nodal point in the web of truth covering the world.

But of more interest in the present discussion is an older, medieval variant of the commentary. I am thinking here of the long-standing medieval so-called *quaestio* tradition which would become prominent in the schools of the twelfth and thirteenth centuries. In this tradition the meanings of the words and sentences were discussed—by comparing established authorities with each other and by making use of logic and semantics—and after a painstakingly precise exposition of what could be said in favor or against the text's claims, the teacher finally cut the Gordian knot and expounded his own opinion.[30] From the later medieval period many of these scholarly commentaries, written down by advanced students and by their teachers, have survived.

Two aspects of this kind of commentary are relevant here. In the first place, the production of such a commentary was essentially a social process and ought to be such: It was believed that the individual mind could easily be led astray, as had become clear from the often idiosyncratic readings of the Holy Scriptures by the Egyptian anchorites and by the Desert Fathers of the fourth and fifth centuries. This was, in fact, one of the main reasons for the institution of controlled teaching, both in the monasteries and, from the twelfth century on, in the cathedral schools and the nascent universities. Controlled teaching in the publicity of the religious community was considered the best guarantee of the uniformity of the interpretation of the text, sacred or not. Hence, there was not believed to be in the depth of the isolated individual some reliable compass that would guide all his intellectual movements when reading a text.[31]

However, this is not the whole truth, and this brings me to a second observation. It should not be inferred from this that the individual's "experience" of the text was always and under all circumstances completely distrusted. In the Middle Ages there was always a powerful undercurrent of the mystical experience of religious truth—an undercurrent occasionally rising to the surface as, for example, in the case of Bernard of Clairvaux. But there were certain more or less well-defined limits to this acceptance of individual experience or inspiration. For example, when writing down his mystic "experiences," Bernard of Clairvaux took care to formulate them in the idiom of Solomon's Song. In this way the "individuality" of his religious experience was attenuated, and this gave to his writings the appearance of merely being a continuation or even an emanation of texts that were already known and accepted by the religious community.

This was not merely a matter of satisfying the rhetorical requirements of the age. More important and relevant here is the medieval conception of the (sacred) text and of its status—a conception that would also prove to be acceptable to most of the humanists of the early Renaissance. Crucial is the idea that the text is the spoken word of God Himself and that it therefore possesses an absolute priority to both reality and the reader of the text. Text and language precede reality since it was the Word of God that created reality; or as Vanderjagt put it, "Language is not metaphorical but the world as we know it is an imperfect metaphor of the real world of the Word."[32] And since the text, in its quality of being God's own Word, is reality *par excellence,* it also has an absolute priority to its reader, for if reality is a representation of the text rather than that the text is a representation of reality, the reader can do justice to the text only by transfiguring the reality of his or her own personality into that of the text. Only the transference and the immersion of the reader's own individuality into the reality of the text can adequately express the recognition that reality, and thus the reader, are mere reflections or representations of the Word.[33] Or, to put it differently, the reader is not allowed—nor *could* the reader even have—any interpretative autonomy with regard to the text. *The text is, so to speak, never a thing in the mind of the reader; it is rather the reverse, the reader is, or ought to be "in" the text.* The text is not an intellectual entity that one can do different things with; when the reader has correctly read the text, he or she "participates" in the text, so to speak, much in the way that Aristotle defined knowledge as an identification of the knowing subject with the known object.[34]

Two consequences follow from this. In the first place we will now understand why Bernard of Clairvaux wished to rely on an existing idiom or vocabulary for expressing or verbalizing his religious experiences. Using the vocabulary of Solomon's Song would take away any obnoxious individuality from his own text—an individuality that might be seen to counteract or even to prevent the immersion or subsumption of its reader in God's Word. In short, all traces that might bespeak the introduction of origins alien to God's Word itself had to be carefully obliterated. The other consequence is intimately related to this. If the text affords room only to Divine individuality (and not to the individual authors of texts), there is one and only one individuality that is shared by all the (religious) texts. But if this is the case, the implication is that there cannot be such a thing as textual "individuality," which might demarcate texts from each other. Text is, so to speak, to the medieval mind a "sortal concept" (denoting substances such as "stone," "gold," or "flesh") rather than a "count noun" (such as "house," "ring," or "human being") that denotes identifiable individual things. Hence, the notion of "the meaning of the text"—as we have learned to understand this phrase and to associate with the individual meaning given to individual texts—will be a term that is absent from the dictionary of medieval semantics. And this means, again, that "interpretation" in our (modern[-ist]) sense of that word will be a practice that is unknown to the medieval mind. There is to the medieval mind just one and only one analogue to what we modern(ist)s call "a text"—and that is the text written by God and manifesting itself in all its many differentiations.[35]

All this changed with the birth of the modern(ist) mind in the course of the seventeenth century—and this brings us to the second phase in the history of textual interpretation. As was so brilliantly shown by Rorty himself in his *Mirror of Nature,* the modern(ist) mind was the result of a movement of withdrawal or *anachoorèsis:* the knowing subject withdrew from its former direct and intimate contact with the world as presented in Aristotle's *De Anima* into the inner sanctuary of the Cartesian and Kantian transcendental self—thus giving rise to all the questions with regard to the relationship between reality and the transcendental self that philosophers since the seventeenth century have so eagerly discussed.[36]

Now, although Rorty does not deal with this issue himself, it should be observed that, in fact, much the same thing happened in the field of the humanities and of interpretation. After the abandonment of Aristotelianism and the introduction of the Cartesian ego in the model used by the West for exploring one's relationship to the world, reading the text could no longer be seen as this immersion or subsumption in the text that reading could still be for sixteenth-century humanists. Reading was now essentially done by a transcendental self, no longer able to lose itself in or merge with the text as the premodern(ist) reader was required to do; reading was now done by a self that would always remain separate from and outside the text. And although the epistemological barrier that was erected between subject and object removed, on the subject side, the subject to a position from where an identification with the text could never be achieved anymore, it resulted, on the object side, in the creation of the (notion of the) meaning of the text. The text obtained an unfathomable depth that, because of its purely philosophical origin, no human mind could ever penetrate. (It took on the features of what Kant would call the noumenal.)

Indeed, as one might have expected, in this way the introduction of the transcendental ego caused much the same problems in the field of the humanities that it had caused in Western epistemology. Just as Cartesianism effected an alienation of daily reality from the knowing subject (an alienation that was, indeed, the condition for the possibility of modern science), so texts now acquired, with their "meaning," an aura of noumenal mysteriousness that they had never possessed before. And it became necessary to develop all kinds of extremely complicated techniques—each with their complicated and often ridiculously overloaded philosophical appendages—to regain access to that strange textual reality that had come into being as a consequence of the anachoorèsis of the transcendental ego into its *forum internum.* Hermeneutics was given the task to explain how, in one way or another, we could get in touch again with the meaning of the text *tant bien que mal.* But just as the alienation of the knowing subject and reality effected by Cartesian and Kantian transcendentalism proved to be irreversible (at least as long as one persisted in asking oneself Cartesian and Kantian questions), so hermeneutics for two centuries attempted to construct a bridge over a gap that it had so carefully made unbridgeable several centuries ago. After all, a noumenon is a noumenon is a noumenon, and so on (to paraphrase Gertrude Stein). And the unintended effort of hermeneutics, semantics, semiotics, and so on has thus been not to show us how we can get access to the meaning of the text but rather why we are always and inevitably condemned to miss that meaning. At the basis (or rather at the end) of all these variants of hermeneutics we will find a "politics of cultural despair," motivated by our impossible desire to jump over our own hermeneutical shadow.

And, as we have seen, all this reached its apogee in the writings of Gadamer and Derrida. Gadamer's *Wirkungsgeschichte* ("effective history") is in the end, if anything, a confession of impotence. No real "directions for the use" of a text follow from it; it merely repeats the undeniable fact that texts have been interpreted differently in the past, and it then recommends us to be happy with that and not to ask for more. Moreover, as we saw in section 2.3, Gadamer's attack on transcendentalism had the unintended result of effecting transcendentalism's ultimate triumph. The unattainability of the *mens auctoris,* which has so eloquently and convincingly been argued by Gadamer, is nothing but the belated echo of the alienation of the text from the reader caused by the embrace of transcendentalism three centuries ago. And Derrida's critique of "the metaphysics of presence," as also expounded in section 2.3, is just one more such echo of this withdrawal of the transcendental self from the world of publicly accessible meaning in which the medieval scholastic and the Renaissance humanist used to experience their so intense and challenging interaction with the text. Indeed, no transcendentalism, no hermeneutics and no interpretation problems; and all our writings and worries about how to interpret texts prove only how much we are still bewitched by the modern(ist) notion of the Cartesian self. When seeing this, we will recognize how much Rorty's recommendation to exchange Descartes and Kant for Gadamer and Derrida has been, in fact, an exchange of the Devil for Beelzebub.

2.5 THE THIRD PHASE:
TRANSCENDENTALISM AND BEYOND

Transcendentalism has come in many guises to the reflection on the humanities—we may think here of hermeneutics, structuralism in all its many variants, semiotics, post-structuralism, deconstructivism, rhetoric, tropological readings, and so on. But all of them had two things in common. In the first place, a distrust of how we might directly experience the text, of how we might read the text in a "naive" encounter with it, an encounter that is not guided by one of the technical apparatuses that had been devised by hermeneuticists and their colleagues in the last two centuries. In the second place, the text was postulated to possess some hidden meaning that one could get hold of only with the help of these technical apparatuses. They would function as a kind of *interface* between the text and the reader where the text would manifest itself to us in a way that made it accessible to rational analysis. So when attacking the transcendentalist tradition here, I am, in fact, proposing to radically do away with this interface, whatever form the transcendentalist tradition may have given to it, and to rely exclusively on how we *experience the text.*

When making a similar proposal a few years ago in an attempt to rescue the notion of experience from the contempt with which it ordinarily is nowadays seen, Putnam said that this would undoubtedly be considered a plea for a "re-infantilization of philosophy."[37] Nor do I expect that my summons to abolish transcendentalism and to relegate hermeneutics, (post-)structuralism, deconstructivism, and so on to the museum of the outmoded intellectual curiosities of the past will be warmly welcomed by most of my colleagues. Undoubtedly they will also want to accuse me of such a re-infantilization of our thinking about the nature of the humanities—a re-infantilization, moreover, threatening to put us all out of work. To which I hasten to add, that at least the latter part of the accusation would be wholly mistaken. Many traditional questions one may ask about the writing of history will even then have lost nothing of their urgency—think, for example, of the issue of the nature of (historical) representation, of historism, of experience (self-evidently!), of subjectivity, of what makes one historical representation of some part of the past into a better one than another, and so on. The only thing to be cut out will be these theories prescribing how the historian should interpret the texts of the past. Historical theorists should not meddle with the historian's activities but accept them as they are and restrict themselves to reflect on these. And this task is ambitious enough—even more so, much work is waiting here that has been postponed for too long already, now that theorists invested all their energies in the construction of these abstract and pretentious fata morganas of how historians *ought* to read their texts.

Furthermore, think of this. It may be that the Kantians are right when claiming that we need some epistemological grid for making sense of nature (although I would venture to say that mathematics would be a far better and more plausible candidate for giving us what we are looking for than what has been proposed to that effect by epistemologists since Descartes—for is mathematics, as Galilei already recognized, not the condition for the possibility of scientific knowledge?). But why should such grids be required for the understanding of texts at all? What makes us look for them *here,* in the world of the humanities? Let us suppose that the transcendentalist is right after all and that such grids giving us the transcendental conditions of all textual meaning would really be there. But if such grids were to really exist, they would be a condition of the understanding of the historian's text about a text from the past, no less than of understanding the historical text in question *itself.* But, as a moment's thought will make clear, only this simple fact is enough for proving the irrelevance of these grids for the understanding of the texts the past has left us. If these grids function in the historical text itself and in the historian's own text in *exactly* the same way (as we must assume to be the case if the universalist pretensions of the hermeneuticists and so on are really legitimate), they can *sui generis* never contribute to the meaning of the historical text—and would thus be completely irrelevant to our effort to understand that meaning.

In order to see this, recall the story about these strangely deformed and elongated figures in El Greco's paintings. Some art historians have argued that this is how El Greco deliberately chose to represent people on his canvases—and this was for them an occasion for discerning some specific meaning in his pictures (a reminiscence of Gothic spirituality in the work of this so deeply religious painter, perhaps). Other art historians, however, proposed the provocatively pedestrian explanation that El Greco had an eye defect which made him see *and* represent people in the way he did. They argued, next, that because of this eye defect El Greco saw the elongated faces depicted on his paintings in exactly the same way as people without this eye defect see the faces of their fellow human beings. So El Greco himself could have no idea that he presented the human face in an odd and unusual way: When looking at his paintings, he saw exactly the same thing we do when looking at the faces of our friends and family. The eye defect therefore functioned as a kind of epistemological grid whose existence El Greco himself could never be aware of, but that *we* perceive, as such, when noting this systematic difference between how we see the human face and how it was depicted by El Greco. And the implication then is that we should be acutely aware at all times of the presence (or not, as the case may be) of such "epistemological grids" and of how they make us look at the world. But, obviously, the argument is wrong. Even if El Greco had this eye defect, it would *also* determine how he saw real human faces (and not only as he had depicted them in his paintings). And then he could not fail to notice that there was a systematic difference between how he perceived real human faces and how he represented them in his paintings. So, it might well be that the eye defect caused El Greco to have mental representations of the human face different from ours—but we could never infer the existence of this difference from how he represented the human face in his paintings. Such "epistemological" differences between people automatically cancel each other out, so to say, in the interaction of the (perception of the) represented and of its representation, and we have, therefore, no real reason to be interested in them.

And so it is with the interpretation (or representation) of texts: If historian A interprets a text by means of the interpretative grid G_A and historian B by means of the interpretative grid G_B, these transcendentalist grids are (contrary to accepted wisdom) as irrelevant with regard to the nature of A's and B's interpretation of the text in question as having El Greco's eye defect (or not) is in a discussion between El Greco and somebody (not having this eye defect) about whether some person was or was not correctly portrayed by him. Of course there may—and in all likelihood will—be discussions about correct interpretation or representation. But these discussions will necessarily be grid-*in*dependent, so to speak. They will be questions concerning differences in how respectively a text or a personality was *experienced* by an interpreter or a painter—and *these differences* could not possibly be reduced to differences in interpretive or representationalist grids.

I am well aware that this unconventional argument will be met with disbelief and resistance. Most of hermeneutics and most of the discussion about the historian's subjectivity have always set great store upon these interpretative grids and upon the gap they were believed to create between the historian and the object of investigation. So one likely rejoinder to my argument would run as follows: We should strictly distinguish between the texts we investigate on the one hand and the texts we write when interpreting them on the other and bear in mind that different semantic "grids" determine their meaning. For example, one could argue that there is an absolutely crucial difference of level, with the text itself being on the object level and its interpretation situated on a meta-level, and that each of these levels possesses a transcendental hermeneutic logic of its own. In that case we would have to take into account the transcendental logic of the text to be interpreted for much the same reason that we should be acquainted with the rule of German grammar if we translate a German text into English. Obviously, this would take the sting out of my El Greco argument of a moment ago, although at the not inconsiderable price of having to sacrifice the universalist pretensions that transcendentalists had always so proudly claimed for their transcendentalist schemes. Furthermore, adopting this strategy would get us involved in the difficult question of what will guide us in our search for the "right" transcendentalist grid after having abandoned this claim of universality. Should we use grid x for an author of the seventeenth century and grid y for an author of the eighteenth century (and probably no grid at all for what we ourselves and our colleagues write about these great dead authors)? Perhaps there should be some "supergrid," or "master grid" for helping us out here? And if so, what would the supergrid look like? More specifically, would it not get us back again to the universalist grid that we had rejected when discussing the El Greco example? And how could we get to know what "local" grid to use, as long as we have not yet applied the "right" local grid to the great dead author's writings? Do we not presuppose, in this way, the possession of the kind of knowledge we can have only after having made use of it? So, as these questions make clear, this will inevitably get us into a swamp of nasty Catch-22 problems.

However, we should now realize ourselves that texts were never written in agreement with such grids—in the way that tonal music before the days of Schoenberg *was* written in agreement with the theory of harmony. I would not know of any text that was written with the explicit purpose of satisfying the grids or rules devised by hermeneuticist or (post-) structuralists, or the adherents of any other literary theory for getting to the meaning of a text. Perhaps an author like Borges might like to do this kind of thing, but such textual parodies are rare and always easy to identify. If we then read the text on the assumption that such grids are present in it, we can conclude only that we then project on it something that is not part of the text *itself.* Put differently, we will then see the meaning of the text as a *function* of the grid we project on it. Interpretation will then be much the same as looking into a mirror—and we will never see anything else other than ourselves, over and over again, whatever text we read. We are then inevitably guilty of the subjectivism that transcendentalists have always so much been the first to decry and for which their own technical schemes were supposed to be the only effective remedy. Admittedly, an illusion of objectivity may then result, since all historians applying the same transcendentalist scheme will then come to comparable if not identical results. But this is, indeed, a mere *illusion,* for what one will then observe over and over again is the unnoticed "content" of the transcendentalist "forms" we use for understanding the past.[38] In this way (hermeneutic) transcendentalism is not the safe road to objectivity it claims to be but is instead, the systematization or codification of one specific variant of subjectivity (in section 2.6 I shall deal more extensively with the objectivity issue).

But let us return to our question of a moment ago and see where we will find ourselves after having shrugged off the transcendentalist approach of the humanities. Well, to begin with, when refusing the gifts that the hermeneuticist had so proudly promised, we will basically be back again where the sixteenth-century humanists had been already—and this is why I started my story of the history of the reading of texts with them. Indeed, if there is no longer this "interface" functioning as an insuperable barrier between ourselves and the text—if there is no longer this transcendentalist diaphragm through which the rays of meaning have to pass before entering the camera obscura of the historian's mind, historians will find themselves "immersed" in the text again; they will be "in" the text, they will experience it like the air all around them, and its meanings will be as diffuse and unstable to them as the forms of the clouds, now that they no longer have at their disposal any foolproof models for bringing order in this kaleidoscopic play of forms. The only thing that historians can be sure of is that they must turn to the best advantage their own subjectivity, that they must rely on their subjectivity as much as possible and, yet, at the same time make it as much invisible to their readers as they can manage to do. More generally, when taking together this double movement of (1) a complete reliance on subjectivity and (2) effacing subjectivity at the same time, the picture is that historians should dissolve their own subjectivity in the text, just like a piece of sugar may dissolve in a cup of tea. This, obviously, is the same picture we encountered when discussing text interpretation in the Middle Ages, where the text is not in (the mind of) the reader but where the reader is "in the text." And since you can dissolve pieces of sugar only if you begin with having them—so it is here as well.

Or, to put it in the language of the transcendentalist, the best instrument for reading the text is *the person that we are*—and we should avoid eliminating a priori any aspect of our personality from our reading of the text. If we really would find it unbearable to wholly discard the transcendentalist's terminology, we might say that the only "transcendental condition" of getting to the meaning to the text is the person we are—but *this* is a variant of "transcendentalism" that we will *never* be able to live up to. Or, rather, we shall recognize that we shall never be able to fully realize the promises implicit in this kind of transcendentalism. We shall see that we will always fail within this variant of transcendentalism, because we are only too painfully aware that our personality could always be richer and more sensitive to all the diversities of the *condition humaine* than it presently is. To return to the metaphor I used a moment ago: It is as if the piece of sugar would never succeed in sweetening all of the cup of tea. But this is something we shall have to live with. So, for better or for worse, *life*, and no fixed transcendentalist scheme, is our best, nay, our only guide for understanding the text—and there is no end and limit to that. And transcendentalist schemes will even be recognized to be counterproductive and to obscure our understanding of the text, for such schemes are like the coatings of individual grains of sugar, in terms of the metaphor that I have been using here, that prevent their solution in the cup of tea.

What this must mean in practice can best be elucidated by having a look at the arts. A work of art can, in many although not all cases, be said to be a representation of how the artist has experienced part of the world— say, a landscape. The painting expresses, or is a representation of the artist's experience of nature, although, if we are as precise here as we should be, it would be more correct to say that the painting is a representation of a landscape expressing the artist's experience of it, for paintings are representations of the world and not of our experiences. Now, within this context the interesting fact is that the landscape could not possibly be said to have a meaning *itself;* meaning comes into being only with the work of art. Only the work of art has a meaning that, for example, historians of art could comment on. It follows from this that the representation of experience as given in the work of art carries us from what still has *no meaning* (the landscape itself) to what *possesses a meaning.* This is, arguably, the most fascinating feature of artistic representation—as it is of representation in general: It introduces us to the domain where meaning emerges from where meaning is not yet. *Representation is the birthplace of meaning—and whoever is interested in the nature of meaning can do little better than to closely investigate representation.*

This may help us understand how experience, representation, and meaning are related when we are dealing with the issue of the reading of texts that is at stake here. First, a comment on terminology. Hermeneuticists ordinarily speak of the *interpretation* of texts and, furthermore, they do not clearly distinguish between the act of interpretation itself and what results from this, that is, the essay or book the historian may write on a (corpus of) text(s). The notion of interpretation is used indiscriminately for both. This, then, is what I would like to avoid. For me there is, first, the *text* we read; second, the *experience of reading;* and, third, the *representation* giving an account of how the historian has read (experienced the text) and, hence, of what the historian takes to be the text's *meaning.* But, once again, just as in the case of painting, the "representation" (third phase) is a representation of the *text* that was read and not of the *experience of reading.* In sum, I am pulling apart two things (that is, "experience" and "the representation of meaning") that are taken together in hermeneutics under the name of "interpretation." Obviously, this gives to "experience" an autonomy it never had under the dispensation in which "experience" and "the representation of meaning" were always indiscriminately lumped together.

This will give us a different picture of the reading of texts. To begin with, modeling the reading of texts on aesthetic representation will help us recognize that reading (also) makes us move from the domain of what has not yet meaning to what has meaning, that is, from the text itself to the representation given to it by the historian. You have meanings only if you have representations. The crucial implication is that meaning should never be ascribed to the text we read *itself* (as if the text consisted of words, sentences, and so on while there is, apart from these things, still some extra thing in it—although difficult to locate—that we may refer to with the phrase of "the text's meaning"). Meanings come into being only when we experience the world—or a text—and then go on to represent the world, or the text, as is suggested by our experience of it. I am well aware that this may seem odd to many people and will meet with great resistance. "Surely," one may feel tempted to exclaim, "the text *does* have a meaning. How could one possibly deny this?" Well, in a way, one *can* say that the text has a meaning, but one should be aware that this "having" should be read, if one wishes to be precise, as "having provoked in us"—which removes meaning from the text to our minds. Next, it will probably be objected that my modeling of the text on the landscape to be represented by the painter misconstructs the issue, since texts have meanings, whereas landscapes are devoid of meaning. But this objection is easily overcome with the argument that we can divide all things in the world into two categories: (1) the category of things (such as landscapes) lacking the explicit purpose of the production of meaning, although they may give rise to a process of meaning-making, as when landscapes come to be represented by painting; or (2) the category of things whose *raison d'être* is almost exclusively the production of meaning, and this obviously is the category to which texts do belong. But what both categories share (landscapes *and* texts)—and this is what truly counts—is that that they are themselves devoid of meaning.

This may also make clear where the role I have ascribed to the reader of a text differs from the one given to the reader in some hermeneutic theories. In these theories it is often emphasized, too, that readers of the text should not be afraid to involve their own personality in their reading of the text since precisely this may give them access to the text's meaning. The argument that is often given is that there will be a considerable overlap in the personalities of the author of the text and the author's readers—we are all human beings and have a lot of experiences in common.[39] So here the appeal to the readers' personalities and to their life experiences functions as (an albeit complex) transcendental condition of getting to the truth about the text's meaning (and a moment ago, when commenting on theorists with a nostalgia for transcendentalist terminology, I said something coming quite close to this). But in my view, if we wish to be careful and precise, we must recognize that there is no such thing as the meaning of the text, although we should try to approximate it as much as possible because the meaning lies hidden somewhere in the text like a valuable pearl in an oyster's shell. So the hermeneuticist's picture of the text's meaning as existing outside processes of reading in the text itself and as something that we could somehow get access to by making (a transcendentalist) use of our own personality and of our life experience, is, within the picture proposed here, fundamentally mistaken. Meaning comes into being only when a reader has read or, rather, "experienced" a text and then gives a representation of the text in agreement with this reading experience (and to which I should add, for precision's sake, that readers give us an account of their representation of the *text* and *not* of their *experience of it*—although their account will be guided by this experience, this will be its *form* so to say).

And that is all there is—and all we need. What traditional hermeneutics sees as "the meaning of the text" is an ontologization of how I propose to look at this concept; and hermeneuticists always felt the need for such an ontologization in order to provide themselves with an anchor for text interpretation and for the complicated hermeneutic machineries they had developed for the reading of texts. But all this is mere intellectual overhead—and we should ruthlessly cut it out. Textual meaning is "heterotopic," as I would formulate it in order to please literary theorists with the penchant for Greek terminology characteristic of that discipline. We ascribe it to *texts,* but it *exists* only in our minds. And as soon as we see this, we will recognize once more that transcendental hermeneutics is simply useless: It promises to give us access to something that does not even exist.

2.6 SUBJECTIVITY AND OBJECTIVITY

Let us return for a moment to the issue of subjectivity briefly hinted at earlier when discussing the pseudo-objectivity that transcendentalism so alluringly dangled before our eyes. It might be objected that my experience model of the reading of texts is, in fact, nothing but an open invitation to subjectivism. Well, the accusation is correct.[40] But I hasten to add that both the accusation and the recognition of its correctness are, in fact, quite empty declarations; these are seemingly violent movements in a space where nothing is hit but empty air. The accusation could make sense only if there exists such a thing as an *objective* interpretation of a text, hence an interpretation where the meaning given to the text by the reader agrees with an antecedent meaning somehow embodied in the text itself. But there simply is nothing in the text itself that the meanings we give to it could or could not correspond with. Thus, if texts do not have a meaning *themselves* in the true sense of the word, the very notion of an "objective interpretation" is a contradiction in terms. So the claim that interpretations of texts are necessarily and always subjectivist is wholly true, but at the same time a wholly undramatic and innocuous observation as well.

Nevertheless, even then many people will not be quite happy with it,

I expect. Does this not imply that interpretation may now go "wherever the wind bloweth us"? Should we then not say that each interpretation is as good as any other and that historical writing has now been wholly abandoned to the whims of subjectivism? Well, this inference does not follow, as will become clear if we consider painting again. We will all agree that the great artistic genius is the artist who teaches us to see reality as we never saw it before, and, next, that the artist's achievement can best be formulated in terms of experience: The artist has experienced the world, nature, or some aspect of social reality in a quite specific way; this gave us the painting; and when looking at it, this may change something in how we ourselves experience the world. Think of somebody who, after having visited an art gallery displaying seventeenth-century Dutch landscape paintings, next decides to takes a walk through the woods and then sees the trees, the bushes, and the clouds in the way that Jacob van Ruisdael, Allaert van Everdingen, or Jan Hackaert saw them three centuries ago. But not all artists will be capable of effecting this in us. We know that it is only the really great painter who may succeed in opening us to such new ways of experiencing reality. Indeed, these are the kind of painters whose aesthetic genius and whose personality is much more clearly present in their paintings than in the case of their less gifted colleagues. And in *this* way their paintings can properly be said to be "subjective." But would this imply that we should no longer strive for "objectivity" and acquiesce in all the manifestations of subjectivity?

I hope to show in what follows that this would be an overhasty conclusion. In order to make this clear, a few remarks on the relationship between experience and representation are indispensable. To begin with, we should recognize that experience has *sui generis* a most important role to play when representation is the instrument we rely on for making sense of the world. As I have shown elsewhere, the nature of representation can best be analyzed by contrasting it to description. In description you can always distinguish between reference (this is done by the subject term of a description) and predication (the task performed by the description's predicate term); but no such distinction is possible in the case of representation. Think of a portrait, for example; then you cannot say of certain parts of the painting that they exclusively refer, whereas others exclusively attribute, a property to the painting's alleged object of reference. It can be shown that because of this there is an indeterminacy in the relationship between the represented and its representation not having its counterpart in description.[41] To put it metaphorically, in the case of description the subject term (reference) and the predicate term (predication) function as two "screws" firmly tying language and the world together. Because of the absence of such screws representation possesses an autonomy with regard to the world that is absent in the case of description.

This is why tradition can be so very important in representation (whereas the notion makes no sense if applied to description) and why it may sometimes even begin to function as a quasi-transcendental condition of understanding the world. Think of how a painting can always be situated in one of the pictorial traditions in terms of which art historians write the history of art. Think, next, of how the tradition of socioeconomic historical writing was presented by some of its practitioners (such as Braudel) as the only legitimate way of doing history. Indeed, as soon as we have to do with representation, tradition will immediately assert all its rights. The explanation is that there is an indeterminacy in the relationship between the represented and its representation not having its counterpart in description—and because of this indeterminacy the forces of tradition are in the case of representation often stronger than those of the object. Precisely this raises the obvious question of whether we might ever hope to succeed in breaking through the magic circle of representation and the traditions governing it. Surely all seeing of the world and all artistic representation of the world by the artist are mediated by tradition; surely theorists of art like Goodman and Gombrich were right when attacking in Ruskin "the myth of the innocent eye." However—and here lies the rub—the imperialism of tradition has not in the least prevented the history of art from being more variegated and richer in sudden and unexpected evolutions than almost any other history. So, it may well be the case that the constraints of tradition are stronger in fields governed by the logic of representation (such as the arts and historical writing) than anywhere else, but it is precisely this which has made artists (and historians) so eager to escape from these constraints. Where tradition is strongest, the challenge to break with it will be strongest as well.

And this is where experience comes in, for it is only in the name of experience that representation and representationalist traditions can be attacked. Experience relates to representation in much the same way as falsification relates to theory. There is, therefore, an elective affinity between the notion of representation and that of experience[42]—the difference being, though, that in the case of a conflict between theory and an experience, the nature of the conflict is completely clear; if not, there simply *is* no conflict. However, in the case of a conflict of representation and experience there is no common basis in terms of which the exact nature of conflict can be defined. The explanation being that any such definitions would inevitably force us to abandon the domain of experience for that of a language in terms of which the nature of the conflict can, if only tentatively, be defined. So conflict would be possible only after experience has been translated into language and representation. And, indeed, it may happen that some crucial experience is recognized as such and immediately caught in a linguistic and representationalist formulation. But *then* we no longer have a conflict of representation and experience but a conflict of representations—which is an altogether different problem.

This may also explain why no deep claims can be made about conflicts of experience and representation. The only thing one can say is that in general the stakes will be in favor of representation since it has all the support (and the deadweight) of a representationalist tradition behind it— a tradition, moreover, having (unlike theory) no *fundamentum in re* and which is, therefore, paradoxically, all the more resistant to the impact of experience. Paradoxically, tradition is so strong precisely because of its weakness; because it has no foundations, there are no foundations to be shaken. Experience, on the other hand, merely has the privilege of authenticity— and authenticity is desperately hard to recognize for others than the person having had an authentic experience of the world. In this way experience is no less helpless if measured with cognitivist criteria than representation is. So the conflict of representation and experience will amply display all we associate with a *dialogue des sourds.* Nevertheless, if others recognize this authenticity (and this *is* decisive), this can and will be decisive, despite the fact that both experience and representation belong to so very different spheres. If we try to imagine the nature of this strange conflict between experience and representation we had, perhaps, best think of the picture of a tiny bullet (that is, experience) that is fired at a stone wall (that is, representation). In almost all cases the bullet will have no effect: It will simply be flattened by the stone wall's surface and then take *its* form. Tradition has then been triumphant, as it ordinarily is. But it may happen that others will recognize the experience's authenticity—and it will then be as if the bullet hit the stone wall at an already existing crack. And then an old world will fall apart and a new world of experience (and of representation) will announce themselves.[43] But all this is mere description—and no explanation; so when I use the term *authenticity,* the term is modestly meant to fit into a descriptive scheme and not have any explanatory pretensions. Authenticity is a useless notion from the cognitivist's point of view, as I shall be the first to admit.[44]

If the artist (or the historian) actually succeeds in hitting the crack in the stone wall of representation and tradition, this is ordinarily seen as their greatest achievement. We then praise them for having taught us to see the world with different eyes. Thus, new developments in the history of art often have their origin in a new way of experiencing the world—the rest is pure arbitrariness and ordinarily a temporary aberration soon to be corrected or forgotten again by later artists. And so it is in historical writing: As we shall see in the last chapter of this book, the most decisive transitions in the history of historical writing had their origin in how a recent and ineluctable past had been experienced. In such situations we can no longer separate the experience from what it is an experience *of:* The past then comes into being only because a certain social and mental world is experienced *as* past. That is to say, there is not, first, a past, and next, an *experience* of this past (in the way that there *is,* first, this chair and, next, my experience of it). The experience of the past and the past itself (as a potential object of historical research) are born at one and the same moment, and in this way experience can be said to be constitutive of the past. This is how the past comes into being. So, condemning experience as an invitation to an unfettered subjectivity would require us to do away with what truly has been the most powerful motor in the evolution of historical writing all through the centuries and would blind us to all that the writing of history is about.

Returning to the artist, we know that it is in the artist's *subjectivity,* hence in what makes the truly great artist into the artist he or she is, and in all that makes the artist's work so clearly different from other painters that the artist's *objectivity* has its sole and exclusive origin. Subjectivity here is the only way to objectivity, to the world of objects.[45] To return to the example mentioned just now, it is precisely where Ruisdael's paintings express a unique experience of nature apparently not shared by any of his contemporaries that the experience of having seen *his* pictures may make us receptive to a new, richer, and more complete experience of nature. So, once again, we see that here the most pronounced subjectivity is the condition for the highest degree of objectivity; the "objective" artist, the artist who presents to us the world in a way that the world is seen by all of us, is an uninteresting and boring artist.

But an important qualification of these views must be added. It may well be that the uninteresting and boring artist nevertheless gives us a fairly reliable representation of a landscape, a city, or an individual sitter; undoubtedly the mediocre artist who had been properly instructed about the laws of perspective, how to use color, how to effect the illusion of transparent or shining surfaces, and about spherical perspectivism will be more successful than the untalented and untrained amateur. So where does this leave us with regard to subjectivity and objectivity?

On the one hand, one could certainly say that the subjective personality of the painter will be more obviously visible in the case of the amateur than in that of the mediocre artist carefully and diligently applying all the rules that he or she has been taught without adding anything of the artist's self to that. Psychologists even use drawings of trees and so on by their patients in order to get a first impression of their psychopathology, and Anton Ehrenzweig has elaborated on all this for great art as well in a justly famous study.[46] On the other hand, we may well feel that the "subjectivity" of the amateur is mere clumsiness and idiosyncrasy. More specifically, the way that a child draws a landscape may give us some Piaget-like information about how children perceive reality and in what way the cognitive apparatus they use for processing the data of experience may differ from that of the adult. And a good psychologist might perhaps even discern in the child's drawing the first announcement of some psychopathology. But, as will be clear from all this, in all these cases the information we may derive from the subjectivity of the painter and what the painter adds to the data of objective reality may increase our understanding of the painter's personality rather than that of represented reality.

So it may seem that there are, in fact, *two* regimes of the subjectivity versus objectivity opposition, instead of just one. There is the kind of subjectivity (which we may find in the work by the great artist) that will teach us some new and deep truths about *reality;* but next to this there is the "bad" kind of subjectivity (to be found in poor art) that will invite only speculations about the *personality* of the painter (if we would happen to be interested in this; for example, because we wish to explain the painter's weaknesses as an artist). I would not wish to imply that there could be no overlap between the two regimes: It may be that the new experience of nature that we become capable of after having "undergone" Ruisdael's "portraits of trees" will also tell us something about Ruisdael himself—although I would venture to say that these insights into the personality of the painter will concern truths about how nature or reality in general was experienced in the historical period in which the artist lived and worked rather than about his own psychology. The painting is, here, I would say, an "exemplification" (in Goodman's sense of that word) of an age rather than of an individual person, and we may even discern here a valuable source for the history of mentalities.

To take an example from one specific region, there is in Dutch landscapes from the middle of the eighteenth century a suggestion of transparency, of clarity, of a contrast between the openness of the country and the density of the woodland scenery, and a cool windiness that one will not even observe in the serenest landscapes of seventeenth-century painters such as a Cuyp, Pijnacker, or van der Heyden.[47] This peculiar atmosphere we will find in paintings and engravings by Troost, Goll van Frankenstein, Keun, Pronk, Bulthuis, or Vinkeles. In seventeenth-century paintings human beings still experience themselves as part of nature, whereas a century later the landscape acquired a new objectivity and became a mere stage on which human activities were enacted. Certainly, we may discern here an experience of nature exemplifying much that we have learned to associate with the Enlightenment: The artist and the spectator no longer experience themselves as part of the world, for they have withdrawn themselves into the seclusion of a transcendental self, to put it in the terminology that has been adopted throughout this chapter. Or, to take a quite different example, if we compare the, in themselves, meaningless ornamental figures of the age of Louis XV to those of *Jugendstil*, it is clear that in both cases vegetative forms are the source of inspiration—but what difference there is between the natural elegance, the perfect equilibrium, and compact harmony of the Louis XV ornament and the weak, elongated, and faded forms that our grandparents apparently found so interesting![48] The former are a respectful tribute to the beauties of nature, but the latter are a nasty and cruel caricature of it. I opted for this perhaps slightly peculiar example because of my conviction that ornament might well prove to be a most valuable source for a history of the experience of nature—as I hope to show in Chapter 7.

This brings me to the last stage of my argument here. In the introduction to this chapter I pointed out that changes in how people in the past experienced their world can be perceived only if they somehow have a resonance in how historians experience their world. In this way, there is a continuity between past and present, an overflowing of the former into the latter, if experience is to play the role I have assigned to it here. Put differently, the loss of a previous way of experiencing the world, the awareness of one way of experiencing the world having been exchanged for a new and later one, must have lost nothing of its drama, if not of its tragedy if enacted on the strictly private scene of the historian's own mind. This dimension of drama or of tragedy will be increased beyond measure if these two coincide—that is, when the story the historians are telling about this transition from one way of experiencing the world to a later one is a story taking place in the historians' own lifetime. In such cases the historians' story is a story about themselves and their own lives are a parable of the course of history: *fabula de te narratur.* All the pain occasioned by the loss of a previous world, of a world about to be superseded by a new one, a world that is still unknown but feared to be pregnant of unfathomable social disasters may then become the historians' own pain. As we shall see in the last chapters of this book, it is under such circumstances where our entry into a new world will also present us with a new kind of historical writing. This is what took place in the minds of sixteenth-century historians such as Machiavelli and Guicciardini and in that of the greatest of the French and German historians in the wake of the French Revolution.[49]

2.7 CONCLUSION

This chapter mainly has been a summons to eliminate transcendentalism and all its traces from both historical theory and from historical writing itself and to do so in the name of experience. Next, it follows that we should also ruthlessly do away with all these useless and cumbersome products of transcendentalist bureaucracy, such as we may find these in semiotics, hermeneutics, structuralism and post-structuralism, tropology, deconstructivism, textualism, contextualism, and so on. It is time we begin to recognize that over the last five decades we have been bombarded with an almost endless series of transcendentalist monstrosities, each of them even more difficult to grasp and more ambitious than its competitors, and that these monstrosities did, in fact, little more than to perversely draw attention to themselves instead of opening our eyes to the sublime mysteries of the past. So let us throw open the windows of this narrow and stuffy room that we have been living in for the last fifty years—and let us breathe again the fresh air of the outside world! This may seem—to echo Putnam—a plea for a re-infantilization of our reflection about the nature and the purpose of historical writing. Perhaps it is—but it may, at times, be necessary (and even demand the greatest effort) to regain something of the child's innocent naivete and to be wholly open to what the world has to offer us. And I believe that the notion of experience is best suited for discarding the Schillerian "sentimentality" of "theory" and for regaining this blessed state of "naivete" So let us try to become a little more "naive" than we used to be, and let us acknowledge that much of historical truth and objectivity has often been, in fact, the historian's variant of Schillerian sentimentality.

When saying this, I do not in the least wish to belittle, let alone condemn, much of the work that has been done in the name of the transcendentalist idols from a more remote or recent past. On the contrary, I am convinced that underneath many, if not all, of the monuments erected in honor of these idols, an authentic experience of the past or of the text can, in the end, be discovered. For example, we have every reason to be deeply impressed by how Roland Barthes has made us look in a new way at the texts that were written by Balzac, Flaubert, or Michelet or at the banalities of daily life that he had so brilliantly unmasked in his *Mythologies.* Did the twentieth century ever produce a more original, profound, and more acute reader of texts than Barthes? However, if Barthes discovered in the writings of the authors studied by him things that had never been noticed before, this is not because he had previously discovered a superior kind of structuralist semiotics and applied, next, this theory to the texts that were written by the authors investigated by him. It is the other way round: Barthes had a unique capacity for *experiencing* those texts in a new and unprecedented way. And only after his having had this reading experience, and on the basis of it, was he able to develop some new semiotic or hermeneutic theory. But the interest of these theories is negligible since they were never more than the codification of a unique reading experience. Or, to take an example from historical theory, much the same is true of Hayden White's so extremely influential and powerful rereading of nineteenth-century historians. It is in these rereadings of those historians themselves where all the force of *Metahistory* should be situated, whereas the introduction and conclusion to the book only present us with a codification of these results. And the theories presented there would be singularly unconvincing in the absence of these rereadings themselves. Good interpretations are not the spin-off from good hermeneutics, but good hermeneutics merely is a spin-off from good interpretations. So let us thus wave good-bye to hermeneutics, deconstructivism, semiotics, tropology, and so on and see, next, in what way the notion of experience can take their place.

3

HUIZINGA AND THE EXPERIENCE OF THE PAST

> Apparently this historical experience is so essential, that it has always
> been believed to be the true moment of historical knowledge.
> —(Huizinga) [1]

3.1 INTRODUCTION: SCIENCE, HISTORY,
THE CRAFTSMAN, AND THE POLITICIAN

All our knowledge of reality has its ultimate source in experience. This is evidently true of the knowledge we have of our daily world: It is thanks to visual experience that we know how to find our way in a building that we enter for the first time; it is thanks to experience that we discover that our car has run out of gasoline. It is mainly this kind of experience that enables us to act as predictable and responsible human beings and that ensures that our behavior reflects a reality that we all share. Our behavior is socially meaningful to the degree that it mirrors this shared reality and experience is the indispensable *trait d'union* between reality and behavior. So much for the Davidsonian charity principle. It is true, however, that the reality underlying our speech and behavior may be subject to certain reductions and transformations. For example, each profession will bring to the foreground a certain conception of reality that tends to exclude others or to push them over the horizon of the relevant. In this way one might well say that reality is not like a solid block of concrete, as suggested by the cruder kind of metaphysics (which we may find in Descartes or Spinoza), but rather a mosaic of which each individual piece of marble corresponds to a certain profession, artistic skill, and so on. We could go on from there and cut the mosaic pieces down to the size of each of our daily occupations or even beyond this, if we should wish to—and it would certainly be an interesting question of where the process would necessarily have to stop.

When taking into account how experience makes us divide the world into a mosaic of individual pieces, we can discern an interesting difference between the scientist and the craftsman. Scientists undoubtedly have their own piece of the mosaic: There is a part of the world of which they have a unique and unchallenged expertise. However, what they can tell us about their field of expertise will have its implications for all of us, whether we are aware of this or not. But this is of no specific interest to them: They do science and how this may affect the world is for others to decide. In this way the scientist's experience of the world has unleashed a tremendous potential of social and political change that exceeds by far the narrow circumscriptions of the scientist's own mosaic piece. A potential of change thus came into being that is outside anybody's control (for we could not possibly expect such a control from the nonscientist). Or, to put it somewhat more dramatically, with the Enlightenment's discovery of science an unprecedented potential of social and political change had been set loose and it has, since then, been allowed to run wild. One need only be a computer user to be acquainted with the exasperating consequences that have so nicely been summed up in the dictum "that progress has not yet overtaken progress."

Now consider craftsmen and what different kind of change is to be associated with their way of experiencing the world. Just like scientists, craftsmen have a superior talent for dealing with a well-defined and specific part of daily reality; think of carpenters or bricklayers. So, just like scientists, craftsmen live on their own metaphysical mosaic piece. But, as different from the scientists' case, change somehow remains wholly encapsulated within the kind of experience craftsmen have of the world. Change is emphatically *not* set loose here but is always carefully controlled because it never goes beyond what the craftsmen do with the wood, stone, or iron they are working on. Their experience of the world therefore is, unlike that of scientists, always strictly change related. That is to say, their experience of the world, or their "expertise," as we would preferably call it, is always related exclusively to the many individual changes that they effect in their material. This, then, is where experience shades off into expertise—and of expertise we may say that it is the true and full knowledge of change. Science could never produce expertise, since scientific knowledge is not born within the context of the production of change.

What is basically at stake here has best been captured in Marx's notion of practical knowledge (his variant of the notion of expertise). The idea is, roughly, that the woodcarver's "practical knowledge" of wood is not expressed in terms of his *scientific* knowledge of, for example, the specific gravity of wood or of its chemical properties, but rather makes itself felt in how a piece of wood reacts to his effort to make a piece of furniture or a sculpture. Science has no role at all to play in his expertise—or would even be counterproductive.

And all this has its exact analogue in politics, as would be argued by Marx (and by Gadamer "bien étonnés de se trouver ensemble"). Political knowledge or experience is not to be found in the kind of data that political scientists and statisticians are interested in and that are so eagerly collected nowadays but in what happens when the politician, just like the craftsman, tries to *change* existing political reality (and although I am not a Marxist, I have always found this to be one of Marx's more impressive arguments). How political reality *reacts* to the politician's effort to change it, what potential of resistence it may then develop, this and only this gives us access to knowledge of what political reality is like. Political knowledge is a variant of expertise; it has its proper model in how the craftsman experiences the world and not in that of the scientific research. So, one of the most worrying evils of our contemporary political culture is that we tend to forget about this, to celebrate the scientist and not the craftsman as the true politician's model, and to see in statistics, opinion polls, econometrics, or political science in general the only sound basis for political decision making. So, in politics one has also become enchanted by the transcendentalist "interface" between subject and object (which I already put in the pillory in the previous chapter). This had two consequences that mar contemporary political culture. In the first place, an unbridgeable gap between the politician and the public came into being, each of them living on their own side of this interface separating the two of them, which put an end to any real interaction between the politician and the public. In the second place, social and political change were also allowed to run wild—as in science. The control of change was considered just as dangerous and counterproductive—once again, as undoubtedly is the case in science. This is technocratic government—and bureaucracy has been the main beneficiary of it all.

Obviously, history and historical experience belong to the domain of the craftsman and of the (good) politician rather than to that of the scientist. Is there not a striking similarity between what was said just now about the continuous interaction between the craftsmen and their materials, on the one hand and, on the other hand, the abolition of the interface between the historian and the past that was demanded in the previous chapter? Indeed, for craftsmen all that is of interest takes place *on the surface,* where they and their material "meet each other," so to say; and they will produce nothing of value as soon as they move away from the surface and get lost in meditations on themselves or on the (physical) nature of their material. And so it is, again, in history and historical experience: Historical experience and knowledge are "impressionist" in the sense of having their natural habitat on the *surface* of things, on where they come closest to each other, on where they reach out for each other—and *not* on where they tend to turn away from each other and hide themselves from us in their own fathomless depths.

3.2 CONSTRUCTIVISM

But despite their differences, all sciences share with our dealings with daily reality the dependency on experience. It is true that in sciences like physics the relation between empirical fact and theory has become so complicated that its articulation required the effort of several generations of philosophers of science. And even they have never succeeded in defining the nature of that relationship in a way that is satisfactory to all of them. Nevertheless, without experience, without empirical data, science could never go beyond mere mathematical redescription—however useful such redescriptions may sometimes be.

Nevertheless, even though experience plays in science a role that is different from the one assigned to it in history (and in the humanities), no sensible person would deny that experience is conditional for the possibility of historical knowledge as well. The coming into being of "scientific history" has been attributed to many historians from Thucydides to Braudel or the cliometricians. But each of these proud attributions was supported by the claim that the historian, to whom the honor of having founded "scientific history" was granted, should have been the first to discover a solid experiential basis for historical writing. Ranke, whom many see as the founder of modern historical writing, may well illustrate the point. According to Ranke, the historian should possess a "pure love of truth," and that would require the historian to engage in a "documentary, penetrating and profound study" of the past.[2] For Ranke historical documents, such as the *Relazioni,* that is, reports by ambassadors or statesmen, and so on, provide the historian with the solid *experiential* basis for the science of history. This program, as Ranke did not tire to point out, implied a rejection of speculative philosophy of history—which Ranke mainly associated with Fichte. In Ranke's view philosophy of history relates to the science of history as pure mathematics relates to the empirical sciences (surely a most flattering picture of the Fichtes and the Hegels!), for in both cases deductive truth would vanquish empirical truth with the result that (in the case of history) "all that is typically interesting in history would disappear."[3]

But there is a problem here that Ranke failed to see. One may well say that the documents that the past has left us constitute the experiential basis of all sound historical knowledge. However, these documents do not provide us with an experience of the past itself, that is, with the reality of a world of centuries ago. Insofar as experience has a role to play here, we could properly say that historians have an "experience" of the documents they find in the archives but not that they have therewith an "experience" of the past. Documents are clues that may enable the historian to formulate hypotheses with regard to what the past has actually been like, but neither documents nor hypotheses can be identified with the past itself. To put it differently, the experiential basis that documents undoubtedly present permit the historian to develop a construction of the past but not a *re*-construction of the past (as it actually has been). It may function as *evidence* for a certain conjecture of what the past may well have been like but can never amount to a revelation of its actual nature because we can never check these conjectures against the past itself.

This is the thesis that has been most convincingly argued by the so-called historical constructivists, theorists like Oakeshott, Meiland, and Goldstein.[4] For the constructivists we cannot have experience or experiential knowledge of the past itself for the simple but decisive reason that the past could not possibly be an object of experience because it no longer exists. We can experience in the true sense of the word only what is given to us *here* and *now.* All that historians have at their disposal here and now are the documentary *remains* that the past has left us (we can have experience of *these*)—so all that historians can meaningfully do is to develop on the basis of these documentary remains the most plausible hypothesis with regard to what the actual past *may* have been like. But whatever the hypothesis historians come up with, it can never be checked by comparing it with the past *itself*—for, once again, the past no longer exists. So these hypotheses necessarily must remain mere constructions—and this is why people like Oakeshott, Meiland, and Goldstein are called constructivists. And the crucial conclusion is that plausibility is the only workable criterion for assessing the merits of historical accounts and not historians' experience of their subject matter (that is, the past itself), for no such experience of the past is possible.

In many respects the constructivist's argument is a most convincing account of the nature of the historian's relationship to the object that is studied. It certainly does most adequately explain a large part and of the practice of history. And the more responsible variants of so-called narrativist historical theory are, essentially, an elaboration of the constructivist's position. But we cannot fail to note and be amazed by the fact that this account of the practice of history effectively rules out the possibility of any experience that historians might have of their object of investigation, that is, of the past *itself.* Even in the most esoteric parts of contemporary theoretical physics such a state of affairs would be the cause of epistemological alarm. It may well be that the link between theory and empirical fact has become extremely tenuous and complicated in physics because of the abstractions of theory, yet even here the link between theory and empirical fact about the object of investigation is never completely severed—as the constructivist quietly requires us to do as a matter of course for the practice of history. Taking into account all this, we get the puzzling picture of history as a science founded on experience, but we can never acquire experiential knowledge of the object of investigation itself.

Let us have a closer look at the constructivist's case. Decisive is the constructivist's argument that we can experience only what is given to us here and now, and next, that the past is not given to us here and now and that, thus, no (direct) experience of the past is possible. When dealing with the constructivist argument I propose to distinguish between (1) the question of whether the constructivist gives a correct account of the historian's epistemological predicament and (2) if so, whether the constructivist's (philosophical) assessment of the historian's predicament is valid.

To begin with the first question, it is by no means as self-evident as the constructivist believes that no experience of the past should be possible.

As we shall see in this chapter, Huizinga had his historical experiences when looking at paintings of the Van Eycks or of Rogier van der Weijden. Bachofen had his when entering an Etruscan burial chamber. For Goethe and Mario Praz a historical experience could be provoked by a piece of furniture or a room that was left unchanged for centuries, and Herder, Prescott, and Burckhardt had theirs when assisting at the enactment of an ancient ritual or when looking at a certain city scene. It seems to be a perfectly reasonable assumption that in these objects a *Hauch* or aura of the past *itself* has been preserved all through the centuries and that the subject of the historical experience suddenly becomes aware of it.[5] Put differently, in such cases the past *itself* can be said to have survived the centuries and to be still present in objects that are given to us here and now, such as paintings, burial chambers, pieces of furniture, and so on.

Hence, the notion of historical experience does not necessarily require a sudden disappearance of the dimension of time or some mystical union with the past (as was assumed by Meinecke[6]), for the past can properly be said to be present in the artifacts that it has left us. They are protuberances, so to say, of the past in the present—and, as such, there is no more mystery about them and about their being the potential objects of an experience of the past than about a traveler visiting different countries and then having an experience of a country that is different from his own. Indeed, these objects are like travelers through time (and they have now reached us on their journey), although always bearing in themselves the signs of their origin—and this is why they have this capacity to provoke a historical experience in those who are singularly sensitive to the complex meaning of those signs. It is true that our experience itself of this kind of object should not be confused with the kind of *inferences* that we might make about certain aspects of the past on the basis of visual evidence provided by paintings. For example, one might use Gabriel Metsu's painting *The Sick Child* (ca. 1655) in an argument about Philippe Ariès's famous thesis on family life in early modern Europe—and then go completely astray if Metsu happened to have manipulated the details of daily life in this painting. But there is one thing that Metsu could *never* have manipulated, namely, that this is a painting from the middle of the seventeenth century, bearing testimony to what we might call the style, *Hauch,* or aura of that quite specific period in history. And it is *this* that I have in mind when speaking about how we may experience the past by looking at a painting.[7]

In sum, the notion of historical experience does not in the least necessarily involve the epistemological acrobatics of having to obliterate or transcend forbidding time barriers. In the kind of cases mentioned just now the notion of historical experience is as straightforward and as pedestrian as the notion of the experience that I now have of the computer on which I am presently typing this text. However, the constructivist would be right in pointing out that this may well be true for the art historian (although not even all of them), but that this will be of little comfort to the historian who has to develop a hypothesis about what the past may have been like on the basis of the evidence the past has left us—and is then confronted with the situation that no artifact (painting, piece of furniture, or whatever you have) that the past has left us can meaningfully be related to the hypothesis in question.

I believe that the constructivist is right in arguing that our experience of a work of art is a quite specific situation and fundamentally different from the epistemological situation that historians will normally find themselves in when having to develop the most plausible hypothesis about what has happened in the past. So this rejoinder by the constructivist will now require us to consider the second question that was mentioned a moment ago, namely, the question of whether the constructivist's skepticist argument is correct that such hypotheses could not possibly have their basis in *experience* since we can experience in the proper sense of the word only what is given to us here and now.

As is so often the case, we see in the constructivist's position how a variant of skepticism (that is, the claim that experiential knowledge of the past is impossible) results from imposing unrealistically high demands on what is to count as knowledge. Why should we restrict, as the constructivist requires us to do, the domain of reliable experiential knowledge to what is given us here and now? Recall the trite argument of the astronomer who has experiential knowledge of a past, which is sometimes up to several billion years old, when looking at the sky (even more so, when we look at the sun ourselves, we *see* [experience] a past that is eight minutes old). Next, as soon as we accept the astronomer's telescope and the biologist's microscope as enabling the astronomer and the biologist to gain experiential knowledge of what they see through these instruments (as seems to be a reasonable thing to do), why should we stop there and not accept the physicist's knowledge of the behavior of, say, electrons and photons as "experiential"? Because no physicist ever "actually saw" an electron or a photon? But did the astronomer or the biologist ever "actually see" themselves what they observed through their telescopes and microscopes? In fact, you can only correctly say that they really "saw" these stars and microbes on the assumption that the laws of optics that were used for building these instruments do hold. So when accepting what the astronomer and the biologist see as experiential knowledge, all knowledge based on observation and reliable inference should count as experiential knowledge as well. But then it will no longer be clear why the constructivist skeptic is making such a fuss about our not being able to experience the past. What the historian writes about the past, insofar as it is based on solid documentary evidence and sound reasoning, is then epistemologically just as robust as what the astronomer, the biologist, and the physicist claim to be the case on the basis of their observations.

I expect the constructivist not to be wholly convinced by this argument and to riposte that in the sciences the chain from observation to conclusion is so far more stronger and solid than in history. Indeed, the constructivist will be ready to admit that you must have confidence in the laws of optics if you decide to attribute to the astronomer experiential knowledge of some galaxy. But, the constructivist will go on to say, you have nothing like this in such a notoriously uncertain and disorderly discipline as the writing of history. And this is why, in history, you can have experiential knowledge only of what is simply and unproblematically given to you—the documents in your hands, for example, for as soon as you really start to *think* and to make inferences on the basis of this documentary evidence, you will undoubtedly stray from the right path sooner or later.

Now, there is a whole nexus of interesting philosophical problems involved in this—for example, is experiential knowledge the kind of thing that could *ex hypothesi* never misguide us? But what then about fata morganas, delusions of sight, and so on? Surely these things are given to us experientially, and yet they invite mistaken beliefs about the world. But I shall leave these issues aside and focus, instead, on another interesting hidden assumption of the constructivist's argument. This is the assumption that experiential knowledge, what we believe to be true about the world on the basis of experience, always possesses what one might call an atomic or elementary character. The domain of experience is thus reduced to these atomic and tiniest building blocks of knowledge. Hence, the suggestion always is that you begin with these tiny packages of experiential knowledge and that, next, something "great" or more complex, a scientific theory of historical narrative, can perhaps be built out of these elementary building blocks. And precisely this is where things ordinarily go right in the sciences but tend to go wrong in history and why the constructivists are so skeptical about the possibility of an experiential knowledge of the past itself, whereas they are so much less likely to cherish such defeatist worries about scientific theories. In sum, the constructivist's argument both presupposes and enhances the assumption that experiential knowledge always comes to us in these tiny packages and that we could never have experiential knowledge of something that is complex, comprehensive, and overwhelming. This is, of course, a typically positivist dogma and the kind of intuition of which you may expect to find variants in the writings of any positivist philosopher.

But as soon as the nature of the dogma is clearly written down, you will immediately become aware of its being, indeed, a mere dogma. Suppose you encounter a person. Is a person not a most complex and comprehensive object? Or think of what you are actually seeing when looking at the sky at a clear night or of what you are doing when reading a book. In all these cases you will have to do with complex objects. And apart from the scientific experiment, complexity seems to be the rule rather than the exception in our experience of the world. Perhaps the positivist will now riposte that the object you see may well be complex but that our *experience* of it would or, rather, should be quite simple and elementary. So, according to the positivist, we mistakenly tend to project the complexity of these objects of experience on our experience of them. Although not being a phenomenologist à la Husserl, I must confess that I would not feel myself capable of making much of this objection. This distinction between "seeing complex things" on the one hand and the "complexity of seeing things" on the other seems to me to serve no other purpose than to save the skin of the positivist's *Weltanschauung*—for this is what it is, in the end.

But even if this were to be granted to the positivist, I would like to ask about our experience of painting, of music, of art in general. Surely, such experiences are experiences in the most dramatic sense of the word, but we know that the experience of a work of art cannot be taken apart into a multitude of experiences of all its constituent components. When looking at a painting, you do not see, first, myriad tiny individual brushstrokes that you, next, somehow put together again; you see the painting as a whole, in its totality, and experience it *as such*. There is an instructive anecdote about Clement Greenberg: When wishing to make up his mind about a painting, he walked up to the painting with his hands before his eyes. When standing right in front of the painting he dropped his hands and the immediate impact the painting *then* had on him would be decisive for him. Obviously, the procedure was intended to take in *the painting as a whole* and to avoid the temptation to somehow put it together out of its component parts. In sum, let us look with the greatest suspicion at philosophical accounts of experience ruling out a priori that experience could be something complex. More specifically, as long as we allow ourselves to be seduced by the positivist's dogma of the nature of experience, we shall never be able to make any sense of historical experience. Theories of "sense data" are our worst guide if we wish to get a grasp of what goes on in history and in the humanities in general. As we shall see, historical experience is, just as it is in the arts, always most complex. In fact, in history it is just the other way around than is suggested by the positivist's *Weltanschauung*. In history you move toward abstraction—and to doubtful intellectual construction—when moving away from complexity to what is allegedly basic and elementary. History comes to us in wholes, in totalities, and this is how we primarily experience both the past itself and what it has left us—as is the case in the arts and in aesthetic experience. The explanation is that history does not rise up before our minds from data found in the archives in the way that a detective may infer from the relevant data who committed a murder: It is, instead, a "displacement" of the present as dictated by these data, and, as such, it is experienced as a totality no less than is the case with the present. This, then, is what we always must bear in mind when thinking of the notion of experience and especially when considering what has been said on the notion by Huizinga—to whom I shall now turn.

3.3 HUIZINGA ON HISTORICAL EXPERIENCE

Historical experience has rarely attracted the attention of historians and has only rarely been discussed by historical theorists. What is, in my view, still the best account of historical experience can be found in Huizinga's collected work, where the notion is discussed on two occasions, albeit tantalizingly briefly. Although the phenomenology of historical experience presented here by Huizinga is deplorably sketchy, I believe it to be fundamentally correct in the sense of projecting on it all the right associations with the right dosage. We might even conjecture it to have been a blessing in disguise that Huizinga never managed to write more than these meager two to three pages on historical experience. He is quite explicit about how important the notion is to him, and the brevity of his exposition may therefore have forced him to remain as close as possible to his intuitions and to what the notion truly meant to him. If Huizinga's fascination for the notion had tempted him to write some lengthy treatise on it, the clear contours of what we now find in his writings on historical experience might well have been lost. The passage in which Huizinga most fully summarizes his intuitions about historical experience runs as follows:

This brings us to the essence of the issue. There is in all historical awareness a most momentous component, that is most suitably characterized by the term historical sensation.[8] One could also speak of historical contact. Historical imagination already says too much, and much the same is true of historical vision, insofar as the cognate notion of visual representation suggests a degree of determinacy that is still absent here. The German word "Ahnung" that had already been used by Wilhelm von Humboldt in this connection would almost express it if only the term had not lost its precise meaning by its use in another context. This contact with the past that cannot be reduced to anything outside itself is the entrance into a world of its own, it is one of the many variants of ekstasis, of an experience of truth that is given to the human being. It is not like the enjoyment of the work of art, nor a religious affect, nor a trembling before the confrontation with nature, nor the recognition of a metaphysical truth, but yet a member of this series. The object of this sensation are not individual human beings, nor human lives or human thoughts insofar as these possess discernible contours. It can hardly be called an image what the mind forms here or undergoes. Insofar as it takes on any distinct form at all, this form remains composite and vague: an "Ahnung," just as much of streets, houses and fields, of sounds and colors as it is of human beings structuring their lives and being structured by it. This contact with the past, that is accompanied by the absolute conviction of complete authenticity and truth, can be provoked by a line from a chronicle, by an engraving, a few sounds from an old song. It is not an element that the author writing in the past deliberately put down in his work. It is "behind" and not "in" the book that the past has left us. The contemporary reader takes it along with himself in his encounter with the author from the past; it is his response to his call. If this truly is an element of historical understanding, which many have referred to with the term "Nacherleben," then this term is completely mistaken. "Nacherleben" is too much suggestive of a psychological process.

Historical sensation does not present itself to us as a re-living, but as an understanding that is closely akin to the understanding of music, or, rather of the world *by* music.[9] (my translation)

When trying to understand what Huizinga has in mind here, we had best begin by looking at what he considers to be the "typical" object of historical experience or sensation. As becomes clear from the quote, this object is nothing very specific: We should not relate it to the doings or the thoughts of individual human beings. Neither is it some deep structure that one might discern in it. The object of historical experience is given to us prior to conscious reflection by the historian; it is not to be related to any process of thought, to how the historian may combine the evidence the past has left us in order to devise the kind of hypotheses about the past that the constructivist we discussed a moment ago always had in mind. It is to be related, rather, to what happens between the historian and the past, to what happens on the interface between the two of them, and not where we will find ourselves when moving away from the interface, either toward the dark and hidden recesses of the past itself or toward the historian's cognitive machinery. Huizinga speaks here of *ekstasis,* hence of a movement by the historian with which he moves outside himself and reaches for the past, so to say. This is where Huizinga's historical experience comes close to Nietzsche's *Rausch,* a word without its exact equivalent in English, perhaps best described as a moment of enrapture and of being carried away by the intensity of experience. Its meaning and effects can best be elucidated by Nietzsche himself: "Die Raum- und Zeitbedingungen sind verändert; ungeheure Fernen werden überschaut und gleichsam erst wahrnehmbar; die Ausdehnung des Blicks über grössere Mengen und Weiten" ("The determinations of space and time have changed; immense distances are grasped within one single overview and become only now perceivable; it offers an expansion of view comprising many things both close and remote" [my translation]).[10] All spatial and temporal demarcations have momentarily been lifted; it is as if the temporal trajectory between past and present, instead of separating the two, has become the locus of their encounter. Historical experience pulls the faces of past and present together in a short but ecstatic kiss. Historical experience is, in this way, a "surface" phenomenon: It takes place on the surface or interface where the historian and the past meet each other. But this certainly does not imply that we have now entered the domain of mysticism and irrationality.

This can be made clear when we focus on the notion of *Ahnung* that Huizinga associates with historical experience. Admittedly, there is no satisfactory equivalent for the German word *Ahnung* in English. Close to it come verbs like *to surmise* and *to conjecture,* but these words suggest a clarity and certainty about *what* is surmised and conjectured which is absent in the case of *Ahnung.* The word *Ahnung* is, in this respect, closer to the verb *to intimate* where we cannot be sure about the exact nature of *what* is intimated. This is left indeterminate in the case of intimation, and the word is meant to do just this. The difference between *Ahnung* and *intimation* being, of course, that *Ahnung* is something that *comes* to us, whereas when intimating, we *bring* something to others. Both words suggest a movement in the opposite direction, so to say. But yet, if one has an *Ahnung* of something, this is not completely random, and it is certainly suggestive of an intuition of how things are, or will be. So how do we sort out this strange mixture of determinacy and indeterminacy that is part of the logic of the words *Ahnung* and intimation?

The aspect of the meaning of the word *Ahnung* that is at stake here can best be clarified in terms of the difference between seeing, on the one hand, and hearing (or smelling), on the other.[11] When seeing things, we can always distinguish between (1) seeing two different specimens of the same type of thing (for example, when we see two different specimens of the same type of automobile) and (2) seeing twice the same specimen of the same type of thing (when we see twice the same car of the same type). This distinction makes no sense in the case of hearing: When hearing on two different occasions a C, we hear twice the *same* C, although on different occasions. So, identity is peculiarly "incomplete" or "truncated" in the case of hearing in a way not having its equivalent in the case of seeing. Individuation seems to be peculiarly incomplete in the case of hearing if compared to what happens to be the case with seeing. And yet, it is not *actually* incomplete or deficient, since it succeeds in doing perfectly well what is expected from it. So much becomes clear already from the fact that individuation in the case of hearing should not be thought to imply any vagueness or imprecision—at least not necessarily so: On the contrary, our certainty about hearing a C may even be greater then the certainty we have about the things we see. It just takes more to individuate the identity of the things we see than of the sounds that we hear.[12]

This is, then, what we should associate with the word *Ahnung,* and the suggestion is that with *Ahnung* we experience the objects of the world when robbed of the articulate identity we "normally" ascribe to them.[13] It is as if we would have to find our way around in the world of the things we see with nothing else to go on than the sounds we hear or the odors we smell: We would feel awfully handicapped and terribly uncertain about all that we are doing. But our relief about living in a world of things that we can see should not make us forget that we are also the inhabitants of the world of sounds and of smells. Moreover, as we know from music, the world of sounds may sometimes give us an understanding of the *condition humaine* that we can never expect from the world of visual forms. This, then, should invite some more respect for *Ahnung* and for its cognate notion of historical experience than many nowadays would be willing to credit it with. Indeed, in agreement with the logic of the word *Ahnung,* as expounded a moment ago, we could say that the objects of historical experience are rather "heard" than "seen"—but that, as such, their existence can be doubted just as little as the historical existence of Napoleon or of the Treaty of Versailles.[14]

If we recognize all this, it is easy to see (1) why the notion of historical experience may provoke in historians and historical theorists these associations with the irrational and with mysticism and (2) what is wrong with such overhasty intuitions. Intuitions like these originate from our unreflected conviction that the past is there for us only to be "seen" and that it is not something that can be "heard" or "smelled" (for much of what I have been saying about hearing is true about the sense of smell as well). It is as if we were saying, well, we all know that the world is made up of individual objects that we can see and that we can most truly and accurately depict with pencil drawings, whereas the world of colors, of the sounds we hear, and of smells is inevitably a hopeless chaos compared to the contours of objects that we can "objectively" capture with the pencil drawing. Elaborating on this metaphor, we could say that the resistance against historical experience originates from the assumption that the past (as a potential object of historical investigation) is the kind of object corresponding to the cognitive operations that have so convincingly been described by the constructivist—that is, to a past whose individual objects we can see with the constructivist's eyes and that permit of clearly delineated pencil drawings of the past only. And since it is believed that this is all there is to historical writing, both our hearing or smelling of the past is automatically excluded together with the past objects that we hear or smell.

The professionalization of historical writing, distrusting each relationship to the past that cannot be expressed in constructivist terms, has strongly contributed to reducing historical experience to the *nomen nefandum* that it presently is. But this is to be regretted for two reasons, both of them suggested by this distinction between seeing and hearing the past. In the first place, seeing always places us at a distance from the object we see, whereas in the case of hearing and smelling we have a direct contact with the object of experience. There is no clear separation here between the object and the subject of experience: As in Aristotle's account of experience given in *De Anima,* there is a continuity between subject and object that all of the epistemological tradition since Descartes has always wanted to deny.[15] The sound we hear is in our ears. And much the same is true of the sense of smell and of the sense of touch. And because of this continuity, we could agree with Aristotle's suggestion that in perception we become ourselves more or less like the object of perception, just as the sand of the beach may take on the form of our feet. By presenting us with such an "imprint" of the past in our mind, historical experience provides us with a source of truth and authenticity that will never have its equal in a historical writing carefully respecting the restriction of constructivism (and of seeing the past). In the second place, this may also explain why historical experience may, at times, be such an immeasurably stronger determinant of how we conceive of the past than constructivist historical writing. Indeed, as we shall see in a moment, historical experience may sweep away with one simple majestic gesture all that had been built up by generations of historians. The true revolutions in the history of historical writing and in historical awareness in general have been provoked by shifts in historical experience and not by the polemics of constructivist historical writing or by the reactions it elicited. Constructivism always respects these forces of tradition discussed at the end of the previous chapter.

Next, if such revolutions occur, we undoubtedly have to do with conceptions of the past that no longer fit within the patterns of the gradual evolution of historical insight. Put differently, the revolutionary insight provoked by historical experience transcends contextualization: It is a rupture with the context we had inherited from the past of historical writing for discussing a certain topic. Huizinga explains why this must be so when criticizing the hermeneutic notion of *Nacherleben* or of reliving. Huizinga rejects this notion since it seems to leave no place for the (Aristotelian) interaction between the past and the historian that he deems to be so crucial to all historical experience. Historical experience is the historian's "response" to "the call" of the past, as Huizinga formulated it. There is in the case of historical experience a "communication" between the historian and the past excluding all that is not part of this most private and intimate communication. Several consequences follow from this. In the first place, we can now understand how this decontextualization I mentioned a moment ago could come about. "Normally" our conceptions of the past are no less the expression or the product of a historiographical tradition within which the historian writes than of data that had been discovered about the past. But this dimension of "horizontality" (connecting through time the different phases of a historiographical tradition) is suddenly eliminated, and all that then remains is the "vertical" relationship between the historian and the past. When responding to "the past's call," the historian momentarily "forgets" the historiographical context within which he normally operates. For a moment there is only the past itself, revealing to him its quasi-noumenal nakedness with an unusual directness and immediacy. And the same can be said for the past, the object of historical experience: It hurries toward the historian with the same eagerness to rupture its ties with what surrounds it, as is the case with the historian. When taking into account this double movement of decontextualization, we are reminded of how Romeo and Juliet could achieve the intimacy of their being together only after having freed themselves from the influence of their families, the Montagues and the Capulets:

> O Romeo, Romeo! Wherefore art thy Romeo?
> Deny thy father and refuse thy name;
> Or, if thou wilt not, be but sworn my love,
> And I'll no longer be a Capulet.[16]

Indeed, as will be argued in the next chapter, historical experience and contextualization mutually exclude each other, and it is certainly true that the contemporary cult of the context has blinded us more than anything else to the notion of (historical) experience. Think of Jonathan Culler's "meaning is context-bound, but context is boundless," ruling out all directness and authenticity in our contact with the world of meaning and history.

This may explain one further feature Huizinga attributes to historical experience. Huizinga emphasizes that a historical experience will ordinarily be provoked by relatively uninteresting objects that the past has left us: a line from a chronicle, an engraving, or a few sounds from an old song.

Elsewhere Huizinga confesses that the engravings of people moving their things to a new house by the seventeenth-century artist Jan van der Velde (which Huizinga recognizes to be wholly devoid of any art-historical significance) could nevertheless provoke in him a historical experience:

What am I enjoying here. Art?—Yes, but something else as well. It is not a scientific pleasure: for, to say the truth, the history of people moving to a new house at the beginning of the seventeenth century has no secrets that attract me. "These are merely antiquarian interests of a lower order," comments the art-historian.— OK. If only I am allowed to claim that for me this inferiority in comparison with the enjoyment of the engraving as a work of art has no role to play. Yes, I go further, for it may well be that such a historical detail, in an engraving, or in a notarial act for that matter, while it may be indifferent to me, may suddenly give me the conviction of an immediate contact with the past, a sensation as profound as the profoundest enjoyment of art, an (don't laugh) almost ekstatic experience of no longer being myself, of a flowing over into a world outside myself, of a getting in touch with the essence of things, of the experience of Truth by history.[17] . . . It is a pathos, an ebriety of the moment . . . . It is familiar to you, is it not?, for it has been suggested as a motive in thousands of sonnets. This is the nature of what I call historical sensation.[18] (my translation)

The paradox is, of course, that none of Huizinga's own historical experiences has left deeper traces in his writings than the one he underwent when visiting the exhibition of the Flemish primitives in 1902 in Bruges. This was the historical experience from which *The Waning of the Middle Ages* was born. And, obviously, the Van Eycks, van der Weijden, Campin, van der Goes, and so on were anything but minor painters, and their paintings clearly are among the most auratic objects that have ever been made in the history of mankind.

But the paradox is not difficult to dissolve and its solution will bring us closer to an understanding of historical experience. We should realize ourselves, to begin with, that great art is covered by such a thick layer of centuries of historical interpretation, is so much an exponent of the whole history of art, that decontextualization is well-nigh impossible to achieve. We cannot see a painting by Leonardo, Rembrandt (whom Huizinga, by the way, firmly disliked because of his un-Dutch propensity to drama and theatricality), or Goya without being aware of their place in the history of art and of how their paintings have been seen by many generations of art historians. These paintings are all covered by a thick crust of interpretation, and this prevents us from getting access to where these paintings are emanations of the past that had produced them and, hence to these paintings as objects that may trigger a historical experience. This is different with the minor work of art, say, the engravings by a Jan van der Velde illustrating the activities of his fellow countrymen for each of the twelve months of the year. Here we still possess a complete openness to how the past reveals itself to us in the guise of these unpretentious registrations of daily life in Holland at the beginning of the seventeenth century and of what it must have been like to have lived then.

But this does not imply that it would under all circumstances be impossible to scrape off the crust of interpretation sedimented on the great work of art and to experience it as if a whole civilization saw it for the first time. This is what took place when Huizinga had his historical experience of the late Northwest European Middle Ages when visiting with his friend André Jolles at the 1902 exposition in Bruges. The historical experience he then had cut right through the crust of interpretation on the surface of these paintings obscuring the past underneath it as a varnish yellowed by age. The life of these late Middle Ages, its fierceness, its fascination with extremes, its unwillingness to discover new forms behind these extremes, all this now sprung onto him and overwhelmed him as we may be overwhelmed by music, say, by Bach's *Hohe Messe* or Beethoven's *Missa Solemnis*. This is what made Huizinga write *The Waning of the Middle Ages*— although the road from historical experience to the historical text and the historian's language still is a tortured and most complex one, as we shall find in the remainder of this chapter. In this way one can say that a historical experience may lay at the basis of the most revolutionary historical writing. Or, to put it in Kuhnian terms, a historical experience may function as the "anomaly" that is excluded by a "period of normal science" and that may trigger a "scientific revolution." Here the past itself, a past that is not contaminated by the "paradigms" of "normal science," functions as the corrective of our most general and formal intuitions about what the past is like. Hence, the interest for the notion of historical experience is not only justified by our desire to break out off the prisonhouse of language discussed in the chapters 1 and 2, but also by our wish to perfect our understanding of the development of historical writing over the last few centuries. And at the end of this book we shall encounter a variant of historical experience that has even been far more decisive in this than the kind of historical experience discussed here.

I close this section with the discussion of two last features of historical experience mentioned by Huizinga. Because of its being decontextualized on the level of the subject, historical experience is a gift of the moment; it comes unannounced and unexpectedly and cannot be repeated at will. Huizinga described it, as we have seen, as "an ebriety of the moment": It is something that suddenly happens to the historian (or not, of course) rather than something the historian could deliberately provoke. Finally, historical experience should be distinguished from historical intuition, or insight. With regard to historical intuition one may think here of how Huizinga himself, during one of his walks along the canals in his birthplace Groningen, suddenly conceived of the late Middle Ages as an ending rather than as a proto-Renaissancistic promise of a new beginning. It is true, in both cases, whether we think of historical experience or of historical intuition, that we have to do with sudden revelations. But there is a difference in the nature of these two kinds of revelation and in the level where we should situate them. Historical experience is primarily "receptive," whereas the sudden intuition of how to give form to a complex past is predominantly a matter of an "active" projection. Put differently, whereas in the case of historical experience the historian's mind is formed by the past, historical insight is, on the contrary, a giving of form to the past by the historian. Recognizing the difference between historical experience and historical intuition does not exclude, of course, that in practice there will an intense interaction between the two, for what is more natural and self-evident than using what has been given to the historian in terms of historical experience to also guide him in his exposition of the past?

3.4 HUIZINGA ON LANGUAGE AND HISTORICAL EXPERIENCE (SENSITIVISM)

In the two preceding chapters we have commented lengthily on the issue of how experience, as understood in this study, and language are related to each other. To put it in the terms of section 3.3, how can or should we translate the sound or the smell of the past (*Ahnung*) into the visual imagery of the historical text? One of the most interesting things about Huizinga is that he was profoundly sensitive himself to precisely this issue. And he was far more prolific about this issue than about historical experience itself. Indeed, the problem of translating the data of (sensory) experience into language belongs to one of Huizinga's oldest and most persistent preoccupations. When discussing Huizinga's views on the writing of history, one should never forget that Huizinga was trained as a linguist, not as a historian, that he began his scholarly career as a Sanskritist, and that his doctoral dissertation was devoted to the role of Vidusaka in Indian comedy.

What most deserves our attention here is Huizinga's initial plans for a doctoral dissertation. Huizinga makes a short comment on this abortive project in his autobiography, and he writes there that it had been his aim to investigate the expressions for the sensory perception of light and noise employed in the Indo-Germanic languages.[19] Huizinga's biographer, Wessel Krul, informs us that Huizinga wanted to demonstrate in his thesis that the words we use for expressing sensory perception are formed by a "direct lyrical formation" or "by the lyrical metaphor of an already existing word for expressing feeling or sensation."[20] Such words originally express a feeling, a mood, an atmosphere, and not a well-defined concept. Huizinga clarified his ideas with the help of the example of the synesthetic metaphor of "the red sound of a trumpet." Huizinga argued that this metaphor has a peculiar plausibility that we can explain only by assuming that there is a word that may express what we associate with both seeing something red and hearing the sound of a trumpet. For Huizinga this is the word *fierce* (*fel* in Dutch). And it follows that we can say of the word *fierce* that it expresses something that seeing and hearing do apparently have in common. And what both have in common, in this case, is apparently not yet differentiated, or pulled apart, in correspondence to the nature of these two senses and, therefore, necessarily refers us to a level in our contact with reality that is prior to or deeper than both seeing and hearing. Hence the word *fierce* has a more intimate and direct relationship with sensory experience than words giving us literal descriptions of what we either see or hear. *Fierce* therefore belongs to the category of words that express the most intimate and direct experience we can have of reality. Here we really have reached a point where the epistemological barriers between language, experience, and reality begin to give way and where the three seem to merge into each other. But this most intimate contact is not achieved, as in Gadamer's case, by an intertwining together of reality, experience, and language but by a contact among the three where the individual nature of each of them is carefully respected despite the most intimate relationship that has been effected between them.

Now, in his autobiography Huizinga wrote at the end of his life he tells his reader that the Ph.D. project for a dissertation was the result of literary influences that he had been exposed to in his youth rather than of some research program already existing in the linguistics of his time. For a correct understanding of Huizinga's intentions and of his conception of historical experience, it is of the greatest importance to closely investigate these literary influences. Crucial for Huizinga was the work of the novelist and literary theorist Lodewijk van Deijssel (pen name of K. J. L. Alberdink Thijm [1864–1952]) for whom Huizinga had a profound admiration in his student days.

Van Deijssel distinguished among "observation," "impression," and "sensation" to express three different degrees in the intensity of our contact with reality. "Observation" denotes the kind of objectivist interest we have for reality, as is exemplified in the statements that historians make about the past on the basis of documentary research. "Impression" already suggests a greater intimacy with reality, but even here reality still has to submit to the subject's mental makeup. We have opened ourselves here to reality but are susceptible only to what can "impress" us, hence to where reality may succeed in penetrating the innermost reaches of our minds. "Sensation," on the other hand, expresses the most intimate contact with reality that we can have, and here subject and object are in complete equilibrium[21]—this is the highest stage in our encounter with the world. Sensation is, so to say, a mutual embrace of subject and object in which each gives itself completely and unreservedly to the other, without any reluctance. Once again, think of the embrace of Romeo and Juliet. In continuation with the metaphor of this loving embrace, sensitivism was also intended to be suggestive of how we experience reality in the sense of touch—for love is something that you do with your fingers, your mouth, and so on, isn't it? Whereas the eye is the most "transcendentalist" of our senses, to adopt the terminology of the previous chapters. The eye perceives the world while always keeping a safe distance from it; it will never be guilty of such a vulgarity as getting into actual contact with what it perceives, as is the case with the sense of touch. Indeed, as soon as the eye comes too close to what it perceives, everything becomes an indiscriminate blur. This is precisely why Van Deijssel—just like the Aristotle of the *De Anima* mentioned in section 3.3, for that matter—so much wishes to privilege the sense of touch to the eye. Moreover, unlike the eye, the sense of touch really *adapts* itself to what it experiences. Think again of feeling the form of a vase that we hold in our hands: We then feel the vase's form because our own hands take on the very same form as the vase's. We are *formed* by what we perceive, what we perceive leaves its indelible traces on us—and this, too, is a very Aristotelian reflection.

Van Deijssel hoped that this distinction between observation, impression, and sensation would help literature out of the impasse in which it had maneuvered itself in the *fin de siècle.* Like the French symbolists of roughly the same time,[22] Van Deijssel was also disappointed by what had, in the end, been achieved by naturalism or literary realism. Like the symbolists he felt that realism had not succeeded in its main aim, that is, to bridge the gap between language and the world. In order to remedy this, literature should not be content, in his view, to merely give us a believable and "realistic" account of what our social world actually is like but aim to impart to the reader of a novel what one might call "the feel of reality," with all the connotations of sensory perception implicit in that notion. And this is where Van Deijssel's sensitivism, that is, his theory on the kind of experience of the world that is promised by sensation, comes in. Literature should give us a sensation of the world. So, both in the case of the symbolists and in that of Van Deijssel, there is an awareness of the gap between language and reality that literary realism had vainly attempted to bridge. But whereas symbolists tended to fall back on a hermetic idealism in order to penetrate the secrets of reality that realism had remained blind to, Van Deijssel opted for the opposite route by radicalizing realism, and he did so by focusing on our most direct and immediate sensory experience of reality.

In opposition to Mallarmé's well-known "le monde est fait pour aboutir à un beau livre" ("the world was made in order to end up as a beautiful book"),[23] the sensitivist wants to "creep into" reality and to overcome all boundaries between the self and the world. Thus when Herman Gorter (the undisputed literary genius among the sensitivists) could look at the colors of the evening sky and then feel affected by the silence of its clouds, this was to him a subconscious recognition of having become himself part of these clouds and of participating in their majestic silence.[24] Surely, this is sensitivist experience *par excellence* (and, of course, Aristotle all over again). Symbolism represents a movement toward the abstract; it has an elective affinity with idealism (think of Mallarmé's Hegelianism); sensitivism, on the contrary, is a movement toward the concrete or even an attempt at identification or at a quasi-mystical unification with reality. It is, in fact, the *ne plus ultra* of empiricism, since it wishes to do away with all that might stand in the way of a direct and immediate contact with the world itself; it wishes to lose itself in the world; it assigns to itself the paradoxical and self-destructive task of trying to overcome with (literary or poetic) language the barriers between language and the world inevitably created by language. In sum, it looks for the language to undo all language.

Kemperink gives a succinct synopsis of the characteristics that Van Deijssel attributed to sensation in his multivolume and rampant collected literary critiques. Sensation is momentary and has little or no duration; it is abrupt and cannot be predicted. It is accompanied by a sense of anxiety and of alienation: The direct experience or sensation of reality provokes a loss of the naturalness of even the most trivial objects. This explains why sensation is so enigmatic and why the right words seem to fail us for describing its content: Experience here precedes language and the whole complex web of associations embedded in the semantics of our language. There is, furthermore, a feeling as if space had suddenly acquired extra dimensions, a different awareness of colors and, connected with that, a propensity to synesthesia in which the fullness of sensory experience causes an overflowing of the senses into each other. And the result of all these elements of sensation is that the customary demarcations between self and external reality momentarily disappear; this identification with reality is, however, not a triumph of the self over reality but rather a "pathos,"[25] a passive submission and complete receptivity to it. But what is, perhaps, most striking in Van Deijssel's account of sensation is the disruption of temporal continuity and of the normal sequence of before, now, and afterward. The sensation therefore produces in us the conviction that its content is a repetition of something that has happened in precisely this same way maybe centuries ago. Sensation effects a fissure in the temporal order so that the past and the present are momentarily united in a way that is familiar to us all in the experience of déjà vu.[26]

Much, if not all, of what Van Deijssel ascribed to sensation returns in Huizinga's observations on "historical sensation."[27] Indeed, Huizinga's conception of the "historical sensation"—as expounded in section 3.3— can best be seen as an application of Van Deijssel's ideas to the domain of history. And that Huizinga had attempted to do just this is obvious already from the fact that he explicitly avoided the term *historical experience* but adopted the peculiar technical term *historical sensation*.[28] This must make us all the more eager to see how Van Deijssel's sensitivism influenced both Huizinga's views on historical experience and his historical writing itself. To this we shall now turn.

3.5 THE WANING OF THE MIDDLE AGES

It has been observed that Huizinga's best known book, *The Waning of the Middle Ages,* is stylistically quite different from anything that he wrote before or after it.[29] Indeed, syntax sometimes deliberately deviates from what Dutch grammar would prescribe, there is often something strangely archaic about the book's prose, it contains many neologisms, and the book is written throughout in a style that is literary and poetic rather than what one would expect from historical writing. Surely, the text does have a decidedly odd ring in the ears of a speaker of the Dutch language. It is a well-known fact about Huizinga that he was no less careful about matters of style and wording than historians such as Tacitus, Gibbon, or Mommsen. So, when Huizinga adopted a style for *The Waning of the Middle Ages* so different from the one we will find in his other writings, we obviously have a question that needs to be answered.

I shall argue in what follows that the peculiarities of the style of *The Waning of the Middle Ages* can be explained on the basis of the assumption that Huizinga attempted to "translate" into historical language a historical experience of his.[30] This is why the prose and the style of *The Waning of the Middle Ages* are so strikingly different from the more conventional way of writing we find in what he wrote before and after his magnum opus. The most telling evidence for this contention is the fact that Huizinga used in *The Waning of the Middle Ages* the "sensitivist" style to be associated with Van Deijssel and the most prominent authors of the literary movement of the 1880s (of the Tachtigers, as they are known in the history of Dutch literature). And as we saw in section 3.4, these were precisely the poets, novelists, and literary theorists always focusing on the problem of how to bring language as close as possible to the world, to our most direct and immediate experience of it. These were the theorists of literary language who were fascinated by the problem of what language to adopt if we wish to circumvent language's innate propensity to withdraw into a world of its own and to relinquish the world that it was meant to give us access to. It is, thus, a most plausible hypothesis that Huizinga adopted this style of the Tachtigers in order to give expression to a historical sensation or experience—a sensation that he apparently had not felt, or felt with less intensity, when writing his other major works.

And, indeed, the relatively few remarks that Huizinga devoted in his autobiography and elsewhere to the inception of *The Waning of the Middle Ages* suggest that the Middle Ages had for him a meaning quite different from that of all other topics that he studied in the course of his career as a historian. If, then, we read Huizinga's own declarations about how deeply impressed he had been by Huysman's *La bàs,* but, above all by the Bruges exposition in the summer of 1902,[31] it seems likely that we will find in the latter the historical experience that inspired *The Waning of the Middle Ages.* It was the van Eyck exposition, as he himself stated, that satisfied his yearning for a direct contact with past reality, a direct contact that the visual arts, more than anything else, may bring about. In an chapter on the art of the van Eycks that Huizinga wrote in 1916 and that is a prelude to the ideas to be developed in *The Waning of the Middle Ages* of three years later, Huizinga adds that in our relationship to the past, reading, which traditionally gave us access to the past, will have to yield its privileged position to seeing. "We want," wrote Huizinga, "half dreamt, unclearly delineated images, leaving free play to our imagination and this need is better satisfied by a visual than by an intellectual apperception of the past" (my translation).[32] Self-evidently, this must remind us of what we have learned to associate with *Ahnung.*

We should note, furthermore, that there is a persistent tendency in *The Waning of the Middle Ages* to contrast the present and the medieval past again and again and to actually present the Middle Ages to the readers in terms of only *that* difference—one need only think here of the well-known first sentence of the book: "When the world was five centuries younger, all events had much sharper external forms than now." The whole of history lying between the Middle Ages and our own present seems to have been forgotten or obliterated momentarily, and in this the directness of historical experience is suggested by the text itself. This directness also effects the decontextualization of the past we discussed in section 3.3. Even more so, the fact that Huizinga does not tell us a *story* in *The Waning of the Middle Ages* with a beginning and an end but presents us, instead, with a synchronic section perpendicular on the movement of time, shows that decontextualization manifests itself no less in the form than in the content of his book. Both the content and the form of Huizinga's study exemplify its resistence to subsumption either within the context of the past itself or within the context of historical writing. Therefore, here we have again the embrace of Romeo and Juliet.

And that naturally brings me to the question how Huizinga sought to translate historical experience into language. The authors belonging to the movement of the Tachtigers developed an idiom that they believed capable of realizing their sensitivist aspirations. It was an idiom that one could best characterize as a de-intellectualization or materialization of language. Language should be "pulled back within reality," as it were, and thus had to cast off all intimations, reminiscences, or suggestions of abstraction and of what cannot be reduced to sensory perception, as best exemplified by the sense of touch. Neologisms were coined to produce a language that was permeated through and through by all that we associate with sensory experience, with feeling, and with emotions. All the possibilities of synesthetics were greedily explored in the attempt to absorb language in the concrete realities of sensory experience. It was as if language had become a sense organ like the eye—or, rather, like the sense of touch—and as if reality had been discovered and explored anew with the help of this extra and most refined sense organ.

We will find all this in the dense and amazingly rich prose of *The Waning of the Middle Ages*. We need only read how Huizinga writes in the preface in what mood he had written it: "When writing this book it was as if my gaze was directed into the depths of an evening-sky,—but a sky full of a bloody red and angry with a threatening led-grey, full of a false cupper shine."[33] That is how Huizinga, as expressed in one single, profoundly impressionistic sentence, had experienced, in the most literal sense of that word, "the atmosphere" of the late Burgundian Middle Ages. And where we cannot read such a passage without feeling the shiver that it sends down our spine, we will realize the power of Huizinga's language to evoke this atmosphere in which late medieval life must be situated and its unequaled capacity to translate historical experience into words, into a historical text. Form and content once again mutually reinforce each other here. When Huizinga writes about medieval man that "all experience had yet to the minds of men the directness and absoluteness of the pleasure and pain of child-life," he attributes to medieval man a contact with reality that is both the subject of his book and how he himself attempts to account for that subject. Huizinga attributes here to medieval man a contact with reality that is structurally similar to his own experience of the medieval past investigated by him. There is a deep and meaningful resemblance between medieval man as depicted by Huizinga and the sensitivism of the movement of the 1880s.

Next, we shall not be surprised by Huizinga's eager exploitation of the possibilities promised by synestheticism. Recall the Ph.D. project I discussed at the beginning of section 3.4 and Huizinga's search for words preceding our differentiation of language into what belongs to the eye, the ear, or the sense of touch exclusively. These are the words that will bring us back to reality and synesthetics will tell us how and where to find them. Words for colors, especially *black* and *red,* had Huizinga's special attention in this context. And, indeed, as was pointed out by Jansonius in a learned essay, numerous parallels of these synesthetic experiments can be discovered in the writings of Van Deijssel, Gorter, and other prominent exponents of that movement of the Tachtigers. No less frequent is the use of words like *high, heavy,* and especially *sharp* that enable Huizinga to mobilize the associations we have with the most elementary sensory perceptions in order to resuscitate the past.[34] The title of the first chapter—"The Fierceness of Life"[35]—almost suggesting the transformation of the abstracted life into a material object, is an example in point. What is abstract and might move us away from the blunt directness that life in the Middle Ages shared with how Huizinga chose to present it to his audience is rendered on the level of language in the most concrete terms. The perennial propensity of language for abstraction is continuously and systematically resisted by Huizinga: Language is deliberately and consistently tied as closely and firmly to reality as possible. Historical Truth is achieved not by "saying true things about the past" because precisely the correspondence of the true statement and the past that it is true of would expose how much the two belong to different realms. Historical Truth had better be contended by obstinately refusing to language any opportunity to move away from reality and from how it had been experienced by the historian (so that, ultimately, language and the world would come so infinitesimally close to each other that questions of truth and falsity could even no longer be asked).

Last, many neologisms were created by Huizinga by transforming a substantive into a verb or vice versa. The effect is the suggestion either of movement or of checking movement, and, in both ways, abstract terms are forced to descend from the sphere of the idea to that of what our eyes can see and, especially, what our fingers can touch. This is not merely a matter of presentation but was no less inspired by Huizinga's conviction that the deepest truths can be found by always exploiting associations of concreteness we may have with the words and concepts we use. In each word or concept a key is hidden to the secrets of reality that especially historians should always be eager to discover because of its promises for the execution of their task. We may see here an amazing parallel between Huizinga's own intuitions about language and relevant conceptions of the late medieval mentality that were so much the subject of his book. Kamerbeek has drawn our attention to a passage in which Huizinga concurred with the medieval realist when holding that beauty, tenderness, and whiteness, in the end, have the same origin. Beauty is what whiteness is—because of a deeper "philosophical synesthetics" shared by both, so to say. Truth is in reality, not in what we say about it; it is to be found in the movement toward reality and not in the movement toward abstraction that is the perennial seduction of language. Surely, this is a quite different kind of truth than the one theorists of the correspondence or the coherence theory of truth are interested in. It is a truth that arises from a quasi-mystic union with the world that no longer allows itself to be enchanted by the abstractions that we all so unproblematically use.[36] It is a mysticism that does not put us at a distance from reality but that brings us to its very heart.

3.6 CONCLUSION

History is an empirical discipline in two respects. First in the more trivial sense that the historian has to deal with the data that the past has left us and that can empirically be verified or falsified. But history is also an empirical discipline in the sense that it can be seen as aiming at the expression of a historical experience of the past. As such, the writing of history can be seen as being a continuous experiment with language; as a never-ending experiment in how to relate language to the world. Admittedly, this kind of experiment is not peculiar to history: The sciences have developed their own artificial languages in order to meet the challenge. But the option of the sciences is not open to history. If historians cease to speak ordinary language, a language accessible to all our civilized fellow citizens, they betray their cultural duty and responsibility. The implication is that historians will have to somehow construct out of the ordinary language available to them a quite specific vocabulary for each of their historical experiences. And experience is their only reliable guide when trying to do so. So language will have to follow experience here, rather than the reverse (as is the case in the sciences). In this way we can say that the historian is in a position not unlike that of the novelist—and we know that the novel has had a complex and variegated history and that the effort to reduce the distance between language and the world as much as possible has contributed not unimportantly to this history. This is what I have in mind when arguing that the history of historical writing could be seen as a series of experiments with language (and why we should regret that historians have become so reluctant to experiment with language since the professionalization of history).

I should emphasize again that no a priori restrictions can or should be made on the nature and number of such experiments with language. On the contrary, the more we have of them and the more variegated they are, the better it will be. It is true that philosophers of a more meddlesome transcendentalist orientation will always feel tempted to dream up such restrictions and, by doing so, lay down the law to the historian. In the preceding chapter we argued that the philosophers succumbing to this seduction are, in fact, continuing Kantian critical philosophy by replacing the Kantian categories of understanding with language. But we should avoid this linguistic transcendentalism and recognize that there are no a priori schemes for how to relate language to experience and knowledge. Nor should language be seen as a Wittgensteinian tool used for "coping with reality," in the way that the painter uses his brushes for painting a picture. To pursue the latter metaphor, language should be seen on a par *not* with the painter's brushes but with the paint that is not so much *used* as *spent* by the painter. That is to say, in contrast to the former metaphor, language has no existence outside the infinity of concrete instances of its use: Whereas we can always distinguish between the brush itself and the way it is used, this distinction is no longer possible with the picture's paint. If we consider this difference between the way the brush and the paint are used by the painter, it will become clear why the Wittgensteinian proposal of language as a tool gave Kantianism and transcendentalist philosophy of language a new leash on life. The brush is a metaphor of the transcendental self that always accompanies representation but that is never itself *part* of it. But just like the picture's paint, language, so to speak, "spends" or "loses itself" in its use. Again, like the paint used by the painter, language is used to express or to materialize the (aesthetic) experience of the historian—although, of course a tube of paint can be emptied, whereas the stock of language truly is inexhaustible (as we will observe with dismay when participating in board meetings or when listening to political speeches).

Indeed, historians' use of language to this end may be more or may be less satisfactory to the historians themselves and to their audience in individual cases. Even more so, it will rarely meet all the requirements of both the historians and their audience and will most often have the character of an experiment that could, and in all likelihood will, be improved upon by later experiments. But there is nothing philosophically "deep" or "interesting" about these partial successes and failures in the sense that there are aprioristically given criteria that may *explain* success and failure in individual cases. Looking for "depth" here would inevitably entail a return to "the metaphor of the brush" and thus to transcendentalism.

Hence, the relationship between history and philosophy is rather the reverse. The philosopher should consider the history of historical writing as a series of experiments with language and reflect on its successes and failures, not in order to *explain* them but rather to guess what *follows* from them and what they may mean for the relation between language and reality. Philosophy, philosophy of language, should be an aposteriorist rather than an apriorist discipline in the sense of taking its points of departure in what actually takes place in disciplines like history. Philosophy should not have the pretension to offer the *foundations* of knowledge but look, instead, in the opposite direction and concentrate on the *results* of scientific or historical research. If, however, philosophers wish to formulate transcendentalist laws for the proper use of historical language, as is still the case in much of contemporary historical theory, they will blind themselves to much of the "beauty" of the history of historical writing. And I deliberately use here the word *beauty* since the question of how properly to relate language to reality, how to put into words the way reality has been experienced by us, is essentially an "aesthetic" question. And the history of historical writing is, therefore, in the final analysis, a chapter in the book of the history of aesthetics. This is the issue we will address in Chapters 5 and 6.

4 [decorative brick pattern]

FRAGMENTS OF A HISTORY

OF HISTORICAL EXPERIENCE

> This simultaneously presents the primary challenge faced by contem-
> porary philosophy and asserts that it can be met: It is, according to
> the typology of Kantian thought, to undertake the epistemological
> foundation of a higher concept of experience.[1]
> —(Walter Benjamin)

4.1 INTRODUCTION

The history of historical experience is yet to be written, and to do so
is not part of my present enterprise. I shall therefore restrict myself here to
a few more conspicuous moments in that history. Moreover, it would not
be easy to write such a history, and the material on which such a history
will probably have to be found in places that are far from obvious and that
have, up to now, only rarely attracted the attention of the historian of historical consciousness.

So, when thinking of how such a history ought to be written (if ever
it will), our preliminary question will have to be where to look for the material for such a history. Koselleck has presented us with a most welcome
suggestion in a fascinating essay. His hypothesis is "dass von dem Besiegten
die weiterreichenden Einsichten in der Vergangenheit stammen" ("that a
conquered elite is typically capable of the most far-reaching insights in the
past" [my translation]).[2] The idea is, roughly, that the representatives of a
social and political elite that is about to be superseded by a new one are in
the best position to know and to grasp what we stand to lose by our entry
into a new world. They used to rule the world as a matter of course—and
believed to possess the knowledge required for doing so—and now they
are forced to recognize that this knowledge and understanding is of no
use anymore. So when they give an account of the world that *they* have

lost with the emergence of a new social and political dispensation, they are in the best position to measure the distance between past and present. As Koselleck puts it:

It's different with the conquered. For their primary experience is that everything happened differently from what had been planned and hoped for. Hence, when they feel compelled to reflect on their past and to explain why things happened differently from what had been expected, the desire of truth and elucidation must be a particularly urgent one. That may stimulate a search for long-term causes, both transcending by far the level of pure coincidence or of individual setbacks and making it possible to explain them.[3] (my translation)

The elites vanquished by the inexorable course of history will be most open to and most fascinated by historical fate as manifesting itself in the guise of long-term developments. Only these can make these former elites realize why all their wisdom and insight could be so sadly helpless and ineffective against the inexorable course of History. Even more so, one may well surmise that an unusually acute awareness of long-term developments is the indelible sign of the historical consciousness of superseded elites, for they are in the best social position to identify them — and perhaps this fact may reconcile them to a certain extent with their fate. To put it provocatively, the best (and most revolutionary) historian will naturally be the *conservative* historian — which does not mean, of course, that all conservatives should be good historians. Moreover, it goes without saying that Koselleck's thesis exclusively applies to the "interesting historians" in whose writings the drama of history truly resonates and not to the practitioners of a more modestly antiquarian approach to the past (which is, for that matter, by no means a belittling the latter's work). One may think here of a Thucydides, a Tacitus, a Guicciardini, or a Clarendon — and, especially, as Koselleck points out himself, of Tocqueville.[4] For the aristocrat Tocqueville the new post-revolutionary democratic order was something of a sublime reality that he spontaneously rejected but nevertheless was willing to accept because he understood, better than any of his contemporaries, it to be our ineluctable future.[5] Indeed, no bourgeois could ever have been capable of the supreme historical insight as expressed in Tocqueville's historical and political writings. But the historian who fits the bill best undoubtedly is Jakob Burckhardt — as we shall see in due moment.[6]

　　Koselleck's exhortation compels us to focus on historism as a matter of course. Historism — as is universally recognized — is the kind of historical consciousness that came into being in response to the upheaval unparalleled in all of Western history of what Hobsbawm has called "the dual revolution,"[7] that is, of this divine, or devilish, if you will, but in any case most fateful simultaneity of the French and the Industrial Revolutions on the threshold between the eighteenth and nineteenth centuries. This simultaneity may make us muse about what Western history would have looked like if fate had decided otherwise and a century, or perhaps even more, had separated these two paramount progenitors of modernity. But thanks to this coincidence, the Western world changed out of all recognition in the years between 1789 and 1815, and it did so in a way wholly unparalleled in all the history of mankind up to then (and, arguably, even since then). It is true that historical change had sometimes made itself felt with a traumatic intensity in the case of individuals who, like Machiavelli and Guicciardini, had been particularly sensitive to this because they experienced themselves as Atlases carrying on their shoulders the full weight of the past and the present.[8] But that historical fate truly resounded in the collective consciousness of a whole generation, that all the intelligent individuals of a period were intensely aware of the cataclysms of hope and despair of collective fate—in this the years between the Revolution of 1789 and the Restoration of 1815 were—and still are—without precedent. It created an insurmountable barrier between past and present that could impossibly be denied or undone anymore[9]—and this barrier became the clearly delineated face the past had turned toward us. The past had become, for the first time in history, an almost tangible reality—and, therewith, an ineluctable object of investigation.

Think of how Hegel remembered in 1830 the universal ecstasy about the events of 1789:

As long as the sun had stood at the firmament and the planets circled around it, it had never happened that "man stood on his head," that is, that he fully embraced the point of view of the Mind and constructed reality accordingly. Anaxagoras had been the first to say that *nous* governs the world; now, however, man has come to acknowledge that Mind must govern spiritual reality. This was therefore a glorious sunrise. All thinking human beings came together in a celebration of the coming into being of this new era . . . as if the reconciliation of the Divine with the world had only now been achieved.[10] (my translation)

But after this initial belief in a new dawn in the history of mankind, one was thrown into a breathtaking "rollercoaster of terrifying events" (Runia), where each event provoked, in its turn, a new set of nauseating novelties. It was like a nightmare, but, as Runia puts it, "All these flagrant events had really taken place: the storming of the Bastille, thousand-year-old traditions were cast aside in a moment, the execution of the king, the desecration of the Church, the mangling of the clergy, the orgiastic indulgence in political idealism, the regime of virtue and terror, an attempt to start history anew, the acclamation of coups d'etat, wars were fought, a Corsican artillerist became Emperor, and so on" (my translation).[11] As a result of this chain of unheard-of miracles, a yawning abyss had come into being between the past and the present—and insofar as this abyss is the natural biotope of historical experience, the past had become a no less conspicuous object of potential experience than a table or a house.

It was *historism* that met the challenge and proposed how to deal with this, admittedly, quite peculiar object of experience. Moreover, a closer look at historism will make clear to what extent historical experience is truly at its very heart and therefore historism's perennial enticement.[12] Think of this: Becoming aware (with the historist) of the powers of history automatically meant the recognition that things are what history has made them to be, hence of the view that the essence or identity of things lies in their past. But there is a peculiar dialectic in this, namely, that the more this historist thesis is emphasized and the more it is consistently applied, the greater the differences between the individual historical manifestations of a thing will become—and the more these manifestations will tend to isolate themselves from their previous and later ones. Thus, the paradox of historism is that diachronicity produces synchronicity: The emphasis on *diachronic* development through time produces its own opposite, or even denial, namely, a focus on *synchronic* slices of time at the expense of development.[13] This implies, next, that the more radical and consistent one's historism is, the more this paradox will make itself felt by emphasizing the conflict between diachronicity and synchronicity. And emphasizing this conflict means that diachronic and synchronic contextualization will ever more exclude each other until, in the end, each historical event presents itself in a complete contextual nakedness to the historian. As such, the event is no longer a symbol that can be read or be given meaning in terms of something else (that is, its context)—it is just what it is, and nothing else, and therefore only and exclusively a *potential object of experience*. What withdraws itself from context, from all (narrative or contextualist) meaning, from all signification, *what is just there in its semantic nakedness,* can be only an object of experience to us. In this way, historist contextualization will ineluctably tend to destroy itself and be transformed into its opposite: decontextualized experience.

The point is worth stressing since it clarifies where historical experience (as understood here) differs from the dialectical conception of experience, as defended by Gadamer,[14] Adorno, and Walter Benjamin (in some of his writings[15]). This conception of experience is often associated with the German word *Erfahrung. Erfahrung* is etymologically related to the verb *fahren* which means "to go," "to sail," "to travel or to pass through." As such it is suggestive of the kind of encounters or, rather, "adventures" that one may have on a journey, and, more specifically on the journey through one's own life and of all that may enrich and form one's personality. *Erfahrung,* then, is dialectical because something antedating and (logically) previous to experience is enriched by the experience in question. This is, for that matter, where *Erfahrung* contrasts with *Erlebnis,* which is ordinarily (although not always[16]) associated with a direct and immediate experience. As Gadamer put it:

> If a new experience of an object occurs to us, this means that hitherto we have not seen the thing correctly and now know it better. Thus the negativity of experience has a curiously productive meaning. It is not simply that we see through a deception and hence make a correction, but we acquire a comprehensive knowledge. We cannot, therefore, have a new experience of any object at random, but it must be of such a nature that we gain better knowledge through it, not only of itself, but of what we thought we knew before—i.e., of a universal. The negation by means of which it achieves this is a determinate negation. We call this kind of experience *dialectical.*[17]

Obviously, this automatically rules out the immediacy that we attributed to Huizinga, to historical experience. The subject of experience indisputably dominates here the object of experience: It is the subject of experience, *its* history, *its* knowledge, *its* interests, and so on which supremely preside over the process of the dialectics of *Erfahrung,* whereas in the case of historical experience subject and object of experience are equal partners (as we have seen with Huizinga)—and it is only thanks to this that the subject can momentarily "forget" itself, become that pure subject of experience devoid of any content preceding the experience in question that is both the condition and the sure sign of the immediacy of experience.

Where subject and object do *not* match, each of them will be an easy and helpless prey to where the other exceeds it. The same resistance of dialectical *Erfahrung* or experience against immediacy can be discerned in Adorno's openly Hegelian view of experience:

Undamaged experience is produced only in memory, far beyond immediacy, and through memory aging and death seem to be overcome in the aesthetic image. But this happiness achieved through the rescue of experience, a happiness that will not let anything be taken from it, represents an unconditional renunciation of consolation.[18]

Although you may agree with Adorno's claim that consolation is not part of experience, you might wonder how memory and an awareness of aging and death could possibly leave experience "undamaged." Don't we all know now to what extent memory and our existential moods form—and distort—the content of experience? Historical experience, however, as discussed here, is an experience in which the history of the experiencing subject (and the memory thereof) has no role to play—*it is an experience without a subject.* The subject has to divest itself from its *own* history which ordinarily contextualizes and historicizes his or her experience[19]—and in this way there is no preceding subject of experience: The subject of experience comes into being only with and thanks to the experience in question. It is only thanks to this emptying of the subject of any prior structure, content, memory, and so on that we can move on from dialectical *Erfahrung* (and thus from Gadamer and Adorno) to the sublimity of historical experience.

4.2 FRAGMENTS OF A HISTORY OF HISTORICAL EXPERIENCE (α): EICHENDORFF

As historical time began to gain speed in the course of the eighteenth century, historism and the historist experience of the past made their entrance before Hobsbawm's dual revolution itself. We may think here of Herder. As a young man Herder participated in 1765 in the feast of Saint John, celebrating the beginning of the summer near Riga. Seeing these "lebendige Reste dieses alten, wilden Gesanges, Rhythmus, Tanzes unter lebenden Völkern" ("the living remains of these ancient savage songs, of rhythmic movement and dance still present in a people living now" [my translation]), Herder felt an immediate contact with a world that seemed to be lost and forgotten forever. And Meinecke describes the meaning of this historical experience for the formation of Herder's mind with the following words: "dies vielleicht einmalige, blitzartige Erlebnis, aus dem die Urzeit sprach und das nun aber lebenslang in ihm nachzitterte" ("this flash of experience (perhaps only on one single occasion) that spoke to him of the past and continued to flicker all his life long" [my translation]).[20] One may think next of Goethe's *Kölner Dom Erlebnis* and a similar experience that Goethe had when visiting the house of the Jabach family, both events taking place only a few years later than that of Herder. In both cases Goethe had "die Empfindung der Vergangenheit und Gegenwart in eins" ("the experience/sensation of a union of past and present" [my translation]) and he emphasized at the end of his life that the experience had profoundly impressed him and left many traces throughout the whole of his oeuvre.[21]

We are all acquainted with David Lowenthal's so very fortunate metaphor that "the past is a foreign country,"[22] suggesting that we experience the past as we might experience a foreign country. It follows from this that we will be most open to historical experience when the experience of the past is reinforced by the experience of a foreign country actually *representing* (in the etymological sense of that climactic word) part of the past. And this will invite us to have a look at the historist's historical mind's encounter with Italy—undoubtedly a kind of physical protuberance of the Antiquity's and the Renaissancist's past into the present and mutually reinforcing more than any other country what is both temporally and geographically remote and foreign.[23] German travelers from the eighteenth to the twentieth century were no less sensitive to Italy's past than to where its nature, its population, and its way of life differed from what one was accustomed to north of the Alps. The journey to Italy, therefore, was to them a journey to the past as well—and in this way the phrase "the experience of the past" could acquire for them an almost literal meaning. These journeys are, consequently, a most suggestive and most illuminating metaphor of the experience of the past and a most appropriate example for exploring its nature.

All the elements of the German historist historical experience find themselves miraculously combined in Joseph von Eichendorff's novella *Das Marmorbild* (1819), which is, in fact, a historical experience expanded into a novella. The novella was an outstanding success (inviting Eichendorff to repeat the formula in his later *Aus dem Leben eines Taugenichts* of 1829); apparently it most happily expressed the historical consciousness of

Eichendorff's generation. When discussing Eichendorff's novella, I should emphasize that its interest lies in how it defines the *structure of historical experience* and not in presenting an account of some specific historical experience itself, for this is not what the novella attempts to do. In this way the novella can be said to give us the matrix within which we can locate historical experience all the more satisfactorily.

The novella is situated in an indefinite past; and in this way all emphasis has (deliberately or not) been taken away from how the history of the present (of the subject) may co-determine historical experience. Gadamerian *Wirkungsgeschichte* ("effective history") is, so to say, wholly absent in the novella; or, to put it more solemnly, historical experience is cut loose here from its contextualist roots in the present and in the subject's (individual or collective) past. And, as we have seen, this is exactly how it is with historical experience. Nevertheless, from Eichendorff's description of the clothes worn by his *dramatis personae* one may gather that the novella should in all likelihood be situated sometime in the Renaissance. And since the book deals with an experience of classical antiquity, it could be seen as an attempt to depict the Renaissancistic experience of Antiquity. These intimations of historical decontextualization are repeated in the main character of the novella, a young knight called Florio. It must strike the reader that Florio really is the flattest character one could think of; he is robbed by Eichendorff of any specific personal characteristics; moreover, nothing at all is said about his history, his nationality, his family, and so on. He is a pure psychological void—once again, the kind of void that is typically required for having a historical experience. No less interesting is the following. Right at the start of the novella, Eichendorff has Florio declare:

I now chose for traveling and feel as if released from prison, all my old wishes and pleasures have now been set free. When growing up in the quiet calm of the countryside, I always looked yearningly to the distant blue mountains; especially when spring made it way through our garden like an enchanting musician and when it enticingly sang of the beauties of distant countries and of immeasurable lust.[24] (my translation)

So, insofar as Florio's past has any role to play at all, it does not function as a tie between his present and former self but is instead completely irrelevant to the formation of his identity—even more so, his past preordained paradoxically his complete emancipation from it.

Eichendorff's Florio stands here in a marked contrast to previous descriptions of the encounter with the past in Italy. Think, for example, of Goethe's immensely influential account of his Italian journey in 1787 and 1788—which was published (in a strongly retouched form) only some thirty years later. Goethe undertook this journey in order to escape from the personal and artistic impasse in which he had maneuvered himself in Weimar;[25] it was therefore a journey which was meant to get in contact with his true self again. Or, as Goethe put it himself in a letter, dated January 25, 1788, to his sovereign master the Duke of Saxen-Weimar, it was his aim "um mich an den fremden Gegenständen kennen zu lernen" ("to learn to recognize myself again in a strange world"); the Italian journey was to him a *Bildungsreise*, a journey back to his own soul by means of Italy (as was also the case with his friend and traveling companion in Rome, Karl Philipp Moritz[26]). And as Goethe exultantly declared during his stay in Rome, "In Rom hab' ich mich selbst zuerst gefunden" ("In Rome I have found myself for the first time"); Rome was to him the eagerly hoped for encounter with "seinem eigenen Wesen" ("his own essence" [my translations])[27] and as such was an indispensable catalyst, as we would nowadays put it. And this is crucially different with Florio: Not only does his historical experience of Antiquity leave his personality unaltered (or, rather, whether this actually is or is not the case is wholly irrelevant here), but, as the passage just quoted suggests, all his travels have effected in Florio only an openness to new experiences without channeling these experiences into one direction rather than into another, hence without interfering with this openness, as typically was to be the case in Goethean *Bildung*. Put differently, Goethe's (and Moritz's) experience of Italy nicely fit within the model of *Erfahrung,* as defined by Gadamer; it is dialectical and recognizes to what extent experience is always limited by the (history of) the subject, whereas Eichendorff's account suggests a (Leibnizian) "experience without a subject" thanks to Florio's psyche being a tabula rasa.

Upon his arrival in Lucca—which is the scene of the novella— Florio meets with two young knights, Fortunato and Donati. Fortunato symbolizes the present and a life uncontaminated by the unsettling mysteries of the past. He is cheerful and uncomplicated. Donati, on the other hand, represents the past; his presence is surrounded by mysteries, his presence provokes in everybody the shudder of the uncanny. "Eine ängstliche Störung, deren Grund sich niemand anzugeben wusste, wurde überall sichtbar" ("An oppressive disturbance, whose causes nobody could explain, was now felt by everyone"),[28] Eichendorff comments on Donati's intrusion into Fortunato's clear and transparent world.[29] It need not surprise us that there is little sympathy between Fortunato and Donati or that Fortunato explicitly associates Donati with the night, with "butterflies of the night," with alarming nightmares and eerie appearances. And it is interesting that these attacks by Fortunato on Donati are never answered by Donati: The past seems incapable of the kind of animosity that the present may feel against the past. The past just *is* and therefore is supremely indifferent with regard to the present—and this indifference of its progenitor toward itself apparently is already more of a frustration to the present than it can cope with. True enough, of course.

The plot of the novella centers around Florio's encounter with an antique statue of Venus. The Venus theme is an old and venerable one in the history of German literature, going back to Tannhäuser (ca. 1205–after 1266) and continuing right down into the nineteenth century in the poetry and music of Heine and Wagner. In the late Middle Ages songs of penance were ascribed to Tannhäuser; Tannhäuser was believed to have lived a life of erotic debauchery—"in the Venus mountain"—and then to have traveled to Rome in the vain effort to be absolved from his sins by the Pope. But after the Pope's refusal, the Pope's crosier sprouts a wonderful flower signifying God's remission of Tannhäuser's sins. So in this tradition Venus and the Venus mountain stand for the sins of the flesh, and there is no specific relationship with Italy. In fact, insofar as Italy has to play a role here, it is papal Rome and not the Rome of classical antiquity, for Venus symbolizes only sin and she is, because of this, not to be related to any specific time or place. Venus is wholly contained within the symbolic and semantic universe of the Christian Middle Ages. This still was the case in Ludwig Tieck's novella *Der getreue Eckart und der Tannenhäuser* of 1799. The Venus mountain is described there as follows:

To this Mountain have the Devils fled, and sought shelter in the desert center of the Earth, as the growth of our Holy Faith has cast down the idolatrous worship of the Heathen. Here, they say, before all others, Lady Venus keeps her court, and all her hellish hosts of worldly Lusts and forbidden Wishes gather round her. (my translation)

And when the question is asked where the Venus mountain is located, the answer is that nobody knows: "Das is das Geheimnis . . . dass dieses niemand zu sagen weiss" ("There is the secret, . . . that no one can tell this").[30]

Although, admittedly, Eichendorff's novella retains the opposition between pagan antiquity (Venus) and Christian devotion (Maria), the story is no longer a story of sin and redemption but essentially one of an encounter with the pre-Christian past. Put differently, the novella is like a palimpsest where a new meaning is inscribed over an old one; and this may go a long way to explaining the immense success of the novella at the time. Eichendorff succeeds in his effort to rewrite the old story so by emphasizing concrete (historical) detail at the expense of the universal moralist message of the old Tannhäuser theme. The novella no longer tells us about the timeless and universal struggle of temptation and redemption but is unambiguously located in Italy, near Lucca; and the encounter with the remains of classical antiquity (that is, a statue of Venus) is the event that dominates all of the story. The symbolism of the Tannhäuser story thus had to make room for a historical reality that was only obliquely hinted at in the original story used by Eichendorff. In this way Eichendorff succeeded in encapsulating all the force of the old story of fall and redemption in a story about an uncanny and most unsettling encounter with the past. Moreover, whereas Christian redemption always is an undoing of the past, since our past sins are "wiped away" by it, Eichendorff freezes, so to say, the encounter with the past and thus succeeds in transforming the old Tannhäuser theme into its very opposite and in rephrasing it into a celebration of the past.

Florio's first encounter with the Venus statue takes place when he has left his inn at night (of course) and gets lost in the woods around Lucca; he then suddenly sees the statue at the edge of a pond whose dark waters mirror the statue. He is immediately fascinated by the statue's beauty (and is, self-evidently, much ridiculed for this by Fortunato on the morning after the experience). The next day Florio rides out on his horse, gets lost once more, but then miraculously arrives again at the same place of the night before. This time, however, he does not see the statue itself but instead a lady closely resembling her. The lady plays a guitar and sings a song whose implicit sexual meaning verges on the obscene:

> Die Rose seh' ich gehn aus grüner Klause,
> Und, wie so buhlerisch die Lüste fächeln,
> Errötend in die laue Luft sich dehnen

> > I see the rose emerging from its green enclosures,
> > and, as lusts may shimmer lasciviously,
> > she unfolded, blushing in the tepid air.[31] (my translation)

Florio's fascination for the Venus statue (that is, the past) explodes into an insatiable love and desire—a desire that is all the more intense since it is to Florio as if he had always known the object of his love and as if his love is, in fact, a memory of a remote and indefinite past: "Florio stand in blühende Traume versunken, es war ihm, als hätte er die schöne Lautenspielerin schon lange gekannt und nur in der Zerstreuung des Lebens wieder vergessen und verloren" ("Florio was standing, sunk in blossoming dreams; it was to him as if he had known the beautiful lute player for a long time already and had then forgotten and lost her again in the diversions of life"). And a moment later Venus explicitly says herself that she is well aware that this is what she provokes in people seeing her: "Ein jeder glaubt, mich schon einmal gesehen zu haben, denn mein Bild dämmert und blüht wohl in allen Jugendträumen mit herauf" ("Everybody believes to have already seen me before, for my image gleams and blossoms in all the dreams of youth").[32] As we shall see in a moment when discussing Benjamin, this is a truly crucial aspect of historical experience. Historical experience always contains an element of recognition, the suggestion of something coming to life again that we had known all of the time but were no longer aware of.

And there is one more aspect of Florio's experience of the past that will be repeated by Benjamin. This is the profound insight that this experience must be situated not in the depth of either the subject or the object of experience but that it has, instead, its natural locus on the surface, where subject and object meet, where they lightly touch each other in a most tactful gesture respecting both, so that a momentary mutual embrace of past and present is possible without a selfish touching of even the tenderest members of each other. It is a gesture of the subtlest and most delicate love—and, as such, the metaphor of an encounter with the past is totally different from the brute and necessarily egocentrist questions by means of which the scientist tries to pilfer his objects of its secrets. When Florio insists that Venus should no longer hide herself from him and reveal to him her name so that her lovely appearance would never be lost again (as typically is the case with scientific knowledge in contrast to the most ephemeral and transient "knowledge" of the experience of the past), Venus mildly reprimands Florio: "'Don't,' she replied musingly, 'take the flowers of life cheerfully, just as the whim of the moment may give them, and do not look for their roots in the soil, for there is no joy and only silence there.' Florio looked at her in astonishment; he did not understand how such mysterious words could come to the mouth of this cheerful girl" (my translation).[33] And as such a delicate embrace has its natural temporal setting in the charms of the moment, it does not allow itself to be commanded even by the most intense desire or *Sehnsucht*. Here the desire of repetition is wholly helpless, if not counterproductive: The past presents itself only when least expected and certainly not at our bidding. Florio also recognizes himself when he begins to realize that for one reason or another he is never successful in his attempts to retrace the route to Venus's strange country house; when he arrives there at all, it always is by some unintended coincidence or when Donati, the past's emissary (and certainly not a personification of anything so earth-bound as the historian), leads him there.

And then the novella comes to an unexpected and symbolic climax. Donati had introduced Florio to Venus's country house. After an intimate tête-à-tête between Venus and Florio in the country house's wonderful pleasure garden, Venus invites him to a room in the innermost halls of the country house. But at the moment when their union, hence of present and past, seems at hand, Florio confusedly utters to himself the fatal words:

"Oh Lord, do not allow me to get lost in this world." He had just spoken these words to himself, when outside a drizzling wind, like from a gathering thunder-storm coming nearer, arose and confusingly blew around him. At the same time he noticed at the window sill, grass and some growths of herbs as on old ruins. A snake came hissing out of it and threw itself with its green-golden tail, twisting, down into the abyss.[34] (my translation)

With these words, with which Florio resists the loss of himself in the past and cuts himself loose from it, the spell is finally and irrevocably broken. Venus changes again into the chilly and forbidding white marble statue that Florio had seen near the garden's pond only a few nights before; the country house itself quickly turns into a place of horror from which Florio escapes in the greatest confusion.

The next day the present triumphantly reasserts all its claims: Venus's country house had changed into a repugnant and lugubrious ruin, Donati's proud mansion was transformed overnight into a decrepit little farmhouse, Fortunato sings his songs always so full of life, and Florio himself feels as reborn after having escaped from the dark temptations of the past and falls in love with the beautiful and uncomplicated Bianca. And the past itself? Eichendorff does not say: It has become so irrelevant as not to deserve any mention anymore. So things are in the world of those living in the present. The experience of the past leaves no traces in their present. "Und so zogen die Glücklichen fröhlich durch die überglänzten Auen in das blühende Mailand hinunter" ("And so the happy pair descended cheerfully through the sunny and shining fields down to blossoming Milan").[35]

Let's take a step backward and ponder Eichendorff's deeply meaningful story. We should observe, to begin with, that there has been no actual union of Venus and Florio, of past and present; both have preserved their preunitary integrity, so to say. Indeed, their identities did come as close to each other as possible, without actually attaining a fusion of identities (or of "horizons," as Gadamer would have put it). Significantly, when such a fusion became an actual possibility, Florio recoiled and he did so precisely for fear of losing his identity.

Eichendorff's construction here is of so much interest since nineteenth-century historists would always argue that we acquire our identity only through and by the past: We *are* what our history is like. So both historism and Eichendorff closely relate history and identity to each other, but they do so in quite different ways. Whereas historism discusses the *acquisition* of identity, Eichendorff emphasizes the danger of *losing* it in our contact with the past. Recall that Florio was well aware of losing his identity in his encounter with Venus; it was precisely this that made him shrink away from her *au moment suprême.* This state of affairs suggests that the historist and Eichendorff move in opposite directions when thinking about how we relate to the past. The historist moves along with the stream of history and time and hopes to find his or her identity in this way. Florio, on the other hand, seems to possess an identity preceding history but risks it when moving in the opposite direction, hence from the present to the past.

But this is not yet all. In contrast to historism, where we have only this level of how the present has grown out of the past, two levels should be discerned in Eichendorff's more subtle account of how we relate to the past. The first level is the one we discussed just now and where we have seen the historist and Eichendorff moving in opposite directions. And this level is certainly predominant in *Das Marmorbild,* for this is where we should situate the substance of the story. But there is one more level in Eichendorff that does not have its counterpart in the historist definition of how we relate to the past. In order to identify this second level recall the famous lines of Goethe:

Wär' nicht das Auge sonnenhaft,
Die Sonne könnt' es nie erblicken,
Läg nicht in uns des Gottes eigne Kraft,
Wie könnt" uns Göttliches entzücken?

> Was not in the eye something of the sun itself,
> It could never behold the sun,
> Was not in us part of God's own power,
> How could the Divine enchant us? [36]

Goethe wishes to say with this that what may seem, at first sight strange, alien, or perhaps even a threat to us, in fact, part of our identity. Something of the Sun or of God must always have been part of who we are, for if this were not the case, we could never be overwhelmed so completely by their beauty and power. This must of course remind us of a famous Platonist topos, where Plato suggests in the *Meno* that all knowledge is, in the end, a matter of remembering of what had always been in our mind already but without our being aware of it. So it is in love: The beloved has a profound and powerful resonance in the heart of the lover; in this way love aims at the reunification of what had inadvertently been pulled apart (as is the message in Plato's myth of the origin of the sexes). And so it was in the love that Florio felt for Venus, for recall that Venus told Florio that his love for her was born from *recognition:* She had been in the depth of his heart all the time; his love for her was a remembering of what he had forgotten because of all the distractions offered to him in Fortunato's clear and transparent world of the present. And this recognition, as the quote from Goethe suggests, is the recognition of a shared identity—a recognition that is, however, both a promise and a threat. It is, on the one hand, a promise of union by offering the prospect of an obliteration of all that separates the past from the present; but it is a threat since this obliteration, if becoming reality, would also involve a loss of identity. By so indissolubly linking together promise and threat, we may get here a first inkling of the sublimity of historical experience, which will be more amply discussed in the last chapter.

We cannot praise Eichendorff enough for this account of the nature of historical experience (and this is why he actually is the hero of this chapter). His account admirably shows that our encounter with the past—as exemplified by historical experience—is not a movement in agreement with the course of history itself. This is how historism presented it. No, it is a movement into the opposite direction, a movement from the present toward the past. Or, to give to it the right connotation, it is a movement of decontextualization, a movement taking away all the context, and all the contextualist accretions gathered over the centuries and standing in the way of a direct and immediate experience of the past. Only then can we recognize the past in ourselves and ourselves in the past, as Eichendorff has Venus explain to Florio. And we shall see in what follows that exactly the same insight was expressed by Burckhardt and by Walter Benjamin, both of whom also suggest the existence of a level of timelessness not preceding history, as one might have expected, but to which we can get access only after contextualization and historicization have first done all that is in their power to do. As such, therefore, this domain of the timeless presupposes contextualization and historicization, for without contextualization there is no decontextualization and thus no historical experience.

We can now also understand why this love affair of Venus and Florio, of the past and the present, must necessarily remain so "superficial": There is nothing underneath the surface that might unite the two of them for the simple reason that all that might be underneath it has to be discarded in order to achieve this most subtle and gentle mutual embrace of past and present that historical experience essentially is (we will find this same theme of the superficiality of historical experience in Benjamin again). So historical experience, as exemplified by Florio's encounter with Venus, is like the most absorbing and total love affair that one may think of, while remaining completely chaste and hence without offspring, without something that is being born from it. Or, as one might also put it, the union or fusion is postponed forever, like a promise always ardently striven and hoped for, but that will never be fulfilled, as an object of *Sehnsucht* or yearning; it is as if an emptiness has been created that can never be filled up, as if a negativity has been absorbed and transformed into a positivity, as if absence, with a softening gesture of acquiescence has been altered into presence. *Sehnsucht* always creates the awareness of a "not here," a "not now," and may do so with such force as to intimate a temporal order that could never coincide with that of this world. A striking illustration is the poem titled "An die Ersehnte" by Nicolaus Lenau (1802–1850):

"Umsonst! Du bist auf immer mir "In vain! You are lost to me forever!
  verloren!
Laut rufend in den dunkeln Wald des Calling loudly in the dark wood of
  Lebens   life

Hat ohne Rast die Sehnsucht dich
  beschworen;
Ihr Ruf durchklang die Einsamkeit
  vergebens.

Tief ist mein Herz erkrankt an einer
  Ahnung,
Von der ich nimmer wohl genesen
  werde,
Es flüstert mir mein Herz die trübe
  Mahnung:
Noch ist sie nicht geboren dieser Erde!

Die Stunden, die mit frohen
  Wandersängen
Das Mädchen einst durch's Erdenthal
  geleiten,
Die schlummern in der Zukunft
  Schattengängen
Bei ihrer Bürde noch von Seligkeiten;

Von Seligkeiten, die mit leichten
  Händen
Die wachen einst entgegenstreuen
  Allen,
An welche sie die schöne Gunst
  verschwenden
Mit ihrer Königinn vorbeizuwallen.

Die eine aber von den Schläferinnen
Wird locken sie zur Kühle von
  Zypressen,
Und führen sie, versenkt in stilles
  Sinnen,
An deinen Hügel, moosig und
  vergessen.

Dann irrt dein Geist um deine Asche
  bange,
Dann zittern Geist und Staub, sich zu
  vereinen;

"Sehn sucht" has restlessly cast a
  spell on you
Its call resounded in vain in your
  solitude.

My heart deeply suffers of an
  intimation
From which I shall never be cured,

My heart whispers in me the dark
  message:
She was not yet born to this world!

The hours that once accompanied
  with cheerful songs
The girl through the valleys of this
  earth,
These hours are still asleep in future's
  darkness
Together with its wealth of joys;

Of joys, that waking hours
  lighthandedly
Throw to all of those

They privilege with the august favor

Of passing them by together with
  their Queen.

One of the sleepers, however,
Will allure her to the coolness of the
  cypresses
And lead her, sunk in silent musing

To your burial mound, mossy and
  forgotten.

Then errs your spirit anxious for your
  ashes,
Then spirit and dust will shiver for
  reunion;

Das Mädchen aber wird am Grabeshange,	The girl, however, will mysteriously be moved,
Geheim ergriffen, stille stehn—und weinen.[37]	She will stay with the grave—and weep.

(my translation)

The poet confesses to have been caught by a sudden strange obsession, namely, the conviction that the encounter with the girl he loves—*die Ersehnte*—is a figure of the future, not of the past, as our use of the category of time would require to be the case. He invokes the image of "the Queen of time" who passes along us together with the "hours" that constitute her empire. Some of these hours are "awake"—this is the past whose "hours" had accompanied him with his beloved through the valleys of this world. But then the poet recognizes that the "hour" of the actual encounter with the beloved is one of the "hours" that is still "asleep" and that thus belongs to an indefinite future. But when this "hour" will come about, the poet will be dead and buried in a grave to which the beloved will be gently led by time. In this way the conflict of actual time with that of *Sehnsucht* is revealed to the poet—and nothing will ever achieve a "fusion" of these two orders of time.

This is, then, where historical experience (as exemplified by *Sehnsucht*) so crucially differs from Gadamerian *Horizontsverschmelzung*, or "fusion of horizons" and where such a fusion of past and present actually comes into being and where, moreover, the present, because of the Gadamerian mechanism of the *applicatio*, always is the dominant partner in the interaction of the past and the present. It is this mechanism guaranteeing the "closure" of the Gadamerian *Erfahrung*, or experience of the past, even though "closure" for Gadamer is always temporary and transient since it merely is just one more phase in the *Wirkungsgeschichte* of our encounters with the past. In this way historical experience is, once again, similar to the sublime, insofar as the sublime also announces a cognitive impasse and of which we can say that the sublime is there as long as the impasse is maintained (as in the Lenau poem), whereas the sublime disappears at the moment of closure when the sublime is reinterpreted as granting us some new insight about the world or about the self. This is paradigmatically the case when dialectical Gadamerian *Erfahrung* teaches us something new about the world—or when the Kantian sublime finds its final closure and transcendence in the subject's awareness of his moral destination.[38]

Furthermore, we cannot fail to notice how strongly Eichendorff associates the past with ahistorical nature and where Florio's experience of the past takes on the character of *myth* (myth in the sense of being a paradoxical return to the dimension of transhistorical nature that always accompanies precisely the strongest efforts at historicization). The suggestion can already be discerned in this sexualization of the relationship between past (Venus) and present (Florio), hence in Eichendorff's modeling of this relationship on how we relate to the time-transcending domain of (the desire of) love and sexual fulfillment. Even more obvious is the metamorphosis of Venus's world after Florio's shrinking away from a union with the past out of fear of a loss of identity: Venus's beautiful country house suddenly is the victim of decay; it falls into ruins and returns to the timeless state of nature—and so does Venus herself—she becomes a piece of marble again. Another sign is Eichendorff's placing the statue of Venus near a pond where it seems to be lost in a narcissistic love of itself, hence in a kind of loop not accessible to anybody or anything outside itself.[39] Here the past is locked up within itself as much as nature typically is. This link between the past and nature is all the more appropriate since the Renaissance (in which the novella is situated) preferably expressed its historical consciousness in terms of the eternal struggle between *virtù* and the Goddess Fortuna. The Goddess of Fortune here symbolizes the invincible forces of decay (of entropy, as we would nowadays say), of all things human finally returning to the domain of nature again, and *virtù* is humanity's strenuous but ever only partial and temporary success in overcoming Fortune and nature. In this way the notion of historical experience is most intimately and directly related to this Renaissancist historical consciousness that was so magisterially depicted by John Pocock in his magnum opus.[40]

This construction of how nature and history are related has two consequences. In the first place, the domain of history is now wholly absorbed by the historical subject: There is no history outside the subject, and all history is the history of the subject. History is not a predicate of the things of the past themselves (such as the Venus statue), as we would naively have surmised—for these things do rather belong to the domain of nature. No, history is a category of the historical subject itself. In the second place, precisely this grants to the subject's encounter with the past the aura of the uncanny that is so explicitly projected by Eichendorff on the world of Venus and of Donati. It is uncanny since here the world hides in a guise preventing a meaningful contact with the subject: for here the subject (= history) encounters the past as its radically "other"—as nature. Here the past is the domain of what transcends time and is uncanny because of this.

Hence, the sublimity of the paradox of historical experience insofar as it seeks to grasp in terms of the historical what has now assumed the ahistorical appearance of nature. The subject seeks to embrace the historical, but when attempting to do so, it sees itself confronted with the ahistorical. The past escapes from us in a guise that is essentially different from that under which we had hoped and expected to recover it, that is, in that of nature. This also explains why historical experience is always accompanied by a sense of loss, whereas, in fact, nothing is lost that had ever been in one's possession. This sense of loss seems indeed to correspond (or to suggest) a loss of the past; but what is lost is *not* the past—which anyway is a reality that we could never have been in the possession of and could therefore not possibly lose. So that we should have lost something is, in fact, a myth. *And it is a myth* in a peculiar double sense of the word. First, it is a *myth,* in the sense that we did not lose anything that we had ever possessed. Second, it *is* a myth, in the sense that myths are those parts of nature we grant the honor of being part of our history. Needless to say, the kind of "nature" discussed here is not the kind of nature which is investigated in the sciences— it is rather what remains after the world of history has been robbed of its attribute of "being history." In this way, *this* kind of "nature" *presupposes* history and is a product of historical awareness—arguably, of even the most refined form of historical awareness. Before the advent of historism, *this* kind of nature did not and could not exist.[41] And the illusion of loss has its origin in our vague and indeterminate elegiac intimation that history (something we can identify with and believe to be part of ourselves and hence something that we can lose) has been transformed into nature (which we can neither possess nor lose and which is inexorably alien). This is the profoundest and saddest tragedy in our relationship to our past and where we can only weep the tears of a civilization which has made this tragedy into the ultimate truth about itself.

4.3 FRAGMENTS OF A HISTORY OF HISTORICAL EXPERIENCE (β): BURCKHARDT

Several of these elements of historical experience can be found in Burckhardt, whose relationship with Italy could best be described in

Eichendorffian terms as a lifelong love affair—with all its ups and downs, its joys, and its disappointments. He made his first journey to Italy in July 1838 with his nephew Jakob Oeri—so even before his decision in favor of the career of the historian. The journey was like a revelation to him, and his openness to the historical experience of the past becomes abundantly clear from his ecstatic account of what he felt when the silent beauty of Pisa's architectural treasures blended with the mysteries of the evening sky:

> I was standing on the marvelous green field, from which arise the Dom, the Battisterio, Campanile, and the Camposanto, and was drawing while leaning against the wall of the seminary. . . . The sky was a deep dark blue, the Apennines were violet in the luster of the early evening; below me the Arno murmured, and I could have wept like a child. All my heroism vanished.[42] (my translation)

Note the most peculiar "all my heroism vanished." What could this be other than a sign that each effort or even each desire of a mastery of the past was momentarily exchanged for a submission to the spell of the moment? A submission guaranteeing the openness to the past which is so essential to historical experience and where Burckhardt found himself in exactly the same position as Florio just before his so fatal exclamation. Burckhardt has, for that matter, always been an ardent admirer of Eichendorff's *Das Marmorbild,* and he regarded the novella as a most subtle expression of the experience of the mysteries of the Italian past. Next, no less reminiscent of Eichendorff's introduction of the element of the uncanny into historical experience (and with more than a hint of the sublime) is Burckhardt's description of his fortuitous first visit to the Santa Croce in Florence. Without knowing what building he was actually entering, he fled during a violent thunderstorm into what proved to be a huge church and was overwhelmed by the combination of the church's sinister darkness and the fierce flashes of lightning outside:

> It was a kind of holy fright I experienced when contemplating this House of God and when lightning momentarily illuminated the marvelous glass paintings, and when, while I was looking at the Giotto frescoes in the choir, thunder made clatter the glass discs; I then mused what great men had crossed the threshold of this church either dead or alive. Here strode Arnolfo [the church's architect] up and down amidst his collaborators. . . , here once stood Dante while looking at the artists decorating the glorious church with their works. And now the graves! At the front at the left of the entrance lies world-weary Galilei. . . . Then I perceived a large drapery from under which a marble pedestal protruded. I went at it, lifted

the drapery a little and took fright when I read the inscription: NICOLAO MACHIAVELLIO etc. . . . . Rain went on and lightning increased. It became darker and darker, and all the more fiercely the white marble graves lit up by the flashes of lightning; the rumble of thunder resounded majestically through the church's high nave; I, however, moved from painting to painting, from grave to grave and celebrated in my mind many masses for the dead.[43] (my translation)

And just as Florio experiences his encounter with Venus as a coming to life again of a remote personal past, so it is with Burckhardt:

Yes, there is Praedestinatio duplex; some are destined to see the Divine in Italy, others are not. I hope that I belong to the first category. . . . At this place and time the idea really came to my mind that I might have been born here. Heine would say: I am the son of a sea nymph of the Mediterranean that had been exposed in a fragrant night with clear moonlight on the pier of an Italian palace and subsequently had been carried away by compassionate-cruel people to Basel so that I could get a practical education.[44] (my translation)

Even more so, the Eichendorffian theme of Venus coming to life again at night also makes its appearance in Burckhardt's fantasy of what might happen at midnight in the *Tribuna* of the Uffizi between the statue of the Medici Venus and those of the two wrestlers, of the dancing Faun, and of Apollo.[45] And there is one more similarity between Eichendorff and Burckhardt which is of specific interest. I am thinking here of the link between how Burckhardt conceived of the relationship between the classical and the romantic (or between Antiquity and the Gothic Middle Ages) on the one hand and that between the ahistorical and the historical on the other. We may discern here a shift repeating a similar shift in Goethe, insofar as both moved from a romantic adoration of the Middle Ages and of the Gothic cathedral to a privileging of the Classical. And in both cases this shift expresses or extols an exchange of the historical in favor of the ahistorical. But in neither case is this the return to an anti-historist rejection of the past. It rather is a synthesis of the historical and the anti-historical in which even Meinecke discerned the highest stage of historism and where Goethe had already transcended, according to him, all that historism would achieve in the course of the nineteenth century. What Goethe had in mind here is explained by Meinecke with the help of God's words at the end of the prologue to Faust:

Das Werdende, das ewig wirkt und lebt,	The creative essence, which works and lives through all time,

Umfass euch mit der Liebe holden Schranken,	Embrace you within the happy bounds of love;
Und was in schwankender Erscheinung schwebt,	And what hovers in changeful seeming,
Befestigt mit dauernden Gedanken.[46]	Do ye fix firm with everlasting thoughts.[47]

So the idea is that behind the manifold of historical change and behind the endless play of historical forms a time-transcending truth may manifest itself, but this is a truth that requires and presupposes this manifold in order to express itself. In this way one could argue that history gives us the means for transcending history and why Goethe's conception of history is both the fulfillment of historism and its transcendance.[48] This is Meinecke's argument—and where we may agree with him. However, we should not forget that this Goethean conception of the past has its origins in Goethe's neo-Platonism: "alles Vergängliche ist nur ein Gleichnis," as he puts it right at the end of *Faust II;* that is, all the transient phenomena of this world are merely the reflection of the timeless Platonist ideas.

But when Burckhardt shifts from the historical to the ahistorical, he may well have had something quite different in mind—and it is much to be regretted (and even somewhat surprising) that Meinecke in his vast oeuvre only incidentally discusses Burckhardt's conception of history, despite its being so very close to his own and in spite of his being a no less great admirer of Goethe than Burckhardt.[49] It is true that we may find statements in Burckhardt's writings that seem to hark back to Goethe, such as his statement in the introduction to the *Weltgeschichtliche Betrachtungen:* "Philosophers of history look at the past as if it were in opposition to, and a mere preliminary to us as fully developed people; we, however, consider the recurrent, the constant, the typical, as what has an echo in us and can be understood" (my translation).[50] No commentator on Burckhardt has failed to wrestle with this enigmatic pronunciation: It is universally recognized to be a most important key for an adequate understanding of Burckhardt's historical thought, but each writer has interpreted it differently. So I may be forgiven for adding here one more item to the list. I had best take my point of departure in Jörn Rüsen's most perceptive analysis of Burckhardt's thought. Rüsen demands that we read Burckhardt's statement together with the one immediately preceding it: "Our starting point is what is, to us, the only possible and lasting center, namely, that of the suffering, striving, and acting individual, of what he is, always was, and will be; in this way our observations will be, to a certain extent, pathological" (my translation).[51] Rüsen discovers here what he refers to as the "anthropological foundation" of Burckhardt's historical thought.[52] Rüsen's argument is that for Burckhardt the life world of the human individual is not an abstraction from the manifold that history presents us with—that this life world is not something we can get access to only after having taken in all that history teaches us about human suffering and about the hopes and efforts of human individuals—but that it is precisely the other way round, since this life world is the condition of the possibility of all true historical insight. The unchanging and ever-recurring components of historicity are to be found in the life world of the ever striving and suffering human individual; and these components are the source not only of historical change itself but also of all the meaning that the historian may give to the past.[53]

Much is to be said in favor of this anthropological approach to Burckhardt's historical thought. We need only recall the chapter titled "The Individual and the Universal" in *Weltgeschichtliche Betrachtungen* to recognize to what extent the human individual—its joys and, above all, its sufferings—is for Burckhardt the alpha and omega of the substance of the past. It is certainly true of Burckhardt himself in the sense that his own personality has its resonance in all of his work and can be said to determine its tonality and rhetoric. Especially from the perspective of this book, that is, from that experience, we cannot fail to notice the significance of the statement with which Burckhardt began the short autobiography he wrote at the end of his life: "His first grief in life was brought about by the death of his sweet mother on March 17, 1830, a year of many illnesses as well. This imprinted upon him the transience and uncertainty of all earthly things, even though his frame of mind was otherwise inclined to cheerfulness" (my translation).[54] Burckhardt's pessimism,[55] his tendency to cast all of history in the mood of a history of an irremediable loss, undoubtedly has its origins here—and Jörn Rüsen has convincingly shown in a recent publication that for Burckhardt history is, essentially, a history of loss.[56] Hence Burckhardt's conviction that the moment of death—when we are on the point of losing everything—is when we will achieve the fullness of meaning.[57] Hence his fascination for the time of Constantine the Great, the subject of his first book, where he describes the loss of Greek and Roman culture and its metamorphosis (*Verpuppung*) into a Christian world. Hence his lifelong fascination for the Italian Renaissance, which meant to him the loss of a world of unparalleled beauty but that, paradoxically, also contained in itself the seeds of its decay into modernity and all its ugliness, such as railways, democracy, industrialization, and "business." For Burckhardt the present is essentially defined by what it has lost to the past by becoming the present—in a way that anticipates Benjamin's notion of the aura, to be discussed later in this chapter. And, more generally, Burckhardt would strongly disagree with Ranke's pathetic exclamation "ich wünschte mein Selbst gleichsam auzulöschen, und nur die Dinge reden, die mächtigen Kräfte erscheinen zu lassen" ("I wished to efface myself, as it were, and to call upon the things, and the powerful forces of the past themselves to speak")[58] and in which Ranke so explicitly avows the scientistic objectivity whose rejection would be the guide of Gadamer's hermeneutics a century later. For Burckhardt the historian should not hesitate to see the past from the perspective of the present: "Our topic is a past which is clearly connected with the present and with the future. . . . Actually, one ought to stress especially those historical realities from which threads run to our own period and culture. There are more of them than one would think" (my translation).[59]

I do nevertheless have my hesitations about Rüsen's anthropological interpretation of Burckhardt's historical thought. When Burckhardt expresses his interest for the recurrent, the constant, and the typical, he does not do so in the context of an exposition of how the human individual has given form to the past but of an exposition of the interaction among state, church, and culture. And this interaction will resist a reduction to anthropological factors; nor does Burckhardt ever attempt such a reduction. I would therefore propose to relate Burckhardt's apparently so unhistorical interest for the recurrent, and so on to what he considered to be the aim of his book: "We do not proudly lay claim to 'world-historical ideas,' but are satisfied with individual observations and to offer cross-sections of the past, in as many directions as possible" (my translation).[60] This certainly is an adequate characteristic of how he deals with state, church, and culture in the substance of the *Weltgeschichtliche Betrachtungen*. When asking himself what this may tell us about Burckhardt's relationship to the past, Runia suggests the following. In the first place, Runia calls attention to Burckhardt's pretension of modesty: He denies having in mind anything "systematic"; the rejection of "(world-) historical ideas" undoubtedly is a nasty dig at historists like Ranke or Boeckh, and, above all, nothing could be further removed from his agenda than what philosophers of history like Fichte and Hegel had been doing. Nor is it his intention to propose a historical methodology, for "wir sind 'unwissenschaftlich' und haben gar keine Methode, wenigstens nicht die der andern" ("we are 'unscientific,' and we do not have any method at all, at least not that of the others").[61] But it is (feigned) modesty rather than any argument, either factual or theoretical, that Burckhardt opposes the latter. Runia not unamusingly compared Burckhardt's way of dealing with his historicist and Hegelian opponents to what psychiatrists call a *Todstellreflex,* that is, an attempt to sham death in order to avoid an open confrontation with an opponent perceived to be all-powerful.[62] And this is certainly part of the truth. But there is more, even much more to the Burckhardtian notion of the *Querschnitt,* or cross-section. In order to see what Burckhardt had in mind, we had best start with having a look at Löwith's comment:

In order to prevent the illusion of a progressive development that is suggested by the chronological order, Burckhardt not only considers history in terms of "longitudinal sections," but especially in those of "cross-sections," that reveal to us, at right angles to the progression of time, "the recurrent" and which is, at the same time, "what is understandable for us and possesses an echo in ourselves.[63] (my translation)

Hence, historical understanding is not achieved by placing something within a chronological and narrative context but by decontextualizing and subsuming these decontextualized elements within these cross-sections that Burckhardt had in mind. As might be expected, Burckhardt has been severely criticized for this, at first sight, so unhistorical approach to the past. Croce discerned here a failure to appreciate the most fundamental truth about all of history and of historical writing, namely, that history is evolution, development, and genesis.[64] And even more hostile is Burckhardt's biographer Wenzel—which should not surprise us of someone looking at Burckhardt from a Marxist point of view. Wenzel accuses Burckhardt's cross-sectional approach of transforming the past into an idle and useless speculation (a *Wolkenkuckucksheim*), effectively making any genuine historical insight impossible.[65] Much the same criticism, although formulated in a more interesting way, was expressed by Burckhardt's former student Dilthey:

Now that the mutual interlockings of the temporal and causal aspects of a past event have been dissolved, history seems to fall apart into atoms, at best into atoms that are grouped together from a certain perspective. . . . This is not the promise of a new way of dealing with the past, but rather the dissolution of all of history.[66] (my translation)

The paradox of Dilthey's critique is, however, that, on the one hand, it correctly explains why Burckhardt's way of dealing with the past is at odds with our intuitions, whereas, on the other hand, it is of so much interest from the perspective of the experience of the past. It is only thanks to this dissolution of the past into individual "atoms" that the past can become an object of historical experience. As long as these atoms have their fixed place in the endless chain of events reaching from the past to the present, as long as we can get access to them only by carefully following this chain itself, all contact with the past will be indirect and mediated by this chain of events. The event, or the past, is then a product or function of the chain of events, and we will never succeed in disentangling it from the cloak of what surrounds it. Only a radically decontextualized past can be an object of historical experience. And precisely this is what Burckhardt wanted to achieve with his cross-sectional *Querschnitte,* for this was an attempt to liberate the event from its ties with what surrounds it (and from what historiographical tradition has been saying about this).

It need now no longer surprise us that the work of art has been so much more important to Burckhardt than any other kind of artifact that the past left us. Surely, we can wrap the work of art in all the historical and cultural traditions we might wish to associate with it. But although we may succeed by completely hiding all other kinds of artifacts underneath these historical and cultural wrappings, we will never be wholly successful in this with the work of art. There is in the work of art a presence, an authenticity, a self-centeredness, a power to resist each effort to dissolve it into its historical and cultural context. It is *there,* in front of us, a product of the past, of history—who would doubt this?—but the pull of its own gravitational field of meaning is so strong that its meaning will never surrender to the powers of history. It is a kind of black hole in the historical or cultural universe—and it is the marvel of historical experience that it enables us to momentarily overcome the laws obtaining in this historical or cultural universe and to enter or to identify with the black hole of the work of art. In this way there is a most intimate relationship between this property of the work of art and Burckhardt's *Querschnitte:* What we may expect to find on these cross-sections will ordinarily be a work of art.[67] We have every reason, therefore, to agree with Runia's observation that for Burckhardt "the past was not a set of longitudinal sections, but a set of cross-sections—not a set of dramas unfolding themselves in time, but 'eine Reihe der schönsten malerischen Compositionen,'" a set of the most beautiful painterly compositions, in Burckhardt's own words.[68]

Or, to put the same point differently, Burckhardt's past is a past denuded of the protective shell of narrative in which nineteenth-century historism had always wrapped it; it is a past that we encounter as we look at a painting and where all that truly counts happens between the painting and ourselves—and not on a trajectory either beyond the painting or in the innermost recesses of our mind when contemplating the painting. Narrative, either the narrative of the past or of our own soul, is the natural ally of these trajectories so much to be avoided according to Burckhardt. Now, insofar as narrative gives us the story of a development, of a becoming, we can agree with Croce, Wenzel, and Dilthey when criticizing Burckhardt's conception of history as ahistorical or perhaps even as anti-historical. Do we not see it as the historian's main task to tell us the narrative of how something developed into something else? Is history not before and above all the organization of what we have discovered in the past into a temporal order, running from a beginning through a middle to an end? And does it not follow from this that Burckhardt, by doing away with narrative and with development, also reduced history to the timeless order of nature? So, did Burckhardt not repeat Goethe's transcendence of history with his attack on narrative? Yes and no. Yes, insofar as Burckhardt shared with Goethe this interest for the ahistorical (or the "natural," as understood in section 4.2), which Meinecke had so very perceptively discovered in Goethe. But no, insofar as Burckhardt's devaluation of narrative and history was not motivated by a Goethean neo-Platonist metaphysics but rather intended to be an undoing of the cognitive scheme of narrativist, Rankean historism. It is the result of an epistemological rather than a metaphysical strategy.

Next, there is something peculiarly parasitic about this strategy in the sense that it truly feeds on narrativist historism: It really requires an initial acceptance of narrativist historism so that it can be rejected at a later phase. Without Ranke, Burckhardt would have made no sense (as Burckhardt well realized himself). Two consequences follow from this. In the first place, the ahistorical that fascinated Burckhardt is not simply nature, human nature, or the time-transcending nature of state, church, and culture as expounded in the posthumous *Weltgeschichtliche Betrachtungen.* This is, again, where I would disagree with Rüsen's anthropological interpretation of Burckhardt. It is ahistorical in the truest sense of the word: One first has to historicize everything with the historist, so that one can make, with Burckhardt, this movement of dehistoricizing what was historicized—where the latter movement always presupposes the memory of the movement it attempts to undo. This is the heart of the Burckhardtian conception of historical experience, where it repeats Eichendorff's striking insight that in historical experience present (subject) and past (object) meet each other cleaned of all their historical denominations, as expounded at the end of section 4.2, and where it embodies the historical sublime, as it will be investigated more closely in the last chapter of the present volume.

No analysis of the Burckhardtian experience of the past would be complete without relating it to his contempt for and disgust of the arid and unwieldy products of so-called scientific, professionalized historical writing in which nineteenth-century German historians (and their successors down to the present day) saw the impressive and convincing proof of their triumphs over the mysteries of the past. As Gossman comments, Burckhardt would have agreed with Machiavelli and Guicciardini that historical writing must bear the stamp of having been written *by* citizens *for* citizens:

Burckhardt, the citizen of Basel, thought of himself as writing a more meaningful and usable history—history by citizens for citizens—than the ponderous volumes of the German scholar-bureaucrats of his day, even when he presented his work only in the form of lectures to his fellow citizens at Basel. His devastating comment on the *viri eruditissimi,* as he liked to call the philologists, is well known: "In front of them a mountain of history; they dig a hole in it, create a pile of rubble and rubbish behind themselves, and die." [69]

And on his frequent visits to Italy Burckhardt always carefully avoided the contact with the historians and philologists doing their research in Rome and elsewhere, because he was well aware that their loquacious and obtrusive pedantry might well spoil the "virginity of his vision" of the past.[70] This is why he felt so uncomfortable in his contacts with the academic historians of his time: "Die Menschen dort haben ein gewisses Etwas, wogegen ich mich hilflos fühle und konkurrenzunfähig bin" ("These people over there have something, against which I feel completely helpless and with which I am unable to compete").[71] Indeed, these scholar-bureaucrats had little affinity with and certainly no susceptibility to historical experience.

They would undoubtedly have condemned it as being at odds with the high requirements of a truly "scientific" historical writing. Telling is the fact that Ranke, who had visited Italy several times and who was by no means a narrow-minded philistine, never informs us about his having had a historical experience. Much the same is true of Theodor Mommsen, although his romanticism made him not wholly unamenable to it, as may be clear from his biographer's remark that for Mommsen Italy was "das Land der Sehnsucht und des wissenschaftlichen Interesses" ("the land of *Sehnsucht* and of scientific interest").[72] But although the poems in which Mommsen celebrated his joyful discovery of the Mediterranean world still betrayed their Eichendorffian inspiration,[73] Italy was, in fact, for him the country satisfying his *wissenschaftliches Interesse* rather than his *Sehnsucht.* Even more so, whereas Burckhardt played with the idea of having been born in Italy, of having been a Mediterranean *Meernix,* Mommsen had to fight off the pangs of nostalgia for his beloved Hamburg while in Florence.

This, then, is the appropriate place to add a few comments on the more theoretical issue of the relationship between historical experience and the professionalization of historical writing in the course of the nineteenth century. Against the background of the above-mentioned we may be tempted to see an unbridgeable gap between professionalized historical writing and historical experience and all that we have learned to associate with both. Does not historical experience aim at the union of subject and object, of present and past, whereas professionalized historical writing stakes everything on pulling them apart as much as possible?

Professionalized historical writing has two strategies at its disposal for doing so: the contextualization of the object and the contextualization of the subject. The contextualization of the object has, of course, been the crown jewel of historism: Historism always urged us to see each historical phenomenon as part of an encompassing historical process. The assumption being that the meaning or the essence of each historical phenomenon could be established only against this background. With hermeneutics this requirement of contextualization was complemented with the requirement that the historical subject should be contextualized as well—the assumption being, this time, that the idea of a time-transcending historical subject makes no sense in the humanities, where all knowledge is no less historically situated as what it is knowledge of. In this way historicization (or contextualization) propelled a *double* movement away from the interface between subject and object. Historism accentuated the trajectory from this interface to some unfathomable depth lying behind it on the side of the object. Hermeneutics achieved the mirror image of this on the side of the subject by pulling the subject away from this interface into the precincts of its own prejudices and historical determinations. Both movements away from the interface between subject and object resulted in the Gadamerian "effective history," where the contact between subject and object has become as tenuous as that between the South Pole and the North Pole of our globe (where *Horizontverschmelzung* is ruled out by the laws of geometry, as we know). It resulted, even worse, in the irresponsible extravagances of deconstructivism, where worries about the relationship between subject and object were scornfully and disdainfully derided as the antiquated remnants of the shallowest of positivisms. In sum, are hermeneutics and deconstructivism, as both the loyal and the *dis*loyal allies of professionalized historical writing, not the implacable enemies of historical experience and its foes with whom no reconciliation could ever be possible?

So it may seem; and this certainly is what the facts seem to suggest. Where nineteenth-century historians remained so close to the interface between subject and object, between present and past, as to retain at least a memory of historical experience, the notion (and all that we should associate with it) was lost without leaving a trace in how twentieth-century historians conceived of their relationship to the past. Admittedly, there have been a few exceptions to this rule of the disappearance of historical experience, such as Johan Huizinga, Friedrich Meinecke, and Mario Praz; but their voices were rarely heard, and if they were heard, they were not taken seriously. And who could put the explanation of the death of experience more aptly and eloquently than Burckhardt's pupil Friedrich Nietzsche:

And now take a quick glance at our time! We fly back in astonishment. The clearness, naturalness, and purity of the connection between life and history have vanished; and in what a maze of exaggeration and contradiction do we now see the problem! Is the guilt ours who see it, or have life and history really altered their conjunction and an inauspicious star risen between them? . . . There is such a star, a bright and lordly star, and the conjunction is really altered—by science, and the demand for history to be a science.[74]

And Nietzsche's Burckhardtian observation is no less correct for the French as for the German historical tradition. Whereas the first generation of historians since the French Revolution was still fully absorbed by the Herculean task of integrating the terrible events of the revolution in some way or another into the collective consciousness—an effort requiring the involvement of all their powerful personalities—since 1870 professionalized historical writing was no less victorious in France, thanks to Gabriel Monod, Ernest Lavisse, Charles Seignobos, and so on than it had been half a century before in Germany.[75] Michelet still felt no reluctance to recount his historical experience of the *fête de la Fédération* of July 1790 in the introduction to his *Histoire de la Révolution Française:* "Chaque fois qu'à cette époque de l'année mon enseignement me laisse, et le travail pèse, et la saison s'alourdit. . . . Alors je vais au Champ de Mars, je m'assieds sur l'herbe séchée, je respire le grand souffle qui court sur la plaine aride. Le Champs de Mars, voilà le seul monument qu'a laissé la Révolution" ("Always when at this time of the year teaching allows me to do so, when work is difficult and the weather oppressive. . . . I go to the Champs de Mars, I sit down on the dry grass, I breathe the hot wind blowing over the arid plain. The Champs de Mars, the only monument that the Revolution has left me" [my translation]).[76] And then Michelet sees before his mind's eye again the miraculous and brotherly reunification of the French nation that was for him so much the symbol of the Revolution and in which it took together all of History's promises to France and to mankind in general. But this so intense and personal relationship with the past then had to give way to Seignobos's famous claim that "l'histoire se fait avec des documents," urging the historian to strive for a total epistemological abstinence. And this abstinence would mean the death of historical experience in France no less than had been the case in Germany.

So if the professionalization and the disciplinization of history dealt the deathblow to historical experience, no compromise between the two seems to be possible. Where we have narrative, experience is impossible; and experience excludes narrative. Either we allow ourselves to be carried away by the time-transcending revelations of historical experience, or we comply with the requirements of the narrativization of the past by scientific historical writing. *Tertium non datur.* I do not doubt that this is how the historians and men of letters discussed here would look at the issue, if its nature had been properly expounded to them. But this is not the position I will defend here—and throughout this book. To put it provocatively, it is precisely the radical incommensurablity of experience and narrative, of Classicism and Romanticism, of nature and history (and what these stand for) which compels us to make use of the positions at both sides of the great divide.[77]

The crucial step toward this apparently impossible position was already made when we observed a moment ago this peculiarly *parasitic* character of Burckhardt's extolling nature above the historical—parasitic in the sense that it presupposes a previous movement of historicization that can be "undone" or invalidated in a second movement. Hence, without historicization, there is no historical experience; and historical experience is a return to the authenticity of the past, which is possible only on the condition of a preceding movement of alienation from the past by history (and Romanticism). This is also, for that matter, why the issue of historical experience is such an appropriate topic at the present juncture. Are we not placed by it at a vantage point which is ideally suited for establishing the ravages wrought by the pompous pedantries of so-called scientific history, the aimless somnambulism of hermeneutics, and the impudent absurdities of deconstructivism—all three of them united in an unholy alliance against the "virginity of vision" and the past's authenticity? It is here that the notion of historical experience may suggest a more fruitful attitude toward our past than we are presently capable of and how we may retrace a route that we have been following far too long already.

The all-important lesson we must learn from Burckhardt's so strangely ambivalent attitude toward professionalized historical writing is that we should not reject or sacrifice it in favor of historical experience: The notion of historical experience makes sense only and exclusively against the background of professionalized historical writing. Before and without professionalized historical writing, historical experience is just as meaningless a notion as the notion of conservatism would have been before the French Revolution. From this perspective Burckhardt's conception of history should not be interpreted as a reactionary critique of professionalized historical writing, as a recommendation to return to a conception of history antedating professionalized historical writing, but instead as a drawing-up of the balance sheet after having seen what professionalized historical writing did and did not give us. Or, to continue this metaphor, the professionalization of historical writing has "revolutionized" it—and surely this was a good and necessary thing. No sensible person would wish to return to "prerevolutionary" historical writing. Nevertheless, we should be more aware of the historical world we lost when revolutionizing historical writing with its professionalization than we have been up to now. And this is where the notion of historical experience comes in. But if we should be prepared to recognize this creative interaction of professionalized historical writing and historical experience, we should by no means underestimate the dramatism of the opposition that is somehow to be reconciled. The logic of professionalized historical writing on the one hand and that of historical experience on the other truly are incommensurable. Hence, although the two mutually exclude each other, the historian must try to build this exclusion into the heart of his writing.

Now, this is what sublimity is all about. We encounter the sublime, as defined by Burke or by Kant (to mention the two most influential theorists of the sublime), when the epistemological instruments we ordinarily use for making sense of the world suddenly prove themselves to be no longer equal to the task. This happens when pleasure and pain, which normally exclude each other within the Lockean epistemology adopted by Burke, paradoxically go together in our experience of the world (Burke) or when the imagination suddenly sees itself confronted with epistemological challenges that only Reason would be able to cope with (Kant). Obviously, this is also the situation when we have to negotiate some *juste milieu* between such irreconcilable enemies as narrative (or professionalized historical writing) and experience.

Having introduced the notion of the sublime, we should now ask ourselves how this notion could help us further. We should observe, in the first place, that the very existence of this philosophical category (assuming that good reasons can be given for its meaningfulness—but a discussion of *this* issue is clearly beyond the scope of the present investigation) will permit us to place this issue of a creative interaction between narrative and experience on the theorist's agenda. Without the category of the sublime, we could say only that narrative and experience are incommensurable and mutually exclude each other—and that would then have to be the end of it. But now we have, with the sublime, a philosophical category legitimating the question of how to conceive of this apparently impossible creative interaction of narrative and experience. Next, we can make a most trivial but nevertheless momentous observation about this creative interaction. The observation in question is that such a creative interaction could never be reached when we have either only narrative (and no experience) or only experience (and no narrative). This creative interaction always and necessarily is some *mixture* of the two of them. However, no rules are available for fixing this *juste milieu.* Suppose we had such rules. In that case these rules could be said to be a *tertium comparationis* of both narrative and experience. And if such a *tertium comparationis* would exist, narrative and experience would no longer be incommensurable—and this would be in contradiction with our premises. It follows that if we accept the category of the sublime as a meaningful category, a creative interaction of narrative and experience must exist, although we will never be able to figure out a priori where to find it. It is the kind of thing that we just hit upon—and more cannot be said about it. We can only just *observe* or *establish* that some *optimum* or creative interaction has been achieved in the relationship between narrative and experience, without our being able to deduce this observation from the application of some set of rules for how to negotiate between the two. This, for that matter, does certainly not imply that such observations would be wholly arbitrary and irrational: only a Cartesian believing that all truth is deducible from indisputable first principles could be tempted to such defeatist conclusions.

At this stage a comparison with mathematics may be helpful. Think of the equation $f(x) = \frac{1}{3}x^3 + \frac{1}{2}x^2 - 12x$; differential calculus shows that this function will have a local maximum for $x = -4$ and a local minimum for $x = 3$. In this way differential calculus can be said to perform what, analogously, could not possibly be performed for the relationship between narrative and experience. So one might say that historical writing is in much the same situation as mathematics was before the discovery of differential calculus by Newton and Leibniz. Before this discovery there was something "sublime" about the question of where the equation $f(x) = \frac{1}{3}x^3 + \frac{1}{2}x^2 - 12x$ would attain its local optimum and minimum: One could only hit on it experimentally (that is, by simply trying out different values for x), but no adequate explanation could be given for this. It has been Newton's and Leibniz's feat of genius to reduce what was "sublime" to what could be figured out, or to reduce what was incommensurable to what could be made commensurable thanks to the magic of differential calculus, whereas this is not (yet) possible in the domain of historical writing. I would like to add here that Leibniz's theory of the substance (which is in many respects the ontological counterpart of his mathematics[78]) may also show us what such a "differential calculus" for the humanities would probably have to look like and how we could thus eliminate sublimity from the humanities—although this will remain in all likelihood a merely theoretical rather than an actual possibility.

But at the present stage I wish to conclude with one last remark on the sublimity of (historical) experience. It will need no clarification that narrative stands for language and experience for reality: We need *language* for telling a narrative about the past, and experience is essentially an experience of *reality*. So most of the foregoing could be rephrased as a theory about the relationship between language and reality in historical writing (and about their incommensurability). Now, speaking about "reality" in general undoubtedly is too vague and imprecise here, for this is not how the relationship between reality and language and its problems ever announce themselves in the practice of historical writing. Here the real issue always is what chunk of language had best be coupled with what chunk of language[79]—and then we always have to do with a series of chunks of language on the one hand and a series of chunks of historical reality on the other. If phrased in this way there is something reassuring and pleasantly undramatic about the problem; it seems merely to be a matter of finding the right or most appropriate definition of some part of the world or of finding the right words for expressing the nature of some vague but strongly felt emotion. And if this definition or these words have been found, there has been, so to say, a comical solution to it all.

But this is different with the relationship between language and reality which is at stake here, for here this relationship is truly tragic rather than comic. The relationship is such that the triumphs of the one are necessarily the defeats of the other: The successes of language are at the expense of experience, and those of experience inevitably dull language. This may explain why historical experience always essentially is, as we have seen, an experience of *loss*. Our initial intuition will be that loss here primarily is the loss of the past—and this is certainly part of it[80]—but apart from this, the feeling of loss mainly originates in the awareness of a loss of transparency in the relationship between language and reality. Insofar as we still can trust language, we have lost part of reality; and insofar as we have access to reality, we have lost language as our trusted and reliable mirror of nature and reality.

Even more so, it might well be that this is really what is at stake in our despair about the loss of the past as such. This loss of transparency in the relationship between language and reality should not merely be a *sign* of our loss of the past, as if language, by a kind of Pavlovian association of language with reality, makes us aware of a loss of the past—where reality is what truly counts. No, it is rather the other way round, the loss of the past *is* this loss of transparency in the relationship between language and reality: When we hit upon this sublime indeterminacy in the relationship between language and reality, at that very moment the past makes its entrance in our minds. The past does not exist prior to this sublime indeterminacy, the past does not *cause* this indeterminacy—the past *is* this indeterminacy, the past *constitutes* itself in this indeterminacy; and temporal distance is, therefore a merely accidental and additional property of what we experience *as* past. In this way historical experience transcends—as is proper to the category of the sublime—time as the Kantian *Anschauungsform* defining our relationship to the past. And in this way there can be no closure of historical experience, since it situates us in a transcendental domain beyond the temporal determinations implied by the notion of closure.

Next, a recurring element in all accounts of the sublime is the paradoxical union of the feeling of pain and of pleasure. And so it must be with historical experience: Because of the tragic interaction of language and reality, the joy we may feel about the optimum that has momentarily been achieved in this interaction is necessarily accompanied by a painful awareness of what has *not* been achieved. It is inherent in the notion of the optimum (so singularly present in the sublimity of the experience of the past) that the optimum is the measure of its own success and of its own failure at one and the same time. They are the two sides of one and the same coin. Hence, the inexplicable gift of what is given to the historian by historical experience (at the moment of this supreme revelation of the past) is, at the same time, counteracted by a no less intense awareness of loss. And, once again, we should not mistake this for the loss of something that was previously in our possession: The past is not an object of possession; we never possessed it in the way we may possess a house or even a beloved.

As we have seen, this is the deep insight that was already so tactfully and wisely expressed by Eichendorff when he took care to separate Florio and Venus at the moment when their union so much seemed to be the natural and inevitable next step. Indeed, the experience of the past is like the most intense love, but one that never reaches its natural climax, though coming "infinitesimally" close to it—and in this way possession always is a promise rather than actuality. A more powerful and suggestive metaphor of this going together of pleasure and pain in the sublimity of the experience of the past will not be easy to find. But if we would nevertheless prefer to cash in the metaphor in a less poetic and more theoretical terminology, we could say that loss here is epistemological rather than metaphysical: It expresses a despair about our relationship to the world, to the past, about their unattainability at the moment when the world and the past seemed nearer to us than ever before, and not a despair about our loss of part of the world or of the past that formerly used to be our securest possession. Indeed, sublimity is an epistemological rather than a metaphysical notion. And this feeling of despair is all the more intense, for although it may have been occasioned by a work of art, a poem, or by what has provoked a historical experience, all of these are at the same time experienced as a reminder of the unattainability of all of the world and of the past. These objects then *exemplify* this sad feature of our *condition humaine,* and with the unfulfilled promise of this painting, of this poem, we weep the loss of all the world and of all that the world had promised us when it presents itself to us in its attire of sublimity.

I add one last comment on the sublimity of historical experience. As was observed a moment ago, there are two strategies for desublimating it. There is the historist strategy, which robs the past of its sublimity by contextualizing all that took place in the past. This strategy has given us professionalized historical writing. Next, we may contextualize or historicize the historical subject itself—and this is the strategy of the (Gadamerian) hermeneuticist. And to which we should add that, although the first strategy may be adopted without adopting the other, the second will rarely, if ever, go unaccompanied by the former. In fact, it will not be easy to think how one could propose the contextualization of the subject without also doing this for the object. Now, as Gadamer himself made abundantly clear, the historist strategy can well be seen as the historist's counterpart of Kantian epistemology (think of Dilthey's claim that he was doing for history what Kant had done already for the sciences). Next, as we all know, the Kantian system still left at least some room for the notion of sublimity, although even in Kant sublimity is marginalized by its being merely an occasion for our becoming aware of our moral destination. But when we radicalize historism in the way proposed by Gadamer's hermeneutics, even an already marginalized Kantian sublimity is shown the door. Kantian sublimity will then be unmasked as the typically Enlightened secularization of the religious origins of moral obligation. Historicization will then blow away the last remnants of sublimity as the wind may chase away the last leaves of autumn. In this way there is a truly paradoxical relationship between history, historicization, on the one hand and historical experience on the other; and this may explain why historicization always undoes historical experience and why historical experience, in its turn, undoes historicization and why sublimity is so much built into the very fabric of history, of historical writing, and of all historical consciousness. This will also remind us, once again, of the fact that Gadamer's hermeneutics is not the attack on (Kantian) epistemology that has often been attributed to it, but is in fact its logical fulfillment and completion.[81]

It follows from this that the (sublime) historical experience of the past can never be part of a history of experience, as so magisterially codified in Gadamer's notion of *Wirkungsgeschichte;* we can *sui generis* not conceive of a historical explanation of what it may reveal to us about the past. It may well be that a historical account can be given for its occurrence, in the sense that certain historical conditions will have to be fulfilled for historical experience to be possible. Who would deny that historical experience requires a certain amount of historical knowledge, a historical awareness, or a susceptibility of the historian for a certain historical period? I have even argued—with Burckhardt—that these things are conditional for the possibility of historical experience. The crucial datum is, however, that such explanations will never succeed in penetrating the very content of historical experience, what is actually given to the historian in and by historical experience. There is no history into which such an explanation could be embedded or within which it could be contextualized. The implication is that to the historians actually having a historical experience, this experience must appear as having come out of nowhere, of being inexplicable and not repeatable even by the strongest effort of the will. It will be a kind of secular revelation; and in a peculiar way beyond their grasp, although, on the other hand, this could only happen to *them*—which suggests a mastery of part of the past that nobody else will or could be capable of. But this suggestion of mastery is an illusion: Historical experience just befalls the historian, or it does not. Historians cannot command or enforce it; the only thing historians can do is decide whether they wish to be open to it or not. Hence, the suddenness, the directness, and the immediacy that are always associated with the experience of the past.

4.4 FRAGMENTS OF A HISTORY OF HISTORICAL EXPERIENCE (γ): BENJAMIN

Taking into account the antithesis between professionalized historical writing on the one hand and historical experience on the other observed in section 4.3, it need not surprise us that few twentieth-century historians have shown any interest in the notion. The only noteworthy exception is Huizinga, as we have seen in the previous chapter. But, on a closer look, Huizinga is a confirmation rather than an exception to this rule. Huizinga was, no less than Burckhardt and Nietzsche, quite skeptical about professionalized historical writing and the quasi-scientific results it promised to achieve. One more counterexample might be Simon Schama's *Landscape and Memory,* where Schama openly takes his point of departure in his most personal experience of the landscape in which he grew up as a child.[82]

Much the same is true for contemporary historical theory. Historical theorists in the twentieth century were either adherents of, first, the covering law model, next, hermeneutics, and, most recently, variants of (post-) structuralism; and if any system can be discerned in how each of these stages succeeded the other, the system could well be characterized as a moving ever further away from historical experience and from all that one may associate with this. I would therefore expect theorists to be even more hostile to the notion of historical experience than historians themselves are already. This may explain why the most profound twentieth-century account of historical experience is to be found neither in the writings of a historian nor in those of a historical theorist but in those of the philosophers Walter Benjamin and Gadamer (whom we shall discuss in the next chapter). Unlike twentieth-century historians, for whom the notion of historical experience could become an issue only to the extent that they were willing or capable of conceiving of our relationship to the past from a perspective beyond professionalized historical writing (and we can only admire Huizinga's courage to embrace such a perspective), Benjamin was not encumbered by disciplinary limitations. He could address the issue of historical experience from the perspective of the whole tradition of Western philosophical reflection on the notion of experience.[83]

Now, if one wishes to get hold of Benjamin's view of historical experience, his comments on the photography of Eugène Atget must first come to mind.[84] Atget used to be an actor "der, angewidert vom Betrieb, die Maske abwischte und dann daran ging, auch die Wirklichkeit abzuschminken" ("who, disgusted with the profession, wiped off the mask and then set about removing the makeup from reality too"), as Benjamin pithily put it.[85] Atget made photographs of the Paris of the beginning of the twentieth century, admittedly a period that could hardly have been ancient history for Benjamin himself (who was born in 1892). Nevertheless, Atget managed to do something with his photographs which triggered a historical experience in Benjamin's mind. When explaining Atget's photography, Benjamin begins with a remark about photography in general. Photographers feel an almost natural compulsion to give the kind of meaning to their photographs with which painters self-evidently endow their pictures. Is photography not a "painting with the camera," so to speak; are not both the painting and the photo aesthetic representations of the world? Surely, there is much truth in this; and no sensible person would contest that photography is an art in its own right. Nevertheless, there are differences as well. Each brushstroke of the painter and all that we see on the painting are there because the painter wanted it to be there. Even if the painter has deliberately forsaken a perfect control of what manifests itself to us on the canvas (as with Pollock and so many others since him), even then this "abandon" has its exclusive origin in the painter and not elsewhere. If one recalls Barthes's distinction between "prediction" (the plot of the novel) and "notation" (the irrelevant details in the naturalist novel mentioned in order to achieve a reality effect [an *effet de réel*]), one might say that in painting, even in the weirdest abstractionist painting, everything is "prediction." But this inevitably is different with photography; however much a photographer may wish to manipulate his pictures, there will always be traces or reminiscences of the real escaping his control. That is simply part of the medium. And in this way the tension between what is made and what is found (which will ordinarily disappear in painting) will always present itself in photography. Or, rather, it is a tension that can be exploited better and more naturally by the photographer than by the painter. And it is precisely because of this tension that "the real" stands a better chance of surviving representation by the photograph than by painting: "The real" is accentuated and, so to say, "enlisted" by the traces of the photographer's presence in a way that could never be possible in painting. Now, Atget, in Benjamin's eyes, had been more successful than any other photographer in saving "the real" in his photographs of the Paris of the end of the nineteenth century:

No matter how artful the photographer, no matter how carefully posed his subject, the beholder feels an irresistible urge to search such a picture for the tiny spark of contingency, of the Here and Now, with which reality has, so to speak, seared the subject, to find the inconspicuous spot where in the immediacy of that long-forgotten moment the future subsists so eloquently that we, looking back, may rediscover it.[86]

In sum, Benjamin's argument is that the openness or indeterminacy that is the heart and the essence of the present is, somehow, preserved in the photograph, so that the photograph effects in us a conviction of being momentarily contemporaneous with the scene depicted by the photograph. And Benjamin adds that the reality of the past is so marvelously preserved, almost "fossilized" in Atget's photographs because of the absence of any traces of human activity, it is as if we succeed in reaching the past through some time-indifferent layer that is typically devoid of all time-bound human projects and planning:

Remarkably, however, almost all these pictures are empty. Empty the Porte d'Arceuil by the Fortifications, empty the triumphal steps, empty the courtyards, empty, as it should be, the Place du Tertre. They are not lonely, merely without mood; the city in these pictures looks cleared out, like a lodging that has not yet found a new tenant.[87]

It is thanks to this atmosphere of an uncanny forlornness and desertion that the "real of the past" succeeds in overcoming the noisiness of historical change and in making itself heard—much in the same way that "the demon of noontide" may reveal to us nature and the world in its quasi-noumenal state in the eerie silence of siesta time.[88] And it is therefore most appropriate that Benjamin emphasizes in another context how Atget's photographs may perturb us: They seem to isolate us from the world in which we are living, to confront us with reality as it is without ourselves, which requires an effort on our part if it is to reveal itself to us: "Sie beunruhigen den Betrachter; er fühlt: zu ihnen muss er einen bestimmten Weg suchen" ("They stir the viewer; he feels challenged by them in a new way").[89]

One more aspect of Atget's photographs is of interest in the present context. This has to do with his much cherished notion of the aura. Benjamin links Atget's photographs and aura in the following passage: "He looked for what was unremarked, forgotten, cast adrift, and thus such pictures too work against the exotic, romantically sonorous names of the cities; they pump the aura out of reality like water from a sinking ship. What is aura, actually? A strange weave of space and time: the unique appearance or semblance of distance, no matter how close the object may be."[90] Now, aura is one of Benjamin's most fascinating notions, and his appeal to it in this context may help us to explain his conception of historical experience as exemplified by Atget's work. The paradox of being both remote and close can be achieved by the work of art when we become aware of the many layers of meaning that it may have, layers that are more accessible and those that will demand an effort or perhaps even the greatest sophistication on behalf of the spectator. A work of art may acquire aura in the course of time and thanks to there being a history of how it has been seen and experienced through the ages. Self-evidently, the great works of art from the past have been most successful in collecting aura.

But there is a further paradox about aura. We can become aware of aura only when the work of art is on the verge of loosing it—and Benjamin wants to maintain in his famous essay on the work of art in the age of its technical reproducibility that this is what has happened because of this reproducibility of the work of art.[91] So the reproduction of works of art does not one but two things at one and the same time: It takes away the aura from the work of art, *but precisely because of this makes us aware of the fact that the work of art possessed this aura at all.* So we have lost what we now have seen for the first time, although it had always been there but was simply not noticed by anybody. The insight is expressed most convincingly by Benjamin when he points out that the human face possessed an aura that was lost by the photograph: The human face used to be the unique mirror of a human being's soul, and now this mirror could suddenly be reproduced in any number in newspapers, films, and so on. *But it was only the discovery of the photograph which made us aware of the existence of this aura.* Hence this aura made its existence felt only *in* and *by its being lost forever.* As Nicholsen forcefully put it, "Photography, which made the ubiquity of images possible, helped to destroy the unique photographic aura of the face and the world in which it flourished."[92] This also makes clear that the essence of the face (its *photographic* aura) could *sui generis* not reveal itself before the era of photography, so that, paradoxically, something's essence is to be situated in what it possesses *no longer.* And in this way we can only dream of what is essential to our present life, which only the future can and will reveal. This, then, is how it is with aura: We can become aware of it only after having lost it, since it belongs to this quite peculiar category of things for which pastness is a condition of their existence.[93] Hence, by pumping aura out of reality like water out of a sinking ship, Atget's photography makes the past contemporaneous with us again: It is robbed of its pastness, and the gap between past and present is momentarily bridged. We are caught up, so to speak, in the historical moment when the photograph was made—as if we were to return to the scene of a crime, in Benjamin's own memorable metaphor[94]—and it is as if we were invited to join into the complex interweavings of the stream of time of that specific moment.[95] And these photographs present us with such an invitation because they create in us, first, a certain disturbance, which, second, requires us to find our way into it: "They stir the viewer; he feels challenged by them in a new way," to repeat the quote of a moment ago.[96]

The momentary disappearance of aura, this momentary lifting of the veil of Maya normally separating past and present and enabling the past to reveal itself to us in its quasi-noumenal manifestation, may direct our attention to another feature of historical experience. Recall that Huizinga had observed that historical experience is typically provoked by minor works of art, works of art incapable of gathering aura—hence, by the work of art not giving rise to deep questions about its meaning, about how it should be located into some history of art or of aesthetic expression. They simply are what they are, in the same way that the brushstroke in modern art is not suggestive of something beyond itself (for example, the painting's overall meaning or what it represents)—it simply is a brushstroke and aspires to being nothing more than this. (In this way the interest in historical experience can be said to embody the modernist or abstractionist phase in our awareness of the past.[97]) The implication is that all "depth," everything suggestive of what is "hidden" or "behind" the work of art as it presents itself to us, is eliminated—there is just the surface and nothing but the surface.

Benjamin himself, however, links the conception of experience at stake in this context not to modernist abstract art but rather to impressionism—and his reason for doing so is quite illuminating:

The technique of Impressionist painting, whereby the picture is garnered in a riot of dabs of color, would be a reflection of experiences with which the eyes of a big-city dweller have become familiar. A picture like Monet's *Cathedral of Chartres*, which is like an ant heap of stone, would be an illustration of this hypothesis.[98]

Impressionism was unreservedly "phenomenalist"; it wanted to show the world as it presents itself to us; it is interested in the movement of a tree's leaves or of the waves on a pond and in how the light plays with them and not in the leaf or the wave itself. It wants to capture the *surface of things* and is, as such, a movement toward us and away from the things themselves. In this way impressionism and how it experiences the world has its social counterpart in the flâneur or the dandy (as typically exemplified by Baudelaire, Benjamin's Virgil on his journey through the secret caverns of urban modernity): The flâneur is not involved, neither committed nor engaged; he simply *looks*—and his gaze is all the more penetrating, direct, and pitiless since it is never led astray by any interest, by any program, hope, or even preceding question. The eye operates here like the sense of touch— the eye then firmly resists the tendency so natural to it of searching for truths behind how the world appears to us. The flâneur knows that the great truths are always the most obvious truths, but precisely because of this they are the most difficult to identify since they require from us the unnatural and almost superhuman effort to stay at the surface and to avoid approaching them with a set of preconceived questions.[99] Human beings are, by instinct, "radicophiles," always in search of the roots of things, and they therefore automatically turn their gaze away from the surface. This is also where Benjaminian experience most pronouncedly differs from the scientific experiment since the latter is intended, and ordinarily even deliberately devised, to get hold of a reality lying underneath or beyond it.[100] The scientific experiment has an instrumental function, it mediates between us and the knowledge that we hope to gain access to thanks to the experiment.

It is in this respect that the scientific experiment comes close to what German theorists since the end of the nineteenth century were in the habit of contrasting as *Erlebnis* to *Erfahrung*.[101] Think of Ernst Jünger's *Der Kampf als inneres Erlebnis* (1922), where Jünger explains in what way his experience, his *Erlebnis* of the trenches of World War I had taught him some deep insight into human nature in general and into his own nature in particular. Just as in the scientific experiment *Erlebnis* is a passage to something else—and this is different in the case of Benjaminian *Erfahrung*, where the *Erfahrung* itself, and nothing outside or beyond it, *is all that counts*.[102] We can now also understand why, for Benjamin, this notion of experience transcends or overcomes the split between subject and object[103] and why experience presupposes, testifies to, expresses or suggests an intimacy between subject and object that is inconceivable in both *Erlebnis* and in the Kantian model of experience. In Benjaminian experience there is "a mutual recognition of the perceiver and the perceived" (Eichendorff!) that Benjamin found most aptly and succinctly expressed in his friend Hessel's statement, "We only see what sees us," to which Benjamin adds the following comment: "No one has more deeply understood the philosophy of the flâneur than has Hessel in these words."[104] This most intimate relationship of subject and object, not having its equal anywhere else in our transactions with the world, can come into being only because subject and object see in each other only either object or subject and not the mere mask of some deeper reality behind the mask.

And, moreover, the argument expounded a moment ago about aura makes clear what is the mechanism behind this mutual recognition of subject and object. Think of a snowball falling apart into two halves A and B—and, obviously the two halves fall apart precisely where the forces of cohesion were weakest.[105] Next, imagine that half A represents the subject (or the present) and the other half, hence B, represents the object (or the past). This, then, is a most suggestive model of what happens in the case of Benjaminian experience (or, in that of historical experience[106]). When aura becomes visible, this is like our seeing from A's perspective that side of B (that is, aura) which is moving away from us when the snowball breaks apart. So we can become aware of it only at the moment when it no longer glues together "subject" and "object." As long as subject and object are fixed to each other in the snowball, there is no surface of fissure—and the whole idea of aura makes no sense at all. There is just the snowball—and neither halves nor a line of fissure between them.

But even more important in this context is the following. When the snowball breaks apart into "subject" and "object," so to say, the surfaces are each other's *negatives,* each bearing the imprint of the other half. One could imagine somebody putting the two halves together again—and then the two halves would fit together perfectly. In this way one might well say that the two halves, the subject and the object of Benjaminian experience, the present and past, "recognize each other" and/or that "we can see only what sees us." This may also explain the paradox of closeness and distance which is always part of Benjaminian experience: Closeness is suggested by the fact that subject and object of experience here are each other's "negative," so to say, and distance is suggested by the fact that what recently still was an undifferentiated whole has now split into two parts, forever separate even though always retaining the memory of each other. And, as so often is the case with Benjamin, the notion of aura is most illustrative here again. The aura of the human face (as discussed a moment ago) is lost (distance) at the very same moment when it manifests itself (closeness) with the first photograph that was made of the human face. As Nicholsen put it: "The aura as Benjamin defines it in the 'Short history of photography' is a kind of container or husk that creates the sense of distance in time and space, despite all closeness and presence. It signals, one might say, the illusion of distance in closeness." [107] This is what one might well call *the sublimity of the aura*. And thanks to the auratic sublimity of the photograph of the human face, past and present articulate themselves by opposing themselves against each other in the way that two skaters may push each other away on the ice, where the movement of each has its origin in the opposite movement of the other. Or, as Kafka described his own literary effort, "We photograph things in order to drive them out of our minds. My stories are a way of shutting my eyes." [108]

In what is, arguably, one of the best essays he ever wrote, the essay on Baudelaire, Benjamin adds a fascinating extra dimension to all this. The point of departure here is Proust's distinction between *la mémoire involontaire* and memories that we knowingly and deliberately invoke. In the latter case we find in the present the occasion to remember something from our past; for example, we try to remember a vacation with our parents in our youth or the joys and the miseries of a first love affair. In such cases our memory will always be tainted by what made us wish to remember this specific part of our past—we will necessarily see it under the perspective of the present and the event of the past is thus reduced to being an annex of the history of the present. This is different with the *mémoire involontaire*— Proust's memories of Combray as provoked by the taste of the madeleine being the paradigmatic (and hackneyed) example—here the past suddenly presents itself like a meteoric invasion by the past into the present. Everything surrounding us in the present is pushed aside and the whole of the world is reduced to just ourselves in this specific memory—where the memory sees us, so to say, and we see only *it*. The past event in question can present itself with such an unusual intensity when it was in one way or another incompletely and not fully experienced when it actually took place: We finish, so to say, in the present a task that we had prematurely laid down in the past itself. This is, as Benjamin is at pains to point out, what the *mémoire involontaire* shares with the remembrance of traumatic experiences: These experiences were too terrible to be admitted to consciousness when they took place and therefore were provisionally shelved and put away for later inspection: "Only what has not been experienced explicitly and consciously, what has not happened to the subject as an experience, can become a component of the *mémoire involontaire.*" [109] Benjamin's most challenging insight is, however, to attribute to experience the features of Proust's *mémoire involontaire*—hence, the suggestion is that experience in the Benjaminian sense possesses a component of *memory.* There is a structural resemblance between Benjaminian experience and this sudden irruption of the past into the present: Our truest and most authentic experiences present us with something that will appear to us as something that had been inscribed into our minds a long time ago already. [110] Obviously, this goes a long way to explaining the fusion of subject and object that was mentioned a moment ago as one of the characteristic features of Benjaminian experience. It is as if an aspect of one's personality or identity suddenly appeared before the footlights and is shown to be what it is: a forgotten part of the self. Benjamin illustrates this aspect of experience by means of the fourth poem of Baudelaire's *Les fleurs du mal,* titled "Correspondances." [111] According to Benjamin "Correspondances" epitomizes (together with "La vie antérieure") what Baudelaire had wanted to express with *Les fleurs du mal,* namely, the fading memory of a world that we have lost with the emergence of modernity. [112] Baudelaire figures so prominently in Benjamin's Arcades project since Benjamin considers him to be the threshold between two ages, between the age of tradition and continuity and the age of modernity. Baudelaire is, so to say, to be situated at the place where the two halves of this snowball of a moment ago break apart from each other. The notion of the "correspondance" expresses, first, a relationship to the world that we have lost—a relationship where subject and object, we and the world, still recognize each other and where "we only see what sees us," where the temple of nature still speaks to us and looks at us with a familiar gaze. [113] And, second, there is a "correspondence" between the objective fact of a rupture with the past and how this rupture is experienced by the human individual Charles Baudelaire.

Obviously, this world that we have lost is not a historical world, it is a mythical world, more specifically, a mythical past not temporally preceding history in the way that the world of the prehistorical cave dweller precedes that of historical man but rather in the sense that "paradise" precedes history.[114] It is a mythical past that arises with history itself; it is history's "other," what is pushed away and aside by history, the negative trace of history itself in which the loss of a previous, prehistorical past announces itself to us, as beings determined by the course of history. As Benjamin comments: "The *correspondances* are the data of remembrance—not historical data, but data of prehistory. What makes festive days great and significant is the encounter with an earlier life. . . . [They] rise from the warm vapor of tears, tears of homesickness."[115] But it is with this experience of a mythical, prehistorical past as it is with the notion of aura as discussed a moment ago: It can come into being only as a figure of loss.[116] As long as this mythical past or aura are still present, there is simply nothing to experience; they make themselves felt and may become a potential object of experience only in their absence, that is, in their being part of a world that is forever and irrevocably outside our reach. And this is the deep insight that Benjamin (and Baudelaire) allows us in the nature of historical experience: the insight that life, history (and narrative) move in a direction *opposite* to how we experience them. "Normally" experience and the knowledge gained through it run parallel to each other: We have an experience and can express the content of experience in terms of the knowledge that it has given us of the world. This is how it is in science and in most of daily life. But it is the other way around with historical experience (and in what forms our identity as individuals). In the Baudelairean correspondence we experience the past in terms of what it is *not*—that is, the prehistorical past that has been discarded by the past and by the modernity (which has given us the past). It also follows from this that historical experience essentially is a dissolution of knowledge (and, as such, a variant of forgetting), not in the familiar sense of substituting inadequate knowledge with a more successful insight, but rather in the sense of a process of *an undoing of knowledge,* of an "unknowing" the past, if I may introduce this oxymoronic neologism. It is like transforming light into darkness.[117] And in this way historical experience is fundamentally tragic—truly a *fleur du mal.*[118]

4.5 CONCLUSION: FOR A ROMANTICIZED HISTORICAL THEORY

This book deals with the conflict of language (and truth) and experience. In order to identify the deepest roots of the conflict, we have investigated in the previous chapters how the transcendentalist legacy was carried over to twentieth-century philosophy of language and how it even infected hermeneuticist and post-structuralist patterns of thought that have often been applauded for their alleged anti-transcendentalism. This chapter has added an extra dimension to this triumphant history of transcendentalism by showing how it also stimulated the disciplinization and professionalization of historical writing and how it motivated all the efforts of the last two centuries to change history into a "science." Transcendentalism and the ideal of "history as science" have proven to be powerful allies in the last two centuries. Although transcendentalism originally was a philosophical analysis pretending to merely make us acquainted with the epistemological *facts* about knowledge and experience, in history it almost automatically became a highly *prescriptive* enterprise, attempting to lay down the law to historians, to show them how to mend their terrible ways and how they ought to proceed if they wished to be taken seriously by their colleagues in other academic departments. Nevertheless, all these efforts have dismally failed up to now, and history has stubbornly remained what it had always been, namely, something halfway between a craft and an art—and we should praise historians for not having lost their heads because of all these ambitious scientistic attempts to violate the nature and the purpose of historical writing. Anyway, one would hope that the fact will discourage positivist and scientistically minded theorists and make them recognize that they had better devote their energies to more useful intellectual enterprises.

However, the argument in this chapter has not been a summons to do completely away with disciplinary historical writing as it came into being over the last two centuries. It may be that Nietzsche would have been willing to sacrifice historical writing, although without being very clear about what should take its place. And it would, by the very logic of the case, be far from easy to think what the alternative should or even could be. There is something deeply problematic, if not outright contradictory, in the position of saying, with Nietzsche, (1) that history is not a science and (2) that it should stop being the science that nineteenth-century historism had made of it. If history is not a science, you could not realistically ask it to stop being a science. You cannot stop being what you are not. This is why the more ambiguous position of both Burckhardt and Huizinga with regard to professionalized historical writing is far more subtle and of more practical significance than Nietzsche's position. They did not want to do away with disciplinary historical writing, as it had come into being in the course of the nineteenth century, but wished to inculcate in the minds of their colleagues that one should not ape the sciences by positioning oneself on the place of a quasi-transcendental self. On the contrary, as a historian you should make use of all of your personality when writing history and not allow any part of it to be sacrificed on the altar of some misguided scientistic delusion.

"L'histoire se fait avec des documents"—indeed, but *also* with historians. How historians relate to their own time, what are their innermost feelings and experiences, what have been the decisive facts in their own lives—these are all things that should not be distrusted and feared as threats to so-called historical subjectivity but cherished as historians' most crucial asset in their effort to penetrate the mysteries of the past. Of course, these most personal feelings can and should never be an *argument* in a historian's account of the past—we wish to read about the past and not about its historians—but they are absolutely indispensable for historians' being open to the experience of the past, which is, in turn, the bridge to the past for both the historians and their readers. The historians' own sentiments, their convictions and feelings, provide them with the fertile ground on which historical experience can flourish. In this way the present study can be seen as an attempt to "romanticize" historical theory again after the "rationalism" of the linguistic approaches to historical writing of the recent past.

More specifically, this also is why I have highlighted and openly welcomed the allusions to sexual love that Eichendorff was most explicit in associating with historical experience. Quite natural, of course, for has our experience of the world not its natural center of gravity in what love may give us? Indeed, when exchanging language for experience, the result can only be a "romantic" historical theory also taking most seriously *this* aspect of the *condition humaine*. In this way, thinking about historical experience will result in a kind of theory that is far more "exciting" (in all the connotations of the word) than we have encountered in the arid and formalist speculations of linguistic transcendentalism. As we shall see in Chapter 8, though, the notion of (historical) experience may also bring us to the worst that we ourselves, or humanity in general, may sometimes have to go through. Love may extol us to the highest degree of happiness and perfection, but it can also throw us into the deepest abyss of distress and despair.

5

GADAMER AND HISTORICAL EXPERIENCE

The other sense-organs seem to perceive *by* touch, but *through* something else, touch alone being thought to do so through itself.[1]

5.1 INTRODUCTION: EXPERIENCE, TRUTH, AND LANGUAGE

In *Philosophical Investigations* Wittgenstein deals with sensations and pain on several occasions. At a certain stage of his argument he asks himself the question of whether I can meaningfully be said to *know* that I am in pain if I am in pain:

When I say "I am in pain," I do not point to a person who is in pain, since in a certain sense I have no idea who is. And this can be given a justification. For the main point is: I did not say that such-and-such a person was in pain, but "I am. . . ." Now in saying this I don't name any person. Just as I don't name anyone when I *groan* with pain. Though someone else sees who is in pain from the groaning. *What does it mean to know who is in pain?* [my italics] It means, for example, to know which man in this room is in pain: for instance, that it is the one who is sitting over there, or the one who is standing in that corner, the tall one over there with the fair hair, and so on.—What I am getting at? At the fact that there is a great variety of criteria for personal "identity." Now which of them determines my saying that "I" am in pain? None.[2]

When discussing these sections on pain in *Philosophical Investigations*, John Cook takes up Wittgenstein's question of what it means to *know* to be in pain, more specifically, the question of whether it makes sense at all to say, "I know that I am in pain" (if one is in pain). Can one truly say that the utterance is *an expression of certainty*—as in saying, "I know that it is raining now"? According to Cook there is a difference between the utterance (1) "I know that I am pain" and (2) "I know that it is raining now." The difference is that we use the phrase "I know that *p*" only in contexts in which I could, in principle, be mistaken about the truth of *p*. As Cook puts it, "For 'I know that . . .' to be an expression of certainty, it is at least necessary that the sense of the sentence filling the blank allow the speaker to be ignorant in some circumstances of the truth value of statements made by means of the sentence (or equivalents thereof)."[3] And this condition is clearly not satisfied in the case of pain: One cannot be mistaken about one's being in pain. It follows that the phrase "I know that I am in pain" is not an expression of certainty. This conclusion is expressed by Wittgenstein himself in the section I quoted just now, when he insists that the utterance "I know that I am in pain" could be exchanged by a simple *groaning* from pain, where the groaning certainly does not have the pretension to express a certainty or true belief, although others might correctly infer from either the utterance or the groaning that somebody is in pain—and who this somebody is. But from my perspective the crucial fact is that I do not intend to make any statement by my groaning; the groaning may simply have escaped from me and taken place involuntary. It is almost as if the pain has given voice to itself by the groaning and as if the groaning is the speech of the experience of pain itself. Experience is talking to us here, so to say.

This has an interesting implication for the relationship between experience and truth. Normally, truth is based on experience: We have the experience of rain and express the experience by means of the true statement "it is raining now." But in the case of the experience of pain the statement expressing the experience—although it seems to give a correct description of a certain state of affairs—has, in fact, the same status as an inarticulate *groan*. All that we normally associate with true statements and what true statements may express about what they are true of is then most misleadingly relied on if we try to read in statements such as "(I know that) I am in pain" *more* than the inarticulate groan. But the groan does not express a truth; and because of the equivalence of groan and the statement "(I know that) I am in pain," the same is true of the statement, despite what it seems to say. *So, we should argue precisely the other way around: The groan does not belong to the logic of the statement, but the statement belongs to the logic of the groan.* However, this does not imply that the groan should be meaningless—far from it! Its meaning is more intense, may have a more profound impact on us, and may impress us deeper than most true statements—the implication merely is that its meaning cannot be rephrased in terms of what can be either true or false. In sum, Wittgenstein's argument demonstrates that the criteria of truth and falsity have no application to a large part of our dealings with the world (and ourselves, for that matter) and to how these are expressed in language or otherwise. This, then, is where Wittgenstein's analysis of the experience of pain should invite us to question the bonds between experience, truth, and language that structure the empiricist's mental universe.

Wittgenstein discussed the experience of pain and of statements about our being in pain in the context of his argument against private languages. Pain does belong to a private world, to a world that is and could only be mine. As Wittgenstein puts it, "In what sense are my sensations private?—Well, only I can know whether I am really in pain; another person can only surmise it."[4] And he then goes on to argue that to this division of the world into a public world and one that is strictly private does not correspond to a parallel division of language into the domain of public language and one of a strictly private language. All language necessarily is "public" language.[5] It follows that if we turn inward, if we turn to the sphere of our innermost feelings and sensations, there will not be a corresponding shift from public to private language when we express our feelings and sensations. So our conclusion—certainly surprising for the poets among us—must be that language is strangely indifferent to whether it is used for speaking about ourselves or about trade deficits and molecules.

We might infer from this that Wittgenstein's argument could not possibly have any significance for the issue of historical experience. Is historical experience not an experience of the past, of an object, that is of a reality outside ourselves, outside the historian? Hence, does historical experience not invite a movement into a direction that is opposite to the one we follow when focusing on our sensation of pain? More specifically, if Wittgenstein distinguishes between statements like "This cat is black" (that is, statements about an objective reality outside ourselves) on the one hand and "I am in pain" (that is, the groans discussed a moment ago) on the other, does historical experience not correspond to the former rather than to the latter? Is the past not an "objective reality" no less than the black cat? So, should we not infer from all this that historical experience is a variant of empiricist experience rather than of the kind of experience involved in situations in which we tend to utter the words "I am in pain"?

So it may seem. But think now of a civilization, a culture, or a historical epoch as if it were some strange and hybrid creature, a creature reminiscent of what Schopenhauer had in mind with his notion of a Will preceding the stage in which the *principium individuationis* has started to perform its tasks. Such a creature would be "strange and hybrid" in the sense of being, on the one hand, far more than what *we* are and, on the other, far less—"more" in the sense of comprising, in some way or other, all the individuals that are part of this civilization, and so on but "less" so in the sense that its level of self-awareness is far less developed and far less articulate than usually is the case with us as normal, waking human individuals. Moreover, think of this strange creature to consist of nothing but these vague and inarticulate sensations, moods, and feelings. It lacks a "self" tying them together; these creatures *are* only these fleeting sets of sensations, moods, and feelings. In this way these creatures are sets of experiences without there being a *subject* of experience. Suppose, furthermore, that, for all their so very weak or, rather, nonexistent capacity of self-awareness, these strange creatures may nevertheless sometimes become conscious of themselves, of their pains and sensations, although *even then* there is no "I" to which (the awareness of) these pains and sensations could meaningfully be attributed. What could this entity possibly be? The paradox of a self-awareness without self-awareness could then be solved by saying that the presence of these pains and sensations articulates itself only in the minds of some of the great poets, novelists, or historians living and writing in a certain civilization or culture. The job of self-awareness has been delegated, so to say, by these creatures to certain "subsystems" of theirs—to use Niklas Luhmann's vocabulary—such as poets, novelists, and historians (and we may envy them for their capacity for doing this, for how more pleasant would human life be if we could do the same!). These poets, novelists, and historians are the creature's "nerves," so to say (although in order to make the metaphor work, we should attribute to these nerves also the capacity for translating the firings of these nerve cells to the level of consciousness). In that case the disjunction of experience from truth and language would hold also for what these "enthusiastic" (to use the most appropriate adjective here) poets, novelists, and historians say about their civilization, and so on. And the implication would be that we should not try to fit their writings into the discourse of truth (as exemplified by statements such as "This cat is black"); instead we should see them as the *groan-*

ings of this civilization. That does not imply, however, that they should be meaningless to us. Once again: Far from it! These groanings may overwhelm us with an unequaled force and intensity, and they may be perceived in the *basso continuo* accompanying all that a civilization thinks and does. It means, rather, that we should not interpret them *as being about something else* in the way that the true statement is about some state of affairs in the world. We should take them for what they *are,* that is, as the groanings of a civilization, as the texts in which the pains, the moods, and feelings of a civilization articulate themselves. *In this way these groanings are essentially poetic; just like a poem they do not aim at truth but at making experience speak. And this is how we should read them.*[6]

No analysis of the writing of history by a contemporary theorist has come closer to the picture I drew up a moment ago with Wittgenstein's help than Hans-Georg Gadamer's profound and magnificent *Truth and Method* (*Wahrheit und Methode*). In the first place, historism has found in this work its ultimate perfection. Before Gadamer historists had historicized truly everything, but they never even considered the possibility of historicizing themselves as well. The transcendental historical subject thus continued to stand like a solid rock in the raging seas of historicization. Even more so, historists such as Ranke or Dilthey used history to give to this rock a solidity it had never possessed before: For them it is History that will teach us the final Truth about the past and about ourselves. History was thus presented as the very crown on all the epistemological enterprise: It completed the philosophical torso that had been wrought by Descartes, Kant, and so many others in their wake. When Gadamer took the extraordinary step to historicize the historical subject itself, this was not merely to make the trivial and pedestrian point that our conceptions of the past are just as much subject to historical change as anything else in history. This kind of skepticism would still be an indelible part of the epistemological approach to historical writing; skepticism is, after all, a word in the epistemologist's dictionary, and it has its use and meaning only in this dictionary's philosophical language. So with such skepticist conclusions Gadamer would still have remained tributary to the epistemological tradition. However, Gadamer inferred from his radical historism the far more important conclusion that we should think of historians and their writings not in *epistemological* but in *ontological* terms. That is to say, he urges us to surrender all attempts to project epistemological hierarchies on the relationship between subject and object (regardless of whether the subject or the object is believed to be the stronger partner of the two) and to exchange this for a relationship of pure *contiguity* between the two, in the way proposed by Heidegger in his *Being and Time* (1927). That is to say, the historian (subject) and the past (object) should be recognized to have a shared ontological status, and the historian should not be situated in some transcendental realm outside or beyond this shared ontological domain. It is, therefore, the historical theorist's main task to take into account and to elaborate all the far-reaching consequences of this Heideggerian insight—and this is exactly what Gadamer had wanted to do in his *Truth and Method*.

Self-evidently, this is in agreement with my Wittgensteinian picture of historians expressing the pains, moods, and feelings of their civilization and its past and hence with an account of historical writing in which the ties between experience and Truth have unsparingly been cut. Truth is the implacable enemy of contiguity and of an ontological negotiation of the claims of subject and object. And where the severing of these ties is neither an embrace of nor an invitation to irrationality or arbitrariness, but is inspired by the recognition that questions of truth and falsity are meaningless as soon as we have to do with historical experience, so the main question to be addressed in this chapter is what gains may be expected for our understanding of the notion of historical experience from the ontological approach to experience that has been advocated by Gadamer in his magnum opus.

In the course of this chapter we shall discover, however, that Gadamer's oeuvre, for all its outstanding originality and immense erudition, remained an unfulfilled promise from the perspective of historical experience. It surely is a promise since Gadamer freed experience from the fatal embrace of a positivist (and/or neo-Kantian) conception of experience and thus rendered to it its autonomy with regard to language and knowledge. But the promise remained unfulfilled, as we shall find, since Gadamer, in the end, enclosed experience in the reassuring and irenic matrix of *Wirkungsgeschichte* ("effective history"). And this made (historical) experience subservient again to a new god; namely, the god of (effective) history. Historical experience thus lost its autonomy to effective history: All historical experience should now be seen as being merely a phase in a text's effective history. In essence: *Effective history is the main notion in Gadamer's oeuvre and rival concepts, such as experience are subordinate to it. In this way*

Gadamer did not give us "the experience of historicity" but instead "the historicity of experience."

The result has been just one more domestication of experience in the name of Truth, which, on the level of the text, seemed to repeat the same movement that has so often been associated with Ranke's conception of the past. Ranke exchanged the Enlightenment's trust in the triumphant march of world history toward scientific and moral perfection for an openness to drama of all that the past presents us with: To the individual historical epoch he rendered its autonomy with regard to the whole of historical human history. Nevertheless, to put it in Hayden White's quite appropriate terminology, the result was a "comic" interpretation of the past; the past was cast in the mode of a comedy with a happy ending after all the misunderstandings and false starts that so much preoccupied the *dramatis personae* of the past itself. And so it is with Gadamer: He courageously and unhesitatingly threw aside all the transcendental schemes we may still find in traditional historism and, more important, in Dilthey. The experience of text and past seem to have been freed from its transcendentalist fetters. But a quasi-Rankean trust in the benefactions of effective history was appealed to in order to give us, again, the desired intellectual mastery of the text and the past. And the end result is that the political promises Ranke had expected from the past thus have their (historiographical) counterpart in the promises that Gadamer expected from "effective history," where the realization of the goals of history implicitly suggested by Ranke's comic conception of the historical process has its counterpart in the realization of interpretative Truth that is implicit in Gadamer notion of "effective history."

In this chapter, then, I shall try to go beyond Gadamer by cutting the ties between Truth and experience—and I shall unhesitatingly embrace the anti-cognitivist implications following from this.

5.2 GADAMER ON AESTHETIC EXPERIENCE AND TRUTH

But let us now have a look at *Truth and Method* itself—and start with the "emancipatory" part of Gadamer's hermeneutic message. *Truth and Method* is, essentially, a book on how we read texts and on hermeneutic truth—hence the book's title. The book wants to make clear how texts are interpreted and, more generally, how understanding comes into being in the humanities and, especially, in the writing of history. So much is clear already from the book's title, for *Wahrheit,* "Truth," refers to what truth is in the humanities. Nevertheless, as all readers of *Truth and Method* discover to their amazement, the first 100 pages of the book are devoted to aesthetic experience, hence to a topic that has, at first sight, little or nothing to do with text interpretation or with how to write history.

So, why is this? The explanation is given by the title of the first part of Gadamer's masterwork: "The Rehabilitation of the Question of Truth by Means of the Experience of Art."[7] The idea here is both historical and systematic. From a historical point of view Gadamer argues that philosophy since Descartes has, for all its successes, essentially been a history of loss (obviously, an emplotment of philosophy's past that is wholly consonant with the inspiration of this book, where the main message also is that history is the history of loss). What we lost, according to Gadamer, has been a certain conception of experience and truth that the Aristotelian tradition had still been able to account for but no longer fitted within the scientistic worldview that came into being with and since Descartes. But *what* is this conception of truth we have lost when moving from Aristotle to Descartes? This brings us to the systematic component of Gadamer's argument. The point Gadamer wishes to make here is twofold. First, that *art and aesthetic experience* can give us access again to these two (most intimately related) notions of experience and truth. And, next, Gadamer claims that this will also enable us to explain how truth is achieved in the humanities, in the interpretation of texts, and in historical understanding (although, as we shall see, *Truth and Method* does not *really* tell us how to move from aesthetic experience and truth to historical experience and truth). So it was *aesthetic* truth that we lost with Descartes.

How the recovery of these two notions would exactly fit within the modern, post-Cartesian worldview is a question that Gadamer does not address. That is to say, he does not explain whether his rehabilitation of them is intended to be merely a supplement to the scientistic and epistemological account of experience and truth, whether they should replace them, or, to mention a third possibility, whether he aims at some kind of synthesis of a pre-epistemological and epistemological conceptions of experience and truth. But since Gadamer nowhere explicitly deals with science or with the question of how philosophy should account for science and since he even seems to believe that "method" is all right for science and for the epistemological analysis of scientific knowledge, the first possibility seems to be closest to his intentions. And it would follow, for that matter, that

Gadamer would in all likelihood not agree with the argument of Rorty's *Philosophy and the Mirror of Nature* that *all* theory of knowledge will have to be radically de-epistemologized.[8] There is in Gadamer an implicit dualism that is patently absent from the essentially monistic pretensions of Rorty's thought as expounded (and criticized) in Chapter 1.

Anyway, if we wish to regain what has been lost since Descartes, we will have to start, according to Gadamer, with making clear to ourselves how epistemological thought since Descartes succeeded in so thoroughly discrediting the notions of (aesthetic) experience and truth in art. If we know what went wrong there, we may be able to undo the damage, to make these two notions philosophically respectable again, and, finally, to come to an adequate understanding of what goes on in the humanities. When making clear the havoc that has been wrought by epistemological thought, not Kant but Schiller is Gadamer's main culprit.[9] Gadamer has in mind here Schiller's *Letters on the Aesthetic Education of Mankind* (1795). He points out that Schiller emphasized and radicalized here those aspects of Kant's aesthetics that tended to place art outside the domain of (scientific) truth. As we all know, when Kant used the notion of a "transcendental aesthetics" in the first Critique, he was not thinking of art but of how space and time prefigure our experience of the world. Moreover, although Kant distinguished between the faculties of knowing and of judgment, there is no clear separation between the two; in fact, it has often been argued that the third Critique should be seen as achieving the final synthesis of the first two. So in Kant there still is no unbridgeable gap between art and aesthetics on the one hand and the domain of cognitive truth on the other.[10] But this is different with Schiller, as Gadamer insists:

As we know, an education by art becomes an education to art. Instead of art's preparing us for true moral and political freedom, we have the culture of an "aesthetic state," a cultured society (*Bildungsgesellschaft*) that takes an interest in art. But this raises a new obstacle to overcoming the Kantian dualism of the world of the senses and the world of morality, as they are overcome in the freedom of aesthetic play and the harmony of the work of art. . . . Thus beneath the dualism of "is" and "ought" that Kant reconciles aesthetically, a more profound, unresolved dualism opens up. The poetry of aesthetic reconciliation must seek its own self-consciousness against the prose of alienated reality.[11]

In sum, Schiller effected a rearrangement of the Kantian system that radically and irrevocably placed art, aesthetic experience, and aesthetic truth

outside the domain of cognitive truth and experience. Thus came into being what Gadamer refers to as the "aesthetic distinction" ("ästhetische Un-
terscheidung") and "aesthetic consciousness" ("ästhetisches Bewusstsein")
for which the very notion of an "aesthetic truth" would be a *contradictio in
adjecto;* nor could aesthetic experience even be expected to contribute to
insight and truth. (Cognitive) truth and aesthetics were now completely
separate domains—truth was no longer to be found in art, and beauty was
no longer to be found in science. Surely, one might sometimes elevate art
far above the pedestrian world investigated by the scientist; one might even
attribute to art a universality and a freedom of reflection that is not to be
found elsewhere. But this universality and this freedom never truly encounter the resistance of the universality and freedom embodied by other
works of art;[12] and in this way art has been relegated to the domain of
Hegel's "bad infinite" and from which truth is never to be expected.[13]

When thinking over Gadamer's argument, we cannot fail to be struck
by an oddity in his strategy. In his book Gadamer wishes to tell us about
hermeneutic and historical understanding. So when trying to deal with the
obstacles preventing us from getting a proper grasp of hermeneutic and historical understanding, we would have expected him to explain to us why
and how epistemology since, say, Descartes, Kant, or perhaps Schiller has
robbed us of the intellectual instruments that are needed for this. But instead of this we get an exposition about art, aesthetic experience, and aesthetic truth. It may well be that truth in the humanities and aesthetic truth
have suffered much the same fate at the hand of epistemology, but as far as
I can see, that this should have been the case is suggested rather than demonstrated in *Truth and Method.* Even more so, when Gadamer comes close
to suggesting something like this at the beginning of the second part of
Truth and Method, he uses the notion of playing ("das Spiel") in order to
bridge the distance between art and hermeneutic understanding. This is all
the more amazing since Schiller in his *Letters on the Aesthetic Education of
Mankind* had used this *same* notion of play for achieving art's autonomy
with regard to the domain of truth that Gadamer had so much objected to.
So, in order to rehabilitate aesthetic truth, Gadamer made use of exactly the
same notion that, according to him, had led to the demise of aesthetic truth.

Moreover, it is not in the least as obvious as one might have hoped
(and expected) that Gadamer uses the play metaphor much differently
from Schiller. Gadamer is interested in the metaphor since when playing a

game, the game becomes something serious to us; we immerse ourselves in the (new) reality of the game, so to speak.[14] And precisely this is why Gadamer believes the play metaphor capable of bringing art to reality again and of undoing the dualism created by epistemological thought. But is this, in the end, really so much different from what Schiller had in mind with his play drive ("Spieltrieb")? Play drive is for Schiller the synthesis of the drive to form ("Form-Trieb") and the material drive ("Stoff-Trieb") that will be our incentive to realize a new and more humane political order. Indeed, not only the *Letters* but also much of Schiller's thought is aimed at overcoming the problem of *akrasia* occasioned by Plato, and more important, by Kant's ethics. That is, the problem that we may well know the good but lack an incentive, drive, or desire to live accordingly. From this perspective, the parallelisms of Schiller's and Gadamer's thought are, in fact, more striking than their differences.[15] And, finally, even if we grant to Gadamer the similarities between playing and the aesthetic experience of art, we may remain unconvinced, in the end, by his claim that the former may significantly contribute to a better understanding of the latter.[16]

But to return to the main issue, why move to art if having to deal with experience and truth in the humanities? Is this not a most counterintuitive strategy? From whatever angle we look at the humanities, at the problem of the interpretation of texts and of historical understanding, there will be nearly unanimous agreement that truth has a more important role to play there than in the arts. There is nothing particularly outrageous in saying that historians discuss what is the most "truthful" interpretation of Hobbes's *Leviathan* or of the French Revolution, however much historical theorists may disagree about what exact meaning should be given to the term "truth" in this context. Whereas the notion of truth will make little or no sense if used with regard to arts such as architecture or music, admittedly, we can meaningfully speak of "the truth" of a painting or of a novel, for example, when a portrait rightly renders the personality of the sitter (or not) or if a novel succeeds in expressing some profound truth about the *condition humaine* (or not). But it cannot be doubted that this is a far more problematic version of truth than the one that we may associate with the practice of the humanities or the writing of history. Take portrait painting. If we would have to decide about "the truth" of Hyacinthe Rigaud's picture of Louis XIV, what else do we have to go on than what historians have written about Louis XIV? Or think of the novel. When confronted with the question of "the truth" of Emile Zola's *Les Rougon-Maquart,* we would probably start by listening to what historians like Theodore Zeldin or Peter Gay have said on the French bourgeoisie during the Second Empire. And we would be in an even more difficult predicament when having to decide about the truth of a novel by, for example, Dostoyevsky that does not aim to depict a certain society in a certain historical period. History would be of no help here. So where should we turn instead? To psychology, anthropology, to sociology perhaps? But this would certainly be a move in the wrong direction from Gadamer's perspective, for this would invite a return to all the scientistic and epistemological demons that he so much wishes to exorcise from hermeneutics and historical thought. Taking all this into account, we can only be amazed by Gadamer's appeal to the arts, to aesthetic experience and aesthetic truth, in order to account for truth in the humanities. If anything, the reverse would seem to be the more natural course to follow.[17]

Indeed, we need only think here of Gadamer's own account of painting to recognize how close his aesthetics is to historical theory and how much his own position invites us to exploit the fruits of historical thought for solving the mysteries of aesthetics. This can best be clarified by focusing on Gadamer's claims about the ontological status of the work of art—which is of central importance to both his aesthetics and his hermeneutics. The claim is, roughly, that a representation has, from an ontological point of view, the same status as what is represented by it and, next, that only thanks to this the work of art can express a truth about the world, that is, about what the work of art represents, that would not be available to us in the absence of the work of art. Hence, the validity of Gadamer's claim of aesthetic truth (which is the basis of his attack on epistemology) depends, in the end, on this argument about the ontological status of the work of art. When dealing with the issue, Gadamer distinguishes among (1) mirror images, (2) *Abbilder,* such as passport photographs, and (3) *Bilder,* such as painted portraits. Only the last items are "works of art" in the true sense of the word. According to Gadamer the mirror image possesses no ontological status of its own apart from what it is a mirror image of. As Gadamer puts it: "Es [the mirror image] hat wirklich ein verschwindendes Sein; es ist nur für den, der in den Spiegel blickt, und ist über sein reines Erscheinen hinaus ein Nichts" ("Its being really does disappear; it exists only for someone looking into the mirror, and is nothing beyond its mere appearance").[18] This is different with *Abbilder,* such as passport photographs, which should, according to Gadamer, be granted an ontological status of their own. But even then their ontological status is, so to say, merely subservient to that of what they depict or represent. This is so because the *Abbild* is a mere means to the identification of the original, and it "abolishes" itself as soon as this goal has been achieved. It is true, as Gadamer admits, that we might, under certain circumstances feel compelled to compare the *Abbild* with its original; but in such a case we ask ourselves whether it properly does what it is expected to do. Put differently, we then consider it only as an instrument, only as a means for a certain purpose (such as identification), but not for what it may teach us about what it represents. You do not expect a passport photograph to convey information about the psychology of whom it represents. It is typical, therefore, of the *Abbild* that it modestly effaces itself behind what it represents.

And this is different with the *Bild,* with the representation that we consider to be achieved by the work of art. Ontologically, the *Bild,* or work of art, truly is on a par with what it represents, with its *Urbild,* as Gadamer calls it. Here the representation truly attempts to be interchangeable with what is represented by it. The explanation is, according to Gadamer, that the *Bild* really *interacts* with what it represents, hence with reality itself, and this can happen only when the *Bild* and what it represents are ontologically each others' equals. This interaction between the *Bild* and what is represented by it ordinarily takes the form that the *Bild* completes the *Urbild* in the sense of adding to it something that was not yet in the *Urbild* itself. This is where the *Bild* differs from the *Abbild.* The *Bild* emphatically does not abolish itself: "On the contrary, it is by affirming its own being that the picture enables what is depicted to exist. . . . Without being imitated in the work, the world does not exist as it exists in the work. It is not there as it is there in the work, and without being reproduced, the work is not there. Hence, in presentation, the presence of what is presented reaches its consummation."[19] In this way we can say that the *Bild,* the representation, contains or expresses "the truth" about what it represents, a truth, that is, that we can find only in the *Bild* or the representation and *not* in the represented itself. We really need the painting, generally speaking, the work of art, in order to get access to the kind of truths about the world that the epistemological tradition is so sadly oblivious of.[20] And this is what makes aesthetic truth so vitally important and why we need aesthetics to be reminded again of an experience of the world and of a truth that was lost with the victory of epistemology over its Aristotelian ancestry.

Even more so, in this interaction of *Urbild* and *Bild* the latter may sometimes prove to be the stronger partner. In a certain sense, reality, the represented, or the *Urbild* really needs *being represented* for fully expressing its ontological status. Think, for example, of Rigaud's portrait of Louis XIV, which was mentioned a moment ago, or of Baron Gros's *Napoleon*. In such cases we would not say that the painting makes its subject appear in a new and unexpected way, in the same way that you may increase your knowledge of a building by looking at it from different points of view. Knowledge and insight are then produced by (activities) of the subject, of ourselves; by our moving around the observed object, for example. But here it is rather the reverse. These paintings convince because they express a truth about Louis XIV or Napoleon to which we can get access only by the painting and not by merely adding new knowledge about Louis XIV and Napoleon to what we do know about them already. These paintings reveal an aspect of their personalities that we would never have surmised and would always have remained blind to in the absence of these *paintings*. As soon as there is the painting, we *recognize* its truth (as if we had known about this truth all along but had never been aware of it). In this way, representational truth is a *recognized* truth. So in cases like these insight becomes possible only thanks to the representation, but the truth or the adequacy of the insight does not have its origin in the subject (that is, the painter or ourselves) but in the object. It is not the subject but the object, that is, the sitter of the portrait, that makes the painting true, but, once again, we can become susceptible to *this* truth only thanks to the representation. Truth comes here, so to say, from "the inside," from the object, and not from "the outside," that is, from the subject, as would be the case in simple description. And in this way the ontological status of the portrait can be said to feed on what is depicted by it, that is, on its *Urbild*.

However, as Gadamer goes on to say, there is a turning point here in the sense that the heroes depicted in these paintings, such as Louis XIV or Napoleon, will have to satisfy the expectations raised by these paintings. The hero must, "when he shows himself, . . . fulfill the expectations that his picture arouses. Only because he thus has his being in showing himself is he represented in the picture. First, then, there is undoubtedly self-presentation, and, secondly, the representation in the picture of this self-presentation. Pictorial presentation is a special case of public presentation. But the second has an effect on the first."[21] In this way the representation can become more powerful than the represented (to put it in a way that might please Baudrillard), and in situations like these one might properly grant to the representation a higher ontological status than to the represented itself.[22] And Gadamer ends this exposition with a fascinating speculation about what this may clarify about the history of the Western visual arts. In the first place the ontological rivalry of the represented and its representation will allow us to understand the iconoclastic tendencies that the West had inherited from the Old Testament prohibition on image making. But, second, we shall now recognize that there also is another side to this. Precisely, this ontological rivalry allowed the representation to function as a fulfillment, or (Derridean) "supplement," to the represented—which was indispensable for revealing the represented's ultimate meaning. And it is precisely this that made possible the triumph of Western art: "In their overcoming the ban on images we can see the decisive event that enabled the development of the plastic arts in the Christian West."[23] The image of the divine no longer parasitized ontologically on the Deity itself—which was the iconoclast's perennial fear—on the contrary, the image could from now on be seen as its continuation or emanation and, perhaps, even as the perfection of the message of the Gospel.[24]

Now, all this undoubtedly is wonderful, and no reader of these passages in Gadamer can fail to be struck by the scope of his argument and the profundity of his insights. But this does not alter the fact that Gadamer's claims can be far more easily and more unproblematically shown to be true by looking at historical writing—and the implication is (again) that Gadamer's route from aesthetics to hermeneutics and history is an unnecessary and even dangerous detour—dangerous since these speculations about the ontological status of *Urbild, Abbild,* and *Bild* will probably not convince theorists who are (rightly) scared of ontological arguments. It is not unlikely that such theorists will resist ontological hierarchies; they will probably argue that a mirror image is no less real than a passport photograph, a portrait painting or what is represented by them and that it is (perhaps) the cognitive psychologist's task to explain if and why we tend to react differently to seeing either of these and to project unwarranted ontological hierarchies on them. But this has little, if anything, to do with the philosopher's professional concerns.

But the theorist skeptical of ontological hierarchies will not be able to ignore likewise the ontological problems occasioned by historical writing: There is an aspect to Gadamer's speculations that we cannot fail to take into account. I would like to remind the reader, in this context, of what was said in Chapter 4 about constructivism. The gist of the constructivist's argument is (1) that we cannot doubt the reality of the past but (2) that we can no longer get access to this past, so (3) all that historians can meaningfully do is discuss the relative plausibility of the "constructions" of the past proposed by them on the basis of available evidence. Narrativist historical theorists inferred from this that the historian's narrative should not be seen as a kind of mirror image, or Gadamerian *Abbild* of past reality; indeed, it is the positivist's or the empiricist's naivete to define the historian's task in this way.[25] Instead, to historical narrative should be attributed the kind of autonomy with regard to the past itself that Gadamer had associated with the *Bild*. More specifically, in the "interaction" between the past itself and historical narrative it is the latter that has an epistemological priority to the former. And this is not so because we can unfortunately never compare the historian's narrative to the past itself. This would amount to falling in the positivist or the empiricist trap again. The explanation is, rather, that the past is not an "untold story" or narrative itself, to put it in Mink's terminology, but that we can make sense of the past only in terms of "narrative."[26] Narratives are the cognitive instruments we rely on for understanding the past, and we should avoid the realist seduction to elevate them into the linguistic mirror images of past reality itself.

But this instrumentalist modesty is not in the least an unwarranted embrace of historical skepticism: The narrativist historical theorist will appeal here to the constructivist's argument in order to emphasize that an open and rational discussion is always possible about the merits and shortcomings of individual narrative representations of the past—as is, of course, unambiguously clear already from the very practice of historical writing itself. Hence, even though historical narratives share with Gadamer's *Bilder* (1) the property of not having a counterpart in reality itself and (2) of giving form to reality, they are nevertheless "real" enough in the sense of being the stake, and product, of rational debate. In this way they could be said to be a "virtual reality." And when using this term, this is not meant to be a concession to the idiom lately made fashionable by postmodernism. I am referring, rather, to how the word is used in optics. For example, a convex mirror may project of an object a "virtual image" that seems to be behind the mirror's surface, although it could of course not possibly be there; and yet optics can determine with mathematical precision the place and properties of this virtual image, to which nothing corresponds in the actual world. In sum, when taking our point of departure in historical writing, we can account for all that Gadamer attributed to *Bilder*, to the interaction of *Bild* and *Urbild*, and to the autonomy of the *Bild* in its relationship to the *Urbild* without ever having to appeal to anything so questionable as Gadamer's ontological hierarchies. And our conclusion should be that we had better deal with the mysteries of aesthetic truth with the help of what we can say about truth in historical writing, instead of the other way around.[27]

As I said at the outset of this discussion of Gadamer, the notion of aesthetic truth was of so much importance to him since only this notion can smooth the way for a hermeneutics and a historical theory free from epistemological schemata. Aesthetic truth exemplifies, for Gadamer, what truth is or, rather, ought to be in hermeneutics. Think of the "truth" about the harsh and bitter realities of peasant life so movingly expressed by Van Gogh's painting of the pair of peasant shoes and to whose message Heidegger had been so much susceptible.[28] This is also the kind of truth which is at stake in hermeneutics and in historical understanding—and it hardly needs saying that the epistemologist's schemata will forever be blind to this kind of truth. It is a truth that will strike us when being confronted with the painting (or not, if we are, for one reason or another, insensitive to the sad aspects of human existence so powerfully evoked by Van Gogh). It is a truth requiring for its recognition the involvement of all our own personality and not merely those structures of our cognitive apparatus that have always interested the epistemologist. It is a truth that should be situated in human existential time and that reveals itself with "sudden lightning" to us, to use Dostal's apt words[29]—but, once again, only if we happen to be susceptible to this truth. It is, in sum, a truth that is given to us in our experience of the work of art in question. And this is how aesthetic truth and aesthetic experience hang together; this is, then, how we should move from truth to experience if we wish to understand the role of experience in hermeneutics and in historical understanding.

Nevertheless, if we turn to *Truth and Method* with this in mind, we cannot fail to be disappointed in the end. As we shall find in a moment,

Gadamer's account of experience does insufficient justice to the promises of his so magnificent and powerful analysis of aesthetic truth. And we are left with the uncomfortable conclusion that there is an unfortunate imbalance in *Truth and Method* in how it deals with truth and experience and where the victories over epistemology fought in the name of truth are lost again by the defeats of experience.

5.3 GADAMER ON DILTHEY

When dealing with Gadamer's theory of historical experience, we had best start with the relationship between Dilthey and Gadamer— for undoubtedly Grondin is right with his observation that "Dilthey is in may respects the main interlocutor and principal adversary in *Truth and Method.*"[30] Gadamer agrees with Dilthey when the latter is fully aware of the challenges of history and of how history and historical awareness had shattered in the course of the nineteenth century all traditional foundations of Western thought. With the recognition of the powers of history a fundamentally new phase had begun in how Western man conceived of himself and of his world. Since the French Revolution one had discovered in History a new dimension of human existence, and the problem was how to fit it into a rational and comprehensive worldview. The Enlightenment had succeeded in developing such a rational and comprehensive account of man and his world in which everything could be assigned its proper place. But History and the chaos and irrationality that so much seemed to be part of it had irrevocably destroyed this order. Gadamer proposes to discern between two ways of how these challenges posed by History were met. On the one hand there was the reaction of Fichte and Hegel, and on the other hand, there were historists such as Ranke and Dilthey. Fichte and Hegel had tried to neutralize the problems posed by History by presupposing the rationality of History itself. They attempted to do so by appealing to a Stoic correspondence of Logos and Being which (as Dilthey so perceptively demonstrated in his writings on the intellectual history of the seventeenth and eighteenth centuries[31]) had never been completely abandoned in the Enlightenment. So here the idea is that a certain rationality is present and active in the historical process itself and that it is the philosopher's task to find out about this rationality by looking at the past from the perspective of Reason.

But this philosophical route had, in fact, already effectively been cut off by Kant's critical philosophy and the critique of metaphysics expounded in it. So, in fact, no room was left anymore for this Stoic correspondence of Logos and Being. Fichte's and Hegel's philosophies of history were thus outmoded already before they were written.[32] The only realistic alternative was to work out some kind of reconciliation between Kant and History. This was the strategy that had been adopted by historism: Historism had wished to avoid the dogmatic historical rationalism of Fichte and Hegel and proposed to reconcile History and Reason on the level not of history itself but on that of historical writing and of historical understanding. Nevertheless, historism never fully developed an alternative to Hegel's historicization of Stoic rationalism and, as Gadamer demonstrates, Ranke's worldview remained, in fact, quite close to Hegel's.[33] And this was still even more the case with Droysen. So when Dilthey started to write, the reconciliation of Kant and History was a task that still awaited its proper execution. As Gadamer characterizes Dilthey's position: "So next to Kant's answer to the question of how a pure science of nature is possible, Dilthey now had to find an answer to the question how historical experience can become science."[34]

As Dilthey realized quite well, this demanded a theory of historical experience, for if Kant had developed a critical philosophy of our experience of physical reality as described by the sciences, a critical philosophy of *historical* experience would have to be constructed. And such a philosophy would have to account, in one way or another, for the *historicity* of experience, for only a reflection on the historicity of experience can give us the historicist supplement to Kantian criticism that is needed. As Gadamer comments on Dilthey's endeavor:

He considered neo-Kantian critical philosophy itself to be dogmatic, and he was equally correct in calling British empiricism dogmatic. For the structure of the historical world is not based on facts taken from experience which then acquire a value relation, but rather on the inner historicity that belongs to experience itself. What we call experience (*Erfahrung*) and acquire through experience is a living historical process; and its paradigm is not the discovery of facts but the peculiar fusion of memory and expectation into a whole.[35]

So what Dilthey attempted to do was to find the *juste milieu* between a Hegelian Logos philosophy on the one hand and an empiricist or neo-Kantian theory of experience, ignoring the historicity of experience, on the other.

Gadamer has two main problems with how Dilthey negotiated his *juste milieu*. One of them has to do with how Dilthey deals with the difficulties encountered on his journey toward a critical philosophy of historical experience. And the other concerns the very idea of such a critical philosophy of historical experience itself. In order to appreciate the nature of the first problem, we should start with Dilthey's notion of experience (*Erlebnis*). This notion is one of the three among which all of Dilthey's hermeneutics moves—the other two being *Ausdruck* and *Verstehen*. The understanding of a text's meaning (*Verstehen*) is achieved by reconstructing what experience of the world (*Erlebnis*) is expressed (*Ausdruck*) in the text or a work of art. This is, basically, how the three hang together. Obviously, from the perspective of a critical philosophy of historical experience *Erlebnis* will require our special attention.[36] Dilthey's account of *Erlebnis* can be summarized in the following two claims. First, *Erlebnis* is essentially historical since all of our experience—*Erlebnis*—is a fusion of past, present, and future. We do not experience the world as a series of Cartesian moments but as a continuously shifting connection (*Zusammenhang*) of past, present, and future. So this is how historicity and history get into our experience of the world. And one might well say that this notion of *Zusammenhang* is the truly transcendental category in Dilthey's philosophy of the historicity of *Erlebnis*. Second, the construction of such a connection of past, present, and future is essentially interpretive, or hermeneutic (I shall leave aside here the problem of how Dilthey in his later writings used Husserl's *Logische Untersuchungen* in order to work this out in detail). And in this way hermeneutics can be said to be part of both the object and the subject of hermeneutics and of historical understanding. Dilthey liked to express, at this stage of his argument, his agreement with Vico's well-known dictum that *verum et factum convertuntur;* that is, we can understand the historical world since we have made this world ourselves. And in this way an important step has been made toward a critical philosophy of historical experience explaining how historical understanding is possible. So far, so good.

But the problem is, as Gadamer points out, how to get from how the individual experiences his or her world to historical connections that are no longer experienced by human individuals. The problem is all the more urgent since historians only rarely deal with the past in terms of the life stories of human individuals and since they preferably conceive of it in terms of the histories of peoples, nations, social classes, and so on. Dilthey was well aware of the problem himself, but although wrestling with it for the greater part of his life, he never succeeded in finding a satisfactory answer to it. When trying to deal with it as well as he could, he ordinarily relied on the Hegelian notion of the Objective Spirit. In terms of this notion Dilthey staked out a domain beyond that of the individual human being but where the transcendental category of connection (*Zusammenhang*) could nevertheless be put to work again, for in agreement with traditional hermeneutics this category requires us to understand the whole (for example, of a text) in terms of its parts, and vice versa. And, as Dilthey would argue, if we avail ourselves of this notion of the Objective Spirit, thanks to it, we will dispose of the means to move from the level of the individual (that is, the parts) to that of the collectivity (that is, the whole) with the help of this transcendental category of connection (*Zusammenhang*). In this way Dilthey hoped to solve the problem of how to move from the domain of the individual to that of the collectivity. However, as Gadamer objects, we will then be confronted with connections (*Zusammenhänge*) that were never experienced as such in terms of any individual's *Erlebnisse*. So how to account for these connections in terms of Dilthey's hermeneutics? Obviously, when attempting to answer this question, we shall have to move beyond the borders of the domain within we should remain according to Dilthey's own transcendental deduction of historical experience.

And this brings me to the second and more important problem that Gadamer has with Dilthey's hermeneutics. After this exposition of the problems occasioned by Dilthey's notion of the Objective Spirit, Gadamer teasingly asks the question of whether we could not also find in his writings an equivalent of the Hegelian Absolute Spirit, hence an allusion to the possibility of perfect, time-transcending truth and knowledge. And then the amazing answer is, yes! This *is* in Dilthey, too: For Dilthey we *can* achieve perfect and final truth in the humanities:

For Dilthey there is no question that it exists and that what corresponds to this ideal is historical consciousness, not speculative philosophy. It sees all the phenomena of the human, historical world only as objects by means of which the spirit knows itself more fully. Understanding them as objectifications of spirit, it translates them back "into the mental life whence they came." Thus for historical consciousness the forms that objective spirit takes are objects of this spirit's self-knowledge. . . . *It is not in the speculative knowledge of the concept, but in historical consciousness that spirit's knowledge of itself is consummated.*[37] (Gadamer's italics)

Hence, the main insight is that the challenges presented by History (to Reason and perfect timeless knowledge) *are overcome by History itself.* History is the quasi-homeopathic remedy for the epistemological illnesses that it causes itself! History is now no longer the challenge to truth and knowledge that it was believed to be since Romanticism and down to all our contemporary worries about historical relativism and historical skepticism — on the contrary, History was now presented by Dilthey as the grail of perfect knowledge. The Enlightenment, rationalism, empiricism *e tutti quanti* had always striven for absolute knowledge, but all the attempts foundered, since they failed to make use of the ultimate and strongest instrument we possess in our quest for Truth, that is, History itself. So this is how the Enlightenment should be perfected: *"Die Aufklärung vollendet sich hier als historische Aufklärung"* (*"The Enlightenment reaches its consummation as historical enlightenment"*).[38] History simply is the last and final chapter of the Enlightenment's cognitive triumph; for both the historism and Dilthey History is, paradoxically, the crown on all the Enlightenment's aspirations.[39] History is not the threat to absolute knowledge that we had always conceived it to be but, on the contrary, is its *fundamentum inconcussum*.[40] And, finally, in this way Dilthey's hermeneutics should not be seen as a move against the Enlightenment and against epistemology but as their very perfection and ultimate promise.

Although Gadamer was as deeply impressed by the daring of Dilthey's strategy as I expect anybody else to be, he remained unconvinced — and for good reasons. Think of this. As we saw a moment ago already, Dilthey still embraced (like Gadamer himself, for that matter) the old hermeneutic rule that one must understand the whole in terms of its parts and vice versa. It will immediately be clear that on the basis of this rule a perfect and final understanding of the past will never be possible. The search for historical meaning will oblige us to situate the object of historical understanding in ever more comprehensive contexts. And perfect and final meaning will then be possible only if we can get access to the context of all possible contexts. But, obviously, no such thing will ever be possible. As Gadamer insists, we human beings — whether we are historians or not — are finite beings, and the infinity that is irrevocably part of this notion of "the context of all contexts" will thus forever be outside our reach. It is true that Dilthey had proposed a number of attempts to tackle this problem. For example, there is the suggestion that History comes to insight into itself that was mentioned a moment ago; next, he played with the idea of a historicist "philosophy of philosophy" breaking through the barriers of the infinite; and, finally, he speculated about the possibility of achieving prefect knowledge at the end of history, just as the meaning of our life can be said to be revealed to us only at the moment of our death.[41] The latter option will, of course, be of little solace to historians not given to apocalyptic speculations about their own time.

Gadamer's critique of Dilthey as expounded just now is, in fact, the heart of his own hermeneutics. In opposition to Dilthey Gadamer believes it to be an illusion that we shall ever be able to transcend the limits of our finitude; and that means, for Gadamer, that we shall never be able to overcome our historicity: However much we may try to do so, we shall always find ourselves blocked by a history eluding us. Think of a person wading through the water of a lake and trying to get a grasp on all the ripples in the water caused by her. Each attempt to grasp with her fingers the ripples of water will merely cause new ripples beyond her reach; and the more desperately she tries to get hold of them, the more ripples she will cause escaping her grasp. So it is with history and with historical meaning: We live in a sea of historical meaning, and the more we try to domesticate history and to appropriate historical meaning, the faster both will move away from us and from our "cognitive fingers." This is, of course, the very antithesis of Dilthey's so overly optimistic picture.

Even more so, this is precisely how Gadamer would actually *define* history and historical meaning. History is, essentially, the world in which we are embedded and that manifests itself to us in its success to resist domestication and appropriation. Here Gadamer clearly is in agreement with Heidegger's exchange of epistemology for ontology, with his notion of our *Geworfen-sein*, which will, in the end, wreck all the epistemologist's efforts. Or, as Gadamer puts it, "*Geschichtlichsein heisst, nie im Sichwissen aufgehen*" (Gadamer's italics) ("*To be historically means that knowledge of oneself can never be complete*").[42] We can never move beyond History and obtain a point of view outside it, where we could have a secure grasp of its course and of how its details hang together.[43] Wherever we move, History is always around us; or, as Gadamer summarizes it all in a most effective one-liner: "In Wahrheit gehört die Geschichte nicht uns, sondern wir gehören ihr" ("In fact, history docs not belong to us; we belong to it").[44]

This, then, is the source of Gadamer's famous notion of *Wirkungs-*

geschichte ("effective history"), which is, arguably, the most important theoretical instrument in all of his hermeneutics (and it certainly is so within the context of the present discussion). He defines effective history as follows:

Real historical thinking must take account of its own historicity. Only then will it cease to chase the phantom of a historical object that is the object of progressive research, and learn to view the object as the counterpart of itself and hence understand both. . . . I shall refer to this as "history of effect." *Understanding is, essentially, a historically effected event.*[45]

The notion is meant to express that all historical understanding will always be part of a *history* of historical understanding. But as such it is not a necessary supplement to historical understanding in the sense that only thanks to it a clarification can be achieved about the interpreter's situation that will place the interpreter's findings in the proper light. Effective history is not a kind of commentary on interpretation that will yield truth in conjunction with what it is a comment on. As Gadamer emphasizes himself: "We are not saying, then, that history of effect must be developed as a new independent discipline ancillary to the human sciences, but that we should learn to understand ourselves better and recognize that in all understanding, whether we are expressly aware of it or not, the efficacy of history is at work."[46]

In several ways this is a statement that should make us halt for a moment. In the first place it is a striking example of Gadamer's habit throughout his book of wrong-footing his readers and of saying, in an ingenuous kind of way, things with the most far-reaching implications while most innocently pretending not to be aware of this himself. Among the truly great contemporary philosophers one will find few such subtle and accomplished actors as Gadamer (and this is why one may like him all the more—as I happen to do). But in the second place (and in continuation with what I said just now) we should not be lulled into forgetting how outrageous the statement really is. The astounding paradox of the statement is that we should realize ourselves that each interpretation merely is a new phase in an interpretation history, but that we should, at the same time, discourage eager advocates of this view to see in this an indispensable auxiliary discipline for all historical understanding (think of, for example, Hans Robert Jauss's reception aesthetics). Apparently, it has merely been Gadamer's intention to remind us of the existence and possibility of such an auxiliary discipline, only in order to reject it at once as the most naive and useless of intellectual enterprises. And, indeed, as is the case with all paradoxes, a moment's thought will make us see that a profound truth is hidden under the paradox, for since effective history is *sui generis* also a *history* (even though on a meta-level, so to say), it will give rise to exactly the same problems again as history (on the object-level) itself. So, from here an infinite regress will start—pulling away any *fundamentum inconcussum* from under our feet. History cannot be cured by history—and hermeneutic interpretation cannot be given a secure basis in the industrious mappings of effective history. And this means the end of Dilthey and of all attempts to lock history within the epistemologist's schemata.

5.4 HISTORICAL EXPERIENCE VERSUS DIALECTICAL EXPERIENCE

I shall now turn to my criticism of Gadamer's historical thought—although *criticism* is probably not the right word. I had better speak of a profoundly respectful interaction with his ideas. When defining my own position with regard to Gadamer, I shall begin with the concept that is at stake throughout this book, that is, the concept of historical experience. Gadamer discusses historical experience in the second part of *Truth and Method,* although the notion occasionally returns in the last, and third, part of the book. Unfortunately he never informs his readers of how *historical* experience is related to *aesthetic* experience, as expounded in the first part of the book and as discussed earlier. This is to be regretted since Gadamer makes use of Hegel's conception of dialectical experience for developing his own notion of historical experience. And there is nothing obviously Hegelian about aesthetic experience as this notion was defined in the first part of *Truth and Method.* In fact, my main reason for feeling disappointed about Gadamer's theory of historical experience is that he did not try to integrate his most valuable insights into aesthetic experience (as obtained in the first part of *Truth and Method*) into his account of the nature of historical experience given in the second part.

When Gadamer discerns in the Hegel of the *Phenomenology of the Mind* the basis for his conception of historical experience, two aspects of Hegel's conception of dialectical experience will demand our attention. In the first place, experience (*Erfahrung*) is presented in the *Phenomenology* as the motor moving the Spirit to ultimate self-insight in the course of the history of its self-unfolding.[47] In this way Hegelian experience is indissolubly linked to the speculative and rationalist dimensions of his thought. That is to say, experience is, for Hegel, instrumental in how the Spirit in its "subjective" manifestation recognizes itself (*Anerkennung*) in its "objective" manifestation in order to achieve the final phase of the Absolute Spirit. But since this speculative aspect of Hegelian dialectics is at odds with Gadamer's recognition of the finitude of all human understanding[48] (recall his criticism of Dilthey here!) and, more important, since it would be hard to grant to the kind of self-insight that Hegel had in mind an important place in hermeneutics and in how we come to understand texts, this aspect of Hegelian experience remains virtually absent from Gadamer's own account of historical experience.[49]

So let us see how Gadamer defines historical experience after having cut out the speculative dimension from the Hegelian concept of dialectical experience. This results in the claim that experience essentially is a *process* and that this "process of experience" is essentially negative and dialectical in the sense that, in the course of a dialectical shuttling between subject and object, imperfect knowledge is continuously improved (!) by the subject's *experience* (*Erfahrung*) of the object:

> If a new experience of an object occurs to us, this means that hitherto we have not seen the thing correctly and now know it better. Thus the negativity of experience has a curiously productive meaning. It is not simply that we see through a deception and hence make a correction, but we acquire a comprehensive knowledge. We cannot, therefore, have a new experience of any object at random, but it must be of such a nature that we gain better knowledge through it, not only of itself, but of what we thought we knew before—i.e., of a universal. The negation by means of which it achieves this is a determinate negation. We call this kind of experience *dialectical*. . . . In fact, as we saw, experience is initially experience of negation: something is not what we supposed it to be.[50]

After having climbed the dizzying heights of Hegelian *Erfahrung*, there is something peculiarly plain and down-to-earth about this conception of experience, where it gives an unexpected directness to Gadamer's thought— a directness, if I am permitted this aside, that is reflected in Gadamer's prose. No reader of Gadamer can remain insensitive to the sweet reasonableness of his argument, to the easy and powerful flow of his writing, to its affinity with the concrete, to what our hands can touch, and where it so strikingly contrasts with the "Heideggerei" that has made the prose written by German philosophers so odious to their Anglo-Saxon colleagues. The problems of Gadamer's text will typically be occasioned by how the larger parts of his writings hang together rather than by what is said at the level of the sentence or the paragraph, for at the latter level an absolute transparency reigns in his text.

Nevertheless, I am afraid that the concreteness of the passage quoted just now is not merely a matter of style but of content as well. It cannot fail to strike us that little of Gadamer's insights into the nature of aesthetic experience and truth have been preserved in dialectical experience as defined a moment ago. Characteristic is that Gadamer himself has compared his concept of experience to Popper's dialectic of *trial and error*.[51] And it may well be that he wished to distinguish his own concept of dialectical experience from Popper's by pointing out that in Popper clarity is achieved about falsification or a not yet having been falsified, whereas even this (negative) kind of certainty is never attained in hermeneutics.[52] But even so, does this not move hermeneutics and historical understanding closer to science than one would have expected from a philosopher who is, like Gadamer, so much intent upon removing all traces of Cartesianism and of epistemology from his thought?[53] Furthermore, Weinsheimer also recognized (and emphasized) the similarities of Gadamer's dialectical notion of experience and the role of experience in the sciences. In both cases knowledge comes into being in the course of a process where we move from expectation, by means of a disappointment of mistaken expectations, toward improved knowledge. As Weinsheimer puts it: "In Gadamer's view this continuing cycle constitutes the nature of experience. If *wirkungsgeschichtliches Bewusstsein* is not pure self-contemplation and formal speculation, it too learns from experience, namely the experience of the past and the interpretation of history. No less than the natural sciences, the human sciences are dependent on experience."[54] It will be very hard to discover in this still a challenge to the epistemological tradition.

Taking all this into account, we may well begin to wonder whether there are not many more traces of transcendentalism in Gadamer's hermeneutics. Think, for example, of his embrace of the hermeneutical rule to understand the components of a text against the background of the whole and vice versa. Were Schleiermacher and Dilthey so much mistaken in seeing here the heart of a hermeneutical "epistemology"? Think, moreover, of Gadamer's notorious concept of the "Vorgriff der Vollkommenheit" ("preconception of completeness"), which is defined by Gadamer as:

a formal condition of all understanding. It states that only what really constitutes a unity of meaning is intelligible. So when we read a text we always assume its completeness, and only when this assumption proves mistaken—i.e., the text is not intelligible—do we begin to suspect the text and try to discover how it can be remedied.[55]

How could we interpret this *Vorgriff der Vollkommenheit*[56] as anything other than as what we may describe as a "transcendental category of the hermeneutic understanding," as explaining how historical knowledge is possible?[57] Next, when Gadamer relates the hermeneutic circle to this notion of the *Vorgriff der Vollkommenheit* in order to explain what methodological mechanism must guide our dialectical experience of the text, his most acute commentator, Grondin, explicitly discerns here a return to epistemological concerns.[58] And against the background of what was said just now, we have every reason to agree with Grondin's observation that Gadamer himself can be accused of what he criticizes in nineteenth-century hermeneutics, namely, the tendency to transform hermeneutics into a method.[59]

This must also have its unfortunate consequences for Gadamer's notion of "effective history" (*Wirkungsgeschichte*). As we have seen, the notion is meant to emphasize that history is always "larger" than us, that it will always extend beyond ourselves, that it will never fully be domesticated by us, and that, because of this, the epistemological schemata of our cognitive apparatus will always be helpless against this *sublime* reality (to use the most appropriate adjective in this context). And this will have its implications for historical experience as well. As Gadamer puts it: "Erfahrung ist somit Erfahrung der eigene Geschichtlichkeit" ("Experience is, at the same time, an experience of one's own historicity").[60] And this means, again, that all historical experience and all historical understanding is embedded in a *history of its own,* that is, in an interpretation history and should be understood accordingly: "Die hermeneutische Erfahrung hat es mit der Überlieferung zu tun. Sie ist es die zur Erfahrung kommen soll" ("Hermeneutical experience is concerned with *tradition.* This is what is to be experienced").[61] This is, essentially what effective history is all about.

However, in Gadamer's historical thought the "sublimity" of historical experience is wholly absent—and we can now understand why. Recall that within the framework of Gadamer's dialectical conception of historical experience, experience is essentially our recognition that until now we did see things wrongly and that we shall therefore have to adapt our ideas to what we have just now perceived to be the case. As Grondin points out, this will necessitate us to accept, in some way or another, the venerable but thoroughly unspectacular notion of truth as "adaequatio rei et intellectus."[62] We can recognize a previous intuition of what is the case to be wrong only when seeing that a new and later one is more in agreement with what the world, or a text, for that matter, is like. Admittedly, Grondin emphasizes that final truth will never be attainable because of the finitude of all human understanding that Gadamer upholds against Hegel (or Dilthey). But this does not make Gadamer's conception of historical experience and truth any bit more interesting. The same is true in the sciences; think, for example, of Popper's claim about scientific theories as being "approximations of the Truth." So, no epistemological theorist would need to have any insurmountable problem with this kind of assessment of the nature of historical knowing.

However, it might now be objected that there is a difference, after all, between the sciences and the humanities. The difference is that we may approach Truth asymptotically in the course of time both in the sciences and in the humanities—but that History is not an ingredient in the sciences, whereas it *is* in the humanities. In the sciences History simply is the time that is needed for the refinement of our insights, but History is no ingredient itself in this process of refinement. And this would be dramatically different in the humanities, where History is like the spear of Amfortas that causes wounds but also is the only remedy for curing them.[63] That this is how Gadamer looks at history is argued by Grondin:

> Our Reason is to be identified with the Reason of History in a way that cannot be misapprehended. The consciousness of effective history should therefore not only be taken as a *genetivus objectivus* (i.e., *our* consciousness of effective history), but also a *genetivus subjectivus:* i.e., the consciousness, or rather: the Reason, that we must attribute to effective history. History obeys a permanently unfolding logic, and that is the foundation of our understanding. Human society and intersubjective understanding are only possible thanks to this logic. The changeable and by no means absolute Reason of effective history is essentially identical with our Reason with which tradition conflicts and against which it measures itself.[64] (my translation)

This is a most momentous insight into the nature of Gadamer's hermeneutics, *for it makes clear how close Gadamer still is, in the end, to both Dilthey and Hegel.* Gadamer's *Wirkungsgeschichte* functions in his hermeneutics in a way that does not differ fundamentally from what Dilthey expects from the Objective Spirit. And Gadamer comes uncannily close to Hegel as well. It may be true that we can never objectify effective history, that it will forever escape our grasp, and that this ties all understanding to ontology and prevents us from having access to the level of epistemological truth. But the essentially dialectical character of historical truth gives it the aura of Hegel's "cunning of Reason" in the sense that historical understanding makes use of finite efforts of the historian in order to move itself ever further into the direction of perfect historical understanding. In this way effective history functions like a Janus in Gadamer's hermeneutics. On the one hand it is meant to underline the historicity of all understanding and of all historical experience; but on the other hand the notion *itself* is a transhistorical category—and in this way is suggestive of transhistorical Truth about the past. Historist, and Rankean "comedy" has thus most insidiously hijacked the enterprise of Gadamerian hermeneutics. And by doing so, it succeeded in effectively frustrating all of Gadamer's so very commendable aspirations to overcome epistemology and transcendentalism in the humanities.

5.5 EXPERIENCE, TRUTH, AND LANGUAGE

So, what went wrong? Why did Gadamer, on the one hand, see why we should overcome transcendentalism in the humanities and what would be necessary for achieving this, whereas, on the other hand, he was a no less easy victim to it than his great predecessor Dilthey? The answer is that he—unlike Dewey[65]—could not summon the courage to cut the ties between experience and truth.[66] Not only in his account of dialectical experience but even in his most daring writings about aesthetic experience and truth, experience and Truth were always each other's closest companions. And Truth is a most jealous god. As soon as it makes its entrance, no room will be left for any other god. And then, sooner or later, science, epistemology, and transcendentalism will make their entrance, too. So if we wish to reinstitute "polytheism" in philosophy again, so to say, we shall have to radically cut the bonds between experience and Truth. This is what I wish to do here in terms of the notion of a "(sublime) experience without a subject of experience"—albeit with the proviso that I am not developing here an alternative epistemology. That is to say, I shall not deny (for could one possibly do so!) that experience often serves the cause of Truth and that this is where the positivist and Gadamer—"bien étonnés de se trouver ensemble"—are undoubtedly correct. With regard to the positivist, think of how experience presents itself in the form of the experiment in the sciences.[67] And with regard to Gadamer, his dialectical experience is certainly part of the truth on how our ideas about, for example, Locke's *Two Treatises on Government* have continuously been refined ever since the book's publication. And whether this refinement has been the result merely of a more careful reading of the text itself or of the insights offered by Gadamerian *applicatio* is of no relevance here.[68] But there is a different kind of experience, the one to be dealt with in this section, that does not humbly fall prostrate before Truth as its only god. This kind of experience, which is its own god, we encountered already as "sublime experience."

We normally conceive of the world as consisting of two parts: There is the part of which we have knowledge, and there is the part of which we have no knowledge as yet or of which our conceptions are still inadequate. And we find it impossible to conceive of a relationship to the world that could, albeit with some makeshift arrangements, not be made to fit within either of these two categories. I shall be the first to recognize the plausibility of this view as soon as we assume that there is or should always be a subject of experience and of knowledge and that there could be no experience or knowledge without there also being somebody or some person having this experience or knowledge. That there always should be such a subject of experience and knowledge was most categorically asserted by Kant:

Through this I or he or it (the thing) which thinks, nothing further is represented than a transcendental subject of the thoughts = *X*. It is known only through the thoughts which are its predicates, and of it, apart from them, we cannot have any concept whatsoever, but can only revolve in a perpetual circle, since any judgment upon it has always already made use of its representation.[69]

Hence, each thought (whether provoked by experience or being a matter of rational inference) is necessarily accompanied by a transcendental subject of understanding whose presence is as indisputable as that there could not possibly be predicates without there also being a subject whose predicates they are. But that we might doubt the ineluctability of the Kantian transcendental self is already clear from the no less well-known statement by David Hume about personal identity:

For my part, when I enter most intimately into what I call myself, I always stumble on some particular perception or other, of heat or cold, light or shade, love or hatred, pain or pleasure. I can never catch *myself* at any time without a perception, and can never observe any thing but the perception. When my perceptions are removed for any time, as by sound sleep, so long am I insensible to *myself,* and may truly be said not to exist. And were all my perceptions removed by death, and could I neither think, nor feel, nor see, nor love, nor hate, after the dissolution of the body, I should be entirely annihilated, nor do I conceive what is farther requisite to make me a perfect nonentity.[70]

So where Kant and Hume agree is that we will peer into an empirical vacuum when looking at the self; but whereas Kant postulates the transcendental self to give coherence to our experiences and knowledge, the notion of the self, or of personal identity falls victim to Hume's relentless skepticism. In what follows I shall side with Hume rather than with Kant—with the all-important proviso that when doing so, I have a quite specific kind of experience in mind—namely, sublime experience. It is therefore by no means my intention to take a stand in the conflict between Hume and Kant about personal identity, nor in the two centuries of discussion provoked by this conflict insofar as this discussion is informed by reflections on our "nonsublime experience" of the world. Finally, I shall discuss sublime experience within both the context of the human individual and within that of a collectivity, that is, the self-interpretation of a culture or civilization, a historical epoch, and so on.

I begin with the context of the individual human being and start with an asymmetry between how we speak about knowledge on the one hand and about our moods and feelings on the other.[71] In most languages we say that we *have* knowledge, whereas we say that we *are* (un)happy, cheerful, tired, and so on. Knowledge is something we possess; it is an article that we may acquire or lose again much in the way that we may acquire or lose money at the stock exchange. With regard to knowledge we are much like Neurath's ship, which remains the same, whereas the timber, the ropes, and sails of which it consist may all be replaced by new timber, ropes, and so on in the course of time. We may acquire new knowledge because this knowledge is, in one way or another, indispensable to us for the tasks we are expected to perform in our lives. And we may lose this knowledge when it has, again for some reason or another, become irrelevant to us. So we are like the captain of Neurath's ship continuously making decisions about the proper construction of our ship if it is to be capable of facing the challenges it can be expected to encounter.

But this is different with our moods and feelings:[72] They just happen to us; we do not own them in the way that we own our knowledge. Our moods and feelings follow each other in the haphazard way so nicely suggested by Hume: "If any impression gives rise to the idea of a self, that impression must continue invariably the same, through the whole course of our lives; since self is supposed to exist after that manner. But there is no impression constant and invariable. Pain and pleasure, grief and joy, passion and sensations succeed each other, and never exist all of the time."[73] Moods and feelings come and go at their own will and are ordinarily beyond the influence and domination of our will. They seem to lead their own life and not to heed us in their continuous metamorphoses. We do not possess or own them, as we can be said to own our knowledge; rather, if anything, they seem to own *us.* So precisely because of this, we should say that we *are* our feelings and moods rather than that we *possess* them, for there is an intimacy and directness—the intimacy of being what you feel—in the relationship between ourselves and our feelings and moods that is fully absent in the case of the knowledge we possess. We are not what we possess—we are not our houses or our bank account—but we *are* our feelings and moods. And nothing beyond this, for what could properly be said to be more than this falls in the category of what we *possess.* But, conversely, being your feelings and moods also implies that your identity *dissolves* in them; this should be taken quite literally in the sense that, insofar as we could metaphorically ascribe a movement to identity, it has the tendency to move away from anything so unitary and cohesive that we might associate with personal identity and toward its dispersal and full dissolution in this continuous metamorphosis of moods and feelings. If you *are* your moods and feelings—and truly nothing beyond or apart from them— there is not an identity of yours outside and beyond these moods and feelings in which these moods and feelings could be said to inhere like flowers in a vase or like the pages of a book in the book's cover. If you are your moods and feelings, then you *are* your moods and feelings—and nothing more is needed.

Now, sublime experience is closer to moods and feelings than to knowledge; like them it is ontological rather than epistemological, and sublime experience is to be defined in terms of what you *are* rather than in terms of what you know, what knowledge you *have.* Sublime experience— and historical experience—do not aim to satisfy our thirst for knowledge.

It does not serve any purpose at all, although its appearance may have its consequences for somebody having the experience—consequences that one might express in terms of an elucidation of whom one is, of what the now wholly forgotten German philosopher Karl Jaspers (1883–1969) once referred to with the most appropriate term of *Existenzerhellung* (that is, an elucidation of existence). And where one is typically *changed* by the experience—which further contributes to the claim that there is no stable subject of experience in the case of sublime experience—one's individuality gets lost in the experience.

So let us now look at what picture results when we see experience in the light of what was said just now about our moods and feelings. In the first place, there is a peculiar deaf-mutism about our moods and feelings where they so conspicuously differ from our beliefs and convictions. Moods and feelings are, typically, speechless, and this is what they share with aesthetic (and sublime) experience. This observation is common and uncontroversial enough; even the philosophically illiterate are acquainted with the fact that one may stand in front of a painting or listen to Bach's *Partitas* or his *Hohe Messe* and simply be *speechless*. As we then like to say, we lack the words for expressing our experience of the painting or of the music. But this has nothing to do, at least not primarily so, with the complexity or the overwhelming beauty of the painting or the music. It is not simply a matter of our incapacity of finding the right words in such cases, as we might feel that our vocabulary for colors lacks the right word for the color of this particular rose. Nor is our bafflement "epistemological" in the sense that we feel driven to take a position outside language and the world in order to discover the epistemological relationship between the two. Rather, the problem is, to put it paradoxically, that there is *no* problem, for as we saw a moment ago, the peculiar fact about moods, feelings, and aesthetic or sublime experience is that "what" or "who" we are is temporarily wholly subsumed in them. We *are* the feeling or the experience—and then the problem of what could or should be said about the feeling or experience makes just as little sense as to ask a stone what it is like to be a stone. The problem of how to put a mood or an aesthetic or sublime experience into language arises only *after* we have become (again) our "normal" self, the person with a certain name, a certain history, profession, and so on. *But then the problem has taken a significantly different form already, for now the question will be what it is for this person, the person with this identity, this name, history, profession, and so on to have (had) such and such a feeling or experience.* This is a question different from the one we had wanted to ask: Then we asked a question about our feelings and experiences—and now we get an answer (if we get one) to *what it is for a certain person* to have a certain feeling or experience. The emphasis will shift from the experience to the issue of how to couple it to a certain person. The problem arises, in sum, from the fact that feelings, moods, and aesthetic or sublime experiences are all *experiences without a subject,* whereas all sensible statements about their nature will be statements about what it is *for a certain subject* to have these experiences.

To put it all into one phrase: When having to put into words a mood, feeling, or the aesthetic or sublime experience of a work of art, *our bafflement is not epistemological but ontological.* The problem is not what words we should use in order to do justice to our experience of the world, for this is an epistemological problem. The problem is, rather, that there is no longer anybody there to speak, since experience will then be all that is left to us. When we are speechless after having seen or heard a great work of art, the explanation is, quite simply, *that there is nobody to speak.* And this confronts us with an ontological problem: *Who, what being,* on this indefinite trajectory between my "ordinary" self and this experience so eagerly absorbing all identity into itself is entitled to speak? Or, if anything, is not this experience, itself situated at the end of this trajectory, the only proper candidate for speaking here? But can experiences speak? Perhaps one could say that it is the strange talent of truly great poets "to make experience speak" and to lend their mouth to an experience that they are not but try to become or to identify with as much as possible. And the problem that poets have to face under such circumstances is, again, ontological and not epistemological. They must shed their former identities and become an experience, "an experience without a subject of experience," for that matter.

And this is neither easy nor pleasant and certainly not something that one could learn.[74] It is not easy, since one should have the (probably innate) talent of having the capacity to reduce one's identity to just *this* experience. It demands, therefore, the talent of *dissociation,* of being able to momentarily discard from yourself all that you think to be essential to you and to your identity. It need not surprise, furthermore, that the sublime—so close to experience as meant here—always is the result of a movement of dissociation, as we shall see in Chapter 8. It is not pleasant, since dissociation is one of the most unnatural things that we human beings can be asked to do. The art of being human is, to a large extent, the art of association; our identities, all our conceptions of the world, of history and historical writing, for that matter, are all the product of association. Leave the human mind to itself for a moment, and it starts to associate; it will do so as naturally as a stone will obey gravitational pull as soon as we drop it. Association is the big law of the human mind, as the English philosophers of the eighteenth century and their French disciples from Condillac down to the *idéologues* knew so well already. This is also, partly, why mathematics is so difficult to most of us: It is difficult not only because of the supreme intelligence it demands but also because it is so unnatural to us to dissociate all material content from our thought in order to attain the domain of pure mathematical abstraction. From this perspective there is a striking affinity between poetry and mathematics and why we could speak of "the poetry of mathematics" and why some poets (like Mallarmé) may appear to us as being "mathematicians of language."

But dissociation is not only unpleasant by being so utterly unnatural: It is also a premonition of death and foreshadows the end of our existence. Think again of the passage from Hume that I quoted a moment ago: "When my perceptions are removed for any time, as by sound sleep, so long am I insensible of *myself*, and may truly be said not to exist. And were all my perceptions removed by death, and could I neither think, nor feel, nor see, nor love, nor hate, after the dissolution of the body, I should be entirely annihilated, nor do I conceive what is farther requisite to make me a perfect nonentity." And precisely this is when dissociation momentarily overcomes the gravitational pull of the law of association, when our identity momentarily dissolves into an experience without a subject—although this loss of self may be compensated by the extreme intensity of the experience. *We die a partial death at such moments since all that we are is then reduced to just this feeling or experience.* And it need therefore no longer surprise us that theorists of the sublime have often related the sublime experience to death; think of Burke:

Whatever is fitted in any sort to excite the idea of pain and danger, that is to say, whatever is in any sort terrible, or is conversant about terrible objects, or operates in a manner analogous to terror, is a source of the *sublime*. . . . So death is in general a much more affecting idea than pain; because there are very few pains, however exquisite, which are not preferred to death; nay, what generally makes pain itself, if I may say so, more painful, is, that it is considered as an emissary of this king of terrors.[75]

Nor need it surprise us that French writers such as Georges Bataille and Maurice Blanchot believe unsupportable pain, a pain excluding the possibility of feeling anything else or of thinking of anything else, to be the ultimate experience.[76] Insofar as there is, in such cases, only the experience of pain, we may see here the same movement toward an experience without a subject of experience—and which is at the heart of sublime experience.

I readily admit that the notion of an experience without a subject of experience will be looked at suspiciously by many readers: Surely, it will be pointed out, there always has to be *somebody* to whom the experience is or can be ascribed; experiences are not like autumn leaves that the storms have torn from the trees. I would like to make two comments. First, with regard to human individuals the problem can be solved by saying that the notion should be understood in a *liminal* sense. Normally the subject will be there as subject of experience, but it may gradually lose all content and, in the end, be virtually absent from the experience. This would give us sublime experience, although it would also follow that pure sublime experience can be approximated only asymptotically. Second, and more important, at the level of how an epoch or a civilization relates to its past, the notion of experience without a subject of experience will encounter significantly fewer difficulties (and then pure sublime experience is a possibility or even simply the thing to be expected, as we shall see in a moment). The difference arises from the fact that we may well say that an epoch or a civilization *is* nothing but such experiences. Epochs or civilizations are not, first, autonomous entities in the manner of individual human beings to whom we may attribute, next, certain moods, feelings, or experiences. They *are* these moods, feelings, or experiences—and nothing but them—so that what is merely a liminal case when we think of individuals is normal for them.

One had best explain this in terms of the distinction between two kinds of identity: one kind that we typically ascribe to human individuals and another type that we attribute to epochs, civilizations, and so on. And where the human individuals have a coherence and solidity that is wholly absent in epochs, civilizations, and so on, the parts of a person's identity closely hang together; they all seem to be attached firmly to *this* person and to whom he or she is. We can even make certain predictions about certain parts of a person's identity on the basis of what we know about him or her already. And this is completely different with epochs and civilizations. Everything is fluid here and in a constant flux; sometimes an identity may even disappear from the scene only to make its comeback centuries or even millennia later—think of Antiquity and its alleged "rebirth" in the Renaissance; think of Poland since the partition treaties of Russia, Austria, and Prussia in 1772, 1793, and 1795; think of the triumphant return of all these nationalist feelings on the Balkan and in the former Soviet Union that had so ruthlessly been suppressed there for decades. On the other hand, where is Egypt since the end of the Ptolemaic dynasty in 30 B.C., what are the continuities and the discontinuities of Imperial and Papal Rome or of the first German empire (843–1804) and the second empire that came into being in 1870? And what about the relationship between India before the arrival of the Dupleix and Clive in the eighteenth century on the one hand and contemporary India on the other? Here everything is up for grabs, and sound arguments can be found for each position.

One might, in a metaphorical sense, speak of two "states of aggregation of identity": one for human individuals and another one for those strange and elusive entities that are the historian's professional concern— where the former is comparable to that of solid matter, whereas there is something peculiarly "gaseous" about the latter. And the difference between these two states of aggregation of identity may strongly remind us of the disagreement between Kant and Hume about personal identity discussed a moment ago. It is as if we have in the first state of aggregation of identity a transcendental self—itself without any empirical content—but around which an individual human being's identity is firmly and coherently organized. However, in the latter state of aggregation of identity we merely have an ever-changing flow of fleeting moods, feelings, and experiences without a subject organizing them and fixing them into a coherent whole (as was suggested already in the introduction to this chapter). Or, to put it in the terms of our present argument, in the latter we have moods, feelings, and experiences without a subject of experience.

And we should, at all times, avoid the reductionist strategy of postulating such a subject of experience in either the people of the past itself or in that of the historian. With regard to the former option, these experiences are scions of the venerable family of the unintended consequences of intentional human action; they have their source and origin in the interaction of people and not in people themselves. These experiences are not an attribute of individual people. It is the other way round: People are an attribute of these moods, feelings, and experiences and possess, in this way, an autonomy of their own which resists reduction to the level of the individual. With regard to the second option, it has been the perennial temptation provoked by the notion of the Objective Spirit to discover in these moods, feelings, and experiences a subject of experience with which the historian's transcendental self should achieve a "fusion of horizons," to use Gadamer's terminology. The mechanisms of historical empathy required for this task have been defined in many different ways by historical epistemologists—but that need not concern us here. What counts is that these theories about the Objective Spirit were all meant to demonstrate how historical knowledge is possible. But they all suffer from the same defect, namely, their failure to recognize that the Objective Spirit (surely a most useful and even indispensable notion!) is an ever-changing amalgam of moods, feelings, and experiences—*and nothing but this.* Here we meet these moods, feelings, and experiences in their complete nakedness, without the loincloth of a transcendental self (however defined). Here, then, we meet the past in its sublimity—and it need not surprise us, therefore, that moods and feelings will dominate the scene when I give examples of sublime historical experience in the next two chapters.

Sublimity will, by its very nature, teach us no truths about the past, for from the perspective of cognitive truth this kind of encounter with the past simply does not and cannot exist. Sublime experience lives in a universe different from that of truth—*and* of falsity, as I would like to insist. All attempts to wring from this sublime encounter of the past some payoff for our knowledge of the past are therefore doomed to failure. As we have seen when discussing Burckhardt and as will be elaborated later, the sublime experience of the past can be constructed as a tacit comment on what has been achieved in the field of the acquisition of cognitive knowledge of the past. But this truly is a *tacit* comment and cannot be translated in terms of a meaningful debate between the sublime experience of the past on the one hand and historical knowledge on the other. The latter has nothing to say or to add to the former. In this way one might say that, in fact, historical experience has the last word here and is, in this way, superior to the other.

This may, again, be interpreted as a plea in favor of a Romanticist conception of our relationship to the past—a conception seeing in moods, feelings, and the experience of the past the highest stage of historical consciousness. This is, finally, where and why it surpasses the Enlightened rationalism of contemporary "Theory," whose arid abstractions have so much dominated historical thought in the last decades; this is where it can, at least, be seen as a correction of all the hermeneuticist, (post-)structuralist, tropological, or narrativist theories of history and in terms of which we used to conceive of the past and of what it must mean to us. It is open, again, to the profound and fascinating mysteries of the past and considers it to be historical theory's main task to rekindle our sensitivity to these mysteries, instead of surrendering to intellectualist fashions from which the reality of the past, its hopes, its catastrophes, its joys and miseries, has so completely been banned.

Bearing all this in mind, we can now see what went wrong in Gadamer. We must admire him for following Heidegger when urging us to replace epistemology with ontology. But he has been insufficiently consistent himself in applying this recommendation to both his aesthetics and his hermeneutics. He stopped halfway on the road to the realization of his aims. Gadamer nowhere suggests the possibility of an experience without a subject of experience. As a consequence, in all his writings the presence of a transcendental subject of experience is still presupposed. And this means, again, that the real motor in the epistemological machinery was left intact in his hermeneutics; in the end he does not differ that much from Dilthey (or Ranke). As is suggested already by the quiet and conciliatory tonality of his prose, he nowhere makes the impression of being dissatisfied with how things are in the practice of historical writing; and no practical indications for historical practice seem to follow from it. Apparently "whatever is, is right" no less in Gadamer's hermeneutics than in Pope's cosmic Toryism. The implication is that there exists no open conflict between Gadamer's hermeneutics on the one hand and the openly epistemological and transcendentalist aspirations of contemporary historical writing on the other. It follows from this, again, that Gadamer, despite his attempt to rehabilitate aesthetic experience and truth, made them subservient again to the quest of (epistemological) truth that he had so much condemned in Ranke and Dilthey.

The explanation is, as we saw at the beginning of this section, that Gadamer never envisaged the possibility of disconnecting experience and truth. But as long as we stick to truth, and as soon as the notion of truth is appealed to, experience will have to surrender to it and be content with the modest role of being the humble and obedient servant of truth. And then all the transcendentalist demons that Gadamer had so much wished to exorcise (with Heidegger) will inevitably make their glorious return to the scene. But we must avoid making experience into the servant of truth, or, rather, this is not how it is with these sublime encounters with the past that I have in mind when discussing historical experience in this book. *Sublime experience is sovereign master in its own territory and no longer subject to the epistemological legislation of truth (as experience is in its more trivial form that we know as the scientific experiment). It therefore makes no sense to ask for "the truth of (sublime) experience" or for what might or should (in)validate historical experience.* And this claim is less odd than it may seem at first sight. In the first place, even with regard to more pedestrian variants of experience, it makes no sense to ask whether an experience is true or not. Questions of truth and falsity arise only when we ask whether the experience has been correctly described or, perhaps, whether the experience is in agreement with what the world is actually like. This last option is not unproblematic: Suppose somebody gives a correct description of the fata morgana of an oasis he saw on a trip through the desert. Then we might probably say that the description was true to fact, whereas we would characterize the experience itself as a "delusion" rather than as "false" because, again, we use the terms *true* and *false* with regard to language and not for experiences. Experiences just *are*.

But whatever one might decide with regard to the truth and falsity of this kind of experience, it makes no sense to ask for the truth of historical experience. Even more so, not only should we grant full sovereignty to sublime experience over its own domain in its relationship to truth; it may even demonstrate a certain aggression with regard to truth. Think of historical experiences such as we may associate with authors like Guicciardini, Machiavelli, Tocqueville, or Burckhardt (whose writings will be discussed in the last chapter). It would be nonsensical to ask whether their experience of the past as a history of loss is true or false; only a narrow-minded philistine (such as a Behan McCullagh, perhaps) could hit upon the naive idea to look at their writings with this kind of question in mind. It makes no sense to analyze historical consciousness or awareness in terms of truth and falsity. Or, rather, the relationship between truth and the criteria of truth seem to be strangely reversed here; the writings of the kind of authors I just mentioned and the experience of the past that is expressed in them (I return to this notion of "expression" in a moment) define criteria of truth rather than being subject to such criteria. With these authors a new historical consciousness came into being and, in its wake, a new way of writing history; darkness fell over a large part of what used to be historical Truth until then and held out the prospect of a new day in the history of historical writing. In this sense one might say that historical experience is, in fact, an *"unknowing of the past"* and therefore a movement against Truth rather than in agreement with it or indifferent to it.[77] Admittedly, a new world of historical Truth may arise from this.

But before making myself guilty of this notion of a "new world of historical Truth" of the same kind of quasi-Rankean disciplinary optimism that Gadamer had accused Dilthey of and of which I had accused Gadamer himself, I hasten to point out that the relationship between historical experience and language is not one of *meaning* but merely *causal.* In order to appreciate the significance of this observation, note that this would certainly be an odd thing to say about the prototypical epistemological experience, that is, the scientific experiment. Needless to say, the scientific experiment always has a meaning, namely, the description given to it on the basis of the scientific theory it is meant to test. If the relationship between experience and language would merely be causal, science—and, for that matter, a great deal of normal human communication as well—would become impossible. This is, of course, what Rorty had in mind with his thesis "language goes all the way down," which was discussed in Chapters 1 and 2.

This is different with historical experience. Cognitively historical experience is simply *nothing,* it has no *raison d'être* from a cognitivist point of view. And if only because of this, it can never be summoned to the court of justice of epistemic truth. But although the words *true* and *false* do apply as little to historical experience as the words *green, sleep,* and *furiously* do to the notion *idea,* a historical experience may *cause* a historian to look at the past in a certain way, just as a gunshot may cause us to look in a certain direction. But this unassuming causal relationship is all there is to it, and, as we saw when discussing what Huizinga had done with his historical experience when writing *The Waning of the Middle Ages,* there are no epistemological rules or schemata for how to tie historical experience to historical language and truth.[78] Just as it needs the poet's talent "to make experience speak," there is in the experience itself no meaning silently awaiting its expression by the poet; so it is in history. In this way Guicciardini, Tocqueville, Michelet, Burckhardt, or Huizinga can be said to have been the great "poets of historical writing," since they succeeded in giving speech to their sublime experience of the past. And we have every reason to regret them, now that contemporary historians have left it to sociologists (such as Bauman), novelists (such as Coetzee), or political commentators (like Fukuyama) to give voice to the experience of the past.[79]

Needless to say, Gadamer's "effective history" leaves no room for such a merely *causal* relationship between (reading) experience and language since all reading of texts is contextualized here in the deeply *meaningful* relationship between previous and later readings of texts. Gadamer himself is quite explicit about this. The third part of *Truth and Method*, titled "Speech as Guiding the Ontological Turn in Hermeneutics," openly aims to accomplish the exchange of epistemology for ontology in the domain of language and speech. Gadamer is a linguistic transcendentalist here no less than Derrida or Rorty by his repeated insistence that both experience and *Verstehen* ("historical understanding") are intrinsically *linguistic* phenomena; again and again we encounter Gadamer's conviction (inspired by Heidegger) "that tradition is essentially verbal in character."[80] Obviously, insofar as the historian interprets texts, Gadamer's statement is reasonable enough; however, when he goes on with the far bolder claim that "it is not just that sources are texts, but historical reality itself is a text that has to be understood,"[81] we apparently have to do with a 100 percent epistemological claim. The attack on epistemology in the name of ontology resulted here in a return to epistemology by presenting language as the condition of the possibility of hermeneutic understanding. Text, language, and, more specifically, "effective history"[82] have become another set of transcendental categories for historical experience and understanding—as Gadamer is fair enough to recognize himself:

Experience is not wordless to begin with, subsequently becoming an object of reflection by being named, by being subsumed under the universality of the word. Rather, experience of itself seeks and finds words that express it.[83]

In other words, there is no prelinguistic or preverbal experience and all experience is already structured by language, with the corollary that a direct and immediate experience of the past, an experience that is *not* mediated by language or the text, is impossible.[84] So, Gadamer not only embraces transcendentalism but even a *linguistic* transcendentalism (that is, precisely the kind of transcendentalism most to be feared from the perspective of experience); and the third part of *Truth and Method* is even explicitly based on "the fundamental claim according to which language is both the object and the medium in which understanding is achieved."[85] Moreover, whereas Gadamer in his account of aesthetic experience in the 1960s had still been very much aware of how experience may challenge the domination of language, even this awareness disappears from his later writings. For example, when commenting (in 1985) on the "Grenzen der Sprache," that is, on the limits of language, it is no longer experience he has in mind but our failure to find the right words for what we wished to say:

Finally the profoundest of all problems has to be mentioned, i.e. the problem that the limits of language are, so to speak, "innate" to language itself. The problem manifests itself in the awareness of each language-user that he is always looking for the right word—i.e. the word that may attain others—while, at the same time being aware of the inadequacy of the words that were used.[86] (my translation)

Hence, the limits of language are for Gadamer, again, linguistic limits, that is, limits that are, so to speak, made of language and therefore part of the world of language; and when we try to get a glimpse of what lies beyond language, we will run up against a *linguistic* wall. In the end, the (historical) world is a text for Gadamer, and the openness to the existential fullness of the world that one still found in Heidegger's *Time and Being* is now reduced to the reading and understanding of language. One is reminded here of Odo Marquard's famous quip that Gadamer had replaced Heidegger's "Sein-zum-Tode" by a "Sein-zum-Text."[87]

Nevertheless, Gadamer *recognizes* the existence of these linguistic limits. Unlike, for example, Rorty, he is clearly willing to acknowledge that "language does *not always* go all the way down" and that there is *not always* this complete match of language and experience as suggested by the Davidsonian and Rortyan picture of language. How else could we interpret his statement that "the inadequacy of the words that were used" and "the problem of the limits of language" are "the profoundest of all problems to be mentioned" with regard to language? And yet, in the end he would agree with them that the limits of language are the limits of the world. The explanation is, probably, that Gadamer is unaware of the capacity of *language itself* to transcend its own limits and to achieve the sublime *itself*. This might explain why, according to him, we could never get across this linguistic wall I mentioned a moment ago.

However, Burke had already unreservedly attributed to language this capacity, and he had even insisted that language is more successful in achieving the sublime than painting because it possesses a greater autonomy with regard to the world than we can grant to painting:

For we find by experience that eloquence and poetry are as capable, nay indeed much more capable of making deep and lively impressions than any other arts, and even than nature itself in many cases. . . . In painting we may represent any figure we please; but we never can give it those enlightening touches which it may receive from words. To represent an angel in a picture, you can only draw a beautiful young man winged; but what painting can furnish out anything so grand as the addition of one word, "the angel of the *Lord*"? It is true, I have here no clear idea, but these words affect the mind more than any sensible image did, which is all I contend for. A picture of Priam dragged to the altar's foot, and there murdered, if it were well executed would undoubtedly be very moving; but there are very aggravating circumstances which it could never represent. *Sanguine foedantem quos ipse sacraverat ignes* ("fires which he had sanctified with his own blood," Virgil, *Aeneid*, ii, 502).[88]

So language itself can be a source of the sublime; language may transgress its own limits. The sublime—and where the sublime transcends the limits of language—is in such cases not a reality preceding all language. It is not a variant of the Kantian *noumenon;* it is, instead, an "unsayable" *presupposing* language and the sayable in order to truly be a sublime "unsayable." It is not "before" but "beyond" language.

Perhaps a more appropriate model would be the Lacanian triad of the Symbolic, the Imaginary, and the Real. And where the Real is a product of the Symbolic order—that is, of language—but at the same time "the irremediable and intractable 'outside' of language; the indefinitely receding goal towards which the signifying chain tends; the vanishing point of the Symbolic and Imaginary alike. As a result of this view the Real comes close to meaning 'the ineffable' or 'the impossible' in Lacan's thought."[89] We happily and comfortably move in the Symbolic order in the firm conviction that nothing has been lost, since we will find a counterpart in the world for all that we have been and will be saying. But then we may come across a piece of language, such as Burke's "the angel of the Lord" or the lines he quoted later from Virgil or Milton in order to recognize the sublimity of this piece of language. At such moments we are open to a sublime experience—and it is true: We need language for being open to it. Only language can bring us to a stage where we can see what we have lost by entering the Symbolic order and by being satisfied with the substitutes of the Real that it offers. No language, no loss—and then no sublime experience, either.

Thinking this over, one cannot fail to be struck by how close

Gadamer really came to what was said in this book about historical experience. With his argument about the limits of language, all real obstacles between his and my position have, in fact, been removed. It is only a word—the sublime—that still separates the two positions from each other.

5.6 CONCLUSION

There is a painting by the sixteenth-century artist Giuseppe Arcimboldo (1527–1593), titled *The Librarian,* in which the artist had applied the method that had made him famous in the courts of continental Europe—and especially at the court of that most peculiar monarch of the time: the Hapsburg Emperor Rudolph II.[90] This method consisted in painting the human face as if it consisted of plants, vegetables, leaves, or animals such as fishes or mussels. The effect was "uncanny" in the real sense of the word since these paintings suggested that we are, in fact, made up from quite different materials than our trustworthy human flesh. It is as we had been taken over by an order that we normally consider to be alien from us, if not worse—for nobody can fail to be sensitive to the suggestion of decay that always is so powerfully present in Arcimboldo's paintings. So it is with the librarian in Arcimboldo's portrait: He is made up of books, of a book's pages, its covers, bookmarkers, and so on. In fact, the painting is a most appropriate allegory for Gadamer's hermeneutics. Gadamer could be compared to the person who saw in the painting nothing but books and texts and no human face. He will therefore be insensitive to the uncanny message of the painting, for it is only sublime experience—metaphorically speaking, of course—that may make us see that there is a human face in the Gadamerian pile of texts and books where the Lacanian Real (the face) differs from the represented (the books). And, indeed, if we had initially looked at the painting in the Gadamer manner, it would come as a nasty shock to us—as a sublime experience, again—that we should be open to the unwelcome and unsettling idea that we consist of inhuman material or, worse still, of material in a state of decay. A trick has been played on how we conceive of our identity: We dissolve into an amalgam of the most disparate components and are anything but the transcendental self's orderly and well-kept garden that we had always believed to be. So Hume, not Kant, was right after all.

And there is one more conclusion we may infer from the foregoing.

Our discussion with Gadamer has taught us to disconnect truth and experience, if we wish to come to a satisfactory understanding of historical experience. The momentous implication is that truth is not always our best (and only) guide in our effort to map all the ramifications of how we relate to our past. I insist most emphatically that this should under no circumstance be interpreted as an attack on truth. Truth is our only criterion when we have to decide about what is said about the past in terms of singular statements. Nothing in my argument would compel us to question this absolutely basic fact about the writing of history, and I have no ambition to dispute most of what empiricists have said about this. Where truth has its role to play, we should under all circumstances most dutifully respect its rights. But two circles can be drawn around truth—and where the powers of truth rapidly diminish. The first circle can be associated with representation. The relationship between (a historical) representation and what it represents cannot be reduced to or explained in terms of truth. Nevertheless, we can meaningfully ask for the adequacy of historical representations of the past—and the issue of the criteria for the adequacy of historical representation undoubtedly still has a strong reminiscence of what is at stake in the discussion of (historical) truth.

But around this circle we can draw the still wider circle of (historical) experience. And then even the issue of adequacy will have lost its relevance. Adequacy still presupposes the distinction between world, past, and object on the one hand and text, historical writing, and representation on the other. But this distinction vanishes with historical experience. Then there is only experience; the object and subject (and all that we may associate with these two terms) then are merely the spin-off of experience. We then begin with experience; the subject, the object—and truth!—must then be the protagonists of an essentially later dispensation. So what our analysis of Gadamer has made clear—apart from what it has taught us about history—is an awareness of the limitations of the discourse of truth and that the movement toward experience, as meant here, is a movement *away* from truth (although not *against* it). There is a dimension of meaning in human existence—as exemplified by (the writing of) history and by how we relate to our (collective) past—where truth has no role to play. And since history is so deeply rooted in all of human existence, we can be sure that this must have its implications for other aspects of human existence as well.

6

(PRAGMATIST) AESTHETIC EXPERIENCE
AND HISTORICAL EXPERIENCE

> We might say that esthetic experience is pure experience. For it is experience freed from the forces that impede and confuse its development as experience; freed, that is, from factors that subordinate an experience as it is directly had to something beyond itself. To esthetic experience, then, the philosopher must go to understand what experience is.[1]

6.1 INTRODUCTION

One important question raised by Gadamer's oeuvre still is unanswered. The reader will recall that we began our analysis of Gadamer's writings with a discussion of his notion of aesthetic experienc and truth in the expectation that we might move on from there to historical experience. However, it became clear that Gadamer exchanged aesthetic experience for dialectical experience when addressing historical experience in the second part of *Truth and Method.* So we still have to deal with the issue of the relationship between aesthetic and historical experience and, more specifically, with the question of whether any help is to be expected from existing accounts of aesthetic experience in order to deepen our insight into the nature of historical experience. This will be the topic of this chapter.

Aesthetic experience has never been much of a subject in twentieth-century aesthetics. The explanation is the predominance of analytic philosophy in contemporary aesthetics: As the term *analytic philosophy* already suggests, analytic philosophy was *sui generis* little inclined to recognize, or even to deal with, the complexity that is so much part of all aesthetic experience. "The analytic program," observes Shusterman, "was launched under the aegis of logical atomism, the idea that there are at least some logically independent facts or things in the world (even if these be only sense data), which constitute an immutable foundation for reality, truth, and reference, and which are somehow represented to us in experience through our conceptual scheme"[2] and, as Shusterman goes on to say, this effectively blinded analytical aesthetics to the phenomenon of aesthetic experience, more specifically, to a kind of experience of the world that could impossibly be dissolved into its individual components as the program of logical atomism would require us to do. Both the experience of the world itself, which is expressed in the painter's painting, and our experience of the world are essentially something more than a buzzing confusion of sense data. And whoever wishes to understand experience here in terms of these atomistic sense data has just as little chance of success as the hermeneuticist believing that a book's meaning should be explained in terms of the book's individual words and sentences. Because of this really frontal confrontation of aesthetic experience on the one hand and the program of logical atomism on the other, it will not be hard to see that the logical atomists could do either of two things: (1) simply ignore all of aesthetic experience or (2) dogmatically ignore the challenge that it poses to logical atomism. It need not surprise us, therefore, that in an influential essay J. O. Urmson, when investigating the notion of aesthetic experience from the perspective of analytic philosophy of language, finally came to the disappointingly philistine conclusion that it is impossible to distinguish aesthetic experience from other modes of experience and therefore that we have no reason to believe that there is such a thing as aesthetic experience at all.[3]

6.2 PRAGMATIST AESTHETIC EXPERIENCE

Shusterman recommends us to turn to pragmatist aesthetics since pragmatism, not being handicapped by an a priori adherence to methodological atomism and thanks to its being even explicitly hospitable to holistic patterns of argument, is better equipped to deal with the challenges posed by aesthetic experience. Moreover, in the last few years pragmatist aesthetics seems to have surpassed analytical aesthetics in scope, interest, and significance; so my appeal in the present context to pragmatist aesthetics surely is far from being a relapse into a forgotten and obsolete phase in the history of twentieth-century aesthetics. So I shall follow Shusterman's advice in the remainder of this chapter; all the more so since pragmatist aesthetics is far more explicit on this issue of the directness and immediacy of experience than any other variant of contemporary aesthetics. And—as we will recall from our discussion of Huizinga—precisely this is the feature of historical experience that so decisively and irrevocably placed it outside the scope of more traditional (empiricist) accounts of experience and that therefore made us look for help from aesthetics.

I shall now proceed with giving a picture of the pragmatist conception of aesthetic experience by presenting the views of different theorists as if they were contributing to one single consistent view of (pragmatist) aesthetic experience (PAE). Of course, the contributions of these theorists widely differ in scope and purpose. Dewey, whom one might well see as the founder of the notion of PAE, devoted two lengthy books to it;[4] Beardsley, on the contrary, drawing heavily on Dewey, has in a few short but elegant and well-argued publications,[5] in the words of John Fisher, "probably come as close to developing a theory of pragmatist aesthetic experience as anyone."[6] Harold Osborne focuses on what one might call the susceptibility or capacity of aesthetic experience,[7] while Ciaran Benson is mainly interested in the phenomenon of a temporary loss of the self in the object of aesthetic experience;[8] and Shusterman, lastly, attempts to show how PAE is exemplified by our experience of several forms of art and artistic production.[9] I am well aware that presenting these authors as if they were contributing to one shared enterprise will inevitably result in a certain amount of historical distortion, but, for my present purpose, such distortion seems permissible to me. I shall also refer to a well-known and influential 1912 paper on aesthetic experience by Bullough since it is often mentioned by pragmatist theorists;[10] on the other hand, I shall not deal with Dufrenne's work on aesthetic experience because of its background in phenomenology,[11] even though (or, rather, precisely because) Dufrenne's conclusions come so remarkably close to those that have been reached by the pragmatists.[12]

If we wish to grasp the nature of PAE, it will be best to start with some remarks on Dewey's notion of experience. The notion is of central importance in Dewey's pragmatism, and one may well agree with Bernstein's statement that "the key concept in Dewey's philosophy is experience."[13] The explanation is that for Dewey experience is a philosophical category preceding the more intensively researched categories of the knowing subject and the object. What is, in the end, at stake here has been well expressed by Shusterman when he writes: "In Dewey's pragmatism experience rather than truth is the final standard."[14] Needless to say, this is exactly what we need at this stage of our argument and why much is to be expected from pragmatism if we wish to penetrate the secrets of experience, *for whereas Gadamer shrunk away from radically cutting the ties between experience and truth—and thus could not be the guide for understanding historical experience that we are looking for—Dewey is prepared for this jump into the philosophical dark.*[15] Moreover, Dewey is ready for this jump for precisely the same reason that made us disconnect experience and truth in the previous chapter. Crucial there, as we will recall, was the notion of experience without a subject of experience, because only on the basis of this notion could we grant to experience its autonomy with regard to truth that the epistemological tradition had always denied it. And, once again, so it is with Dewey. Here the main idea is, too, that experience precedes the categories of subject and object, hence a partitioning of the given into these two categories that are necessarily presupposed as soon as we start asking ourselves the question of the origin of the *true* beliefs that a subject may have of an object—with the result that in Dewey's pragmatism experience precedes truth (understood in the sense of the correspondence theory). Put differently, what is primarily given to us is experience, and what we come to see, at a later stage, as subjects and objects ought to be derived from experience; and it is not the reverse. So Dewey is to whom we should turn after having reached the point where Davidson, Rorty, and Gadamer cannot help us further.

Self-evidently, pragmatism, as summarized just now, seems to be at odds with the routine realities of daily life where the demarcation line between subject and object seems to be wholly unproblematic. This commonsense intuition gives us the familiar picture of a subject having an experience of some object where, next, the experience in question is the source of empirical truth. But although it follows from this that experience and truth are always a function of what prior decisions had been made about this demarcation line between subject and object, this implication has never attracted a great deal of attention from philosophers. And quite understandably so. In practice, our intuitions about this demarcation line seem to leave very little room for dispute: Is the demarcation line between the knowing subject on the one hand and what it has knowledge of on the other not wholly unproblematic in the case of statements such as "The cat lies on the mat"? And think of science, that prototypical form of knowledge. Even the staunchest defender of the thesis of the theory-ladenness of empirical fact will never see in this thesis an occasion for believing in the blurring of the demarcation line between subject and object or in some kind of fusion of scientists with what is investigated by them.[16] And if we might nevertheless have our worries about the correctness of all our commonsense intuitions about this, we can turn to epistemology for an explanation of their soundness.[17]

However, we need only think of ourselves as historical beings and of the humanities to realize ourselves that this familiar picture is far from being universally correct, as we might at first sight assume. Where does "I" (or the historian) stop and "history" and "culture" (as objects of historical investigation) begin? That is clearly impossible to say. And this is not all yet. We may now ask ourselves how far and how deep "history" and "culture" penetrate into daily life. History and culture are not realities merely for the historian: They are an integral part of daily life, no less than tables, trees, and dogs are. We live in a world that is formed by history, culture, and tradition. In this way these systematic uncertainties about the demarcation line between subject and object may begin to invade daily life as well. And then experience will acquire a freedom of maneuver and an autonomy with regard to subject and object that empiricist accounts of experience had always inadvertently denied to it. Finally, whereas under the dispensation of epistemology truth marginalizes experience, it will now be experience's turn to marginalize truth (and falsity), for in the name of what (transcendental) subject could truth be claimed?

Several conclusions follow from this. In the first place, we should acknowledge that (much of) epistemology is based on an ontological prejudice—namely, the prejudice that the world is made up of "middle-sized dry goods" (as Austin once put it) like tables, trees, and dogs and that all the other things that we might wish to add to the inventory of the world are, in one way or another, mere abstractions from this elementary set. In the second place, this prejudice compelled us to embrace a certain conception of experience (the one that is investigated by epistemology) as the *only* one that is worthy of philosophical investigation. And third, this is why the notion of historical experience will make no sense to most of us insofar as we are naturally inclined to fit historical experience within the epistemological framework. Indeed, historical experience must seem a philosophical monstrosity if seen from the perspective of positivist experience (and the reverse is no less true, for that matter!). None of the precise and technically sophisticated questions formulated on the basis of the positivist matrix of the relationship between subject and object can meaningfully be asked if we have to make do with historical experience. Think of the question of how Guizot or Tocqueville "experienced" the French Revolution. According to the positivist the word *experience* is used here, at best, metaphorically, and, at worst, in a profoundly misleading and silly way. We can experience tables, trees, and dogs in the proper sense of the word, but what could one possibly mean by saying to have had an "experience" of such most dubious "things" as the French Revolution (and yet, I would not hesitate to say that all that makes *De la démocratie en Amérique* into the fascinating book that it is down to the present day has been its author's *experience* of the French Revolution[18])? We should not be surprised, therefore, that historical experience was left unexplored by philosophers. In the fourth place, this is all the more to be regretted since the gap between the notion of historical experience and contemporary philosophy of language is less deep than one might surmise. Taking historical experience seriously will require us (as we just saw) to reject any fixed schemata for how to relate the subject (and its true statements on the objects of this world) and the objects of which these statements are true. Now, as we found in Chapters 1 and 2, precisely this had attracted philosophers like Donald Davidson and, especially, Richard Rorty to pragmatism: Both writers reject the notion of an a priori scheme that underlies the relationship between language (corresponding to the subject) and the world (corresponding to the object) in terms of which both can meaningfully be compared and that functions in this way as the (indispensable) background for ascertaining truth.[19] So if they would have linked their sympathy for pragmatism to the realities and the practice of the humanities, this might have given to their thought a scope that it now unfortunately lacks. They cleared the way for a new understanding of the humanities but refrained from realizing the promises of their most revolutionary innovations.

But it should be conceded, in all fairness, that one could hardly expect them to undertake what even for historical theorists proved to be a bridge too far. Think, again, of Gadamer. One of the outstanding features of Gadamer's hermeneutics is that it proposes an ontological context for historical understanding that could metaphorically be compared to a rope in which the world (of objects), (the subject's) language, and the subject's experience of the world are the individual strands, which are all intertwined so closely and so intimately with each other that no one could tell them apart anymore. This comes close, of course, to the (pragmatist) rejection of these schemata underlying language and the world that had been proposed by Davidson and Rorty. However, in the end (or, rather, in the third part of *Truth and Method*) Gadamer makes experience subservient to language again. In 1960, two decades before the linguistic turn in the humanities, this certainly was a breathtaking and most courageous innovation. Nevertheless, from the perspective of the present, we will take a different look and deplore that it resulted in the emasculation of historical experience that Gadamer had *also* so clairvoyantly put on the philosopher's agenda. Next, take narrativism. Narrativism argues that initially the world is given to us in such a way that the distinction between language and the world cannot be made. Then, after a typification process has taken place, "the buzzing confusion" of experience crystallizes out into the individual things that constitute the world and the names and descriptions we use for referring to and describing these individual things.[20] So, just like pragmatism and Gadamer, narrativism takes its point of departure in a situation in which the world has not yet been divided into subject and object and where truth is not yet required for building a reliable bridge between the two of them. But, until now, narrativist historical theorists have been even less sympathetic to the notion of (historical) experience than either Gadamer or philosophers such as Davidson and Rorty. In sum, one could hardly refuse to Gadamer the honor of having at least been sensitive to the issue of historical experience (especially in the first part of *Truth and Method*); and the robust common sense of theorists like Rorty prevented them from removing the category of experience altogether from their philosophical vocabulary. But language has nowhere been more triumphant than in the writings of narrativist historical theorists such Hayden White and his followers. Here literally everything dissolves into language.

If we are willing to abandon, for a moment, our habit of linking the term *epistemology* exclusively to the enterprise that Descartes and Kant had put on the philosopher's agenda, one might say that there are, in fact, *two* kinds of epistemologies. There is, indeed, in the first place the modernist variant that came into being with Descartes and Kant that attempts to satisfy the analytic philosopher's fascination with how we may acquire true beliefs about these "middle-sized dry objects." This is the kind of epistemology asking itself difficult questions that nobody asks himself in daily life: Who would doubt that the chair you see there is really there? This is the kind of epistemology in which the imperialism of either subject or object (or of both of them) left no room for experience as a philosophical category in its own right. Indeed, the issue that now wholly disappeared from the scene is the problem of experience, for what chances are left for experience if subject and object are so successful in dividing the business of cognition between the two of them while excluding any rivals? Philosophy then becomes the familiar seesaw of realism and idealism, where realism puts all its cards on the object whereas idealism favors the subject. The discourse of truth is the discourse in terms of which the battle between realism and idealism is fought, for both agree that truth is the issue of their debate. This automatically marginalizes experience, for insofar as experience has any role to play in this struggle, it can have this role only thanks to its alliance with either object or subject and by assuming the role of the humble satellite of a more prestigious power. Indeed, where truth is, experience is not, and vice versa.[21]

But there is another kind of epistemology which is free from the polarization between subject and object—an epistemology respecting the situation in which we unproblematically "interact" with the world and where a certain amount of fusion of self and world is natural. This brings us to the world in which most of our life is enacted—and where truth has little or no role to play. Where is truth in matters of culture and tradition? This is the kind of epistemology having an elective affinity with the kind of experience investigated in this book, and with daily life, with social interaction, with how we account for these things in informal speech, in representation, above all, and hence with the writing of history. This is the kind of epistemology suggested more than 2,000 years ago in Aristotle's theory of sensory perception, since for Aristotle knowledge of the world results from our *interaction* with the world as embodied by experience, and not from looking at the world (with the Cartesian and with the analytic tradition) from the point of view of the moon. Characteristic is the way Aristotle privileges the sense of touch over the other senses, since, unlike the eye, the sense of touch really interacts with what it perceives:

For without touch it (i.e. the animal's body) can have no other sense, every ensouled thing being, as we said, a tactile body, and, while the other elements apart from earth might be sense-organs, they would produce sensation by indirect and mediate perception, whereas touch consists, as its name suggests, in contact with objects. The other sense-organs seem to perceive *by* touch, but *through* something else, touch alone being thought to do so through itself.[22]

Interaction, the direct and immediate contact with the objects of perception, the subject's being actually formed by the object (think again of how your hand and your fingers take on the form of the vase that you have in your hand)—these are what this kind of epistemology is all about. In this Aristotelian "model" of experience, there is, first, the experience, and, next, the subject is formed by the experience, whereas the object has no existence outside and beyond its formative role. There is, so to say, only the *surface* of the experience—and object and subject are merely its obedient shadows.

Now, let us ask the artist and the aestheticist which of these two epistemologies they would prefer. Asking the question is, self-evidently, answering it. What could the artist say if confronted with the epistemological queries of the Cartesian or of the Kantian? She will point out that the problems of the Cartesians and of the Kantians are so remote from her work as to be wholly irrelevant to it.[23] What interests the Cartesians and the Kantians is how we can have experience and knowledge of the objects of the world, whether of works of art or of what is represented by them. And the answers the artist hopes to find for these questions will be just as effective for the work of art as for what it represents. From the perspective of the epistemologist the difference between the work of art and what it depicts, between representation and the represented, is impossible to substantiate; the relationship between experience, representation, and the represented can *sui generis* not be operationalized within the framework of epistemology. The distinction between the represented and its representation— which is absolutely crucial in art and aesthetics—is wholly useless for the epistemologist since epistemological schemata could not and should not differentiate between the two. The epistemologist's schemata should be just as effective for our perception of representations as they are for what representations represent; epistemology is indifferent to the issue of representation, since both the representation and the represented are part of the inventory of the world and therefore cannot be fitted within the framework of the relationship between language and the world, which is the epistemologist's major concern. Similarly, representation is indifferent to whether the world is represented in terms of language or by artifacts such as paintings or sculptures that the epistemologist will see as belonging to the world of things. So the epistemologist's opposition between language and the world is fundamentally different from the aestheticist's opposition between the represented and its representation. Hence, whoever tries to solve the mysteries of representation with the instruments of epistemology is like someone looking in the Bible for information about Zeus. Epistemology is indifferent to representation, to art, and to aesthetic experience—and this is as it should be, for as soon as epistemology leaves any room for an analysis of the relationship between experience, representation, and the represented, it would fail to do what we expect from it.[24]

But the artist and the aestheticist will feel much sympathy for the Aristotelian interaction variant of epistemology. They will emphasize that all that is of importance in art takes place in the interaction between the work of art and the spectator: The artist hopes to captivate the spectator with her work of art, and the spectator, in his turn, will not feel tempted to strive for a transcendentalist detached conception of the work of art since he knows that this would make him insensitive to all that the work of art is about. Not the Cartesian *anachoorèsis* we discussed in Chapter 1 but the interaction with the work of art will make him recognize its beauty and its secrets. Interaction and aesthetic experience are his guides in the world of art. All that counts then takes place on the surface where subject and object meet and interact with each other. From this perspective it need not surprise us that for Dewey aesthetic experience is our best point of departure for obtaining an optimal insight into the nature of experience in general. As he explicitly states himself: "To aesthetic experience, then, the philosopher must go to understand what experience is."[25] And Dewey even goes on to claim that the merits of each philosophical system can best be judged by seeing what it does with aesthetic experience.

Dewey's theory of PAE has best been summarized (and elaborated in certain respects) by Monroe Beardsley. Beardsley ascribes the following features to PAE. First of all, "an aesthetic experience is one in which attention is firmly fixed upon heterogeneous but interrelated components of a phenomenally objective field."[26] A comment on this seemingly innocuous statement is worthwhile in the context of the present discussion. What is given to us in PAE is the *whole* of the picture (if I may restrict myself here to painting); we do not first see the details and only then the whole. It is the reverse. Illuminating here is how the art historian Kenneth Clark once described aesthetic experience. According to Clark, the art historian:

identifies a recurrent pattern he characterizes as impact, scrutiny, recollection, and renewal. During the impact phase the picture is seen as a whole. A general impression of the picture forms that depends on the pictorial qualities of area and tone, shape and colour. This precedes any identification of the subject of the picture. During the next phase, that of scrutiny, critical powers come into play and he finds himself looking for the central idea of the picture. Significantly, he observes that he cannot enjoy what he calls "a purely aesthetic relationship" with a picture for longer than he can enjoy the smell of an orange,[27] which is about two minutes.[28]

In short, there is a relatively short moment, to be identified with the PAE, during which one passively "undergoes" the picture and when it has on us its greatest "impact"; then the mind takes over, so to speak, and only then do we become aware, by power of abstraction, of the details of the picture and, perhaps, of their art-historical significance. This later phase, this phase of what one might call "erudite scrutiny," is the one we may associate with Gadamer's hermeneutics. It has been suggested that the "impact" of the initial phase is even felt in the case of figurative paintings if they are presented to us top down or on their side—a fact that may well demonstrate the extent to which PAE is prior to and independent of interpretation and of erudite scrutiny. And, once again, the paradoxical message is that in aesthetic experience the whole is the given and the detail is a (mental) construction.

Second, as Beardsley emphasizes, "aesthetic objects give us a concentration of experience":[29] When having an experience of a work of art, we concentrate only on what we see or hear and ignore everything else. Here we encounter, obviously, Dewey's formulation of the decontextualization claim that we discuss in this chapter and that I have referred to on several occasions already with the help of the metaphor of the embrace of Romeo and Juliet. In section 6.3 this feature of aesthetic experience will be elaborated. Third, PAE is "an experience that hangs together, or is coherent, to an unusually high degree." Or as Beardsley puts it a moment later, "It is an experience that is unusually complete in itself. The impulses and expectations aroused by elements within the experience are felt to be counterbalanced or resolved by other elements in the experience, so that some degree of equilibrium or finality is achieved and enjoyed."[30] Obviously, this feature of PAE is intimately related to the priority of the whole to the part in PAE. And no less interesting are two other characteristics of PAE. Aesthetic objects, the objects causing PAE, are described by Beardsley as "objects *manqués,*" that is to say, "there is something lacking in them that keeps them from being quite real, from achieving the full status of things."[31] Apparently, Beardsley would agree with Gadamer's argument, as given in the previous chapter, that paintings lack the "ontological fulness" of what they represent. The objects of PAE seem to remain content with their ephemeral ontological status and thus illustrate the thesis defended earlier that in PAE the interaction between subject and object is emphasized at the expense of the object (and the subject). Moreover, this may also explain why the pragmatist account of aesthetic experience is little interested in a philosophical investigation of the nature of the aesthetic object that customarily is the point of departure in analytical aesthetics. Once again, the (Eichendorffian and Benjaminian) message is "to stay at the surface" and to avoid moving away from where subject and object interact.

Finally, if we consider the features that Beardsley ascribed to PAE, we cannot fail to be struck by the extent to which these features coincide with what we have learned from Huizinga to associate with historical experience. In both cases experience is something that is undergone rather than an (active) violation of the object of experience by any cognitive schemes or categories existing in the subject's mind. It possesses all the characteristics of a revelation, which is, in both cases, described in wordings sometimes bordering on the mystical. In both cases experience is accompanied by the conviction of having a completely *authentic* contact with (past) reality, a contact that is not tainted by any previous contacts or by any knowledge or theories that we might have had already of the object of experience in question.[32] And, most important of all, in both cases it is the complex or the whole that is given and concrete, whereas parts and components belong to the abstract.

6.3 PRAGMATIST AESTHETIC EXPERIENCE AND HISTORICAL EXPERIENCE

There is one feature that Dewey repeatedly ascribes to PAE and that I only briefly hinted at in section 6.2. At several places in *Art as experience* Dewey speaks of PAE as "an immediate experience" whose value is "directly fulfilling" and not deferred for some other end or experience.[33] It is an experience having an unusual independence from its context; it is a "decontextualized" experience. Dewey claims for PAE the directness and immediacy which, as we have seen, is also such an important property of historical experience and where both aesthetic and historical experience are most conspicuously at odds with more traditional (empiricist) accounts.

The explanation is that this directness and immediacy testifies to aesthetic and historical experience's indifference to the epistemologist's transcendental schemata for relating language to the world. Think of the scientific experiment and of the thesis of the theory-ladenness of empirical facts: Existing scientific theories will rob experience of directness and immediacy, and all experience is then "mediated" by these theories. And we need only recall Gadamer's notion of effective history to recognize that resistance to the directness and immediacy of (historical) experience is no less widespread among historical theorists willing to respect its so very special status. So, apparently, this is a feature of (aesthetic and historical) experience with which even the most open-minded theorists feel ill at ease.

Shusterman's book on pragmatist aesthetics is a good example. A large part of Shusterman's argument aims at a reconciliation of Dewey's analysis of PAE with deconstructivism and current theories of interpretation.[34] And one might well argue that deconstructivism, if we recall what was said about it in Chapter 2, is, in fact, a hitherto unparalleled celebration of the *in*directness of textual experience. One may surmise that Shusterman has been misled here by Rorty's attack on anti-foundationalism that is so unreservedly endorsed by him. With, once again, the kind of consequences that we have already mapped in Chapter 2. On the one hand, anti-foundationalism certainly is critical of transcendentalist attempts to found scientific experience and knowledge in the *data for* (as opposed to the *content of*) sensory experience (and here anti-foundationalism and pragmatism still travel the same route), but on the other hand, as we found in Chapter 2, especially Rorty's variant of anti-foundationalism mistakenly infers from this that we are irrevocably enclosed within the prisonhouse of language and that there are no foundations of experience and knowledge outside language (and this is where my account of PAE and of historical experience and anti-foundationalism take different roads). "Language goes all the way down," doesn't it?

On the other hand, it is true that Shusterman is more prepared than Rorty (and other anti-foundationalists) to recognize the possibility of direct, unmediated experience. Thus Shusterman opposes "understanding" to "interpretation," and he uses the first term to refer to a prelinguistic awareness of (textual) reality. The objection that all knowledge or understanding necessarily is linguistic is rejected by Shusterman: "Even if we grant that linguistic understanding is always and necessarily interpretation, it still would not follow that all understanding is interpretive. For that requires the further premise that all understanding and meaningful experience is indeed linguistic. And such a premise, though it be the deepest dogma of the linguistic turn in both analytic and continental philosophy, is neither self-evident nor immune to challenge."[35] Shusterman then mentions examples of experience and understanding that do not involve language; thus the dancer understands "the sense and rightness of a movement or posture proprioceptively by feeling it in his spine and muscles."[36] And it will not be difficult to think of other, less contrived examples; who would wish to doubt that animals like dogs or horses or children, before having acquired speech, would be incapable of meaningful experience? It certainly needs the philosopher's propensity to dogma and to intellectualization to sincerely believe that a pre- or nonlinguistic experience of reality would be impossible. As Shusterman most preceptively comments:

We philosophers fail to see this because, disembodied talking-heads that we are, the only form of experience we recognize and legitimate is linguistic: thinking, talking, writing. But neither we nor the language which admittedly helps shape us could survive without the unarticulated background of pre-reflective, nonlinguistic experience and understanding.[37]

I could not agree more, although I would not go along with Shusterman's tendency to deintellectualize experience. We need only think of historical experience in order to see that experience may be an intellectual achievement of the highest order. And meaning is certainly not the victim of the disjunction of truth and experience (as pragmatists with a nostalgia for Truth are likely to believe).

So we have no reason to doubt the possibility of a direct and immediate experience of reality for the single categorical reason that all experience is mediated by language.[38] But might one not try another strategy and argue that experience is always mediated by previous experience, by the kind of person that we are, by our psychological constitution, by social conditioning, and so on? Moreover, Dewey often emphasizes that all experience is context-bound, and it seems likely that he would hold this true of PAE as well. Thus Shusterman summarized Dewey's position as follows: "Though it may *appear* [my italics] spontaneous in its immediacy, aesthetic experience (as Dewey himself insists) always depends on a background of prior perceptions, prestructuring orientations, and funded meanings which themselves entail background practices."[39] However, in my view both claims about the nature of PAE are incompatible if stated without crucial qualifications, and it will, therefore, be necessary to investigate the relationship between immediacy and context in the case of PAE.

In order to do so, I shall start with Bullough's influential essay on aesthetic experience of 1912. It was commonplace in eighteenth-century aesthetics to see aesthetic experience as isolated from the human concerns that occupy us in daily life;[40] the commonplace was codified by Kant's well-known characteristic of aesthetic experience as exemplifying a "disinterested interest." Elaborating on this insight, Bullough introduces the notion of "psychical distance"; psychical distance "is produced in the first instance by putting the phenomenon [that is, the work of art], so to speak, out of gear with our practical, actual self, by allowing it to stand outside the context of our personal needs and ends—in short, by looking at it 'objectively.'"[41] Although Bullough's essay cannot be considered part of the pragmatist tradition in aesthetics, his views are often appealed to by pragmatists and used for an elaboration of PAE. Thus Beardsley emphasizes that PAE "detaches itself, and even insulates itself, from the intrusion of alien elements." It is thanks to this decontextualization that PAE has the intensity that is so much part of its impact. As Beardsley amusingly puts it: PAE "does what whisky does, only not by dulling sensitivity and clouding the awareness, but by marshalling the attention for a time into free and unobstructed channels of experience."[42] In sum, PAE tends to isolate itself from our other experiences, and the impact it has on us is proportionate to its success in doing so.

But there is another element in Bullough's argument that brings us closer to a solution of our problem. Bullough introduces the notion of "the antinomy of (psychic) distance." With this notion Bullough suggests that aesthetic experience always requires a *balance* between "underdistance" and "overdistance."[43] In the case of overdistance the work of art produces in us "the impression of improbability, artificiality, emptiness or absurdity"— the work of art has moved, so to speak, outside the range of our meaningful experience. However, a greater threat to PAE is underdistance; as an example, Bullough mentions a spectator of *Othello* who distrusts his wife of adultery, is therefore inclined to identify completely with Othello, and thus is unable to avoid the intrusion of all kinds of irrelevant "contextual" elements in his experience of the play.[44] PAE is not a form of empathetic understanding, nor an attempt to relive part of the past, be it the emotions of the artist or as displayed in the work of art; PAE does not present us with a "fusion of contextual horizons," as in the case of Collingwood or Gadamer, but of what is *enclosed* within context. And this brings us to the heart of the matter. Certainly, PAE can occur only in an appropriate context of experience of a capacity of aesthetic experience—if such a *context* is absent, overdistance prevents the work of art from having any impact on us. *But the presence of such a context does not in the least imply that PAE is necessarily tainted or colored by it.*

The following simile may make my intention clear. Compare the subject of PAE to a person in an airplane looking to the countryside deeply below him. Often clouds will prevent him from seeing the ground or will distort his view of it; but when there is an opening in the clouds, he will have an unobstructed look at it. This is how it is with historical experience. Most often the clouds of tradition and context prevent us from seeing the past itself or distort our view of it, but that does not exclude the possibility of a view of the past itself in a momentary absence of these "contextualist" clouds. In that case one may justifiably say that the clouds—that is, context in this simile—determine *that* he can see anything at all (I shall be the first to concede this) but not *what* he will actually see below him. In this way context both determines and does *not* determine what we see—or experience. This unwarranted shift from the "that" to the "what" is the non sequitur that we may discern in many contemporary argumentations in favor of the inexorably context-bound character of all experience. Thus, no one can doubt that Huizinga could be open to his so crucial historical experience in 1902 only because of what he already knew of the late Middle Ages in northwestern Europe nor that he could have this knowledge only thanks to all that had already been written on the subject by others—and in *this* respect context is, indeed, conditional for the possibility of historical experience—but *what* Huizinga actually saw or experienced in 1902 when looking through this opening in the contextualist clouds is *not* determined by context. In sum, however crucially important context (that is, the opening in the clouds) may undoubtedly be, we should avoid the transcendentalist temptation to grant to context a permanent capacity to determine the *content* of experience (and of knowledge). And this implies that a recognition of the role of context (as defined just now) does not prevent us from being capable of having a direct and immediate contact with reality; a contact in which (past) reality reveals itself with the same unexpected suddenness as the landscape below to the traveler in the airplane. If we relate this insight into the nature of PAE to Heidegger's etymological speculations about the Greek word for truth—*alètheia*—or *Unverborgenheit,* one might be justified to say that the ultimate truth we can have of the world is a truth in which the world "exposes" itself to us free from context. And this truth is, paradigmatically, an aesthetic truth as we find it in PAE and in historical experience.

The simile of the airplane suggests a further determination of under what conditions we may escape from the transcendentalist conditions of the possibility of experience and knowledge. In the first place, the *Unverborgenheit* of the landscape is not a matter of discovering some "deep" and final truths about an object that we had been investigating all the time. We had not been looking at these (contextualist) clouds in the hope that something could be learned from them about the landscape below it. The truth about the landscape is not to be found in these clouds: They were simply in the way between us and the landscape—and as soon they momentarily disappeared, the landscape was just there for us to look at. Our "direct" perception of it became possible because of the sudden absence of the "intermediary" clouds. And then there is only us and the landscape. Obviously, here our simile has made us repeat Benjamin's argument about the "impressionism" of historical experience, where Benjamin insisted that direct experience is something of the "surface," something taking place in the interaction of subject and object that is lost immediately as soon as one starts to dig into the "depth" of the object or that drifts away into speculations about the nature of the subject. So, what historical experience has to offer to the historian will not have the character of a deeper penetration into or extrapolation from knowledge of the past already existing (that is, what is given by context), but it will predominantly be a matter of an "impression" of the past on the historian's mind. And the search for "deep" or "final" truths and for "essences," either on the side of the object or on that of the subject, will at all times be fatal for direct experience.

Next, we can see the ground from the airplane only when the airplane (and we ourselves) are located above an opening in the clouds. Similarly, the past can be experienced only when there is a certain "harmony" between the relevant part of the past itself and the subject of experience. In order to flesh out this metaphor of a "harmony" between subject and object, we had best turn, again, to Dewey. Dewey distinguishes between two extremes in our experience of reality. On the one hand we may impassively and stolidly undergo reality in the way that a stone may roll down a hill without "being aware of" what happens to it. The other extreme is when we react to reality with a "mechanical efficiency"—that is, when the impulses reality transmits to us are "read" by us as if they were mere symbols or signs of the presence of some state(s) of affairs in reality. In that case reality disappears, so to speak, behind the "screen" of symbol or sign. In the first case the *subject* of experience is reduced to irrelevance; at the other extreme the *object,* or reality, becomes a mere irrelevance, a mere *occasio,* to use Malebranche's terminology, of subjective processes.[45] Dewey now stresses (in a way closely similar to the Aristotelian notion of *mesotès*) that aesthetic experience can come into being only when the right balance between these two extremes has been struck. One is reminded here of the fact that the communication between partners who are socially each other's equals is far more complex and far richer than that between master and slave. Similarly, both aesthetic and historical experience can come into being only when neither reality nor the subject is the absolute master in their relationship (as, needless to say, paradigmatically is the case in all variants of transcendentalist theories of experience and knowledge, where the subject is the sovereign master of experience).

At this stage of my argument a last feature of PAE, which was mentioned already on several occasions in my exposition, acquires a sudden significance. We must recall that what is given in PAE and in historical experience is complex: The concrete should not be identified with the constitutive components of experience in which transcendentalist, analytical accounts of experience dissolve the unity of experience, but with the rich and variegated content of our experience of the work of art (or of the past). This is why Dewey, as we saw a moment ago, proposed to distinguish PAE from contextualized experience by its "internal integration and fulfillment."[46]

This has an important implication, namely, that PAE (and historical experience) are highly resistant to metamorphosis—such as may be effected by interpretation. The content of aesthetic and historical experience is always quite complex and substantial; it therefore possesses a considerable amount of inertia when coming into collision with other data of experience or of knowledge. It is therefore not easily pulled out of its own orbit, so to say, and will not in the least allow subsumptions within schemata ignoring or even violating its own nature. This is where the content of aesthetic and historical experience most conspicuously differs from that of the kind of experience discussed in the empiricist tradition. Think of empiricist accounts of experience, as we may find them in theories on sense data, on what is described by statements about individual states of affairs, in *Protokollsätze,* and so on. Surely, these experiential data are so featherlight, so easy to displace, so gregarious, so much willing to join with others with whom they share a certain affinity, that one can fit them in many different schemes. They are experiential data "without chests"; but what is given us in aesthetic or historical experience is data with *thumos,* so to say; this is experience at its proudest, experience that does not even fear to face the solid and massive block of well-confirmed theory (or narrative). In case of a conflict of theory and this kind of experience, it ordinarily is theory that will be worsted. Experience in the empiricist tradition is pointlike, whereas aesthetic and historical experience should rather be compared to surfaces or, even better still, to volumes. This is also why aesthetic and historical experience sometimes do not shy away from confronting even powerful and respected representationalist traditions and may remain wholly indifferent to the kind of contextualization that is prescribed by these traditions.

If this harmony, this equal relationship between the subject and object of experience, has not been realized, if experience is unlike the embrace of Romeo and Juliet, if either the subject or the object is the stronger partner — this will result, on *both* the side of the object and that of the subject, in a loss of the authenticity of experience. Now we can comprehend what motivates the almost universal and near unanimous contemporary resistance to the very idea of a direct experience of reality. Indeed, when experience is exclusively related to the most simple components of experience, to our most elementary perceptions, to sense data, as Western epistemology was in the habit of claiming since Descartes's "resoluto-compositorical" method, then it need not surprise us that experience completely collapses beneath the heavy load of tradition and context that has gradually hardened into theory or prejudice. Indeed, the "indivisible atoms" of elementary *Protokollsätze,* sense data, immediately lose their inner structure (insofar as they have such a structure at all) when they have to be reduced to the already existing categories, theories, narratives, languages, and so on. However, if the content of experience has the character of a surface or a volume rather than that of a point, it will be able to successfully resist the powers of language, tradition, and so on and retain its identity.

Hence, the direct contact with the past that is offered by historical experience is possible only thanks to the *complexity* of the content of experience. And the paradox thus is that *direct* experience of reality is exclusively possible in the case of a *complex* contact (which may initially seem to favor context and tradition), whereas a *simple,* or pointlike, experience will yield unhesitatingly to the pressures of context and tradition and give us an *indirect* experience of the world. The modernist's reduced and simple atoms of experience are not the natural enemy of context and tradition but, in fact, its best friend. We always associate the attack on context and tradition with science and grant to these atoms of pointlike experience the aura of being revolutionary. But it is precisely the other way around: Science is extremely traditionalist, whereas art and history are in a permanent revolution.

6.4 CONCLUSION

The main effort of this chapter and the previous one has been to claim for historical experience a place of its own where it cannot be reduced within the matrix of traditional accounts of experience. Gadamer was right when expecting that aesthetic experience might help us to see how to achieve this aim. But by exchanging aesthetic experience for dialectic experience, Gadamer failed to cut through the ties between experience and truth. And where you have truth, epistemology is never far off. Consequently, for all his criticism of Dilthey, Gadamer remained closer to the transcendentalism of his so very eminent predecessor than he himself liked to believe. And this confronted us with the question of how to continue where Gadamer (and so many others, like Derrida or Rorty) made such a sudden stop.[47] When addressing this question, we investigated, first, what the consequences will be if experience and truth are disconnected. And, second, in this chapter we have asked ourselves what lessons we can learn from the pragmatist account of aesthetic experience in order to achieve a better understanding of historical experience.

Our main conclusion can best be formulated in terms of a contrast. Think of the commonsense intuition that knowledge always has to do with, essentially, three things: (1) the subject, (2) the experiences this subject has of the world, and (3) the objects of the world that are given to the subject in and by experience. Epistemology has always been a search for the (transcendental) schemata underlying both the subject and the object. Experience was more or less "crushed," so to speak, by these schemata tying the subject and the object as closely together as possible. In fact, the history of epistemology could be seen as one sustained attack on experience, for any autonomy granted to experience would automatically ruin the epistemologist's neat schemata for how the subject (and language or knowledge) and the object are related. Put differently, epistemology being what it is, it simply had to be the epistemologist's continuous effort to divide the realm of experience into a part that should be delegated to the subject and another part that should be assigned to the object.[48] Ideally, therefore, no room would be left anymore for experience as an independent ingredient in the process of the acquisition of knowledge. Experience was thus reduced to being a mere "moment," namely, the infinitesimally short moment of the transition from object to subject, or vice versa. And experience survived only in the perennial seesaw of realism (empiricism) and idealism (transcendentalism) in the guise of the question of where, on the trajectory from subject to object, this "moment of transition" should be located exactly. Experience was the shadow cast by this debate, and it was experience's fate that it could never be more than a mere shadow in this debate. A different account of experience was presented in this chapter. As soon as experience is freed from the deathly embrace of truth, it can regain its autonomy with regard to both the subject and the object. It can then fully exploit again its strategically favorable position of being situated between the subject and the object. Even more so, it can then reassert itself as being the principal agent in the interplay of subject, object, and experience and reduce the first two to the status of being mere functions of itself.

Self-evidently, when drawing up this contrast between epistemology and the rehabilitation of experience attempted in this chapter, it has always been the writing of history (and the humanities in general) that I had in mind. Whether epistemology is the best way to understand how knowledge is acquired in the sciences is an issue that I have neither the ambition nor the expertise to pronounce upon. But epistemology completely and irreparably fails to do justice to all the problems raised by historical writing, by how we read texts, and more generally, by how we relate to the past. Here, this "moment of transition" between the subject and the object is anything but infinitesimally short; in fact, this is where all that truly counts in history and in the humanities happens. The trajectory between the subject and the object (which I identified with historical experience), this trajectory between the historian, or the citizen of the contemporary world that

we are, on the one hand and the past on the other hand is where all historical consciousness and all historical writing originates. We have no a priori
certainties about where "I," the historical subject, stops and where the past,
the object, begins. Everything is fluid and uncertain here; and precisely this
fluidity and uncertainty define the territory in which history and historical
writing can thrive. This is the territory of historical experience.

I end with a brief comment on the contemporary fascination for
memory, remembrance, commemoration, and so on—in sum, all these aspects of our relationship to the past that have so intensively been discussed
since the publication Pierre Nora's massive *Les Lieux de Mémoire*.[49] Nobody can fail to be impressed by the work that has been done in this field:
A new domain of historical investigation had been discovered, and the research of this domain has already yielded the most valuable insights. Nevertheless, from the more theoretical perspective of what has been discussed
in this chapter, there is room for ambivalence. On the one hand, we should
rejoice in the embrace of this notion of memory. Undoubtedly (as I
pointed out in the Introduction to the present study) the category of memory is far more congenial to historical experience than what we are accustomed to from traditional historical writing and traditional historical theory. Are our memories not the most obvious place to look if we wish to get
access to how we experience the past? And in this way it cannot be doubted
that Nora has made us take seriously that trajectory between the historical
subject and the past that is the territory of historical experience. We cannot praise him enough for this. On the other hand, immediately after having identified this territory of historical experience, Nora transformed it
into a new domain of (traditional) historical research. That is to say, he immediately left this trajectory again for the safe and so reassuring position of
the historical (or, rather, ahistorical) transcendental self investigating how
previous generations of Frenchmen had experienced their past. Perhaps
this is what we should have expected from a historian educated in the
strongly scientistic traditions of the Annales school. But then all that had
initially been gained for historical experience, will be lost again.

How to avoid this will be the topic of the last two chapters of
this book.

SUBJECTIVE HISTORICAL EXPERIENCE:

THE PAST AS ELEGY

> Glass / is to be given
> an image
>
> Of what it has
> never / kept behind.
> —(Hanneke van Brakel, *Juxtapositions* [unpublished manuscript])

7.1 INTRODUCTION

Up to now we have discussed historical experience mainly from a philosophical point of view and only rarely have we asked ourselves what role historical experience may actually play in the writing of history itself. And this is, of course, not satisfactory. Not theory but only the practice of our interaction with the past can be decisive in making up our minds about whether historical experience deserves more attention than theorists presently pay to it. Moreover, restricting my argument to an exclusively philosophical and theoretical exposition might all too easily invite us to fall into the trap of prescriptive historical theory, for that kind of exposition always automatically makes us move from a theory about what allegedly are the facts about historical writing to how history ought to be written. And no historical theory is more hostile to this move from the "is" to the "ought" than the kind of theory on historical experience defended in this book. In agreement with its anti-transcendentalism, my account of historical experience requires us to suspend the transcendental, theoretical, linguistic, tropological, or semiotic schemata that we are tempted to project on the past and in terms of which "theorists" have always formulated their prescriptions to historians, as we have seen in Chapter 2. My theory is a theory against theory—although I am well aware of the painful irony of the fact that a profoundly theoretical book is needed for this rejection of theory. My only excuse would be that as soon as there is theory, you will need theory in order to get rid of it again and no amount of practice will be sufficient for the task.[1]

Before discussing the realities of historical experience in this chapter and the next, I propose to distinguish between (1) objective historical experience, (2) subjective historical experience, and (3) sublime historical experience. I shall use the term *objective historical experience* for referring to how people in the past itself—thus in what is the object of historical investigation—experienced their world themselves. As was pointed out in the introduction to Chapter 2, objective historical experience has captured the interest of historians at least since historism; and even such maverick sixteenth-century historians as Étienne Pasquier and Lancelot Voisin de la Popelinière were already sensitive to this dimension of the past.[2] So there is no need to draw the historian's attention to this kind of historical experience, or to urge the historical theorist to investigate its theoretical problems. This is a domain or aspect of historical writing that has been well explored already, and this is why I have left objective historical experience out of my exposition.

So that leaves us with subjective and sublime historical experience. Subjective historical experience should primarily be situated in a context in which the past has already acquired its independence from the present: There is a past that is investigated by the historian and, then, suddenly, seemingly out of nowhere, may arise this sudden fusion of past and present suggested by the image of the embrace of Romeo and Juliet. I call this *subjective* historical experience since it is an experience of the past by the historian, viz. the historical subject. This is the kind of historical experience that Huizinga had in mind and that we investigated in Chapter 3. In this chapter I shall give two examples. With the first example we shall remain fairly close to Huizinga's intentions and discuss a painting that is not of great art-historical significance but that nevertheless (or, as Huizinga would probably prefer to say, precisely because of this) may give us "the feel" of some historical period. The painting in question will be the capriccio by Francesco Guardi depicted on the cover of this book; I hope to suggest in what way the capriccio may give us access to eighteenth-century Venice. In my second example the situation is somewhat more complex in the sense that the distance or difference between past and present is also part of the experience in question. Historical experience, then, is a direct encounter not only with the past in its quasi-noumenal attire but *also* with the aura of a world we have lost. As an illustration of this quite intense kind of subjective historical experience I shall discuss rococo ornament.

But in both these cases historical experience takes place in a context in which past and present are separate categories already. And this is different in the case of sublime historical experience: It is a radicalization of the second variant of subjective historical experience in the sense that sublime historical experience is no longer an experience of the distance between past and present—where the distance between past and present is presupposed. The situation here is rather the reverse, in the sense that in sublime historical experience the past comes into being only thanks to and by historical experience. I remind the reader of the snowball metaphor I used when discussing Benjamin (and of Plato's myth of the origin of the sexes referred to in the second epigraph of this book): Sublime historical experience is the experience of a past breaking away from the present. The past is then born from the historian's traumatic experience of having entered a new world and from the awareness of irreparably having lost a previous world forever. In such cases the historian's mind is, so to say, the scene on which the drama of world history is enacted. The fate of a civilization will then have its resonance in the historian's mind—and, as we shall see in the next chapter, instances of sublime historical experience have been decisive in the evolution of the West's historical consciousness (and hence in the writing of history itself). "The wisdom of the world" is then primarily expressed by historians, and their own personal mental struggles with the historical world that they are living in will then be of no less interest than the problems of this world itself. The historian then is a civilization's Delphic oracle through whose mouth the gods announce their will and speak to all who try to recover their way in the present. These are the most tragic moments for historians, but also the moments of their greatest triumphs. Historians will then feel themselves part of what they are describing—viz. this divergence of present and past—and their desperation about the loss of a familiar world will then motivate their writing and inspire in them their profoundest thoughts. What they then write about their civilization's fate, about its having been thrown into a vortex of unfathomable powers, is then, in the last analysis, an expression of the historian's own experience (of the past). Because of this, we may say that sublime historical experience is, basically, a fusion of the objectivist and the subjectivist experience of the past.

In agreement with this last observation I wish to emphasize that a clear and watertight distinction among these three variants of historical experience cannot be made. In fact, they may easily shade off into one another. For example, objective historical experience may so fascinate historians that it begins to have its resonance in their own minds and thus provokes a subjective historical experience. Next, subjective historical experience may well give rise to a feeling of loss and disorientation—and then some of the sublimity of the third type of historical experience will be imparted to subjective historical experience. This was certainly the case with Huizinga. And last, since sublime historical experience is a going together of objective and subjective historical experience, it even necessarily contains in itself the other two, although the drama of sublime historical experience exceeds by far what one might have expected from a combination of objective and subjective historical experience. It is much like the fusion of two chemical ingredients that may be fairly innocent in isolation from each other but whose mixture is highly explosive.

7.2 A HISTORICAL EXPERIENCE (GUARDI)

Let us consider Francesco Guardi's (1712–1793) painting *Arcade with a Lantern*. It is a so-called capriccio, a genre that is hard to define. Guardi painted many of them in the second half of his long life, after the death of his older brother, Gianantonio, in 1760.[3] Iconographically the painting is not of much interest. The architecture depicted in the painting has in all likelihood been inspired by an engraving by Canaletto that was quite popular in the Venice of the time.[4] And people dressed up like comedians during carnival are also a favorite theme in eighteenth-century Venetian painting. Carnival was stretched almost indefinitely in Venice, so that the masquerades and theatrical disguises were the rule rather than the exception in Venetian public life of the period. The comedians in Guardi's painting are dressed as Pulcinellas. Pulcinella is a figure from the Italian, especially the Neapolitan, commedia dell'arte. He has a hunchback and is pot-bellied; he wears a white costume, a conical cap, and a mask with a hooked nose, whose sexual connotations are too obvious to point out. His is an unpleasant and malicious personality; he is quick at repartee, but is vulgar and egoistic and has an insatiable appetite. This explains why the Pulcinellas have been rendered here by Guardi while they are cooking, eating, and drinking—as also is the case in a very similar painting by the twenty years older Giambattista Tiepolo.[5] And, more generally, Pulcinella is to be associated with the basic needs and processes of the human body, and the many different ways in which these needs and processes make themselves felt may explain the extreme changeableness and mobility of the Pulcinella figure.

The protean form of this character, his capacity to adapt to all situations but all the while remaining true to himself—i.e., the irreducible quintessence of energy enabling him to be reborn from his own ashes—has brought him fame during the 18th century: in popular terms he was the very image of that restlesness, the readiness to set off on a new adventure at the drop of a hat, typical of the spirit of his time. Umpteen plays based on this mask have titles like *Punchinello the Charlatan, Punchinello Triumphs, Punchinello's Ninety-Nine Disasters, Punchinello Goes Hunting, The Birth of Punchinello, Punchinello's Impish Spirit,* etc. (. . .) He [Pulcinella] is man's eternal double, representing vital instinct beyond all the changing fashions.[6]

No less important is the way in which Pulcinella mingles with "ordinary" people—with people "like us." Indeed, sometimes an individual Pulcinella may lose himself in the multitude crowding the streets (and Pulcinella certainly is a forerunner of the Baudelairian dandy)—as is the case, for example, on that most mysterious fresco titled *The New World* that Giandomenico Tiepolo (the son of Giambattista and nephew of Guardi) had painted in 1793 for his own country-house, and that is now in the Cà Rezzonico in Venice. And, indeed, since many people wore the Pulcinella mask during Carnival there is nothing necessarily unnatural about this. In eighteenth-century Venetian painting, however, the Pulcinellas generally prefer to seek each other's company, as if they badly needed each other's presence to counterbalance the otherwise overwhelming presence of "ordinary" people. Put differently, these groups of Pulcinella's are meant to make a statement about "normalcy," and this they can succeed in doing only by suggesting that they belong to a world of their own and that this world truly has an existence, a substance of its own. There really is a Pulcinella world, or a Pulcinella reality, so to say.

It is in this tension between "normalcy" and the world of Pulcinella that much of the secret about Pulcinella lies. The double bottom of their appearance and behavior is that they are both *comic* figures taken from the commedia dell'arte, but, at the same, succeed in *ironizing "normalcy"* (and the exhibition in September 2004 in Venice on the Pulcinella theme in Giandomenico Tiepolo's painting was therefore most appropriately named *Tiepolo. Ironia e comico* [*Tiepolo. The ironical and the comical*]). Thus, the paradox is that Pulcinella is a figure taken from the stage, although, precisely, he is meant to make us aware of the dimension of stage in so-called "normal life." As Goethe has Pulcinella say in the first act of *Faust II:* "Ihr seid die Toren, / Gebückt geboren. / Wir sind die Klugen, / Die nie was trugen; / Denn unser Kappen, / Jacken und Lappen / Sind leicht zu tragen (. . .) Ihr mögt uns loben, / Ihr mögt uns schelten, / Wir lassens gelten" ("You are the fools, / Born to prostrate yourself. / We are the smart ones, / Who never wore anything; / For our conical hats, / Our rags and overalls / Are easy to wear (. . .) You may praise us, / You may abuse, or rail at us, / But we couldn't care less"). And Pulcinella's aim to reveal truth by irony is nowhere more obvious than in Giandomenico Tiepolo's "Punchinello's swing" in the Cà Rezzonico, where we see a Pulcinella on a rope against a blue sky, just as his father, Giambattista, used to depict the gods and the goddesses on his huge and sublime frescoes in Würzburg and Madrid.

The magic of the Guardi capriccio lies in what Guardi does with these well-known topoi. Let us first focus on the painting's form. This form is illogical for several reasons, and it therefore generates a number of frictions. In the first place there is the contrast between the extraordinary heavy mass on the painting's upper side on the one hand and the lower side, which is almost transparent owing to the open doorways and the light colonnade. Because of this, one feels tempted to turn the painting upside down—and, indeed, if one does so, the painting's logic seems far more satisfactory to us. The distortion of the composition is further reinforced because the wall on the left side seems to be pulled away in the direction of the little cupola in the background; the wall on the left appears to be further removed from us in the direction of the painting's vanishing point than the wall on our right. This Escher-like effect is all the more remarkable because everything is, in fact, wholly in agreement with the laws of perspective, as one will find out when putting one's ruler along a few of the composition's main lines. Here we encounter for the first time what one might call the painting's "improbable probability"—a strangeness that turns out not to be strange but wholly in order upon a closer look. Perhaps Venice itself best exemplifies this "improbable probability," for what is more improbable than this work of art that was built in the shallow waters of the lagoon—and yet this city is a reality.

This last friction has a parallel elsewhere, namely, in the difference between the perspective from which the spectator sees the arcade on the one hand and how the spectator is placed in the space which is suggested by the painting on the other. This tension becomes clear if we observe that the spectator seems to have been located quite near the wall on the right— but the painting shows far less of the opposite, left wall than one would have expected from this placing. This shortening of the left wall would be understandable only if we were far closer to it than the painting's perspective allows. Put differently, the painting's vanishing point, which is accurately determined by its perspective—and which is situated where the ship's mast cuts through the horizon—is not in agreement with our being pulled, as it were, into the left part of the painting's space. It is as if our feet are on a place that is a few yards to the left of where our eyes are. In an almost identical representation in the Hermitage in St. Petersburg the effect is even more pronounced than here. And, once again, the origin of the friction is difficult to define and turns out to be a matter of an optical illusion rather than of some compositional inconsistency.

And there is a third inconsistency. The interaction of the arcade and of the walls on the left and the right side is strongly suggestive of a tunnel. Now, one of the paradoxical peculiarities of tunnels is that they suggest a great distance or depth but, at the same time, seem to move the vanishing point closer to us. If we look into a tunnel, the tunnel undoubtedly defines the vanishing point, but we also tend to situate it somehow within the architecture of the tunnel itself so that it could hardly be further away from us than the tunnel's backside. So tunnels effect a conflict between optical *extension* and the *reduction* of depth (an effect that one will find quite often in Guardi's paintings, by the way). Turning to the capriccio, then, the distance between the cupola in the background and the lantern in the foreground seems to be much shorter than it must be "in reality"—an effect that is all the more striking since Guardi placed the two quite close to each other in the painting. Put differently, tunnels may undo, more than any other kind of architecture, the difference between three-dimensional space itself and its projection in the two-dimensional space of a painting. Compositions with tunnels confound our intuitions about what is far off and nearby and thus confound the difference between three-dimensional space and two-dimensional space—an effect that has most eagerly been exploited by Guardi's contemporary Piranesi and that we will also observe (as we shall see later in this chapter) in rococo ornament. But, again, this "improbable probability" nowhere sins against the laws of perspective.

Up to now we have been analyzing the more formal and structural features of the painting. Let us now see whether the frictions we have noted there also have their counterpart in the painting's semantics. Two such frictions demand our attention, and I shall start with the less important of the two. Figures taken from the commedia dell'arte are often depicted in French and Italian engravings and paintings from the eighteenth century. Three levels can be discerned: in the first place, the world of the theater itself from which these figures had been taken; in the second place, "normal" social reality; and, third, a level somehow combining these two, that is, the level of the carnivalist masquerade, of the theater on the street, as it were. The painter can freely play with these three levels, and this is why the genre was so popular in the eighteenth century, a period in which theater and "the real world" were far closer and much more intimately intertwined than at any time before or since. This created the atmosphere in which the most sensitive minds of the period could achieve deeper insights into the nature of social life than was possible in any other period.

Now, if we look at the paintings and engravings by Claude Gillot, who was among the first to experiment with the genre in France, we are clearly expected to take his representations quite literally.[7] The Arlecchinos, the Scapinos, the Pantaleones, the Pulcinellas, or whatever their names may be are really here in the theater's scene. Gillot's successors, Lancret, Pater, or, to mention the most famous of them all, Antoine Watteau, broke with this literalness. They placed, so to say, an imaginary frame around these commedia dell'arte characters so that they are now clearly isolated from the other figures in "normal" dress that the painters, unlike Gillot, also included in their representations. In this way their representations evoke a tension between theater and reality—all the more so, since their commedia dell'arte types are not simply masked people, "normal" people dressed like Arlecchino, Pulcinella, and so on, but clearly still people from the theater. In this way this intertwinement of theater and "real" life—hence, the third level I mentioned a moment ago—is realized. The tension between people representing "real" life and those symbolizing theater that is so deliberately and artfully constructed in these engravings and paintings is strongly reminiscent of the kind of tension produced by the deviant use of language as we find it in metaphor. And, indeed, these compositions are meant to express a metaphor—namely, the metaphor that life is a comedy, hence the metaphor of the *theatrum mundi*. Unlike Lancret and Pater, though, Watteau's singular genius enabled him to express at the same time something about the personality of the person depicted as a character from the commedia dell'arte—and thus to accomplish the amazing feat of producing literalness within metaphor.

Guardi goes beyond all this. The imaginary frame of Watteau *cum suis* separating the theatrical world of the painting from the "normal" world is dramatically absent in Guardi's capriccio; there is in the painting a return from metaphor to literalness. This painting is not a pictorial equivalent of the *theatrum mundi* metaphor. But this does not mean that the six Pulcinellas enclosed within the circle of the five people in normal eighteenth-century clothing would have also become ordinary people who have merely dressed up as Pulcinellas for carnival. This is as little the case here as with Lancret, Pater, and Watteau. The crucial fact in this context is that these people are not simply dressed as Pulcinellas but also do the kinds of things—eating, drinking, peeing, being vulgar, and so on—that one associates with Pulcinella. Now, it undoubtedly is true that many Venetian men dressed like Pulcinella for carnival, but, obviously this did not oblige them to a theatrical performance on the street. So, just as in Watteau *cum suis* there is an interaction of the world of theater and the "real" world in Guardi's capriccio, but Guardi's trope is much different from the one used by Watteau, for the provocative and prosaic vulgarity of these cooking, drinking, and peeing Pulcinellas has absolutely nothing in common with the mild metaphorical allegories of a Watteau or a Lancret. In essence, Guardi does not opt for metaphor but for paradox: There is now a direct and frontal clash between theater and the "real" world. It is as if the theater had integrally been taken out of its proper context and as if it had brutely and unashamedly been thrown right down into "real" life itself—without any of the mitigating devices used by Guardi's less cynical predecessors. The message of his painting is therefore a quite different one: He does not invite us to see the "real" world *as if it were* a theater (as in the *theatrum mundi* metaphor); no, he wants to inculcate in us the truth that life is *both*—real life sometimes is what it seems to be, but at other times it is a harsh comedy in the quite literal sense of the word. And it is the tension between the two, between its being sometimes this and at other times the other, which gives to his message its poignancy. Or, put differently, the world of the theater (and of representation) is in the most *literal* sense part of our daily reality—and representation can thus be said to have invaded the world (of the represented) itself. Representation and the represented are taken together here in a way that we will encounter again in rococo ornament, to be discussed in the second part of this chapter.

I now come to what is, to me, the most important semantic friction in the painting—and I explicitly acknowledge that this is how I experience the painting, and I am fully aware that others may have a completely different emotional reaction to the painting. This is the friction to be related to the feeling of boredom, or ennui. The feeling of boredom is provoked, in me, by the fierce Mediterranean sun that is seen in the background and that yet does not succeed in penetrating the dark foreground; this gives me the feeling of having been enclosed within the narrow impasse of the arcade and of being unable to attain the free and real world behind the arcade. This feeling is emphasized by the oppressive weight of the high ceiling of the arcade and the heavy vertical wall above it—and the three formal frictions mentioned earlier add still further to this impression of having been locked in a narrow space, where one can hardly move and where one is far removed from the sunny world beyond it, where the joys and pleasures promised by public life are all to be found. The frictions seem to define the walls of a prison within which our feelings have been incarcerated and to effectively prevent any escape from it.

Surely, there is much movement in the painting, as suggested by the Pulcinellas in the foreground, but their movements are as useless, pointless, and meaningless to us as all of life must seem to us when being in the state of boredom or ennui. And, indeed, as the object relations psychologist[8] Kernberg has said, boredom results from a temporal incapacity to enter into a meaningful relationship to the outside world and what is contained by it.[9] And his interpretation of boredom is here fully in agreement with what in antiquity and in the Middle Ages was described as "the demons of noontide" and as *acedia*.[10] Even more important is that psychologists agree that boredom is always the result of an internal conflict, of internal "frictions," and in this way the frictions of the painting can be said to channel our response to it into the direction of boredom. Thus the Freudian Otto Fenichel wrote in the first clinical treatise on boredom that boredom typically comes into being in case of a conflict of the desires of the *id* and the rejection of these desires by the ego. The ego denies to the individual the aims in which the *id* might have found its satisfaction; in short, "die Triebspannung ist da, das Triebziel fehlt" ("The instinctual tension is present, the instinctual aim is missing").[11] This conflict is suggested by the austere indifference of the capriccio's background (sun, church, sea, ship) to the obsessive manifestations of the id by the Pulcinellas in the foreground, resulting in a suffocating awareness of having hopelessly gotten stuck in something. Quite illuminating is also Kernberg's observation that boredom betrays a feeling of inner emptiness, a "subjective experience of emptiness" and that one ordinarily tries to hide oneself, as Healy comments, by "a peculiar restlessness: children wriggle, adults may literally writhe as in agony, or merely fiddle, fidget, jitter . . . eat compulsively and without appetite, or chain-smoke."[12]

Next, Pulcinella's white costume—so provocatively devoid of all the finery and ornament of which the ancien régime was always so fond, a mere overall, so to say—expresses the inner emptiness of boredom. One should know that Pulcinella symbolizes a "larva," the soul of a deceased person,[13] which is condemned in popular culture to a meaningless and purposeless wandering about and thus to a permanent boredom.[14] No less striking is that Pulcinella is in the commedia dell'arte the most elusive character; he has no fixed role; he manifests himself now in this way, then in another, so that the heart, or the common denominator, of his theatrical personality is as empty as his costume is white.[15] His fidgety impatience, his continuous agitation, his always varying occupations, the compulsive eating of the already quite corpulent Pulcinella, are in complete agreement with the urge (which was mentioned a moment ago) to suppress boredom with excited and exaggerated behavior. In sum, Pulcinella represents boredom, and, indeed, already in 1628 Cecchini described him as the theatrical figure "who dissipates boredom or bans it for a long time."[16] What better way to ban the boredom provoked by the *theatrum mundi* metaphor than to objectify it and to move, by doing so, by means of boredom to a position beyond it?

It is here that the Guardi's capriccio gives us access to what one might call "the mood" of the ancien régime, or at least one of its moods, which is no less essential to a historical period, such as the ancien régime, as our own

moods are to ourselves. Our moods are the frame within which all our experiences of the world are enclosed, and so it is with historical periods. I
call to mind here my comment on Huizinga's notion of historical experience in Chapter 3: We observed there that the objects of historical experience are heard or smelled rather than seen. And, surely, the mood of a time
is an impossible object of historical investigation, as long as we adopt the
historical discourse of the positivist or constructivist historian for whom all
that we can meaningfully say about the past is the result of deduction from
evidence. Then the notion is utterly hopeless. But the mood of a time is
something we can only hear and not see—although it is no less real for
this. We can hear it because its impact on us is so much more direct than
that of the things that we may see in the past—the objects we see are at a
distance from us, whereas the sounds we hear are right in our ears. So when
a painting, such as the Guardi's capriccio, has its "resonance" (to use the
most appropriate metaphor here) in a mood of our own, our own mind
will find itself in agreement with the sound timbre or color of a historical
period, and then we are closer to it than we can ever come; we then truly
are where Florio was at his so fateful last meeting with Venus. This is the
kind of "intellectual experience" I referred to in the introduction to this
book; and this is where the "mood" of a painting may strike us far more directly and with much greater intensity than anything we actually *see* in it.
We here encounter the painting as if it were a piece of music.

And, indeed, Guardi's capriccio and the Pulcinellas depicted in it
symbolizing boredom and the effort to overcome it bring us right into the
heart of eighteenth-century public life and to its fascination for the *theatrum mundi* metaphor and to the boredom inevitably resulting from living in agreement with this metaphor. Let us listen to Richard Sennett in
his brilliant *The Fall of Public Man:*

There is a final question to ask about the public realm in the 18th Century. What
kind of man inhabited it? The people of the time gave a clear answer to this question: he was an actor a performer. . . . The image, two centuries ago, of public man
as an actor was a very definite identity; precisely because it was so forthrightly declared, it serves in retrospect a valuable purpose.[17]

Indeed, under the ancien régime acting was not restricted to the theater,
but it was part of behavior in public, on the street, in the coffeehouses of
the time, and even at home. The complicated eighteenth-century dresses
gave both men and women the possibility to use their clothing as costumes

for a theatrical performance, as it were. One often was made up, once again, both men and women; and the beauty spots one put on one's face were intended to indicate what "role" one wanted to play in the theater of society. People belonging to the high society in all European capitals—and especially in Venice—were fond of masquerades and of the most elaborate disguises. In this way Guardi's paradox of the combination of normal life and the theater had become a reality on the eve of the French Revolution.

Next, as La Rochefoucauld had already observed at the end of the seventeenth century, this extreme theatricalization of life (reaching its culmination at Versailles) would inevitably create a sentiment of boredom in all people now finding themselves as remote from their real sentiments as the actor is removed from the person he is outside the theater.[18] Marie du Deffand, in whom the *ver solitaire* (as she described her ennui) actually took on the proportions of a veritable depression, understood quite well the mechanism: Boredom results from the suppression of emotions that eighteenth-century social life required (and against which Rousseau would revolt). Ennui "c'est la privation du sentiment avec la douleur de ne s'en pouvoir passer," as Deffand wrote in a letter to her friend, the Duchesse de Choiseul.[19] And this is the mood of Guardi's capriccio, a mood that is expressed in it with a singular force enabling it to overcome the barriers of time and of the centuries separating us from the world of eighteenth-century Venice.

7.3 DECONTEXTUALIZATION AND AUTHENTICITY

But what has all this to do with historical experience? In what way does my discussion of Guardi's capriccio differ from what historians normally do? Is this explication of Guardi's capriccio, of how it fits within a tradition comprising Gillot, Lancret, Pater, or Watteau, and of the role of Pulcinella within the commedia dell'arte not exactly the kind of thing we would expect from a wholly conventional "contextualizing" analysis of this work of art? Is all of this not in complete agreement with what an *Erlebnis* à la Dilthey would make us do with the painting? So where is the extra that historical experience seemed to promise?

In order to answer this question I propose to focus on what has been, for me, when looking at the capriccio, the "opening in the contextualist clouds," to use the metaphor adopted at the end of the previous chapter. This has been, in my experience of the painting, the opposition mentioned already between, on the one hand, the serenity of the lagoon in the background and the fierce summer sun on the little cupola so strongly suggestive of a still wider world and, on the other hand, the ostentatious and bustling excitement of the Pulcinellas in the narrow and confined space underneath the arcade. Of special importance was the streak of sunlight on the lower left of the arcade's ceiling: This truly was to me the semantic heart of the painting (and that it must have been important to Guardi as well is suggested by the fact that one will discover exactly the same streak on the closely similar painting in the Hermitage). We should realize ourselves, then, that this streak will narrow down in the course of the day when the sun approaches the horizon—and in this way the streak is a kind of natural sundial objectively and impassively registering the regime of day and night that is supremely indifferent to all human action and endeavor as symbolized by the cooking, eating, and drinking Pulcinellas below it. This is what so overwhelmingly struck me when seeing the capriccio and where it obliterated, in my experience of the painting, the barriers separating me from the end of the eighteenth century when it came into being and where it effected in me the paradoxical feeling of a recognition of what I had somehow always known, but forgotten, and of a confrontation with what was both strange and alien to me.

Now, these aspects of the painting are, in themselves devoid of any historical or art-historical interest. No historical knowledge, no knowledge of the history of art, is needed for becoming aware of them—an ignorant but intelligent and observant child might be struck by them no less than I have been. Moreover, for the historian there is no real need to pay any attention to them, since they do not really contribute to the painting's art-historical meaning—if there is such a thing;[20] they are purely accidental. Nobody will feel fascinated by them, as I have been, unless these features happen to have, for some quite irrelevant reason or another, a certain resonance in oneself. In my own case, perhaps some vague and unspecified childhood experience triggered my openness to the experience of this specific aspect of Guardi's painting. For example, I may (subconsciously) recall having seen such a streak of sunlight[21] as is depicted on the Guardi capriccio on the floor of some room in the house where I grew up and to have experienced this with great intensity at the time, that is, with the kind of intensity that may, in some indefinite way, determine the mood of one's personality for the rest of one's life. *But I do not mistrust my reading of the painting because of this; on the contrary, the forgotten childhood experience is precisely what gave me an access to the picture that others, not having had this childhood experience, would lack; it thus enabled me to say something about the painting, and the past it exemplifies, that others may not see in it.*

Admittedly, although these aspects of the painting could have been noticed by anybody, my being susceptible to them can undoubtedly be related to details of my personal history mentioned just now. Speaking generally, such forgotten parts of our personal past may justify some "contextualist" explanation of why we have proven to be so strangely sensitive to some feature of a painting (or of a text) that may well be so clearly of only minor importance to the painting or the text if seen or read by others. And, needless to add, the same would be true of all that we have read and already know about some historical period. But, as we saw in section 6.3 of Chapter 6, although this may explain *why* "the clouds of context" open up at a given moment and then enable us to have a view of the past itself, it does not follow that the content of historical experience *itself* should be tainted or distorted by what made it possible. Contrary to common wisdom, contrary to the epistemologist's argument about how the formal, theoretical, linguistic, narrative, and historically determined schemata of thought frame experience, historical experience may succeed in escaping these determinations. Even more so, as we have seen when discussing Eichendorff, Burckhardt, and Benjamin, historical experience *even needs and presupposes* such determinations. Only in a thoroughly historicized world, only after the past itself and the historical subject have lost their contours and have been reduced to being mere moments in a Gadamerian effective history, only then will it be possible to break through the thick crusts of effective history and meet history in its quasi-noumenal nakedness. You need these crusts to be able to break through them. *Historical experience is not the return to a state of primeval innocence, to a state preceding all historical writing—it should be situated, instead, in a realm after or beyond all historical writing. Sublimity enters the scene only after all has been said and done; it has no affinity with beginnings, foundations, first principles, and so on. It is the sign that something has come to an end.*

Common wisdom and the epistemologist are right with regard to the elementary data of experience: These are helpless against the violence of the schemata of thought. But the congruence of subject and object of historical experience is possible only in a mind permeated by history, that is, in a mind possessing a kaleidoscopic variety of forms of which one suddenly matches one of the past itself. And when saying this, I hasten to reject any objectivist or subjectivist interpretations of what takes place in historical experience. We have learned from our discussion of Gadamer that in historical experience subject and object dissolve into experience itself. However difficult and unnatural this must seem to us, we must abandon the so familiar picture of an object (such as a tree or a table) that is given to the subject in experience. In historical experience there is only the experience; and then the domains of both subject and object fall away behind *its* horizon and momentarily lose their logical priority to experience. Subjectivist or objectivist accounts of historical experience are out of the question for the simple reason that they are in flat contradiction to its essence. So, if this congruence of the past and ourselves and our own feelings has suddenly and unexpectedly come about in and by historical experience, all of ourselves and of the past will momentarily be lost in an axis tying past (object) and present (subject) together. At such a moment everything outside this axis—such as our personal past or the art-historical context in which the painting in question should be located—will lose presence and meaning to us. As the reader will recall from our discussion of pragmatist aesthetic experience (PAE), this is what Dewey had described as the "concentration of experience" and what Beardsley had in mind when writing of aesthetic experience that it is "an experience that is unusually complete in itself." [22] There is only the painting and how we experience it; and the two are wholly lost in their mutual Romeo-and-Juliet-like embrace.

But what we then see through this opening in the contextualist clouds will come as no less than a *revelation* to us; it will come to us with the suddenness of a revelation for which we were completely unprepared. Hence, we also have the conviction of authenticity that Huizinga had claimed for historical experience. And I would propose to define authenticity in agreement with what we should, according to Dewey and Beardsley, associate with aesthetic experience—hence with its capacity of subsuming all sources of its meaning in itself, to be "complete in itself," and, thus, of being wholly free from the suggestion of a context also contributing to its meaning. Context kills authenticity. If authenticity is understood as proposed here, it can, indeed, never be achieved under so-called normal circumstances, that is, under the dispensation of the distinction between object and subject that is presupposed by all epistemology.

In order to see this, let us investigate the role played by context under "normal" circumstances. "Normally," that is, in daily experience, in experience in the sciences and even in most of our dealings with the past, subject and object are logically prior to experience. Characteristic of this "normal" situation is, furthermore, a systematic "inequality" in the relationship between subject and object: an inequality in which ordinarily either the object or the subject has an overwhelming predominance over the other. It is hard, if not impossible, to think of situations in which subject and object are equally strong. I must confess to being unable to conceive of an example myself. However, the object and the subject *themselves* are not responsible for this systematic imbalance in their relationship. The notions of subject and object themselves are flexible enough. The subject may expand over a great deal of the terrain that we would preferably, or at first sight, assign to the object—think of the nation or the civilization with which I may identify myself. Or to take an even more impressive (and worrying) example, think of how, according to mass psychologists, such as Gustave Le Bon, Gabriel Tarde, or Freud himself in his *Massenpsychologie und Ich-Analyse* (1921), the individual may completely lose his identity in the mass. And, conversely, the object may sometimes claim for itself part of the world that more or less naturally seems to belong to the subject—think of the body. Through the body, much, if not all, of the subject can be attributed to the world—and there is little that can effectively resist this onslaught on the subject by the object, or the world. So the notions of subject and object themselves are open to consider any compromise between them. They are not the problem. It is not *they* but *context* that makes them into such intransigent notions, for as soon as context comes into play and has attached itself to either subject or object, it will in no time succeed in completely draining the other of all content, so that, in the end, little or nothing will be left of it. Once again, take an object, such as a table or even your own body, and start contextualizing it: The object will immediately undergo the immense gravitational pull of the context of all of physical reality. And in the blink of an eye the subject will shrink to a mere transcendental self at best, or at worst, wholly disappear in a mist of neurophysiological data. But now take the subject as your starting point for contextualization. Optical perspective may then be the first, still modest, triumph of the subject over the object; next comes (the language of) science, then epistemology, and, in the end, idealism will signal the subject's final victory over the object. The object will then have lost all its autonomy and prerogatives. In sum, object and subject are such self-evident and apparently inescapable categories to us not because of the nature of these two categories themselves but because the *contexts* in which they present themselves are always so dramatically out of pace with each other, so hostile to each other, and so much inclined to marginalize each other. And one might well say that the philosopher investigating the epistemological relationship between subject and object without being aware of the sinister machinations of context is like somebody fighting Al Qaeda without taking into account who finances international terrorism.[23]

Obviously, this must have its implications for experience. In the conclusion to the previous chapter I sketched the model of the trajectory between subject and object and how experience is crushed, so to say, between the two of them within epistemology: All territory that might be given to experience will, in the end, be claimed by either subject or object. Where the subject is victorious over the object and the relevant components of experience, context (in whose name the subject fights its battle against the object) will be victorious, too. That will give us idealist, epistemological, hermeneuticist, or deconstructivist contextualism. But the reverse may be the case as well—and then we will end up with the contextualism of science or of history or the contextualism that is our guide in daily life. But where historical experience marginalizes both the subject and the object, it also marginalizes context, for in the absence of subject and object, context is robbed of the instruments it necessarily has to rely on for making its so very irresistible powers felt. This is why historical experience is so far better equipped to resist context and contextualization than the epistemologist's experience. "Meaning is context-bound, but context is boundless," Culler pithily writes when commenting on Derrida, that contextualist *par excellence.*[24] Indeed, as soon as there is context, meaning is automatically boundless. But the reverse is *not* true: *There is meaning without context.* Context *has* its limits; it is a term belonging to a world containing subjects and objects, and it loses its meaning and significance when there is only experience, as is the case in historical experience. And since historical experience is far from being meaningless, our conclusion must be that there *is* meaning without context. Historical experience gives us the fissures of sublimity in the web of meaning and context—and hence the authenticity of historical experience that Huizinga had so rightly and eloquently claimed for it.

7.4 SUBJECTIVITY AND OBJECTIVITY AGAIN

In section 2.6 of Chapter 2 we discussed the objectivity–subjectivity issue with regard to the interpretation of texts. In this section I wish to add a remark on how to deal with the issue in the context of (subjective) historical experience. I can hardly avoid the issue, for the role assigned to historical experience here will undoubtedly foster the accusation of subjectivism. Did I not unashamedly rely on my quite personal experience of the Guardi capriccio when saying what I felt when looking at it? And have I not shown a complete disregard for what my experience of the capriccio might mean in terms of intersubjective historical truth? Indeed: *this* is what I *felt*, being the person that I am, when looking at this, admittedly, not very important painting. This is where this inconspicuous painting could function for me as a bridge between the present and the world of the ancien régime for which I have had a fascination since early adolescence and which has been to me, ever since, my version of "the world we have lost."[25] This is what I wanted to talk about when commenting on it and where I have, in all likelihood, focused on features of the capriccio that happened to have their effect on me, and probably on me alone.

The accusation is both correct and incorrect. It is correct that my argument questions the traditional wisdom that we, as historians or scientists, should under all circumstances be silent about ourselves. Recall Francis Bacon's "de nobis ipsis silemus"—and he did not even write "de nobis ipsis sile*a*mus," as if he believed his claim to be so obvious that it would be a pointless pedantry to formulate it as an exhortation to the scientist. Admittedly, in the writing of history it is not always so obvious that "le moi est haïssable," as the French put it. Even the scientistic extremists of the Annales school, such as Braudel, Duby, Vovelle, and Le Roy Ladurie, frequently used the word *I* in their writings. But perhaps their "I" merely was a shorthand for what every reasonable historian would agree with. Thus Carrard writes about Le Roy Ladurie: "The intense, highly opinionated, fiercely motivated 'I' which underlies many judgments made in *Le Carnaval de Romans* is that of the Professor at the Collège de France who can take some liberties with the conventions of academic writing. Le Roy Ladurie was not as daring when he was a *lycée* teacher writing *Les Paysans de Languedoc*."[26] Nevertheless, in general, historians will distrust the meddlesome and intrusive "I." And this is where my account of historical experience clearly clashes with the objectivism almost universally embraced by both historians themselves and historical theorists and, hence, where the accusation of subjectivism is undoubtedly correct (although I hasten to add that it is not my intention to contest objectivist convictions with regard to the daily practice of historical writing[27]).

But the accusation is incorrect for historical experience. In the first place, this book is not a treatise on historical methodology. This book is an attempt to come to a better understanding of the notion of experience—especially that of (sublime) historical experience. As such the book can be read as a recommendation to historians to take more seriously than they presently do how the past sometimes may be given to them in historical experience. I am telling them that it may happen to them, no less than to the reader of a novel or to somebody looking at a work of art, that they will feel directly addressed by the past and that this may then have its resonance in their whole being. And I am telling them that *if* this takes place, the worst thing they could then do is to say, "Well, this is how I personally respond to the past, to a work of art, a novel or a historical text—but this should or could, *precisely because of this,* be of no interest to others." And so historians would decide to remain silent about it. But it is precisely the other way around: Their educated and well-considered opinions on a work of art and so on will be something that could, more or less, be predicted on the basis of how we are expected to react to works of art, and so on—and we all know how boring and uninteresting historical writing sometimes may be because of this. Their quite personal response to a painting or to some other historical artifact may reveal to me or to you something that nobody had ever been aware of before and that may redefine our relationship to the work of art in question or to some part of the past. And this "something" reveals itself to them only because they are the kind of people they are and ones in whom this something has a resonance that it will not have in anyone else. It is much like what Nietzsche said about how we should look at the great philosophical systems that have been constructed in the past:

It gradually became clear to me what every great philosophical system up until now, in the end, is: namely a confession of its author and a kind of unintentional and unconscious *mémoires;* similarly, the moral (or immoral) intentions of each philosophy constitute its real germ, out of which the whole plant has grown.[28] (my translation)

Moreover, for Nietzsche, the real driving force and significance of a philosophical system, where it contains a kernel to which philosophers will always return sooner or later and where it has its *raison d'être* apart from what arguments can be found to support or undermine it, is to be situated in this quasi-instinctive dimension. Or, as Nietzsche puts it himself a little later—and with a tacit reference to Apuleius's poem *The Golden Ass*—"in each phi-

losophy is a moment where the 'conviction' ('Überzeugung') of the philosopher enters the scene: or, to put it in the terminology of an old mystery:
adventavit asinus, pulcher et fortissimus"[29] (my translation). Likewise, this
"conviction" has to be situated on a level deeper than that of argument; that
is, it has to be situated on a level *motivating* what takes place on the level of
discursive argument. This is what I have in mind here also: that great and
valuable historical insights will always have their roots in historians' "unintentional and unconscious *mémoires*"—in their *experiences,* as I would put
it—and historians forsake the most valuable instrument at their disposal,
as historians, when they refuse to make use of them. So I am recommend-
ing historians to trust, under such admittedly most unusual circumstances,
themselves rather than *Theory* (and, in order to achieve this, to allow for a
certain amount of *abandon* in their relationship to the past); the profoundest of theories still is an abyss of vulgarity compared to even the simplest of
persons and the full richness of his or her experience of the world. The implications of what I am arguing for in this book for historical practice do
not go beyond this "modest proposal" (of course, I do not have Swift in
mind with this phrase). But the proposal could never be elevated into a
methodology, if only because historical experience is, as we have seen with
Huizinga, something that can never be deliberately produced.

In the second place the accusation is incorrect for the very simple reason that it makes no sense to project the notion of subjectivity (or of objectivity, for that matter) onto historical experience. As we have seen in the
previous chapter, historical experience brings us to a domain that can no
longer be mapped in terms of subject and object. In this way historical experience is neither subjectivist nor objectivist—or both at the same time,
if you would happen to have a penchant for paradox.

For similar reasons one should not consider my account of historical
experience to be just one more chapter in the already long book of heuristics. Heuristics deals with how we arrived at certain insights contributing
to the progress of knowledge. But this is not at stake here for two reasons.
In the first place, the reader should recall here Huizinga's explicit distinction between historical experience on the one hand and the kind of brain-
wave from which new historical insight may result (such as Huizinga's idea
that the northwest European late Middle Ages are the ending rather than
the beginning of a period). The latter can undoubtedly be said to possess a
heuristic significance. But this is different with historical experience.
Heuristics is, if anything, a phase in the trajectory from ignorance to in-

sight or knowledge and is to be defined in terms of what it can contribute to the latter. In this lies its role and function, and this is what defines its place in the logic of scientific discovery. But historical experience is *not* merely such a transitional stage on the route from ignorance to knowledge; it is wholly self-sufficient and truly final in itself. The separation of historical experience from truth defended in Chapter 5 should prevent us from projecting cognitivist pretensions on historical experience. Even more so, as we have seen already when discussing the relationship between (historical) experience and language in the case of Huizinga's *Waning of the Middle Ages* in Chapter 3, we will inevitably lose something when moving beyond experience to, for example, the historical text. In this way, historical experience is *itself* already the highest stage of historical insight (as Huizinga himself had emphasized), and what we might wish to do with it at a later stage will inevitably involve a loss. So, what lies beyond historical experience—the story that the historian will finally tell us about the past and that we can all read—is not its completion but rather its inevitable contamination, although the move beyond it is not always and under all circumstances wholly hopeless. So what we would *really* need, if anything, in continuation with this, would be a kind of "negative heuristics," suggesting how to move, with a minimum of loss, from historical experience to the historical text. This would be a negative heuristics in the sense that it does not show how to *maximize our gains* but merely how to *minimize our losses*.

Finally, I should candidly confess that the Guardi capriccio possesses a number of features that make it an exceptionally suitable object for clarifying the nature of historical experience. Thanks to these features other people may catch a glimpse of what *I* have seen when looking through the contextualist clouds normally obscuring our sight of the world of the ancien régime. And, self-evidently, this is why I took the Guardi capriccio as my example. I remind the reader here of the formal and semantic frictions that could be observed in the painting. As we have seen, from a formal point of view, perspective seems to have involved itself in paradoxes in the capriccio. And a similar tendency to paradox is manifest in the semantics of the painting, if we take into account the opposition between the busy Pulcinellas in the foreground and the impassability of the streak of sunlight on the left wall.

Now, paradox is unique among all other figures of speech by requiring us to abandon the level of representation for that of the represented itself. An instructive example is sometimes more illuminating than a cumbersome argument. So take, for example, Tocqueville's paradox of the post-revolutionary governments compared to those of the ancien régime: "The governments it (the Revolution) set up were less stable ("plus fragiles") than any those if overthrew; yet, paradoxically, they were infinitely more powerful ("plus puissants")."[30] On the level of representation, on the level of the language used by Tocqueville, this surely is a paradox: How could a government be both *less stable* and *more powerful* than those preceding it? Language resists such an untoward construction. Nevertheless, if we cast a look at historical reality itself, we shall see, much to our amazement, that the statement *is* true: These post-revolutionary governments *were* both less stable and more powerful.[31] So language here bears the unmistakable signs of its own insufficiency: In paradox language is used to convey the message that it cannot be trusted anymore and that we must now move beyond it, to the world itself. Language has done all it could, so to say; it now graciously takes its leave from us, recognizes that this is the last thing it could do for us, and leaves us to our own devices. *Language functions here as a kind of tunnel, requiring us to look through it and to focus on what lies at the end of it, or rather beyond it, that is, reality itself—just as the tunnel of Guardi's arcade pulls our gaze to the lagoon. This is what paradox shares with the sublime: In both cases our cognitive instruments, whether language or our epistemological schemes, have demonstrated their inadequacy—and the result is that we stand face to face with reality itself in an encounter with reality that is direct and immediate since it is no longer mediated by the categories we normally rely on for making sense of the world.* And, obviously, this is what paradox also shares with what sensitivists such as Van Deijssel, who were discussed in Chapter 3, had in mind: They were *also* looking for a language to undo all language.

In sum, the relevant formal and semantic structures of Guardi's capriccio happen to be identical with what is the defining feature of historical experience as such—and this explains why this painting is such an excellent example for illustrating historical experience (and why other examples will ordinarily be less suggestive). Indeed, thanks to its formal and semantic frictions, the Guardi capriccio moves historical experience closer to what experience normally is, that is, to what we are all capable of if placed in the right relationship to the object of experience. The Guardi capriccio is an object achieving the rare feat of making historical experience repeatable and "intersubjective." But ordinarily the formal features of historical experience will not match its content so closely. "Ordinarily" historical experience (I apologize for this untoward conjunction of the phrases "ordinarily" and "historical experience") will lack this dimension of intersubjectivity and be far more personal. This is different, I suppose, with the example to be discussed next. So the autobiographical accent will be stronger here than in the case of the Guardi capriccio. I must confess that I feel slightly uncomfortable with the autobiographical style, but one should have at least the courage to practice what one preaches. So there we go.

7.5 EXPERIENCE AND IMAGINATION

I had been a sickly child. With an almost perverse dedication I went through the whole long list of sicknesses that children are apt to fall prey to, while repeating several items on that list over and over again as if to make sure that I had not forgotten or inadvertently skipped them. This regular confinement to bed tended to put me out of touch with things, which led my parents to allow me to travel more or less with my bed through the whole house, which in turn often brought me to their bedroom. Now, despite being ill so frequently, I was a quite active child. So I remember lying in my parents' bedroom painfully aware that, meanwhile, my friends were swimming or playing in the snow. This painful awareness of being excluded from my school friends' games stimulated in me an intense feeling of boredom. Boredom, as we have seen when discussing the Guardi capriccio, is the feeling that brings one closest to the nature of things. In boredom the interactions between ourselves and the world are temporarily suspended; and this suspension invites reality to manifest its true nature, untainted and undistorted by our interests and preoccupations.[32]

Overwhelmed by boredom, I often felt a peculiar fascination for the flower patterns on the curtains in my parents' bedroom. And I am convinced of an intimate connection between those feelings of boredom on the one hand and fascination on the other. The intimacy of this connection is at first sight paradoxical, since boredom seems to exclude us from reality and all that goes on in it, whereas fascination (obviously derived from the Latin *fasces,* meaning "bundle" or "truss") clearly suggests a being tied together of subject and object. So, initially, boredom and fascination seem to travel in diametrically opposed directions. The paradox disappears, however, as soon as we recognize fascination as the tantalizing promise of a fusion between the subject and the object in the *absence* of the intensely desired fulfillment of this promise. Obviously, in fascination the desire of such a fusion can be inordinately strong, precisely because its promises have not yet been fulfilled. And this must provoke, again, an awareness of the unattainability of the object and, thus, of boredom. We are never more sensitive to *both* the desire to fuse with reality (that is, the origin of fascination) *and* the final unattainability of reality (that is, of what causes *boredom*) than when fusion seems so much at hand, so imminent, and so much a natural thing to expect and is yet postponed again and again. Think, for example, of what Narcissus must have experienced when looking, with so much "fascination," at his own image in the fountain: What could still separate the subject from the object when the object is the subject's own reflection? But ultimate closeness also proved to be ultimate unattainability—hence the melancholic expression of boredom on Narcissus's face in Caravaggio's painting that has been so perceptively analyzed by Mieke Bal in her book on that painter of a few years ago.[33]

I recently came to understand the nature of my fascination. My belated revelation came as I read the following passage by Scruton on the aesthetics of music:

Consider the leaf-mouldings in Gothic architecture. There is no doubt that these are of great aesthetic significance: by the use of these mouldings the Gothic architect was able to transform stone into something as full of light and movement as a tree in summer. But the resulting building conveys no thought about leaves. . . . The same is true of the stylized flowers in a dress or a piece of wallpaper. There is all the difference in the world between the pattern of wallpaper and a picture of the thing used in the pattern: even if they look exactly the same. The wallpaper is not asking us to think of the flowers contained in it. Put a frame around one of the flowers, however, and a signature beneath it, and at once it jumps at you, not as a pattern, but as a flower, asking to be understood as such.[34]

Scruton is saying here, I believe, something profound about what is essential to the experience of decoration. We can do, Scruton argues, two things with vegetal ornament: See the stylized leaves or flowers as representations of the real thing, or see them as pure wallpaper patterns, regardless of what the design represents or refers to. In the former case we situate ourselves, as spectators, somewhere in the trajectory between a real flower (the represented) and its depiction (or representation); in the latter, the flowers are drained of their representational content and start to interact freely with each other. Shapes begin to interweave with each other and to acquire new meanings—meanings that may be derived as much from the shapes of the flowers depicted themselves as from the negative spaces between them, that is, from the background of the design or by just any aspect of the wallpaper that may catch our interest. New meaning may even crystallize around imperfections in the wallpaper or the curtain, such as a stain or a tear as long as these incidental qualities interact with the design itself.

And this is not a matter of seeing one thing where we used to see another thing, as in the case of seeing a duck where we used to see a rabbit or the Rorschach pattern that seems to change from a face into a sailing ship or vice versa. In such cases we project a new pattern on what the eye perceives. Here, however, the imagination frees itself from all previous patterns: We no longer ask ourselves what the design *looks like.* Imagination is left to itself, in a free play such as the one Kant attributed to imagination when there is no concept to guide the cooperation between the imagination and the understanding. As Crowther put it when discussing Kant, in these cases the imagination has an unusual freedom to function as "an originator of arbitrary forms of possible intuitions."[35]

Put differently, normally we recognize the things we see (as flowers, as human beings, and so on); we take the things we see apart, first, into the *kind of thing* that they are and, second, into the *properties* that are specific to *this* individual specimen that differentiate it from other specimens of the same kind. The secret of the duck/rabbit drawing and of the Rorschach test is that they can resolve into two or even several familiar patterns. But these patterns exist already in the mind of the perceiver—and it has been precisely the purpose of the Rorschach tests to find out what exists in the mind already. However, in the case of the near fusion of subject and object in the wallpaper design we have been discussing familiar patterns that are *developed* and not *applied.*

This, I suggest, is the closest that we can come to pure experience, to a complete openness to what the senses present to us, for now neither the real world nor our perception of it is forced any longer within preexisting patterns. Admittedly, a psychological explanation may be given of how this most peculiar state of affairs came into being. Perhaps psychological laws can clarify why we may sometimes have these moments of a quasi-Heideggerian receptivity to the world's *aletheia.* And this seems to reduce the conviction of openness to mere illusion. But this conclusion would be invalid. The conclusion would follow only if we embrace two further premises, namely, (1) that there is only *one* way to see reality and only *one* pattern to discover in it and (2) that the laws of cognitive psychology determine and fix this pattern. Only on the basis of these two premises could it be shown that we have clearly mistaken psychological determination for openness. But these two premises ought to be rejected as the codification of the psychologist fallacy that the world is how we perceive it because of our psychological makeup.

In sum, the way of seeing that Scruton has in mind invites a complete free play of the imagination. Compared to how we ordinarily perceive reality, however, this way of seeing is strangely paradoxical. On the one hand it has liberated us from all patterns and structures that require us to see reality in one way rather than in another. This is why reality may manifest to us its quasi-noumenal qualities. But on the other hand, a complete subjectivity of perception must also be diagnosed since nothing in what is seen still guides, instructs, or determines the free play of our imagination. And this condition of subjectivity seems to remove us, again, further from the perceived object than even the most structured perception of it. We will agree with Kant that the workings of such cognitive structures do not in the least exclude the possibility of knowledge of objective reality. So, from a cognitive perspective we always founder when we seem to come closest to our goal. On the one hand, freedom of the imagination may bring us closest to reality and to a direct experience of it, but on the other hand it also takes away all that might put a fix on or give us a firm hold of the object. The greatest objectivity thus gives way to the greatest subjectivity, and vice versa—which is a belated contribution to the argument of section 7.4. And in the process of becoming aware of this distressing dialectic we are removed further from the object the closer we come to it. We will turn away in *boredom,* for what else could our reaction be since reality hides most on the verge of revealing itself? This is the deep truth taught to us by the story of Narcissus—as recounted a moment ago—who so movingly sublimated his boredom in his metamorphosis into a flower.

This, then, is how freedom of the imagination and the paradoxes of experience are interrelated. In Kantian terminology the sublime (in which the paradoxes of experience manifest themselves) does not provoke in us an awareness of our freedom and of moral destination. The reverse happens: Freedom results from our experience of the sublime indifference of reality to the categories and structures that we both so eagerly and so uselessly project on it.

7.6 ORNAMENT

Up to now I have been speaking of ornament and of how ornament may dissolve the structures and conventions determining our perception of the world. I hope that my autobiographical remarks in the previous section may at least have created a certain susceptibility to the idea that ornament is a more interesting category than contemporary common wisdom is prepared to concede.

"Ornament is crime," as many people nowadays tend to say with Adolf Loos—for ornament conceals essence and in doing so is a crime against art's assignment to reveal essence. To be sure, Loos was quite well aware of the seductions of ornament and of the power that ornament consequently has over us. In his famous denunciation of ornament, Loos was prepared to admit that even the most "primitive" people, such as the Papuans, cover everything—their own bodies, their boats and rudders—with decorative tattoos.[36] Loos believed that the passion for decoration is as typically human a property as sexual desire. And precisely this recognition may make us wonder to what extent we should see Loos's attack on decoration as originating from the same deep-seated impulses as the Papuan's desire of ornament. Put provocatively, is Loos's rejection of ornament not a eulogy on the "ornament of the absence of ornament" rather than the attack on ornament that it pretends to be? He certainly seems to have had a pronounced *aesthetic* preference for objects from which ornament was most conspicuously absent. As Rykwert put it: "His passion for smooth and costly objects was an unconscious desire that he rationalized later on."[37] Loos was not an aesthetic Calvinist who rejected ornament with pain in his heart because its attractions might divert our attention away from the essence of things. Loos could love beautiful things no less than the "primitive" Papuans (or ourselves)—but he could love them only on the condition of their being *un*decorated. He simply loved the decoration of being undecorated. And if even the prototypical hater of decoration can thus be shown to be sensitive to the charms of decoration, this may invite us to look with less disdain at decoration than we presently tend to do. I would therefore agree with Gadamer's rehabilitation of decoration:

The argument was more or less that what is only decorative is not the art of genius but mere craftsmanship. It is only a means, subordinated to what it is supposed to decorate, and can therefore be replaced, like any other means subordinated to an end, by another appropriate means. It has no share in the uniqueness of the work of art. . . . We have only to remember that the ornamental and the decorative originally meant the beautiful as such. It is necessary to recover this ancient insight.[38]

Nevertheless, his aesthetic preference for the undecorated object blinded Loos to the secrets of ornament and of decoration.

In order to come to an understanding of these secrets, let us consider a late seventeenth century engraving by Bérain (see Figure 1[39]). The engraving presents us with an elegant arrangement of grotesques. The grotesque, as is of importance to recall in this context, presents us with something that we will not find in actual reality, although not being at odds with logic itself.[40] For example, the grotesque may be part human, part animal, or plantlike (see Figure 2[41]); logic does not forbid the existence of such creatures (as it would forbid the kind of thing we may see in an Escher engraving[42]), although it merely is a contingent fact about the world that it does not contain such creatures. The grotesque thus exemplifies the Kantian free play of the imagination that I mentioned in section 7.5. On the one hand, the grotesque deliberately leaves us in "phenomenal" reality; it carefully obeys all the laws of perspective and of illusion that are characteristic of how phenomenal reality presents itself to us. But on the other hand, the grotesque depicts things that do not really exist and that are the product of the free play of our imagination. In this way the grotesque is a visualization of the Humean distinction between what is empirically and logically true: It respects logic while being at odds with what empirically is the case in our world.

But if we now return to Bérain's engraving, we will perceive here an interesting complication of what was said just now about the grotesque. Even a momentary glance at the engraving will make clear that it is composed of two parts, or elements. Bauer distinguishes between these two elements as follows:

In the grotesque's center we find a small tempietto of Amor—both the engraving's theme and its pictorial condensation. But already in its graphic articulation the tempietto distinguishes itself from the surrounding ornament of grotesques thanks to its heavy, shadowy and pictorial forms. It is, so to speak, truly an object proper

FIGURE I. A late seventeenth century engraving by Jean Bérain (1640–1711) presenting an elegant arrangement of grotesques. By courtesy of the Library of the Humanities of Utrecht University.

for depiction. That is wholly different with the surrounding ornament of grotesques. For this is not situated in a three-dimensional space, as is the case with the tempietto, even though naturalist motives, such as putti and animals have been strewn all through it. For this ornament organizes the two-dimensional space of the page.[43] (my translation)

FIGURE 2. This engraving was taken from: J. W. von Goethe, *Reinecke Fuchs.*
Zeichnungen von Laubach. Gestochen von K. Kahn und A. Schleich, Stuttgart, s.a.: 1.

Hence, the center of the engraving—the tempietto—is intended by the
engraver to be seen by us as the depiction or the representation of a *real*, although imaginary, tempietto that *could* in actual reality be built in a real
three-dimensional world as represented here. This is obviously different
with the richly elaborated framework. Although "reality effects" abound
here as well—consider the shadows and the perspectivalism of the lower
edge—it is clear that the ornamental frame does not depict a three-
dimensional world. It is what it is—an engraving—and this fictive representation does not give the illusion of being anything else. We are firmly
situated in the two-dimensional space of the image itself and nowhere else.
As Bauer succinctly summarizes the status of the grotesque ornamentation:

Its logic is that of depiction, of representation, but the logic of free forms which
are, as such, objects themselves and not represented objects.[44] (my translation)

The convention of a picture representing a three-dimensional world within
a picture frame is familiar enough. And it is widely recognized that picture
frames belong to the semantics of the picture itself. In a famous paper
Meyer Shapiro convincingly demonstrated that picture frames are far more
than the irrelevant ornament that they may initially seem to be: They actually, and even essentially, contribute to the making of meaning that takes
place in paintings and drawings. The picture frame is a "nonmimetic"
component of the painting that instructs us on how to understand its

mimetic components. The picture frame does this by clearly demarcating the painting from the three-dimensional space inhabited by the spectator. The picture frame thus requires us to see the picture differently from the way we perceive our surroundings; it sensitizes us to the illusionist suggestions in the painting, urging us to see something as three-dimensional that, in fact, possesses two dimensions only. In this way, the picture frame makes us see depth as a distinction between foreground and background—and by forcing us to do this, the frame does substantially contribute to the meaning of the painting itself.[45]

But in the Bérain engraving there is something odd about the relationship between the picture frame and what is framed by it. In the first place, the engraving gives us *both* the picture itself (that is, a representation of the tempietto) *and* the picture frame (that is, the framework of grotesques around the tempietto). Hence, it is as if a painting also depicted its own picture frame. So two-dimensionality and (the illusion of) three-dimensionality are *both* present in the engraving. And this makes the structure supporting the tempietto of special interest. This structure, in its turn, rests with four feet on the surfaces of two tables that are part of the ornamental frame. It should be noted, moreover, that the outer left and right feet ought to have been placed *behind* the two inner feet, but are deliberately drawn as if they were actually on either side of them (so that, if the structure were real, it would inevitably fall either toward or away from us).[46] This Escher-like effect (Figure 3)—which could never exist in actual three-dimensional space—marks the transition from the picture center to the ornamental framework. It can be interpreted as a representation of the transition from the two-dimensional space of the ornamental framework on the one hand to the (illusion of) the three-dimensionality of the picture's center on the other. And as such the transitional motif is absolutely crucial to the engraving as a whole: The engraving would be illogical if it failed to recognize the difference between two- and three-dimensional space and if it did not actually represent this transition. Of course, Bérain could have taken care that the picture in the center never came into contact with the ornamental framework—we could imagine the transition from two to three dimensions to take place silently and imperceptibly somewhere in the empty space surrounding the picture center. But since the picture in the center actually blends *into* the framework, it is inevitable that this transition is represented somehow somewhere.

But there is still something more to the engraving. Suppose we de-

FIGURE 3. A detail of a late seventeenth century engraving by Jean Bérain (1640–1711) presenting an elegant arrangement of grotesques. By courtesy of the Library of the Humanities of Utrecht University.

cide to take it out of the book or the portfolio where we found it in order to hang in on the wall. We would then have to frame it—and in order to prevent a conflict between the ornamental order of the engraving and that of the actual picture frame, we would obviously choose a smooth, undecorated picture frame. But the picture frame would, in agreement with Shapiro's argument, be just as necessary as in the case of less unusual pictures or paintings. The engraving represents something—that is, the transition from two to three dimensions (or vice versa, depending on whether one starts with the center or with the ornamental frame)—that is not part of the three-dimensional world in which we are living. (This is true as well for the [illusion of] three-dimensionality inside the picture frame.) In short, the engraving is a representation of dimensional change; it has *dimensional change* as its subject, just as, for example, a portrait has its sitter as its object. And it will therefore require a frame in order to allow us to move from "normal" reality, which, self-evidently, is free from dimensional change, to the picture's reality, in which dimensional change takes place. Put differently, the frame marks the difference between "dimensional change actually taking place" on the one hand and a "depiction of dimensional change" on the other hand: Within the frame we have dimensional change *itself*, whereas the engraving as a whole, that is, center plus frame, is a *depiction* of dimensional change. And it is this philosophically deep difference between the two levels—between object level and meta-level—that is effected by the picture frame.

So far, so good. But now suppose that the ornamental framework of the engraving itself was replaced by (the depiction of) just such a smooth and undecorated picture frame. I shall not consider the question of what then would have to happen to the Escher-like confusion of dimensions taking place where center and frame actually get into contact with each other in this profoundly ambiguous space below the tempietto. But the result would be awkward, if not a destruction of the whole meaning of the engraving, for now it would represent a tempietto and no longer the transition from two to three dimensions and vice versa that is so provocative in the engraving as it is. It follows, then, that in order to represent this change in dimensionality, we really cannot do without the *ornamental* framework of the engraving (replacing it with an undecorated framework would spoil the whole point of the engraving). And this is an important insight, for insofar as this change in dimensionality is an aspect of *all* (figurative) representations of reality and insofar as *all* figurative paintings represent this change, apart from all the other things that they depict, not only will *each* picture require a picture frame (as Shapiro argued), but, more specifically, each picture will require a *decorated* picture frame. Undoubtedly this is why there is something almost inevitable about decorated picture frames. Smooth picture frames are justifiable only when the picture tends to withdraw within its own center and, so to speak, to shun its own borders—as most typically will be the case with portraits.

In sum, Bérain's engraving is a representation of dimensional change, and in this respect it represents what is intrinsic to all figurative painting and drawing. The engraving can effect this dimensional change only on the condition of a formal resemblance between what is depicted by the picture in the center and by the components of the ornamental framework. Without this formal continuity the framework would function like an ordinary picture frame; as such it would certainly *effect* the transition from ordinary space to the space of the picture or painting, but it could then no longer be said to *represent* this transition. And so it is with all pictorial representations of reality. In the case of ordinary paintings and pictures the level of Bérain's ornamental framework is tacitly subsumed, so to speak, in the painting's or the picture's picture frame. Bérain's engraving, in turn, arguably is a depiction of the (secret of the) ornamental picture frame. And the effects that we expect of the picture frame depend on its containing (ornamental) variations of the kind of thing that we may find in the "real" world, as well as the formal similarities between these things as they "really" are and the ornaments of the picture frame.

7.7 ROCAILLE AS REPRESENTABLE REALITY

I started my autobiographical account by mentioning my fascination for the patterns I discovered in the flower design curtains of my parents' bedroom. Whether there is any causal link I do not know, but only a few years later I developed a true love of rococo decoration. From an expert woodcarver I received some instruction in rococo decoration. Even today I start sketching rococo motives when I am idle or bored. Even today I consider rocaille to be the quintessential kind of decoration, unsurpassed in its elegance and in the logic of its forms by any other decorative style. This conviction led to my profound hatred of Jugendstil, which I understand as a stupid, vulgar, and repulsive caricature of rococo's aristocratic elegance. Both styles of ornament draw their primary inspiration mainly from vegetal forms—but what a difference! Compare, for example, the weak, wilted, and elongated flowers of Jugendstil to the vigorous and compact forms of rococo ornament. The subtle balance between imitation and the free play with vegetal forms of rococo is wholly lost in Jugendstil. But insofar as an ornament differs from "real" things—and this is a requirement for all good ornament—the difference testifies to the artist's freedom of imagination and should not give the impression that he or she is simply a bad draftsman. What permits the artist to violate reality in an imaginative and pleasing manner while representing it is the artist's *style,* for style may make the representation more interesting than the represented and an imagined reality more suggestive than reality itself. But this is where Jugendstil sadly fails: Whereas we may prefer a rococo arabesque to a real flower (see Figure 4[47]), real flowers are infinitely better than their insipid Jugendstil counterparts.

In what is arguably still the best book published on rocaille, Bauer explains the evolution of rococo style most strikingly by Figure 5,[48] an engraving taken from Juste Aurèle Meissonnier's *Livre d'ornemens et dessines* (1734).[49] The publication of this book is generally seen as one of the most important milestones in the history of rococo ornament. If we compare

FIGURE 4(A&B). Engravings taken from Juste Aurèle Meissonnier's *Livre d'orne-mens et dessines* (1734). By courtesy of the Library of Groningen University.

this engraving with the one by Bérain that was discussed a moment ago, the most conspicuous difference between them is, according to Bauer, the relationship between the picture center and ornament. Both are clearly and unambiguously separated in the Bérain engraving; and I have argued that this distinction is quite essential to the semantics of the image. But in the Meissonnier engraving ornamental forms have penetrated into the picture center; they are emancipated from the status of being merely decoration and have become *themselves* potential objects of depiction. Quite instructive here is the ornamental line running from the top center to the bottom right of the engraving. At the top and the bottom the rococo ornament around this line has become part of the picture frame. Incidentally, the frame itself is about the least decorative frame that one can think of; for the greater part of the engraving, it is merely a simple straight (!) line. The difference from Bérain's most elaborate grotesque ornament could not possibly be more dramatic. But no less important is the fact that, when this straight line begins to twist and curl over the page, it becomes part of *both* the line demarcating the plane of the engraving itself *and* of the architec-

FIGURE 5. Engraving taken from Juste Aurèle Meissonnier's *Livre d'ornemens et dessines* (1734). By courtesy of the Library of Groningen University.

ture depicted in the engraving. The levels of the represented and of its representation are deliberately confused here.

Sometimes the status of the ornament is plainly ambiguous in the Meissonnier engraving. Obviously the staircase on the left and the portico on the right depict some very weird imaginary architecture—but what about the two C curves on the top right? It is impossible to say whether they are part of the architecture or just mere ornament. This effects something quite unusual—which probably had never been tried before—in artistic representation. Ordinarily it is sufficient to distinguish between medium (painting, engraving, and so on) and what is represented (a "real" landscape, architectural structure, and so on). Think, for example, of Michelangelo's Sistine Chapel ceiling. All that is of (philosophical) interest in the pictorial representation of reality can be expressed in terms of this distinction. But in the case of Meissonnier's engraving we also need to take into account the formal properties of the representation. The engraving is not simply a representation of an (imaginary) piece of architecture (as is the case with "normal" pictures). Here we are required to discern *two* levels in the representation: the level of the picture as representation of a represented (a trait that it shares with all pictures) and the level where the plane surface of the engraving so provocatively and paradoxically mixes with the representation. The engraving also clearly speaks about itself when it seems to speak only of an (imaginary) represented.

In order to correctly appreciate the sheer nerve of this "invention" (to use the most appropriate rhetorical term here), we should recognize that it does not exist even in the work of that greatest of all followers of rococo art, the Dutch graphic artists Maurits Escher (1898–1972).[50] Escher's play with the representation of space always takes place *within* the frames of his pictures—he never involves the frames themselves in his play with spatial representation. His play always resolutely stops as soon as we reach the picture frame within which he always safely contains his dizzying paradoxes, as if to avoid the danger that these paradoxes might infect the "real" world. Meissonnier—and before him Watteau[51]—had no such fears. The explanation is probably that Escher's engravings were meant to be "approximations of infinity":[52] They invite us to extrapolate Escher's spatial experiments beyond what is shown in the engraving itself, rather than to be objectified by a picture frame. You are invited to participate in the space suggested by the engraving and not to move outside it in order to obtain a vantage point from which this space might be objectified, discussed, or analyzed. Put differently, these engravings exemplify a certain spatial paradox but avoid the urge to introduce or suggest the level on which the paradox can become an object of thought or of representation. They are not self-reflexive. However, as I shall show in a moment, the rococo artist's play with space always makes space enclose itself within itself, and it puts an imaginary fence around it in this way.

To express this in a different idiom, Escher's play with space is "totalitarian," in the sense of intimating some universal truth, whereas his rococo predecessors created for themselves a "private" world of their own within which they could move with complete liberty. Or, Escher's play is "serious," whereas that of the rococo artist truly is play and nothing but play.[53]

Bauer summarizes Meissonnier's amazing achievement with the following words:

For Watteau a picture still is a representation of a representable reality. Meissonnier, La Joue, and Mondon went beyond this, for now all of reality had become ornament, or, to be more precise, the grotesque became worthy of being represented. This is only possible on the condition that the representation no longer pretends to be the representation of a representable reality. This is not primarily a question of the object, for until the beginning of the eighteenth century the classical gods and Arcadia were taken as realities. It is, rather, a question of the conception of art. In the eighteenth century the mannerist circle is closed again in which art refers to art and becomes an object to itself.[54] (my translation)

Ornament has invaded representable reality, but, in doing so, it changed the nature of both reality and itself. Ornament transformed itself from being *mere* decoration into a reality as real as real trees and real palace architecture, and, as a result of this ornamental hubris, decorative forms became just as much a potential object of representation as the "normal" objects of perception. Obviously, this did not leave reality unaffected. Reality itself was now forced to adapt to the strange forms of rococo ornament—hence also the perplexing mixture of small-scale ornament with the larger proportions of natural objects or architectural structures, so that the spectator does not know whether they have to do with a monumental macro-world or with microscopic miniatures. Bauer suggestively speaks in this context of the *mikromegalische* ambiguity of rococo art.[55]

Nevertheless, when representable nature had to negotiate its proportions with those of ornament, nature was compensated for this loss by acquiring a freedom of forms that previously was exclusively reserved for the ornament. Forms became possible and perfectly acceptable in representable "objective" nature that were hitherto possible only in the artificial world of ornament. One could now have the best of both the forms presented to us by nature and the formal playfulness of ornament.

It is impossible to say, therefore, which of the two, ornament or reality, is the victor or the vanquished in the process. Probably it is best to say that rococo presents us with a synthesis of the logic peculiar to ornament and with the logic that belongs to representable nature in such a manner that what was prevented by one is now made possible and acceptable by the other. In this way, a *new* imaginary world became possible—a world in which pure elegance is achieved through the transcendence of absurdity and that manifests itself as such. The nostalgic elegance of Watteau's paintings expresses its profound logic in this seemingly so idle play with space.

7.8 THE MEANING OF ROCOCO

One important aspect of rococo decoration has until now been left unaccounted for. One sometimes speaks of the "grammar of decoration," a phrase which suggests that decoration and ornament consist of a number of fixed conventional constants that can be varied by artists and architects.[56] The Doric, Ionic, and Corinthian columns are obvious examples of such constants. One may think of the convention of acanthus leaves, of the stylized lotus leaf of Egyptian decoration; also recall ovolo moldings or the arabesque. Most often ornamental motifs do have their origins in certain organic and vegetal forms; Goethe even argued that this is a necessary condition for all successful ornament.[57] A century later, this view guided Alois Riegl's impressive catalogue of decorative forms:

All art, and that includes decorative art as well, is inextricably tied to nature. All art forms are based on models in nature. This is true not only when they actually resemble their prototypes but even when they have been drastically altered by the human beings who created them, either for practical purpose or for simple pleasure.[58]

But these elementary organic forms can be systematized further. Attempts to do so had been undertaken already by artists such as Dürer or Hogarth. Dürer did so by reducing ornamental forms to three elementary geometric figures: the line, the circle, and the S curve. He did the same for letters of the alphabet, thus adding an unexpected extra dimension to the notion of "the grammar of ornament": Just as letters are the most elementary components of language as the vehicle of meaning, so does ornamental meaning have its "alphabet" in these three simple geometric forms. Hogarth followed another approach, one more suitable to the philosophical taste of his age, by systematizing ornaments in agreement with the feelings they provoke in the spectator.[59]

But in whatever way Dürer's way of cataloguing ornamental forms might be elaborated, it will become clear that the rococo added a new and last item to it. "Rocaille is the last original ornament that the West has developed"[60]—such is Bauer's claim—Rococo was the last truly original addition to the West's repertoire of ornamental forms. And, as I hope to show in what follows, Rococo arguably is its most subtle and sophisticated acquisition as well.

What is at stake here is the following. The primary characteristic of all rococo ornament is referred to as the C curve. The architecture depicted in Meissonnier's engravings shows an abundance of C curves and so do the ornaments connecting the picture to the frame. The rococo C curve is often identified with the scallop shell that had already made its appearance in sixteenth-century decorations. But it differs from the scallop shell in its provocative asymmetry: one end of the rococo C curve, where the C curve curls up into itself, is always smaller than the other. Moreover, in order to negotiate this difference, the flexure of that part of the C curve leading to one end is always slightly different from that leading to the other. When we compare the rococo C curve with its origins in baroque ornament, this asymmetry is most pronounced. Symmetry is the highest law of the baroque and of the style of Louis XIV ornament:[61] Think of Madame de Maintenon's sigh of resignation that "in the end, we shall all have to die symmetrically." Symmetry is the ornamental counterpart to the hierarchical social order during the age of Louis XIV, exemplified in Saint Simon's Versailles.

But rococo asymmetry is far from being mere arbitrariness. On the contrary, although we might be completely incapable of explaining why, we nevertheless feel that ordinarily these C curves are perfectly "right" in one way or another and that they simply are the way they ought to be. With the lines, the circles, and the ellipses of Dürer and the symmetric motifs of other ornamental forms our satisfaction is not difficult to justify; in most cases, it is sufficient to turn to geometry. But with the C curve the impression of perfection is born from a curious combination of a considerable freedom in determining the curve of the C curve on the one hand and the feeling that we are always absolutely sure about whether it has been drawn "right" or "wrong" on the other. Freedom transcends here the application of rules. These curves are far from arbitrary and even seem to exemplify certain rules—although we would be unable to define the nature of these rules (but perhaps an inventive mathematician could help us here).[62] Moreover, insofar as this interplay of rule and freedom can be transposed to ethics, one may feel tempted to ask oneself in what way the secret of the rococo curve could explain or exemplify the nature of free, moral action? Should the C curve require us to ponder an aesthetically inspired ethics? And, if so, could the C curve's inversion of rule and aesthetic freedom be interpreted as a visual analogue to a freedom beyond rules?

There is one more feature of the C curve that we should observe. I mentioned earlier that one end of the C curve has different proportions from the other. This gives an illusion of depth, as if one end of the C curve (the larger one) is closer to us than the other (the smaller one). Hence, the rococo C curve is far more suggestive of depth and of three-dimensionality than the line, the circle, or the S curve of previous ornamental "grammars" (I shall return to this point in a moment). The illusion of depth is accompanied by a suggestion of movement and of mobility—whether we look at a rococo ornament, a rococo interior, or the rococo decoration of an altar, we always have the impression that its components have been caught at one moment in their movement and that they will continue it at the next instant. It is very difficult to explain how this suggestion of movement is actually achieved, but anyone who has ever visited a Bavarian rococo church, such as the Vierzehnheiligen or the Wieskirche near Steingaden (surely the most beautiful of them all), will understand what I have in mind. If we recall, then, that all movement takes place in time, we will recognize that the rococo C curve, unlike any other previous "grammar of ornament," can truly be said to represent the four-dimensional world of length, width, depth, and time that we actually live in. If Newtonian science inspired the Enlightenment's confidence to conquer space and time, rococo ornament is the artistic expression of this confidence.

This becomes clear if we apply one more categorization of ornament to the rococo C curve. I quote Wersin:

In agreement with the two most fundamental impulses of ornament, the manifold of ornamental forms can be ordered within two main groups; the ornament suggestive of a rhythmic repetition of the same act—without beginning or end—and the form of ornament suggestive of a closed ornamental organism whose coherence is dynamic in origin. . . . To the last category also belong the simplest autonomous ornaments . . . that dominate rococo art.[63] (my translation)

Hence, there is the kind of "rhythmic" ornament that could go on without end or beginning, suggesting infinity (think of the geometric style of early Greek amphora) and the "organic" ornament which tends to enclose itself within itself. At first sight the former kind seems to be the more audacious of the two: Whereas the latter suggests a closed world, the former appears to give us an open one. But this intuition is wrong, as we might already expect from the fact that the former kind of ornament is older and more primitive than the latter. The problem with this intuition becomes clear if we recognize that the former obediently fits within space as an order that is given to us prior to the ornament, whereas the latter actually forms space itself. This is what most typically is achieved by the rococo ornament: if we consider Figure 6, the composition and the form of the objects represented within the cartouche, we shall see that the space within which these objects

FIGURE 6. The engraving was taken from W. von Wersin, *Das elementare Ornament und seine Gesetzlichkeit: eine Morphologie des Ornaments,* Ravensburg 1940; 15.

are located is forced to adapt itself to the rococo frame and to the manner in which the frame arranges these objects within the cartouche.[64] Illustrative in this context are also the two extremities of the C curve. It is as if at the two ends of the C curve a line, or the tendrils of a previous ornamentation—which, indeed, could go on indefinitely—are pulled together by the C curve and are curled up in themselves. By rolling up an infinitely long line or tendril, infinity is, so to speak, reduced to what can be surveyed by us finite human beings in a single glance. In this manner, the C curve is suggestive of a victory over space and infinity.

This, then, gives us the "meaning" of rococo ornament. The rococo ornament's first step has been the step from the merely ornamental framework into representable reality itself. The rococo ornament gives us the invasion of reality by ornament: The objects of representable reality now have to adapt themselves to ornament. Ornament superseded itself, so to speak, by becoming part of reality—so that ornament paradoxically disappeared at the very moment that ornament became everything. In this way rococo ornament is both the highest stage of ornament and the death of ornament. Loos and his contemporary disciples are, from this perspective, not the enemies of ornament that they seemed and wished to be: They should rather be seen as the true heirs to (the logic) of rococo ornament. Loos's proposal for the office building of the *Chicago Tribune* of 1923 is a striking example: Just as rococo ornament turned into architectural structures, so did Loos give this building the form of one huge Doric column. The design shows us Loos as having been, in fact, a twentieth-century Meissonnier.[65] But, with a second step, rococo ornament also took possession of space itself, domesticated it, and made it inhabitable for the people of a new era in the history of Western civilization. The Enlightenment's optimism and its conviction that the sciences would make us the victors of the natural world are heralded and expressed by rococo ornament. And this is where its meaning and interest lie. This is, as we have seen, what happened in the Meissonnier engravings, for here ornament left the flatness of the picture plane and invaded three-dimensional space itself. And it did so literally in the splendid kind of ornament to which Bavarian rococo churches owe their justly deserved fame. Here space becomes tangible at our fingertips; and the pleasures that its tangibility inspires in us is the promise of celebrating real pleasures. In this way the rococo ornament is a (homeopathic) cure from boredom and the feelings of an estrangement from reality.

7.9 MOODS AND FEELINGS AS THE LOCUS OF HISTORICAL EXPERIENCE

This is what I find so fascinating about rococo ornament. Apart from its beauty and the very special place it has in the history of ornament, it represents and expresses, for me, a world of moods and feelings. A world of moods and feelings having its deepest resonance in myself—not only because of the nature of these moods themselves but also because their kaleidoscopic interaction, as in the transition from boredom to participation in the world—seems to repeat something that I know from my own experience. Or, rather, I succeeded in recognizing it in myself only after having observed this kaleidoscopic interaction of moods in the past—where, paradoxically, the reverse seems to be no less true as well. Here past (object) and present (subject) merge in pure experience, an experience without a subject of experience, as becomes clear from this subject of experience moving so easily from past to present and vice versa.

A subject of experience that is capable of such drastic dislocations must have become featherlight and, in this way, lost all content. And it is not difficult to account for this, for, as Bollnow marvelously explained, moods and feelings belong to the most elementary and basic category of human existence:

At the deepest level of all of our mental life we will find our "moods," expressing how we feel about life in general. These are the most elementary and basic ways in which human life—albeit always already with a certain bias, tendency and attitude—may become aware of itself.[66] (my translation)

And elsewhere he requires us to accept the paradox that our moods and feelings are, on the one hand, the foundation of all of our mental life ("die tragende Grundlage des gesamten Seelenlebens") but, at the same time, its most volatile and transitory aspect ("das flüchtigste und Unbeständigste . . . was wir am seelischen Leben kennen").[67] Moods and feelings are all-pervasive and determine the color of all our experience. This is also where moods and feelings differ from sensations such as joy or fear, which characteristically have an object.[68] On the contrary, moods and feelings are objectless; they can even be said to precede the differentiation between self and the world, between subject and object: "In our moods the world has not yet become a world of objects" ("Die Welt ist in der Stimmung noch nicht gegenständlich geworden"). And Bollnow quotes S. Strasser when arguing that "in moods in the true sense of the word there is no 'I,' there are no objects, and no borderlines between the self and the objects of the world. One should rather say: the borderlines of the self fade away and disappear in a peculiar way. Self and world are embedded in an undivided totality of experience. Moods are experiences of both the self and of the world." [69] *Because of this moods and feelings have a natural affinity with (historical) experience as discussed throughout this book; and one might well say that sublime historical experience preferably makes itself felt in these moods and feelings.*

But moods and feelings will not lose their power after the differentiation between subject and object, between self and the world, has actually taken place. On the contrary, they will then go on to "color" how we experience the world. However, instead of "the color" of experience we had perhaps better speak of the "key" in which we experience the world. Illustrative here is the German word for moods: *Stimmung. Stimmung* is etymologically related to *Stimme* ("voice") and is suggestive of the pitching of an instrument, for example, of a piano or a violin, and of the *key* in which a musical composition has been written. Taking this into account, we have every reason to agree with Novalis's acute observation "das Wort Stimmung deutet auf musikalische Seelenverhältnisse" ("the word *Stimmung* is suggestive of a musical definition of the condition of our soul").[70] Novalis's association of moods with music may clarify one more feature of the former. The key in which a composition is written will itself convey no information about musical content or about its *style*. Bach, Mozart, Chopin, and so on all wrote compositions in C major, E flat, and so on. So, in a way, the key in which a composition was written will tell us even less about the composition than its style; so, on the one hand, key is a better defined notion than either musical content or style, but it has, on the other hand, even less content than musical form or style. But precisely because of this, just *anything* can musically be said in a certain key, except for what is expressed in *other* keys. If we translate this insight to the world of moods and feelings, we shall recognize that they have no content and even lack the determination of form that we associate with *style*.

Two consequences follow from this. Moods and feelings themselves do not have their origin in "emotional objects," in the events, objects, persons, and so on that will provoke in us certain emotional reactions. They precede these emotional objects, in the way that key precedes musical composition. But they are the landscape in which our emotional life will take place: Our emotional life is the totality of the holes, fissures, local condensations, or patterns in the web within which our moods weave our emotional life. In the second place, moods and feelings are, in the most literal sense of the word, *next to nothing*—and, thus, in terms of them, "next to nothing" will prevent us from moving through the temporal and existential space ordinarily separating the past from the present. Precisely because of this, moods and feelings define the place where the transition from past to present (and vice versa) will preferably be enacted. As soon as content, or form and style enter the scene, a temporal "heaviness" inevitably enters the scene favoring either the past (object) or the present (subject)—and the doors between past and present will then silently but irrevocably be closed. Historical experience is the resonance that the "music of the past," its moods and feelings, may have in the historian whose mind happens to have been written in the same key. And it is the sublime combination of an extreme lightness with all-pervasiveness that has enabled moods and feelings to have this resonance through the centuries. Once again, how can one fail to admire Huizinga for having discovered this relationship of historical experience to music!

In his now so sadly underestimated *Der Untergang des Abendlandes* Oswald Spengler discussed rococo art and ornament of which he was no less a great admirer than I am. In order to appreciate Spengler's comments on rococo, we should place them against the background of one of the book's main theses, namely, the claim that the sciences and, specifically, mathematics are far from being so remote to the arts and the culture of a historical period as we always tend to believe. In order to illustrate his thesis, Spengler asks us to consider architecture. He argues, for example, that the Greek temple is to be related to the Greek abhorrence of a pure mathematics uninterested in its relationship to actual reality. For the Greeks, mathematics should always bear in mind the origins that it allegedly ultimately has in "das Greifbar-Sinnliche," that is, in what we can experience and get hold of;[71] Greek mathematicians would never have been willing to work with so-called complex or imaginary numbers (such $i = \sqrt{-1}$)—hence the "massivity" of the Greek temple and its suggestion of enclosing space within itself; space is made solid and almost tangible by the temple, it does not reach outside itself. The Gothic cathedral, on the other hand, expresses in both its form and ornament the transcendence of this restriction to the sensible; there is in the Gothic cathedral and in the intricacies of late Gothic ornament a suggestion of the infinite and of an effort to escape what we can grasp with our fingers. And Spengler then most surprisingly relates this to the history of mathematics by saying that the late Middle Ages developed an *outillage mental* (as we would nowadays have called it) in which became possible both Gothic architecture and the first anticipations (Spengler had Cusanus in mind here) of the infinitesimal calculus of three centuries later. Pure form had acquired both in architecture and in ornament an autonomy with regard to the sensible that would have been profoundly repugnant to the Greek mind—an autonomy of form corresponding to the liberation of mathematical thought from the realist assumptions unanimously accepted by Greek mathematicians.

But the ultimate triumph of mathematical formalism over a mathematics that still cherished its ties with the sensible would only be achieved by Newton and Leibniz. And once again Spengler sees a profoundly revealing relationship between mathematics and the art of the time (give or take a decade or two), as exemplified, most specifically, by rococo decoration and architecture:

In the façades of palaces and churches straight lines of a still sensory palpability gradually become more and more unreal. The clear determinations of the Florentine–Roman arrangement of columns and stories are now replaced by the "infinitesimal" elements of swinging and flowing structures, of volutes and cartouches. The construction disappears in the fullness of the decoration—of the "functional," in the mathematical sense of the word; columns and pilasters, placed together in groups or in bundles, travel without a resting point, in front of the beholder's eye, over the façade's surface, now moving toward and then away from each other; the surfaces of walls, ceilings, and stories dissolve in a flood of stucco and ornament, disappear and fall apart in a colorful explosion of light. This light, however, playing over the world of the ripe Baroque—from Bernini around 1650 to the Rococo of Dresden, Vienna, and Paris—has become a purely musical element. The *Zwinger* of Dresden is a *Symphony.* Together with mathematics, eighteenth-century architecture developed into a world of forms of an essentially *musical* character.[72] (my translation)

Let me add a few comments on this. In the first place, late Gothic ornament has often been compared to that of rococo, and both have often been accused of an excess of free play, threatening the disjunction of ornament from what it is ornament of. With Spengler we can see what is right and what is wrong with this, for the parallelism of the emancipation of mathematical thought from the sensible, on the one hand, and the free play of form in Gothic and rococo ornament is most helpful in this context. Indeed, form (either mathematical or ornamental) was now freed from content. This is suggestive of an alienation from the world that was associated earlier with the mood of boredom. So this is where the accusation against rococo art of being a mere idle play of forms is undoubtedly correct. But this cannot be the last word. Think of mathematics. Mathematics also gives us a free play of forms and a withdrawal from the world; but, as such, it is, perhaps, the most dramatic example of a *reculer pour mieux sauter* that we can find in all of the history of mankind. In its practical applications in science and technology mathematics gave us an unparalleled grasp of the world. Mathematics is a withdrawal, or alienation, from the world, but only to result in, or to produce, an immersion or penetration into the world that would have been utterly unthinkable without it. And I have tried to tell a closely similar story for rococo ornament. This, then, is where rococo art could be said to guide us back to reality again and to give us the vindication of boredom—and, moreover, where the now so fashionable contempt of rococo art is, if not wrong, at least shallow and misguided.

But second, and more important in the context of the present discussion, we may discern in Spengler's argument about the role of mathematics in a culture an attempt to move beyond what merely are matters of style; that is, an attempt to penetrate to an even deeper level than style itself, and of which style is merely a surface manifestation. This is what made Spengler so much interested in the mathematics of the Greeks, of the late Middle Ages, or of the Rococo period (and we should not forget that Spengler was a mathematician before he started to reflect on history and on the bleak prospects of the West's future). As he put it himself, "The style of a culture is primarily expressed in a world of numbers, and not in how the latter is applied in science."[73] That is to say, behind a culture's style we will find a world of numbers and of mathematics—and in this way mathematics expressed for Spengler much the same of what we discussed in terms of "the moods and feelings of a period." And since these moods and feelings are—as we have seen—just as much devoid of material content as is the case in mathematics, there is a certain theoretical beauty in this parallelism of the two.

Taking Spengler as our guide, we shall be led to acknowledge that there may be a profound relationship between the eighteenth century's moods and feelings, as expressed by rococo ornament, on the one hand and its triumphs in the fields of mathematics and the sciences on the other. We may now be prepared to see that rococo ornament reflects the mood of the Enlightenment's discovery of the physical world and that it celebrates the victory of modern man over physical reality that was so much the Enlightenment's pride. Hence it is also why Enlightenment physicists had no problem with the rococo ornamentation of their instruments that nowadays we find so pathetic or even ridiculous. The use of these instruments was no less a part of the Enlightenment conception of the world as the ornaments adorning them. Indeed, the world of Enlightenment science can be found in rococo ornament no less than in the writings by Newton, Euler, the Bernoullis or d'Alembert. In the Teyler Museum in Haarlem the visitor may admire the electrification machine built (at great cost) by the Amsterdam instrument maker John Cuthbertson between 1783 and 1786.[74] The thing is huge, perhaps the most impressive scientific instrument constructed in the eighteenth century, and it may still fascinate a generation, like ours, that has so much become accustomed to cyclotrons or radio telescopes. But it is hard to decide what impresses us more: its Promethean capacity to imitate the sublimity of flashes of lightning or its elegance and beautiful decoration. And, in the end, we can conclude only that we should avoid opposing science and ornament: Here they are still a transfiguration of each other.

In the third and last place, recall that the Spengler quote was full of explicit references to music. And this is how it ought to be, for does music not lie halfway on the trajectory between mathematics and moods and feelings? All three of them — mathematics, music, and moods and feelings — are rigidly formalist and without substantial content. This is where they are all stations along one and the same trajectory. But music succeeds in combining mathematical abstraction with feeling. So perhaps we can sum it all up in the formula that in historical experience the historian may hear "the music of the past," a formula that would undoubtedly have pleased Huizinga.

7.10 CONCLUSION

Nevertheless, it was not mathematics or music but the paintings by Van der Weyden, Van Eyck, and so on that allowed Huizinga to have his historical experience of the late Middle Ages. And examples taken from the visual arts were also discussed in this chapter in order to contribute to a better understanding of historical experience. It surely is no coincidence that the work of art may be both so singularly effective at provoking historical experience and a better guide for understanding historical experience than mathematics (I may be forgiven to let the issue of music rest here). There is a close similarity between how we experience art on the one hand and the account of historical experience given here, on the other. All that truly counts in aesthetic experience is to be situated in what happens between the work of art and ourselves; as soon as we leave this direct interaction between ourselves and the work of art and either move deeper into the work of art itself or withdraw within ourselves, (objectivist or subjectivist) context takes over—and that will mean the end of the authenticity of aesthetic experience. And so it is with historical experience: We experience the past in the same way in which we may experience the work of art. In both cases we are required to stay "on the surface," so to speak, and to avoid the temptation to look for deeper foundations for what we see and experience either on the side of the subject or on that of the object. Truth has no role to play here.

This assertion should not be misunderstood. In the first place, it is not an embrace of irrationality or skepticism; it is meant only to emphasize the fact that experience has no cognitive function here. However, if one were to insist on relating (historical) experience and truth, I would not hesitate to say that historical experience is not the servant of truth here but rather its guide. A historical writing taking truth as its guide is much like Soviet economy, where one attempted to create economic order by economic planning—and where the paradoxical outcome of the effort was that every increase of planning resulted in an increase of disorder. So it is in historical writing where an exclusive insistence on truth may result in the ultimate stultification of the discipline and in the answering of questions that no sensible person would bother to ask. In economy we should always search for the *juste milieu* between planning and freedom; so it is in historical writing where we also aim at the *juste milieu* between truth and experience and where an excess of one of them sometimes needs compensation by an extra infusion of the other.

This might well be the situation in which historical writing presently finds itself.[75] Think of what historical writing still was in the nineteenth century: A tiny number of professional historians (at least compared to the present) were then investigating a still wholly unexplored ocean of history. The present situation is more or less the reverse: You now have huge armies of historians turning upside down almost every pebble that the past has left us. Most of the "white spots" that were still on the map of the past in the days of Ranke have now been carefully explored and mapped, sometimes even *ad nauseam*. There is now too little past for too many historians, so to say. It is not difficult to figure out what this must mean to historical writing and to the role of historical experience in it. Imagine a discussion between nineteenth-century historians such as Michelet, Lamartine, and Tocqueville on, for example, the French Revolution. We will then realize ourselves that their accounts of the Revolution were so idiosyncratic that such a discussion would be difficult, if not impossible, to realize. Only the assumption of an "objective," shared historical reality could succeed in making their representations of the Revolution more or less commensurable and comparable with each other. Think of different people standing in different positions in front of a mirror; only the assumption that there is a fixed reality mirrored by the mirror may enable them to discuss what they see and to venture some conjectures about how what one of them sees might be related to what the others see. In sum, when you have relatively few historians investigating a still largely unexplored past, you may expect them to feel a strong urge to "fix" the past, to conceive of the past as a solid and objective given.

It is precisely the reverse when our contemporary armies of historians are required to discover something new in a past that has already been painstakingly researched for decades, if not centuries, by their predecessors. There will be an invincible urge to dissolve the solid objective past into an indefinite mist without any fixed or clearly recognizable contours. Only this will enable them to emulate their predecessors and to discover in the past something that they had not yet seen. But to the extent that the past fell apart into myriad incoherent fragments, the necessity arose to "fix" the subject. Now the incommensurability of what historians say about the past and the specter of historical solipsism could be avoided only by a regimentation of the historical subject, of the historians' language, of theories to be employed by them, of the academic institutions in which historians work, and so on. This may explain why the more ambitious contemporary historians, hoping to say something new, have become so much addicted to theory. Theory, not the past, is now the mirror in which historians recognize themselves and each other, and Theory has thus been, for over thirty years, the most powerful instrument for fixing the subject.

Now, as long as few theories were fashionable, fixing the subject by theory was a successful alternative to the by now hopeless strategy of fixing the historical object. But with the proliferation of theories a stage has now been reached where theory contributes to the dissolution of the subject rather than to the fixing of it. If you have many competing theories for how to fix the subject, unfixing the subject can be the only outcome. And, indeed, we now live in an era where each scholar seems to have his or her own theory or epistemological scheme for understanding the past (reducing us to the kind of situation Heidegger had so strikingly depicted in his essay "The Age of the World View")—which must automatically mean the end of the era of "Theory" and of traditional epistemology. This ushers in the stage of historical experience. As we saw in the conclusion of the previous chapter, experience should be situated in the trajectory between the subject and the object. Moreover, it was argued there that traditional epistemology aimed at dividing all of the philosopher's world between the subject and the object, so that experience no longer had any role to play. But if both the strategy of fixing the object and that of fixing the subject have failed, no other alternative is left but to move to (historical) experience— and to see the proliferation of theories (1) as a surrender of the universalism of theory and hence (2) as an embrace of the individual historian's experience of the past. In this way the turn toward historical experience can be said to be the natural result of the development of historical writing over the last one and a half centuries.

SUBLIME HISTORICAL EXPERIENCE [1]

The heart cannot forget
Unless it contemplate
What it declines.
—(Emily Dickinson, *Complete Poems,* no. 1,560)

A Klee painting named "Angelus Novus" shows an angel looking as
though he is about to move away from something he is fixedly contemplating. His eyes are staring, his mouth is open, his wings are
spread. This is how one pictures the angel of history. His face is
turned toward the past.
—(Walter Benjamin, *Theses on the philosophy of history*)

8.1 INTRODUCTION

For many years Kant was dutifully served by the faithful Lampe. But
one unfortunate day Lampe could not resist the temptation to steal something from his master's household. He was dismissed on the spot by his
master, for whom property was sanctified by nothing less than the categorical imperative. Nevertheless, Kant was not at ease with his Roman
severitas, and he kept worrying about poor Lampe. In order to get rid of
this most unwelcome manifestation of *Neigung,* he pinned above his desk
a little note with the stunning text "Lampe vergessen"—"forget Lampe."
There is something pathetic about the naivete of this greatest among all
philosophers urging himself "not to forget to forget Lampe." [2] Obviously,
somebody who requires himself to forget is sure to remember. Or, as Jon
Elster once put it: "The injunction 'Forget it' calls for an effort that can
only engrave what we are supposed to forget more firmly in our memory." [3]

But as we shall see, "not forgetting—or remembering—to forget" is
more than a psychological naivete. More specifically, our attitude to the
collective past may sometimes require us to repudiate part of the past; that
is, to dissociate part of our historical past from our collective self and from

our collective historical identity. And in such situations we find ourselves in the quasi-Kantian position of having to remember, or to bear in mind what is forgotten. We then paradoxically are what we are no longer, in the sense that our identity is then defined by our having repudiated a previous identity.

I hope to demonstrate, next, that in such situations we can speak, from both a material and a formal perspective, of a sublime experience of the past. So much will be clear as soon as we come to see that the sublime is in many, although not all, respects the philosophical equivalent of the psychological notion of trauma. More specifically, although trauma challenges our identity, it does, in the end, respect it, whereas the sublime requires us to abandon a previous identity. This is why trauma serves the cause of memory, and the sublime that of forgetting. It will become clear, finally, that all this may contribute to a better understanding of myth and of the crucial role that myth still plays in our modern(ist) historical consciousness.

8.2 HISTORISM AND NIETZSCHE

Since Cicero's *Historia magistra vitae* many different answers have been given to the venerable question of what are the uses of history.[4] Most convincing still is the claim that our identity lies in our past. Philosophers (since Locke) and psychologists (since Freud) almost unanimously agree that the question of who we are is best answered by an account of our life history (as a *historia rerum gestarum*) and, especially, by our memory of our history (as *res gestae*). And, so the argument continues, having knowledge of one's identity is of the greatest practical importance; all meaningful and responsible action has its origins in this. What would we say of a general who suddenly forgot about his identity and were to behave like a midwife, or vice versa? This is what made the film *Analyze This* into such a hilarious spectacle; we would never expect a Mafia boss to be plagued by the kind of psychological worries that would have sent Woody Allen to his psychiatrist. We attribute to people certain identities and assume their behavior to be in agreement with their identity. Nineteenth-century historists translated this insight into the domain of history: The identity of a nation, of a people, or of an institution lies in the past of this nation, people, or institution, and if we wish to get hold of their identity, we should above all write their histories. This is why the historists had no difficulty at all in answering the question of the uses of history: History, and history alone, will give political and social institutions access to their identity. And this is where they also discovered the condition of all meaningful and potentially successful political action. As Ranke put it in his inaugural address of 1836:

It thus is the task of history to define the nature of the state on the basis of past events and to make this known; it is the task of politics to develop and to bring to perfection the assignment of the past after it has been understood and recognized.[5] (my translation)

Politicians have to begin where historians leave off, and their actions should be a more or less logical continuation of what historians wrote about the nation's past. And even today many theorists still see this as the most convincing and satisfactory characterization of the tasks and the uses of the writing of history.[6] It self-evidently follows that the more we know about our individual or collective past, the better it will be, for the more we know about the past, the clearer the contours of our identity will become and the more adequate our individual and collective action can become.[7] Hence, an overdose of history can hardly be imagined.

As we all know Nietzsche attacked the historist conception of (the uses of) history in his second *Unzeitgemässe Betrachtung*. Nietzsche argued there that *forgetting* is, to a certain extent at least, a condition for successful action—or, perhaps, even for our being capable of any meaningful action at all. Somebody unable to disengage himself from his past and who wishes to relate his actions to the ultimate and finest ramifications of the historical process will never succeed in summoning up the courage for any action:

What deeds could man ever have done if he had not been enveloped in the dust-cloud of the unhistorical?[8]

Knowledge of the past then paralyzes all action; for all action is, to a certain extent, a rupture with what the past has been like and, in that sense, essentially *a-* or *anti-*historical. And Nietzsche then even goes on to say in so many words that you *can* have an overdose of history and that such an overdose will not contribute to an improved awareness of our identity but, on the contrary, to an irremediable *loss of identity:*

The extreme case would be the man without any power to forget who is condemned to see "becoming" everywhere. Such a man no longer believes in himself or his own existence; he sees everything fly past in an eternal succession and loses himself in the stream of becoming.[9]

Obviously, this is the very antithesis of the historist argument.

Now, it must strike us that historism, as defined in the preceding, is, in fact, more consistent and radical than the ordinarily so radicalist Nietzsche. Within Nietzsche's construction you have, first, the individual with his identity and, next, we may ask how much of the past this individual can tolerate before becoming incapable of action. As Nietzsche argues, this is where people may differ: Some people will already be paralyzed by the tiniest bit of history, whereas others can swallow heaps of it without being seriously handicapped by it in their actions.[10] So Nietzsche's argument presupposes the existence of an ahistorical individual, of an individual equipped with an identity logically prior to this individual's history. In this sense Nietzsche seems to preach a return to the ahistorical transcendentalism of the Enlightenment—and this impression is reinforced by his insistence on the dimensions of the unhistorical (human nature) and the superhistorical (the domain of eternal beauty) at a later stage of his argument. Historism, on the other hand, had the courage to completely historicize man and society; and historists therefore could certainly have accused Nietzsche of inconsistency in that he excluded part of our identity from the regime of history.[11] Probably Nietzsche's partial return to the Enlightenment's transcendentalism can be explained by the influence of Burckhardt in particular and by the intellectual climate in Basel in general.[12]

Now, even if we are willing to forgive Nietzsche this inconsistency, we cannot doubt that the historian will prefer the historist position to Nietzsche's, for it is part and parcel of the historical profession to show that what initially may have seemed to be outside the grasp of history is, if one looks well enough, also part of a historical evolution. "Panta rhei, kai ouden menei," to quote Heraclitus. This may explain why neither historians nor historical theorists have ever seen in Nietzsche's diatribe against nineteenth-century historism an occasion to seriously ponder Nietzsche's argument about the necessity of forgetting, for doing so might easily invite awkward questions about why we should be interested in history at all. We will not be in need of historians for forgetting about the past.[13] So historians can be expected to prefer to avoid addressing the issue of forgetting, even if they are willing to recognize that Nietzsche has been up to something. As we all know, sometimes it is prudent to feign agreement with a useful misconception contrary to one's better knowledge and understanding and to sacrifice the lesser truth in order to secure the possession of the greater one.

In order to avoid eventual misunderstandings about what I have in mind here, I would like to point out that I am perfectly well aware that the disciples of Marx and Foucault have written whole libraries about what was marginalized in the past itself, pushed aside deliberately or unintentionally or simply forgotten. But this is not the issue here. So much will be clear as soon as we recognize that these theorists focused on forgetting with no other purpose in mind than to make us remember again the forgotten or repressed past. Consequently, as far as I know, Nietzsche still is the only theoretician who seriously considered the issue of why and when the historian should welcome and contribute to a forgetting of the past—and we should praise him for this. But his analysis of forgetting is incomplete. And in order to remedy this shortcoming, I propose to begin by distinguishing four types of forgetting.

8.3 FOUR TYPES OF FORGETTING

In the first place, as we know from daily life, there is much in our past that we can safely forget since it is devoid of any relevance to our present or future identity. What we had for dinner last Sunday or where we went for a walk with our dog has no consequences for our identity or for the important decisions that we shall have to make in our lives. These are aspects of our existence that we can safely forget about without endangering our mental health—and much the same is true for our collective, social, or political action. This is, in all likelihood, what Nietzsche had in mind and where we can only agree with him. I admit, though, that what initially was irrelevant may acquire an unexpected relevance from a later perspective. Perhaps during our walk with the dog we met somebody who was to make a difference in our lives at some later stage—and then we will have good reasons to remember where we had this walk. Similarly, moving on to the level of the collectivity, thanks to *Alltagsgeschichte,* we have become aware that daily life has a history of its own and that this history may profoundly affect our collective identities.

This automatically brings me to a second type of forgetting. As the example of *Alltagsgeschichte* already suggests, it may be that we have forgotten what truly is relevant to our identity and our actions—but we were simply not aware of this. On the level of the individual we may think of those apparently insignificant details of our lives and of our behavior that psychoanalysis has shown to be of the greatest significance for our personality. Who would have believed that a large part of our personality is revealed by our sexual fantasies (assuming that Freud has been correct about this)? And this has its counterpart in the writing of history. Historians sometimes "forget" what has truly been decisive in the past, not because they deliberately wanted to distort the past but simply because they were ignorant about the significance of certain causal factors. It thus required Restoration historians such as Augustin Thierry or François Guizot, or a Marx and the socialists of the chair, to make historians see that a national history that deals with politics only and that is silent about socioeconomic history must be regarded as seriously incomplete. Because of these thematic shifts in the history of historical writing, this history can well be compared to psychoanalysis, for it makes us aware of the unexpected significance of aspects of the past that were hitherto universally disregarded.

However, there is a third variant of forgetting where we may have excellent reasons for forgetting part of or an aspect of our past—for example, when the memory of it is too painful to be admitted to our collective consciousness. The paradigmatic example is, of course, how in the first two decades after World War II the Holocaust was "forgotten" in Germany and not only there. The memory of it was so threatening and so terribly painful—both for the victims and for the perpetrators (and at times even for the bystanders)—that it was for a long time withheld from conscious memory. The result was repression and the curious paradox that traumatic experience is both forgotten and remembered. It is forgotten in the sense that it can successfully be expelled from conscious memory; it is remembered in the sense that the subject of a traumatic experience will be seriously handicapped by it.

The dissociation of the self into a conscious and an unconscious self guarantees the possibility of a not forgetting to forget. By relegating the traumatic experience to the domain of the unconscious, we can, indeed, forget it. But precisely by storing it there, we will *also* retain it as an unconscious memory. And as an unconscious memory it is a constant reminder that there is something that we should or wish to forget. To return to the Kant example: Kant's problem with Lampe was, so to speak, that he did not succeed in transforming a conscious into an unconscious memory. And the explanation is, in all likelihood, that the whole affair with Lampe, however painful it may have been, was insufficiently traumatic for Kant. Had Lampe done something significantly more painful to Kant, Kant would probably not have needed the note above his desk and would have succeeded in repressing the event from his conscious memory.[14]

Last, we should discern still a fourth type of forgetting that will occupy us for the remainder of this chapter. A few examples may suggest what is at stake here. Think of Europe after the French Revolution, of how the Industrial Revolution profoundly changed the life of Western Europeans in every conceivable aspect, think of what the Death of God must have meant to our *outillage mental.* Undoubtedly these dramatic transformations belong to the most decisive and profound changes that Western man has undergone in the course of history. In all these cases he entered a wholly new world and, above all, he could do so only on the condition of forgetting a previous world and of shedding a former identity. Entering such a new world is, automatically, the abandonment of a previous world, of "a world we have lost" forever, to use Peter Laslett's well-known and appropriate formula. And the latter (forgetting) here always is a condition of the former (the acquisition of a new identity).

In all these cases having had to abandon a traditional and familiar previous world has been extremely painful, and it was always experienced as such. In this way these transitions were no less traumatic than the kind of collective experience we encountered in the previous type of forgetting. But there are no less important differences as well. Crucial is that in the previous type of forgetting closure of the trauma is possible, whereas it remains a constant and permanent presence in the fourth type. The tension between what is present consciously and unconsciously or between remembering and forgetting can always be resolved in the third type—albeit sometimes with the greatest difficulty. As soon as the traumatic experience can be narrativized (as paradigmatically will be the case in the psychoanalytical treatment of trauma), as soon as the traumatic experience can successfully be subsumed in the history of one's life, it will lose its threatening and specifically traumatic character. The traumatic experience has then been adapted to identity, and vice versa. Or, to use the right terminology here, a *reconciliation* of experience and identity has then been achieved, a reconciliation respecting experience *and* identity—and therefore guaranteeing the continued existence of both. It is true that this negotiation of a new balance between the two is possible only at the price of the greatest effort and of a most painful descent into the past of an individual or of a collectivity—but it *.can* be done. And even if this reconciliation is not achieved—although this surely is bad enough already—it need not necessarily imply the loss of one's existing or of one's former identity. As we know from psychopathology, in the worst-case scenario the coexistence of two identities (the former one and a new identity, crystallizing out of the traumatic experience) may be the final outcome. But even then the former identity will remain the dominant one; trauma may shake identity to its very foundations, but it will not result in the abandonment of a former identity for a wholly new one. It *could* not even do so, since trauma is always specific for the identity whose trauma it is—and it therefore necessarily presupposes the continuation of identity.

8.4 THE DESIRE OF BEING AND THE DESIRE OF KNOWLEDGE

And continuation of identity is essentially different with the fourth type of forgetting. The historical transformations occasioning this variant of forgetfulness are always accompanied by feelings of a profound and irreparable loss, of cultural despair, and of hopeless disorientation. In this sense such historical experiences are undoubtedly traumatic too. But the stake of the traumatic experience is far more dramatic in such cases—for here one really loses oneself, here a former identity is irrevocably lost forever and superseded by a new historical or cultural identity. Hence, in cases like these any reconciliation of a former and a new identity is categorically out of the question—and this also means that no room is left for a mechanism that might give us the redemption from trauma. This, then, is the kind of trauma that we will always carry with us after History has forced us to confront it; it is a trauma for which no cure is to be found. The new identity is mainly constituted by the trauma of the loss of a former identity—precisely *this* is its main content, and that this is the ineluctable truth announces itself in the realization (agonizing, resigned, or otherwise) that this loss is permanent and can never be undone. And then trauma is just as permanent as the loss of the former identity is. In this way we can say that our collective identity largely is the sum of all the scars on our collective soul, scars that were occasioned by our forced abandonment of former identities, scars that will never wholly fade and that will cause in us a continuous and enduring pain. Similarly, we may argue that the past will always accompany us as a past love—absent but, precisely because of this, always so very much and so very painfully present. This, then, is what has most appropriately been called "the Pain of Prometheus," in which a civilization is permanently aware of the social idylls of the "lost worlds" that it was forced to surrender in the course of its long history and that will never be returned to it, however strong the nostalgic yearning for these lost paradises may be.

The difference between the third and the fourth type of forgetting can also be explained by emphasizing that in the third variant some specific identity (either individual or collective) is the universe within which a psychological tragedy unfolds itself, while this universe itself is never really at stake in this tragedy. This universe remains intact, together with all the psychological laws and mechanisms that obtain in this universe and that determine what the reaction to a traumatic experience will be like. Precisely because of this and because of the makeup of such a psychological universe, we are allowed to push traumatic loss for some time into the dark background of the unconscious, for the unconscious is an integral part of our identity that may offer us the kind of shelter that we sometimes need more than anything else. But this is different in the fourth type of forgetting since here the *whole* of a previous identity (conscious and unconscious all taken together) is at stake; and then there is no place where we could temporarily shelve a traumatic experience until the moment has come that we can summon up the force to face it. Between identities there is a vacuum— so not even a substrate for the unconscious.

So we should distinguish between *two* kinds of trauma: on the one hand there is the kind of trauma to be associated with the third type of forgetting (trauma$_1$), which, however dramatic, will leave identity intact and, on the other hand there is the kind of trauma to be related to the fourth type of forgetting (trauma$_2$) which involves the transition from a former to a new identity. Here the traumatic loss truly is the loss of one's (former) self. And what loss could possibly be greater—for is this not as close to death as one may come?

So let us now investigate trauma$_2$. Our best point of departure will be the reactionary and the conservative reaction to the French Revolution. When investigating the nature of conservatism Karl Mannheim emphasized the necessity to clearly distinguish between conservatism and traditionalism (a term that was originally used by Max Weber).[15] Traditionalism stands for each human individual's dependence on fixed traditions for his or her orientation in life; and in this sense each human individual is traditionalist (even the revolutionary). Now, according to Mannheim, the French Revolution suddenly made people aware that they had always been living in a world of traditions without ever having been conscious of it, for this was simply how they lived their lives and how they saw their world. But the great Revolution suddenly lifted them, so to speak, out of this world of unreflected tradition and made them aware of these traditions for the first time. Hence, as Mannheim most cogently argues, conservatism has been *the becoming conscious of tradition*—and this may explain the unbridgeable gap between traditionalism and conservatism. Before the Revolution one could not possibly be a conservative; after the Revolution one could no longer be a traditionalist—and it was the Revolution that created an insurmountable barrier between the two.

But the really interesting implication in the present context is that the conservative is no less part of the post-revolutionary order than the revolutionary that he so fiercely opposes. A paradox that Novalis already saw when he jotted down the following profoundly insightful comment after having read Burke's *Reflections on the Revolution in France* immediately after its publication in 1790:

Many contra-revolutionary books were written in favor of the Revolution. Burke has written a revolutionary book against the revolution.[16] (my translation)

So, even for the conservative a return to the prerevolutionary order is unthinkable; and this is why conservatives certainly deeply regretted the Revolution and were adamant that such disasters should *never, ever* happen again, while, at the same time, they were ready to accept the Revolution as an ineluctable fact that we should learn to live with in some way or another. Even the conservatives realized that, however fiercely they might condemn the Revolution, the world had irrevocably and inexorably acquired *a new identity* and that the prudent and sensible person could only acquiesce in this.

Now, part of this is true as well of the reactionary reaction to the Revolution. The reactionaries were no less aware than the conservatives of having been expelled from the idyll of a prerevolutionary and preindustrial world. They were no less aware of living in an essentially post-revolutionary order, and they had therefore moved beyond Weberian traditionalism no less than the conservatives. The fact that we describe their political position as "reactionary" amply testifies to all this. The reactionary position is, after all, a *reaction* to the French Revolution—and therefore presupposes the latter. Each reaction bears the traces of what it is a reaction to. The notion of a prerevolutionary reactionary is therefore just as meaningless as the notion of a married bachelor. Nevertheless, as we know there is a profound difference between the conservative and the reactionary à la Joseph de Maistre or Bonald. And we can explain or clarify the difference in terms of the difference between trauma$_1$ and trauma$_2$.

Although the reactionary reaction to the Revolution is far more vehement and unyielding than that of the conservative reaction, it is the conservatives who lost most and who chose what truly is the *via ardua.* Whereas the reactionaries will experience the loss of the prerevolutionary world in terms of trauma$_1$, the conservatives will undergo their historical predicament in terms of trauma$_2$. Put differently, whereas the reactionaries will not see in the Revolution (and its aftermath) an irreparable rupture with a prerevolutionary identity, the conservatives are aware that the prerevolutionary order is gone forever and can never be reconstituted. So for the reactionaries the prerevolutionary identity can be recaptured again, and their relationship to that past can, therefore, be defined in terms of *being.* The past is an object of the *desire of being*—they want to be(come) again what the past once was like. The conservatives, on the other hand, recognize that they are forever separated from the prerevolutionary past by the abyss between two different historical or cultural identities. Their desire of the past can therefore only be a *desire to know.* They know their lusterless but lofty assignment to be the transformation of (past) *being* into *knowledge*—or, as Burckhardt once so movingly put it: "Was einst Jubel und Jammer war, muss nun Erkenntnis werden" ("What once was joy and misery, must now be transformed into knowledge"). History became an object of knowledge, an object of research forever separated from the world of the subject, of the historian. The past became a world successfully resisting any attempt to restore the union of being and knowledge. It is as in Plato's myth of the origin of the sexes referred to in the second epigraph to this book: All the powerful force of a historical *eros* will never succeed in overcoming the resistance with which the past—now being part of objective reality—will resist this reunification of ourselves with it. To put it quite plainly, "We simply can no longer get into it." [17] We have been ejected, expelled, or exiled from the past; or, rather, because of some terrible event (such as the French Revolution) a world in which we used to live naively and unproblematically fell apart into a past and a present—as the snowball we discussed when dealing with Benjamin. History, as the discipline investigating the past, is therefore the product of the conservative and not of the reactionary reaction to the Revolution and to the loss of the past and of a former identity. Or, we might just as well say that the reactionary lives in the illusion that we may come to know so much of the past that *knowledge* will finally shade off into *being* and that, in this way, we may become the past again.[18] And that would obviously mean the end of trauma$_1$ (which is why the reactionary desires it so much)—although it could never be the end of trauma$_2$ (which is why the conservative accepts the fact of having to live in the post-revolutionary order).

However, a qualification must be added to the acceptance of the present (and the implicit abandonment of the prerevolutionary past) that was attributed to the conservative just now, for this is not an acceptance in the sense that all tension in the relationship with the prerevolutionary past has now disappeared. This will become clear if we recognize that for the conservative—and in the case of trauma$_2$—the opposite will take place of what was said about the reactionary. That is, the *desire of knowledge* will function here as a substitute—or sublimation—of the *desire of being*. And the desire of knowledge will be all the more intense since it can *sui generis* never actually be such a substitute. Hence, trauma$_2$ will never come to a closure, since all that will be told about the past, and all the histories and stories that a culture may wish to tell itself about its past and about what is experienced as traumatic in it, will always be told from the perspective of a modern post-revolutionary identity and, in this sense, reinforce rather than mitigate feelings of traumatic loss. This is, once again, the crucial difference between trauma$_1$ and trauma$_2$: In the case of trauma$_1$ telling the right story about the traumatizing past may, in the end, effect the reconciliation between the traumatic experience and identity. And then trauma$_1$ has been overcome. But such a reconciliation is unthinkable in the case of trauma$_2$, for knowledge can never satisfy the desire of being, although it will naturally have an insatiable urge to do so. In fact, we may locate here the mechanism perpetuating what was called a moment ago "the pain of Prometheus." The historical search for our former identity is motivated by the desire to become this identity again; but each time part of the past identity has, in fact, been recaptured, a new dimension has (unintentionally) been added to the difference between a former and our present identity. So in this way the writing of history must be curiously counterproductive, since the desire of being is continuously betrayed by its own best substitute, that is, the desire of knowledge—but precisely this fact about history will elicit over and over again a renewed effort by the historian to satisfy the impossible requirement of bridging the gap between being and knowledge. In this way the Promethean pain and our wish to assuage this pain keep each other going in a permanent *perpetuum mobile*—and there will be no room for either the temporary calm of repression or for the dissolution of trauma which trauma$_1$ may give.[19]

There is still one more side to all this. The notion of trauma$_1$ was developed by Janet, Charcot, and others in the 1880s to account for certain anomalies in how individual human beings may react to loss or to terrible events. And this puts certain limitations on the proper use of the notion. We may well ask whether we are justified at all in using the term trauma for trauma$_2$ as defined here. More specifically, does this loss of a former identity we encountered in the context of the fourth type of forgetting still sufficiently resemble trauma to warrant the use of the term? Indeed, although we may find the weirdest and most fascinating human psychopathologies in books such as those written by Oliver Sacks, in history still stranger things are possible. What individual psychopathology could, on the scale of the individual, be the counterpart of the history of Poland? Or of Germany? Indeed, centuries of suspended animation, or of being wholly alienated form a former self, or even of the loss of a former identity, interspersed with periods of hyperactivity and of solipsism may succeed each other here in a way which has absolutely no analogue in the vagaries of the human soul. The contours of cultural and historical identities are far more fluid and far less fixed than is the case with individual human beings. Whereas we might compare the contours of human identity with those of trees or houses, the contours of cultural identities are as vague, diffuse, and polymorphic as those of the clouds we see in the sky. (Recall here what was said in section 5.5 of Chapter 5 about different "states of aggregation of identity," where one such state of aggregation was tied to human individuals and another one was tied to nations or civilizations.) This is why the exchange of a former for a new identity may actually take place (although rarely even there) in the world of history and culture, whereas we can say such a thing only in a metaphorical sense about human individuals.

It is difficult, if not impossible, to give a satisfactory answer to the

330 Sublime Historical Experience

question of whether *trauma* is a suitable term for characterizing the loss of cultural or historical identity discussed here. If the term *trauma* is ordinarily used to characterize the incapacity to assimilate loss, then the term is not outrageously inappropriate. On the other hand, since there is no closure for trauma$_2$, it seems to be different in at least one crucial aspect from how trauma is normally understood. Nor is this all. We can only speak of trauma$_2$ in terms of identity: Only the notion of identity may satisfactorily clarify what trauma$_2$ is all about. From this perspective it is worrying (not to put too fine a point on it) that the notion of identity has no role of any significance to play in Freud's writings—he uses the term just once or twice in all his work. The explanation is that the workings of the mechanisms which interested him, as a scientist of the human soul, could always be seen as changes *in,* and not *of,* our identities. Just as the building of new cities or highways are changes *within* the borders of our country, changes that leave these borders themselves unaffected, so the kind of changes investigated by Freud (and psychologists after him) naturally presupposed the persistence of human identity. For this reason the notion of identity has no real job to perform in the field of psychology; what is of interest to the psychologist would immediately lose all its meaning and interest as soon as it was reformulated in terms of identity (supposing that such a reformulation is possible at all). But the borders of identities are continuously at stake and are continuously transgressed in the world of history and culture—and this is why the notion of identity can be so highly useful there. In the world of history and culture tragedies may be enacted which do not have their proper analogue in even the most terrible individual psychopathologies. Our collective psychology knows catastrophes whose proportions exceed by far all that may happen in an individual's psychology—and we can only *decide* whether such catastrophes may still count as traumas since the orthodox meaning of the term is an uncertain guide here.

Anyway, this is the kind of catastrophe which is at stake in the present chapter.

8.5 HEGEL ON THE CONFLICT BETWEEN SOCRATES AND THE ATHENIAN STATE

Hegel's famous analysis of the conflict between Socrates and the Athenian state will prove to be our best point of departure if we wish to deepen our insight into the nature of such catastrophes.

The unparalleled revolution effected by Socrates was, according to Hegel, that he was the first to compel humanity to think rationally and independently of all tradition about questions of good and evil and about what our duties and our obligations are:

In a former time laws and customs were valid unconditionally; human individuality formed a unity with the universal. To honor the Gods, to die for one's fatherland was a universal law and everybody fulfilled this universal content as a matter of course. Then, however, humanity started to inquire whether one should really wish or comply with this content. The awakening of this new principle brought about the death of the Gods of Greece and of moral custom ("die schöne Sittlichkeit"). Thought makes its appearance here as the principle of destruction, that is, as the destruction of natural custom; for because it knows itself to be an independent principle, it establishes principles of reason standing in a critical relationship to existing reality and in opposition to the limitations of natural custom. The former Greeks were perfectly well aware of what custom required them to do under each condition; but that man ought to discover the answer to such questions in himself—that was Socrates' point. Socrates made man aware of his inner self, so that man's conscience could become the measure of what is right and morally true ("Moralität"). This is the contrast between the natural customs of a former time and the moral reasonings of a later time; the former Greeks had no conscience. Socrates is famous as a moral teacher; in truth, however, he was the discoverer of morals. He defined thought as the highest and decisive principle. The Greeks had mere customs; but what are the moral virtues and duties of man, this is what Socrates wanted to teach to them.[20] (my translation)

In this sense Socrates even more than Christ was for Hegel the pivot on which the whole of the history of humanity hinges. History, as conceived by Hegel, is a movement from the objective mind, that is, from a rationality inherent in reality or in the given itself, by means of the subjective mind, that is, the human subject's rational awareness of this objective rationality, toward the absolute mind where objective and subjective rationality finally identify or coincide with each other. Mind first arises out of or dissociates itself from nature; as such it places itself opposite to objectivity, and, finally, it will arrive at a complete knowledge of itself by "recognizing" itself (to use the crucial Hegelian notion) in its previous objective manifestation right at the end of the historical process. And it was with Socrates that the first and decisive step, liberating man from natural and objective necessity, was taken.

But precisely by doing this Socrates shattered the foundations of the

Greek mind; and in this sense Socrates' condemnation by the Athenian state was eminently justified, for the morality of the Athenian state still belonged to the phase of the objective mind. Hence, by condemning Socrates, the Athenian state had condemned its mortal and most dangerous enemy. In this way Socrates' fate was tragic in the true sense of the word: Both parties in the conflict, both Socrates and the rulers of the Athenian state, were right. History was on both their sides. But, and this is crucial, the death sentence of Socrates was also the death sentence that the Athenian state pronounced against itself, for the death sentence was unintentionally a recognition and, in this way, an acceptance of the revolution effected by Socrates. It was such a recognition since it proved that Socrates' principle had already found its way to the hearts of the rulers of the Athenian state themselves. If this had not been the case, they would have cared little, if at all, about Socrates' teachings. They probably would not even have discerned anything subversive in them and probably would have regarded Socrates merely as their wholly harmless village idiot. So Socrates' condemnation made sense only to the extent that it was implicitly a condemnation of the condemners themselves as well. As Hegel comments:

Afterwards the Athenian people profoundly regretted the verdict. . . . They recognized that they were just as guilty or worthy of acquittal as Socrates, since Socrates' principle, namely the principle of subjectivity, had already taken root in their own mind and had already become their own principle.[21] (my translation)

Of the greatest importance here is a recognition of the nature of the relationship between the previous (objectivist) and the new (subjectivist) identity. Ordinarily we will say—with the historists—that our identity lies in our past: Our past will define our identity or will perhaps even be identical with it (if one wishes to avoid the multiplication of theoretical entities *praeter necessitatem*). But under circumstances as sketched by Hegel, this is, paradoxically, both the case and *not* the case. On the one hand it is *not* the case, insofar as the past, the phase of objectivity, has effectively been expelled from a collective identity—obviously so, since Socrates no longer defined humanity in terms of objectivity, but in those of subjectivity, at least as Hegel understood these terms. Within the historist paradigm such a complete erasure of a former identity would, needless to say, be wholly inconceivable. For the historist you are a product of your past; and you may dislike your past, feel unhappy about it, or whatever, but you cannot delete it and become somebody else, somebody who does not have *this* past. All your efforts to get rid of your obnoxious past will only more strongly tie you to it.

On the other hand, however, this is only half the story. Part of the historist view *is* salvaged, after all. It is true that in a certain sense—I emphasize, in a certain sense—the former identity *is* retained. It was retained in the awareness of having surrendered, of having moved beyond it, to a new identity—if we recall the Hegel example, we shall recognize that the realization of being no longer part of the world of objectivity is an integral part of the newly acquired identity of subjectivity. And so it is with all the other examples mentioned: Constitutive of the identity of contemporary Western man is his realization of being no longer part of a prerevolutionary, preindustrial, and still predominantly Christian Europe. To put it in one comprehensive formula: *in all these cases, one has become what one is no longer*—with all the emphasis on the "no longer." What one used to *be*, one's former identity, is now transformed into the identity of the person who *knows* (and no longer *is*) his former identity. One now is what one is, because one no longer is what one was—and this not being any longer what one was, is what one has essentially now become. It is as if something has been turned inside out. One has discarded (part of the) past from one's identity, and in this sense one has forgotten it. But one has not forgotten *that* one has forgotten it, for that one has forgotten precisely *this* is constitutive of the new identity. In this way, then, the desire of being gave way to the desire of knowing, so that one could forget what one knew.[22]

Indeed, the fact that one *could* forget this past at all is constitutive of the new identity rather than the fact of forgetting itself. Not forgetting but *being able* to forget is the real issue here, for we should realize that it is truly part of our identity, of the kind of person that we are, that we are capable of forgetting a certain part of our past (or not). To put it provocatively, we are not only the past that we (can) remember (as the historists have always argued) but *also* the past that we can *forget*. It really requires having a certain personality to be capable at all of forgetting a certain kind of past. For example, it will mean to a former concentration camp victim something entirely different to be able to forget about Auschwitz than to a former concentration camp guard. Or, think of a pair of Jewish twins who survived the horrors of Auschwitz: One is continuously haunted by the memory of the Holocaust, whereas the other has overcome the trauma. Then a crucial part of the difference between their identities must be defined in terms of what they have or have not been able to forget. In this way we can be said to be what we are capable of being no longer—this, then, is the lesson taught to us by the Hegel example.

Last, this may also make clear in what way Hegel's account of Socrates' condemnation upsets both the historist's and Nietzsche's view of forgetting and identity. On the one hand, Hegel would agree with the historist that our identity is exclusively a product of our history, and with Nietzsche that forgetting may sometimes be crucial to our identity. But on the other hand, Hegel's account clashes with that of the historist in that it identifies identity with a *repudiation* of the past, and it clashes with Nietzsche's account where it avoids placing identity outside or beyond history. So we encounter in Hegel a *regime* of our relationship to the past that is fundamentally at odds with the one we discovered in historism and in Nietzsche.

8.6 TRAUMA AND THE SUBLIME

The paradox of a new identity originating in the capacity to forget something brings me to the question of the relationship between trauma and the sublime. It need not surprise that there is a great deal of overlap between the two: In both we have to make do with an experience of the world that is too terrible to fit within the matrix of how we "normally" experience it. But I hope to make clear in this section that there is also an asymmetry between the two.

Let us start with the sublime—more specifically, with Burke's conception of it. Burke takes his departure from Locke's psychology of perception by situating all experience on the axis running from pain or terror on the negative side to pleasure on the positive side. But this "foundation" (to use the appropriate contemporary jargon in this context) of all experience is radically upset by the category of the sublime. Burke observes about sublime experiences that:

they are capable of producing delight; not pleasure, but a sort of delightful horror, a sort of tranquility tinged with terror; which as it belongs to self-preservation is one of the strongest of all passions. Its object is the sublime.[23]

The sublime combines in this notion of a "delightful horror" what is completely incompatible in Lockean psychology—and it is meant to do precisely this. It is as if the axis on which pain and pleasure are each other's opposite extremes has suddenly been turned ninety degrees so that they coincide with each other from this new and unexpected perspective. Lockean epistemology is then just as useless and helpless as the liquefied watches we may find in Dali's surrealist paintings. Think, furthermore, of the Kantian sublime. As Kant explains in the *Critique of Judgment*, when experiencing the sublime, the normal functioning of the categories of the understanding momentarily gives way to a free interaction between Reason and the imagination. And what the categories of the understanding ordinarily do in order to enable us to make sense of the world is temporarily put them into question in the most literal sense of the word. They are weighed and found wanting. So we may observe here the same momentary disruption of our normal cognitive apparatus as in Burke's case, although the technicalities of Kant's account of the sublime are, admittedly, immeasurably more complex than Burke's.

Trauma presents us with a roughly similar picture. The traumatic experience is too terrible to be admitted to consciousness: The experience exceeds, so to speak, our capacities to make sense of experience. Whereas normally the powers of association enable us to integrate experience into the story of our lives, the traumatic experience remains dissociated from our life's narrative since these powers of association are helpless and characteristically insufficient in the case of trauma. And there is one more resemblance between trauma and the sublime that is of relevance in the present context. Characteristic of trauma is the incapacity to actually suffer from the traumatic experience itself (as opposed to the consequences of repression): The subject of a traumatic experience is peculiarly numbed by it; he is, so to speak, put at a distance from what caused it. The traumatic experience is dissociated from one's "normal" experience of the world. A good example is how soldiers suffering from shell shock during World War I dissociated the terrors they had experienced from conscious memory:

Most striking of all, the patient [suffering from shell-shock] would not remember anything about the horrifying events that lay at the origin of his pitiable state. *Dissociation* or *amnesia* was therefore the hallmark of the war neuroses.[24]

Now, much the same can be observed for the sublime. I recall to mind here Burke's statement about the sublime quoted a moment ago. When Burke speaks about this "tranquility tinged with terror," this tranquility is possible (as Burke emphasizes) thanks to our awareness that we are not *really* in danger. Hence, we have distanced ourselves from a situation of *real* danger—and in this way, we have *dissociated* ourselves from the object of experience. The sublime thus provokes a movement of derealization by which reality is robbed of its threatening potentialities. As such Burke's description of the sublime is less the pleasant thrill that is often associated with it than a preemptive strike against the terrible.

Of course, this consideration brings the sublime even closer to trauma, where we can observe exactly the same thing. Since the traumatic experience is not admitted to consciousness but stalled in a directory of the mind (to use computer terminology) specially created for it, it is also temporarily robbed of its threatening features. Consequently, both trauma and the sublime are, if compared to "normal" experience, both extremely *direct* and extremely *indirect.* The sublime or traumatic experience has a *directness* absent from "normal" experience since we must undergo it without the protective mediation of the cognitive and psychological apparatus that normally processes our experience. But on the other hand it is abnormally *indirect* since we cannot face this directness and, precisely because of this, dissociate ourselves from it and thus remain, in a way, external to it. From the latter perspective, both the sublime and the traumatic experience strangely present themselves to us as if they were somebody else's experience.

Perhaps the paradox of the directness and indirectness of this kind of experience is nowhere better exemplified than by the characteristic complaint of patients suffering from derealization or depersonalization when they say that they seem to experience the world "as if from under a glass cheese cover." On the one hand, the experience these patients have of reality is highly indirect in the sense that the glass cheese cover seems to prevent any direct access to reality. They perceive all that we "normally" perceive— truth is just as accessible to them as to "normal" persons—but it nevertheless seems to them as if they see the world in some different way and as if they have begun to live in a world somehow separate from the "normal" world. Some transparent but impenetrable screen seems to have been erected between themselves and the "normal" world. And, indeed, in a certain sense, the illusion is correct, for they *really* inhabit a world that is different from the "normal" world. In this way a *dissociation* of their world from the "normal" world has really been effected. On the other hand, however, this experience of reality has a truly nauseating and most unpleasant directness. The intensity and directness of the kind of experience of the world provoked by derealization found its paradigmatic expression in Sartre's well-known description of how Roquentin, the protagonist of his novel *La nausée,* suddenly became overwhelmed by the presence of the roots of a tree, next to the bench he was sitting on in a park.[25] Suddenly a yawning abyss between himself and the world had come into being—these roots suddenly acquired the threatening strangeness of the sublime and were suddenly *dissociated* from the reassuring continuity of "normal" experience.

Derealization then paradoxically endows reality with a presence that is far more real than reality ever is. Experience can acquire this directness since the protective shield that normally processes our experience of the world and that mediates between us and the world has momentarily been taken away—so that a direct confrontation with the world results—hence the directness and immediacy of the sublime and traumatic experience of the world. So much becomes abundantly clear already from the nature of the experience itself, for, after all, the patient suffering from derealization has become *aware* of the very existence of this glass cheese cover; he really *knows* that he perceives the world through *it*. Whereas in our "normal" relationship to reality, the cheese cover performs its task of processing experience silently and unnoticed; the person suffering from derealization has objectified this cognitive and psychological "interface" between ourselves and the world and thus has reduced it to just one more aspect of the world. Derealization places us, on the one hand, in a realm *beyond* or *outside* the cheese cover, so that we can experience *it* as an objective reality, while, on the other hand we are nevertheless aware that we see the world *through* it. This is the most paradoxical effect the cheese cover experience must have on us. Hence, what is so nauseating in the "cheese cover experience" has its origins in the fusion of an objectification of experience with the object of experience, and not in (aspects of) reality itself (we are momentarily both inside and outside the world, so to say). As the patient suffering from derealization will be the first to admit, the reality perceived through the cheese cover is itself often harmless enough (merely the roots of a tree, for example).

And so it is with epistemology and the sublime. Epistemologists similarly objectify experience; they investigate our epistemological cheese cover and can do so only from a point of view automatically provoking the sublime experience of reality. In both cases the directness and indirectness of experience strangely reinforce each other. So both trauma and the sublime wholly disrupt the normal schema within which we make sense of the data of experience, and they do so by means of dissociation: Trauma dissociates because the traumatic experience is not admitted to "normal" consciousness, and the sublime dissociates since it places us at a standpoint objectifying all experience as such. In sum, trauma can be seen as the psychological counterpart of the sublime, and the sublime can be seen as the philosophical counterpart of trauma.

Two considerations of a more general import can be related to this. In the first place, the foregoing may explain why the sublime and epistemology always tend to go together. Indeed, the category of the sublime was retrieved from 1,500 years of oblivion after Descartes had placed epistemology at the top of the philosopher's agenda. At first sight this might surprise us since the sublime experience (of reality) is an experience which unsettles the epistemologist's account of the nature of experience. So the more ambitious, complete, and comprehensive an epistemology is, the less room it should leave for the anomalies of the sublime. One might argue now that precisely the more ambitious epistemologies must automatically stimulate an interest in experiences (such as the sublime) that do not seem to fit, or that fit only with difficulty, within the epistemologist's matrix, since each philosopher ought to be interested in what seems to conflict with his theories. But this is a rather trivial observation, and there is a stronger and more interesting argument.

Epistemology is an attempt to define the nature of our cognitive apparatus, and therefore it presupposes or effects exactly the same objectification of our cognitive cheese cover that we observed for trauma and the sublime. The logical space enabling the epistemologist to discuss experience and the conditions of the possibility of experience is therefore identical with the one where the experience of trauma and the sublime may manifest themselves. It should therefore not surprise us that epistemology (or transcendental philosophy) and the sublime have a shared fate in the history of philosophy—nor that the period to which Descartes, Locke, Hume, and Kant belong has also been a culmination point in the reflection on the sublime. More generally, insofar as Arthur Danto is right to claim that each philosophy to be taken seriously must minimally be able to explain itself (which is where logical positivism so conspicuously failed[26]), we cannot doubt that the transcendental philosopher *must* be open to the notion of the sublime. All transcendental philosophy is possible only if one places oneself in a position which, if well thought out, also legitimizes the notion of the sublime. In sum, no sublimity without transcendental philosophy—and vice versa. The sublime is the Derridean "supplement," so to say, of transcendental philosophy, in the sense that it speaks "the truth" about transcendental philosophy from a perspective essentially lying beyond it;

just as, for that matter, sublime historical experience is the Derridean "supplement" of disciplinary historical writing. Second, this may also shed some new light on the relationship between the historist, the Nietzschean, and the Hegelian attitude toward the past. The very idea of a historical epistemology makes no sense at all from the historist's point of view—this was Gadamer's profoundest insight, as we observed in Chapter 5. Since for the historist the knowing subject itself was no less taken up in the stream of history than the objects in the past investigated by it, it could never acquire this transcendental position with regard to what is studied by it and what is presupposed by all epistemology. Just as in Aristotelianism, epistemology is impossible, since subject and object cannot be isolated from each other—so it is in historism as well. Small wonder, then, that the intellectual roots of historism are to be found in Aristotelianism: Whereas Aristotelianism was abandoned in seventeenth- and eighteenth-century French and English natural law philosophy, it remained relatively strong in Germany[27] and this is, mainly, why it was in Germany and not, for example, in England where historism could be developed—a fact that may also account, by the way, for the excessively high percentage of German quotes in this book. As we have seen, this was different with Nietzsche: Nietzsche took the historical subject out of the all-embracing stream of becoming where the historists had positioned it and, by doing this, returned to Enlightenment transcendentalism. However, in spite of this, Nietzsche was simply not interested in the development of a historical epistemology. He left this to hermeneuticists such as Droysen or Dilthey. Hermeneuticists opted for a kind of halfway position between the historists on the one hand and a historical epistemology on the other. Some of them, such as Dilthey, tried to move as close as possible to the epistemologists—think, for example, of Dilthey's declaration that he had attempted to do for history what Kant had done for the sciences. Others, such as Gadamer, moved in the opposite direction of historism—recall Gadamer's Heideggerian claim that a convincing account of the nature of historical understanding will require us to abandon epistemology for ontology. And this is, needless to say, once again a very Aristotelian way of looking at how we are situated in the world. It might be argued that this perennial hesitation between the incompatible extremes of historism and epistemology is the source of most of the problems that hermeneutics has become entangled in.

But Nietzsche did not care about epistemological explanations of how historical knowledge is acquired. In his attack on the intellectual bureaucracy of the historical discipline of his time, he was mainly interested in the issue of forgetting, hence in what therapy might save the German culture of his time from the overdose of historical knowledge that historians were poisoning it with. But when dealing with this question, he remained firmly within the epistemological framework: He had lifted the historical subject out of the stream of historical becoming in exactly the same way in which epistemologists always created an unbridgeable gap between the transcendental knowing subject and what it has knowledge of. Nietzsche did so by tearing historical identity loose from the stream of historical becoming. This is why he remained, in the end, vulnerable to a counterattack from his historist *bêtes noires:* Historicization is a very jealous god who usually ends up by appropriating all the territory in the possession of less competitive divinities.[28] As soon as we start to historicize, it is not easy to see where and why we should stop (if at all) and why we should exclude, for example, the transcendental knowing subject from historicization. A total historism then is the inevitable outcome, as Gadamer always liked to point out with so much satisfaction.

And this is where Hegel comes in. Hegel succeeded in combining the total historicization of the knowing subject with the possibility of a dissociation from the past, hence with Nietzsche's forgetting—and thus in transcending the opposition of epistemology and history. He performed this most remarkable feat by involving identity itself in the vicissitudes of history: Just as history may die, so a previous identity may die in cases where, paradoxically, we *are* or have become what we *are no longer.* What Hegel saw and Nietzsche did *not* was that sometimes our identity may be defined by what we are no longer, by what we have forgotten and repudiated. For Nietzsche identity and the past are as independent from each other as the diner and his dinner. We may overeat of the past, and this may cause a kind of intellectual indigestion, but precisely this indigestion can be noticed only on the basis of a sound awareness of what it is like to feel normal and healthy, hence, on the basis of an awareness of who we normally—and *a*historically—are.

8.7   THE SUBLIME DISSOCIATION OF THE PAST

The foregoing remarks on trauma and the sublime may enable us to arrive at a deeper understanding of Hegel's account of Socrates' condemnation. In the first place, there can be no doubt that the event must have meant as traumatic loss to the Athenians. If we follow Hegel's interpretation, they lost nothing less than their previous identity; they must have felt, as Victor Hugo once so forcefully put it, what a tree must feel when it is torn from its roots.[29] This can be elaborated. We saw earlier how Hegel insisted on the propensity to self-accusation of the Athenians after having condemned Socrates. They had condemned Socrates—and then immediately went on to condemn themselves as if this was a matter of course. This kind of reaction is, as Freud has argued, typical of the melancholic reaction to traumatic loss, that is, the kind of reaction which prevents one from overcoming loss (which is the "normal" or healthy way to react to loss and which Freud associates with *Trauer*). The explanation is, according to Freud, that what is criticized in the lost object is transformed into a criticism of the self:

The object cathexis proved to have little power of resistance and was brought to an end. But the free libido was not displaced on to another object; it was withdrawn into the ego. There, however, it was not employed in any unspecified way, but served to establish an *identification* of the ego with the abandoned object. Thus the shadow of the object fell upon the ego, and the latter could henceforth be judged by a special agency, as though it were an object, the forsaken object.[30]

Hence, the lost object is, *first,* pulled within the subject in order to be, *next,* repelled again as a criticized object—while it will, *last,* forever remain part of the subject in this guise. And this is, summarized in one sentence, the entire mechanism I am describing in this chapter (and, even more succinctly, encapsulated in Emily Dickinson's poem that I used as its epigraph).

In order to correctly appreciate Freud's meaning and how it may clarify the nature of Socrates' conflict with the Athenian state and this "becoming what one is no longer," a short remark is in order. The conflict between Socrates and the Athenian state was not merely the lawsuit of a state against one of its citizens who had spoiled one of its most valuable possessions. As Hegel made clear, that would be a naive view of what had happened. Socrates was not like the irresponsible child who gambled away his ancestor's inheritance. In opposition to this simplistic view, Hegel insisted that the condemnation of Socrates was the externalization of a drama that was, in fact, enacted in the mind of the Athenians themselves. They punished themselves for the traumatic loss of the abandonment of a previous world— and Socrates was merely the externalized token of this drama enacted in the Athenian's own inner life. Socrates' fate was, in the end, their own.

If seen from this perspective, Freud's comment is highly instructive. In the first place, "object cathexis" (that is, the tie with a former identity) had already become weak and had "little power of resistance"; the Athenians were already moving into a new world, or, rather into a new phase in the history of humanity. When Socrates entered upon the scene of world history, the new world was already manifest in Greek morality: They lived and acted already as Socrates required them to do. The past was a mere empty shell; but the Greeks could still see only the shell and not yet the new content that had gradually filtered into it already. So Socrates merely made conscious (that is, "subjective" in Hegel's terminology) what had come into being already (in "objective" reality). In the second place, however, this object cathexis was not yet available for projection on a new world, for such a new world had not yet come into being. Before it could take a new form, the break with the old world first had to be final and definitive. And in order to achieve this, the mechanism depicted by Freud was instrumental. Crucial here is the phase of identification mentioned by Freud: The lost object, the abandoned past, had first to be fully present to the self, that is, to the Athenians' awareness of their historical identity. Once again, Hegel acknowledges this as well, for at the end of his account he wrote:

The heart of the world must break, before its higher life and destination can truly make itself manifest. The acceptance [of a new phase in the world's history] first takes place in abstract thought: this was Socrates' achievement. But then it still had to be carried out in Mind [and this could take place only thanks to the "heartbreaking" conflict between Socrates and the Athenian state].[31] (my translation)

Hegel emphasizes here *that we can enter a new world only after having gained a complete and adequate insight into what must be given up.*[32] Transcending the past can take place only on the condition of our being able to tell the final story about what we will surrender precisely thanks to our ability to tell this story—and so it is with the overcoming of traumatic experience. And this final story can come into being, as was recognized by Friedrich Hölderlin (Hegel's close friend and discussion partner during their student days at the Tübinger Stift) only on the condition of a complete openness, of an openness respecting the inexhaustible potential of possible narrative meanings:

If the existing is to be experienced (*empfunden*) in its dissolution (*Auflösung*) and is experienced in *this* way, this dissolution is experienced in terms of the inexhausted and the inexhaustible rather than the reverse; for from nothing [i.e., the dissolution in itself] nothing can originate. . . . But the possible which makes its entry in reality by actually dissolving reality is effective and real. It effects both the experience of dissolution and the memory of what has been dissolved.[33] (my translation)

The dissolution of a previous world can give us a new one only if the test of the confrontation with the inexhaustible fullness of meaning embodied in this previous world has been abided. Put more simply, forgetting is possible only on the condition of a perfect memory (think again of the Dickinson poem). The past first has to be fully admitted to our identity, to be recognized as a world that we have left behind us, and *only then* can it be discarded and give way to a new identity. In continuation with this, Hegel had elsewhere emphasized another aspect of this transcendence of the past by historicization:

This dissolving activity of thought also inevitably gives rise to a new principle. Thought, in so far as it is universal in character, has the effect of dissolving every determinate content; but in this very dissolution, the preceding principle is in fact preserved, with the sole difference that it no longer possesses its original determination. The universal essence is preserved, but its universality as such has been brought out into relief.[34] (my translation)

Hence, not only does historical transcendence reveal the true nature of a previous period, but transcendence also is a dissolution of the previous period and, in this way, the destruction of a civilization by itself. In this sense we should agree with Hayden White when he writes in his most penetrating analysis of this aspect of Hegel's philosophy of history that "the deaths of whole civilizations are more like suicides than natural deaths."[35] The past Hegel has in mind does not simply die off like an obsolete and outmoded tradition, it does not gradually become irrelevant like a practice for which we can find no use anymore. This would be the theoretically uninteresting first type of forgetting, where the content of forgetting is restricted to the kind of thing we had for dinner last week. But from the perspective of the truly interesting fourth type of forgetting, moving to a new and different world really *is* and also *requires* an act of violence, in fact nothing less than an act of suicide—hence also the hostility that Freud recognized in our attitude to the lost object after our having internalized it and made it into a part of our own identity.

The nature of this suicidal act is, to put it into one paradoxical formula, the *association of dissociation*. In order to see this, we should in the first place recall that history and narrative are essentially associative. The historian, when accounting for the past, constructs a chain of associations resulting in what Mink called a "configurational comprehension of the past."[36] What was initially a chaos of disjointed events or of unrelated aspects of the past is now tied together into a coherent historical narrative by means of association. Association therefore gives us our mastery of the past; it is, in this respect, the counterpart in the field of historical writing to what the categories of the understanding are in Kant's theory on how experience and knowledge are possible. History essentially is the art of association. This is also why narrative can be the appropriate cure for trauma$_1$: By narrativizing a traumatic experience, by transforming it into a part of our personal history, we can hope to gain mastery of it and to rob it of its threatening features. Dissociation, obviously, does the reverse and may therefore bring us back to a traumatically experienced (historical) reality. This, then, is precisely what takes place in the repudiation of a past as envisaged by Hegel. This past must first be historicized, transformed by association into narrative understanding, before, with a subsequent gesture, it can be repudiated and thus ensured of entry into a new world—hence with a gesture that *creates* trauma$_2$ instead of *overcoming* it.

Here we will also find the explanation of the sublimity of this experience of the past in question here. As will be clear from the foregoing, the movement of dissociation not only denies the movement of narrative association, which is, to use Kantian terminology, the condition of the possibility of historical understanding, but it self-evidently also presents us with the dissociation that we found to be constitutive of the sublime. The experience of the past, as described in Hegel's account, is a movement both *within* and *against* history: it is, at the same time, the deepest and most intense experience of the past *and* a stepping outside the realm of history. Once again *directness* and *indirectness* coincide and mutually reinforce each other. And, no less obviously, the one is the condition of the possibility of the other.

We may ask, last, how this dialectics of directness and indirectness produced by trauma and the sublime arises out of normal experience. Against the background of what has been said before it is not hard to deal with this question. If the kind of cultural suicide which takes place in historical transitions (as envisaged by Hegel) have the character of the exchange of a former identity for a new one, such transitions can properly be described as seeing the former self as if it were the self of somebody else. Hence, this kind of transition presents us with the baffling situation in which it is as if somebody suddenly becomes somebody else—which would require him to see his former self as the self of some other person. What is at stake in such transitions has been brilliantly analyzed by Arthur Danto in his *Transfiguration of the Commonplace,* undoubtedly his major work. His argument, roughly, is that the *directness* of our "normal" experience will then become *indirect,* or *opaque,* because we have become a different person with a different identity. And he explains the directness of "normal" experience by pointing out that we are never aware of the framework within which we experience the world ourselves, whereas we do not hesitate to assert that how others encounter the world is always determined by such frameworks. How we represent the world to ourselves can never be part of our representations; we see the world *through* our representations of it, but not *them.* "I represent the world, not my representations of the world," as Danto puts it.[37] But we feel no reluctance at all to lock others up within their representational frameworks; we enclose them behind a "shield of representation," which is *their* way of seeing the world in a way we could not possibly do for ourselves. Our own way of seeing the world is, to ourselves, not a way of seeing the world at all, but simply how the world *is.* In this way our own representation of the world remains invisible to us—unless some nauseating experience suddenly makes us aware of the glass cheese cover through which we had always seen the world.

But this is still only half the story. Let us take a closer look at this difference between how we relate to ourselves on the one hand and to other people on the other. Danto describes the difference as follows:

I cannot say without contradiction that I believe that *s* but that *s* is false, but I can say of another person that he believes that *s* but it is false. When I refer to another man's beliefs I am referring to him, whereas he, when expressing his beliefs, is not referring to himself but to the world. The beliefs in question are transparent to the believer; he reads the world through them without reading them. But his beliefs are opaque to others: they do not read the world through these beliefs; they as it were, read the beliefs. My beliefs in this respect are invisible to me until something makes them visible and I can see them from the outside. And this usually happens when the belief itself fails to fit the way the world is, and accident has forced me from my wont objects back onto myself. Thus the structure of my beliefs is something like the structure of consciousness itself . . . , consciousness being a structure that is not an object for itself in the way the things of the world are objects for it.[38]

There is, thus, a peculiar asymmetry in how we relate to our own beliefs and to those of others. Whereas we always perceive those of others as being part of a network of their representations of the world, we think of our own beliefs as being directly related to what they are beliefs about. It is part of what it means to be a person to experience one's beliefs as being transparent with regard to the relevant parts of the world; or, as Danto suggests: "to put it with a certain dash of paradox, we do not occupy our own interiors. We live, rather, naively in the world."[39] And our tolerance of contradiction is the logical test of this difference between how we relate to our own beliefs and to those of others. Whereas we cannot say of our own beliefs that we hold them to be false, such assertions are wholly unproblematic if made by us about those of others. We consider their beliefs primarily as the components, or elements of their representation(s) of the world. And when doing so, we "bracket," so to say, the truth or falsity of their beliefs—which is something that we would never do with our own beliefs. Consequently, when beliefs are thus protected by this shield of representation, contradiction is rendered wholly harmless. Not only may we ascribe to A to believe p while p is false, but we may even ascribe to him to believe both p and *not-p*. Put differently, as soon as we observe this absence of resistance to contradiction, this is a sure sign that this shield of representation has been erected between ourselves and somebody's representation of the world.[40]

Now, this may further contribute to our understanding of the sublimity of the kind of historical experience discussed here. Suppose now that we conflate the person ascribing beliefs and the person to whom beliefs are ascribed into one and the same person—so that this shield of representation is no longer situated *between two different persons* but taken up into one and the same person—for example, in the sense that one of the two persons conflated into one is the person A at a *certain* time, whereas the other is this same person A at some *later* time. More specifically, think of what happens when a person, for whatever reason, suddenly comes to look at his or her former self as if this were *another* person. This would give us a situation that is in agreement with the relevant facts about the sublime, for, as we have seen, the sublime is an experience of the world so shattering that "normal" patterns of experience are disrupted—as becomes clear from the fact that sublime experience confronts us with contradictions, oppositions, or paradoxes that are utterly unthinkable within these "normal" patterns of experience. And this is precisely what becomes a possibility if we erect the shield of representation in ourselves, or, rather between the person we are now and the one we were before. We have then made room in ourselves for the epistemological paradoxes that are the defining characteristic of the sublime.

But in the context of the present discussion we had better turn this around. I mean, we should not begin by considering how the erection of this shield of representation may create in us a susceptibility to sublime experience. We should focus, rather, on the way sublime experience may invite or even necessitate us to erect this shield of representation between a former self and the later self that we have become after and because of our having had a sublime experience. Sublime experience is then the kind of experience inviting or necessitating us to discard or to dissociate a former self from the self that we are after having had the sublime experience in question. Sublime experience then is the kind of experience forcing us to abandon the position in which we still coincide with ourselves and to exchange this for a position where we relate to ourselves in the most literal sense of the word, hence, as if we were *two* persons instead of just *one*. This, then, is how identity, (traumatic) dissociation, and the epistemological paradoxes of sublime experience all hang together.

The crucial question is, then, what happens when we begin to objectify a former self, as if we had suddenly become an outsider to our own (former) self. Now, in order to avoid the dangers of a priori speculation, we had best take our point of departure in a description of what goes on under such circumstances. For that purpose, let us consider the following passage from John Banville's novel *Eclipse:*

It was morning, and the housewives were out, with their shopping bags and headscarves. A questing dog trotted busily past me looking neither to right nor left, following a straight line drawn invisibly on the pavement. The open doorway of a hardware shop breathed brownly at me as I went past. . . . Taking in all this, I experienced something to which the only name I could give was happiness; although it was not happiness, it was more and less than happiness. What had occurred? What in that commonplace scene before me, the ordinary sights and sounds and smells of the town, had made this unexpected thing, whatever it was, burgeon suddenly inside me like the possibility of an answer to all the nameless yearnings of my life? Everything was the same now as it had been before, the housewives, that busy dog, the same and yet in some way transfigured. Along with the happiness went a feeling of anxiety. It was as if I were carrying some frail vessel that it was my task to protect, like the boy in the story told us in religious class who carried the Host through the licentious streets of ancient Rome hidden inside his tunic;

in my case, however, it seemed I was myself the precious vessel. Yes, that was it, it was *I* that was happening here.[41]

The similarities between the experience related in this passage and what Danto had in mind in the passage I quoted a moment ago will be obvious. In both cases the contact that we have with the normal "commonplaces" of daily reality is suddenly "transfigured" (to adopt the terminology which is, strikingly enough, used by both Danto and Banville) into an experience of the self, of a certain mood, being the paradoxical mix of pleasure or happiness and fear or anxiety that is traditionally associated with the experience of the sublime.[42] In both cases nothing in external reality is changed — "Everything was the same as it had been before" — and yet, as Danto puts it in a closely related context, "in whatever small degree a revolution in (historical) reality" [43] is achieved. Furthermore, in both cases this transfiguration of the commonplace results in a blurring of the distinction between subject and object, between ourselves and the world. We are forced, as Danto put it, "from our wont objects back onto ourselves." This is so because the directness between our beliefs and the world is interrupted by our sudden awareness of our own (schema of) representations, so that we momentarily experience ourselves as just one more object in the world.

Or, as Banville sums up the enigma of the experience, it is *myself* that is happening. And there is an important suggestion in this strange locution, for what takes place when I say "I am happening" instead of the regular "something happens"? The locution makes sense only if it is taken to express that "I" have included myself in the world of things, so that I can not only correctly say that something has happened to me but also use the phrase "I am happening" for describing the peculiar nature of my experience. Hence, if we were to metaphorically attribute a movement to the kind of experience in question, it would be a movement *toward* the world, not *away* from it — as the fact that we objectify now our beliefs might (mistakenly) make us believe. These beliefs (and the *me* that they embody) is now part of the world. As a result, I am, as in Danto's description of the experience, both *inside* and *outside* the world. Or, to use the terminology that he proposed elsewhere, the nothingness (this "*rien*") between language (representation) and the world (the represented) is eliminated, so that the self temporarily shares with the world a quasi-noumenal status (as, once again, typically is the case in the experience of the sublime). So what is at stake is, essentially, a fusion of the world and the self: "It involves, rather, the *transformation* of a whole *body* of facts, a simultaneous transformation of oneself and of the world."[44] The awareness of this unusual congeniality with the objects of the world, the awareness of a momentary quasi-mystic union with the world of objects in which they lose their strangeness, must come to us like a revelation. Hence, Banville's suggestion that the experience seems to give "the possibility of an answer to all the nameless yearnings of my life."

Undoubtedly, this is having an experience in the most dramatic sense of the word. Ordinarily, either experiences change our conceptions of the world (as most typically is the case with the scientific experiment) or they change ourselves while leaving these conceptions unaltered (think of a traumatic experience), but here the objectivist and the subjectivist aspects of experience go together and strangely reinforce each other. And, more specifically, this is *not* so because the objectivist dimension of the experience causes its subjectivist counterpart to happen. For example, the traumatic experience of the concentration camps may have caused many of its survivors to have a low opinion of human nature, or a happy mood may cause us to be more susceptible to the more attractive aspects of the *condition humaine*. Rather, both are two sides of the same coin: As Banville's phrase "it was *I* that was happening here" suggests, it is in the experience of what happens in the *world* that a different *self* comes into being. One is reminded here of the crucial single scientific experiment that is so categorically ruled out by the Duhem–Quine thesis, that is, the experiment that would require us to abandon a whole system of scientific beliefs in favor of a new system. The example is illustrative because of its suggestion that one aspect of the world could affect the whole of a scientific world picture, involving both ourselves as cognitive subjects and the world as the source of our experiences.

In sum, it is the kind of experience which involves our identity in the sense that the experience makes us look at ourselves from the perspective of the outsider; we look at ourselves as if we were looking at *somebody else*. Put differently, we suddenly become aware of a *previous* identity of ourselves, of the kind of person that we had been up to now and had never realized that we were, and *this* we can do only thanks to our having acquired a *new* identity. This new identity announces itself in the Banville passage in the feeling of happiness accompanying the "transfiguration of the commonplace," which suggests an answer to all kinds of questions that never

had or never could have been asked. And Danto explains this sudden revelation of a previous, unknown self as follows:

In Sartre's beautiful ontology, there is a moment when the pour soi, as he terms it,
which up till then had been invisible to itself, a pure nothingness, becomes
abruptly an object for itself, at which stage it enters a new stage of being. Less cli-
mactically, there is a stage in the history of each of us when we become objects for
ourselves, when we realize we have an identity to inquire into: when we see ourselves rather than merely see the world. But we also recognize that becoming conscious of ourselves as objects is not like becoming conscious of just another object:
it is a new kind of object, a whole new set of relationships, and indeed all the old
relationships and objects are redefined.[45]

Nothing has changed; everything is "indiscernibly" the same that it had always been.[46] Yet a shift in our level of representation has taken place; we
objectified our previous representations and, by doing so, became aware of
our previous identity—a previous identity that could take on its opacity
only from the perspective of a new identity, which, in its turn, is invisible
to us because of its essential transparency. Identity is like our shadow: always outside our grasp and never coinciding with ourselves. That is its supreme paradox, although in the kind of experience as described by Danto
and Banville we may come infinitesimally close to it. At such moments we
almost *see* it, as it were, jump away from us in the shape of a previous identity. And at such moments it must be to us as if we were moving faster than
time itself, for is there then not a suggestion of seeing *together* what is always *separated* within time itself? And, finally, is being faster than time not
a way of saying that we are outside time itself?

8.8 TRAUMA, SUBLIMITY, AND THE EMERGENCE
OF WESTERN HISTORICAL CONSCIOUSNESS

In the last two sections of this chapter I wish to investigate what our
insight into the nature of the historical sublime and of the sublime dissociation of the past may teach us about (Western) historical consciousness.
When dealing with this question we will naturally focus on those aspects
of the Western past that may have provoked a collective trauma. We have
seen that trauma is the psychological counterpart of the sublime and that
the sublime, in its turn, is the philosophical counterpart of trauma. Now,
collective trauma has recently been discussed by historical theorists, most

notably by Dominick LaCapra. For a correct interpretation of the following it is, therefore, of importance to define where my own position with regard to trauma and the sublime differs from these existing debates about trauma. For LaCapra the subject of trauma is still individual people, although these people may experience trauma collectively, as was the case in the Holocaust that is the main focus of his interest.[47] In my approach, however, Western civilization itself is the subject of trauma; my question is how Western civilization, *as such,* dealt with its greatest crises when it experienced the traumatizing loss of an old world because one was forced to enter a new one. And there is no evidence, as yet, that the Holocaust has been such a traumatic experience in *this* sense—presumably (as we shall see in a moment) because the perpetrators of this unprecedented crime were vanquished in World War II and because their actions did and could not become part of our collective future. This is where the Holocaust most conspicuously differs from crises such as the Renaissance's rupture with the Medieval past or the tragedy of the French Revolution.

The drama of these crises was the fact that the traumatic event could *not* be discarded, could *not* be neutralized by refusing to let it become part of the traumatized subject's present and future identity (in the way that our present civilization could not possibly conceive of the Holocaust as a part of our postwar identity). One knew that "one had to become what one was no longer" and that in this way the past had to be accepted as part of the present. For example, we saw in Chapter 4 that nineteenth-century conservatives were very well aware that the reactionary Metternich-like rejection of the French Revolution would be most unwise and that one should recognize that this, to them, so very ugly and traumatic past had to be accepted as part of the modern moral world. And their trauma—in the sense of trauma$_2$, as I hasten to emphasize—was precisely their recognition that they had to accept what they so much abhorred (Tocqueville's reaction to the French Revolution and to the ensuing birth of "democracy" being the finest example of this[48]). But this is completely different with the Holocaust. What Hitler and his henchmen left to posterity is something that should be avoided forever and ever and that could under no circumstances be a legitimate part of our present and our future. So there is occasion for sadness, desperation, and moral outrage about the unspeakable crimes that were committed by the Nazis—but there is *no* occasion here for a collective trauma. Put provocatively, it would even be a moral infamy if the Holocaust would have unleashed a historical trauma, as I understand this notion, for this would suggest that we had accepted Hitler's legacy somehow.[49]

But I expect that theorists like LaCapra will see this argument as a *reductio ad absurdum;* surely, as they will wish to point out, something *must* simply be wrong with any argument denying the Holocaust the dimension of a collective trauma. If the industrial murder of six million Jews, if this genocide on a hitherto unprecedented scale, if the terrors and the horrors of the concentration camps did not stimulate in us a collective trauma, what else can this be than a sign of our collective moral depravity in general and of people, like me, saying that this is how it ought to be? When attempting to justify myself against this accusation, I wish to emphasize that there is not, as we would have expected, a direct correspondence between the horrors undergone by a human society and its propensity to trauma. One need only look at the relevant facts here: Think of the abject fate of the Aztecs or of the American Indians or of the unspeakable horrors that Mongol rule inflicted on Central Asia, which left no traces in written history; and, when turning to Western history, think of the dissolution of the Roman Empire and the West's return to the chaos and barbarism of the second half of the first millennium, think of the Black Death of 1348 that killed one-third of the European population and instilled an intense feeling of fear, despair, and desolation in the mind of the West for almost two centuries—as has so brilliantly been shown by Delumeau in his *La peur en Occident.* Now, what were the tragedies of sixteenth-century Italy and the French Revolution compared to disasters of this scale? What amount of mass slaughter, of plunder, of killing of innocent people, of violation of women, and so on did these events, terrible though they undoubtedly were, in the end involve? So, if seen from the chilling perspective of what proportions human suffering sometimes took in human history, what were these two events, in fact, but mere ripples on the fate of mankind? Far worse had happened before and, alas, would happen again in the West's history.

Yet, compare the curiously dispassionate accounts that, for example, a Gregory of Tours or a Froissart gave of the history of their own appalling world to the harassed and tormented historical writing of a Guicciardini, of a Machiavelli, or of all those nineteenth-century French and German historians desperately wrestling with the legacy of the French Revolution. And we can only be amazed by the huge discrepancy. Apparently relatively minor collective disasters may, under certain circumstances, prove to be a stronger stimulus of historical consciousness than the worst that humanity has had to undergo in the course of its history. One may wonder about how to explain that tragedy, horror, and human suffering on an unprecedented scale so often tended to fade quietly away in the mists of time, whereas in the West relatively minor historical disasters could suddenly be experienced as the kind of trauma from which Western historical consciousness originated. So why and how did this unique capacity for collective trauma come into being in the West?

When answering this question, we should recognize, then, that the susceptibility to collective trauma should not be explained by considering the quantity of "collective pain" that was inflicted on a civilization or even by the intensity of this pain, for even outright unendurable collective pain only rarely results in collective trauma and in the creation of (a new) historical consciousness. I believe that the explanation is, rather, that in the West a shift may be observed from collective pain to an *awareness* of this pain and that this is how this peculiar Western capacity for suffering collective trauma came into being. I hasten to add the following in order to avoid misunderstanding. When thus emphasizing the significance of the awareness of pain, I do certainly not intend to attack the commonsense and unexceptional view that one cannot be in pain without an awareness of this pain. Certainly, one cannot be in pain without knowing that one is in pain; certainly, I do not want to argue that the Aztecs or, for that matter, fifteenth-century Europeans were singularly unaware of their sufferings and stolidly underwent their historical fate in the way that a rock may tumble down from a mountain.

Actually, what I wish to say is rather the reverse. That is, what is typical of trauma is precisely an *in*capacity to suffer or to assimilate the traumatic experience into one's life history. What comes into being with trauma is not so much an openness to suffering but a certain *numbness*—a certain insensitivity as if the receptacles for suffering have become inadequate to the true nature and the proportions of suffering. In this way a dissociation has come into existence between suffering itself and the *awareness* of this suffering; although the two *always* and inevitably go together, it is here as if, when being in pain, I experience my pain as being a mere, although absolutely reliable, *sign* that someone (that is, myself) is in pain, while not actually feeling the pain itself. While being in pain myself, I now feel tempted, so to speak, to look at myself from a point of view that no longer or at least no longer automatically coincides with myself as the person who *is* in pain. I feel my pain as if it were someone else's pain. The shield of representation mentioned earlier had been erected between the subject suffering from pain and the subject being aware of this.

We have seen that Janet used the term "dissociation" for referring to this numbness to one's own (psychic) pain and the derealization and depersonalization that may result from it. This may help us to come to a better understanding of how civilizations may react to collective trauma. When contrasting depersonalization and derealization to compulsion neurosis, Meyer writes:

> Finally, the disorder in the relationship between self and world can also manifest itself in the form of a splitting of the self (into an observing and an experiencing instance): "a second self is formed. I then see myself as when I am saying: I can still see myself at the time when . . . ." Part of the self is here "exterritorialized" so to speak, it becomes part of the outer world. . . . We see what is shared by depersonalization and by derealization in this isolation of the self, in this thwarting of its communication with the outer world, in its isolation from the world. This becomes clear if one compares the depersonalization syndrome with the compulsion syndrome. What both share is the recognition of the morbidity, the nonsensical and the contradictory of their experience; both are illnesses of reflection, maladies de doute. . . . The compulsion neurotic suffers from his being extradited to the world, from his being "possessed" by the world; whereas depersonalization—as a being separated from the world—stimulates a yearning for reality, for a contact with the world.[50] (my translation)

Following Meyer, one might say that ordinarily collective suffering was undergone in the mood of compulsion neurosis, perhaps precisely because suffering abundantly made clear to what extent one is "handed over" (to use Meyer's terminology) to forces beyond our control. So a will-less surrendering to our collective fate, an abandonment of oneself to the course of History is, in all likelihood, our natural reaction if confronted with the great tragedies of History, although it must immediately be admitted that this is a formulation of the issue that civilizations, having this kind of reaction to their worst disasters, could not themselves be capable of. They are too much immersed in the past, and in history, to be able to achieve the position of autonomy with regard to history that is presupposed in (the possibility) of this description of their predicament. In a way, there is no

History, no past for them, in much the same way that the fish may not know it is living in water until it becomes the fisher's victim.

And this is different with derealization and depersonalization. As Meyer observes, if one feels separated from the world—because of the derealization that is, for example, effected by trauma—we will have a yearning (*sehnen*) for dissociated reality. Here suffering, trauma, has produced a dissociation from the disasters and the tragedies of history; it has compelled the most sensitive minds of the time to proceed to a position from which the past can be objectified. And it is with this movement that the past, as such, comes into being, that is, as an object requiring reflection and even the most strenuous effort of historical understanding. The somewhat unnerving (and Schopenhauerian) implication is that there is a necessary link between historical consciousness and historical writing on the one hand and the worst disasters that may befall humanity on the other. Whereas happiness, success, and social perfection, although being an indubitable aspect of social life as well, do *sui generis* not belong to the substance of history, here one can express only one's agreement with Montesquieu's and Hegel's well-known observation that the happy days of mankind are *eo ipso* the empty pages in the book of history.

Thus, what Kant in his *Der Streit der Fakultäten* (1798) referred to as the "moral terrorist" and the "eudaemonist" conceptions of the past, should not be placed next to each other at an equal level: (psycho-)logically the former really precedes the latter. The past is essentially and primarily a painful, if not traumatic past; and histories rejoicing in, for example, the triumphs of monarchs, soldiers, and heroes will never be able to give us that essence. The great deeds of a nation, of a social class, or of a civilization give it much less of a historically defined coherence and identity than trauma and suffering can achieve, at least if certain circumstances are satisfied; this is probably an explanation of why the victims of history may—once again, under certain and surely not all circumstances—discover in history a far more powerful ally than their victors will ever be able to do. Here Thierry, Michelet, and the Marxists were surely right, with regard to the bourgeoisie, *le peuple,* and the industrial proletariat, respectively, when they showed that their past sufferings had been the condition of the so prominent role they would later play in the history of mankind. History, truly is a "dismal science."

I shall clarify in the remainder of this section these remarks by

focusing on how modern Western historical consciousness came into being in sixteenth-century Italy and how it announced itself for the first time
in the historical writings of Machiavelli and Guicciardini—undoubtedly
the most important historians of that time. Their relationship to their past
was determined by how they experienced the events that had been decisive
for Italy's history since 1494. As the reader may recall, this year marked an
end to the Italy of the Renaissance, to the world of Lorenzo il Magnifico,
to peace, order, and the undisturbed pursuit of knowledge and artistic perfection that we so much associate with the Italian Renaissance. In that year
the Duke of Milan, Lodovico il Moro, fearing for his own position as the
all too obvious usurper of his nephew Giovan Galeazzo's legitimate rights,
succeeded in convincing the French King Charles VIII to invade Italy. Listen to Guicciardini's own bitter comment on this so fateful event, match-
ing in eloquence Hegel when the latter expounded the world-historical
tragedy of Socrates' condemnation by the Athenian state:

For, as it often happens that decisions are taken through fear seem unequal to the
danger to those who fear, Lodovico was not sure that he had found adequate support for his security. . . . He forgot how dangerous it may be to use a medicine
more powerful than the nature of the disease and the constitution of the patient
warranted. As though embarking on greater risks was the sole remedy to present
dangers, he decided, in order to ensure his own security with foreign arms to
do everything he could to persuade Charles VIII King of France to attack the
kingdom of Naples, to which he laid claim through the ancient rights of the
Angevins. . . . The King entered Asti on September 9, 1494, bringing with him into
Italy the seeds of innumerable disasters, terrible events and change in almost everything. His invasion was not only the origin of changes of government, subversions
of Kingdoms, devastation of the countryside, slaughter of cities, cruel murders,
but also of new habits, new customs, new and bloody methods of warfare, diseases
unknown till that day; and the instruments of peace and harmony in Italy were
thrown into such confusion that they have never since then been reconstituted, so
that other nations and barbarian armies have been able to devastate and trample
wretchedly upon her.[51]

Both Machiavelli and Guicciardini saw the devastation of their country;
they were fully aware of its complete helplessness against powers such as
France, Spain, or the German emperor Charles V. But before all they realized that the terrors now beseeching their country were not merely the
whim of blind fate, or of the goddess Fortuna, as they would have put it
themselves, but the result of shortsighted and irresponsible political action.

And they also knew that all this meant the entry into a new world, a world in which these strange and barbarian powers from north of the Alps, such as France and Austria, would determine Europe's fate, hence a world where Italy and all that had been Italy's grandeur in the age of Lorenzo il Magnifico would be wholly irrelevant. They knew that they had entered a new stage in history in which the youthful splendor of the Florentine Renaissance could only be a memory and that what had so cruelly been transformed from actual reality into mere memory would be their present and future identity. And they knew all this better than anyone else, better even than the monarchs ruling these terrible new political powers embodying a new political dispensation, since they were most intensely aware of the fact that *they* had been victimized by this transition from a glorious past to a dismal present. To victims a profundity of insight is given that victors are never capable of.[52] History had chosen *them* to make its terrible powers apparent, *their* personal fate was an emblem of the course of world-history— and they felt all the drama of it with an almost existentialist intensity.

This is especially true of Guicciardini. In his service as Clemens VII's main adviser he had recommended to this most irresolute Medici pope risking a conflict with Charles V—and it was therefore *his* advice that had made possible the sacking of Rome in 1527 and the destruction, plundering, and burning down of the city that he loved more than his own life. The proud and arrogant Florentine patrician, so confident about his own supreme political wisdom, feared and considered with awe by all his entourage, had to recognize that he had harmed Italy no less fatally than Lodovico had done a generation before. This filled his mind with an unendurable pain, remorse, and an intense awareness of the tragedy of history.

Hence the close link between the emergence of historical consciousness on the one hand and the dimension of the unintended consequences of human action. Nothing had been wrong with the intentions of Lodovico and of Guicciardini: They had done what had seemed to be the wisest and most sensible thing to do under the circumstances obtaining then. And yet their actions resulted in the destruction of all that was essential and a life necessity to them. We should recognize that this truly is the heart of modern historical consciousness, of how we relate to our past and why we want to know about it. Modern historical consciousness arises from the experience of this discrepancy between the perspective of the past and that of the present. The past can become a suitable and legitimate object of historical research only if it is seen as essentially different from the present: For whomever this difference is a delusion, the writing of history is like the search for truth in dreams. And it is the recognition of the discrepancy of our intentions (the past's perspective) and their unintended consequences (visible only from the perspective of the present) that drove past and present apart from each other. But this recognition should not be seen as if now something had been discovered that had, in fact, always been there in the way that one may discover a new island in a distant sea. It has its origins in this movement of derealization that we discussed a moment ago: A traumatizing event (past) had been dissociated from our experience of the world and then become the tantalizing object of historical understanding—tantalizing since we will never be able to reestablish contact with it. The desire of knowing will never fulfill the desire of being. In this way the past is a product of the mind having no ultimate basis in "objective" reality.

In sum, Machiavelli's and Guicciardini's experience of the past was traumatic in the true sense of the word in that the pain occasioned by the loss of it was too great for them to permit assimilation in their own minds. A dissociation of the past thus came into being and with this the past itself as a potential object of investigation. At the same time, the nature of this past came to be defined in terms of the discrepancy between intentions and their consequences. And the gap thus created between past and present was as unbridgeable as that between the desire of being and that of knowledge, although the effort to bridge the gap would, from then on, be as permanent as the writing of history itself. More generally, in Western civilization collective suffering took on the features of a reality that continuously is most painfully present to us but that we are, at the same time, unable to assimilate in ourselves: Suffering became strangely and unnaturally abstract, something that is to be explained (historically) but that is not experienced primarily or, at least, not completely exhausted in or by the *experience* of suffering itself. It became an occasion for thought, much in the same way that both Hegel and Freud argued that what distinguishes human beings from animals is that thought places itself between desire and the satisfaction of desire in the case of human beings, whereas animals always look for an immediate satisfaction of their desires. Collective suffering became a part of culture, something that could be expressed in the idiom of that culture, something that one could talk and write about. And in this "hollow" between suffering and the language used for speaking about it a new kind of discourse gradually and gropingly came into being—that is, historical writing—having as its goal to relate this talking and writing about suffering to suffering itself. Historical writing, discourse, and historical consciousness *mediate* between trauma and suffering themselves on the one hand and the objectification of trauma and suffering that is so much characteristic of Western civilization on the other. The historian's language originates in this "logical space" between traumatic experience and a language that still had a primordial immediacy and directness in its relationship to the world—and then, in a gesture of insight into itself, pushes itself aside as being forever inadequate to the task. Historical language is the always defective prophylaxis against the sublime discrepancy between the desire of being and that of our knowledge of the past. It is, essentially, an account of the experiences of rupture with all "the worlds we have lost" in the course of time and of the terrible tragedies occasioning these sublime experiences. Proust marvelously summarized the mechanism as follows:

Ideas are produced by pains; at the moment when they change into ideas, they lose part of their harmful effect on our heart, and yet, initially, the transformation itself suddenly generates a feeling of joy. The succession can be found only in the order of time, for that matter, for it may seem that the idea is prior, whereas the pain manifests itself only after the idea has entered our mind. But there are different families of these ideas—and some of them are joys right from the start.[53] (my translation)

"Ideas" are produced by pains, and the transformation of pain into idea provokes a sentiment of pleasure because of the sense of mastery involved in the transition.

Obviously, one might now take one step further backward and ask oneself how to explain Guicciardini's unprecedented susceptibility to the unintended consequences of his actions. Why did his awareness of what he had done to his country fill his mind with an unbearable and traumatic pain, whereas, for example, less than a century before Philip the Good of Burgundy looked with complete equanimity at the destruction wrought on France because of his self-serving alliance with the England of the Hundred Years War? This insensibility is unsurpassably expressed by Shakespeare in the accusatory words that La Pucelle of Orleans leveled against Philip:

Look on thy country, look on fertile France,
And see the cities and the towns defac'd
By wasting ruin of the cruel foe!
As looks the mother on her lovely babe

When death doth close his tender dying eyes,
See, see the pining malady of France;
Behold the wounds, the most unnatural wounds
Which thou thyself hast given her woeful breast!
(*King Henry VI,* part I, scene III)

I am well aware that asking this question will remove me from the realm of solid argument to that of reckless speculation. Nevertheless, I hazard the following contention. It might well be that for Philip the Good sociopolitical reality would remain fundamentally the God-willed order that it had always been, regardless of the nature of his actions. That is to say, he may have believed that his actions touched upon merely the surface of sociopolitical reality and would be incapable of stirring its depth—supposing that the distinction between its surface and depth would have made any sense to him at all. Put differently, he did not yet have the notion of political action in the real, modern sense of that word, that is, of the kind of public action that truly "makes a difference" to what the world is or will be like. Certainly, that does not in the least imply that he would be incapable of feeling any responsibility for what he did or did not do; but the crucial datum is here that this responsibility regarded only his *own* person and how that person might be seen by the eyes of God. And this was different for Guicciardini, for the responsibility that Guicciardini felt was a responsibility to *the world* (or to Italy) rather than to *God.* This is where Guicciardini had left behind him the medieval conception of the relationship between man and the world and entered the social world in which we still live. This is also where the Renaissance demarcates our own modern identity from that of the Middle Ages and where the loss of the latter identity still resonates in our own in agreement with the mechanism analyzed throughout this chapter. As Stephen Greenblatt (who sometimes comes remarkably close to the discourse of experience proposed in this book) once formulated it:

We sense too that we are situated at the close of the cultural movement initiated in the Renaissance and that the places in which our social and psychological world seems to be cracking apart are those structural joints visible when it was first constructed. In the midst of the anxieties and contradictions attendant upon the threatened collapse of this phase of our own civilization, we respond with passionate curiosity to the anxieties and contradictions attendant upon its rise. To experience Renaissance culture is to feel what it is like to form our own identity, and we are at once more rooted and more estranged by the experience.[54]

But perhaps we should not stop here. It might be helpful to rephrase the contrast between Philip the Good and Guicciardini into the terms of Ruth Benedict's well-known opposition between "shame cultures" and "guilt cultures." Following this lead, one might say that in a certain sense Philip the Good could feel *ashamed* only of himself because he would have somehow messed up his own life; but even if he had done so in his own eyes, the consequences of his actions could, within his conception of the world, never have any real impact on the order that had been willed by God. He could feel responsible only toward himself and for his own salvation. Precisely because he was so much part of reality, so completely submerged in it, so much surrounded by reality on all sides—precisely because of the complete osmosis between himself and reality, a responsibility toward himself was the maximum he could possibly be expected to feel. To feel *guilty,* to feel responsible toward the world, would have been to him a presumptuous and preposterous blasphemy. That would have been as if an ant would have believed itself capable of having caused the death of a whole civilization. And in that sense he could not properly be said to be "guilty" of what he had done, for shame is a private feeling, whereas guilt always has to do with a debt that we owe to the world. So what happened, somewhere between Philip the Good and Guicciardini, is that the individual withdrew from the world (in which Philip the Good still felt immersed to such an extent that he could never isolate his own actions from it) and became enthralled by the idea that, from this vantage point outside reality, we can do things to reality that truly may make "a difference to it" and that may fundamentally alter it.

The paradox is, therefore, that it was a *withdrawal* and not a further *immersion* in it that made modern post-Renaissance Western man exchange shame for guilt and that transformed a fixation on the responsibility for one's own salvation into that for the (historical) world. I would not have hazarded this risky contention if it did not find some additional support in what happened in our relationship to natural reality and in the origins that the sciences have in the same period that witnessed, in the writings of Guicciardini and his Italian contemporaries, the birth of modern historical consciousness. From this vantage point we cannot fail to be struck by what the historical and the scientific revolution have in common. As we have seen in Chapters 1 and 2, the scientific revolution was possible only thanks to the creation of the scientistic, transcendental ego whose philosophical properties were so eagerly investigated by Descartes, Kant, and so many others down to the present day. And, this transcendental ego was, just like historical consciousness, the product and result of a movement of *anachoorèsis,* of a withdrawal of the self from the world itself within an inner cognitive sanctuary which decides about the reliability of the data of experience.[55] Quite revealing here is the *bene vixit, bene qui latuit* ("he has lived well, who knew how to hide himself well") that Descartes took as his device: Scientific truth will never be given to man as long as he fully participates in all the complexities of daily life. Science requires distance, not immersion and participation. The mastery of both the historical and the physical world is, therefore, the miracle wrought by a *reculer pour mieux sauter:* only after having left (historical and physical reality) itself and after having situated itself at an Archimedean vantage point outside reality itself—only after having adopted this paradoxical strategy—could the Western mind gain an ascendancy over historical and natural reality that it had never possessed before. And it is only in this way that what we have come to see as "history" and "science" in the West became possible. So, in this way Guicciardini anticipated the world that would come into being one century later with the scientific revolution and the great philosophers reflecting on this revolution.

I want to add one last remark to this discovery of modern Western historical consciousness. We must not be mistaken about the nature of this discovery. It has, in fact, not been a major event in the West's history impossible to overlook; it has not been something like a war, a revolution, the birth of a new religion, or the discovery of a new and effective weapon. In fact, historical reality as such was not in the least affected by it; it was not even a change in historical reality itself. Rather, it was a change in how Western man decided to *look* at historical reality; it is a change in perspective, while everything that it is a perspective *on* remained the way that it had always been. Yet, these small and immaterial changes may become irreversible and determine the future fate of humanity. They are like a mutation: Somewhere in the union of the genes of one specific animal of a specific genus something may mutate on a microscopic scale, and yet this microscopic event may result in a new phase in the history of evolution and in a new regime between the victims and the victors in this world. And so it has been with the rise of Western historical consciousness. In the minds of authors like Machiavelli and Guicciardini the fate of Italy after 1494 was experienced as an irretrievable, irreparable, and traumatic loss that caused in them an unendurable pain, the deepest regret, feelings of the profoundest guilt, and the cruelest self-reproach. Nevertheless, it was this historically microscopic event, this mutation that would change the face of Western civilization and, by the logic proper to all mutations, several centuries later, of non-Western civilizations as well.

8.9 MYTH AND THE HISTORICAL SUBLIME

There is one last dimension to historical consciousness as it developed in the West that needs our attention and with which I shall conclude this book on historical experience. I must remind the reader in this context of what was said in Chapter 4 about the fascination of Goethe, Burckhardt, and Nietzsche for the unchangeable, for what transcends or precedes all historical change—a fascination that was possible only after all that one could historicize had been historicized. An ahistorical nature thus entered the scene, but it was ahistorical in the sense that it was a movement against history *presupposing* history, and in this way, history was therefore still retained. This is what we ordinarily associate with myth: the mythical past preceding the unsparing storms of historical change when everything was still true to its God-willed nature and before historical change estranged us from the world's timeless essence. So myth must be the last milestone along the long trajectory of historical experience—and to this we shall now turn.

Victor Turner defines myth as follows: "Myths treat of origins but derive from transitions."[56] So surely an important boundary is typically transgressed in myth—as will be the case with all transitions. But the transgression of this boundary is dramatized by myth into a dissociation between pre-historical and historical time. The story of a move from one phase to another—which is the nature of all stories about transitions—is now dramatized into a story of the *birth of time itself.* And with this dramatization all that should be associated with what preceded the transition has been removed outside historical time. It has become part of pre- or ahistorical *nature.* A previously historical development is transformed and immeasurably enlarged into the transition from nature to history. Turner's examples are illustrative, for after the passage I quoted a moment ago, he goes on to write:

Myth relates how one state of affairs became another: how an unpeopled world became populated; how chaos became cosmos; how immortals became mortal; how the seasons came to replace a climate without seasons, how the original unity of mankind became a plurality of tribes or nations; how androgynous beings became men and women, and so on. Myths are *liminal* phenomena; they are frequently told at a time or in a site that is "betwixt and between." [57]

As will be clear from Turner's examples, myths separate a pre-historical world of a perennial and quasi-natural stability from the world of change that we presently live in. So when myths are liminal phenomena, they most typically focus on the boundary separating time from what preceded time. They are no less stories of loss, for they tell us about a quasi-natural paradisiacal past that has been taken away from us with the birth of time. And it would be hard to exaggerate the magnitude of this loss: From a world of perfection and stability we stumbled into the world of history, hence of imperfection and of inevitable decay, of mortality, of death, and of the futility of all human effort. All that had made life worth living had been taken away from us. On the collective scale, for example, for a civilization, this must be the equivalent of what the birth trauma is for the human individual: Here we are really thrown out of the womb of nature into the bleak and hostile world of historical time. Next, from our side of this all-decisive divide we necessarily cannot recall its mythical prehistory: The strange and almost unthinkable story of the myth (who could maintain that he or she really *understands* myth?) is therefore required to inform us about it. Without this story there is absolutely nothing in our contemporary predicament and there is *no* fact about our present dispensation that could possibly remind us of this mythical past. So the mythical past is necessarily a past that has left no traces in our contemporary reality, hence a past that we have wholly "forgotten about" and that is "dissociated" from our present historical world.

Furthermore, never in the life of a civilization does the storm of historicization and narrativization blow stronger then when it passes from its mythical phase into historical time. Think of the Benjamin quote that I used as the epigraph for this chapter. Not only can a mythical narrative history be told about this transition, but, even more so, this story of all stories is also a story about the origin of time itself. In this sense myth is the condition of the possibility of all history and of all historical narrative. In sum, myth confronts us with a past that is completely dissociated from the present, informing us about our pristine identity, an identity that we do not recall and that is yet to be linked to the fiercest storm of historicization or narrativization that we can find in a civilization's history.

And so it is with the historical sublime, as exemplified by Hegel's account of the condemnation of Socrates. The historical sublime is also a liminal phenomenon demarcating the phase of the subjective mind from that of the objective mind. And, as with myth, our crossing of this liminal threshold from the former to the latter is accompanied by a true storm of historicization or narrativization. History then becomes an almost tangible reality: One really feels that from now on one belongs to a different world and that a former part of ourselves has died off and become a lifeless and empty shell. One is reminded in this context of the image of an open bottle while a powerful stream of air is blown across the opening. The stream of air may then suck away all the air in the bottle and create a vacuum there. In a similar way the intense historicization and narrativization taking place at the occasion of a sublime historical event may completely dissolve the historical identity of a previous period and replace it with a new one. And this dissolution of a previous identity may be so complete that there really is nothing to be remembered for those living in a later period; their former identity has been completely dissociated from their own present identity. Or, rather, their own identity has emerged from the death of the former. In this way an emptiness, a historical hole so to say, came to the place occupied by the previous identity; and it is only this storm of historicization and of narrativization that may remind one of its once having been there. The desire of knowledge replaced the desire of being.

Paradoxically, then, we may observe here the concurrence of an extreme of historicization with an event whose historicity was wholly sublimated and that has thus been made to return to the domain of natural and ahistorical phenomena. It is, from this perspective, most appropriate that Hegel should locate his historical sublime at the transition from the phase of the *objective* mind to that of the *subjective* mind, for in the former humanity still dwelled in a state of nature: Self-reflection and, thus, all of history[58] still had to come into being. And it is no less revealing that at the heart of myth—beyond the origin which is, as Turner emphasizes, in fact a moment of transition—we will always find a quasi-natural and paradisiacal pre-historical state.

Precisely this may clarify to what extent myth and the historical sublime are far more omnipresent in our experience of the past than we customarily think. True enough, we may find myth in the cosmological speculations of Antiquity, which we may discuss with a condescending smile;

however, myth is no less present in the mind of modern Western man. We can discern in the history of the West several moments where it radically repudiated its previous past in a movement possessing all the characteristics of Hegel's historical sublime. Think, again, of the French Revolution or of that other tremendous revolution that was occasioned by the transition from an agrarian and feudal society to a modern, industrial society. Few events in Western history have been so intensively discussed by historians (and poeticized by novelists), and few provoked such an avalanche of literature. In both cases these events raised a storm of historicization which blew away all that could possibly be historicized—and in the emptiness or historical vacuum thus created, an idyllic, pre-historical, and quasi-eternal and quasi-natural past came into being. Hence, a past came into being that was ideally suited for idealization, a past that we like to yearn for nostalgically and to dream about in order to momentarily forget the ugly and unnatural historical world of modernity. It is an ahistorical past, beyond time or preceding it, as we have seen, and in this respect it is the kind of past that, according to Freud, the melancholic never succeeds in getting rid of and that is, in this way, no longer part of his *history* but instead part of his *nature*.[59] In this way history may create nature (and myth). This nostalgic yearning for an idyllic past was probably never better expressed than by Burckhardt's lifelong *Sehnsucht* ("strong desire") for "das schöne, faule Süden, das der Geschichte abgestorben ist und als stilles, wunderbares Grabmonument mich Modernitätsmüden mit seinem altertümlichen Schauer erfrischen soll" ("the beautiful, lazy South, that has died to history and that may refresh me, who is so much fed up with modernity, as a silent and marvelous monument to the past with its ancient shiver").[60]

It follows that myth and the historical sublime should not be relegated exclusively to a distant past; myth and the historical sublime accompany us like an ever-present shadow on our path toward modernity. Each time humanity or a civilization enters a truly new phase in its history, a new mythical sublime comes into being as this civilization's cold and fossilized heart that will forever be handed on to those living in all its later phases. And since the history of the West is richer in new and revolutionary beginnings than any other, we may expect Western civilization to have been the unparalleled master in the production of myth and to shelter more myths than any other. So let us not believe that reassuring countermyth according to which Western historical writing has, finally, succeeded in disposing of myth: on the contrary, the more history we have, the more successful, "objective," and scientific it is, the more myth we will have as well. Myth is history's *alter ego,* accompanying it like a shadow wherever it goes: Indeed, paradoxically, myth is the best measure of history's own success.

8.10 CONCLUSION: CIVILIZATION'S COLD HEART

Historical theorists have been much interested in the problem of how historical knowledge is acquired, but they have paid amazingly little attention to the issue of how we disengage ourselves from the past, of how we may forget it and dissociate it from our cultural and historical identity. This neglect is understandable insofar as certain parts or aspects of the past may simply lose their relevance for us; the details of some obscure battle between the French and the English during the War of the Austrian Succession may well be left to rest in peace in the military archives of the two nations involved.

But civilizations will sometimes commit suicide and kill a former identity in order to acquire a new one. We tend to be blind to these suicides, since we naively assume that nothing new could be born from such suicides and that for civilizations suicide means death as it does for us mortal individuals. But the capacity to survive suicide—nay, to arise reborn from the ashes of self-cremation like a Phoenix—is one of the more conspicuous differences between our lives and that of civilizations. Perhaps our own Western civilization has been more suicidal than any other—and this may go a long way to explain its so unique role on the scene of the history of mankind. But the capacity of civilizations to survive their suicides should not invite us to downplay what this may mean to a civilization. The tragedy of such episodes in the history of a civilization and the tragedy of what it may mean for the individuals involved in such tragedies—especially for the best and the most responsible among them, the Socrateses, so to speak—are for a civilization what the experience of a traumatic loss may be for an individual. It compels a civilization to abandon a former self and *to become what it is no longer.* Such episodes in the history of a civilization always involve a movement of dissociation: A former identity is discarded ruthlessly, although with the greatest pain, and transformed into the cold heart of a new identity. In a civilization's later life these discarded identities will remain present only as an absence—much in the way that a scar may be the only visible reminder of an amputated limb. In the history of a civilization such dissociated pasts will ordinarily manifest themselves in what a civilization will tend to mythologize, that is, to associate with an idyllic pre-historical and natural world. Myths are those parts of our collective past that we refuse to historicize: A mythical past is taken outside the course of history and made immune to historical (re-)interpretation. Precisely because of this, it will provoke the strongest efforts at historicization and narrativization. In the eye of the great hurricanes of Western historical writing we will invariably find a pre-historical myth.

Each civilization—and our own probably more than any other—drags along in its wake a number of these mythologized pasts—hence pasts that it cannot historicize and that no less define its identity (although in a peculiarly negative way) than the successfully historicized past. It may and will often attempt to do so—or even find the challenge to do so irresistible—but the result will then invariably be a historicization of how it dealt with these myths instead of a historicization of the myth itself. Historiography then functions as a substitute for history itself (which is, I would not hesitate to say, the very essence and purpose of all writing of history). We may desperately try to talk about this naturalized cold heart of our civilization and to integrate it somehow into our collective history, only to discover over and over again that we got lost in what previous historians have already written about it. Knowledge can never replace being. The cold heart itself of our civilization is therefore forever outside our reach (and that of the historian), for *sui generis* these mythological pasts cannot be historicized since they are *dissociated* pasts, and, as such, beyond the reach of even the most sustained and desperate attempt at historicization. They must be situated in a domain that is outside a civilization's historical time. They possess the highest dignity: They are a civilization's historical sublime.

EPILOGUE: ROUSSEAU AND HÖLDERLIN [1]

> We all follow an excentric course, and no other road is possible from
> childhood to the end. Spiritual unity, Being, in the true sense of the
> word, has been lost by us, and we had to lose it, when we strove for
> it, fought for its possession. We tear ourselves loose from the peace-
> ful "Hen kai Pan" of the world, in order to restore it, by ourselves.[2]
> (my translation)

E.I ROUSSEAU

There is something peculiarly "Rousseauistic" about the account of
sublime historical experience that was presented in this book. It may have
struck the reader that (sublime) experience as investigated in this book has
its obvious counterpart in what Rousseau writes about the state of nature
or the state of "l'homme sauvage," whereas (disciplinary) historical writing,
in its turn, clearly is on a par with Rousseau's so very pessimist account of
civil society. Alienation and inauthenticity result when we move from the
state of nature to civil society—or, as in this book, from (sublime) experience to representation and to disciplinary historical writing. On the other
hand, a direct and immediate access to ourselves and the world is the exclusive privilege of the state of nature—or, again, as in this book, of sublime historical experience. Hence, when I described (disciplinary) historical writing in this book as being incapable of an "authentic" and direct
contact with the past—a deficiency corrected by sublime historical experience—I have, in fact, been repeating for history much the same story that
Rousseau already had told about what it means to live in civil society as opposed to life in the state of nature. The contrast was well summarized by
Horowitz as follows: "In civil society the self-identical subject is necessarily divided not only from other individuals and from society as a whole but
also in his psychic integrity. The ego becomes merely the node of a web of

external forces that were his own to begin with, 'formed from his substance.'"[3] And so it is with historical writing: The historical text has become divided against itself because of the mechanisms of intertextuality so famously and convincingly described by the deconstructivists. It owes its meaning no less to other texts than to what the past has been like; and, consequently, historical texts relate to each other (and to themselves) in much the same way that Rousseau's so sadly inauthentic eighteenth-century contemporaries could define themselves only in terms of (each) other(s). They were forever out of touch with their own selves—as disciplinary historical writing is, forever, out of touch with the past's sublime alterity.

So let us have a closer look at Rousseau's conception of the state of nature and of civil society and see what final lessons we may infer from this idea with regard to (sublime) historical experience. In Rousseau's state of nature this process of the dissemination of meaning I referred to a moment ago had not yet come into being. It is the state of what Derrida scornfully and uncompromisingly rejected as "the metaphysics of presence": Meaning is still tied exclusively to what it is the meaning *of.* And no outside interference can succeed in distorting or confusing the purity and complete self-sufficiency of this relationship—hence the immediacy, transparency, and authenticity of the life of "l'homme sauvage." Or, as Horowitz interestingly characterizes this stage of human history:

Like all other animals he [i.e., natural man] lives entirely in the here and now: "his soul, which nothing disturbs, is wholly wrapped up in the feeling of its present existence, without any idea of the future, however near at hand."[4] There is, as it were, no difference between satisfying the demands of reality and pursuing immediate desires, no distinction between reality principle and pleasure principle, a perfect identity of subject and object, because subject and object do not yet exist.[5]

Although, admittedly, even in civil society we can have such experiences, as we may know from Rousseau himself, I would like to remind the reader here of two episodes in Rousseau's life that he recounted in the second and fifth promenades of his *Les rêveries due promeneur solitaire.* In the second promenade Rousseau tells us how he had been run down by a huge dog, lost consciousness, and then gradually returned to his "normal" self. He describes the experience as follows:

Night was falling. I saw the sky, some stars and a few trees. This first sensation was a delightful moment. My awareness was restricted to just this. I was born to life at that moment, and it was as if I filled with my light aetherial existence all the objects that I perceived. Since I was fully given to the moment, there was nothing that I remembered; I had no clear notion of my individuality, not the slightest idea of what had happened to me; I knew neither who I was, nor where I was; I felt neither pain, nor fear, nor alarm. I saw my blood running, as I might have observed the running of the water of a rivulet, without realizing myself for a moment that this blood was my own.[6] (my translation)

Rousseau recounts a much similar experience in the fifth promenade, although the circumstances provoking it were quite different in this case. He spent some time on the island of St. Pierre in the Lake of Bienne and then experienced moments of this same loss of an awareness of past and future and of any trace of temporal succession that we observed a moment ago. Again, Rousseau depicts here an experience leaving no room but for itself only, but whose complete self-sufficiency is not the result of a strategy of exclusion or of any violence that had been done to either the world or the self. On the contrary, it is the result of an unconditional and total openness, an openness preceding all categorization of the world and of the self (including both these categories of the world [or object] and of the self [or subject] themselves). It truly is *le degré zéro* in our relationship to the world and in which nothing is presupposed. It is as if we reenact in this experience that so fateful moment of millions of years ago when consciousness emerged from mere vegetation. Somewhere, in the depth of our souls we all seem to carry this dark and inarticulate memory with us, and at moments as depicted by Rousseau, it may suddenly make itself felt again. But, above all, the experience is accompanied by a feeling of a quiet but supreme and all-pervasive happiness; or, as Rousseau describes it, the experience "d'un bonheur suffisant, parfait et plein, qui ne laisse dans l'âme aucun vide qu'elle sente le besoin de remplir" ("of a perfect and all-encompassing happiness that left in my soul no place still waiting to be affected by it").[7]

    This is what is lost—or at least expelled—to the ultimate margins of our existence and awareness with our entrance in civil society. It would be most reckless to try to do justice to all the complexities of Rousseau's thought that are of relevance in this context. So I restrict myself here to a no less reckless summary of how the transition from the state of nature to civil society can be explained in terms of the transition from *amour de soi* to *amour propre*. *Amour de soi* represents a relationship to the world that still is prereflective: Its needs, desires, and actions come to the human individual spontaneously, as if his mind and his transactions with the world were the simple expression of the laws of (human) nature. At this stage the human individual does not yet manipulate these laws for some goal; he simply exemplifies them, so to say. One might describe his attitude toward the world and himself as "authentic," although the distinction between "authentic" and "inauthentic" is, in truth, inapplicable to him since it belongs to a fundamentally later dispensation. With the entrance into civil society man becomes aware of other individual human beings, and the necessity of dealing with them provokes a metamorphosis of the *amour de soi* into *amour propre,* for the needs and desires he had in the natural state now become essentially *social* needs and desires that would also now require a *social* articulation.

We should be quite clear about the amazing implications of this transition. It is not a matter, as we might initially expect, of a mere complication of the human individual's interaction with his *Umwelt* because of the presence of these other human individuals (a presence that was, more or less, left out of the picture in the state of nature). The problems caused by the presence of these other human individuals is not the equivalent of some particularly intractable aspect or domain of the state of nature. It is much worse, and in any way far more complex. The decisive datum about the entrance of the social is that it combines these at first sight incommensurable notions of "the other" and of "the same." This has been, in my opinion, Rousseau's truly epochal discovery: the discovery that in the social world we encounter other human beings as an (sometimes even threatening) *otherness,* whereas this also is the world of our *equals.* The scandalous paradox of human existence (in civil society) is that "otherness" and "equality" are indissolubly linked together.

Amour propre is the solution we all adopt for dealing with this paradox: We decide (1) to define *ourselves* (a strategy that would have made no sense in the state of nature) and (2) to do so in terms of *other human beings.* With the entry into civil society, we are compelled to proceed to the *symbolic* level of self-definition and, next, to fabricate at that level a construction of our self that is made up of borrowed material. *Amour propre* is needed for shoring up this shaky and unstable fabrication. *Amour propre* is the set of strategies we appeal to in order to create in ourselves and in others a belief in the solidity of this necessarily always so ramshackle construction. We now define ourselves in terms of others and in that of the social order, so that we become what we are *not.* This is how and why *amour de soi* is exchanged for *amour propre* and, hence, "authenticity" for "inauthenticity"[8]—although with the all-important qualification that it is with au-

thenticity just as with Benjamin's *aura:* You can only become aware of it after you have lost it (that is, after the transition from the state of nature to
that of civil society). Both authenticity and aura can be perceived and can
manifest themselves to us only as an *absence* and in an *awareness of loss.*

This brings me to another, and in the context of this book even more
important aspect of Rousseau's thought. I have in mind here Rousseau's
tragic awareness that there is no way back to the state of nature once we
have entered civil society. Rousseau's crucial insight is, at this stage of his
argument, that any attempt to do so is inevitably tainted by civil society
and is, therefore, condemned to fail. The tragedy is that we may fully realize ourselves what was lost with our entrance into civil society but that each
attempt to undo the loss must fail since it inevitably shares in the imperfections of civil society. Even more so, the ideals in whose name we might
try to regain what was lost will also be tainted by these imperfections, for
why are we interested (in the stage of civil society) in ideals such as virtue,
truth, and freedom? Not because their realization might give us back the
state of nature, for they can have their meaning and practical significance
only in civil society. They belong to civil society, and civil society determines their value and scope. More specifically, now that we have entered a
new world—that of civil society—they may function as a corrective or
palliative for its imperfections. We know that there is no way back to the
state of nature so that the only thing left to us is to fight the evils of civil
society with instruments as hopeless and defective as civil society is itself:

The new state of society became the most horrible state of war: Mankind thus de-
based and harassed, and no longer able to retrace its steps, or renounce the fatal
acquisitions it had made; laboring, in short, merely to its confusion by the abuse
of those faculties, which in themselves do it so much honor, brought itself to the
very brink of ruin.[9]

We need the notion of virtue because civil man has a propensity toward
vice, we need truth because we live in falsity, and we need freedom because
we are unfree. And virtue, truth, and freedom are nothing without their
negative counterparts. Or, to take it all together, in civil society we believe
in the perfectibility of man precisely because we are imperfect in that
state.[10] Our highest ideals are the surest sign of our deepest depravation
and of what we apparently have lost when seeking in them our guides for
thought and action. Hence, it is with virtue, truth, and freedom once again
as with these notions of authenticity and of Benjaminian *aura* I mentioned

a moment ago. That is, we do not recognize them, we feel no need for them, and we do not even know what their meaning might be as long as their meaning is realized or actualized in human action and thought. But as soon as these notions acquire their august meaning for us, as soon as we can therefore no longer live without these notions, we have also lost them forever and are condemned to live without them.

It also follows from this that their practical use is restricted to civil society only; as soon as we live in civil society—and are aware of this—we can stave off the worst if we decide to be virtuous and to serve the causes of truth and of freedom. In other words, although these notions must remind us of the state of nature since they owe their *aura*—certainly the right word in this context!—to (the lost) state of nature, they could never show us how to return to the state of nature. Indeed, the unconditional devotion they demand of us has its foundation in their being the most intense of forceful reminiscence of the state of nature, but they cannot lead us back to what shines in and through them. That is the crucial paradox.

This also suggests what is wrong with the view that is defended by some of Rousseau's commentators and according to which the transition from the state of nature to civil society is a secularized version of the Fall. Admittedly, both share an awareness of the tragic irreversibility of the transition—either from Paradise to this world or from the state of nature to civil society. The difference is, however, that in the case of the Christian conception of the Fall the regime of good versus evil coincides with that of Paradise versus the historical world, whereas Rousseau argues the far more subtle and interesting opposition of a state of nature exemplifying what is good without expressing it versus a civil society in which good and evil compete with each other. A comparison with the Nietzsche of *The Genealogy of Morals* and Freud's *Totem and Taboo* is also illuminating in this context. Once again, there is a structural similarity between the transition from what Nietzsche describes as "the aristocratic Law of the Lord"[11] to the "morality of the slave" of contemporary society and the transition from the state of nature to civil society in Rousseau. The crucial difference, however, is that Nietzsche's attack on the "morality of the slave" in the name of "the aristocratic Law of the Lord" presupposed a commensurability of the two that is characteristically absent in Rousseau. Much the same is true of Freud. One might well see his *Totem and Taboo* as the Freudian variant of the state of nature.[12] But since the story told in that book repeats itself in the life history of each individual, there could not be any incommensurability here either between the state of nature and society. The state of nature is part of our psychology, so to say. It follows from this that Rousseau differs from the Christian account of the Fall and from Nietzsche and Freud in that he constructs the relationship between the state of nature and civil society in a way that comes close to the account of myth given in Chapter 8. In both cases the rupture embodied by the transition from the state of nature to civil society is so total as to create a radical incommensurability of the two.

But one more important implication of the Rousseauism of sublime historical experience demands our attention. Recall that there is for Rousseau in civil society no sure compass to guide us back to the state of nature. Truth, virtue, freedom, Reason, the aspiration of perfection do all have their exclusive *raison d'être* in civil society and must therefore fail us sooner or later as such a guide. It can be explained how we arrived from the state of nature in civil society, but there is no map for the route in the opposite direction. The nature of our predicament can be clarified with the help of the following simile. Think of a huge metropolis; furthermore, if you want to go by car from the west to the east in this metropolis, there is an immense ten-lane highway enabling you to do so most comfortably. However, this highway is a one-way route from beginning to end. This highway, then, can be compared to how we got from the state of nature to civil society: It is so easy as to be almost impossible *not* to make use of this highway and thus to get from the west to the east of the city. So inevitably we all end up, sooner or later, in the eastern part of the metropolis.

But suppose now that you wish to go back from the east to the west again. And then there is *no* highway: There is only an intricate network of crooked little narrow streets, and as soon as you think that one of these little streets goes to the west, it turns to the north, the south, and, ultimately, to the east again. Or worse still, it stretches out most satisfactorily in the right direction from the east to the west for as far as you can see — but then you discover to your dismay that it has become a one-way street and that you are forbidden to enter from the east. This is, more or less, what Rousseau had in mind, especially when writing his *Confessions*. It is true that you may have experiences like those I described at the beginning of this epilogue, where the happiness of the state of nature is momentarily granted to us again. Such moments are like the high points in the metropolis's huge sweep, from where you can survey large parts of the city and even catch a glimpse of what the western part of the city must be like. But ordinarily you have little more to go on than a vague intuition about in what direction the west must lie; just as Rousseau knew that getting to the state of nature meant for him that he would have to retrace his own life history and find all these many places where he went wrong. But doing this is a most difficult and almost hopeless task: Even the greatest effort at complete sincerity would always be an easy victim of the inauthenticities provoked by *amour propre*. Rousseau was well aware of this. He knew quite well that to rediscover the state of nature by retracing one's autobiography was like this moving from the east to the west in this metropolis mentioned just now and that each effort would inevitably result in what we had best describe as a most *"excentric course"* through the huge metropolis of our existence in civil society.

E.2 HÖLDERLIN

Now, the theme of this excentric course is central in Hölderlin's novel *Hyperion: Oder der Eremit in Griechenland* (written between 1792 and 1799 [13]), if not in large part of all of his poetry. The notion is explicitly mentioned in the quote from the preface to the *vorletzte Fassung* of the novel that I used as epigraph for this epilogue. Ryan presents the following comment on this passage:

The human being . . . "tears itself loose" from Spiritual unity. This unity can be conceived of as a kind of "center," as a point of intersection of all Being. The human being awakening to consciousness drops out of this center, out of this peaceful "hen kai pan" and now finds an alternative center in itself; the notion of "excentricity" reflects this defection of "conscious being from direct participation to the fullness of Being." [14] (my translation)

This is much the same story as we found in Rousseau: The peaceful *Hen kai Pan* is Hölderlin's equivalent of the state of nature, and the human individual becoming conscious of himself and erecting in himself a center in opposition to that of the peaceful *Hen kai Pan* referred to by Ryan is Hölderlin's counterpart of Rousseau's civil society (although we shall see later that Hölderlin also uses the formula for expressing his Spinozism). Hölderlin's variant of these Rousseauist themes is even somewhat more dramatic than what we find in Rousseau himself. In Rousseau's case our excentric course can begin only after we find ourselves in civil society; Hölderlin's excentric course, on the contrary, also comprises the transition from the state of nature to civil society and our effort to reconstitute it, for this is how we should read his "*wir reissen uns los* vom friedlichen Hen kai Pan der Welt, *um es herzustellen*" (my italics).

There is another respect in which Hölderlin is more radical than Rousseau: Although both advocate "a return to the state of nature," Hölderlin is more explicit than his great teacher and predecessor about what this should mean. Ryan clarifies Hölderlin's relevant intentions as follows:

The help promised by Nature consists in this, that the excentric course will ever and ever again flow into "the Spiritual unity" that was once lost. This is achieved in those moments of an ekstatic enrapturement, that so much accumulate in the course of the novel [i.e., in *Hyperion*]; ekstasis is a being-outside-oneself, it is a participation in a uniting embrace "in all that lives." One further consequence follows from this. It is true that the human being who has been barred from his excentric aspirations can momentarily emerge in "the center," but he cannot persist in this "blissful oblivion of the self" [think of the experience Rousseau recounted in his *Rêveries,* which was discussed in section E.1]—for then he would lose his identity as a conscious being. So the human individual can be led back to this center, but each time he is destined to obey the centrifugal impulses of his nature and to return again to his excentric course.[15] (my translation)

This is where Hölderlin goes beyond Rousseau. Rousseau recognizes that we have lost ourselves, our identity, and our authenticity when moving from the state of nature to that of civil society. He is fully aware of the tragedy of the transition and profoundly regrets it; but his message is, essentially, that we shall have to learn to live with this. It may be that we have such short ekstatic experiences as Rousseau had had himself at the Lake of Bienne. But for Rousseau these experiences can never be more than mere reminders of what we have lost without actual significance for our present station of life. Think of the resignation of the opening words of the *Contrat Social*—where Rousseau explicitly refuses to consider the possibility of an undoing of the transition from the state of nature to civil society.[16] This is different with Hölderlin, since Hölderlin does discern in these ekstatic experiences the possibility of an, albeit momentary, correction of our "dissemination" of ourselves and of our excentric course. This is where Hölderlin goes beyond Rousseau—and he does so by giving in his novel *Hyperion* actual content to the Rousseauist notion of a "return to nature." When discussing the novel in what follows, we shall see how Hölderlin tries to overcome the dark pessimism of Rousseau's argument.

But let me begin with a few comments on the story that is told to us in the novel.[17] The scene of the events related in the novel can quite accurately be situated in Greece at the time of the war between Russia and Turkey from 1768 to 1774.[18]

This war was partly fought in and around the Greek isles and provoked there the first stirrings of the desire for national independence. If we realize ourselves that the novel is among the most high-pitched eulogies of Greek Antiquity (more specifically, of Athens) ever written, we shall recognize that Hölderlin could not have made the gap between the present (of the novel) and a glorious past deeper and more painful. Could one think of a greater contrast than that between the Athens of Sophocles, Plato, Pericles, and so on, on the one hand and the dismal and shameful reality of centuries of Turkish rule on the other? Needless to say, this prepares the terrain for historical experience. Insofar as historical experience is an experience of the difference(s) between past and present, Hölderlin could not possibly have conceived in his novel of a more appropriate frame for evoking it. Even more so, the experience of the difference between past and present can and will often take the form of a "nostalgic remembrance of the past." *Nostalgia* is a neologism coined by the Swiss physician Johannes Hofer in 1688 consisting of the Greek words *nosteoo* ("to return home safely") and *algos* ("pain").[19] And, indeed, it will not be difficult to model Hyperion's experience of the past on that of a nostalgic remembrance.[20] The *nosteoo* dimension is all-pervasive in the novel (especially in the chapter describing Hyperion's visit to Athens, which is known in the Hölderlin literature as the *Athen-Erlebnis,* that is, the experience of classical Athens); it also has a more practical manifestation, so to say, in Hyperion's desire to achieve for his country a kind of Renaissance of classical Greece. But the dimension in question was most perfectly expressed elsewhere, namely, in the last strophe of Hölderlin's poem *Griechenland:*

Mich verlangt ins bessre Land hinüber	I am yearning for the better country
Nach Alcäus und Anakreon,	For Alcaeus and Anacreon,
Und ich schlief im engen Hause lieber,	And I wished I could sleep in the narrow house
Bei den Heiligen in Marathon;	Close to the holy heroes of Marathon;
Ach! Es sei die letzte meiner Tränen,	Ah! Let it be the last of my tears
Die dem lieben Griechenlande rann,	That was shed for blissful Greece,
Lasst, o Parzen, lasst die Schere tönen,	O, Parcae, let hear your scissors,
Denn mein Herz gehört den Toten an.	For my heart belongs to the dead.[21]
	(my translation)

Next, the "pain" dimension is most powerfully voiced by Hyperion right at the beginning of the novel when he tells us how he thinks of his homeland in its present state:

Fortunate the man whose native country flourishes to rejoice and strengthen his heart! For me, it is as if I were cast into a swamp, as if the coffin lid were being nailed shut over me, if anyone reminds me of mine, and whenever I hear myself called a Greek, it is as if I were being bound with a dog collar.[22]

By the juxtaposition of the two dimensions the tensions between past and present are increased inordinately in *Hyperion*—and it will be obvious that this is a first and necessary step to unglue someone from his own time and make him susceptible to historical experience. So, on the one hand, we have good reasons to be amazed by an author wishing to remind us of, what is for him, the highest stage humanity ever reached and who does so by setting his story at a time that could not possibly be more remote from it. Why not evoke the glories of the Greek past by firmly setting the scene of the novel in that past itself? Is this not the literary strategy almost self-evidently adopted by all (historical) novelists wishing to oppose the greatness of the past to the deceptions of the present? But on the other hand, could one make the past into more of an inevitable reality and into more of an ineluctable object of historical experience—or, rather, into an object of *sublime* historical experience? The juxtaposition of a dismal present and a sublime past, as taken up in the juxtaposition of the "pleasure of homecoming" and the "pain of (temporal) dislocation," cannot fail to remind us of the Burkean sublime as discussed in Chapter 8.[23]

    After having informed the reader about Hyperion's youth and his education by his wise teacher Adamas (clearly modeled on Rousseau[24]), Hölderlin tells us how Hyperion gets in touch (although not without some initial misunderstandings) with Alabanda, a freedom fighter in the tradition of the ancient *clephts* combining patriotism with banditry. After some hesitations, Hyperion decides to join this band of freedom fighters. In the first book of the second volume of *Hyperion* all this ends in a terrible disaster when the "liberation" of Misistra (that is, ancient Sparta) makes the way free for plunder and murder of the conquered city by Alabanda's and Hyperion's motley and ill-disciplined troops. Both turn away in dismay from the enterprise: Alabanda flees in order to seek his death elsewhere, whereas Hyperion flies to Europe and visits Italy, France, and Germany. Later, he returns to Greece from Germany (as "der Eremit in Griechenland") and from there writes the letters to Bellarmin (that is, the "beauti-ful German"[25]) that make up the greater part of the novel. In these letters he tells Bellarmin the story of his life, and instead of ending it (as one might have surmised) with the resignation of a Boethius in the latter's *De consolatione philosophiae,* he concludes his story with the famous *Schel-trede*—which is an attack as vicious as it is lively on late eighteenth-century intellectual life in Germany.[26] But the novel is, above all, the story of Hy-perion's love for classical Greece and for Diotima.

Not coincidentally I name classical Greece and Diotima in one and the same breath, for both their roles in the novel are most closely inter-twined. Two comments are in order in this context. First, this is where we may discern a certain structural resemblance between *Hyperion* and Eichen-dorff's *Das Marmorbild* of some twenty years later. In both cases the theme of how we relate to the past is closely connected to the love between man and woman. But the differences are no less striking. Diotima is a human being of flesh and blood, whereas Venus is a mere symbol or specter of the past. This also explains why *Hyperion* is of more interest than *Das Mar-morbild* in the context of the present study. Diotima incorporates all of the trajectory from the present (of which she is herself such a most conspicu-ous part) to the past (which she symbolizes)—she is both real *and* a sym-bol—whereas Venus never gets us out of the past that we associate with her resurrection. To put it somewhat ungenerously, Eichendorff tells us a ghost story, whereas Hölderlin's Diotima functions as the foil on which all aspects of our relationship to the past—from historical experience, by means of straightforward historical insight, to how the past may affect present and future action—can be projected and investigated in all their complexity.

But, second and more important, the superposition of Hyperion's re-lationship to Diotima and his relationship to Greek Antiquity enables Hölderlin to go beyond Rousseau, for we will readily endow the love of man and woman with the authenticity we associate with Rousseau's state of nature; it truly satisfies all that Rousseau projects on the state of nature. In this way each love undoubtedly is (for the two people involved) either a continuation of the state of nature under the dispensation of civil society or a momentary return to it. And we can therefore only be astonished that Rousseau never really presents the relationship between Julie and St. Preux to his readers in this light. Perhaps it was Rousseau's intention to suggest that the social inequality of Julie and St. Preux prevented them from this return to the state of nature that so much seemed to be the promise of what he had undertaken to do in the novel; or, to mention another possibility, perhaps he wanted to investigate what being true to oneself ought to mean under such circumstances. In both cases we remain within the matrix of civil society. And, in fact, each of the many interpretations of the novel that have been offered in a debate spanning more than two centuries can be seen as one more explanation of why Rousseau avoided framing the love between Julie and St. Preux in terms of the state of nature.

Anyway, the outcome is that the theme of love as an exemplification of the state of nature remained an open and undecided one in Rousseau's writings. But this is different in *Hyperion:* Hölderlin explicitly states that Diotima was Hyperion's gateway to beauty and to Hölderlin's equivalent of the state of nature: "And you, you showed me the way! With you I began. They are not worth speech, the days when yet I knew you not—O Diotima, Diotima, divine being!" [27] And, indeed, one will not come across exclamations like these in *La nouvelle Héloise* or elsewhere in Rousseau's writings; this introduces, therefore, into Hölderlin's discourse a force not having its equivalent anywhere in Rousseau. And this explains, again, why the return to the state of nature (or, rather, what this notion stands for) could be a theme in Hölderlin and not in Rousseau. In sum, the relationship between Hyperion and Diotima also symbolizes Hyperion's relationship to the past; and, even more important, *precisely this parallelism of how Hyperion relates to Diotima and of how he relates to the past enables the former relationship to carry the latter to stages that would have been unthinkable in Rousseau.* If seen from this perspective, the relationship between Hyperion and Diotima is absolutely crucial in the novel, for without it the novel would have lacked the scope and frame needed for formulating its philosophical message. Only Diotima gets Hyperion (and Hölderlin) outside the confines of the Rousseauist framework.

But if Hyperion's involvement with Diotima is an expression of his involvement with the past, this does certainly not imply that evolutions in the latter could simply be read off from those in the former and vice versa. The situation is more complex than that. Admittedly, on the larger scale there is a parallelism between the story of Hyperion's love for Diotima and his involvement with Greece and what that should imply for the present. Hyperion meets Diotima when Adamas's lessons about classical Greece began to carry fruit in his mind, whereas the Misistra catastrophe causes him to abandon his hopes of a Greek renaissance and to bid farewell to Diotima as well (I shall return to this in a moment). And the acme of his love of Diotima coincides with the *Athen-Erlebnis*—which undoubtedly is the climax of the novel as well.

But on a deeper level a significant asymmetry arises, for with and after the *Athen-Erlebnis* Diotima begins to lose her significance for Hyperion. Hence, the decisive event in the complicated dialectics of their relationship is not the Misistra catastrophe—as a superficial reading of the novel would suggest. In fact, this event functions in the novel as merely the codification or the mutual recognition of the inevitability of their separation rather than its ultimate cause.[28] This event makes manifest what had been latent since the *Athen-Erlebnis.* Paradoxically, it was not the *ugliness* of Misistra but the *perfection* of the *Athen-Erlebnis* that placed Hyperion and Diotima apart from each other, as Hyperion realizes himself in the very evening after their visit to Athens: "We returned, as after our first embrace. Everything had become strange and new for us."[29] A new and disruptive reality had crept into their relationship.

The explanation is, essentially, that this unique moment could not last, precisely because of its perfection, for as soon as its perfection became clear to Hyperion, as soon as he understood what this required him to do (and that he would attempt to do in the second book), he had moved *beyond* perfection. The *recognition* of perfection is outside perfection itself— and this is why the decline of Hyperion's relationship with Diotima set in with the *Athen-Erlebnis* and why this decline is indissolubly linked to what the *Erlebnis* meant to Hyperion and what he learned from it. The fruits of perfection are necessarily imperfect themselves, since they belong to the domain in which perfection has been recognized, and they can therefore not be part of it themselves.

Put differently, throughout the novel there is a parallelism (although in opposite directions after the *Athen-Erlebnis*) between Hyperion's own evolution and his relationship with Diotima. As we shall see later when discussing the philosophical meaning of the novel, Hyperion's evolution (in which the *Athen-Erlebnis* is absolutely central) hinges on the discovery of what Hölderlin understands by "nature" and, above all, "beauty" (*Schönheit*). Indeed, the *Athen-Erlebnis* marks the unique moment of a perfect and well-balanced equilibrium in their relationship. But to the extent that Hyperion succeeds in subsuming these concepts in his life and personality, Diotima must necessarily shift to the background.[30] As Ryan puts it:

To the extent that Hyperion realizes himself that his real duties are to "Beauty" and to the extent that he penetrates ever deeper into its secrets, Diotima is robbed more and more of her autonomy and independence, and in the end she almost seems to evaporate in Hyperion's being. Right at the beginning she is like an overwhelming revelation to him, but at the end she becomes his "Muse," giving herself to him even in her death and who then continues to live on, as a transfiguration of herself, in his poetry.[31] (my translation)

In sum, nature and beauty are ever more "internalized" by Hyperion in the course of the novel with the result that Diotima gradually loses her independence with regard to Hyperion and thus becomes, in the end, transformed into a mere aspect of his personality. It is here that Hyperion's relationship to Diotima is both a parable of Rousseau's story of the state of nature and a movement beyond it. In both cases the achievement of perfection is also the destruction of perfection, and in both cases the abyss between the state of nature or of perfection and what lies beyond it is unbridgeable. But Hölderlin is more explicit than Rousseau about the fact that perfection bears the seeds of its own destruction in itself and that the simple fact of the recognition of perfection is sufficient for bringing these seeds to life. Next, Hölderlin is more aware than Rousseau of how and in what guises the state of nature may linger in our minds after we have lost it—think of Ryan's comment about Diotima after the *Athen-Erlebnis* quoted just now. So against the background of Rousseau's thought, Hölderlin presents us with the paradox of both deepening the abyss between the state of nature and history and of indicating how the former may nevertheless live on in the latter. This paradox demonstrates both that Hölderlin's position could not possibly be reduced to Rousseau's (although it has its origins in the latter's thought) and that Hölderlin goes beyond Rousseau, even though he had always revered him as a "demigod."[32]

The *Athen-Erlebnis* is situated at the end of the second book of the first volume (and is recounted in the last letter to Bellarmin); it combines in itself what I have referred to in this book as "subjective historical experience" and "sublime historical experience" and is, as such, an appropriate summary of its argument. There can be no doubt that the visit to Athens— the climax with which the first book of Hyperion ends is constructed by Hölderlin as Hyperion's decisive subjective historical experience. The "ekstatic" features of the experience (which are essential to subjective historical experience) have been recognized by all commentators—to which I should add that the movement of "ekstasis" should be conceived here as a movement outside the sphere to which the excentric course of normal human existence is condemned, and this is why it makes imaginable a return to a source from which this excentric course originates but that is forever outside its reach once we stumble upon the hopeless complexities down its path. The letter in which Hyperion recounts the experience begins with the resounding statement: "Life has great hours. We gaze up at them as at the colossal figures of the Future and of Antiquity."[33] And such "great moments" will elevate us far beyond "das gewöhnliche Dasein"—"the ordinary existence."[34] Hyperion is struck by "das schöne Phantom des Alten Athens" ("the beautiful phantom of ancient Athens") as though it "wie einer Mutter Gestalt, die aus dem Totenreiche zurückkehrt" (as though it was "like the figure of a mother returning from the realm of the dead")[35] and confesses that he "hätte vergehen mögen vor dem mächtigen Anblick" ("could have fainted, so mighty was the spectacle").[36] We are reminded of Hyperion's exclamation in a previous letter that the "terrible magnificence" of Antiquity knocks us down just like a hurricane may do to a stand of young trees and that the victories of that great past resounded in his ears like a "jubilant thunderstorm" ("frohlockend Gewitter")[37]—and in both cases the connotations of the sublime are impossible to oversee. And his wish to become, if only for a moment, a hero of that great past, even at the cost of his life, now seems close to fulfillment, as is suggested by Diotima's exclamation that Hyperion succeeds in bridging the gap between past and present, to carrying himself back to the past.[38]

And here Hölderlin, once again, surpasses Rousseau. Whereas for Rousseau the decisive moment in human history has been the transition from the state of nature to civil society, Hölderlin finds this decisive moment in classical Antiquity.[39] Athens is, for him, what the state of nature has been for Rousseau, and human history since then is for him just as much a history of decline as that of civil society has been for Rousseau. This is where the story that Hölderlin tells us in Hyperion comes closer to my argument about myth and sublime historical experience as expounded in the last chapter of this book than is the case with Rousseau. Obviously, myth as understood there has its counterpart in Rousseau's state of nature—hence, in what lies outside or in what precedes all of human history. So much is true. Hölderlin, however, relates myth to Athens and thus to a phase in human history itself. Put differently, myth is historicized by Hölderlin. And this is in agreement with my argument in the last chapter. Crucial to my argument has been (1) the idea that myth, as the conception of a state of nature, is a product of history and a spin-off of historical thought, of historical writing, and of historical awareness and (2) that, as such, it is the object of sublime historical experience. Since Rousseau squarely opposes the state of nature (myth) and civil society (history), such a historicization of myth would be inconceivable in the intrigue of human history as presented in his writings. For Hölderlin, however, there is no domain outside history, and myth is shown to be a product of history itself. Hölderlin thus succeeds in reconciling the authenticity of historical experience with historicity in a way that would be unthinkable in both Rousseau and contemporary historical thought.

For Rousseau such a reconciliation would be unthinkable on ontological grounds: The nature of civil society leaves no room for authenticity and authentic experience simply because it is the domain of inauthenticity. Within contemporary historical thought the idea of myth as the object of historical experience is for a double reason little less than a contradiction in terms. In the first place, it is rejected on the basis of the epistemological argument that all historical experience is historically situated. And second, and more obviously, all that we have learned to associate with the notion of "myth" excludes already automatically the possibility of myth being a source of authentic experience. Myth is a dream, a delusion, isn't it? So how could it possibly be an object of *authentic* experience? Hölderlin succeeds in overcoming these two objections by "pinching" the two notions of history and of a mythical state of nature as tightly together as possible, *with the result that myth becomes an aspect of history, and vice versa.* Each moment in history then is accompanied with its own mythical heart—and only then does it make sense to say that history gives us access to myth as the object of (authentic) historical experience. It is the ahistorical eye in the hurricane of historicization, as I put it in the last chapter. Or, to express this paradox in a Rousseauist terminology: It is each historical moment's "state of nature":

Like an immense shipwreck, when the gales have been hushed and the sailors have fled and the corpse of the shattered fleet lies on the sandbank unrecognizable, so before us lay Athens, and the forsaken pillars stood before us like bare tree trunks of a wood that at evening was still green and, the same night, went up in flames.[40]

Thus spoke Hyperion when he first set eyes upon Athens. Two things must strike us in this passage. In the first place, it abundantly makes clear that for Hyperion/Hölderlin classical Athens is "the world we have lost"—just as this had been the case with the Italy of Lorenzo il Magnifico for Machiavelli and Guicciardini and with the Middle Ages for so many nineteenth-century historians.[41] In the second place, the metaphors of the fleet destroyed by a storm and of the forest fire for the ruination of Athens are both appropriate and quite compelling, but yet there is something peculiar about them. Both metaphors are suggestive of seeing a previous state in a later one: You see the dilapidated fleet or the forest that was burned down, and then you see the original fleet or forest in it. And in both cases the image of the previous state is stronger and more powerful than the later one. Or, as Diotima puts it a moment later, "Der Künstler ergänzt den Torso leicht" ("The artist can easily restore the torso for himself").[42] There is decrepitude only in order to remind us all the more forcefully of primeval perfection. The metaphors thus invite a way of seeing the world oddly combining the dissolution of an original state with its reconstitution—much in the way that a string may be made brought to vibration (on its excentric course, so to say) only to return to its initial position in the end while remaining all the time the string that it is. The vibrating string clearly is a modification of the string at rest—but it will also return to this state in a moment.

Although this notion of the vibration of a string is in some respects misleading as an account of Hölderlin's intentions (namely, where it implies that the initial and final state are identical), it may shed some light on the heart of the matter and on what is generally recognized to be "the philosophical statement" of *Hyperion*.[43] This philosophical statement is formulated in *Hyperion* in the context of a discussion of how philosophy was possible in Athens: "The great saying, the *hen diapheron heautooi* (the one differentiated in itself) of Heraclitus, could be found only by a Greek, for it is the very being of Beauty, and before that was found there was no philosophy. Now classification became possible, for the whole was there. The flower had ripened; now it could be dissected."[44] In short, philosophy was possible only after the discovery by Heraclitus of this notion of the one that differs in or from itself. Hölderlin obviously refers here to a set of Heraclitean fragments, most prominently the one saying "they do not understand how what differs may agree with itself; just like the returning harmony of a bow or a lyre" (Heraclitus also reminds us here of this idea of the vibration of a string I evoked a moment ago, namely, of the string of a bow or a lyre). Other, closely related fragments are suggestive of a hidden (*aphanè*) harmony that is better (*kreittoon*) to the extent that it is harder to perceive and where the most beautiful harmony (*kallistè harmonia*) arises from the union of differences and contraries.[45] Last, Heraclitus's reference to the harmonious sounds produced by a lyre's vibration is repeated in Hölderlin's often used metaphor of the "resolution of dissonances."[46] Moreover, musical metaphors abound in the text of *Hyperion,* and one might well agree with Walter Silz's observation that "in Hyperion, the art of words seems constantly to be reaching for the immediacy and immateriality of the art of tones."[47]

It should be added, in this context, that the Heraclitean formula of the *Hen heautooi diapheron* has connotations slightly different from those of the *Hen kai Pan* that is used by Hölderlin on similar occasions. The explanation is that for Hölderlin the *Hen kai Pan* had the same meaning as the Spinozist formula *Deus sive Nature*—and much of Hölderlin's thought can, indeed, be seen as a fusion of a pre-Socratic philosophy of nature with Spinozism (I shall return to Hölderlin's Spinozism in a moment). The *Hen kai Pan* is suggestive of a unity in diversity, and, obviously, this is also what Spinoza had in mind with his idea that the multitude of existing forms is a totality of "modifications" of the one substance which is God or nature. But the *Hen kai Pan* is also primarily static and, as such, in obvious agreement with the general atmosphere of the Spinozist system. The *Hen heautooi diapheron,* however, is suggestive of a movement of proliferation and dissemination that we would associate with Leibniz rather than with Spinoza. Movement, change, evolution, and history have little or no role to play in the universe of Spinozistic ontology, whereas Leibniz calls to mind a never-ending process of representations mirroring representations—a continuous kaleidoscopic play guided by the aim of achieving a maximum of harmony. Leibniz's monadology is here undoubtedly closer than Spinoza to what is intimated by the Heraclitean fragments.[48]

In order to come to a better understanding of what Hölderlin had in mind with the *Hen heautooi diapheron,* we had best proceed in two steps. In the first place, we should observe that in the passage quoted just now Hölderlin relates the discovery of philosophy to beauty (*Schönheit*), albeit that the relationship between the two is a hierarchical one, for Hölderlin quite explicitly states that poetry and beauty precede philosophy.[49] Or, rather, all philosophy begins and ends with poetry and beauty so that philosophy is enclosed by beauty as an island is surrounded by the sea. So the

Heraclitean notion of "the One differing in itself" is a truth *about* philosophy, a meta-philosophical statement rather than one belonging to philosophy itself. There is the One and the many disseminations in which it may manifest itself and still be itself within the powerful aesthetic grasp of the poet; and it is, next, the philosopher's task to investigate how these disseminations of the One may mutually relate to each other and to the One. The world investigated by the philosopher is thus the world of fixed forms, of the individual things resulting from the "dissemination" of the original One of the *Hen kai Pan*. It is our world in which we dare not and could not possibly question the powerful presence of these fixed forms and which we accept as a "second nature," a nature that is stronger and more "natural" than the nature of the One. This is what Hölderlin expressed with this "one could now determine the nature of the whole. The flower had blossomed; it could now be dissected and studied in its individual components" that was mentioned a moment ago.

In the second place, in the quoted passage Hölderlin related the principle of the One different from itself to "das Wesen der Schönheit," the essence of Beauty, and more clarity about the nature of their relationship is required. Two passages demand our attention in this context:

O you who seek the highest and the best . . . do you know its name? the name of that which is one and is all? Its name is Beauty.[50]

The first child of human, of divine Beauty is art. In art the divine man rejuvenates and repeats himself. He wants to feel himself, therefore he sets his Beauty over against himself. Thus did man give himself his gods. For in the beginning man and his gods were one, when, unknown to itself, eternal Beauty *was*.[51]

The first passage will need no comment: it explicitly identifies the Heraclitean principle of the One differing in itself with beauty. But the second passage is truly crucial in the context of my argument—and, in fact, it takes together all the themes in Hölderlin's thought that are of relevance in this conclusion. To begin with the end of the passage, eternal beauty, *Schönheit,* was originally *unknown* (*unbekannt*) to itself; it can be recognized only *ex post facto* and when it has been lost already. Obviously, this repeats the mechanism that we first came across when discussing Benjamin's notion of *aura,* which proved to be of so much importance for an understanding of sublime historical experience. This is the mechanism that links the subject and the object of experience together in a mutual embrace so immensely strong so that the very notions of the subject and object of experience lose their significance and so that (authentic) experience is all that is left to us. All that ordinarily separates subject and object (in an epistemological, ontological, spatial, temporal, or causal sense) has momentarily been overcome.

Second, consider Hölderlin's bold assertion that God and Man were originally one. This is a profoundly problematic assertion against the background Hölderlin's well-attested Spinozism (which I referred to a moment ago).[52] In Spinoza God and humankind are entirely different categories: God is infinite, whereas human beings are finite; in contrast to human beings, God acts exclusively in agreement with the laws of his own nature ("ex solis suae naturae legibus"), and this is why finite *modi* such as human beings, and not God, are subject to suffering and, last, why man is dependent of the one substance, whereas God *is* this one substance.[53] It is true that in many places in his poetry Hölderlin respects Spinoza's views of how the human being relates to God and where he rejoices in expressing the "aloofness" of God with regard to humankind.[54] But elsewhere he substantially reduces the ontological distance between God and humankind, as is the case in the quote from *Hyperion* that is under discussion here.[55]

I would not wish to claim, however, that Hölderlin's elevation of humankind to a status close to that of God (or gods) should be wholly at odds with Spinoza's conceptions. It might be argued that Hölderlin's assertion that the gods and human beings share a common origin can be justified in terms of Spinoza's panentheism—and, more specifically, by an appeal to the Janus-faced character of the Spinozist notion of nature, looking both in the direction of God (or gods) and in that of human beings. Whoever embraces the Spinozist formula *Deus sive natura* may feel free to speak of nature without fearing to disparage God by doing so—and, in this way, the notion of nature may be made to do the work originally assigned to the notion of God. Clearly, Hölderlin liked to make use of this possibility—as is suggested by his habit of speaking of the *Hen kai Pan* (in which no explicit reference is made to God) instead of the Spinozist *Deus sive natura*. In sum, there is a tendency in Hölderlin to rephrase the relationship between God (or the gods) and human beings in terms of the relationship between nature and humankind. Two implications of this strategy are of importance in the context of my argument here. In the first place, the strategy must be expected to invite a certain anthropomorphism with regard to nature—or to put it provocatively, to replace the *Deus sive natura* with a

Homo sive natura—for what other result could this focus on the common ground of nature and humankind possibly have? In this way a continuity between nature and humankind comes into being that has inspired a large part of Hölderlin's poetry.[56] And, second, as one might have expected, this could not fail to further invigorate the Rousseauist tendencies in Hölderlin's thought.

This conjecture of Hölderlin's propensity to move from Spinoza to Rousseau, to read and understand Spinoza from a Rousseauist perspective, and to give to nature the aura it has in the *Émile* and in the *Rêveries du promeneur solitaire,* is confirmed by Jürgen Link's recent and profound study of Hölderlin's Rousseauism. Link closely investigates here what he refers to as Hölderlin's *Privatreligion,* hence what the God (and the gods) represented for him and how humankind fits into his conception of the divine. When getting to the essence of Hölderlin's *Privatreligion,* Link writes:

The figure of thought of "Deus sive Natura (sive Potentia)" as a self-less and unconscious *Hen kai Pan* and that of *Natura naturans* and *Natura naturata* presents us with the decisive key for grasping the nature of Hölderlin's private religion. "God" (in the singular) is then identical with the power of determination as such (*Potentia*); more specifically, with how the "fleeting" *Natura naturans* eternally determines the fixed "modi" of the *Natura naturata.* Whereas his "Gods" (in the plural) stand, so to speak, for the "energy" required for the transition from the eternal "substance" of the *Naturar naturans* to the spatial and temporal "modi" of the *natura naturata.*[57] (my translation)

We see here at work the mechanism hinted at in the previous paragraph. That is to say, the argument begins with what undoubtedly are the defining features of humankind—self-awareness and the capacity of speech. Next, nature and humankind are compared from precisely the perspective of these features: It is argued that nature lacks them. And, finally, this lack of self-awareness and of speech is then attributed to the gods. And, in contrast to Spinoza's demand to see everything *sub specie Divinitatis,* we now come to see, with Rousseau and Hölderlin, nature and the Gods *sub specie humanitatis.*[58]

We can now also understand the meaning of another passage in Hyperion's eulogy on Athens, where he presents Athens as the childhood of mankind. When comparing Athens to Sparta, Hölderlin/Hyperion explains Athens's superiority in world history to Sparta's, he urges us to take into account the evolution of the human individual:

Leave the human being undisturbed from the cradle on! Do not force him out of the close-wrapped bud of his being, the small house of his childhood! . . . In short, let him not learn until late that there are men, that there is something else outside of himself, for only thus will he become a man. But man is a god as soon as he is man. And once he is a god, he is beautiful.[59]

We encounter here, once again, this so very un-Spinozist theme of the equivalence of man and God—but, at the same time, the quote makes clear what made Hölderlin deviate from Spinoza here. Hölderlin obviously repeats here the message of Rousseau's *Émile,* where Rousseau insists that education should always aim at respecting as much as possible the child's nature or, rather, where each child is an exemplification of the state of nature. Only on this condition can the child develop into a "god," whose life no less shall be in agreement with the laws of "nature" no less than that of the gods. One can fully become a man only after first having fully been a child. We can therefore observe here, as Link writes, "a transposition of the Rousseauist theory of education (in the *Émile*) from the individual to a collective (a people)" ("eine Übertragung der Rousseauschen Erziehungstheorie [im *Émile*] vom Individuum auf ein Kollektiv ['Volk']," and hence we find the place where Hölderlin's Rousseauism begins to dominate his Spinozism. Much in the way that for Freud the Oedipus complex is a repetition at the level of the individual of the phase humankind went through in the transition from the state of nature as depicted in *Totem und Tabu* to civil society, so is there for Hölderlin a structural equivalence of how humankind evolves from the state of nature (that is, Athens) to its present state—whose utter depravity Hölderlin attacks no less bitterly in the *Scheltrede* against his German contemporaries than Rousseau had condemned the inauthenticity of eighteenth-century French society.

   All these themes are taken together in the discourse of the "wise man" that makes up the substance of the fragment of *Hyperion* that is known as the metric version. Admittedly, the fragment did not find its way to the novel's final version. The explanation is, in all likelihood, that it was written when Hölderlin was trying to overcome the dualisms of Kant's and Fichte's philosophy (which he had discussed intensively with Schelling, his close friend from the days of the Tübinger Stift).[60] But after his "inventive return to Rousseau" (to use Link's terminology) had shown him how to do this, the issue probably lost much of its former urgency to him.[61] So if the passage presenting the "wise man" did not find its way to the final version, this does certainly not mean that Hölderlin had become dissatisfied with the content of the wise man's speech. It might well be that Hölderlin simply found it difficult to fit this part of the metric version in his conception of the final version and that this is why he left it out. Commentators agree that the "wise man" is in all likelihood Hyperion himself after his return to Greece from Germany and after having become a hermit, much like Rousseau in Ermenonville. And that places the passage outside the temporal limits of the story Hyperion/Hölderlin had decided to tell Bellarmin.

But, more important, it is also generally agreed that the wise man's speech has in Rousseau's philosophy of history its point of departure.[62] The wise man gives here a philosophy of history, both in the sense of a philosophical reflection of the history of mankind and in that of what belongs to the essence of historical awareness and writing. The story is, basically, a cosmology combining Spinozist and Rousseauist components in a powerful synthesis, which we may see as a formulation of Hölderlin's philosophy of history. Spinozist is the conception of a "spirit" (*Geist*) as the source of all that the world contains and the attribution to this spirit (that is, God) of the properties of purity (*Reinigkeit*), freedom (*Freiheit*), and being free from suffering (*Leidensfrei*). Decidedly Rousseauist, however, is the association of this primeval Spirit with the absence of consciousness (this Spirit is "sich keines Dings und seiner nicht bewusst, für ihn ist keine Welt, denn ausser ihm ist nichts").[63] This is where this primeval Spirit represents the equivalent of Rousseau's (state of) nature and where the wise man's story turns Rousseauist by expressing the message of the *Rêveries* and repeating Rousseau's account of his "experiences" of a happiness untainted by consciousness—that is, the supreme happiness to be expected from a return to the state of nature. This is where, as Rousseau explicitly states, one finds oneself at a stage prior to the partitioning of the world into a subject and object. At this stage—the state of nature, so to say—there is only the *experience,* where *penser c'est sentir,* to quote Rousseau's slogan.[64] This state of nature is contrasted with the state of the proliferation and dissemination of fixed forms[65]—this is the stage in which experience and what it is experience *of* are systematically out of step with each other, in which consciousness arises in order to bring order and to manage this discrepancy and in which the world, because of this, falls apart in subject and object. It is also the state of historical representation, where representation will create only representeds and not give us access to the world. This state of permanent and relentless dissemination ("der Trieb unendlich fortzuschreiten") is the scene of both the grandeur and the misery of human existence. Its grandeur is that it gives us all that distinguishes life from death—"sich aber nicht zu fühlen, ist der Tod"; its misery is that it binds us to the world of forms that are both fixed and transient, which is the paradox of all history.

But whereas the recognition of these two stages, the stage of nature and that of disseminated forms, is the birthplace of dichotomies such as that of the noumenal versus the phenomena (Kant) or the self versus the not-self (Fichte), *Hölderlin both intensifies and transcends such dichotomies.* This he achieves with his notion of "love" (*die Liebe*), for love can come into being only thanks to the opposition between what is on both sides of the dichotomy ("der Wiederstreit der Triebe"), and the stronger their opposition, the stronger love will be. Love has here the connotation[66] of desire and of *Sehnsucht* ("und es sehnt der Geist zum ungetrübten Aether sich zurück")—and draws all its strength from a recognition of what it is not from what has been lost ("sie trägt der Armut schmerzliches Gefühl"[67]); it originates in the awareness of a "having become what one is no longer," to put it in the terms of the last chapter. But as such it may become an invincible force, obliterating the narrow confines of the present while giving access to both the past and the future ("mit ihrer eignen Herrlichkeit veredelt sie die Vergangenheit, wie ein Gestirn durchwandelt sie der Zukunft weite Nacht"). Love may often lead us astray on its perennial excentric course ("doch irret mannigfaltig auch die Liebe"); but there are moments—not of Truth but of Beauty—where it is its own daybreak (where "nur von ihr die Dämmerung entspringt, die heilig ihr und hold entgegenkommt"). *These are moments of sublime experience.*

One will find all this in the following marvelously elegiac passage from the metric version, fully demonstrating Hölderlin's poetic genius—and while effacing myself behind it, I bid farewell to my readers and thank them for their attention:

Als unser Geist, begann

Er lächelnd nun, sich aus dem freien Fluge
Des Himmlischen verlor, und erdwärts sich,

—When our spirit, he now began smilingly,
Lost itself in free flight from Heaven,

And moved towards the earth

Vom Aether neigt', und mit dem Überflusse	Away from the aetherial skies,
Sich so die Armut gattete, da ward	And poverty thus paired with abundance,
Die Liebe. Das geschah, am Tage, da	Then Love was born. This happened at the day
Den Fluten sich Aphrodite entwand.	When Aphrodite emerged from the seas.
Am Tage, da die schöne Welt für uns	At that day, when a fine world began for us,
Begann, begann für uns die Dürftigkeit	Began for us the penury of life
Des Lebens und wir tauschten das Bewusstsein	And we exchanged our purity
Für unsre Reinigkeit und Freiheit ein.—	And our freedom for consciousness.—
Der Leidensfreie Geist befasst	A spirit free from passion does not care
Sich mit dem Stoffe nicht, ist aber auch	For the realm of matter, but neither is it
Sich keines Dings und seiner nicht bewusst,	Conscious of anything, or of itself,
Für ihn ist keine Welt, denn ausser ihm	For it there is no world, for outside itself
Ist nichts.—Doch, was ich sag, ist nur Gedanke.—	Is nothing.—Yet, what I'm saying, only is an idea.—
Nun fühlen wir die Schranken unsers Wesens	Now we feel the limitations of our being
Und die gehemmte Kraft sträubt ungeduldig	And the inhibited force impatiently wrestles
Sich gegen ihre Fesseln, uns es sehnt der Geist	With its chains, and the spirit yearns
Zum ungetrübten Aether sich zurück.	For the transparent aetherial sky.
Doch ist in uns auch wider etwas, das	And yet, something in us also longs
Die Fesseln gern behält, denn würd in uns	To retain our chains, for if in us
Das Göttliche von keinem Widerstande	The Divine was not bound by any resistance—
Beschränkt—wir fühlten uns und ander nicht.	We would not feel ourselves and others.
Sich aber nicht zu fühlen ist der Tod,	But not to feel oneself is death,
Von nichts zu wissen, und vernichtet sein	To know about nothing, and to be annihilated

Ist eins für uns.—Wie sollten wir den
　Trieb,
Unendlich fortzuschreiten, uns zu
　läutern,
Uns zu veredlen, zu befrein, verleugnen?
Das wäre tierisch. Doch wir sollten
　auch
Des Triebs, beschränkt zu werden, zu
　empfangen,
Nicht stolz uns überheben. Denn es
　wäre
Nicht menschlich, und wir töteten uns
　selbst.
Den Widerstreit der Triebe, deren
　keiner
Entbehrlich ist, vereinigt die Liebe. . . .

Doch irret mannigfaltig auch die Liebe.
So reich sie ist, so dürftig fühlt sie sich,

Je mächtiger in ihr das Göttliche
Sich regt—sie dünket nur sich um so
　schwächer.
Wie kann sie so den Reichtum, den
　sie tief
Im Innersten bewahrt, in sich erkennen?
Sie trägt der Armut schmerzliches
　Gefühl,
Und füllt den Himmel an mit ihrer
　Reichtum.
Mit ihrer eignen Herrlichkeit veredelt
Sie die Vergangenheit, wie ein Gestirn
Durchwandelt sie der Zukunft weite
　Nacht
Mit ihren reinen Licht, und sie vergisst,

Dass nur von ihr die Dämmerung
　entspringt,
Die heilig ihr und hold
　entgegenkommt.

Is one and the same to us. How could
　we abnegate
The desire to progress, to purify
　ourselves,
To ennoble and to liberate ourselves?
That would be bestial. But neither
　should we
Proudly discard the gift of the desire

Of being limited. For this were

Inhuman, and we would murder
　ourselves.
The conflict of desires of which none

Is indispensable, is reconciled by
　Love. . . .

But Love also frequently errs.
As rich as it is, as destitute it thinks
　itself to be,
The more powerful the Divine stirs
In it—the more feeble it believes
　itself to be.
How can it then recognize the wealth

It preserves in the depths of its self?
It carries with it the painful awareness
　of its poverty
But pervades Heaven with its riches.

With its own heavenly bliss
It ennobles the past, like a guiding star
It traverses with its pure light

The spacious night of the future, and
　it forgets,
That the dawn coming to meet it
　gracefully
And comely, originates from itself.[68]
(my translation)

NOTES

Preface

1. As so brilliantly developed in C. A. W. Brillenburg Wurth, *The musically sublime: Infinity, indeterminacy, irresolvability* (Groningen, 2002), Chapter 1.

2. M. Jay, *Songs of experience* (Berkeley, 2004).

3. C. Ireland, *The subaltern appeal to experience: Self-identity, late modernity, and the politics of immediacy* (Kingston and Montreal, 2004).

Introduction: Experience in History and in Philosophy

1. D. Baecker, *Wozu Kultur?* (Berlin, 2000), 22, 23.

2. C. Ireland, *The subaltern appeal to experience: Self-identity, late modernity, and the politics of immediacy* (Montreal and Kingston, 2004), 145.

3. In his recent study of the triumphs of French theory in the United States since the famous conference "The Languages of Criticism and the Sciences of Man" (held at Johns Hopkins University in 1966, where it all began), François Cusset also comments on the resistance it provoked, notably among philosophers. See F. Cusset, *French theory: Foucault, Derrida, Deleuze, and Cie et les mutations de al vie intellectuelle aux États Unies* (Paris, 2004). The philosopher of history will find it hard to repress a wry remark on this. "Theory" could gain such an easy victory in the American academic world because philosophers of language have always, down to the present day, consistently ignored the problem of the text and of how a text relates to what it is about. And nowhere is this problem more acute than in the writing of history where the historian attempts to account for the past by means of a historical text. So if philosophers of language would have taken the problems investigated in philosophy of history more seriously than they did, competition from "theory" and from the departments of literature would, in all likelihood, have been less fierce than it was in the recent past.

4. M. Pickering, *History, experience, and cultural studies* (London, 1997). Pickering correctly points out that "poststructuralism and postmodernism have been critical of conceptions of experience (too often lumped together, holus-bolus, under the cardinally sinful label of humanism) on the grounds that these presuppose

linear and unitary connections between experience and knowledge, assume progressive and cumulative increments of knowledge on the basis of experience or accredited experience, and enact a closure around experience as lived by human subjects because of its taken for granted status. I have tried to show that these claims, amongst others, are unfounded. Their shadow claims derive from linguistic determinism" (p. 242). See also the excellent M. Jay, "Songs of experience," in Jay, *Cultural semantics: Keywords of our time* (London, 1998), 37–47; and my *History and tropology: The rise and fall of metaphor* (Berkeley, 1994), the last chapter, and my *Historical representation* (Stanford, 2001), 139–175.

5. See J. Toews, "Intellectual history after the linguistic turn: The autonomy of meaning and the irreducibility of experience," *American Historical Review* 92 (1987): 879–907; Toews's views were fiercely attacked from a deconstructivist perspective by Joan Wallach Scott. See J. W. Scott, "The evidence of experience," *Critical Inquiry* 17 (summer 1991): 773–797.

6. See my *Historical representation,* Chapter 5.

7. For an excellent exposition of the recent interest for memory in the writing of history, see P. Hutton, *History as an art of memory* (Hanover and London, 1994). One of the strange things to be noted about this book is that one could almost everywhere exchange the word *memory* for the word *history* without the text becoming incomprehensible.

8. For an explanation, see the conclusion to Chapter 7.

9. See, for example, F. Dretske, *Naturalizing the mind* (Cambridge, Mass., 1995); M. Rye, *Ten problems of consciousness* (Cambridge, Mass., 1995); J. Levine, *Purple haze: The puzzle of consciousness* (Oxford, 2002); P. Carruthers, *Phenomenal consciousness: A naturalistic theory* (Cambridge, 2002); M. Rowlands, *The nature of consciousness* (Cambridge, 2002); D. Papineau, *Thinking about consciousness* (Oxford, 2002); and J. Campbell, *Reference and consciousness* (Oxford, 2003).

10. For a few amazing contemporary theories about how language emerged from experience, see G. G. Harpham, *Language alone: The critical fetish of modernity* (London, 2002), 226–237.

11. As is argued by J. Searle, *The rediscovery of mind* (Cambridge, Mass., 1992); needless to say, the claim that there can be no language without consciousness does not entail the inverse claim that there can be no consciousness without language—unless, of course, consciousness is defined in such a way as to make the inverse claim trivially true. This Cartesian view is defended by P. Carruthers, *Language, thought, and consciousness* (Cambridge, 1996).

12. "As I shall say, there are three worlds: the first is the physical world or the world of physical states; the second is the mental world or the world of mental states; and the third world is the world of intelligibles, or *of ideas in the objective sense;* it is the world of possible objects of thought: the world of theories in themselves, and their logical relations; of arguments in themselves; and of problem situations in themselves." See K. R. Popper, "On the theory of the objective

mind," in K. R. Popper, *Objective knowledge: An evolutionary approach* (Oxford, 1972), 154.

13. See C. L. Becker, *The heavenly city of the eighteenth-century philosophers* (New Haven, 1932), Chapter 1.

14. Some elementary variants of intellectual experience are discussed by R. Sheldrake, *The sense of being stared at* (Hutchinson: London, 2003). Sheldrake introduces here the notion of the "extended mind" in order to make sense of a number of phenomena that cannot be accounted for by mainstream science, such as the well-established fact of a kind of telepathic awareness in people of terrible events that have happened to their beloved ones. Accounts of such inexplicable experiences are too frequent and too well documented to be discarded as mere illusions. The present book can be seen as an elaboration of this theme with regard to how we can sometimes relate to our collective past.

15. See Chapter 6.

16. Although the claim has been made by historians. Modris Eksteins, for example, has argued that the contemporary historian should write history "from the border, which is the new center," and that this will reveal to him "the intimacy not of truth but of experience." See M. Eksteins, *Walking since daybreak: A story of Eastern Europe* (London, 2000), xxi. And one might also think, in this context, of S. Schama, *Landscape and memory* (London, 1995), where Schama takes experience and memory as his guide.

17. As I argued in the chapter on Hayden White in my *Historical representation*.

18. This is how White's *Metahistory* is usually interpreted. But an alternative reading of this book is possible as well. In my *Historical representation* I argued that White was interested less in the tropological grid itself than in how the fissures and tensions in that grid could be exploited by the historian to make room for a quite personal relationship to the past. If read in this way, the gap between *Metahistory* and this book is far less deep.

19. And that White was the first to introduce into historical theory. See H. White, "The politics of historical interpretation: Discipline and de-sublimation," in White, *The content of the form* (Baltimore, 1987), especially 71–75.

20. N. Beets, *Camera obscura* (Haarlem, 1952 [1839]), 378.

21. Antoine Compagnon uses an even stronger metaphor when speaking of the *terrorisme intellectuel* of "theory" and when urging us to abandon it for good old "common sense." See A. Compagnon, *Le démon de la théorie* (Seuil: Paris, 1998), 12, 13.

22. Throughout this book, I shall strictly distinguish between the notions of "historism" and of "historicism": the term *historism* refers to the kind of historical theory one may associate with Ranke, Humboldt, or Droysen. The term *historicism* has the meaning Popper gave to it in his *Poverty of historicism* (London, 1954); that is, it will be used for referring to speculative philosophies of history (such as the Hegelian or the Marxist system). See also Chapter 1, note 39.

23. The theme is magisterially dealt with in the first part of W. Schivelbusch, *The culture of defeat: On national trauma, mourning, and recovery* (New York, 2003).

24. This has been the essence of my argument about nostalgia in the last chapter of my *History and tropology;* nostalgia was described there as "the experience of difference (between past and present)" and the writing of history as we know it in the West since, say, 1800, makes sense only after this difference is felt and recognized.

25. See the conclusion to Chapter 5.

Chapter 1: Linguistic Transcendentalism in Extremis:
The Case of Richard Rorty

1. This notion of linguistic transcendentalism in extremis is meant to convey the suggestion of both transcendentalist extremism and a transcendentalism in its death throes.

2. E. S. Reed, *The necessity of experience* (New Haven and London, 1996), 8.

3. Many references to Rorty's writings will be made in this chapter (and the next), in particular: R. Rorty, ed., *The linguistic turn* (Chicago, 1967); R. Rorty, *Philosophy and the mirror of nature* (Princeton, 1979); R. Rorty, *Consequences of pragmatism* (Minneapolis, 1982); R. Rorty, J. B. Schneewind, and Q. Skinner, eds., *Philosophy in history* (Cambridge, 1984); R. Rorty, *Contingency, irony, and solidarity* (Cambridge, 1989); R. Rorty, *Philosophical papers, volume 1* (Cambridge, 1991); R. Rorty, *Philosophical papers, volume 2* (Cambridge, 1991); and R. Rorty, *Philosophical papers, volume 3* (Cambridge, 1998).

4. If one wishes, one may well project onto my more or less accidental use of the term *sublime* here all the technical connotations that were given to this word in the Kantian system. Within this system the sublime brings us to the elevated level of transcendentalism where the capacities and shortcomings of our intellectual faculties can meaningfully be discussed. Indeed, transcendental philosophy is philosophy from the point of view of the sublime, and it thus neutralizes the potential sublimity of experience by hiding this potential within itself in the same way that we become unable to recognize the distance between two points A and B if they are seen from a point lying on the line connecting A and B. The sublimity of transcendental philosophy robs (the experience of) reality of the dimension of the sublime.

5. Rorty, *Philosophical papers, Vol. 1,* 175–197.

6. Aristotle, *De Anima,* 424, a, 17–21.

7. Rorty, *Consequences of pragmatism,* xxxix. What is wrong with claims like these has been pointed out by Putnam: "The key assumption responsible for the disaster is that there has to be an interface between our cognitive powers and the external world—or, to put the same point differently, the idea that our cognitive powers cannot reach all the way to the objects themselves." See H. Putnam, "The Dewey Lectures," *Journal of Philosophy* 91, no. 9 (1994): 453.

8. When speaking here and on several other occasions in this chapter of "pre-Tarskian conceptions of the correspondence theory of truth," I would not wish to imply that Tarski's truth theory could plausibly be seen as a sophisticated variant of the correspondence theory. Tarski's truth theory is applicable to formalized languages only (and, more specifically, to the relationship between the object and metalevels in formalized languages) and it would require some very strong reinterpretation indeed if one were to apply it to the relationship between language and an objective reality of historical states of affairs. In fact, it is quite strange that Tarski's truth theory has become so customarily associated with the correspondence theory of truth; and when I follow this custom here, this should certainly not be taken to mean that there are, in my view, good arguments in favor of it.

The issue is of some importance here, since it will now be clear that the rejection of the correspondence theory in this section should not, in its turn, invite the question of whether the correspondence theory would look any better if reformulated in conformity to Tarski's suggestions, for no such thing is possible.

9. Quoted in Rorty, *Consequences of pragmatism*, xxvi.

10. Rorty, *Philosophical papers, Vol. 1*, 138.

11. "Jener Schatten, welche alle Dinge zeigen, wenn der Sonnenschein der Erkenntnis auf sie fällt—jener Schatten bin ich auch." See F. Nietzsche, "Menschliches, Allzumenschliches, Zweiter Band," in Nietzsche, *Werke I* (Frankfurt am Main, 1983) (Ullstein Materialien), 872. F. Nietzsche, *Human, all too human: A book for free spirits* (Cambridge, 1986), 301.

12. Self-evidently, the physicist's mathematics is no such scheme or *tertium quid,* since mathematics is a language and not a *tertium quid* between language and reality.

13. Rorty, *Philosophical papers, Vol. 1*, 126.

14. Rorty, *Philosophical papers, Vol. 1*, 140, 141.

15. Rorty, *Philosophical papers, Vol. 1*, 10.

16. Rorty, *Philosophical papers, Vol. 1*, 51.

17. For a defense of this view, see, for example, my *History and tropology: The rise and fall of metaphor* (Berkeley, 1994), Chapter 3.

18. Rorty, *Consequences of pragmatism*, 144.

19. Rorty, *Consequences of pragmatism*, 139.

20. My objection would be, though, that this "ontological democratization" of the status of texts to that of lumps (with which I agree) does not in the least imply that the methods for studying lumps are necessarily the same as those for studying texts. Similarly, both a glass of wine and subatomic particles are, ontologically, objects; but it would be ridiculous to infer from this fact alone that the "methods" of the wine taster will be of any help to the theoretical physicist—or vice versa.

21. Rorty, *Philosophical papers, Vol. 1*, 78–93.

22. Rorty, *Philosophical papers, Vol. 1*, 146.

23. Rorty, *Philosophical papers, Vol. 1*, 113–126.

24. Rorty, *Philosophical papers, Vol. 1*, 128.

25. Rorty, *Philosophical papers, Vol. 1*, 10 ff.

26. Rorty, *Philosophical papers, Vol. 1*, 81.

27. Rorty, *Philosophical papers, Vol. 1*, 52.

28. Rorty, *Philosophical papers, Vol. 1*, 145.

29. Rorty, *Philosophical papers, Vol. 1*, 152.

30. Rorty, *Philosophical papers, Vol. 1*, 10. The suggestion to exchange Descartes for Darwin is also present in Popper's philosophy of science when he recommends us to see the evolution of science as a Darwinian "survival of the fittest" scientific theory. Similar suggestions can be found in Dewey's philosophical oeuvre and where Dewey's pragmatism attempts to circumvent transcendentalist accounts of (the acquisition of) knowledge. From this perspective Dewey's reference to Darwin fits well within the framework of the present book.

31. Rorty, *Philosophy and the mirror of nature*, 10.

32. In Derridean deconstructivism the (historical) context, within which historism always embedded the text, has now been absorbed by the text itself—thus effecting that unprecedented interaction of the text with itself, which is deconstructivism's lifeblood.

33. Rorty, *Philosophical papers, Vol. 2*,15.

34. Rorty, *Contingency*, 9.

35. Rorty, *Philosophical papers, Vol. 2*, 62.

36. Rorty, *Contingency*, 7.

37. Rorty, *Philosophical papers, Vol. 2*, 17.

38. Rorty, *Philosophical papers, Vol. 1*, 61.

39. I distinguish in this book between "historism" and "historicism." Historism refers to the kind of historical writing that came into being at the beginning of the nineteenth century and that we often associate with the names of Ranke, Humboldt, and Droysen; I shall use historicism for referring to the kind of speculative philosophies of history that Popper had so famously attacked in his *Poverty of Historicism* (1957). And we should recall that historism and historicism (as defined here) are quite different things: One could argue that historism was born from the rejection of historicism. Little love was lost between Ranke and Hegel.

40. Rorty, *Philosophical papers, Vol. 1*, 81.

41. Rorty, *Philosophical papers, Vol. 2*, 81.

42. That is, *contingent* as opposed to the intentions of the builders of speculative philosophers of history and of the constructors of Lyotard's *grands récits* or *méta-récits*.

43. Rorty, *Contingency*, xvi.

44. Rorty, *Contingency*, 18; Rorty, *Philosophical papers, Vol. 1*, 162–175; Rorty, *Philosophical papers, Vol. 2*, 12–17.

45. I expounded on this admittedly somewhat disparaging interpretation of Davidson's view of metaphor in my "Davidson en Derrida over de metafoor," in R. T. Segers, ed., *Visies op cultuur en literatuur* (Amsterdam, 1991).

46. Rorty, *Philosophical papers, Vol. 2*, 12.

47. Rorty, *Contingency*, 73.

48. Rorty, *Consequences of pragmatism*, 108.

49. Rorty, *Contingency*, 19.

50. A. MacIntyre, "The relationship of history to its past," in R. Rorty et al., *Philosophy in history*, 31–49; and A. C. Danto, "The decline and fall of analytical philosophy of history," in F. R. Ankersmit and H. Kellner, eds., *A new philosophy of history* (London, 1995), 73.

51. Rorty, *Contingency*, 13.

52. For an elaboration of the affinities between historism and postmodernism, see the last chapter of my *History and tropology*.

53. R. Rorty, "On ethnocentrism: A reply to Clifford Geertz," in Rorty, *Philosophical papers, Vol. 1*, 203.

54. Rorty, "On ethnocentrism," 203.

55. Rorty, "On ethnocentrism," 207.

56. Rorty, "On ethnocentrism," 207.

57. For the remainder of my argument in this section I am deeply indebted to Jack Zammito's brilliant and magisterial survey of philosophy of science since Quine to the "science wars" of the 1990s, even though my own view about the relationship between history and science is diametrically opposed to his. See J. H. Zammito, *A nice derangement of epistemes* (Chicago and London, 2004).

58. W. V. Quine, *Word and object* (Cambridge, Mass., 1975), 28.

59. Although Quine refers to a book by the linguist K. L. Pike when dealing with the issue of phonemics and of how to reduce language to writing. See Quine, *Word*, 28.

60. W. V. Quine, "Two dogmas of empiricism," in Quine, *From a logical point of view* (Cambridge, Mass., 1961), 41.

61. W. V. Quine, "On what there is," in Quine, *From a logical point of view*, 13, 14.

62. Quine, *Word*, 51, 52.

63. Quoted in Zammito, *A nice derangement*, 16. And Zammito also mentions here an essay by Gary Hardcastle in which Hardcastle uses Quine for a discussion of the methods of intellectual history (as proposed by Quentin Skinner).

64. D. Davidson, "Radical interpretation," in Davidson, *Inquiries into truth and interpretation* (Oxford, 1985), 129.

65. Davidson, "Radical interpretation," 134.

66. B. T. Ramberg, *Donald Davidson's philosophy of language* (Oxford, 1989), 70.

67. Rorty, *Philosophical papers, Vol. 1*, 160.

68. D. Hume, "An enquiry concerning human understanding," in Hume, *En-*

quiries concerning the human understanding and concerning the principles of morals (Oxford, 1972), 95.

69. This has also been argued recently by Giuseppina d'Oro in an essay in which she opposes the historism of Collingwood to the a- or even anti-historism of Davidson. See G. d'Oro, "Reenactment and radical interpretation," *History and Theory* 43 (2004): 198–209. I quote from the abstract of her essay: "Davidson endorses an extensional semantics that links meaning with truth in the attempt to extrude intensional notions from a theory of meaning. Since radical translation rests on a truth-conditional semantics, it rules out the possibility that there may be statements that are intelligible even though based on false beliefs. Collingwood's account of re-enactment, on the other hand, disconnects meaning from truth, thereby allowing for the possibility of understanding agents who have false beliefs" (p. 198; see also p. 205). Since the historian characteristically brackets, so to speak, the truth of the beliefs of historical agents, Davidson's philosophy of language will be of little use to the historical theorist.

70. A. Cobban, *The social interpretation of the French Revolution: The Wiles lectures given at the Queen's University Belfast* (Cambridge, 1964).

71. See for this my *Narrative logic: A semantic analysis of the historian's language* (Dordrecht and Boston, 1983), especially Chapters 4 and 5.

72. W. B. Gallie, "Essentially contested concepts," in Gallie, *Philosophy and the historical understanding* (New York, 1968).

73. See, for example, P. Kitcher, "Theory, theorists, and theoretical change," *Philosophical Review* 87 (1978): 519–547, and the otherwise sympathetic exposition of Kitcher's views in J. H. Zammito, *A nice derangement*, 75, 76.

74. D. Davidson, "On the very idea of a conceptual scheme," in Davidson, *Inquiries into truth and interpretation* (Oxford 1985), 185.

75. Davidson, "Conceptual scheme," 190.

76. Davidson, "Conceptual scheme," 189.

77. A. C. Danto, *Narration and knowledge* (New York, 1985), 143–183.

78. See my criticism of the empiricist position in historical theory in my *Historical representation*, 49–63.

79. Barrington Moore Jr., *Social origins of dictatorship and democracy: Lord and peasant in the making of the modern world* (Aylesbury, 1969).

80. See my *Historical representation*, 34, 35.

81. N. Rescher, "Conceptual schemes," in P. A. French, T. E. Uehling Jr., and H. K. Wettstein, eds., *Midwest studies in philosophy, Volume V, Studies in epistemology* (Minneapolis, 1980), 340. It should be added, though, that Rescher's argumentation substantially differs from the one I have presented here.

82. Rescher, "Conceptual schemes," 324.

83. This abnegation of historism has also been observed, and sharply criticized, by Zammito. See J. H. Zammito, "Rorty, 'Historism,' and the practice of history," *Rethinking History: The Journal of Theory and Practice* (forthcoming). Zammito's main argument is that Rorty's historism has never been more than a matter of

"keeping up historist appearances," and he illustrates his argument with some very striking examples of Rorty's indeed extremely "Whiggish" interpretation of the history of philosophy.

84. K. Mannheim, "Historismus," in Mannheim, *Wissenssoziologie* (Neuwied am Rhein, 1970), 247.

85. See also Chapter 7, note 24. Another example that may come to mind is Charles Taylor, *Sources of the self* (Cambridge, 1989). Taylor offers in this much-discussed book an archeology of modern identity. As such, the book is impressive proof of what history can and should mean to us. It is all the more striking that the chapter devoted to history (Chapter 11) is the least convincing of the whole book. But, even more so, think of Hayden White, who has done more than any one else to stimulate our awareness of what he once described as "the burden of history" and who yet abandoned, in the end, philosophy of history for comparative literature.

86. Cited by Rorty himself in his *Philosophical papers, Vol. 1*, 157. Further characteristic is Rorty's statement: "To say, as Davidson does, that 'belief is in its nature veridical' is not to celebrate the happy congruence of subject and object but rather to say that the pattern truth makes is the pattern that *justification to us* makes" (Rorty, *Philosophical papers, Vol. 3*, 25). Observe, that the historian—as historian—will emphatically insist that "justification to us" should be replaced by "justification to him" (i.e., the historical agent whose thought and actions are investigated by the historian). To put it in the words of Arthur Danto, the logic of the historian's discourse always is the logic of intensional contexts. See the last chapter of A. Danto, *The transfiguration of the commonplace* (Cambridge, 1983). But for Rorty, the people who lived and thought in the past are essentially living in the same world as we do; despite his profound admiration for Hegel, Gadamer, and Foucault, he nowhere leaves any room for the abyss separating us from those who lived in another age. For Rorty all human beings, since the days of Adam, are essentially contemporaneous. This is an important source of the anti-historism pervading the writings of this otherwise so historically minded philosopher.

87. But no rule is without its exceptions. Think, for example, of Henry Adams, and although Arthur Danto's past is, essentially, the history of Western art of the last half century, his approach to this past is historist through and through.

88. G. F. Handel, the last duet from *L'allegro, il penseroso ed il moderato* (1740).

89. See Rorty, *Linguistic Turn*, passim.

90. Rorty, *Contingency*, 88.

91. Rorty, *Philosophical papers, Vol. 2*, 115, 116.

Chapter 2: From Language to Experience

1. T. W. Adorno, "The experiential content of Hegel's philosophy," in Adorno, *Hegel: Three studies* (Cambridge, Mass., 1993), 53.

406 *Notes to Pages 69–78*

2. J. G. Herder, *Briefe zur Beförderung der Humanität: Herausgegeben von Hans Dietrich Irmscher* (Frankfurt am Main, 1991), 581.

3. Nagel's problem had already been put on the philosopher's agenda by William James: "Were we lobsters, or bees, it might be that our organization would have led to our using quite different modes from these actual ones of apprehending our experiences. It might be too (we cannot dogmatically deny this) that such categories, unimaginable by us today, would have proved on the whole as serviceable for handling our experiences mentally as those we actually use." Quoted in N. Rescher, "Conceptual schemes," in P. A. French, T. E. Uehling, and H. K. Wettstein, eds., *Midwest studies in philosophy, Volume V, Studies in epistemology* (Minneapolis, 1980), 323. On the same page Rescher also mentions a similar example given by the German sociologist Simmel.

4. T. Nagel, "What it is like to be a bat," in Nagel, *Mortal questions* (Cambridge, 1983), 166.

5. Nagel, "What it is like to be a bat," 169.

6. The argument has since then become known as the *qualia* problem.

7. Nagel, "What it is like to be a bat," 179.

8. R. Rorty, *Consequences of pragmatism* (Minneapolis, 1982), xxxv ff.

9. See my *History and tropology: The rise and fall of metaphor* (Berkeley, 1994), introduction.

10. Nagel, "What it is like to be a bat," 171.

11. R. Rorty, *Contingency, irony, and solidarity* (Cambridge, 1989), 94.

12. See, for example, Rorty, *Contingency*, 101. Rorty's dislike of the sublime is also the background of his debate with Lyotard. See R. Rorty, *Philosophical papers, volume 1* (Cambridge, 1991), 214–218.

13. C. Prendergast, *The triangle of representation* (New York, 2000), 12, 13.

14. A fact that is rightly emphasized by Reed. See E. S. Reed, *The necessity of experience* (New Haven and London, 1996), Chapter 6.

15. True, Rorty also mentions Heidegger in this context, but since Rorty's Heidegger is a very Gadamerian Heidegger, I may be forgiven for restricting my discussion here to Gadamer.

16. Elsewhere I have argued that historical representation presents us with such vacuums in the relationship between language and the world. The explanation is that historical representations are, on the one hand, made up of language while being, on the other hand, things from an ontological point of view. They do not fit therefore within the picture, leaving room for language and the world only—which is also accepted within Rorty's pragmatist interaction model of the relationship between language and the world. They are a kind of puncture in the sheet of language, so to speak. See my *History and tropology*, Chapter 3. It follows that representation and experience are the two sides of one and the same coin.

17. Consider, for example, R. Rorty, *Consequences of pragmatism*, Chapter 5,

where experience, as discussed by Dewey, is only tangentially dealt with, even though Rorty's lack of sympathy for the notion is evident.

18. H. G. Gadamer, *Truth and method,* 2nd ed. (New York, 2003), 453.

19. A marvelous illustration is given in Tolstoy's *War and peace.* When Andrej Bolkonski lies mortally wounded on the battlefield of Austerlitz, Napoleon passes by, as chance would have it. Napoleon has a look at him and then mumbles the words "a glorious death." Bolkonksi heard these words but heard them "as he would have heard the humming of a fly. Not only because they were devoid of any interest to him, but he even did not take any notice of them and forgot them immediately. His head was afire, he knew that he was bleeding to death, and he stared in the far, high and eternal sky. He knew that it was Napoleon—his hero—but at that moment Napoleon was to him a wholly insignificant creature, if compared to what happened between himself and that high and infinite sky where the clouds were floating along." Napoleon, the incarnation of History and of all this sublime *narrative* that had started with the French Revolution was reduced to a nonentity compared to the intensity with which the heavily wounded Bolkonski *experienced* his last moments. So, where narrative is, experience is not, and vice versa. See E. Runia, "Het zoemen van een vlieg: Oorlog en vrede in Tolstoj's Oorlog en Vrede," *De Gids* 156 (1993): 646–665.

20. J. Burckhardt, "Weltgeschichtliche Betrachtungen," in Burckhardt, *Gesamtausgabe: Siebenter Band,* ed. Albert Oeri and Emil Dürr (Berlin and Leipzig, 1929), 6, 7.

21. Best formulated in the chapter Gadamer wrote on Dilthey. See H. G. Gadamer, *Wahrheit und Methode* (Tübingen, 1972), 205–229. There is, hence, something profoundly ironic about Gadamer's critique of historism: "It appears that *historicism, despite its critique of rationalism and of natural law philosophy, is based on the modern Enlightenment and unwittingly shares its prejudices"* (Gadamer, *Truth and method,* 270). As we shall find in Chapter 5, exactly the same accusation could be leveled against Gadamer himself.

22. See F. De Saussure, *Course in general linguistics,* trans. and annot. by Roy Harris (London, 1983), 65 ff.

23. See my *Historical representation* (Stanford, 2001), Chapter 1.

24. See my *History and tropology,* 139–144.

25. But this will require a pretty strong instrument that not everyone may be willing or be happy to make use of. The instrument in question is Leibniz's so-called *predicate in notion principle;* this principle fixes the sign's reference in the way proposed by Frege while allowing us to explain its intertextuality (Saussure). For an elaborate defense of this claim, see my *Narrative logic* (Dordrecht and Boston, 1983), Chapter 5; and for a succinct exposition of the same issue see my "Reply to Professor Zagorin," *History and Theory* 31 (1990): 275–297. One of the more momentous implications is that Leibniz's notion of the substance may enable us to show how the world view of the sciences (Frege) and that of the humanities (Saus-

sure) are related, or, to be more precise, to establish on the basis of a Leibnizian common ground where and why both differ from each other, as was suggested eighty years ago in D. Mahnke's brilliant *Leibnizens Synthese von Universalmathematik und Indiivdualmetaphysik* (Halle, 1925).

26. J. Derrida, *Of grammatology*, trans. Gayatri Cakravorty Spivak (Baltimore, 1976), 60. See also 61, 62. I would like to thank Martin Jay for these references. In his forthcoming book *Songs of experience* (Berkeley, 2004) Jay also explains the differences between Derrida and Gadamer with regard to the notion of experience.

27. In his recent book, *Thinking after Heidegger* (Cambridge, 2002), D. Wood argues in favor of "the return of experience" in Derrida. But I would not see in his argument an occasion for reconsidering my claim that Derrida leaves no room for the notion of experience. More specifically, the notion of (historical) experience that I have in mind would certainly be condemned by Derrida as just one more variant of "the metaphysics of presence," although, admittedly, my argument throughout this book is epistemological rather than metaphysical. Rei Terada has also tried to claim a place for experience in Derrida's writings; see R. Terada, *Feeling in theory: Emotion after the "Death of the Subject"* (Cambridge, Mass., 2001). But, again, I would agree with Martin Jay in his forthcoming book on experience when he expresses his doubts about reading Derrida in this way.

28. It should be added, though, that one needs to be a transcendentalist to speak about the "sublimity" of experience. The anomalies we associate with the sublime are such anomalies only to the transcendentalist. No transcendentalism, no sublime—although what we call a sublime experience is of course, itself, wholly indifferent to this fact about it. It exists whether we use this notion or not. This may give us an inkling of the problems in writing a book like this one: One needs the terminology of the (transcendentalist) tradition one wishes to overcome for an exposition of what should replace this tradition. It is as if the French revolutionaries of 1789 could describe what was to be expected from their revolution only in terms of the ancien régime they so much wished to abolish.

29. I would like to thank Professor A. J. Vanderjagt and Dr. B. Roest for their most valuable help with this part of my argument.

30. Dom J. Leclercq, *L'amour des lettres et le désir de Dieu: Initiation aux auteurs monastiques du Moyen Age* (Paris, 1990), 116 ff.

31. It is of interest in the context of this chapter that precisely the same issue was at stake in Descartes's vicious quarrel with the Dutch theologians Voetius and Schoockius—a quarrel that caused Descartes to institute legal proceedings against the University of Groningen, Schoockius's (and my own) alma mater. Voetius and Schoockius argued that the Cartesian *cogito* made theological truth into a plaything of the vicissitudes of the individual human mind. Theological truth was, for them, a public and not a private certainty. Obviously, this was one of the last battles that was fought in the name of Aristotle against the *forum internum* introduced by Descartes and that would again be seriously challenged only three centuries later by Rorty. The historical context is sketched in A. J. Vanderjagt,

"Filosofie tussen humanisme en eclecticisme," in G. A. van Gemert et al., eds., *"Om niet aan onwetendheid en barabarij te bezwijken": Groningse geleerden 1614–1989* (Hilversum, 1989). For a presentation of the material relevant to this momentous debate between the last heirs to 2,000 years of Aristotelianism and Descartes himself, see T. Verbeek, ed., *R. Descartes et M. Schoock: La querelle d'Utrecht—Textes établis, traduits et annotés par Theo Verbeek* (Paris, 1988).

32. A. J. Vanderjagt, "Bernard of Clairvaux and Aelred of Rievaulx," in R. I. A. Nip et al., eds., *Instrumenta patristica XXVIII: Media latinitas* (Turnhout, 1996), 342.

33. Hence the unparalleled elevated status of the book in the Middle Ages: The book is more real than what it is about, in the same way that God's Word is more real than the reality created by the Word. Thus Coletti remarked, "As Curtius's famous survey of the *topos* has shown, figures of the book and of writing appear throughout world literature, but Christianity gave the book 'its highest consecration': its belief in the Bible's absolute totality of divinely inspired meaning sanctioned the use of the book as metaphor for signifying systems." See T. Coletti, *Naming the Rose: Eco, medieval signs, and modern theory* (Ithaca, 1988), 25, 26. This inversion of reality and its (textual) representation clearly announces itself in the well-known formula by Alanus de Insulis: "Omnis mundi creatura / Quasi liber et pictura / Nobis est et speculum." Similarly characteristic of this inversion is the statement by Hugh of St. Victor (died 1141): "This whole perceptible world is like a book written by God's finger . . . , and every creature is like a character, not invented by human choice, but instituted by the Divine will, to manifest and signify somehow God's invisible wisdom"; see J. van Zwieten, *The place and significance of literal exegesis in Hugh of St. Victor* (Amsterdam, 1992), 35.

34. Quite revealing is the idea that reading can be compared to eating. One can think here of the Apocalypse 10.9–10: "And I went to the angel, saying unto him that he should give me the book. And he said to me: Take the book and eat it up. . . . And I took the book from the hand of the angel and ate it up; and it was in my mouth, sweet as honey; and when I had eaten it my belly was bitter." For an early fourteenth-century manuscript illustration of John eating the book, see J. M. Gellrich, *The idea of the book in the Middle Ages: Language, theory, mythology, and fiction* (Ithaca, 1985), 16.

35. Divine wisdom was present in the text and required no interpretation but a being taken up by the reader of the text: "While medieval instructors surely appreciated the distinction between 'reality' and 'semblance'—between Augustine's eternal Text and temporal writing—they nonetheless rigorously tried to locate divine wisdom within the letters of the *sacra pagina*. Instead of a stumbling block to truth, the 'semblance' was its 'revelation' in the Bible, the 'veil' (*integumentum*) or 'mirror' (*speculum*) in which divine wisdom was present, if only readers had 'eyes to see.'" See Gellrich, *Idea of the book,* 33.

36. Obviously, it is not an existential but a cognitive anachoorèsis that I have in mind here. The existential alienation from the world is at least as old as Gnos-

ticism. Gnosticism presented this world as a hell through which the divine spark that some of us have in ourselves (the *scintilla animae*) must pass in order to be reunited with (or in) a primordial fullness (*plèrooma*).

37. H. Putnam, "The Dewey Lectures 1994: Sense, nonsense, and the senses—An inquiry into the powers of the human mind," *Journal of Philosophy* 91, no. 9 (1994): 454.

38. An example would be the tropological reading of historical texts as proposed by Hayden White. See my *Historical representation, 63–73.*

39. This argument was most recently put forth in Mark Bevir, *The logic of the history of ideas* (Cambridge, 1998). For a discussion of the merits and problems of this study, see the debate between Bevir and me in *Rethinking History* 4, no. 3 (2000): 351–373.

40. I should add that I am, perhaps, less afraid of "subjectivism" than most of my colleagues. See my *Historical representation,* Chapter 2.

41. See my *Historical representation,* Chapter 1.

42. This is also why I very much welcome Putnam's and McDowell's attempt to rehabilitate the notion of experience but expect it to remain unsuccessful. Experience can become the philosophical crowbar that it is only if introduced together with the notion of representation. As long as these notions are used without reference to each other, they will remain relatively helpless. They reveal their strength only in close cooperation with each other.

43. See section 4.4 on Walter Benjamin in Chapter 4.

44. See also section 7.3 of Chapter 7.

45. For an elaboration of the thesis that in historical writing objectivity is to be achieved by means of subjectivity, see my *Historical representation,* Chapter 2.

46. A. Ehrenzweig, *The hidden order of art: A study of the psychology of artistic imagination* (Berkeley, 1967).

47. See, for example, illustrations 325, 326, 328, and 330 in W. Stechow, *Dutch landscape painting of the seventeenth century* (London, 1966).

48. For a discussion of how baroque art anticipated the wilder asymmetry of art nouveau, see G. Bazin, *The Baroque: Principles, styles, modes, themes* (New York, 1978).

49. For a further comment on the objectivity/subjectivity issue from the perspective of subjective historical experience, see section 7.4 of Chapter 7.

Chapter 3: Huizinga and the Experience of the Past

1. J. Huizinga, "De taak der cultuurgeschiedenis," in Huizinga, *Verzamelde Werken 7: Geschiedwetenschap, Hedendaagsche Cultuur* (Haarlem, 1950), 72.

2. L. von Ranke, *The theory and practice of history,* ed. G. G. Iggers and K. von Moltke (Indianapolis, 1973), 39.

3. Ranke, *Theory and practice of history,* 36.

4. M. Oakeshott, *Experience and its modes* (Cambridge, 1933); J. W. Meiland,

Skepticism and historical knowledge (New York, 1965); L. J. Goldstein, *Historical knowing* (London, 1976). The constructivist thesis had already been defended 150 years ago by Droysen: "This is the most fundamental theorem of our science, namely, that whoever wants to know something about the past, should not hope to find this in the past itself, for the past itself is no longer available; instead he should hope to find it in what the past has left us, in whatever form, in what is still available and open to empirical investigation" (my translation). See J. G. Droysen, *Historik* (Munich, 1971), 20.

5. For some examples, see R. Lowenthal, *The past is a foreign country* (Cambridge, 1985), 245–249. Lowenthal concludes his exposition with the following words: "Laymen glean little historical knowledge from, say a table that has been in the family for generations." He then quotes D. S. Carne-Cross: "One does not know its history in the way an art historian knows the pedigree of a picture. It brings rather a sense of the past," and comments, "But that tangible sense persuades us that the past we recall and chronicle is a living part of the present." For further examples, see also J. Tollebeek, *De ekster en de kooi* (Amsterdam, 1996), 35–58. The mechanisms of memory that are at work here were analyzed by Freud in his essay on Wilhelm Jensen, *Gradiva: A Pompeiian fancy* (1903). See Lowenthal, *The past is a foreign country*, 255.

6. F. Meinecke, *Die Entstehung des Historismus* (Munich, 1965; 1st ed., 1936), 465.

7. Simon Schama's marvelous *Embarrassment of riches* provoked a great deal of debate about these issues. See, for example, F. Haskell, "Visual sources and *The Embarrassment of Riches,*" *Past and Present* 120 (1988): 216–226, and Haskell, *History and its images: Art and the interpretation of the past* (New Haven, 1993).

8. See sections 3.4 and 3.5 for a clarification of Huizinga's use of the word *sensation* instead of *experience*.

9. J. Huizinga, "De taak der cultuurgeschiedenis," 71, 72.

10. "Die Raum- und Zeitbedingungen sind verändert; ungeheure Fernen werden überschaut und gleichsam erst wahrnehmbar; die Ausdehnung des Blicks über grössere Mengen und Weiten." Quoted in F. O. Bollnow, *Das Wesen der Stimmungen* (Frankfurt am Main, 1956), 88; elsewhere Bollnow comments: "In *Rausch* the human being is torn from his isolation and made part of a larger community embracing him" (my translation) (Bollnow, *Das Wesen*, 86).

11. See Lowenthal, *The past is a foreign country*, 203. Lowenthal observed here that "it is not introspection that yields these heightened recollections [of the past], but the chance reactivation of forgotten sensations, commonly *a touch or smell or taste or sound*" [my italics]. Like nostalgia's alpine melody, the village bell was Cowper's mechanism:

> Clear and sonorous, as the gale comes on!
> With easy force it opens all the cells
> Where mem'ry slept. Wherever I have heard

A kindred melody, the scene recurs,
And with it all its pleasure and pains."

The paradigmatic example is, of course, Proust's much discussed madeleine.

12. And one might even conjecture that precisely because of this, successful individuation and precision is easier to achieve in the domain of sounds and of music than in that of visual form and painting. The more the need for individuation, the sooner things may be expected to go wrong. And, indeed, music is closer to mathematics than painting. Obviously, considerations like these are at odds with the vagueness that Huizinga himself projected on historical experience.

13. This relationship between experience and identity implied by *Ahnung* will provide us with the background of the notion of sublime historical experience, to be discussed in the last chapter of this book. In the case of sublime historical experience we, or a civilization, undergo an experience provoking the shift from one historical identity to another, and this shift requires us to move through a sphere where identity is momentarily held in abeyance in the way suggested by *Ahnung*, as analyzed here. See also my *Narrative logic: A semantic analysis of the historian's language* (Boston and The Hague, 1983), 196.

14. And I remind the reader of the fact that at the end of the passage I quoted, Huizinga himself relates historical experience to music. And this does not substantially alter the picture I have sketched when speaking about sound. Suppose we hear two different performances of the same Beethoven sonata. In that case we do not hear the same sonata twice—for what would be the allegedly unchangeable identity of the sonata? Suppose we would decide to ascribe this identity to the score written by Beethoven—as would probably be our natural reaction when confronted with this question of the identity of the sonata. But *this* is not what we *hear:* We listen to music and not to scores, even though the sonata is played on the basis of what we find in the score. So we encounter here again the same indeterminacy with regard to identity that was discussed in the previous note. Last, Huizinga's remark—unfortunately not elaborated by him—that *Ahnung* in history comes close to "an understanding of the world by music" must remind us of Schopenhauer's view that music brings us to the world in its quasi-noumenal stage where the *principium individuationis* has not yet given form to our representations of the world, a stage that Schopenhauer explicitly relates to the sublime, as I shall also do in the last chapter to this book.

15. "And, in the way we have said, the sense faculty is like the actual sense object—it is affected as being unlike but on being affected it becomes like and is such as what acts on it" (Aristotle, *De Anima*, 418, a). Aristotle's claim of the continuity between subject and object of experience invites him to privilege the sense of touch to that of seeing (see Aristotle, *De Anima*, 435). Surely this epitomizes the unbridgeable gap between Aristotelian epistemology and Western epistemology since Descartes. And it is precisely for this same reason that Aristotle is

a so much better guide for understanding history and the humanities than Western epistemology.

16. W. Shakespeare, "Romeo and Juliet," in Shakespeare, *The complete works of William Shakespeare: Comprising his plays and poems* (Spring Books: Middlesex, 1958), 901.

17. Huizinga's wordings here are reminiscent of Hugo von Hofmannsthal's characteristic of an experience of the world that is not or no longer mediated by language. I discussed the implications of Hofmannsthal's conceptions for the notion of historical experience in my *Historical representation,* 140–144.

18. J. Huizinga, "Het historisch museum," in Huizinga, *Verzamelde Werken 2: Nederland* (Haarlem, 1950), 566.

19. J. Huizinga, "Mijn weg tot de historie," in Huizinga, *Verzamelde werken I* (Haarlem, 1948), 23.

20. W. E. Krul, *Historicus tegen de tijd: Opstellen over leven en werk van Johan Huizinga* (Groningen, 1990), 132.

21. M. G. Kemperink, *Van observatie tot extase* (Utrecht, 1988), 87 ff.

22. And like the German and Austrian poets and novelists (such as Hugo von Hofmannsthal) undergoing at this same time their so-called language crisis.

23. It is possible to see much of contemporary French literary criticism and philosophy, as exemplified by *Tel quel* or by Derrida, as an elaboration of the philosophical intuitions underlying Mallarmé's "pure poetry." Mallarmé would have agreed with Derrida's "il n'y a pas dehors texte"; the extravagancies of poststructuralist French philosophy and its peculiar disregard for the real is, to a large extent, a repetition of how nineteenth-century symbolism reacted to literary realism and naturalism. And this is where sensitivism and symbolism are diametrically opposed to each other.

24. See E. Endt, *Herman Gorter: Documentatie 1864–1897* (Amsterdam, 1986), 179. I am referring with this example to a passage in Gorter's rejected doctoral dissertation of 1888. Gorter's *Verzen,* published two years later, are, probably, the best and purest expression of sensitivism in Dutch literature.

25. Kemperink, *Van observatie tot extase,* 85–88.

26. L. van Deijssel, *Verzamelde opstellen: Tweede bundel* (Amsterdam, 1897), 185, 298, 299.

27. For a more elaborate discussion of Huizinga's conception of historical sensation or experience and for where this notion differs from the notion of *Erlebnis* in German hermeneutics, see my *De historische ervaring* (Groningen, 1993). References are also give there to what other historians have written on the subject of historical experience.

28. The fact is all the more significant since the Dutch equivalent of *historical experience* would be *historische ervaring,* and since this term in Dutch has exactly the same connotations as the German *Erfahrung,* it would, in fact, have been a most suitable candidate for the job. It would be even more suitable, since in Dutch

ears the word *sensatie* immediately calls to mind something that is "sensational"—
and there can be no doubt that nothing could be further removed from Huizinga's
intentions here than this.

29. F. Jansonius, "De stijl van Huizinga," *Bijdragen en mededelingen betreffende
de geschiedenis der Nederlanden* 88 (1973): 196.

30. As I deliberately suggest with the word *attempt,* the possibilities for solving
the problem of how to translate experience into language may be as numerous as
the varieties of historical writing. Other possibilities (which will not be discussed
here) would be Ginzburg's proposal to use ekphrastic poetry as a model for the historian's language. See C. Ginzburg, "Ekphrasis and quotation," *Tijdschrift voor
filosofie* 50 (1988): 3–19, or Hayden White's suggestion that the middle voice may
diminish the distance between the past itself and the historian's language. For an
exposition of White's proposal and for the relevant references to his work, see my
Historical representation, Chapter 9. Elsewhere I have used Tocqueville's political
and historical writings for demonstrating how the trope of paradox may effect a direct contact with past reality. See my *Aesthetic politics: Political philosophy beyond
fact and value* (Stanford, 1997), Chapter 6.

31. Huizinga, "Mijn weg tot de historie," 32, 33.

32. J. Huizinga, "De kunst der Van Eyck's in het leven van hun tijd," in
Huizinga, *Verzamelde werken 1* (Haarlem 1948), 436.

33. This is my translation from the preface to the Dutch edition (the preface
to the English edition is not a translation of the original Dutch preface). It must
be observed that almost all the features of Huizinga's style that are discussed here
are absent from the English translation (which is, moreover, also a much abridged
version of the Dutch version). Although it may readily be conceded that it would
be well-nigh impossible to preserve Huizinga's most idiosyncratic use of the Dutch
language in the English translation, it should never be forgotten that the English
translation is a mere shadow of the book that Huizinga originally wrote and that
it fails to do justice to what are precisely its most interesting properties. But I suppose one had best say that the book is, in fact, untranslatable, for it would be impossible to retain the sensitivist allusions without producing a text that would simply sound ridiculous to the English reader. For an exposition of the literary
antecedents of the sentence from the preface that is quoted in my text, see W. E.
Krul, "In de schaduwen van morgen," in R. T. Segers, ed., *Visies op cultuur en literatuur* (Amsterdam, 1991).

34. Jansonius, "De stijl van Huizinga," 198 ff.

35. Although "the fierceness of life" surely is not an entirely satisfactory
translation of the far more dramatic Dutch of *'s levens felheid,* since *fel* is semanti-
cally somewhere between *sharp* and *fierce,* this translation is nevertheless to be
preferred to the peculiarly inept and impotent "the violent tenor of life" of the English translation.

36. J. Kamerbeek Jr., "Huizinga en de beweging van tachtig," *Tijdschrift voor
geschiedenis* 67 (1954): 150.

Chapter 4: Fragments of a History of Historical Experience

1. "Damit ist die Hauptforderung an die gegenwärtige Philosophie aufgestellt und zugleich ihre Erfüllbarkeit behauptet: unter der Typik des kantischen Denkens die erkenntnistheoretische Fundierung eines höheren Erfahrungsbegriff vorzunehmen." See W. Benjamin, "Über das Programm der kommenden Philosophie," in Benjamin, *Gesammelte Schriften II, 1,* ed. Rolf Tiedemann and Hermann Schweppenhäuser (Frankfurt am Main, 1977), 160. W. Benjamin, "On the program of the coming philosophy," in Benjamin, *Selected writings, volume 1, 1913–1926* (Cambridge and London, 1999), 102.

2. R. Koselleck, "Erfahrungswandel und Methodenwechsel," in Koselleck, *Zeitschichten: Studien zur Historik* (Frankfurt am Main, 2000), 68.

3. Koselleck, "Erfahrungswandel und Methodenwechsel," 68.

4. Koselleck, "Erfahrungswandel und Methodenwechsel," 75 ff.

5. For an exposition of the roles of paradox and the sublime in Tocqueville's political and historical writings, see my *Aesthetic politics: Political philosophy beyond fact and value* (Stanford, 1997), Chapter 6.

6. As Rüsen put it, Burckhardt's "critical abnegation of the novelties of the present enabled him to achieve powerful insights into their eviscerating consequences, insights that the political historism of his own time, unproblematically presupposing the possibility of rendering the secrets of tradition and of emancipation, had remained blind to" (my translation). See J. Rüsen, "Der ästhetische Glanz der historischen Erinnerung: Jakob Burckhardt," in Rüsen, *Konfigurationen des Historismus* (Frankfurt am Main, 1993), 280. See also p. 302.

7. "This book traces the transformation of the world between 1789 and 1848 insofar as it was due to what is here called the 'dual revolution'—the French Revolution of 1789 and the contemporaneous (British) Industrial Revolution." See E. Hobsbawm, *The Age of revolution 1789–1848* (London, 1969), xv.

8. See Chapter 8 for an elaboration of this.

9. As Burckhardt expressed it, "The fact that since the last century everything in state, church, art and life changed so radically, has poured such a horrible amount of consciousness in all the relevant minds, that a recovery of the previous tutelage is wholly out of the question" (my translation). Quoted in E. Runia, *Waterloo, Verdun, Auschwitz* (Amsterdam, 1999), 80.

10. "Solange die Sonne am Firmamente steht und die Planeten um sie herumkreisen, war das nicht gesehen worden, dass der Mensch sich auf den Kopf, das ist, auf den Gedanken stellt und die Wirklichkeit nach diesem erbaut. Anaxagoras hatte zuerst gesagt dass der *nous* die Welt regiert; nun aber ist der Mensch dazu gekommen, zu erkennen, dass der Gedanke die geistige Wirklichkeit regieren sollte. Es war dieses somit ein herrlicher Sonnenaufgang. Alle denkende Wesen haben diese Epoche mitgefeiert . . . als sei es zur wirklichen Versöhnung des Göttlichen mit der Welt nun erst gekommen." See G. W. F. Hegel, *Vorlesungen über die Philosophie der Weltgeschichte, Band II–IV* (Felix Meiner Verlag: Hamburg, 1976), 926.

11. Runia, *Waterloo, Verdun, Auschwitz,* 86 (my translation).

12. When dealing with Burckhardt in this text, I shall add an even more dramatic dimension to this curious relationship between "historism as the narrative story of the past" on the one hand and "history as historical experience" on the other. We shall see that the two both exclude and presuppose each other, and that in this fact the sublimity of the past announces itself.

13. See my *Historical representation* (Stanford, 2001), 132–134.

14. For a more detailed account of the Gadamerian view of *Erfahrung* and historical experience, see section 5.5 of Chapter 5.

15. See, for example, W. Benjamin, "Erfahrung und Armut," in Benjamin, *Walter Benjamin: Gesammelte Schriften II, 1,* ed. Rolf Tiedemann and Hermann Schweppenhäuser (Frankfurt am Main, 1977), 213–219. Experience in this essay clearly has all the connotations of "expertise" and so of the knowledge of *how to do certain things* that we may accumulate in life or in some practice. But, as we shall see when dealing with Benjamin, his most interesting reflections on experience present us with a conception of experience that is essentially different from the Gadamerian, dialectical conception.

16. For example, Dilthey attributes to *Erlebnis* what is here ascribed to *Erfahrung.*

17. H. G. Gadamer, *Wahrheit und Methode* (Tübingen, 1972), 336. Gadamer, *Truth and method,* 2nd ed. (New York, 2003), 353. For a further discussion of Gadamer's notion of dialectical experience, see section 5.4 of Chapter 5.

18. T. W. Adorno, "On Proust," in Adorno, *Notes to literature, Volume II,* trans. Shierry Weber Nicholsen (New York, 1991, 1992), 317. Quoted in M. Jay, "Is experience still in crisis? Reflections on a Frankfurt School Lament," in P. U. Hohendahl and J. Fisher, eds., *Critical theory: Current states and future prospects* (Berghahn: New York, 2001).

19. The requirement is, needless to say, an intolerable heresy from the perspective of the almost unanimously held belief that we can never isolate ourselves from our history. For a recent statement of the orthodox view, see D. Simpson, *Situatedness: Or, why we keep saying where we are coming from* (Durham, 2002); and for a psychological approach to the issue, see M. Kusch, *Psychological knowledge: A social history and philosophy* (London, 1999). Simpson's book was critically reviewed by Martin Jay in the November 28, 2002, issue of *The London Review of Books.*

20. F. Meinecke, *Die Entstehung des Historismus* (Munich, 1959), 366, 367. F. Meinecke, *Historism: The rise of a new historical outlook* (London, 1972), 305.

21. For a sample of the relevant references to Goethe's writings, see the most useful compendium of F. Wagner, *Geschichtswissenschaft* (Munich, 1951), 140–151.

22. Which is a quote from L. P. Hartley's *The go-between,* as Lowenthal writes. See D. Lowenthal, *The past is a foreign country* (Cambridge, 1985), xvi.

23. I am deeply indebted here to the research of Henk de Jong for his book on

the German nineteenth-century experience of Italy. The draft of his dissertation on this topic has been my main and indispensable guide here, and many of the insights proposed here will be elaborated in his forthcoming book.

24. "Ich habe jetzt das Reisen erwählt und befinde mich wie aus einem Gefängnis erlöst, alle alten Wünschen und Freuden sind nun auf einmal in Freiheit gesetzt. Auf dem Lande in der Stille augewachsen, wie lange habe ich da die fernen blauen Berge sehnsüchtig betrachtet, wenn der Frühling wie ein zauberischen Spielmann durch unser Garten ging and von der wunderschönen Ferne verlockend sang und von grosser unermesslicher Lust." See J. von Eichendorff, "Das Marmorbild," in Eichendorff, *Eichendorffs Werke in vier Bänden,* ed. Wilhelm von Scholz (Stuttgart, 1924), 343, 344.

25. A pattern that would repeat itself all through the nineteenth century, from Goethe down to Rilke and Hofmannsthal; there is a conjunction of a personal and intellectual crisis, expressing itself in an oppressive awareness of not being able to get to the heart of things, of being trapped in a self-created impasse, of a being locked-in within oneself, within a prison with glass walls, within language and its treacherous pseudo-transparency—and then there is the elation and the liberation occasioned by the *experience of Italy,* by its nature, its history, and its promises of happiness and fulfillment.

26. See K. P. Moritz, *Über die bildende Nachahmung des Schönen* (1788/1789) and his autobiographical novel *Anton Reiser* (1785–1790).

27. J. W. von Goethe, "Italienische Reise: Zweiter Teil," in *Goethes sämtliche Werke, volume 27* (Stuttgart und Berlin, n.d.), 249.

28. All translations into English of *Das Marmorbild* are my own.

29. Eichendorff, "Das Marmorbild," 350; see also p. 352.

30. "In diesen Berg haben sich die Teufel hineingeflüchtet, und sich in den wüsten Mittelpunkt der Erde gerettet, als das aufwachsende heilige Christentum den heidnischen Götzendienst stürzte. Hier, sagt man nun, soll vor allen Frau Venus Hof halten, und alle ihre höllischen Heerscharen der weltlichen Lüste und verbotenen Wünsche um sich versammeln." See L. Tieck, "Der getreue Eckart und der Tannenhäuser," in Tieck, *Werke in vier Bänden: Mit Nachworten und Anmerkungen versehen von Marianne Thalmann, Band II* (Munich, 1963), 35. L. Tieck, "The trusty Eckart," in T. Carlyle, ed., *Latter-day pamphlets and tales by Musæus, Tieck, Richter* (London, 1897), 165.

31. Eichendorff, "Das Marmorbild," 360.

32. Eichendorff, "Das Marmorbild," 377.

33. " 'Lasst das,' erwiderte sie träumerisch, 'nehmt die Blumen des Lebens fröhlich, wie sie der Augenblick gibt, und forscht nicht nach den Wurzeln im Grunde, denn unten ist es freudlos und still.' Florio sah sie erstaunt an; er begriff nicht, wie solche rätselhafte Worte in den Mund des heitern Mädchen kamen." See Eichendorff, "Das Marmorbild," 369.

34. " 'Herr Gott, lass mich nicht verloren gehen in der Welt.' Kaum hatte er die

Worte innerlichst ausgesprochen, als sich draussen ein trüber Wind, wie von dem herannahenden Gewitter, erhob und ihn verwirrend anwehte. Zu gleicher Zeit bermerkte er an den Fenstergesimse Gras und einzelne Büsche von Kräutern wie auf altem Gemäuer. Eine Schlange fuhr zischend daraus hervor und stürzte mit dem grünlichgoldenen Schweife sich ringelnd in den Abgrund hinunter." See Eichendorff, "Das Marmorbild," 378.

35. Many of these themes were taken up again by Eichendorff in his immensely successful *Aus dem Leben eines Taugenichts* (1826); but in this book all the dramatism of the encounter with Italy's past has been eliminated.

36. J. W. von Goethe, "Die zahme Xenien III," in Goethe, *Goethes Sämtliche Werke, Vierter Band, Gedichte, Vierter Teil* (Stuttgart and Berlin, n.d.), 59, vv. 724–728. Nietzsche turned Goethe's Platonist conception topsy-turvy when, right at the beginning of the book, he makes Zarathustra say to the sun the following words: "Du grosses Gestirn! Was wäre dein Glück, wenn du nicht die hättest, welchen du leuchtest!" ("O, ye great constellation! Where were your happiness if you did not have those that you can shine upon!" [my translation]). See F. Nietzsche, "Zarathustra," in Nietzsche, *Friedrich Nietzsche: Werke II*, ed. Karl Schlechta (Munich, 1984), 551.

37. N. Lenau, *Nicolaus Lenau's sämtliche Werke in einem Bande*, ed. ed. E. Emil Barthel (Leipzig, 1883), 11 (my translation).

38. This is most convincingly and forcefully argued in the first chapter of C. A. Brillenburg Wurth's *The musically sublime: Infinity, indeterminacy, irresolvability* (Groningen, 2002).

39. As is observed by Henk de Jong in his forthcoming book on the nineteenth-century German experience of Italy.

40. J. G. A. Pocock, *The Machiavellian moment: Florentine political thought and the Atlantic republican tradition* (Princeton, 1975), 31–49.

41. And as we shall see in Chapter 8, it is to be identified with the mythical.

42. "Ich stand auf der schönen, grünen Wiese, wo sich Dom, Battisterio, Campanile und Camposanto erheben, und zeichnete, an die Mauer der Seminarium gelehnt. . . . Der Himmel war ganz dunkelblau, der Apennin stand violett im Abendglanz; unter meinen Füssen rauschte der Arno, und ich hätte weinen mögen wie ein Kind. All mein Heroismus verschwand." Quoted in W. Kaegi, *Jacob Burckhardt: Eine Biographie I* (Basel, 1948), 474.

43. "Es war eine Art von heiligem Schrecken, den ich während der Betrachtung dieses Gotteshauses empfand, wenn die Blitze die herrlichen Glasgemälde auf Augenblicke erhellten, wenn ich, die Fresken des Giotto im Chore betrachtend, beim Donnern die Scheiben klirren hörte und dabei bedachte, welche Männer die Schwelle dieser Kirche tot oder lebend überschritten haben. Hier schritt Arnolfo zwischen seinen Arbeitern auf und nieder . . . , hier stand einst Dante und sah den Künstlern zu, die den Prachtgebäude mit ihren Arbeiten schmückten. Und nun vollends die Gräber! Vorn links vom Eingang ruht der lebensmüde Galilei. . . . Da

bemerkte ich eine grosse Draperie, unter welcher ein Marmorpiedestal hervorschaute. Ich ging drauf zu, hob das Tuch etwas auf and erschrak, als ich die Inschrift las: NICOLAO MACHIAVELLIO etc. . . . Der Regen dauerte fort und das Gewitter ward noch stärker. Düstrer ward es, und um so heller schienen, wenn es blitzte, die weissmarmoren Gräber zu leuchten; das Tosen des Donners wallte majestätisch durch die hohen Schiffe der Kirch; ich aber schritt van Gemälde zu Gemälde, von Grab zu Grab und hielt im Geiste manche Totenmesse." See J. Burckhardt, *Gesamtausgabe, Erster Band, Frühe Schriften* (Berlin and Leipzig, 1930), 42, 43.

44. "Ja, es gibt eine Praedestinatio duplex; die Einen sind bestimmt, in Italien das Heilige zu sehen, die Andern nicht. Ich gehöre hoffentlich zu den Ersten. . . . Es ist mir an Ort und Stelle wirklich der Gedanke durch den Kopf gegangen, ich sei vielleicht hier geboren. Heine würde sagen: ich sei der Sohn einer Meernixe aus dem Mediterraneum, in einer duftigen, mondhellen Nacht auf der Landungstreppe eines Italienischen Palastes ausgesetzt und von mitleidig-grausamen Leuten einer praktischen Erziehung wegen nach Basel transportiert." See Burckhardt, *Gesamtausgabe, Erster Band,* xxiii.

45. "Um Mitternacht, wenn die Kustoden längst zu Bette gegangen sind, in der Zeit des Vollmondes, wenn derselbe schön blendend durch die hohe Fenster auf die Venus scheint erhält dieselbe nach und nach lebendige Farbe und einen lebendigen, süss schmachtenden Blick (einst nannten es die Griechen: das Feuchte); sie entschwebt dem Piedestal und berührt sanft die beiden Ringer. . . . Die Göttin aber schreitet zum Apollino hin und lispelt süss und leise: Apollon! Er wird lebendig und reibt sich lange die Augen und weiss nicht, wie ihm geschieht; sie aber küsst ihn auf die Stirn, und nun erst richtet er sich auf in seiner ganze Herrlichkeit und folgt der Venus, die nun anfängt, sämtliche Kunstwerke zu erläutern." See Burckhardt, *Gesamtausgabe, Erster Band,* 46.

46. J. W. von Goethe, "Faust: Eine Tragödie," in Goethe, *Goethes Sämtliche Werke, Dreizehnter Band, Erster Teil* (Stuttgart, n.d.), vv. 346–349.

47. J. W. von Goethe, *Faust* (Paddington, 1977), 24.

48. Such is the thesis of Meinecke's magisterial discussion of Goethe's conception of history; see Meinecke, "Die Entstehung des Historismus," 445–585.

49. In his review of Burckhardt's *Weltgeschichtliche Betrachtungen* of 1906, Meinecke is content to show to what extent Burckhardt has been an outsider in the German historical tradition. However, at the end of his career, when reacting to the German catastrophe, Meinecke sees in precisely this a suggestion for how German historical writing had best reorient itself: "Will Burckhardt not be more important than Ranke in the end, for us and for future historians?" (my translation). See F. Meinecke, *Ranke und Burckhardt: Ein Vortrag* (Berlin, 1948), 4. No less astonishing is Gadamer's almost complete lack of interest in Burckhardt.

50. "Die Geschichtsphilosophen betrachten das Vergangene als Gegensatz und Vorstufe zu uns als Entwickelten; wir betrachten das *sich Wiederholende, Konstante,*

Typische als ein in uns Anklingendes und Verständliches." See J. Burckhardt, *Weltgeschichtliche Betrachtungen: Gesamtausgabe, Siebenter Band* (Berlin and Leipzig, 1929), 3. The statement is flatly contradicted, for that matter, by Burckhardt's assertions a little later that change is the essence of the past ("das Wesen der Geschichte ist die Wandlung"). See Burckhardt, *Weltgeschichtliche Betrachtungen,* 19.

51. "Unser Ausgangspunkt ist der vom einzigen bleibenden und für uns möglichen Zentrum, vom duldenden, strebenden und handelnden Menschen, wie er ist und immer war und sein wird; daher unsere Betrachtung gewissermassen pathologisch sein wird." See Burckhardt, *Weltgeschichtliche Betrachtungen,* 3.

52. J. Rüsen, "Der ästhetische Glanz der historischen Erinnerung," 292.

53. Rüsen, "Der ästhetische Glanz der historischen Erinnerung," 292 ff; see also 305, 311. And see J. Rüsen, "Historisches Denken als Trauerarbeit: Jakob Burckhardts Antwort auf eine Frage unserer Zeit," in Rüsen, *Geschichte im Kulturprozess* (Cologne, 2002), 74.

54. "Das erste Leid im Leben brachte der Tod der lieben Mutter am 17. März 1830, in welchem Jahr das Haus auch durch Krankheit heimgesucht war. So machte sich bei ihm schon frühe der Eindruck von der grossen Hinfälligkeit und Unsicherheit alles Irdischen geltend, und dies bei einer sonst zur Heiterkeit angelegten Gemütsart." See J. Burckhardt, "Autobiographische Aufzeichnungen," in Burckhardt, *Gesamtausgabe: Erster Band, Frühe Schriften* (Berlin and Leipzig, 1930), vii.

55. Still further stimulated by his reading of Schopenhauer, of whom he was a great admirer. The similarities between Schopenhauer's speculations on the Will on the one hand and Burckhardt's fascination for the workings of all-encompassing impersonal historical forces on the other will need no elucidation.

56. Rüsen, "Historisches Denken als Trauerarbeit," especially pp. 81 ff. See also R. Stepper, *Leiden an der Geschichte: Ein zentrales Motiv in der Griechischen Kulturgeschichte Jacob Burckhardt's* (Bodenheim, 1997).

57. For an analysis of this theme in Burckhardt's (and Dilthey's) thought, see J. Grosse, "Letzte Stunden: Zur Analogie von Welt- und Lebensgeschichte bei Wilhelm Dilthey und Jacob Burckhardt," *Storia della Storiografia* 37 (2000): 67–101.

58. L. von Ranke, "Englische Geschichte," in Ranke, *Sämtliche Werke, Band 15* (Leipzig, 1867), 103.

59. "Unser Gegenstand ist diejenige Vergangenheit, welche deutlich mit Gegenwart und Zukunft zusammenhängt. . . . Eigentlich sollte man vor allem diejenigen Tatsachen hervorheben, von welchen aus die Fäden noch bis in unsere Zeit und Bildung hineinreichen. Dieser Fakta sind mehr, als man denken sollte." See J. Burckhardt, "Historische Fragmente aus dem Nachlass," in Burckhardt, *Gesamtausgabe, Siebenter Band* (Berlin and Leipzig, 1930), 225. J. Burckhardt, *Judgments on history and historians* (Boston, 1958), 1.

60. "Wir machen keinen Anspruch auf 'Weltgeschichtklichen Ideen,' son-

dern begnügen uns mit Wahrnehmungen und geben Querschnitte durch die Geschichte, und zwar in möglichst vielen Richtungen." See Burckhardt, *Weltgeschichtliche Betrachtungen*, 1.

61. Quoted in Rüsen, "Historisches Denken als Trauerarbeit," 290.

62. Which is how historians down to the present day still tend to react to theory and historical theorists, as I can tell from my own experience.

63. K. Löwith, *Jacob Burckhardt: Der Mensch inmitten der Geschichte* (Luzern, 1936), 77.

64. B. Croce, "Jakob Burckhardt," *Neue Schweizer Rundschau* 6 (1938/1939): 606.

65. J. Wenzel, *Jakob Burckhardt in der Krise seiner Zeit* (Berlin, 1967), 125.

66. "Indem das Zeitliche und ursächliche Ineinandergreifen der Momenten einer Begebenheit aufgelöst wird, scheint die Geschichte in Atome, im beste Falle in unter allgemeinen Gesichstpunkte gruppierte Atome zu verfallen. . . . Diese Manier ist nicht der Anfang einer neuen geschichtlichen Behandlung, sondern die Auflösung aller Geschichte." See W. Dilthey, *Gesammelte Schriften, Band XI* (Leipzig and Berlin, 1921), 71, 72.

67. And for much the same reasons, things apparently so small and insignificant that they had, until now, escaped subsumption in historical narrative: "This perfect being [i.e., the being of the past] did Burckhardt not only discern in the most powerful creations of the great artists, but also in the smallest and humblest things with which the daily life of a great culture surrounds itself. In contrast to those people, whose gaze is reduced to the printed word and whose eyes have become tired by overworking, Burckhardt still had the openness and susceptibility of someone for whom the whole visible world is full of enchantment and who therefore can also take pleasure in the most insignificant things, in some form, in some small vivid beauty, in some perfect utensil" (my translation). See Löwith, *Burckhardt*, 326.

68. Runia, *Waterloo, Verdum, Auschwitz*, 65.

69. L. Gossman, *Basel in the age of Burckhardt: A study in unseasonable ideas* (Chicago, 2000), 284. The superiority of a direct experience of the past to the labors of the philologist was expressed by Burckhardt in the account he wrote of his first visit to Italy: "Who takes better care of his mind, the person who sits for days at his writing desk making excerpts, or the person who spends his time in a wonderful city by a lively intercourse with a so very talented, and in many respects unique population, by daily visits to the greatest works of art of a both more remote and more recent past, and by learning from a direct encounter of these" (my translation). See Burckhardt, *Gesamtausgabe, Erster Band*, 40, 41.

70. For this most apt metaphor "virginity of vision" and for what it may explain about Burckhardt's conception of the past, see Runia, *Waterloo, Verdum, Auschwitz*, 61 ff.

71. Quoted in Wenzel, *Jakob Burckhardt*, 84.

72. L. Wickert, *Theodor Mommsen: Eine Biographie II* (Frankfurt am Main, 1959), 51, 52.

73. For example, when describing a nightly tour through Florence in his diary.

74. F. Nietzsche, *The use and abuse of history*, 2nd ed. (New York, 1957), 22.

75. For a characteristically voluble account of the professionalization of French historical writing, see P. den Boer, *Geschiedenis als beroep: De professionalisering van de geschiedbeoefening in Frankrijk (1818–1914)* (Nijmegen, 1986).

76. J. Michelet, *Histoire de la Révolution Française I* (Paris, 1952), 1.

77. When associating here Romanticism with narrative and with history, I am well aware that this seems to contradict our intuition that *experience,* hence *not* narrative, is Romantic. But this intuition is wrong. *In historicis* Romanticism has been the application of the epistemological way of thinking, inherited from the Enlightenment, to the field of historical writing, as has been shown by Gadamer.

78. Such is the thesis of D. Mahnke, *Leibnizens Synthese von Universalmathematik und Individualmetaphysik* (Halle, 1925).

79. An issue that I have related elsewhere to Quine's notion of "semantic ascent"; see my *Historical representation,* Chapter 1.

80. See the end of section 4.2.

81. As was already pointed out in Chapters 1 and 2.

82. S. Schama, *Landscape and Memory* (London, 1995), 3–23. Schama undoubtedly belongs to the most daring innovators of contemporary historical writing.

83. Right from the start of his intellectual career Benjamin was looking for a notion of experience that might correct the Kantian scientistic conception of experience. See W. Benjamin, "Über das Programm der kommenden Philosophie," 157–171.

84. Benjamin scholars might be surprised by the fact that I shall not deal here with Benjamin's notion of the *Jetztzeit* ("now-time"), as developed in his *Arcades-Project* and as suggested in the posthumous *Theses on the philosophy of history.* It might well seem that this notion is the obvious point of departure for investigating Benjamin's notion of historical experience. But there is a decisive difference between the two. In the *Theses* Benjamin defines the notion of *Jetztzeit* as follows: "History is the subject of a structure whose site is not homogeneous, empty time, but time filled by the presence of the now [*Jetztzeit*]. Thus, to Robespierre ancient Rome was a past charged with the time of the now which he blasted out of the continuum of history. The French Revolution viewed itself as Rome reincarnate. It evoked ancient Rome the way fashion evokes costumes of the past." See W. Benjamin, "Theses on the philosophy of history," in Benjamin, *Illuminations* (New York, 1968), 263. Hence, *Jetztzeit* certainly is suggestive of a union of the present and the past—as also is the case in historical experience as understood throughout book—but the nature of this union is the very opposite of what is the case in historical experience. *Jetztzeit* comes close to Auerbach's notion of *figura,* which relates two separate events in history in such a way that the former is the promise

of the latter and the latter is a fulfillment of the former. Think, for example, of the Jews crossing the Red Sea and Christ's baptism by St. John. *Jetztzeit* is essentially Messianist; it is a reconciliation of past and present, a momentary overcoming of what is separate in the past itself, whereas historical experience—as discussed in the present study—is an experience of loss. In historical experience the past is presented to us in a moment of disunion, whereas *Jetztzeit* unites what was disunited.

Put metaphorically, the union of past and present is approached from opposite directions in *Jetztzeit* and historical experience. *Jetztzeit* is a movement toward union. Historical experience is a movement away from union, although, as such, it presupposes a moment of union. Disunion, that is, the separation of past and present, and the experience of (the loss of) the past are a falling apart of what was a unity. *Jetztzeit* is a moment of fulfillment, of joy and reconciliation; historical experience is a moment of an often traumatic loss, of the dissolution and disruption of identity. For the Messianist dimensions of Benjaminian *Jetztzeit*, see I. Wohlfahrt, "On the Messianistic structure of Walter Benjamin's last reflections," *Glyph* 3 (1978): 148–212; and R. Tiedemann, "Dialectics at standstill," in W. Benjamin, *The Arcades Project*, trans. H. Eiland and K. McLaughlin (Cambridge, Mass., 1999), 929–946.

85. W. Benjamin, "A small history of photography," in Benjamin, *One-way street and other writings* (New York and London, 1997), 249.

86. Benjamin, "A small history of photography," 243.

87. Benjamin, "A small history of photography," 251.

88. For this topos of the demon of noontide and for what it may mean for the notion of historical experience, see the last chapter of my *History and tropology: The rise and fall of metaphor* (Berkeley, 1994). It should not surprise us that Burckhardt knew the experience. See J. Burckhardt, "Bilder aus Italien," in Burckhardt, *Gesamtausgabe, Erster Band* (Berlin and Leipzig, 1930), 32.

89. W. Benjamin, "Das Kunstwerk im Zeitalter seiner technischen Reproduzierbarkeit," in Benjamin, *Illuminationen: Ausgewählte Schriften* (Frankfurt am Main, 1955), 158. W. Benjamin, "The work of art in the age of mechanical reproduction," in Benjamin, *Illuminations* (New York, 1968), 228.

90. "Er [i.e., Atget] suchte das Verschollene und Verschlagene, und so wenden auch solche Bilder sich gegen den exotischen, prunkenden, romantischen Klang der Stadtsnamen; *sie saugen die Aura aus der Wirklichkeit wie Wasser aus einem sinkenden Schiff.*—Was ist eigentlich Aura? Ein sonderbares Gespinst von Raum und Zeit; einmalige Erscheinung der Ferne, so nah sie sein mag" (my italics). See Benjamin, "Kleine Geschichte der Photographie," in Benjamin, *Gesammelte Schriften II, 1*, ed. Rolf Tiedemann and Hermann Schweppenhäuser (Frankfurt am Main, 1977), 378. Benjamin, "A small history of photography," 250.

91. One could read Benjamin's later writings on Baudelaire as suggesting that the work of art may retain its aura even in the age of the reproduction of the work of art; I owe this information to the Finnish Benjamin expert Kia Lindroos.

424 *Notes to Pages 183–185*

92. S. W. Nicholsen, *Exact imagination: Late work—On Adorno's aesthetics* (Cambridge, Mass., 1997), 191.

93. This category of things will be more closely discussed in the last chapter of this book.

94. Benjamin, "Das Kunstwerk im Zeitalter," 158.

95. It is hard to overlook the similarities between Benjamin's argument here and what Barthes would refer to as the *punctum* of a photograph: "This second element which will disturb the *studium* I shall therefore call *punctum;* for *punctum* is also: sting, speck, cut, little hole—and also a cast of the dice. A photograph's *punctum* is that accident which pricks me (but also bruises me, is poignant to me)." See R. Barthes, *Camera lucida* (New York, 1981), 27.

96. Benjamin, "Das Kunstwerk im Zeitalter," 158.

97. Modernist or abstractionist in the sense expounded in Clement Greenberg's seminal *Towards a newer Laokoon* (1948), in which Greenberg contrasts modern art with traditional figurative painting by pointing out that modern art radically abandoned (since Cézanne and Matisse) the illusionism of traditional figurative painting and celebrated unashamedly the brushstroke and the materiality of the modernist painting. We are now no longer invited to look *through* the painting to an imaginary virtual reality behind it but *at* the painting itself.

98. W. Benjamin, "On some motifs in Baudelaire," in Benjamin, *Illuminations* (New York, 1968), 199.

99. In his reading of Hölderlin's and Goethe's poetry Benjamin even constructs a hermeneutics out of this conception. We should avoid making use of any hermeneutic "machinery" that has been invented by philosophers or literary theorists and be content to derive our means for understanding poetry exclusively from the poem itself. These hermeneutic machines, as developed from Schleiermacher to Derrida, always aim to discover some alleged secret of the poetic text— but by making us do so, they merely transform the poem into a helpless mirror confronting us with the mirror image of the hermeneutic machinery we have been employing. Thus the deconstructivist approach to texts does nothing more than debase all poetry and literature into an endless repetition of its own deconstructivist message. Once again, *stay at the surface* and *then* the poem will tell us what it has to tell us; and as soon as we think we have discovered its secret, we may be sure that we have merely been looking at our own boring selves. This is explained in H. Caygill, *Walter Benjamin: The colour of experience* (London and New York, 1998), 36 ff. For a much similar criticism of hermeneutics, see Chapter 2 of the present volume, where I argued against the transcendentalist seduction of hermeneutics to which even Gadamer succumbed.

100. And right from the beginning of his intellectual career Benjamin had opposed this, in his eyes, most regrettable mutilation of the richness of experience in the name of science. Think, for example of W. Benjamin, "Über das Programm der kommenden Philosophie," 157–171. Illustrative is his scathing condemnation

of the Kantian notion of experience: "This experience, however, as already indicated, was unique and temporally limited. Above and beyond this form, which it shares with every type of experience, this experience, which in a significant sense could be called a *world view,* was that of the Enlightenment. But in its most essential characteristics, it is not all that different from the experience of the other centuries of the modern era. *As an experience or a view of the world, it was of the lowest order*" (my italics). See Benjamin, "On the program of the coming philosophy," 101.

101. For Benjamin's critique of Jünger's notion of *Erlebnis,* see W. Benjamin, "Theorien des Deutschen Faschismus," in Benjamin, *Gesammelte Schriften III,* ed. Rolf Tiedemann and Hermann Schweppenhäuser (Frankfurt am Main, 1977).

102. In fact, things are somewhat more complicated. Benjaminian *Erfahrung* unfortunately still retains something of the dialectical notion of experience, where experience is part of a larger history of experience (determining to a certain extent its "content"). Insofar as I am allowed to criticize Benjamin, I would say that this is where his conception of experience is still insufficiently consistent with itself— insufficiently consistent since the whole revolutionary drift of Benjaminian experience is to get rid of this contextualization of experience. This is why in this book experience is always associated with the notion of the sublime, since this notion is the most powerful brake on any attempt to contextualize experience.

103. As is most compellingly argued by Martin Jay. See M. Jay, "Experience without a subject," in Jay, *Cultural semantics: Keywords of our time* (London, 1998), 51 ff.

104. Quoted in the excellent Caygill, *Walter Benjamin,* 68.

105. Obviously my story here is a pedestrian variant of the one told by Plato about the origin of the sexes, which I used as an epigraph for this book.

106. One is reminded, in this context, of why Burckhardt saw the migration of the Germanic peoples as the greatest crisis in world history: "But to return to Rome, the real crisis here has been the migration of the nations. This can, above all, be characterized as follows: the fusion of a new material force with an older one, and where the latter, in a spiritual metamorphosis, having changed from state into church, managed to live on. This crisis is quite unlike any that we know of and is unique, as a crisis" (my translation). See Burckhardt, *Gesamtausgabe, Siebenter Band,* 128. The Roman Empire and Papal Rome were like the two halves of the snowball—the latter seeming to be a mere metamorphosis of the former and retaining the former's form. On the other hand, its material content could not possibly be more different. And so it is with the two halves of the snowball: On the one hand there is a complete formal agreement, but no molecule of one half of the snowball is also part of the other half. For Rüsen's comments on Burckhardt's view of history as "ein wundersames Prozess von Verpuppungen" ("a miraculous process of metamorphoses"), see Rüsen, "Der ästhetische Glanz der historischen Erinnerung," 278, 282, 283.

107. Nicholsen, *Exact imagination,* 194; see also 205 and 206.

108. Quoted in Nicholsen, *Exact imagination,* 200, 201.

109. "Bestandteil der mémoire involontaire kann nur werden, was nicht ausdrücklich und mit Bewusstsein ist erlebt worden, was dem Subjekt nicht als Erlebnis widerfahren ist." See W. Benjamin, "Über einige Motive bei Baudelaire," in Benjamin, *Illuminationen* (Frankfurt am Main, 1955), 206, 207; Benjamin, "On some motifs in Baudelaire," 162–163. Fascinating is no less how Benjamin links the experience in question to artistic and intellectual creativity. The insight here is that creativity is not, as we might be inclined to think at first sight, the sudden mastery of some problem that had hitherto successfully resisted all our attempts to cope with it; on the contrary, creativity is rather a matter of a surrendering oneself to the challenge posed by the problem, of the shock and fright involved in the recognition of how it transcends our grasp. "Baudelaire has portrayed this condition in a harsh image. He speaks of a duel in which the artist, just before being beaten, screams in fright. This duel is the creative process itself. Thus Baudelaire placed the shock experience at the very center of his artistic work." See Benjamin, "On some motifs in Baudelaire," 165.

110. One is naturally reminded here of Plato's argument in the *Meno* that the acquisition of knowledge is a becoming aware of what we had, in fact, always known already—and is therefore structurally similar to memory. For an account of how the Platonist thesis on the origins of knowledge can be related to aesthetic experience, see P. Fisher, *Wonder, the rainbow, and the aesthetics of rare experience* (Cambridge, Mass., 1998), 67–79.

111. "Correspondences":

La nature est un temple où de vivants piliers
Laissent parfois sortir de confuses paroles
L'homme y passe à travers des forêts de symboles
Qui l'observent avec des regards familiers.

Comme de longs échos qui de loin se confondent
Dans une ténébreuse et profonde unité,
Vaste comme la nuit et comme la clarté.
Les parfums, les couleurs et les sons se répondent.

Il est des parfums frais comme des chairs d'enfants,
Doux comme les hautbois, verts comme les prairies
—Et d'autres, corrompus, riches et triomphants,

The pillars of Nature's temple are alive

And sometimes yield perplexing messages:
Forests of symbols between us and the shrine
Remark our passage with accustomed eyes.

Like long-held echoes, blending somewhere else
Into one deep and shadowy unison
As limitless as darkness and day,
The sounds, the scents, the colors correspond.

There are odors succulent as young flesh,

Sweet as flutes, and green as any grass,

While others—rich, corrupt and masterful—

Ayant l'expansion des choses infinies,
Comme l'ambre, le musc, le benjoin et
l'encens,
Qui chantent les transports de l'esprit et
des sens.

Possess the power of such infinite things
As incense, amber, benjamin and musk,

To praise the senses' raptures and the
mind's.

For the translation, see http://www.geocities.com/Paris/Metro/1301/corre.htm

112. See also A. Benjamin, "Tradition and experience: Walter Benjamin's 'On some motifs in Baudelaire,'" in A. Benjamin, ed., *The problems of modernity: Adorno and Benjamin* (London, 1991), and K. Lindroos, "Scattering community: Benjamin on experience, narrative, and history," *Philosophy and Social Criticism* 27 (2001): 19–47.

113. As is also argued in T. Weber, "Erfahrung," in M. Opzitz and E. Wisla, eds., *Benjamins Begriffe: Erster Band* (Frankfurt am Main, 2000), 230–259.

114. For a further development of this notion of a mythical time underlying our experience of the past, see the last chapter of the present volume.

115. "Die correspondances sind die Data des Eingedenkens. Sie sind keine historischen, sondern Data der Vorgeschichte. Was die festlichen Tage gross und bedeutsam macht, ist die Begegnung mit einem früheren Leben. . . . Sie heben sich aus dem warmen Dunst der Tränen, welche Tränen des Heimwehs sind." See Benjamin, "Über einige Motive bei Baudelaire," 228. Benjamin, "On some motifs in Baudelaire," 184.

116. I should be clear about where I draw my own line with regard to Benjamin's thesis on nostalgia and the tears with which we may remember the past. I can agree with Benjamin here insofar as he wishes to emphasize that our experience of the past is essentially an experience of loss. But I feel no affinity with his tendency to move from here to an idealization of the past—as Benjamin (and Adorno, for that matter) is in the habit of doing when claiming that we should have lost an openness to experience (*Erfahrung*) that people still possessed before modernity and the emergence of modern technology. It must be added, though, that Benjamin is of two minds about nostalgia: On the one hand there is the nostalgic Benjamin regretting this loss of experience he thinks to be such a sad characteristic of our time; but on the other hand we have the Benjamin who most eagerly awaits the kind of experience that the future seems to promise us.

117. See note 2 in Chapter 8.

118. And one might add that from the same perspective historical narrative is essentially *comic*.

Chapter 5: Gadamer and Historical Experience

1. Aristotle, *De Anima (On the soul)*, trans. and introduction and notes by Hugh Lawson-Tancred (London, 1986), 220 (Aristotle, *De Anima*, 435, a, 12–13).

2. L. Wittgenstein, *Philosophical investigations*, trans. G. E. M. Anscombe (Oxford, 1974), section 404.

3. J. W. Cook, "Wittgenstein on privacy," in G. Pitcher, ed., *Wittgenstein: The philosophical investigations* (London, 1966), 291, 292.

4. Wittgenstein, *Philosophical investigations,* section 246.

5. In M. Tournier, *Les Météores* (Paris, 1975) we may find a fascinating example of the "private language" developed by a twin. Since the two twins are as close to each other as to meld almost into one single person, one is tempted to see here a refutation of Wittgenstein's argument against the impossibility of private languages.

6. When commenting on Hölderlin's "Öfters hab' ich die Sprache. . . . Öfters hab'ich Gesang versucht, aber sie hörten dich nicht" ("From time to time I attempted language. . . . From time to time I attempted song, but they didn't hear you"), Frey emphasizes that Hölderlin wishes to suggest with the verb *attempt* the submission of language to experience. This is what I have in mind here as well. See H. J. Frey, "Hölderlin's marginalization of language," in A. Fioretos, ed., *The solid letter: Readings of Friedrich Hölderlin* (Stanford, 1999), 361. For a fascinating comment on the Romanticist discovery of the incommunicability of moods and feelings (as discussed in this chapter and in Chapter 7), see N. Luhmann, *Liebe als passion: Zur Codierung von Intimität* (Frankfurt am Main, 1982), Chapter 12.

7. "Freilegung der Wahrheitsfrage an der Erfahrung der Kunst." See H. G. Gadamer, *Wahrheit und Methode* (Tübingen, 1960), 1.

8. R. Rorty, *Philosophy and the mirror of nature* (Oxford, 1980), 313–395.

9. There is a striking similarity between Gadamer's argument here and Dewey's exposition in his *Art and experience*—with the difference, though, that Dewey takes Kant to task for this separation of knowledge and aesthetic experience: "Kant was a past-master in first drawing distinctions and then erecting them into compartmental divisions. The effect on subsequent theory was to give the separation of the esthetic from other modes of experience an alleged scientific basis in the constitution of human nature." See J. Dewey, *Art as experience* (New York, 1980), 252.

10. Needless to say, this should not tempt us to see in Kant a precursor of contemporary philosophers, such as Nelson Goodman, who favors a cognitivist approach to the arts (in his *Languages of art*). Goodman wishes to bridge the gap between cognitive truth and the arts. But for Kant there was still no gap to bridge at all. Unlike Kant, Goodman wrote from a post-Schillerian perspective, to put it in Gadamer's terminology.

11. H. G. Gadamer, *Truth and method,* 2nd ed. (New York, 2003), 83.

12. Gadamer comes close here to what Carl Schmitt had referred to as Romanticism's "occasionalism," that is, its tendency to see in the most insignificant things an "occasion" for the most far-reaching and universalist speculations. In order to illustrate what he had in mind with this, Schmitt quoted Novalis: "Alle Zufälle unseres Lebens sind Materialien, aus denen wir machen können, was wir wollen, alles ist erstes Glied einer unendlichen Reihe, Anfang eines unendlichen

Romans." See C. Schmitt, *Politische Romantik* (Berlin, 1992), 121. ("All the accidents of our life are materials of which we can make whatever we want. Everything is the first term in an infinite series, the beginning of an endless novel" [my translation]. See C. Schmitt, *Political romanticism* [Cambridge and London, 1986], 74.)

13. Gadamer summarizes it all in a wonderful paradox: It had now become easy to write a good poem, but precisely because of this desperately hard to become a poet (Gadamer, *Truth and method,* 91). To move away from the pedestrian world of daily reality to that of art and poetry is extremely difficult, but once this step has successfully been made, one has entered a world in which everything is permitted.

14. Gadamer speaks in this context of the "medial" character of play. The word *medial* is derived from the Greek "middle voice": in the aorist the Greek language has *elousamèn* ("I washed myself") next to the active *elousa* ("I washed") and the passive *elouthèn* ("I was washed"). Because of this, the middle voice is suggestive of a relationship to the world that is neither active nor passive but rather an immersion or participation in it. Since Emile Benveniste and Roland Barthes and down to Berel Lang and Hayden White, many theorists have made use of this notion of the middle voice in order to characterize situations in which we can be said to become what we are doing; Roland Barthes, for example, discusses a writing in which the writing involves the writer's identity or personality.

15. Although Gadamer devotes quite some attention to the play metaphor, it is not easy to see what job precisely the metaphor is expected to perform within the whole of his hermeneutics and aesthetics. Illustrative is that the metaphor is dealt with in the first part of *Truth and Method* but is never taken up again in the remainder of the book.

16. Thus Grondin summarizes Gadamer's relevant views as follows: "The spurring effect of truth and the work of art most clearly manifests itself in play. Truth is not something dead, but something that is very much alive and stimulating. But the concept of play especially accounts for the phenomenological features of the occurrence of truth" (my translation). See J. Grondin, *Hermeneutische Wahrheit: Zum Wahrheitsbegriff Hans Georg Gadamers* (Königstein, 1982), 105. But I must confess that I find questionable this idea of "a truth" to be found in playing, and even more so as a category that might reveal to us something about art, aesthetic experience, and truth. For example, in play we should always distinguish between the play itself—its own reality, its rules, and so on—and those people *with whom* we play the game. This is absolutely crucial for play since only it does justice to the play's capacity for creating a new reality for itself that is of so much importance in Gadamer's argument. But how do we operationalize this distinction in art and in aesthetic experience?

17. As Gadamer suggests himself when pithily declaring *"Aesthetics has to be absorbed into hermeneutics"* (his italics) (Gadamer, *Truth and method,* 164). The implication here is that aesthetics must be clarified from the perspective of hermeneutics. But the suggestion is complicated by Gadamer's comment a moment later

that "conversely, hermeneutics must be so determined as a whole that it does justice to the experience of art" (Gadamer, *Truth and method,* 164). And then the implication is that aesthetics is the ultimate test for hermeneutics. This would privilege again aesthetics above hermeneutics or historical theory.

18. Gadamer, *Truth and method,* 138.

19. Gadamer, *Truth and method,* 140, 137.

20. As Grondin makes clear in his excellent book on Gadamer, Gadamer had been inspired here by Heidegger's famous essay on Van Gogh's painting of the pair of peasant's shoes. "Think, for example, of van Gogh's painting of the peasant shoes that so powerfully affected Heidegger. The painting gave to these shoes an unusual presence (an increase in Being) when transforming them into a representation. . . . Far from having an autonomous reality, the painting always reflects a reality or a model, that acquires in this way a 'valency of Being.' This notion of an increase in Being is all the more appropriate here because the represented Being only becomes real thanks to its representation (think of the shoes of Van Gogh or of the portrait giving us an inkling of the true nature of the sitter). Gadamer's thesis is even more provocative here: what attains representation in the painting, is not an arbitrary Being, but a Being possessing a representative function itself and whose Being the representation renders adequately, because it so well represents this representation" (my translation). See J. Grondin, *Einführung zu Gadamer* (Munich, 2000), 63, 75. See also J. Grondin, *The philosophy of Gadamer* (Chesham/Bucks, 2003), 49–50.

21. Gadamer, *Truth and method,* 142.

22. For a marvelous illustration of Gadamer's insight here, I would like to refer my Dutch readers to M. Toonder, "De Kiekvogels," in Toonder, *Ach Mallerd* (Amsterdam, 1979).

23. 134. Gadamer, *Truth and method,* 141.

24. The theme has been developed further in a fascinating study by Hans Belting. See H. Belting, *Bild und Kult: Eine Geschichte des Bildes vor dem Zeitalter der Kunst* (Munich, 1990).

25. As I have argued on several occasions. See, for example, my *Historical representation* (Stanford, 2001), 49–63.

26. Thus Mink urges us to abandon "the remnant of the idea of Universal history that survives as a presupposition, namely, the idea that there is a determinate historical actuality, the complex referent for all our narratives of 'what actually happened,' the untold story to which narrative histories approximate." See L. O. Mink, "Narrative form as a cognitive instrument," in Mink, *Historical understanding* (Ithaca and London, 1987), 202. A similar argument was defended already by Munz: "For the truth of the matter is that there is no ascertainable face behind the various masks every storyteller, be he a historian, poet, novelist, or mythmaker, is creating. He is telling a story and the story is all we have. . . . The ineluctable truth is that that there is no face behind the masks and that the belief that there is one is an unsupportable allegation. For any record we could have of the

face would be, precisely, another mask." See P. Munz, *The shapes of time* (Middletown, 1977), 16, 17. All wisdom about the nature of historical writing starts with the recognition of the truth of insights like these.

27. Others have doubted as well, although for reasons different from those expounded on here, whether Gadamer really succeeded in his effort to rehabilitate aesthetic experience and truth. Thus Karl Albert said, "However one may judge Gadamer's inquiry into the 'experience of art' . . . , it did not achieve a clarification of the question of truth to the extent that art is concerned by it, nor did it demonstrate that it represents a specific mode of knowledge that would bring about any kind of essential knowledge." Quoted in J. Grondin, "Gadamer and the truth of art," in M. Kelly, *Encyclopedia of aesthetics, volume 2* (Oxford, 1998), 269. In this entry Grondin himself writes that Gadamer's acceptance of a neo-Platonic or Plotinian ontology has been the root of the trouble (Grondin, "Gadamer and the truth of art," 269).

28. M. Heidegger, "Der Ursprung des Kunstwerks," in Heidegger, *Holzwege: Gesamtausgabe V* (Frankfurt am Main, 1977). For an exposition of the impressive "effective history" of Heidegger's famous essay, see W. E. Krul, *Onzuivere Kunst* (Amsterdam, 1999), 16 ff.

29. R. Dostal, "The experience of truth for Gadamer and Heidegger," in B. R. Wachterhauser, ed., *Hermeneutics and truth* (Chicago, 1994), 47–67.

30. Grondin, *Philosophy of Gadamer,* 66.

31. W. Dilthey, "Die Funktion der Anthropologie in der Kultur des 16. und 17. Jahrhunderts," in Dilthey, *Gesammelte Schriften, II, Band* (Leipzig and Berlin, 1921), 416–494. The Stoicism of sixteenth- and seventeenth-century natural-law philosophy was also emphasized in Q. Skinner, *The foundations of modern political thought, 2 vols.* (Cambridge, 1978).

32. And much the same can, paradoxically, be said of Kant's own philosophy of history, as expounded in I. Kant, "Idee zu einer allgemeinen Geschichte in weltbürgerlicher Absicht," in Kant, *Kleinere Schriften zur Geschichtsphilosophie, Ethik und Politik* (Hamburg, 1973), 3–21.

33. Gadamer, *Wahrheit und Methode* (Tübingen, 1960), 191–205.

34. Gadamer, *Truth and method,* 221.

35. Gadamer, *Truth and method,* 221. Within the context of this book it is of special interest to note what kind of experience Gadamer was primarily thinking of here. He then goes on to say: "Thus what preshapes the special mode of knowing in the historical sciences is the suffering and instruction that the person who is growing in insight receives from the painful experience of reality" (Gadamer, *Truth and method,* 222).

36. It is tempting to explain Dilthey's notion of *Erlebnis* in terms of the notion of moods and feelings that will be discussed in the last sections of the next chapter.

37. Gadamer, *Truth and method,* 229.

38. Gadamer, *Wahrheit und Methode,* 226. Gadamer, *Truth and method,* 239.

39. We should realize ourselves, *"that historicism, despite its critique of rationalism and of natural law philosophy, is based on the modern Enlightenment and unwittingly shares its prejudices"* (Gadamer's italics) (Gadamer, *Truth and method*, 270).

40. Gadamer, *Truth and method*, 238.

41. Historical meaning "is a relationship which is never quite complete. One would have to wait for the end of a life, for only at the hour of death could one survey the whole from which the relationship between the parts could be ascertained. One would have to wait for the end of history to have all the material necessary to determine its meaning" (my translation) (W. Dilthey, *Selected writings* [Cambridge, 1979], 236).

42. Gadamer, *Wahrheit und Methode*, 285. Gadamer, *Truth and method*, 302. This is why we should disagree on two counts with Kessler's comment: "Because he [i.e., Gadamer] identifies Hegel's negation with hermeneutic experience, he robs the former of its speculative character and equates overhastily dialectical experience with experience in life. By identifying experience with the self-knowledge of the individual human being in the context of its historically determined prejudices, he eliminates the critical dimension of experience focusing on its correspondence with an object. He thus throws out the child of dialectical thought with the bathwater of the absolute mind" (my translation). See A. S. Kessler, "Erfahrung," in H. Krings, H. M. Baumgartner, and C. Wild, eds., *Handbuch philosophischer Grundbegriffe I* (Munich, 1973), 384. But Gadamer recognizes both that hermeneutic understanding should aim at being "adequate" to its object (see note 62) and that absolute self-knowledge in Hegel's sense is unattainable.

43. Optical metaphors tend to invite epistemological schemata, as was already pointed out by Count Yorck von Wartenburg in his correspondence with Dilthey. See Grondin, *Einführung zu Gadamer;* 115. And from this perspective there is ample reason to be worried about the prominent role played in Gadamer's hermeneutics of such an unashamedly optical metaphor as that of the *Horizontverschmelzung:* "In the sphere of historical understanding, too, we speak of horizons, especially when referring to the claim of historical consciousness to see the past in its own terms, not in terms of our contemporary criteria and prejudices but within its own historical horizon" (Gadamer, *Truth and method*, 302).

44. Gadamer, *Wahrheit und Methode*, 261. Gadamer, *Truth and method*, 276.

45. Gadamer, *Truth and method*, 299–300.

46. Gadamer, *Truth and method*, 301

47. Hegel is quoted by Grondin as follows: "Diese dialektische Bewegung, welche das Bewusstsein an ihm selbst, sowohl an seinem Wissen als an einem Gegenstand ausübt, insofern ihm der neue wahre Gegenstand daraus entspringt, ist eigentlich dasjenige, das Erfahrung genannt wird (PhG 78)." ("This dialectical movement, which consciousness carries out on itself, both on its knowledge and on the object of knowledge, insofar as a new object of knowledge originates from this, is, in fact, what is called experience" [my translation].) See Grondin, *Hermeneutische Wahrheit*, 55.

48. As Teichert put it: "He [Gadamer] rather aims—in opposition to Hegel—at an emancipation of the notion of experience from such an overrating of itself" (my translation). See D. Teichert, *Erfahrung, Erinnerung, Erkenntnis: Untersuchungen zum Wahrheitsbegriff der Hermeneutik Gadamers* (Stuttgart, 1992), 120.

49. Without, however, being wholly absent from it. As Grondin comments: "The process of experience brings about 'an inversion of consciousness,' i.e. consciousness achieves a stage at which it recognizes itself as this process of inversion, of continuous change and evolution. . . . Insofar as it recognizes its own philosophical character, Hegelian dialectics and philosophical hermeneutics culminate in the self-knowledge of the experiencing subject. . . . The heart of this truth is that the subject recognizes the essence of its experience" (my translation). See Grondin, *Hermeneutische Wahrheit*, 56. But, as will be clear from this quote already, the recognition of the speculative dimension of *Erfahrung* will have its significance for a theory of hermeneutic understanding rather than for its practice.

50. Gadamer, *Truth and method*, 353–354.

51. For a discussion of Gadamer's appeal to Popper, see Grondin, *Einführung zu Gadamer*, 130, 187.

52. Grondin, *Einführung zu Gadamer;* 187.

53. It is a sobering insight that contemporary post-Kuhnian philosophy of science is, in fact, more historist than even Gadamer, even though most experts will probably acclaim his writings as the still unsurpassed culmination point in the history of historism since Herder or Ranke. The orderly and gradualist development of *Wirkungsgeschichte* does not leave any room for anything so dramatic as Kuhn's paradigm changes or for anything so completely enclosing a historical period (of scientific or of historiographical practice) within itself. And the fact that Kuhn's historicization of science most dramatically announced itself in the radical gaps and fissures he believed to separate successive paradigms may give us an inkling of what the consequences might and ought to be of a consistent rejection of transcendentalist patterns of thought. Indeed, the cognitive ruptures suggested by Kuhn's scientific revolutions seem to have their counterpart in the way historical experience breaks through the historiographical context within which it takes place and in its supreme indifference, or even blindness, to all that is outside it.

54. J. C. Weinsheimer, *Gadamer's hermeneutics: A reading of* Truth and Method (New Haven and London, 1985), 202.

55. Gadamer, *Truth and method*, 293–294.

56. The notion has often been compared to Davidson's "charity principle." See, for example, R. J. Dostal, ed., *The Cambridge companion to Gadamer* (Cambridge, 2003), and J. Malpas et al., eds., *Gadamer's century: Essays in honor of Hans Georg Gadamer* (Cambridge, Mass., 2003).

57. And indeed described by Grondin as a "transzendentale Bedingung des Verstehens." See Grondin, *Hermeneutische Wahrheit*, 143.

58. Grondin, *Einführung zu Gadamer*, 133.

59. Grondin, *Einführung zu Gadamer*, 143.

60. Quoted in Grondin, *Einführung zu Gadamer,* 143.

61. Gadamer, *Wahrheit und Methode,* 340, 341. Gadamer, *Truth and method,* 358.

62. "The notion of *adaequatio* is indispensable here, since there are obviously also *inadequate* representations, renderings or statements, and where the object resists one-sided approaches and statements." See Grondin, *Philosophy of Gadamer,* 86.

63. One is also reminded here of Hölderlin's characteristic of language as "der Güter Gefährlichstes," that is, as "the most dangerous of goods." Quoted in Frey, "Hölderlin's marginalization of language," 362.

64. "Unsere Vernunft ist in einem nicht zu missverstehenden Sinne mit dem Vernunft der Geschichte gleichzusetzen. Das wirkungsgeschichtliche Bewusstsein meint somit nicht nur ein *genetivus objectivus* (*unser* Bewusstsein der Wirkungsgeschichte), sie erweist sich auch als ein *genetivus subjectivus:* das Bewusstsein, oder besser: die Vernunft, die die Wirkungsgeschichte hat. Die Geschichte gehorcht einer sich ständig bildenden Logik, auf der unser Verstand ruht. Sie macht Gemeinschaft und intersubjektives Verständnis möglich. Die wandelbare und keineswegs absolute Vernunft der Wirkungsgeschichte ist mit unsere Vernunft, auf die die Tradition stösst und an der sie sich misst, im Grunde identisch." See Grondin, *Einführung zu Gadamer,* 147, 148.

65. In the next chapter we shall discuss Dewey's destruction of the link between experience and Truth.

66. This is not an attempt to reinstate the separation between the domain of aesthetics and that of cognitive truth that Gadamer sought to undo in terms of his notion of the "aesthetic consciousness." Gadamer's (most commendable) effort presupposes a clarity about the demarcation between the two that is questioned throughout this book. For example, in the writing of history we shall find a fusion of the domains of truth and of aesthetics successfully challenging all overhasty intuitions about the borderline between the two domains.

67. The scientific experiment is, of course, the last thing one should think of in order to get a grasp of the notion of experience under investigation here. From this perspective we should agree with Bollnow: "What is being done in the experiential sciences is, above all, *research,* and we should, for clarity's sake strictly distinguish between experience and research. For whereas experience in the sense meant here is always the plaything of fate and of the incalculable incident and where the human individual is primarily passive, research always is, on the contrary, an arrangement that has been carefully and purposefully planned by the scientist in order to achieve well-defined and intersubjectively communicable results" (my translation). See F. O. Bollnow, "Was ist Erfahrung?" in R. E. Vente, ed., *Erfahrung und Erfahrungswissenschaft* (Stuttgart, 1974), 22, 23.

68. According to Gadamer, the hermeneutic understanding of a text also requires a *subtilitas applicandi,* which he defines as follows: "In the course of our re-

flections we have come to see that understanding always involves something like applying the text to be understood to the interpreter's present situation." And he deeply regrets that this dimension of *Verstehen* was lost with the attempt to find an epistemological foundation for hermeneutic understanding. See Gadamer, *Truth and method*, 308.

69. I. Kant, *Critique of pure reason* (New York and Toronto, 1965), 303. "Durch dieses Ich, oder Er, oder Es (das Ding), welches denkt, wird nun nichts weiter, als ein transzendentales Subjekt der Gedanken vorgestellt = *X*, welches nur durch die Gedanken, die sein Prädikate sind, anerkannt wird, unn wovon wir, abgesondert, niemals den mindesten Begriff haben können; um welches wir daher in einem beständigen Zirkel herumdrehen, indem wir uns seiner Vorstellung jederzeit schon bedienen müssen, um irgend etwas von ihm zu urteilen" (Kant, *Kritik der reinen Vernunft*, B 404, A 346).

70. D. Hume, "Of personal identity," in J. Perry, ed., *Personal identity* (Berkeley and London, 1975), 162.

71. For a continuation of my discussion of moods and feelings and of how they relate to (sublime) historical experience, see section 7.8 of Chapter 7.

72. For a more elaborate account of the (psycho-)logical status of moods and feelings—and of their crucial role in historical experience, see section 7.9 of Chapter 7.

73. Hume, "Of personal identity," 162.

74. As Bollnow puts it: "The experiences one has always are *painful* experiences. Experiences are always unpleasant. Pleasant experiences do not exist. For that would be a *contradictio in adjecto*. This may sound like an arbitrary exaggeration. But this is only so because the word *experience* has been blunted by injudicious use" (my translation). See O. F. Bollnow, "Was ist Erfahrung?" 20.

75. E. Burke, *A philosophical enquiry into the origin of our idea of the sublime and the beautiful* (Oxford, 1990), pt. I, sec. VII. For similar statements, see pt. II, sec. VI, and pt. IV, secs. III and VII.

76. For these two French authors, see Chapter 9 of Martin Jay's forthcoming book on experience. What Bataille referred to as "inner experience" comes close to what I have in mind here with aesthetic experience, experience without a subject of experience. I quote from Jay's book: "Like Montaigne, albeit without his great predecessor's personal equilibrium, Bataille knew full well that the limit of experience was met only in death that was both impossible to incorporate in life and also its most intense, ecstatic, profound moment." And Jay then goes on to cite the following from Bataille's *Inner experience* (1943): "By inner experience I understand that which one usually calls mystical experience: the state of ecstasy, rapture, at least of meditated emotion. But I am thinking less of confessional experience, to which one has had to adhere up to now, than of experience laid bare, free of ties, even of an origin, of any confession whatever. This is why I don't like the word mystical. . . . What characterizes such an experience, which does not proceed from

revelation—where nothing is revealed either, if not the unknown—is that it never announces anything reassuring." No less appropriate in the context of my exposition is the passage Jay quotes from Rebecca Comay's essay on Bataille: "Erfahrung: The experience lost is nothing other than the experience of loss."

77. See also Chapter 4, at the end of section 4.4, for this notion of "unknowing" the past.

78. Causality is an ontological category insofar as causes and their consequences belong to the inventory of the world. Indeed, in my account of sublime historical experience I have reduced experience to an exclusively ontological category by taking away all its epistemological connotations and by insisting that it is what remains of us—as an object in this world—when the sublimity of experience has wholly enclosed us in the experience itself. Next, insofar as historical experience can be said to cause a historical narrative to come into being, it should be pointed out that narrative, although consisting of language, nevertheless is an ontological category as well. See my *Historical representation,* 137, 138.

79. One might place all of contemporary historical writing along the two axes of (1) traditional historical writing and (2) what is new and fashionable. In traditional historical writing historians discuss the history of a nation, of social classes, of ideas, and so on. There is nothing wrong with this kind of historical writing— and this is the kind of thing that will always be needed. Worrying, however, is the kind of historical writing having the pretension to be the avant-garde of the discipline. The urge to discover new domains of historical investigation has prompted these pretentious and assuming historians to move in exactly the wrong direction and to discover the new not in what is important but in what used to be left aside because of its all too obvious irrelevance. The cult of the new has all too often become the cult of the irrelevant.

80. Gadamer, *Truth and method,* 389.

81. Gadamer, *Truth and method,* 198.

82. We cannot fail to be struck by the fact that Gadamer's *Wirkungsgeschichte* has in his hermeneutics a function that is exactly similar to, for example, the categories in Kantian transcendentalism. In both cases we have to do with an a priori structure that (1) is the condition of the possibility of knowledge while (2) effectively preventing a direct and immediate contact with what is given to us in experience. *So* Wirkungsgeschichte *is Gadamer's transcendental condition for the possibility of all historical understanding.* We should note here, more specifically, that Gadamer's notions of tradition, or *Überlieferung,* and of *Wirkungsgeschichte* are, like the Kantian categories, empty and formal principles guiding experience and knowledge. We tend to forget this, since the word *Wirkungsgeschichte* sounds so reassuringly anti-transcendentalist and is so suggestive of the idea that here all transcendental schemes dissolve in the fullness of history. But here our critical sense has been lulled to sleep, for just as the notion of length does not have a length itself, so is the notion of *Wirkungsgeschichte* outside history itself. So, despite the fact that these two notions seem to refer to or to be full of an empirical historical content,

Überlieferung and *Wirkungsgeschichte* are strictly formal in the sense that they have as little affinity with one specific content or another as have the Kantian categories.

83. Gadamer, *Truth and method,* 417. Unfortunately Gadamer does not tell us how experience succeeds in doing this.

84. One is strongly reminded here of Richard Rorty's "language goes all the way down" with which Rorty, in his debate with Thomas Nagel, expresses his own variant of linguistic transcendentalism. See the discussion between Rorty and Nagel recounted in Chapter 2.

85. Grondin, *Philosophy of Gadamer,* 125.

86. "Endlich sei auf das tiefste der Problemen hingewiesen, die der Grenze der Sprache wesenhaft eingeboren sind. . . . Es ist das Bewusstsein, dass jeder Sprechende in jedem Augenblick, in dem er das richtige Wort sucht—und das ist das Wort das den anderen erreicht—, zugleich das Bewusstsein hat, dass er es nicht ganz richtig trifft." See H. G. Gadamer, "Grenzen der Sprache," in Gadamer, *Gesammelte Werke 8: Ästhetik und Poetik I* (Munich, 1993), 361.

87. When dealing with Marquard's criticism, Gadamer emphasized how far and deep language penetrates into human existence while avoiding, again, the recognition of a "dehors texte." See H. G. Gadamer, "Rhetorik, Hermeneutik und Ideologiekritik," in Gadamer, *Gesammelte Werke 2: Hermeneutik II* (Munich, 1999), 233.

88. E. Burke, *A philosophical enquiry,* pt. IV, sec. VII (pp. 158 and 159).

89. M. Bowie, "Jacques Lacan," in J. Sturrock, ed., *Structuralism and since* (Oxford, 1979), 134.

90. For an account of Arcimboldo and his many followers throughout Europe, see M. Brion, *Jenseits der Wirklichkeit: Phantastische kunst* (Vienna, 1962), 124 ff.

Chapter 6: (Pragmatist) Aesthetic Experience and Historical Experience

1. J. Dewey, *Art as experience* (New York, 1980), 274.

2. R. Shusterman, *Pragmatist aesthetics: Living beauty, rethinking art* (Cambridge, Mass., 1992), 5.

3. J. O. Urmson, "What makes a situation esthetic?" in J. Margolis, ed., *Philosophy looks at the arts* (New York, 1962).

4. J. Dewey, *Experience and nature* (La Salle, 1971), and Dewey, *Art as experience.* The prolixity so much characteristic of Dewey's style of writing makes it difficult to summarize his argument. This is why I shall so much rely on what others have written on Dewey's aesthetics.

5. M. C. Beardsley, *Aesthetics: Problems in the philosophy of criticism* (New York, 1958), 527–535.

6. J. Fisher, "Beardsley on aesthetic experience," in Fisher, ed., *Chapters on aesthetics: Perspective on the work of Monroe C. Beardsley* (New York, 1983).

7. H. Osborne, "What makes an experience aesthetic?" in M. H. Mitias, ed., *Possibility of aesthetic experience* (The Hague, 1986).

8. C. Benson, *The absorbed self: Pragmatism, psychology, and aesthetic experience* (New York, 1993).

9. Shusterman, *Pragmatist aesthetics.*

10. E. Bullough, "Aesthetic experience as mental distance," in E. J. Coleman, ed., *Varieties of aesthetic experience* (Lanham, 1983).

11. Self-evidently this would oblige me to discuss the question of what light phenomenology might shed on the notion of historical experience. I wish to restrict myself here to the observation that phenomenology's tendencies to break with epistemology were fully realized only by Heidegger and, insofar as this has its implications for the humanities, by Gadamer. Consequently, a discussion of phenomenology would, at the present stage of my argument, serve no purpose since it would carry us back to a territory that we have already left behind us.

12. M. Dufrenne, *The phenomenology of aesthetic experience* (Evanston, 1973).

13. R. Bernstein, "John Dewey," in P. Edwards, ed., *The encyclopedia of philosophy, volume 2* (London, 1967), 381.

14. Shusterman, *Pragmatist aesthetics,* 18.

15. When Rorty is like Moses leaving us to ourselves at the moment when we are about to actually enter the promised land of post-epistemological philosophy, this is because he refuses to grant to experience the role Dewey gave to it.

16. I shall not venture to pronounce here on how this picture might be complicated by developments in theoretical physics, such as Heisenberg's uncertainty principle.

17. For example, by explaining the differences between this "fusion" of scientists and their object of investigation on the one hand and how they manipulate this object of investigation in the scientific experiment on the other.

18. As I have tried to explain in my "Metaphor and paradox in Tocqueville's political writings, in my *Aesthetic politics: Political philosophy beyond fact and value* (Stanford, 1997).

19. See Chapter 1.

20. See my *Narrative logic: A semantic analysis of the historian's language* (The Hague, 1983), 155–169, my *History and tropology: The rise and fall of metaphor* (Berkeley, 1994), 75–97, and my *Historical representation* (Stanford, 2001), 80–88.

21. See Chapter 2, note 19).

22. Aristotle, *De Anima (On the soul),* trans. Hugh Lawson-Tancred (London, 1986), 220 (Aristotle, *De Anima,* 435, a, 12–13).

23. Although, as always in the humanities, there are exceptions to this rule. There have undoubtedly been artists wishing to raise with their work Kantian or epistemological questions about art. Magritte would be an obvious example. And one could also think of Duchamp. See T. de Duve, *Kant nach Duchamp,* (Munich, 1993).

24. See also my *Historical representation,* 11–13, 82–86, and 223–225.

25. Dewey, *Art as experience,* 24, 25.

26. Beardsley, *Aesthetics,* 527.

27. One is curiously reminded here of Mozart's information that he had had one of his most brilliant musical inventions (the theme of Don Giovanni's "Là ci darem la mano, là mi dirai di si") while eating an orange. And what is striking in both cases is the link between aesthetic experience and what is given to us by smell or taste.

28. Quoted in Benson, *The Absorbed self,* 2.

29. Beardsley, *Aesthetics,* 527.

30. Beardsley, *Aesthetics,* 527, 528.

31. Beardsley, *Aesthetics,* 529.

32. When using here the notion of "authenticity," I should remind the reader of my argument in the previous chapter about the disjunction of experience and truth. So "authenticity" is certainly not to be taken here as a privileged access to truth, as is the case with the kind of authors Adorno had in mind when speaking about "the jargon of authenticity." I therefore have no wish to disagree with Adorno's criticism of authenticity as expressed, for example, in aphorism 99 of his *Minima Moralia.*

33. Dewey, *Art as experience,* 87, 91, 120–126.

34. See especially Shusterman, *Pragmatist Aesthetics,* Chapters 3 and 4.

35. Shusterman, *Pragmatist aesthetics,* 127.

36. Shusterman, *Pragmatist aesthetics,* 127.

37. Shusterman, *Pragmatist aesthetics,* 128.

38. And as we saw in Chapter 3 when dealing with the sublime, even language is less hostile to the idea of direct experience as the transcendentalist wishes us to believe.

39. Shusterman, *Pragmatist aesthetics,* 47, 48.

40. As is argued by Osborne, "What makes an experience aesthetic?" 120 ff. The separation of life from disinterested art was challenged not only by Deweyan pragmatics but by the entire avant-garde, as Peter Bürger demonstrated in his *Theorie der Avant-Garde* (Frankfurt am Main, 1981).

41. Bullough, "Aesthetic experience as mental distance," 60, 61.

42. Beardsley, *Aesthetics,* 528.

43. And, once again, we are reminded of how for Aristotle sensory perception is always a balance, a mean (*mesotès*) between warm and cold, wet and dry, and so on.

44. Bullough, "Aesthetic experience as mental distance," 68 ff.

45. Dewey, *Art as experience,* 278.

46. Dewey, *Art as experience,* 42, 45, 63.

47. When taking Gadamer, Derrida, and Rorty together here, I do not wish to suggest that there should be no huge differences between the contextualism of each of them. For an exposition of these differences, see M. Jay, "The textual approach to intellectual history," in Jay, *Force fields: Between intellectual history and culture critique* (New York, 1993).

48. An illustrative example comes from Schopenhauer: "They limit each other immediately; where the object begins, the subject ceases." See A. Schopenhauer, *The world as will and representation, volume 1* (New York, 1969), 5. And, indeed, experience has no role to play in Schopenhauer's system.

49. P. Nora, ed., *Les lieux de mémoire*, 3 vols. (Paris, 1984–1992).

Chapter 7: Subjective Historical Experience: The Past as Elegy

1. There is a marvelous illustration of this. When the historist Justus Möser (1720–1794) wanted to reject the claims made for "theory" by Kant in his essay "Über den Gemeinspruch: Das mag in der Theorie richtig sein, taugt aber nicht für die Praxis" (1793), he answered Kant with an erudite account of the history of feudalism in his native Hannover. In a way this was admirable: Möser realized himself that a "theoretical" rejection of Kant's argument would automatically have transformed him into an adherent of the very position he had wanted to criticize and that, therefore, only something like this would do. On the other hand, however, one can well imagine that Möser's readers will have asked themselves in desperation what to make of Möser's so curiously inapposite rejoinder. Indeed, it is the handicap of all "theory against theory" that it cannot avoid weakening its own position by adopting the language of the enemy.

2. For these authors, see D. R. Kelley, *Foundations of modern historical scholarship: Language, law, and history in the French Renaissance* (New York, 1970). It has often been argued that Vico can well be seen both as a precursor of nineteenth-century historism and as the heir of proto-historist sixteenth-century historical writing—and this can only enhance our respect for the achievements of these sixteenth-century "proto-historists."

3. "A capriccio is a view in which the fantasy has an interior meaning," wrote V. Mischini, *Francesco Guardi* (London, n.d.), 32. For Guardi's relationship to his less-talented older brother, see M. Goering, *Francesco Guardi* (Vienna, 1944), 12 ff.

4. Mischini, *Guardi*, 32; see also J. Adhémar, *Meesters der prentkunst van de achttiende eeuw* (The Hague, 1963), 77.

5. I have in mind here Tiepolo's painting *Pulcinella,* which is in the collection Cailleux in Paris.

6. A. Mariuz, *Giandomenico Tiepolo: The Zianigo frescoes at Cà Rezzonico* (Venice, 2004), 27.

7. M. Florisoone, *La peinture Française: Le dix-huitième siècle* (Paris, 1948), 35.

8. Object relations psychology is a scion of Freudian psychoanalysis focusing especially on "exploring the relationship between real external people and internal images and residues of relations with them and the significance of these residues for psychic functioning"; see J. R. Greenberg and S. A. Mitchell, *Object relations in psychoanalytical theory* (Cambridge, Mass., 1983), 12.

9. O. F. Kernberg, *Borderline conditions and pathological narcissism* (New York, 1985), 213–224.

10. For a brilliant exposition of the history of boredom and ennui, see R. Kuhn, *The demon of noontide: Ennui in Western literature* (Princeton, 1976).

11. Quoted in S. D. Healy, *Boredom, self, and culture* (London, 1984), 47, 48. O. Fenichel, "On the psychology of boredom," in Fenichel, *The collected papers of Otto Fenichel: First series* (New York, 1953), 293.

12. Healy, *Boredom,* 42.

13. R. L. Erenstein, *De geschiedenis van de* commedia dell'arte (Amsterdam, 1984), 104.

14. See for these traditions in popular culture E. Le Roy Ladurie, *Montaillou: Een ketters dorp in de Middeleeuwen* (Amsterdam, 1984), 446–466, and C. Ginzburg, *De kaas en de wormen* (Amsterdam, 1982), 127 ff.

15. Erenstein, *Geschiedenis,* 109.

16. Quoted in Erenstein, *Geschiedenis,* 106.

17. R. Sennett, *The fall of public man* (New York, 1978), 107.

18. Healy, *Boredom,* 21.

19. W. Klerks, ed., *Madame du Deffand: Essai sur l'ennui* (Leiden, 1961), 48.

20. I remind the reader here of what was said in Chapter 2 on "the meaning of a text."

21. There is a most effective illustration of what such a streak of sunlight on the floor of a room may emotionally do to us in Claude Monet's *Coin d'appartement.*

22. See for references Chapter 6.

23. Take, for example, the correspondence theory of truth. The trouble with this theory has always been that it is by no means clear about what it means to say that a statement "corresponds" to actual fact. On the one hand, you have a chunk of the world and, on the other hand, a chunk of language: So, what could we possibly have in mind when saying that two such very different things "correspond" with each other? The only solution is to conceive of some scheme encompassing both the object and the subject's true statement about the object, in terms of which this "correspondence" can be both defined and established. But, as we have seen already in Chapter 1, no such schemata exist: There is just language and the world, and that is all we have (and all we need, as Davidson and Rorty would argue). As we all know, Tarski solved the problem by distinguishing between the object level of the true statement ("snow is white") and the meta-level of speaking about how the object level is related to the world ("snow is white" is true if and only if snow is white). In this way the problem of the correspondence of language and the world was circumvented by transforming it into a relationship between meta-level and object level. This is a relationship that makes sense, and we possess the instruments for adequately dealing with it. But is this not a solution of the epistemological problem of "truth as correspondence" in terms of the distinction of different *contexts*—that is, the context of object language and that of meta-language? So the problem of truth as correspondence can be solved only if we appeal to *context*— which suggests, once again, that context is the truly decisive factor in epistemological issues.

24. J. Culler, *On deconstruction: Theory and criticism after structuralism* (London, 1985), 123.

25. The transition from childhood to early adolescence on the one hand and this nostalgia for the eighteenth century on the other are, for me, most intimately linked. I must have transferred my feelings about the loss of my happy childhood days to 1789–, and I am well aware of what things made me do this at that time in my life. Undoubtedly this is why I can now still feel the awareness of what we lost in 1789 with the intensity with which one experiences the great losses in one's personal life and why, for me, 1789 is still the historical event par excellence. This also molded my relationship to the past, and this book is, in fact, an attempt to come to terms with the pain I can still feel about 1789. Needless to say, I fully recognize that all this is peculiar to me and that I will not share my attitude toward the past with many others. On the other hand, was *History,* as we presently know it, not born from the rupture of the great revolution from the West's childhood days of the ancien régime? Is *History*—again, as we presently know it—not the offspring of the unhappy marriage of past and present that was celebrated in 1789?

Perhaps one more admittedly quite personal effusion will be allowed to me. Is History not something that we predominantly have on the European continent, which has gone through the experience of the French Revolution and its aftermath but that is much less of a presence in the Anglo-Saxon countries, where both in how people behave and in politics the ancien régime clearly still persists? We, on the European continent are therefore in a certain sense people of a fundamentally *later* stage in history because of all the unprecedented disasters that we have had to go through here in the two centuries between 1789 and 1989, where *later* certainly does not mean "more modern" or "better." Quite the contrary—as the brute facts of two world wars, a near third one, and of a Holocaust sufficiently suggest. It is true that the French Revolution has given us social democracy, or, rather, a moral involvement with the fate of our less successful fellow citizens that one will encounter less frequently in the United States. But it also gave us Hitler and communism—and the permanent possibility of their return, sooner or later. The European continent is traumatized by its terrible past and stands with its back to the future—and the pathetic helplessness of the European Union, that is, of the institution symbolizing how we try to overcome our dismal past, epitomizes it all.

Or, to put it all in different terms, Bauman was essentially right with the assessment of modernity he gave in his *Modernity and the Holocaust.* But he forgot to mention that there are *two* modernities: the one that went through the experience of 1789 and the one that did not. And there are strange ironies in the relationship between these two modernities: One might well say that the present predominance of the United States is, in fact, the final and belated victory of the ancien régime over the revolution. Anyway, this might well be our big divide for the foreseeable future. All the more so since the mental gap between the Anglo-Saxon countries on the one hand and the European continent on the other seems to grow only deeper with time—all the more so because of the amazing paradox that the more "modern," post-revolutionary variant of modernity (i.e., the European continent) has less of an orientation on the future than the "ancien régime" variant (i.e., the United States). This is also why I expect that this book's message will probably sound a lot stranger in the ears of an Anglo-Saxon than in those of a Continental audience. Historical experience, and the experience of an irreparable cultural loss that is so much part of it, is closer to how the people of the European continent relate to their past than to how the Anglo-Saxons relate to theirs.

And when restricting our gaze to continental Europe, there is one more amazing paradox. The formation of modern Western historical consciousness has been a matter of a mere ten years. It came into being in the decade between 1790 and 1800 in the thought and writings of Herder, Kant, Schiller, Goethe, Fichte, Klopstock, Novalis, the Schlegels, and the three angry young men at the Tübinger Stift: Hegel, Hölderlin, and Schelling. Before 1790 all the options were still open—and after 1800 nothing of any substance was ever added to the matrix of Western historical consciousness. But why did this happen in Germany, in that most backward nation of Europe? More specifically, why not in France, where the Great Revolution had opened up a more threatening abyss between the world of the present and that of the past than the West had ever experienced before? But asking the question is already answering it, for a new historical consciousness also emerged in France. This is the historical consciousness we may associate with Constant, Barante, Lamartine, Guizot, and Tocqueville (and, in England, with Carlyle). But *this* was a historical consciousness quite different from the German one: It was, essentially, the *participant's* historical consciousness, whereas its German rival was the *onlooker's* or the *spectator's* historical consciousness. That is to say, even though they wrote a generation later than the Germans I mentioned a moment ago, these French authors (and all of them were great politicians as well!) still experienced themselves as the potential participants of the sublime tragedy of the Great Revolution. But with the death of Michelet—its last great protagonist—the spectator's historical consciousness, as developed in Germany, gained its final victory over its French competitor, and since then it has conquered all of continental Europe. It even found its way to the Anglo-Saxon academic world, although without ever reaching its deeper mental layers. And, indeed, of what use could the spectator's historical consciousness possibly be for a hegemonic power such as the (contemporary) United States?

26. P. Carrard, *Poetics of the new history: French historical discourse from Braudel to Chartier* (Baltimore and London, 1992), 99.

27. So this book is not a recantation of what I have said in previous publications about historical truth and, more specifically, about what criteria to adopt for deciding about the adequacy of narrative representations of the past. This book simply deals with a different topic.

28. "Allmählich hat sich sich mir herausgestellt, was jede grosse Philosophie

bisher war: nämlich das Selbstbekenntnis ihres Urhebers und eine Art ungewollter und unvermerkter *mémoires;* insgleichen, dass die moralischen (oder unmoralischen) Absichten in jeder Philosophie den eigentlichen Lebenskeim ausmachten, aus dem jedesmal die ganze Pflanze gewachsen ist." F. Nietzsche, Jenseits von Gut und Böse, in id., *Friedrich Nietzsche Werke III. Herausgegeben von Karl Schlechta,* Frankfurt am Main 1983; section 6, p. 571. See also section 3.

29. "In jeder Philosophie gibt es einen Punkt, wo die 'Überzeugung' des Philosophen auf die Bühne tritt: oder, um es in der Sprache eines alten Mysteriums zu sagen: *adventavit asinus, pulcher et fortissimus.*" See Nietzsche, *op. cit.;* section 8.

30. A. de Tocqueville, *The old regime and the French Revolution,* trans. Stuart Gilbert (Doubleday Anchor Books: New York, 1955), 9.

31. For a more elaborate exposition of this argument, see my essay on Tocqueville in my *Aesthetic politics* (Stanford, 1997), 332–336.

32. The feeling of boredom has its paradigmatic manifestation in what has come to be known as the "demon of noontide." In southern European countries objects tend to coincide with their shadows at noontide and this may provoke in us an awareness of the objective nature of reality, which is inaccessible to us when things and their shadows intermingle. See for this R. Kuhn, *Demon of noontide.*

33. M. Bal, *Quoting Caravaggio: Contemporary art, preposterous history* (Chicago, 1999), 241.

34. R. Scruton, *The aesthetics of music* (Oxford, 1997), 121.

35. P. Crowther, *The Kantian sublime: From morality to art* (Oxford, 1991), 56.

36. A. Loos, "Ornament und verbrechen," in Loos, *Trotzdem* (Vienna, 1982), 78 ff.

37. J. Rykwert, *Ornament ist kein Verbrechen: Architektur als Kunst* (Cologne, 1983), 109.

38. Gadamer, *Truth and method,* 2nd ed. (New York, 2003), 158–159.

39. H. Bauer, *Rocaille: Zur Herkunft und zum Wesen eines Ornament-Motivs* (Berlin, 1962), Figure 1.

40. The grotesque in art and literature can be defined as "the unresolved clash of incompatibles in work and response." See P. Thomson, *The grotesque* (Norfolk, 1972), 27. But Vitruvius had already offered the following characteristic of the grotesque, which is most appropriate in the present context: "Our contemporary artists decorate the walls with monstrous forms rather than producing clear images of the familiar world. Instead of columns they paint fluted stems with oddly shaped leaves and volutes, and instead of pediments arabesques; the same with candelabra and painted edifices, on the pediments of which grow dainty flowers unrolling out of robes and topped, without rhyme or reason, by little figures. The little stems, finally, support half-figures crowned by human or animal heads. Such things, however, never existed, do not now exist, and shall never come into being. . . . For how can the stem of a flower support a roof, or a candelabrum bear

pedimental sculpture? How can a tender shoot carry a human figure, and how can bastard forms composed of flowers and human bodies grow out of roots and tendrils?" Quoted in W. Kayser, *The grotesque in art and literature* (Bloomington, 1963), 20. For the Renaissance, especially for Pirro Ligorio's authoritative conception of the grotesque, see D. Summers, *Michelangelo and the language of art* (Princeton, 1981), 496, 497.

41. J. W. von Goethe, *Reinecke Fuchs: Zeichnungen von Wilhelm von Kaulbach* (Stuttgart, n.d.), 1.

42. Which has the interesting implication that what is logically impossible can, nevertheless, be depicted.

43. Bauer, *Rocaille,* 4, 5.

44. Bauer, *Rocaille,* 4, 5.

45. M. Shapiro, "On some problems in the semiotics of visual art: Field and vehicle in image-signs," *Semiotica* 1 (1969): 224, 225.

46. This feature of the engraving is not mentioned by Bauer.

47. N. Pevsner, *Rococo art from Bavaria* (London, 1956), Figure 110.

48. Bauer, *Rocaille,* Figure 45.

49. For Meissonnier, see the elaborate thesis by P. J. Fuhring, *Un génie du Rococo: Juste Aurèle Meissonnier (1695–1750)—Orfèvre, dessinateur, architecte* (Paris, 1994).

50. Escher's play with spatial dimensions has its antecedents in Giambattista Piranesi's *Carceri.* And Escher's deep admiration for this prototypically rococo artist is well attested. See, for example, J. L. Locher, "Het werk van M. C. Escher," in Locher, ed., *De werelden van M. C. Escher* (Amsterdam, 1975), 24.

51. See, for example, O. T. Banks, *Watteau and the North* (New York, 1977), Figure 102. Where Meissonnier makes ornament into part of represented reality, the tree above the couple of lovers is presented here as ornament. Hence, we may observe here the same ambiguity between ornament and represented reality, although Watteau exploits this ambiguity differently from Meissonnier.

52. M. C. Escher, "Oneindigheidsbenaderingen," in J. L. Locher, *De werelden van M. C. Escher* (Amsterdam, 1975), 40–44.

53. Needless to say, I am thinking here of Huizinga's conception of play as developed in his "Homo Ludens": "The game creates, temporarily and locally, its own, exceptional, enclosed world within our wonted world, in which the players can move in agreement with a coercive law of their own, until this law itself releases them again" (my translation). See J. Huizinga, "Homo Ludens," in Huizinga, *Verzamelde Werken 5* (Haarlem, 1950), 5.

54. Bauer, *Rocaille,* 38.

55. Bauer, *Rocaille,* 20, 21.

56. The phrase had already been used by O. Jones in his *Grammar of ornament* (London, 1856).

57. As is explained in A. Wanerberg, *Urpflanze und Ornament: Pflanzenmor-*

phologische Anregungen in der Kunsttheorie und Kunst von Goethe bis zum Jugendstil (Helsinki, 1992).

58. A. Riegl, *Problems of style: Foundations for a history of ornament* (Princeton, 1993), 14.

59. G. von Graevenitz, *Das Ornament des Blicks: Über die Grundlagen des neuzeitlichen Sehens—Die Poetik der Arabeske und Goethes "West-östlichen Divan"* (Weimar, 1994), Chapter 2.

60. Bauer, *Rocaille*, 49.

61. Illustrative here is Bérain's engraving, even though careful investigation will bring to light certain imperfections in its symmetry.

62. It might be interesting to hear from mathematicians about the C curve.

63. W. von Wersin, *Deas elementare Ornament und seine Gesetzlichkeit: Eine Morphologie des Ornaments* (Ravensburg, 1940), 15.

64. Wersin, *Deas elementare Ornament*, 15.

65. What certainly is a most ironic observation about an author who took pride in writing: "Ich schreibe nur für Menschen, die modernes Empfinden besitzen. Für Menschen die sich in Sehnsucht nach der Renaissance oder dem Rokoko verzehren, schreibe ich nicht." Quoted in W. Benjamin, "Erfahrung und Armut," in Benjamin, *Walter Benjamin: Gesammelte Schriften II, 1, Herausgegeben von Rolf Tiedemann und Hermann Schweppenhäuser* (Frankfurt am Main, 1977), 217. "I write only for people who possess a modern sensibility. . . . I do not write for people consumed by nostalgia for the Renaissance or the Rococo." Quoted in W. Benjamin, "Experience and poverty," in Benjamin, *Walter Benjamin: Selected writings, volume 2, 1927–1934* (Cambridge and London, 1999), 733.

66. "Als die unterste Stufe liegen dem gesamten seelischen Leben die 'Lebensgefühle' oder 'Stimmungen' zugrunde. Sie stellen die einfachste und ursprünglichste Form dar, in der das menschliche Leben seiner selbst—und schon immer in einer gefärbten Weise, mit einer bestimmt gearteten Wertung und Stellungnahme—inne wird." See O. F. Bollnow, *Das Wesen der Stimmungen* (Frankfurt am Main, 1956), 33.

67. Bollnow, *Stimmungen*, 57, 58.

68. Although the two can be related to each other—and Bollnow does so by making use of an appropriate musical metaphor: "If moods and feelings constitute a musical composition's steady and uniform *basso continuo*, then sensations are the ever-changing and variegated melodies that have been constructed on this basis" (my translation). See Bollnow, *Stimmungen*, 36.

69. "Es erscheinen in den echten Gestimmtheiten überhaupt kein Ich, kein Gegenstand, keine Grenze zwischen Ich und Gegenstand. Man müsste im Gegenteil sagen: die Grenzen des Ichs verschwimmen und verschwinden in eigentümlicher Weise. Ich und Welt werden in ein ungeteiltes Totalerleben eingebettet. Stimmung ist Ich- und Weltgefühl zugleich." Quoted in Bollnow, *Stimmungen*, 40, 41.

70. Quoted in Bollnow, *Stimmungen,* 38. For an elaboration of the relationship between music and *Stimmung,* see L. Spitzer, *Classical and Christian ideas of world harmony: Prolegomena to an interpretation of the word* Stimmung (Baltimore, 1963).

71. O. Spengler, *Der Untergang des Abendlandes, volume 1* (Munich, 1923), 87.

72. Spengler, *Der Untergang des Abendlandes,* 117.

73. Spengler, *Der Untergang des Abendlandes,* 78.

74. For a description of the machine, see L. H. Count Schimmelpenninck, ed., *"Teyler" 1778–1978: Studies en bijdragen naar aanleiding van het tweede eeuwfeest* (Haarlem, 1978), 122–124.

75. For a further development of this theme, see my "Invitation to Historians," *Rethinking History: The Journal of Theory and Practice* 7 (Winter 2003): 413–439.

Chapter 8: Sublime Historical Experience

1. I would like to express my gratitude to Jaap den Hollander for his most valuable comments on a previous version of this chapter.

2. But perhaps one must be a philosopher to be capable of this naivete. The philosopher, with his love of distinctions, will argue that the notion of "forgetting *p*" does not necessarily presuppose the knowledge that *p.* The former merely is an operation that should be executed on *p* and its meaning is, as such, independent of the knowledge that *p.* So there is no contradiction between the command to forget *p* and not knowing that *p.* But in real life the notion of forgetting *p* is transparent with regard to *p,* so that, paradoxically, we cannot forget *p* unless we know that *p.* Of course that is the point of Dickinson's poem quoted at the beginning of this chapter.

As Elster has shown, the distinction can be formalized in terms of the distinction between internal and external negation. If we have the proposition "*s* believes that *p,*" its internal negation is "*s* believes *not-p,*" whereas its external negation is "it is not true that *s* believes that *p.*" If applied to forgetting, the distinction is described by Elster as follows: "L'oubli ou l'indifférence est une négation externe, la simple absence de conscience de **x**, tandis que la volonté d'oublier requiert la conscience de l'absence de **x**, et donc de **x**. Vouloir oublier, c'est comme si l'on se décidait à créer l'obscurité par la lumière." See J. Elster, *Psychologie politique (Veyne, Zinoviev, Tocqueville)* (Paris, 1980), 82. "Forgetting or indifference is an external negation, a mere lack of awareness of *x,* whereas the desire to forget presupposes a representation of the absence of *x* and hence of *x* itself. Trying to forget is like using a flashlight to create darkness." See J. Elster, *Political psychology* (Cambridge, New York, and Oakleigh, 1993), 82. For a psychological analysis (as detailed as it is disappointing) of this paradox of not being able to forget what one wishes to forget, see E. W. Rassin, *Limitations of the thought suppression paradigm as a model of obsessive intrusions and memory loss* (Maastricht, 2000).

3. "Le commandement 'oublie-le' exige un effort qui ne peut que graver dans

la mémoire l'object qu'on est supposé oublier." See J. Elster, *Psychologie politique*, 81. Elster, *Political psychology*, 81.

4. For a magisterial exposition of the history of this topos, see R. Koselleck, "Historia magistra vitae: Über die Auflösung des Topos im Horizont neuzeitlich bewegter Geschichte," in Koselleck, *Zur Semantik vergangener Zeiten* (Frankfurt am Main, 1979).

5. "Demnach ist es der Aufgabe der Historie, das Wesen des Staates aus der Reihe früheren Begebenheiten darzuthun und dasselbe zum Erkenntnis zo bringen, die der Politik aber nach erfolgtem Verständnis und gewonnener Erkenntnis es weiter zu entwickeln und zu vollenden." See L. von Ranke, "De historia et politices cognatione atque discrimine oratio," in Ranke, *Sämmtliche Werke, Band 24* (Leipzig, 1872).

6. For a modern defense of this view, see the influential writings by, among others, Hermann Lübbe and Jörn Rüsen. On several occasions I have expressed my agreement with it. See for example the last chapter of my *Historical representation* (Stanford, 2001).

7. I deliberately said "can become" and not "will become," for although knowledge of one's identity undoubtedly is a *necessary* condition, it is not a *sufficient* condition for successful action. We may derive mistaken or inadequate maxims for action from our knowledge of our identity. For example, somebody who knows himself to be a relatively weak-willed person may suddenly display an unreasonable stubborn behavior in his reaction to people that he believes to be inclined to exploit his pliability. And with states or nations it is no different.

8. F. Nietzsche, *The use and abuse of history*, 2nd ed., trans. Adrian Collins (New York, 1957), 8.

9. Nietzsche, *Use and abuse of history*, 6.

10. Nietzsche, *Use and abuse of history*, 7.

11. Admittedly, this may put nineteenth-century historism in too favorable a light, for, as we saw with Gadamer in Chapter 5, nineteenth-century historists (unwittingly) adopted Kantian transcendentalism when firmly excluding the historical knowing subject itself from historical change. Indeed, the historists historicized everything except themselves—and precisely this confirmed them in their conviction that objective knowledge of the past is, in the end, possible. However, as the quote from Ranke makes clear, we get a fundamentally different picture when we move from the historical knowing subject to the collective individuality of a nation, a people, or a state. Then the kind of historical knowledge that should inspire political action is always fully contextualized historically by the historists. And then the transcendental knowing subject is abandoned by the historists. Hence, at *this* level—which is the level Nietzsche was thinking of when attacking the historist dive into the past—the historists were undoubtedly more consistent than their angry and short-tempered opponent.

12. For the view that "Basel" can be conceived of as a kind of missing link be-

tween the Enlightenment and German historism, see L. Gossman, *Basel in the age of Burckhardt: A study in unseasonable ideas* (Chicago, 2000).

13. Or so it may seem. As we will see in the course of this chapter, things are, in fact, more complicated.

14. This does raise the question of what happens when a memory is relegated to the unconscious. More specifically, in what way does a conscious memory differ from an unconscious one? An unconscious memory is, so to speak, a package that we put away on a shelf unopened, whereas the conscious memory is like a package that we have opened in order to see what it contains. To put it more precisely, conscious memory is transparent with regard to its contents in the sense that the object of memory is not memory itself but what is remembered, that is, remembered experience. However, unconscious memory is merely the memory$_1$ (memory about memory) of a memory$_2$ (memory itself) in which the actual *content* of memory$_2$ remains unarticulated. This may help us to understand the paradox of our being both unable to forget and to remember a traumatic experience. A traumatic experience is not forgotten insofar as it may occasion a memory$_1$ of a memory$_2$; however, it is forgotten as far as the content of memory$_2$ is concerned. And in this way the seeming contradiction of a forgetting and remembrance at one and the same time can be solved satisfactorily. For a further analysis of the different levels of forgetting, see Elster, *Psychologie politique,* 74 ff.

15. K. Mannheim, "Das konservative Denken," in Mannheim, *Wissenssoziologie* (Neuwied am Rhein, 1970), 408–509.

16. "Es sind viele antirevolutionäre Bücher für die Revolution geschrieben. Burke hat ein revolutionäres Buch gegen die Revolution geschrieben." See Novalis (pen name of the poet Friedrich von Hardenberg), *Blüthenstaub I* (Heidelberg, 1953), 340.

17. Generally speaking, one might agree with Bollnow when he defines reality as the domain of resistance against our effort to achieve a reunification of what has fallen apart into a world of the subject and another one of the object: "These considerations have to do with the fact that absolute certainty about the existence of a reality outside the human being cannot be achieved by theoretical speculation. This certainty is given to us, however, prior to all theoretical speculation in an original experience at a most elementary level of life: the urge for the development and unfolding of life hits upon something outside it, and in which life discovers its borders, it hits upon a resistance restraining and limiting it. And all later certainty about a reality outside ourselves is based on this original experience of resistance" (my translation). See Bollnow, *Stimmungen,* 112, 113. This is the trauma of birth coloring all of human existence and experience.

18. The desire is, strangely enough, both natural and perverse. Think of the story of Plato about the origin of the sexes that I used as an epigraph for this book. One might then say that sexual desire is both natural—as being a desire of fusion with somebody of the opposite sex—but perverse in the sense of expecting from

this union the abolishment or overcoming of sexual differentiation. A similar story could be told about History: We live in the gap between present and past that History created in 1789, and this is why we write history. But this writing is never wholly free from the desire to make this gap disappear by writing.

19. I shall return to this issue when dealing with myth at the end of this chapter.

20. "Früher galten die Gesetze unbedingt, die menschliche Individualität stand in Einheit mit dem Allgemeinen. Die Götter ehren, für das Vaterland sterben, war ein allgemeines Gesetz, und jeder erfüllte den allgemeinen Inhalt ohne Untersuchung. Da aber ging der Mensch in sich, fing an zu forschen, ob er sich dem Inhalt fügen wollte und müsse. Dieser erwachte Gedanke brachte den Göttern Griechenlands und der schönen Sittlichkeit den Tod. Das Denken erscheint also hier als das Prinzip des Verderbens, und zwar des Verderbens der schönen Sittlichkeit; denn indem es sich affirmativ weiss, stellt es Vernunftprinzipien auf, die in einem wesentlichen Verhältnisse zur vorhandenen Wirklichkeit und im Gegensatze gegen die beschränkende Sitte stehen. . . . Die Griechen wussten wohl was sittlich war in jeder Beziehung; aber das der Mensch dies in sich suchen und aus sich finden müsse, das ist der Standpunkt des Sokrates. . . . Sokrates hat die Innerlichkeit des Menschen zu seinem Bewusstsein gebracht, so dass in dem Gewissen das Mass des Rechten und Sittlichen aufgestellt wurde. Darin lag der Gegensatz des bisherigen Sittlichen zu dem der folgenden Zeit; die früheren Griechen hatten kein Gewissen. Sokrates ist als moralischer Lehrer berühmt; in Wahrheit aber ist er der Erfinder der Moral. Er hat den Gedanken als das Höchste, als das Bestimmende ausgesprochen. Sittlichkeit haben die Griechen gehabt; aber welche moralische Tugenden, Pflichten usw. der Mensch habe, das wollte sie Sokrates lehren." See G. W. F. Hegel, *Vorlesungen über die Philosophie der Weltgeschichte, Band II–IV* (Felix Meiner Verlag: Hamburg, 1976), 640–644.

21. "Nachher hat das Athenische volk das Urteil bereut, und auch das war gehörig. . . . Sie sahen ein, dass sie ebenso mitschuldig oder freizusprechen seien, weil das Prinzip des Sokrates bei ihnen schon feste Wurzel gefasst habe, schon ihr eigenes Prinzip geworden sei, nämlich das Prinzip der Subjektivität." See Hegel, *Vorlesungen über die Philosophie, Band II–IV,* 646.

22. Insightful as always, Michelet had already surmised the significance of this relationship to the past, as we may gather from the following note in his diary in 1841: "In order to be fully himself, man must no longer be himself. But must die, must undergo a metamorphosis." Quoted in J. Tollebeek, " 'Renaissance' and 'fossilization': Michelet, Burckhardt, and Huizinga," *Renaissance Studies* 15, no. 3 (2001): 360, 361.

23. E. Burke, *A philosophical inquiry into the sublime and the beautiful* (Oxford, 1992), 123.

24. R. Leys, "Shell shock, Janet, and the question of memory," in P. Antze and M. Lambek, eds., *Tense past: Cultural chapters in trauma and memory* (New York,

1996), 104. For a clinical definition of dissociation, see E. Cardeña, "The domain of dissociation," in S. J. Lynn and J. W. Rhue, *Dissociation: Clinical and theoretical perspectives* (New York, 1994): "In its broadest sense, 'dissociation' simply means that two or more mental processes or contents are not associated or integrated. It is usually assumed that these dissociated elements should be integrated in conscious awareness, memory or identity." In the 1880s Pierre Janet had already lengthily commented on how traumatic experience may give rise to a dissociation (or *désagrégation* as he called it) of the memory of trauma from normal memory. See also R. Leys, *Trauma: A genealogy* (Chicago, 2000), and the seminal discussion of trauma and experience in C. Caruth, *Unclaimed experience: Trauma, narrative, history* (Baltimore, 1996).

25. Admittedly, as an existentialist Sartre phrased in ontological terms what is discussed here in epistemological terms. And it should be added that an ontological definition of the sublime is not easy to imagine.

26. Since the statements defining logical positivism wholly failed to satisfy the logical positivist's own criteria for what is to count as a meaningful assertion. So logical positivism is nonsense if measured by its own standards.

27. See my "Burke and historism," in my *Political representation* (Stanford, 2001).

28. See also note 11.

29. V. Hugo, *Oeuvres Complètes, Volume XIII, Quatre-vingt treize* (Paris, n.d.), 419: "Il sentait en lui quelque chose comme ce qu'éprouve l'arbre où on l'arrache de sa racine." Nietzsche happened to use exactly the same metaphor when describing what he referred to as "critical history": "Its past is critically examined, the knife put to its roots, and all the "pieties" are grimly trodden under foot" (F. Nietzsche, *Use and abuse of history*, 21). From the perspective of the contrast between Nietzsche and Hegel that was discussed earlier, it is of interest that Nietzsche explicitly says here that one cuts *oneself* loose from one's roots—and that he does not present this as something that history may force us to do. Obviously, this suggests again how much Nietzsche (unlike both the historists and Hegel) is inclined to place the self in the position of a historical transcendental ego that is itself outside or beyond history.

30. S. Freud, "Mourning and melancholia," in Freud, *The standard edition of the complete psychological works of Sigmund Freud, Volume XIV* (London and Toronto, 1981), 249.

31. "Erst muss das Herz der Welt brechen, ehe ihr höheres Leben vollkommen offenbar wird. Die Versöhnung ist deshalb zuerst nur im abstrakten Gedanken: so hat Sokrates sie erfasst. Aber sie musste dann erst noch im Geiste geschehen." See Hegel, *Vorlesungen über die Philosophie, Band II–IV*, 647.

32. Hegel's point has been most forcefully put by Arthur Danto in his claim about what makes a historical period into what it is: "Something of the same sort is true for the historical period considered as an entity. It is a period solely from

the perspective of the historian, who sees it from without; for those who lived in the period it would just be the way life was lived. And asked, afterward, what it was like to have lived then, they may answer from the outside, from the historian's perspective. From the inside there was no answer to be given; it was simply the way things were. So when the members of a period can give an answer in terms satisfactory to the historian, the period will have exposed its outward surface and in a sense be over, as a period." See A. Danto, *The transfiguration of the commonplace* (Cambridge, Mass., 1983), 207.

33. "Wenn also das Bestehende in seiner Auflösung empfunden werden soll und empfunden wird, so muss dabei das Unerschöpfte und Unerschöpfliche, der Beziehungen und Kräfte, und jene, die Auflösung, mehr durch diese empfunden werden, als umgekehrt, denn aus Nichts wird nichts. . . . Aber das Mögliche, welches in die Wirklichkeit tritt, indem *die Wirklichkeit sich auflöst,* dies wirkt, und es bewirkt sowohl die Empfundung der Auflösung als die Erinnerung des Aufgelösten" (Hölderlin's italics). See F. Hölderlin, "Das Werden in Vergehen," in Hölderlin, *Sämtliche Werke: Herausgegeben von Friedrich Beissner* (Frankfurt am Main, 1961), 1,004.

34. "Die Auflösung durch den Gedanken ist nun notwendig zugleich das Hevorgehen eines neuen Prinzips. Der Gedanke als Allgemeines ist auflösend; in diesem Auflösen ist aber in der Tat das vorhergehende Prinzip erhalten, nur nicht mehr in seiner ursprünglicher Bestimmung vorhanden. Das allgemeine Wesen ist erhalten, aber seine Allgemeinheit ist als solche herausgehoben worden." See G. W. F. Hegel, *Vorlesungen über die Philosophie der Weltgeschichte, Band 1, Die Vernunft in der Geschichte* (Felix Meiner Verlag: Hamburg, 1970), 165. G. W. F. Hegel, *Lectures on the philosophy of world history: Introduction—Reason in history* (Cambridge, 1975), 147.

35. H. White, *Metahistory: The historical imagination in nineteenth-century Europe* (Baltimore, 1973), 117.

36. "But there is another way in which a number of things may be comprehended, as elements in a single complex of concrete relationships. It is in this way that we see together the multiple images and allusions of a poem, or the combination of influences, motives, beliefs and purposes which explain a concrete historical action. It is not as instances of a theory but as centers of concrete relationships that we understand ourselves and others, and one may say that there is also a kind of *configurational* comprehension." See L. O. Mink, "Modes of comprehension and the unity of knowledge," in Mink, *Historical understanding,* ed. Brian Fay, Eugene O. Golob, and Richard T. Vann (Ithaca and London, 1987), 39.

37. Danto, *Transfiguration of the commonplace,* 206.

38. Danto, *Transfiguration of the commonplace,* 206.

39. A. C. Danto, *Narration and knowledge* (New York, 1985), 339.

40. For a similar argument, see my *Narrative logic: A semantic analysis of the historian's language* (Dordrecht and Boston, 1983), 137, 138.

41. J. Banville, *Eclipse* (London, 2000), 32, 33. One is tempted to compare this passage to Hugo von Hofmannsthal's famous *Der Brief des Lord Chandos,* in which Hofmannsthal describes how the distrust in the capacity of language to represent the world may grant to experience the force of a sublime revelation of the world. See H. von Hofmannsthal, "Ein Brief," in Hofmannsthal, *Sämtliche Werke, Volume XXXI, Herausgegeben von Ellen Ritter* (Frankfurt am Main, 1991), 45–56.

42. The issue of the sublime in art is never addressed by Danto, although he comes quite close to it in his discussion of "disturbatory art." See A. C. Danto, *The philosophical disenfranchisement of art* (New York, 1986), 123 ff. Of specific interest in the present context is Danto's observation that "the disturbatory artist aims to transform her audience into something pretheatrical, a body which relates to her in some more magical and transformational relationship than the defining conventions of the theatre allow. And she means to achieve this by some transformation of herself, which consists in taking off the protective and powerfully dislocative atmosphere of theatrical distance and making contact with a reality" (*Disenfranchisement,* 131).

43. Danto, *Narration and knowledge,* 327.

44. Danto, *Narration and knowledge,* 289.

45. Danto, *Disenfranchisement,* 205.

46. The notion of identity is one more striking example of how Danto's method of the indiscernibles (which he so famously and successfully applied in the case of Warhol's Brillo Box) can be used for obtaining an answer to some of the most difficult and most stubborn philosophical problems. There may be no discernible difference between the self before and after the kind of experience discussed here—and yet this enables us to clarify the notion of identity. For a discussion of the method of indiscernibles, see my "Danto on representation, identity, and indiscernibles," *History and Theory, Theme Issue 37: Danto and his critics* (1998): 44–71.

47. See, for example, D. LaCapra, *History and memory after Auschwitz* (Ithaca and London, 1998), and D. LaCapra, *Writing history, writing trauma* (Baltimore, 2001).

48. Tocqueville hated or, better, feared democracy, but at the same he recognized that democracy was our inevitable fate and that it would realize the equality that "the Creator and Preserver of man has set as man's highest historical goal." See A. de Tocqueville, *Democracy in America, Part II* (New York, 1946), 351.

49. The great crises in Western civilization often compelled it to redefine its relationship to its past, hence a new historical consciousness and a new kind of historical writing to do justice to this new relationship. But up to now no new historical consciousness and no new kind of historical writing emerged in reaction to the Holocaust. So what must we conclude from this about how deep the Holocaust affected the West's historical consciousness? See for this E. Runia, *Waterloo, Verdun, Auschwitz: De liquidatie van het verleden* (Amsterdam, 1999), 9 ff.

50. "Schliesslich kann die Störung der Beziehung zwischen Ich und Welt auch als Spaltung des Ich (in eine beobachtende und eine erlebende Instanz) hervortreten: 'Es bildet sich ein zweites Ich. Ich sehe mich dann so, als wenn man sagt: ich sehe mich noch wie damals . . . .' Hier wird also ein Teil des Ich gewissermassen exterritorialisiert, wird zu einem Stück Aussenwelt. . . . Wir sehen das Gemeinsame von Depersonalisation and Derealisation in der Isolierung des Ich, in der Erschwerung seiner Kommunikation mit der Aussenwelt, in der Abgeschiedenheit der Welt. Das wird vollends deutlich, wenn man das Depersonalisations-Syndrom met dem Zwangs-Syndrom vergleicht. Beiden gemeinsam ist die Einsicht in das Krankhafte, Unsinnige und Widerspruchsvolle ihres Erleben, beide sind Reflexionskrankheiten, maladies de doute. . . . Der Zwangskranke leidet durch sein an der Welt Ausgeliefertsein, an der 'Bessessenheit' von der Welt, während sich der Depersonalisierte von der Welt abgeschieden fühlt, sich nach der Realität, nach Kontakt mit der Wirklichkeit sehnt." See J. E. Meyer, *Die Entfremdungs-Erlebnisse: Über Herkunft und Entstehungsweisen der Depersonalisation* (Stuttgart, 1959), 4, 5.

51. F. Guicciardini, "History of Italy," in P. Gay and V. G. Wexler, eds., *Historians at Work, Volume II* (New York and London, 1972), 50, 61.

52. I remind the reader here of Koselleck's insight mentioned at the beginning of Chapter 4.

53. "Les idées sont des succédanés des chagrins; au moment où ceux-ci se changent en idées, ils perdent une partie de leur action nocive sur notre coeur, et même, au premier instant, la transformation elle-même dégage subitement de la joie. Succédanés dans l'ordre du temps seulement, d'ailleurs, car il semble que l'élément premier en soit l'idée, et le chagrin, seulement le mode selon lequel certaines idées entrent d'abord en nous. Mais il y a plusieurs familles dans le groupe des idées, certaines sont tout de suite des joies." See M. Proust, *À la recherche du temps perdu, Volume III, Texte établi et présenté par Pierre Clarac et André Ferré (Bibliothèque de la Pléiade)* (Paris, 1954–1962), 906 (with thanks to Malcolm Bowie).

54. S. Greenblatt, *Renaissance self-fashioning: From More to Shakespeare* (Chicago and London, 1980), 174, 175.

55. I am deliberately using the theological term *anachoorèsis* to suggest what might be considered to have been the religious origins of modern science and historical writing.

56. V. Turner, "Myth and symbol," in D. Sills, ed., *International encyclopedia of the social sciences, volume 9* (New York, 1968), 576.

57. Turner, "Myth and symbol," 576.

58. And, as Hegel insists, both in the sense of *historia* and in that of *historia rerum gestarum*. See Hegel, *Vorlesungen über die Philosophie, Band 1*, 164.

59. In his essay "Mourning and Melancholia," Freud distinguishes two ways of dealing with loss: In mourning loss is overcome, and in melancholia loss in never really worked through and in this way is taken out of time.

60. Quoted in J. Wenzel, *Jakob Burckhardt in der Krise seiner Zeit* (Berlin, 1967), 75.

Epilogue: Rousseau and Hölderlin

1. This epilogue should be read in conjunction with my "The ethics of history: From the double binds of (moral) meaning to experience," *History and Theory* 43 (Theme issue) (2004).

2. "Wir durchlaufen alle eine exzentrische Bahn, und es ist kein anderer Weg möglich von der Kindheit zur Vollendung. Die selige Einheit, das Sein, im einzigen Sinne des Worts, ist für uns verloren und wir mussten es verlieren, wenn wir es erstrebten, erringen sollten. Wir reissen uns los vom friedlichen 'Hen kai Pan' der Welt, um es herzustellen, durch uns selbst." See F. Hölderlin, "Hyperion: Die vorletzte Fassung," in Hölderlin, *Sämtliche Werke: Herausgegeben von Friedrich Beissner* (Frankfurt am Main, 1961), 717.

3. A. Horowitz, *Rousseau, nature, and history* (Toronto, 1987), 127.

4. J. J. Rousseau, "Discourse on the origin of inequality," in Rousseau, *The social contract and discourses*, trans. G. D. H. Cole (London, 1968), 172.

5. Horowitz, *Rousseau, nature, and history*, 69.

6. "La nuit s'avançait. J'aperçus le ciel, quelques étoiles, et un peu de verdure. Cette première sensation fut un moment délicieux. Je ne me sentais encore que par là. Je naissais dans cet instant à la vie, et il me semblait que je remplissais de ma légère existence tous les objets que j'apercevais. Tout entier au moment présent je ne me souvenais de rien; je n'avais nulle notion distincte de mon individu, pas le moindre idée de ce qui venait de m'arriver; je ne savais ni qui j'étais, ni ni où j'étais; je ne sentais ni mal, ni crainte, ni inquiétude. Je voyais couler mon sang comme j'aurais vu couler un ruisseau, sans songer seulement que ce sang m'appartînt en aucune sorte." See J. J. Rousseau, *Les rêveries du promeneur solitaire* (Gallimard: Paris, 1972), 48.

7. Rousseau, *Rêveries*, 101.

8. See for this M. Berman, *The politics of authenticity* (New York, 1970).

9. J. J. Rousseau, "Discourse on the origin and the foundations of inequality among mankind," in Rousseau, *The social contract and the first and second discourses* (New Haven and London, 2002), 123–124.

10. "It would be a melancholy necessity for us to be obliged to allow that this distinctive and almost unlimited faculty is the source of all man's misfortunes" (Rousseau, "Discourse," 96).

11. F. Nietzsche, "Zur Genealogie der Moral," in Nietzsche, *Werke II, Herausgegeben von Karl Schlechta* (Frankfurt am Main, 1984), 219, 224.

12. See Chapter 3 of my *Political representation* (Stanford, 2002).

13. Thus Hölderlin's work on the novel spans more than half the period of his literary activity. Moreover, it was the only substantial text Hölderlin published during his lifetime.

14. L. Ryan, *Hölderlins "Hyperion": Exzentrische Bahn und Dichterberuf* (Stuttgart, 1965), 12.

15. Ryan, *Hölderlins "Hyperion,"* 12.

16. "L'homme est né libre, et partout il est dans les fers. Tel se croit le maître des autres, que ne laisse pas d'être plus esclave qu'eux. Comment ce changement s'est-il fait? Je l'ígnore. Qu'est-ce qui peut le rendre légitime? Je crois pouvoir résoudre cette question." ("Man was born free, and everywhere he is in chains. Many a one believes himself the master of others, and yet he is a greater slave than they. How has this change come about? I do not know. What can make it legitimate? I believe I can settle this question.") See J. J. Rousseau, "The social contract," in Rousseau, *The social contract and the first and second discourses* (New Haven and London, 2002), 156. Of course Rousseau's "je l'ignore" should not be taken literally but read rather in the sense of a "this is not the place for a discussion of this issue."

17. I shall leave wholly aside here the structural peculiarities of this extremely complex and intricate epistolary novel, even though I am well aware of the significance of this aspect of the novel for the historical theorist.

18. This certainly does not mean that *Hyperion* is "realistic" in the way this could be said of the historical novel since Scott. On the contrary, especially the events recounted in the book's first volume are dreamlike rather than part of a believable reality.

19. For a discussion of the nostalgic yearning for the past and of why the experience should be taken more seriously than we are presently inclined to do, see my *History and tropology* (Berkeley, 1994), 199 ff.

20. As was recently demonstrated by John Boardman, the nostalgic remembrance of the past did certainly have its antecedents in Greek antiquity itself. See J. Boardman, *The archaeology of nostalgia: How the Greeks re-created their mythical past* (London, 2003).

21. F. Hölderlin, "Griechenland," in Hölderlin, *Sämtliche Werke* (Frankfurt am Main, 1961), 145.

22. "Wohl dem Manne, dem ein blühend Vaterland das Herz erfreut und stärkt. Mir ist, als würd ich in den Sumpf geworfen, als schlüge man den Sargdeckel über mir zu, wenn einer an das meinige mich mahnt, und wenn mich einer einen Griechen nennt, so wird mir immer, als schnürt' er mit dem Halsband eines Hundes mir die Kehle zu." See F. Hölderlin, "Hyperion," 491 (German ed.). F. Hölderlin, "Hyperion," in Hölderlin, *Hyperion and selected poems* (New York, 1990), 2.

23. Similarly, much later in the novel, Diotima will emphasize that Hyperion had a rare capacity for recognizing the sadnesses, the disappointments, and the abjections of his own time: "Es ist so selten, dass ein Mensch mit dem ersten Schritt ins Leben so mit Einmal, so im kleinsten Punkt, so schnell, so tief das ganze Schicksal seiner Zeit empfand, und dass es unaustilgbar in ihm heftet, dies Gefühl,

weil er nicht rauh genug ist, um es auszustossen, und nicht schwach genug um es aus zu weinen." See Hölderlin, "Hyperion," 612 (German ed.). "It is so seldom that a man, at his first step into life, has at *once* so suddenly, so minutely, so quickly, so deeply felt the whole inevitable course of his time, and that this feeling is so ineradicably fixed in him because he is not rugged enough to cast it out and not weak enough to weep it away" (Hölderlin, "Hyperion," 107 [English ed.]).

24. J. Link, *Hölderlin–Rousseau: Inventive Rückkehr* (Opladen, 1999), 179.

25. Bellarmin (to whom forty-five of all the sixty of the novel's letters are addressed, the remaining fifteen being letters exchanged between Hyperion and Diotima)—who never manifests himself in the book—should certainly not be associated with Galilei's nightmare, the Cardinal Robertus Bellarmin (1542–1621). Wolfgang Binder has convincingly argued that the name Bellarmin had best be read as "the beautiful German": "beautiful in the sense of the novel's doctrine of beauty; German in the sense of the Germans' hero celebrated in the extensive Arminius literature of the eighteenth century." Quoted in E. Pankow, "Epistolary writing, fate, language," in A. Fioretos, ed., *The solid letter: Readings of Friedrich Hölderlin* (Stanford, 1999), 158. With regard to the name Hyperion we should recall that this is the name of the father of the sun, or sometimes (as in Homer) of the sun itself (because the sun is moving [*ion*] above [*hyper*] everything. Diodorus makes Hyperion into a brother of Saturn, the god of the sky, and about whose supreme status—compared to that of Zeus—Hölderlin is quite explicit in the ode "Natur und Kunst oder Saturn und Jupiter" (F. Hölderlin, *Sämtliche Werke: Herausgegeben von Friedrich Beissner* [Frankfurt am Main, 1961], 254, 255). For an explanation of Hölderlin's respect for Saturn, see W. F. Otto, *Der Griechische Göttermythos bei Goethe und Hölderlin* (Berlin, 1939), 13 ff. All this is suggestive of a close link between Hyperion and Apollo, the Greek god for whom Hölderlin felt a special affinity. Last, the etymological meaning of Diotima is "she who fears the gods (or, rather, Zeus)" and the name Diotima will, of course, also call to mind the Diotima teaching to Socrates the secrets of love in Plato's *Symposium*.

26. There is an obvious parallel between Hyperion's state of mind as "der Eremit in Griechenland" and that of Boethius when writing his so tremendously influential book in Theodoric the Great's prison.

27. "Und du, du hast mir den Weg gewiesen! Mit dir begann ich. Sie sind der Worte nicht wert, die Tage, da ich dich noch nicht kannte—O Diotima, Diotima, himmlisches Wesen!"

See Hölderlin, "Hyperion," 537 (German ed.). Hölderlin, "Hyperion," 42 (English ed.).

28. After Misistra Hyperion writes to Diotima the following: "Ich habe gezaudert, gekämpft. Doch endlich muss es sein. Ich sehe, was notwendig ist, und weil ich es so sehe, so soll es auch werden. Missdeute mich nicht! verdamme mich nicht! ich muss dir raten dass du mich verlässest, meine Diotima. Ich bin für dich nichts mehr, du holdes Wesen." See Hölderlin, "Hyperion," 602 (German ed.). "I have

hesitated, I have struggled. But now at last it must be. I see what is necessary. And since I see it, it shall come to pass. Do not misunderstand me! Do not condemn me! I must advise you to give me up, my Diotima. I am nothing more for you, lovely being!" See Hölderlin, "Hyperion," 98 (English ed.). And Diotima expresses her agreement with Hyperion's decision in her *Schwanenlied* (Hölderlin, "Hyperion," 627 ff [German ed.]).

29. "Wir gingen zurück, wie nach der ersten Umarmung. Es war uns alles fremd und neu geworden." See Hölderlin, "Hyperion," 573 (German ed.). Hölderlin, "Hyperion," 74 (English ed.).

30. It is, therefore, difficult to agree with Silz's strange claim that Diotima, not Hyperion, should be seen as the real hero of the novel. See W. Silz, *Hölderlin's Hyperion: A critical reading* (Philadelphia, 1969), 48.

31. "In dem Masse, wie Hyperion sich der 'Schönheit' verpflichtet weiss und tiefer in deren Verständnis eindringt, wird Diotima ihrer Selbständigkeit beraubt, ja sie scheint fast in Hyperions Wesen aufzugehen. Am Anfang ist sie ihm eine überwältigende Offenbarung, am Ende wird sie ihm zur 'Muse,' die sich im Sterben weitergibt und in verwandelter Form in seinem Dichten weiterlebt." See L. Ryan, "Hölderlins 'Hyperion': Ein 'romantischer' Roman?" in J. Schmidt, ed., *Über Hölderlin* (Frankfurt am Main, 1970), 194, 195. For a similar observation, see M. Wegenast, *Hölderlins Spinoza-Rezeption und ihre Bedeutung für die Konzeption des "Hyperion"* (Tübingen, 1990), 182.

32. See for this theme Link, *Hölderlin–Rousseau,* 121–155.

33. "Es gibt grosse Stunden im Leben. Wir schauen an ihnen hinauf, wie an den kolossalischen Gestalten der Zukunft und des Altertums." See Hölderlin, "Hyperion," 560 (German ed.). Hölderlin, "Hyperion," 62 (English ed.).

34. Quoted in Ryan, *Hölderlin's "Hyperion,"* 150.

35. Hölderlin, "Hyperion," 567 (German ed.). Hölderlin, "Hyperion," 69 (English ed.).

36. Hölderlin, "Hyperion," 568 (German ed.). Hölderlin, "Hyperion," 70 (English ed.).

37. Hölderlin, "Hyperion," 502 (German ed.). Hölderlin, "Hyperion," 10 (English ed.).

38. "Kannst du so dich in die alte Zeit versetzen, sagte Diotima" (Hölderlin, "Hyperion," 568 [German ed.]). "'Can you thus transport yourself to ancient times?' asked Diotima" (Hölderlin, "Hyperion," 69 [English ed.]).

39. The significance of Rousseau for Hölderlin's thought was first demonstrated in A. Buck, *Rousseau und die deutsche Romantik* (Berlin, 1939), and was fully investigated later on in G. Raynal-Mony, *Hölderlin et Rousseau* (Paris, 1975).

40. "Wie ein unermesslicher Schiffbruch, wenn die Orkane verstummt sind und die Schiffer entflohn, und der Leichnam der zerschmetternde Flotte unkenntlich auf den Sandbank liegt, so lag vor uns Athen, uns die verwaisten Säulen standen vor uns, wie die nackte Stämme eines Waldes, der am Abend noch grünte,

und des Nachts darauf im Feuer aufging." See Hölderlin, "Hyperion," 568 (German ed.). Hölderlin, "Hyperion," 70 (English ed.).

41. Especially illuminating in this context is S. Bann, *Romanticism and the rise of history* (New York, 1995).

42. Hölderlin, "Hyperion," 569 (German ed.). Hölderlin, "Hyperion," 70 (English ed.).

43. "So wird Hyperions Athener Rede tatsächlich immer wieder als *das philosophische 'statement'* des Romans . . . interpretiert." ("Thus Hyperion's Athenian speech is always interpreted again as the novel's main philosophical statement" [my translation].) See Wegenast, *Hölderlins Spinoza-Rezeption,* 183.

44. Hölderlin, "Hyperion," 67 (English ed.).

45. The relevant fragments are the fragments 75, 78, 80, and 124 in C. H. Kahn, *The art and thought of Heraclitus: An edition of the fragments with translation and commentary* (Cambridge, 1979). The fragment quoted in the text is fragment 78.

46. The metaphor occurs right at the beginning of the preface, and the book ends with it as well.

47. W. Silz, *Hölderlin's* Hyperion, 97.

48. Think, for example, of Leibniz's "since everything is connected because of the plenitude of the world, and each body acts on every other more or less, depending on the distance, and is affected by the reaction, it follows that each monad is a living mirror, or a mirror endowed with an internal action, and that it represents the universe according to its point of view and is regulated as completely as is the universe itself." See G. W. Leibniz, "The principles of nature and grace, based on reason," in Leibniz, *Philosophical papers and letters: A selection translated and edited with an introduction by Leroy E. Loemker* (Dordrecht, 1976), 637. It should be added that Hölderlin had been an eager reader of Leibniz during his years at the Tübinger Stift; see for this P. Kondylis, *Die Entstehung der Dialektik: Eine Analyse der geistigen Entwicklung von Hölderlin, Schelling und Hegel bis 1802* (Stuttgart, 1979), 72–77. It might well be that the Leibnizian antecedents in Hölderlin's thought have, up to now, remained underexposed in Hölderlin scholarship.

49. "Die Dichtung, sagt ich, meiner Sache gewiss, ist der Anfang und das Ende dieser Wissenschaft [i.e., of philosophy]." See Hölderlin, "Hyperion," 564 (German ed.). "'Poetry,' I answered, confident of my argument, 'is the beginning and the end of philosophical knowledge.'" See Hölderlin, "Hyperion," 66 (English ed.).

50. "O ihr, die ihr das Höchste und das Beste sucht . . . , wisst ihr seinen Namen? Den Namen des, das Eins ist und Alles? Sein Name ist Schönheit." See Hölderlin, "Hyperion," 536 (German ed.). Hölderlin, "Hyperion," 41 (English ed.).

51. "Das erste Kind der menschlichen, der göttlichen Schönheit ist die Kunst. In ihr verjüngt und wiederholt der göttliche Mensch sich selbst. Er will sich selber fühlen, darum stellt er seine Schönheit gegenüber sich. So gab der Mensch sich

seine Götter. Denn im Anfang war der Mensch und seine Götter Eins, da, sich selber unbekannt, die ewige Schönheit war."

See Hölderlin, "Hyperion," 563 (German ed.). Hölderlin, "Hyperion," 65 (English ed.).

52. Hölderlin's Spinozism—especially in *Hyperion*—has been expounded with an unparalleled erudition and perspicacity in Wegenast, *Hölderlins Spinoza-Rezeption,* although I shall question—with Link—her conviction that Spinoza and late eighteenth century Spinozism offer all the variables we need for satisfactorily clarifying the philosophical statement of *Hyperion.*

53. For an exposition of the ontological differences between God and humankind, see A. Bartuschat, *Spinozas Theorie des Menschen* (Hamburg, 1992), Chapters 1 and 8.

54. As is expressed in the following lines from the elegy *Brot und Wein:* "Mein Freund! Wir kommen zu spät. Zwar leben die Götter / Aber über dem Haupt droben in anderer Welt. / Endlos wirken sie da und scheinen es wenig zu achten, / Ob wir leben, so sehr schonen die Himmlischen uns. / Denn nicht immer vermag ein schwaches Gefäss sie zu fassen, / Nur zu Zeiten erträgt göttliche Fülle der Mensch." See F. Hölderlin, "Brot und Wein," in Hölderlin, *Sämtliche Werke* (Frankfurt am Main, 1961), 297. "But, my friend, we have come too late. Though the gods are living, / Over our heads they live, up in a different world. / Endlessly there they act and, such is their kind wish to spare us, / Little they seem to care whether we live or do not. / For not always a frail, a delicate vessel can hold them, / Only at times can our kind bear the full impact of gods." See F. Hölderlin, "Bread and wine," in Hölderlin, *Hyperion and selected poems* (New York, 1990). This is also how Hölderlin depicts the relationship between the gods and humankind in the *Schicksalslied* in *Hyperion* (p. 626 of the German edition).

55. It should be admitted, though, that this does have its antecedents in Spinoza's earliest writings, where Spinoza (under the influence of Leone Ebreo and the neo-Platonist Renaissance philosophers Marsilio Ficino and Pico della Mirandola) still believed in the possibility of a union with God. But he completely and unequivocally rejected any such views in his *Ethica.* See for this W. Bartuschat, *Baruch de Spinoza* (Munich, 1996), 40. Nevertheless, the *scientia intuitiva,* which is the third kind of knowledge Spinoza discusses in his *Ethica,* is still reminiscent of a route from the finite *modi,* such as human beings, back to God. See also the epigraph to the introduction of this book.

56. Think, for example, of the initially somewhat odd assertion: "Von Pflanzenglück begannen die Menschen und wuchsen auf, und wuchsen, bis sie reiften; von nun an gärten sie unaufhörlich fort, von innen und aussen, bis jetzt das Menschengeschlecht, unendlich aufgelöst, wie ein Chaos daliegt, dass alle, die noch fühlen und sehen, Schwindel ergreift; aber die Schönheit flüchtet aus dem Leben der Menschen sich herauf in den Geist; Ideal wird, was Natur war." See Hölderlin, "Hyperion," 547 (German ed.). "Men began and grew from the happiness of

the plant, grew until they ripened; from that time on they have been in ceaseless ferment, inwardly and outwardly, until now mankind lies there like a Chaos, utterly disintegrated, so that all who can still feel and see are dizzied; but Beauty forsakes the life of men, flees upward into Spirit; the Ideal becomes what Nature was" (Hölderlin, "Hyperion," 51 [English ed.]). For a similar statement, see p. 528 of the German edition: "Was ist der Mensch? konnt ich beginnen; wie kommt es, dass so etwas in der Welt ist, das, wie ein Chaos, gärt, oder modert, wie ein fauler Baum, und nie zu einer Reife gedeiht? Wie duldet diesen Herling die Natur bei ihren süssen Trauben?" ("What is man?—so I might begin; how does it happen that the world contains such a thing, which ferments like a chaos or moulders like a rotten tree, and never grows to ripeness? How can Nature tolerate this sour grape among her sweet clusters?" in Hölderlin, "Hyperion," 35 [English ed.]).

57. "Die Gedankenfigur von 'Deus sive Natura (sive Potentia)' als ichlos-unbewussten Hen kai Pan und die von Natura naturans und Natura naturata liefert geradezu einen definitorischen Schlüssel zu Hölderlins 'Privatreligion.' Danach ist 'Gott' (im Singular) mit der Determinationskraft als solcher (Potentia), d.h. der ewig determinierend in die Natura naturata 'fliessende' Natura naturans identisch, während seine 'Götter' (im Plural) sozusagen die 'Übergangsenergie' von der ewigen 'Substanz' der Natura naturans zu den raumzeitlichen 'Modi' der Natura naturata benennen." See Link, *Hölderlin–Rousseau*, 122, 123.

58. Or, to put it differently, where the gods *need* humanity. There is a marvelous comment on Hölderlin in Coetzee's most recent novel. He begins with what one might call the Spinozist definition of the relationship between the gods and humankind that is, admittedly, to be found in many places in Hölderlin's poetry (see note 55). Coetzee criticizes Hölderlin for this and proposes an alternative view: "We think of them as omniscient, these Gods, but the truth is they know very little and what they know, they know only in the most general of ways. No body of learning can they call their own, no philosophy, properly speaking. Their cosmology an assortment of commonplaces. Their sole expertise in astral flight, their sole homegrown science anthropology. They specialize in humankind because of what we have and they lack; they study us because they are envious." See J. M. Coetzee, *Elizabeth Costello: Eight lessons* (London, 2003), 189. But, as we are now in the position to acknowledge, this alternative view is not so alien to that of Hölderlin himself.

59. "Lasst von der Wiege an den Menschen ungestört! Treibt aus der engvereinten Knospe seines Wesens, treibt aus dem Hüttchen seiner Kindheit ihn nicht heraus! . . . Kurz, lasst den Menschen spät erst wissen, dass es Menschen, dass es irgend etwas ausser ihm gibt, denn nur so wird er Mensch. Der Mensch aber ist ein Gott, so bald er Mensch ist. Und ist er ein Gott, so ist er schön." See Hölderlin, "Hyperion," 562 (German ed.). Hölderlin, "Hyperion," 64 (English ed.). And Link shows that the passage quoted here is an almost verbatim translation of a passage in the *Émile;* see Link, *Hölderlin–Rousseau*, 183.

60. Wegenast, *Hölderlins Spinoza-Rezeption*, 88–96.

61. As Wegenast fails to recognize. Thus Link: "zu recht sieht sie (i.e. Wegenast) daher auch im *Hyperion* ein spinozistisches 'Natur'-Konzept; eine 'Engführung' zwischen Spinoza und Rousseau hätte allerdings die aktuellen Konnotationen des Romans (die Wegenast häufig fehldeutet) adäquater erschliessen können." ("She (i.e., Wegenast) correctly discerns in *Hyperion* a Spinozist concept of nature; but a focus on what Spinoza and Rousseau share and on where they differ might have re-sulted in a more adequate assessment of the real meanings of the novel (and that Wegenast misses all too often).") See Link, *Hölderlin–Rousseau*, 122.

62. See, for example, U. Gaier, *Hölderlin: Eine Einführung* (Tübingen and Basel, 1993).

63. Other influences may have to be taken into account as well, if we think of the fragment "Urteil und Sein," which probably reflects (a stage in) Hölderlin's struggle with Fichte and Schelling. Hölderlin contrasts here Being (*sein*) with judgment (*Urteil*). When doing so, he takes his point of departure in the etymol-ogy of the word *Urteil: Urteil* is a primeval (*Ur*) division (*Teilung*) of what pri-marily was one (i.e., Being) into subject and object—a division from which all self-consciousness and all the fixed forms of this world arose. See F. Hölderlin, "Urteil und Sein," in Hölderlin, *Sämtliche Werke* (Frankfurt am Main, 1961), 947, 948. For a comment on this fragment and on when it was probably written, see D. Henrich, "Hölderlin on judgment and being," in Henrich, *The course of re-membrance and other essays on Hölderlin* (Stanford, 1997), 71–90.

64. This is also, as Hölderlin would insist, a moment of complete forgetfulness and hence of transcendence of history: "Es gibt ein Vergessen alles Daseins, ein Verstummen unsers Wesens, wo uns ist als hätten wir alles gefunden. Es gibt ein Vestummen, ein Vergessen alles Daseins, wo uns ist als hätten wir alles verloren, eine Nacht unsrer Seele, wo kein Schimmer eines Sterns, wo nicht einmal ein faules Holz uns leuchtet." See Hölderlin, "Hyperion," 526 (German ed.). "There is a forgetting of all existence, a hush of our being, in which we feel as if we had found everything. There is a hush, a forgetting of all existence, in which we feel as if we had lost everything, a night of our soul, in which no glimmer of any star nor even the fire from a rotting log gives us light." Hölderlin, "Hyperion," 32 (English ed.). The first is the highest and most supreme experience that we are capable of as human beings; the other brings us to the darkest realms of human existence.

65. Hölderlin's conception of history as a play of fixed forms continuously re-placing each other should be placed in the context of "the also for Hegel decisive opposition of the 'positive' and the 'negative.' All evolution has, as is the case in the Rhine hymn, its source in pure negativity, i.e. in a still chaotic phase in which all is available for the creative process, and from whence the 'positivity' of all fixed forms and ties originates. In the middle between these two extremes is the phase of historical fulfillment, of a harmonious reconciliation of the finite and the infi-nite that Hölderlin mystifyingly refers to as the marriage feast of the Gods and hu-

manity" (my translation). See J. Schmidt, *Hölderlins geschichtsphilosophische Hymnen "Friedensfeier"—"De Einzige"—"Patmos"* (Darmstadt, 1990), 3.

66. Henrich also links the "wise man's" conception of love to Schiller's synthesis of what he considers to be the two fundamental human drives, the material drive and the drive of form. See Henrich, *Hölderlin,* 78. And it is of interest, in this context, that Schiller attributes to such a synthesis the capacity to transcend time, that is, "die Zeit in die Zeit aufzuheben, Werden mit absolutem Sein, Veränderung mit Identität zu vereinbaren." See F. von Schiller, "Ueber die aesthetische Erziehung des Menschen," in Schiller, *Sämtliche Werke in zwölf Bänden, Zwölfter Band* (Stuttgart, n.d.), 41. That is, "annulling time within time, reconciling becoming with absolute being and change with identity." See F. Schiller, *On the aesthetic education of man* (Oxford, 1967), 97.

67. Recall, in this context, the passage in Plato's *Symposium* where Diotima explains to Socrates that Love was born from the union of Resource and Poverty. See Plato, *Symposium,* ed. and trans. C. J. Rowe (Warminster, 1998), 203.

68. Hölderlin, "Hyperion," 675, 677 (German ed.).

INDEX

Cultural Memory | in the Present

Ian Balfour, *The Rhetoric of Romantic Prophecy*

Martin Stokhof, *World and Life as One: Ethics and Ontology in Wittgenstein's Early Thought*

Gianni Vattimo, *Nietzsche: An Introduction*

Jacques Derrida, *Negotiations: Interventions and Interviews, 1971–1998*, ed. Elizabeth Rottenberg

Brett Levinson, *The Ends of Literature: The Latin American 'Boom' in the Neoliberal Marketplace*

Timothy J. Reiss, *Against Autonomy: Cultural Instruments, Mutualities, and the Fictive Imagination*

Hent de Vries and Samuel Weber, eds., *Religion and Media*

Niklas Luhmann, *Theories of Distinction: Re-Describing the Descriptions of Modernity*, ed. and introd. William Rasch

Johannes Fabian, *Anthropology with an Attitude: Critical Essays*

Michel Henry, *I am the Truth: Toward a Philosophy of Christianity*

Gil Anidjar, *"Our Place in Al-Andalus": Kabbalah, Philosophy, Literature in Arab-Jewish Letters*

Hélène Cixous and Jacques Derrida, *Veils*

F. R. Ankersmit, *Historical Representation*

F. R. Ankersmit, *Political Representation*

Elissa Marder, *Dead Time: Temporal Disorders in the Wake of Modernity (Baudelaire and Flaubert)*

Reinhart Koselleck, *The Practice of Conceptual History: Timing History, Spacing Concepts*

Niklas Luhmann, *The Reality of the Mass Media*

Hubert Damisch, *A Childhood Memory by Piero della Francesca*

Hubert Damisch, *A Theory of /Cloud/: Toward a History of Painting*

Jean-Luc Nancy, *The Speculative Remark: (One of Hegel's bon mots)*

Jean-François Lyotard, *Soundproof Room: Malraux's Anti-Aesthetics*

Jan Patoçka, *Plato and Europe*

Hubert Damisch, *Skyline: The Narcissistic City*

Isabel Hoving, *In Praise of New Travelers: Reading Caribbean Migrant Women Writers*

Richard Rand, ed., *Futures: Of Jacques Derrida*

William Rasch, *Niklas Luhmann's Modernity: The Paradoxes of Differentiation*

Jacques Derrida and Anne Dufourmantelle, *Of Hospitality*

Jean-François Lyotard, *The Confession of Augustine*

Kaja Silverman, *World Spectators*

Samuel Weber, *Institution and Interpretation: Expanded Edition*

Jeffrey S. Librett, *The Rhetoric of Cultural Dialogue: Jews and Germans in the Epoch of Emancipation*

Ulrich Baer, *Remnants of Song: Trauma and the Experience of Modernity in Charles Baudelaire and Paul Celan*

Samuel C. Wheeler III, *Deconstruction as Analytic Philosophy*

David S. Ferris, *Silent Urns: Romanticism, Hellenism, Modernity*

Rodolphe Gasché, *Of Minimal Things: Studies on the Notion of Relation*

Sarah Winter, *Freud and the Institution of Psychoanalytic Knowledge*

Samuel Weber, *The Legend of Freud: Expanded Edition*

Aris Fioretos, ed., *The Solid Letter: Readings of Friedrich Hölderlin*

J. Hillis Miller / Manuel Asensi, *Black Holes / J. Hillis Miller; or, Boustrophedonic Reading*

Miryam Sas, *Fault Lines: Cultural Memory and Japanese Surrealism*

Peter Schwenger, *Fantasm and Fiction: On Textual Envisioning*

Didier Maleuvre, *Museum Memories: History, Technology, Art*

Jacques Derrida, *Monolingualism of the Other; or, The Prosthesis of Origin*

Andrew Baruch Wachtel, *Making a Nation, Breaking a Nation: Literature and Cultural Politics in Yugoslavia*

Niklas Luhmann, *Love as Passion: The Codification of Intimacy*

Mieke Bal, ed., *The Practice of Cultural Analysis: Exposing Interdisciplinary Interpretation*

Jacques Derrida and Gianni Vattimo, eds., *Religion*

CPSIA information can be obtained
at www.ICGtesting.com
Printed in the USA
LVHW090734161220
674238LV00007B/197